AGAINST AUTONOMY

Cultural Memory
in
the
Present

Mieke Bal and Hent de Vries, Editors

AGAINST AUTONOMY

Global Dialectics of Cultural Exchange

Timothy J. Reiss

STANFORD UNIVERSITY PRESS

STANFORD, CALIFORNIA 2002

Stanford University Press
Stanford, California
© 2002 by the Board of Trustees of the
Leland Stanford Junior University

Printed in the United States of America
on acid-free, archival-quality paper

ISBN 0-8047-4349-5 (alk. paper)—
ISBN 0-8047-4350-9 (pbk. : alk. paper)

Original Printing 2002

Last figure below indicates year of this printing:
11   10   09   08   07   06   05   04   03   02

Typeset by BookMatters in 11/13.5 Adobe Garamond

For friends, colleagues,
Ngũgĩ wa Thiong'o and Kamau Brathwaite,
whose explorations and discoveries
of voice are central to
many identities

and for
Patricia J. Penn Hilden,
second nature,
who knows what it is
to inhabit two minds

Contents

Acknowledgments xiii

Introduction 1

1 Uses of Autonomy: Nostalgias, Prescriptions, and the Fictive Imagination 29

2 Mapping Identities, Othering Cultures 68

3 The Law, the Tragic, and Cultures of Dissonance 108

4 Disjunctive Culture, Representation, and Mimetic Ends 150

5 Denying Body, Making Self? Histories and Identities 184

6 Dreams of Science, Science of Dreams: Selves and Reasons 219

7 Disordering Narrative Grasp 258

8 Reclaiming the Soul: Poetry, Autobiography, and the Voice of History 296

9 On Languages, Flowers, and Geography: Outsmarting Sisyphus, Amending Eldorado, Writing Caribbean 329

10 Caribbean Knights: Quijote, Galahad, and the Telling of History 360

11 Urban Imaginings: Histories and Geographies of Place 405

Notes 443

Works Cited 469

Index 509

we not knowing that the literature and history, even the grammar we learning in school is part of the contour map of we own geography of exile.
—Marlene NourbeSe Philip, *Frontiers*, 10

My thought swims the river only quite slowly,
Heavily burdened by clothes men have made it wear.
I try divesting myself of what I've learned,
I try forgetting the mode of remembering they taught me
And scrape off the ink they used to paint my senses. . . .
—Alberto Caeiro, *The Keeper of Sheep* XLVI, "One way or another,"
  Fernando Pessoa, *Poems*, 24–25

Once upon a time, our King, Dom João the Second, known as The Perfect King and in my opinion the perfect wit, made a certain nobleman a gift of an imaginary island, now tell me, do you know of any other nation where such a thing could happen, And the nobleman, what did the nobleman do, he set out to look for it, now, what I'd like to know is how you can find an imaginary island.
—José Saramago, *The Stone Raft*, 48

What kind of bad-minded snake that, that could sit down for all these years fool people that it is log; make us wash on it, talk round it, invite we friends to sit down on it, take it make prekkeh in every kind of way, then after all this time, decide to make a move?
—Velma Pollard, "Parable I," *Considering Woman*, 1–2

Acknowledgments

For the occasions that provoked the first versions of what are now the greatly rewritten chapters of this book, I am indebted to many people. Chapter 1 started life as a lecture for a conference on "Aesthetics and Politics" in October 1994 at Michigan State University, thanks to Judith Stoddart and William S. Penn III. It used extensive passages from an earlier Columbia University seminar in criticism given at the behest of Michel Beaujour and others. Benefitting from Arnold Krupat's talk at the former conference, it appeared as "Autonomy, Nostalgia, and Writing for the Aesthetic: Notes on Cultures and Exchanges" in a special issue of *Centennial Review* edited by Stoddart (39, no. 3 [fall 1995]: 513–36). The present reworking was especially helped by Stanley Corngold's and Ngũgĩ wa Thiong'o's attentive and generous readings.

Chapter 2 results from a request by Gordon Hutner and Art Casciato for a multibook review essay that appeared in *American Literary History* (4, no. 4 [November 1992]: 649–77). In good part, this invitation, coming at the time when I was writing the epilogue to *The Meaning of Literature*, provoked the work to which this present book—and eventually a companion one on European writing—are a first response. That epilogue, replete with what I was then able to make only as vague remarks implying a possibility of some new (or just different) functions and global practices of cultural production in general and imaginative writing in particular, cried out for wider and more thorough thought and attention. Reading and writing in reply to Casciato's and Hutner's invitation revealed much about the failures of "metropolitan" critical thinking, its reasons, and the need to understand European culture in a global and cosmopolitan context. The use Patricia Penn Hilden and Shigehisa Kuriyama made of this published text in an Emory University seminar produced essential conversations. At the same time, Monique Moser and Marshall Brown gave further occasion to consider and debate these issues, notably—but not only—as they concern themes of *Meaning*, with Marc Angenot in *Études Littéraires* (25, no. 3 [winter 1992–1993]: 162–71) and Anthony Cascardi in *Modern Language Quarterly* (54, no. 3 [November 1993]: 393–418). Later correspondence and conversations with Gregory Jusdanis apropos of this and more, and still later discussion with Vangelis Calotychos, also provoked further consideration. All these have affected what follows.

Chapter 3 began with Christopher Prendergast's invitation to participate in a seminar series at King's College, Cambridge, in April 1995 on the general subject of tragedy. Early in its preparation, I profited from a conversation with Wladimir Krysinski. Remarks and questions during the seminar by Simon Goldhill, Istvan Hont, Éric Méchoulan, and others unknown to me were especially helpful. At the generous request of Alessandro Briosi and Siena's Associazione—Simbolo, Conoscenza, Società, its first published version appeared in *Symbolon* (1, no. 1–2 [July–December 1996/January–July 1997]: 179–219). Sandro's too-early death is a grievous loss. Over years of correspondence and conversation, Harold Donohue gave me reactions and information that have found their way into this and probably other chapters. Vassilis Lambropoulos' careful reading of its earliest published version made me rethink aspects of its argument. It is likely that memories of Keith Hansen's 1990 New York University doctoral dissertation on Miguel de Unamuno and Albert Camus (*Tragic Lucidity*), now a book, may have inflected my thought about the former and his contemporaries of the Generation of '98.

A question from and talk with Chris Prendergast at the original seminar led to several pages of my Introduction and the elucubrations of Chapter 4—also affected by correspondence over the years with Sandro Briosi. I first offered these publicly at the "Congreso Internacional de Estudios Ingleses: pasado, presente y futuro" at the Universidad de Almería in October 1997 at the invitation of Emilio Barón-Palma and Miguel Martínez López, and in a slightly different version in February 1998 at the University of Oregon thanks to George Sheridan and Alexander Murphy. Members of both audiences engaged in rich and provocative exchanges and enabled me to hone its arguments considerably. After reading this lecture, Daniel Javitch—as is his wont—provided me with a wealth of further insight and information. The resulting text appears both in the selected *Acta* of the Almería conference, edited by Carmen Portero Muñoz, and, with her permission but in a much extended version, in a special issue of *Diaspora*, edited by Roland Greene (8, no. 1, 2000). Ngũgĩ then again provided me with a fruitful further reading. John T. Hamilton added his insights to some of the Greek material. Jenine Abboushi Dallal was generous beyond request with her time, ideas, and book and article finding, allowing me to be relatively precise and accurate in adding Arab matter to my argument. That on Chinese recalls years when I guided Lu Tonglin's master's thesis on *The Story of the Stone* and certain eighteenth–nineteenth-century French novels and followed its growth into a Princeton doctoral dissertation and a book, and when I codirected, for institutional more than scholarly reasons, Marie-Claire Huot's Montreal doctoral dissertation on Chinese calligraphy—to her is due my acquaintance with Liu Hsieh and others. To both—especially the former, who continues to keep me informed of ongoing thinking—is due a longer interest in Chinese letters. Close involvement with dissertations by Jiao Xiao-xiao and Wang Ping at New York University has (I hope) deepened consideration.

Early thoughts for Chapter 5 were stirred by a request from Michel Beaujour (again) and Ralph Heyndels for a brief conference talk in March 1992. In that version, it appeared as "L'oubli à la lettre: Descartes," in *Francographies*, no. spéc. 1–2: *Création et réalité d'expression française*, 2 vols. (1993) 1: 163–70. Opportunity to expand this was made by Joseph Fracchia. A comment by Alex Murphy at the resulting University of Oregon lecture in April 1993 was particularly useful. In varying forms, this talk was afterward given at several universities. On two of these occasions, it was helped by queries from Jacqueline Lichtenstein and Andrea Loselle and, on a later written draft, by questions from John Sutton to the form in which it was brought by Donald R. Kelley into the pages of the *Journal of the History of Ideas* (57, no. 4 [October 1996]: 587–607). A new and recontextualized version is here because the relation of "self" to history and memory and to notions of "scientific" understanding in Western thought over the past three centuries and the ways in which these relate to the West's exchanges with different cultures is centrally engaged in subsequent chapters. Sutton's correspondence and his now-published book on memory have helped me further tune aspects of arguments to my purpose here.

Chapter 6 began as a few pages in my 1982 *Discourse of Modernism*. As a result of an invitation from Bernard Beugnot and Jean-Claude Guédon to contribute to a special science issue of *Études Françaises*, it grew to the form in which it there appeared in fall 1983: "Science des rêves, rêves de la science" (19, no. 2: 27–61). Chantal Saint-Jarre and Marielle Baillargeon were responsible for reminding me of some material it uses. The former especially brought many issues and writings to my attention. I once thought to expand its concerns to book length but will never do so. As this book progressed, though, I realized that this writing's concerns were further and much trammeled in this work, not just in Chapters 5 and 7, but in matters of identities and their relation to history, geography, and culture that recur earlier and later in the book. This now further elaborated chapter's tracking of analyses of selfhood and identity, individuality and community in a particular European history as well as its fitting of those analyses into that history's tradition of scientific discourse echo in many ways the historical and instrumental concerns of preceding chapters and help understand aspects of these issues as they are raised in following ones, approaching cultures where such a European notion of selfhood may appear and be felt as a particular kind of imposition (a matter further explored especially in the Introduction and *passim* in my *Mirages of the Selfe*).

Chapter 7, founded on writing by a Polish exile in France embedded in a quarter century's earlier exile in Argentina, is the only other chapter with as long a history. Its earliest version was in the *Canadian Journal of Semiotics* (8, no. 1–2 [winter 1980–1981]: 29–64). Sophia Janik and Wladimir Krysinski then readily replied to endless queries about the Polish language of Witold Gombrowicz's *Kosmos*. I revised this essay for inclusion in my 1988 *Uncertainty of Analysis*, but for various reasons chose to omit it. A third revision was published in *Discours Social/Social Discourse* (4, no. 1–2 [winter–spring 1992]: 117–46). Since then, I have benefitted from the doctoral work of and conversations with Krystyna Lipinska-Illakowicz. The reasons for its reincarnation are several. Gombrowicz's critique of European culture are one. His move from what he called a European periphery to Latin America and its impact on his writing are others. Close connections between the essay's preoccupations and those of what are now earlier chapters of this book are yet another. That the novel it examines seems to me to exemplify a sense of how a certain kind of (European) writing fails is a fourth. This last is not, of course, to argue that the novel itself "fails" (whatever that might mean). Rather, it shows the inadequacies and aporias of an individual's efforts to order, impose on, and possess actuality, or, in broader terms, to make a generalizable rational history. It shows how knowledge and action need different kinds of writing and rely on different kinds of relation. I propose *Cosmos* as a kind of fictional limit case of the sorts of failure examined in earlier chapters, a call for instrumental restraint and curb. It is a natural pendant to the preceding stories of "metropolitan" cultural instruments and their uses: singular forms of ordering, imposition, and possession. At the same time, via its author's biography as well as the author's preoccupations, it leads to the Western Hemispheric, though chiefly Caribbean, emphases of the final chapters.

Chapter 8 began as a contribution to an autumn 1994 special issue of *World Literature Today* (68, no. 4: 683–90) at the request of Djelal Kadir. Its present reworking was helped not just by companion essays in that journal but materially by three occasions when I was honored to be asked to introduce public appearances by Kamau Brathwaite: once by him at New York University, once by Silvio Torres Saillant and Daniel Shapiro at the Americas Society in New York, and once by Alfred Arteaga and David Lloyd at the University of California, Berkeley. A shorter version of this reworking is the introductory essay to *For the Geography of a Soul: New Perspectives on Kamau Brathwaite* (Trenton, N.J., and Asmara: Africa World Press, 2001). Chapter 9 was originally the concluding essay of a double issue of *Annals of Scholarship*, edited by Brathwaite and myself: *Sisyphus and Eldorado: Magical and Other Realisms in Caribbean Literature* (12, no. 1–2, 1997: 217–34). A second, revised, edition of this collection was published by Africa World Press in 2001.

Chapter 10 was first written at the request of Brian May for a special number of *Studies in the Novel* (29, no. 3 [fall 1997]: 297–322). Ana Dopico was thoughtful and generous in glossing both these last. Christopher Winks directed me to a nice comment about publishing in Cuba; Maarten van Delden and Jason Weiss went out of their way to try and answer queries from a nonspecialist about specific relations between writers in the Americas, France, and Spain in the 1930s. Chapter 11 resulted from an invitation by Clint Goodson to respond to a paper by Jean Franco at a conference at Michigan State University in October 1997. Reworked and elaborated far beyond its conference brevity, it appeared in a special issue of *Centennial Review* (42, no. 3 [fall 1998]: 437–56), edited by Ralph Bauer. Jean Franco was generous in keeping me apprised of the development of her own essay. As a mark of what it owed her and as a small recognition of her life's work in bridging north and south, the original essay was dedicated to her. I would have retained this dedication, but the chapter has been further reworked, expanded, and moved in different directions in light of the chapters preceding it.

I am deeply grateful to all these friends, colleagues, and editors, who provoked, helped, and commented directly on particular parts of this book, and who in the last case have permitted me to reuse material. The names of many of those who commented after lectures and seminars are omitted because I failed to note everyone. I hope a blanket word of thanks will not affront them. For diversely time-consuming bits of help, I also thank Michelle Knight at Central Missouri State University, Elaine Maruhn at the University of Nebraska Press, Susan Protheroe in Comparative Literature at New York University, Ruth Backer in Comparative Literature at the University of Oregon, Neal Bruss and Louise Smith at the University of Massachusetts, Boston, and L. T. R. McDonald and Joy Dufour in English at Carleton University. Other punctual acknowledgments are in notes, but for help with information that cannot be so referenced, I thank Rolena Adorno, Peter Berger, V. K. Chari, Isis Costa, Nicholas Dirks, Geoffrey Hartman, Richard Lanham, Emerson Marks, Mark McWatt, Walter Mignolo, Chris Miller, Mervyn Morris, Velma Pollard, John Searle, Julie Solomon, Robert Stillman, Mick Taussig, and Kendall Walton.

Much writing often starts less formally as graduate and undergraduate teaching, which can be probing tests. That has not really been the case here, save in the long-ago case of the *Cosmos* chapter (at the Université de Montréal)—less precisely, in that of some of the material of Chapter 10 that benefitted from exchanges in a series of undergraduate seminars ("Caribbean Writing: Histories of Exile, Geographies of Home") given at the University of California, Berkeley, in July 1996, and rather more in that of some of Chapters 8 through 10 used in a graduate–undergraduate seminar at the University of Oregon at a time, however, when the book was virtually done. From this last, it may be pernicious to name some and not others among an often forcefully questioning group of students, but I would like to thank Alain-Fleury Ekorong, Beth Hege, Enrique Lima, and Joshua Dean Morse for making me rethink elements of my argument. Many aspects of what follows were worked and thought through more carefully in such exchanges as well as in those with students in various seminars at New York University over the past years and at Berkeley in 1996–1997. I thank all of these people, as well as those of the Montreal *neiges d'antan*, for giving these opportunities and possibilities for thought. To Haun Saussy and Vassilis Lambropoulos, press readers *extraordinaires*, who gave forcefully bountiful and generously careful readings of the typescript, gratitude is best recorded by my having tried to respond to their suggestions and to meet their wider expectations (without making the thing even longer). I also thank Helen Tartar for her determined faith, enthusiasm, and concern, Karen Hellekson for the gentle and careful copyediting, and Elizabeth Berg for patiently shepherding a long book through the production process. I am also grateful to the office of the Dean of Humanities at New York University for a publication grant.

Many more friends have given me the profit of debate and correspondence over the last years on matters touching this work. The names of some are more appropriately attached to other writing, but here I thank those who further pushed me overall with this work or with whom exchanges have been so ongoing as to make precision impossible: Kamau Brathwaite, John Chioles, Harold Donohue, Ana Maria Dopico, Roland Greene, Peter Haidu, Tim Hampton, Patricia Hilden, Daniel Javitch, Peter N. Miller, Sylvia Molloy, Ngũgĩ wa Thiong'o, Julio Ramos, Domna Stanton, George Szanto, and Silvio Torres-Saillant. In years of correspondence (and finally in person), Nuala Ní Dhomhnaill has been generous in making me more attentive to how languages, persons, cultures, and cultural creation need particularizing as wholes; Cees Nooteboom has often made me think more about art and history, geography and cultural exchanges, about European margins, metropoles, and impositions. Pamela Mordecai's reading of Chapter 5 forced me to clarify the purpose of the entire book. Because grounding concerns of this book are relations between discursive practices and orders of power and between different cultural "regimes" and different "realities on the ground," I must also acknowledge several decades' engagement with the writings of Michel Foucault especially, as well as with those of Michel de Certeau. In particular, many talks with both in Montreal and elsewhere in the mid- and late 1970s are memories of friendship cherished as having fundamentally inflected my ideas on the issues with which they were concerned. Matthew Reiss has given diverse important and generous sorts of sustenance; Suzanna Reiss poses questions overlapping those asked in this book in ways that keep the mind alive. I thank her, too, for the wonderful cover design. And as if this weren't already enough, I owe her as well for directing me to the critical and political writings of M. NourbeSe Philip, whose grand fiction and poetry had nonetheless not readied me for the pellucid and uncomfortably barbed rigor of her judicious and shrewd critical work and activist cultural commentary. Since then, I am grateful to be able to add her name to those of other friends whose conversation has mattered in particular to what follows and in general to ongoing work.

Singling out three of these as dedicatees of this volume, I acknowledge those whose work I have known the longest (in Ngũgĩ's case, it has mattered to me for more than thirty-five years, in Brathwaite's for some twenty-five) and to whom I am closest. But I owe further thanks to Patricia J. Penn Hilden, not only for her reading and criticism of versions of most of these chapters but also for our thinking and talk about the many issues they discuss and for her pushing me to new connections and different imaginings. Her work on American Indian cultures, histories, and politics and in indigenous education—but also her *being* in them—has deeply changed my efforts to understand these complex issues and what ways may be found from the pernicious binds explored by many contemporaries and evident in our day-to-day world. It has also taught me more than peace of mind would have liked about evil and bitter conflicts (the adjectives fall short) fracturing still colonized cultures and colonized minds and the manifold ways in which this internal destructiveness is exploited by those within and without (by no means all colonizers). Without her work, her comments, our conversation, and her practice, much of what follows would have been stillborn.

Introduction

What the book owes to happenstance and to personal and intellectual relations, however, is not more than its debt to the cultural, political, and academic conflicts of the past few years, which seem to grow more numbingly bitter with every passing day. These conflicts oblige those engaged in teaching and researching the "humanities" to think more deeply than we otherwise might about the nature of these areas of work, about their relation to other disciplines and those professing them, and, most crucially (no doubt), to the larger society that must maintain and benefit from the critical institutions in which these activities occur. At their best, these (academic) institutions are critical in several senses. Absent the knowledge their members continuously exchange, acquire, and pass on, the public sphere must ultimately collapse through ignorance and a stultifying simplism that reduces living complexities to trivial dualisms. Absent their attention to ordered ways of thought (which does not mean *one* way of thought, prescribed by one culture), the public sphere must tumble into confusion. Absent their questioning of opinion and claim, the public sphere is unable to renew itself, and rote repetition of the past makes a desolation. That the ideal, as in most human endeavors, may be rarely achieved, does not make the institutions and their activities any less essential.

All the following chapters began, then, as responses to particular requests, events, or queries, but they react to these wider conditions. They do so by addressing dilemmas whose shared focus can be sardonically signaled by words like "Eurocentrism," "multiculturalism," "postmodernism." I say "sardonically" because these are just catchphrases that help us recognize an arena but not the game played within. If these chapters start with issues raised by such terms, they aim further.

They seek to show ubiquitous standard categories of western thought and practice—what I call *cultural instruments*—in their history, development, use, reason, and action: Latin *ratio* better names the extent and complexity of their role, naming not just human "reason" but these histories, developments, uses, causes, and actions *as* rationally constructed. These *rationes* or instruments (or *rationes* that *become* instruments) are forms of analysis and practice, normative ways of thinking and doing, apparently central to western culture—western as far as these chapters are concerned—which in the course of a particular history then came to offer means of understanding and controlling other different cultures—hence my choice of the word "instruments." These include such disparate categories and artifacts as notions of *autonomy* and division of intellectual, social, cultural, and aesthetic practices; ideas of *otherness*, taking forms like *Gemeinschaft/ Gesellschaft, organic/mechanistic, négritude*, afrocentrism at cultural and political levels, or opposition to a self at a narrower, "personal" one; such "conflictual" concepts as fiction and real, truth and falsehood; certain modes of history and memory; cultural and aesthetic categories like *tragedy, mimesis, self, mind/body*; particular forms of discourse like *science, philosophy, aesthetics, literature*. . . .

Many of these *rationes*, like the notion of "otherness" explored especially in Chapter 2, have had evident effects on and in cultures the West has sought to dominate. Romila Thapar and Bipan Chandra have spent forty years showing how western prejudice created the image of an India as somehow the West's Other, either as a utopia to be glorified or as a dystopia to which the West brought a beneficial "progress"—itself another instrument of the kind I envisage. This image long guided not just western policy but Indians' own writing of their history, their economic and social policies, and their political strategies and purposes (Thapar, "Communalism," *Past*; Chandra, "Historians," "Colonialism," and *Nationalism* generally). Equally clear in material practice are the doctrines, actions, and results of free trade and its twin, "political liberalism," Britain's "major export product" of the nineteenth century, to cite André Gunder Frank (*Capitalism*, 67); nationalism as a European export to the rest of the world (Chatterjee, *Nationalist*, 1–53); progress as "'Industrial Revolution' development" and attendant "'capitalism,' 'technology,' and even [Enlightened] 'rationality' ," as Stathis Gourgouris has it, citing Cornelius Castoriadis (*Dream*, 64); private property in Ranajit Guha's analysis of Britain's efforts to impose it on Bengal (*Rule*)—an analysis easily repeated, with needed local diversity, on colonial oppressions from the Indian Americas to East Africa. Other instruments are narrower, like the disciplines of modern western knowledge and their divisions probed by Ellen Messer-Davidow, David Shumway, David Sylvan, and others in their home context (*Knowledges*) and in a colonized one by Partha Chatterjee and others (*Texts*). All these instruments imply, depend on, and reinforce one another.

The chapters of this book further efforts to show how such instruments or categories of thought, analysis, and praxis (thus *rationes*) evolved over time for ends internal to European culture. They try to show how these *rationes* have been applied outside that culture to and by different places and cultures, and to what ends and effects. In this, the book has little more originality than that of the *rationes* discussed and the effort to set them deep in their history. It has affinities with works like those of Guha or Chatterjee, Edward Said's *Orientalism*, or Christopher Miller's *Blank Darkness*, probing import and imposition of cultural instruments. It differs from the former in starting its critique *inside* the culture that made the instruments. It includes their long historical making as a main part of their present and past action, though, unlike *Orientalism*, it sees their modern action as following earlier *reinvention* of that history, not in stable continuum with a culturally distinct Greek antiquity (Reiss, *Meaning*, 226–62; see below especially Chapters 3 and 4, and aspects of others). Too, because it sees this long history as at least western-European wide, it brings in many people and explores a large gamut of writings.

Nonetheless, a book like this must obviously offer exemplary cases rather than attempt exhaustive analysis. Too, given my own areas of expertise, *Against Autonomy* stresses "literary" work, which I prefer here to call that of the "fictive imagination." I use this term because I have argued, especially in *The Meaning of Literature*, and now take for granted that "literature" is itself the product—the *ratio*—of a particular western sociohistorical context and that its meaning(s) are delimited by that history and cultural context. "Fictive imagination" refers to particular forms of cultural production that in the West are called *art* (literature included) but that in different cultures take different names and may well serve quite different purposes. To use the word "literature" in ways implying its universality would prevent one from seeing that it, too, is a *ratio*→cultural instrument. Its use would merely repeat the kind of imposition already mentioned and disable any analysis (for example) of how such instruments get "turned" by, precisely, different fictive imaginations. It would disable one from seeing and participating in those mutually recognizing intercultural "exchanges" respectful of specific "natures" that Wilson Harris has called "mutualities" (*Womb*, 13, 18). Literature, of course, like History, *has* had such disabling effects. Because of its importance throughout the chapters of this book, I shall come back a little later in this Introduction to the *ratio* that is literature.

As my understanding of these categories, these *rationes*, grew clearer, I realized (1) that they were linked in complicated but quite straightforward ways, (2) that they shared western histories of both *longue durée* and short, (3) that they were indeed among concepts and practices central to what one might call western culture's "self-understanding," and (4) that they also became ways of grasping—in the several meanings of that word—different cultures. What was needed, then, was to understand how certain major ones had historically come about and developed. More precisely, since my interest really lay in their modern use and action, I needed to explore how they had been enabled by their particular histories and common interconnections to function in particular ways over the past few centuries and in the present. But most especially, I became concerned to examine how these *rationes* became ways through which western culture claimed to "understand" different cultures with which it came in contact or, usually and more bluntly, whose places it invaded and whose peoples it sought to dominate. One needed then to explore how these *rationes* became instruments of understanding, indeed, but of understanding as a process of control, dominance, and oppression. Their history became also their history as cultural instruments of domination.

So the original essays could now all be linked to make coherently successive chapters of a book each of which shows these three aspects: (1) internal historical development, sense, and action of *rationes*, going back in some cases to Greco-Latin antiquity, in others only to the early Enlightenment; (2) reasons for and meaning of their instrumental transformation, usually in the nineteenth and twentieth centuries, coeval with the industrializing West's growing technological power, rapidly increasing colonial expansionism—at least in Africa and the Far East—and need (?) for cultural imposition; (3) analysis of their "reuse" by the different cultures they sought to control and organize. At the same time, the book as a whole could and does develop from an emphasis on the first two to an emphasis on the third, thus passing, too, from Europe to Africa, the Caribbean, and Latin America.

For now different histories intervened. Cultures in which these *rationes*, instruments, willy-nilly had a place could "make them over," turn them in new ways, turn them indeed *against* the western instrumentality they served. These histories also became essential aspects of such *rationes*—no longer just western. It was necessary to ask how different cultures adapt them to other goals, how they "spill over their colonial embankments to proliferate in the native quarters," as Chatterjee writes of late nineteenth-century Bengal. In Calcutta, its capital, "energized by the desires and strategies of entirely different political agendas, the intellectual project of [western] modernity found new sustenance in those densely populated parts; in the process it took on completely new forms" ("Disciplines," 8). Nationalism, for instance, became different from the West's (*Nationalist*, 41–43, 85–166). Leopoldo Zea earlier wrote analogously of a Latin American scene where colonized peoples' "nationalism reworked the colonizers'" (*Role*, 78–81). Tapati Guha-Thakurta, too, shows how such nationalisms and native artistic traditions reworked western aesthetic and art ideals (*Making*, 118–225). As I insist later in this Introduction and throughout the book, these are not, and are not to be lumped into, some homogeneous hybrid. They must be seen as unique wholes in an embracing world system.

An interestingly accurate image of such reworkings was recorded during early European trade on the "Guinea Coast" of Africa. This trade was never one-sided, and John Thornton, for example, shows that the amount of cloth imported from Europe in the sixteenth and seventeenth centuries was roughly equal to that exported from Africa. Nor was this just an exchange between "Europe" and "Africa." French, English, Dutch, and Portuguese traded up and down the coast from Senegal to Angola and from there across the Atlantic. In this context, Thornton quotes the English captain John Phillips, a 1694 visitor to the kingdom of Allada—in modern Benin—observing that most European cloths "they sold [there] were unraveled and then rewoven into their own cloth and resold in other parts of Africa." European sailors shared in this reselling, and not just in Africa or in Europe, "for Phillips noted that they fetched a crown each in Barbados" (Thornton, *Africa*, 52; the captain is called Thomas Phillips, not John Phillips, in the later edition that I have seen of this work). Reweaving European "says and perpetuans" to be recirculated as superior Allada cloth to other parts of Africa, to the Americas, and back to Europe offers a wonderful image of the complexities of Harris' mutualities. It becomes even better when one knows that these "European" cloths were often "re-exports of textiles . . . from India and China" (Frank, *ReOrient*, 71).

For these instruments do not function only in one direction. So this book complements its exploration of their historical making by showing how their unmaking and reforging by diverse cultures are essential to present and future exchanges. Its chapters suggest how this past and present have to be incorporated in any critical stance and in any hope of widening cultural attentions. Later ones try to offer a sense of how this is being achieved, with whatever difficulty. For it is hard to perceive these changes and perhaps harder still, Nicholas Dirks adds, "to recognize the ways in which specific cultural forms [of the colonizing culture are] themselves constituted out of colonial encounters" (introduction to *Colonialism and Culture*, 4): the other side of the effect observed in the last paragraph. The reworking is not just that of the colonized. The "internal culture" of the colonizer is also, Ashis Nandy observes, deeply changed: the social Darwinian idea of the "fittest" bringing progress to others, for instance, itself developed from the colonizing experience (*Intimate*, 32). But neither is it just in their *later* adaptation that these *rationes* are reforged. They are surely modulated from the first by the impact and imposition (*not* Dirks' and others' "encounter," whose euphemistic implication of equality and serendipitous meeting hides violent invasion and conquest, marks instrumental forgetting, and enables anthropological seizure). Although it tries to do so in the present, what follows does not much explore how Europe's *rationes* may have thus been forged from their "start" (or from their reinvention) out of such violence in their more or less distant past. But the question is not one to be eluded.

How, for example, would knowledge of Europe's Renaissance and Reformation change if one showed that a major reason for Henry VIII's disavowal of Catherine of Aragon and Catholic authority was not just dynastic, religious, diplomatic, or personal, but to be free of Spanish Pope Alexander VI's 1493 bull and the 1494 Treaty of Tordesillas dividing the lands "west and south" of the Azores between Spain and Portugal (and of the 1455 bull, *Romanus Pontifex*, giving Portugal rights to Africa)? The king's failure to form a company for exploration and exploitation in the face of English apathy in 1521 (from letdown at John Cabot's relatively dull northern lands "found" on a voyage licensed by Henry VII under a grant designedly avoiding Vatican and Iberian interests, from the brisk Flanders trade, from fear of

Iberian reaction) would have led directly to his 1533 schism, fixing of his full rule over the English Church and resultant traffic free of Vatican authority, including profitable trade like William Hawkins' with Brazil in 1528 and the early 1530s. Was this why Richard Hakluyt insisted both that Hawkins was "for his wisdom, valour, experience, and skill in sea causes much esteemed, and beloved of King Henry the Eighth" and that such voyages were "in those days very rare, especially to our nation" (*Voyages*, 51)? Historians' silence on such a hypothesis suggests that most would find it perverse (it would demand archival research beyond the scope of this book). But my point is that it would transform understanding of at least the English Reformation, inverting Max Weber's thesis in *The Protestant Ethic and the Spirit of Capitalism* (1904) and grounding something like its reversal in R. H. Tawney's *Religion and the Rise of Capitalism* (1926) not in earlier capitalism but in the invasion of the Americas. No one doubts that European natural rights theories were essentially inflected by debate about relations between indigenous American peoples and their invaders. This hypothesis proposes that the invasions marked Anglo-Protestantism and its resultant culture no less profoundly.[1] In *ReOrient*, Frank argues that the invasion was just an element in Europe's joining an Asian economic system, providing the silver that alone made its participation possible (4–5 and *passim*). Cultural *rationes* may always and only have come from elsewhere.

This is not James Froude's argument of English Renaissance and later culture as affirming itself through wise imperialist strength and moral values. Nor is it therefore countered by certain contemporary denials of Froude's assertions on the grounds that English colonial efforts were half-hearted and inefficient compared with those of the Spanish. It is not the now fairly common argument that this same culture is just deeply marked by these efforts—which seems at some level a truism, even if the detailed demonstration is a necessary one. It is the stronger proposal that without the invasions, that culture and its successors would not have become at all what they did.

This particular hypothesis can play, as I say, no part in this book. But (perhaps lesser) movements from making to unmaking to reforging characterize the book as a whole and their elements are present in each chapter. Their movement in the book is one of relative weight, not of distinct moments. In various forms, alone or together, these concerns are shared by many contemporaries (which is one reason why my bibliography is only a checklist of works cited—the other being the effort to embed these *rationes* in their history: long as it is, it could be quite disproportionate). This is a contribution, at times polemical, to these widening debates.

The book focuses on, although not only on, what the modern West has called "literature," that accumulation of artifacts in which, Peter Haidu suggests, a society explores and transforms its ideational and experiential conflicts; in which, I. A. Richards averred, "we" do not "copy life" but "restore life itself to order" (as known by a particular society, he should have added); which offers, Wole Soyinka urges, "visionary projection of society," "visionary reconstruction . . . for the purposes of a social direction"; or in which, says Marlene NourbeSe Philip, "a society continually accepts, integrates and transcends its experiences" (Haidu, "Politics"; Richards, *Philosophy*, 134; Soyinka, *Myth*, 64, 106; Philip, *She Tries* 14). Literature names an arena of issues I explored historically in *The Meaning of Literature*, at the same time showing its complex ties to a certain order of polity. Whatever else it does, literature enacts the play among a "political and economic arrangement" and "the spirit and the values governing human relationships," to cite Ngũgĩ wa Thiong'o as another witness (*Homecoming*, xvi). Or again, if he will forgive my adapting one other of his many such statements, literature, as a product of the "intellectual and imaginative activity" of men and women in society, "is thoroughly social" and "embodies in word-images the tensions, conflicts and contradictions at the heart of a community's being and becoming" (*Writers*, 4). What may startle in this consensus is that these witnesses otherwise disagree considerably.

But what has been called literature since early in the European eighteenth century has in fact been tied chiefly to one western set of ideas and practices of polity and indeed its imposition elsewhere: that marked by instruments like those named earlier: "nationalism," "progress," "free trade," "liberalism," "capitalism" and others. This is a reason why, as Ngũgĩ further remarks, the Ugandan linguist and critic Pio Zirimu coined the word "orature" to name other kinds and contexts of verbal "creative expression" (*Homecoming*, 70; the issue returns in Chapter 4). It is why many have questioned whether one can speak historically of Chinese "literature." It is why Aijaz Ahmad stresses the difficulty of fixing a category called "Indian Literature" (*In Theory*, 243–85). It is why many have queried the extent to which theoretical and critical tools developed to discuss literature can be unconstrainingly or unrepressively applied to nonwestern creative forms.[2]

This is a further reason why I prefer now to call wider experiences and ideas of the sorts of activity literature names (in *its* place) the "fictive imagination" and avoid any idea that these (or "it") can be easily compartmentalized or separated from other human experiences and practices (Chapter 1 especially treats this issue). For the matters treated here, the "literary" does pose dilemmas, not least because the West universalized literature, shaped to needs of a given time and place, as intrinsic to what it was to be human—and civilized—at all. The West depicted cultures "lacking" what it called literature as less *advanced*, even juvenile, primitive, or savage. But literature is just one manifestation of the human fictive imagination.[3] It is an oppression to demand that all cultures do alike, to assert that *we* (whoever and wherever the speaker may be) own the single truth of humanness. Let us not forget, writes the Guadaloupean Saint-John Perse: "Étroits sont les vaisseaux, étroite notre couche. Immense l'étendue des eaux" ("Narrow are the vessels, narrow our bed. Immense the expanse of waters"; *Amers, Collected Poems*, 450). There is no ready scale to judge ourselves the universal measure.

Two centuries ago, Johann Wolfgang von Goethe opined, "National literature is no longer of importance; it is time for world literature, and all must aid in bringing it about" ("On World Literature," 224). In our time of growing concern with and debate about culture and globalization—culture and *its* globalization—Goethe's plea has become a catchphrase. As such, it has lost the precision of its ties to its own context and the particular ambiguities those ties allowed. For Goethe's world was one where people still imagined themselves in a network of local cultures; where Frankfurt and Venice—Weimar and even Paris—were equal nodes in one great net.[4] And of all European places, Italy not excepted, Goethe's German lands were no doubt still the most culturally splintered. Perhaps that was why his was a first modern voice to claim that "literature" needed to be thought of as a single, worldwide activity, bearing universal values, taste, and common participation in "the true progress of mankind" ("On World Literature," 227). But for him, such values depended still in some way on being bound to localities. Goethe did not so direct it, but the issue could have been the play between those localities and the world: two centuries, no less, before Stuart Hall.[5] Even in his own day, Goethe's voice was not alone, for if the chief era of *nationally* focused and determined cultural imposition still lay largely ahead, England and France had begun the great game of cultural competition in open political (even military) and commercial terms at least by the end of the seventeenth century. Immediately later inventions of literary traditions already served both to legitimate particular nationhoods and to establish a specifically European historical identity, one supposed to have perdured from Greek and Judaic antiquities via pagan and Christian Latinity to the present (Reiss, *Meaning*, chapters 3–8).

Goethe himself was ambivalent about the relation between a putative *Weltliteratur* and the cultures of the "various nations" ("On World Literature," 227), between the "cosmopolitan" and the "national" (228). Not unlike Edward Gibbon in his earlier remarks about what Europe could learn from the Iroquois (see Chapter 2), Goethe felt that the mutual "foreignness" of cultures would make each "aware of intellectual needs previously unknown" (228). But he also thought that "the world at large, no matter how vast it may be, is only an expanded homeland and will actually yield in interest no more than our native land" (227). Ultimately there would be one world literature. It would be achieved "mainly when the disputes within one nation are settled by the opinions and judgments of others" (228). And there's the rub. He was certain where the center was, where the groundwork of universal progress was being laid: most solidly in his time, he felt, "in the French nation" (225), but also in German, English, and Italian literatures, proving their place in this pantheon by showing the same rational authority, ethical values, aesthetic taste, and political ideals (226–27).

So it was also clear who was to settle cultural disputes, both as to foreign literatures and cultures and one's own. If progress had its center, the center had its progressive duties to others less fortunate—such as the producers of those "Indian fables" marred, as we see in Chapter 3, by "specters hostile to art" (*Dichtung*, 9:537). Written in 1812, the belief was soon paraphrased by the actual "coloniser's verdict on the 'monstrous' Hindu divinities" and by the colonized's agreement that "the idols we worship outrage taste, as the worship itself outrages all reason" (Guha-Thakurta, *Making*, 127, citing *The Hindu Patriot*, May 4, 1854): a typical example of that internalized prejudice which Thapar and others have shown to guide what historical analysis reveals as a wholly false image of oneself as someone's "other." But that someone had managed to make itself the universal standard of progressive humanity. So those elites wishing to forge a world *literature* had to be sure it was grounded in the center's values and ideals. That was why its arbitrating leaders, too, Goethe insisted, had not to please the inevitable lowest common denominator of mass culture but to "form a silent, almost secret congregation" (227).

Sharers in the literary tradition such views typify *did* create that ostensibly universal value system whose latest virulent strain is linked in the United States to the names of William Bennett, Allan Bloom, Dinesh D'Souza, Roger Kimball, and others. Their owners are self-proclaimed "defenders of advanced civilized culture," adopting the essentially Euro-American idea that such an ideal universal literature is representative of and for all humans. Among others, Miguel de Unamuno long since criticized, if ambiguously, the false nostalgia of such views and oppressive imposition they express (we'll see soon why I mention this neglected figure in English-language writing, who will reappear often). But these new mandarins take possessively manichean pride in believing other cultural traditions not only futile in their differences, but fundamentally lesser in whatever "successes" they may be granted. For it is not only "easy" but essential for these defenders of a culture "to maintain the absolute value," Ananda Coomaraswamy once observed, of their taste, their ethical system, their political processes, their art (*Dance*, 38). To get beyond such closure not only "demands a greater effort than most are willing to make" but questions the hegemonic surety they feel in their own history and place, and creates, as Philip remarks, "the fear, *as they perceive it*, that, given half a chance, we [from a different culture] will replace them in all fields" (*Frontiers*, 21). We see here, and will again, a kind of deep cultural psychological insecurity, although that "psychology" (if such it is) should not sidetrack us from its being used to justify political and economic dominations—of which it may also be a symptom.

For, taking their own tradition one-sidedly, these defenders of their faith value its culture only inasmuch as it has won some competitive race. Samuel P. Huntington's clamor about "the clash of civilizations" and the hearing his ideas about cultural differences producing inevitable global wars (for which we must pick up steam in readiness) have received in the mainstream U.S. press show the political import of such views. With all its poverty, this six-gun conception of culture is not easily overcome. Its proselytizers tap a powerful vein. For divers historical reasons—including long-lived strains of U.S. anti-intellectualism, enduring xenophobia, and racism (not limited to North America), various versions of the "white man's burden" applied to indigenous and other peoples in "our backyard," the pressures of a global economy—as well as the facilities of a demagoguery pitting "elites" against "real working people," this conception of culture has tied itself to political campaigns of exclusion, as villainous in claiming value when it means power as vicious in pretending empowerment when it means plunder.[6] This campaign is on the airwaves and in print media, in churches and school boards, in Congress and state houses.

The campaign wants to freeze what it likes to perceive as a universal culture based, it delights in saying, on "absolute moral values." Entirely cynical about the relation between words and deeds, between argument and act, those behind it are in fact fairly open that they place myth in service of self-interest and want dominion to satisfy material greed. They are in every way to be identified as what Frantz Fanon called "bourgeois society," adding, "What I call bourgeois society is any society that becomes rigidified in predetermined forms, forbidding all evolution, all gains, all progress, all discovery. I call bourgeois a closed society in which life has no taste, in which the air is tainted, in which ideas and men are corrupt" (*Black Skin*, 224; translation mildly corrected). This definition is as much about attitude and action as it is about class (if they can be separated). Its difference from familiar political–economic ones is useful precisely because it specifies questions about cultural and aesthetic closure to which I'll return. In North America, at least, the statement applies in all its details: the demand for a single culture, indeed, "English only," now embodied in California's Proposition 227 and similar laws in other states, is Fanon's first "forbidding"[7]; California's Propositions 187 and 209 and analogous initiatives in Texas, Florida, and elsewhere, seeking to exclude a diversity of immigrants and minorities, underscore Fanon's "closed society"; endless instances of the hypocrisies and venalities of official life index the taints and corruptions.

In contemporary life, the ranting clamor to impose one set of cultural values is curiously belied by what seems to be the other side of the same coin, the idea that history has ended in the "victory" of these values. If so, then the clamor seems hardly necessary—perhaps it represents an urge for a last clean-up. But a conquering culture that values itself only in terms of competitive inequalities and dominance *has* to maintain its expansive impositions. That is why it has to perceive cultures or "civilizations" different from it as somehow its "other" and so able to be grasped in its terms, defeated in them, and used in them. For these inequalities, dominance and impositions have been, after all, integral to this conquering culture's self-understanding.

"Literature" is still a fundamental source of anxiety for those who think this way. Obvious and notorious—or celebrated, depending on one's views—are works like Allan Bloom's *Closing of the American Mind* or

Harold Bloom's *Western Canon*.[8] More insidious, I think, is a work like Michael Valdez Moses' *The Novel and the Globalization of Culture*. Using Thomas Hardy's *Mayor of Casterbridge*, Joseph Conrad's *Lord Jim*, Chinua Achebe's *Things Fall Apart* and *No Longer at Ease*, and Mario Vargas Llosa's *War of the End of the World*, Moses wants to show the operation of a cultural second law of thermodynamics (my analogy, not his): the advent of cultural entropy revealed through its fictional effects. He argues that "modernization" has been thematized by these novelists and others named but not glossed: Salman Rushdie, Shusaku Endo, Brian Moore, Tahar Ben Jalloun, Ngũgĩ. By "modernization," he means something like the Final Accomplishment of Enlightened Reason and economic capitalism across the globe. According to Moses, these novelists use similar but not identical forms of thematization, each inflected by particular social, political, and cultural conditions in which novel and author are embedded. Each novel differently shows a greater or lesser tension between a place's and a time's past and a present that is, precisely, the posthistorical modernity of a hegelian historical process that has now become Francis Fukuyama's visible experienced *Endpunkt* of the entire globe. Goethe might have enjoyed this: the disputes of one culture would indeed have been settled by the imposed opinions and judgments of others—although Goethe might have worried about the disappearance of local specificities. No longer would we be caught in the tragic agon of history (Moses' term), trapped by unmakeable choices between opposing visions of the world, history, and society: according to this apocalyptic vision, one vision is victorious. Novelists are left to show and clean up the disparities of separate pasts.

This is again, of course, to put things in the very terms familiar to the western culture that thinks it has "won" in this manner, terms of competition and conflict, of cultural otherness and sameness, of nature and nurture and any number of other dichotomies. Gyan Prakash notes how ideas that capitalism and the modern nation-state have won (or are winning) over the Other's cultural forms occupy the same teleological history as that which sets Enlightened western reason and progress against the spirituality of India or the "blank darkness" of Africa. The same is true of discussion of these and other places in terms of "aborted or failed modernity" or indeed of "incomplete or underdeveloped development" ("Writing," 367, 369). Such exegeses, contestatory as they are in certain circumstances and certain hands (on "development," one thinks of Frank's influential work on Latin America, Walter Rodney's on Africa, and Chandra's on India), can also fail to query teleological colonizing history itself. Uncritical in this measure, they continue—or risk continuing—cultural colonizations. Their recent material consequences are manifest enough in the collapse of Asian, Latin American, and ex-Soviet economies to the advantage of those of the United States primarily and of Europe secondarily—achieved, precisely, by the imposition of a particular kind of "free capital flow" that underdeveloped with a vengeance.

Popular discourse does not fail to reveal the procedures at work, taking them as no less *natural* than universal. Thus a report in the *New York Times* rather surprisingly discussed free capital traffic and its results under a headline catching western aggression, presumably unwittingly, in properly sexualized terms: "How U.S. Wooed an Already Yielding Asia to Let Cash Flow In." (This was the run-on, page-wide headline; the front page omitted Asia's collusion.) The essay was the second of four whose overall title implied, however, that no one was responsible: "Global Contagion. A Narrative." Days later, Michael Wines used on another part of the world the same colonizing discourse, not sexualized now but paternalist: "Struggling Ukraine Teeters between East and West." "The *trappings* of a Western democracy are *all in place*," he wrote skeptically but expectantly. "Ukraine can hold free elections *with the best of them*, and *its leaders say* they are committed to laissez-faire capitalism and enlightened self-rule"— save for the indigenous rub: "But too often, it is a shell concealing an Eurasian core" (A1, my italics). One craves ironic parody, down to the masterfully curled lip of that superior *an*. The essay belies the hope. Wines writes of incompetence, of the weight of a controlled economic past, of inability to do "things right" by laissez-faire capitalism and enlightened democracy (A4). The poor benighted heathen can't defeat that Eurasian core. So we have a patronizing tale of a Ukraine striving to hold onto universal natural values benignly offered by the West, yet not quite able to manage because of its people's inherent waywardness. For help, the article begins, they must ask western bearers of the burden. It is not hard to see in all this how the idea of history's end in eventual death of differences is western business as usual. In the West, it is popularly even told as such, triumphally fused with our well-known "exports."

What is clear is that we need to stand both against these sets of ideas and against "this death," to use Fanon's words again (*Black Skin*, 225). The self-evident lie of the cultural claims that accompany the aforenamed forbiddings, closures, taints, hypocrisies, and corruptions only confirms the view of those many, from T. S. Eliot to Aimé Césaire and beyond, who have urged that to seek to destroy cultures different from one's own, or even just to cut oneself off from them, is inevitably to destroy one's own. A culture priding itself on achieving "universal" closure and so wanting to map itself by victorious force onto all others not only murders them. It kills itself. "A people," wrote Unamuno's younger contemporary José Ortega y Gasset, "is a way of life," cultures order "surrounding matter" differently and develop their own "particular energies," each enriching the world in "incalculable" and incalculably diverse ways (*Meditations*, 105–6). And like all living organisms, cultures need interweavings and exchanges with others, in and through their very differences: Harris' "mutualities." "Cultures are constantly challenged, pushed about by other cultures," Achebe writes, and while a momentarily weaker or invaded culture may be changed, "it will modify itself and move on . . . if it is alive" (*Conversations*, 66). So cultures also need the vivacity of their own deep traditions—not sealing them in ever darker myths of self-satisfied universality. "No living culture is ever static," Ngũgĩ adds; it must constantly feed off its own past, present, and future and off those of cultures with which it is always in close or distant contact (*Homecoming*, 4; cf. *Writers*, 3–27). Cultures and their histories are always "relationships and processes that have constructed contingent and unstable identities" (Prakash, 370) in themselves and in their exchanges with different cultures. These things, too, this book hopes at least partly to reflect—in its arguments and in its patchwork.

It may be useful, at this point, to quote some comments on an artwork whose importance, even centrality, to a repoliticized western tradition is not doubted by its overweening proselytizers—although given the work's ambiguities, its *centrality* certainly should be. In Chapter 10, we shall see how this work has been adopted obliquely, so to speak, just to question such centrality. The comments concern the hero's descent in *Don Quijote* into the cave of Montesinos. Slashing with his sword through undergrowth to get to its mouth, he made such a noise that "a huge number of great crows and jackdaws flew out, so thick and fast that they tumbled Don Quixote to the ground." Unamuno saw this scene as an allegory of the effort to get deep into one's traditions, clearing away the undergrowth hiding them, facing the jackdaws and crows who set up as guards of the entrance to their "enchanted abyss." Thence they never sweep down or plunge into its depths, and yet they will dare to caw and cackle about their rights as inhabitants of the interior. The tradition they invoke is not truly traditional; they call themselves the voice of the people, and they are no such thing. The din of their cawing has made the people think they believe what they do not believe, and thus it is doubly necessary to delve into the bowels of the abyss in order to extract from it the living soul of the people's belief.

And before plunging into and burying oneself in the abyss of the true beliefs and traditions of the people . . . it is necessary to hack at and cut down the weeds which clutter and encumber the entrance. When you go to do it, they will tell you that you want to stop up the cave and prevent access to its inhabitants. They will call you a disloyal son, an outcast, and anything else that occurs to them. Turn a deaf ear to all such cawing. (*Our Lord Don Quijote*, 192–93, II.18–23)

The "living soul" of a tradition—need one say?—is by definition in movement, or else it would not be living. "A rounded voice/issues from the deep well of sound," wrote Harris in "The Mute at the Well," "in words of dancing pleasure, the raw scintillating/hush of passion" (*Eternity*, 21). The weeds to be cut down cut off the light and block the entrance. Opened to people's coming and going, the voice of the living soul mixes with other traditions, changes and develops, growing onto new and unwonted paths, which are yet fruitions from its own depths. Unfamiliar to the "crows and jackdaws," they are fearsome. One doubts that Unamuno had much like Goethe's earlier idea in mind. But he was a person of international culture, who would have been as appalled by today's self-elected guardians as he finally was by the Falangist General José Millán Astray's contempt for intellect and encomium of death. The cry "¡Viva la Muerte!" was one that condemned culture and tradition to the cave's deadly darkness. Unamuno refused all it stood for, living "long enough," declares José Saramago, "to see his mistake" if able to do "little to correct it" (*Year*, 327), and soon thereafter dying in grief over his misapprehension of the Falange—an error whose correction meant, *then*, that he could only despair of the future. No culture lives without always evolving. No culture that freezes survives. Most especially, perhaps, as Seneca long ago remarked, is the fictive or creative imagination in constant motion: "Nulla sine motu ars, nulla mutatio est"—"there is no art without movement, no change whatever" (*Epistulae*, lxv.11). What have been thought as European national cultures—even more, as national literatures—marked particular places and peoples at a particular historical moment: one now past, whose crowing is a false nostalgia.

The raucous cawing and cackling are brute noise of panic, dim comprehension that "the Civilized" must learn "to honor, recognize [and] describe the Savage" in terms set by the latter, who could long ago "describe the Civilized"—to adapt James Baldwin. "The only way to prevent this," he echoed others, "is to obliterate humanity" (*Notes*, xiii–xiv). The empire is inevitably fighting back—with the victim's particular advantage, Es'kia Mphahlele agrees, that "we know almost everything about him [the oppressor] and he knows nothing about us" (*Down*, 219; cf. *African Writing*, 12). The victim, Philip adds bitingly, has to be "a Caucasianist": "We who have lived in the belly of the whale—shark is maybe more accurate a symbol—for so long, surely . . . *we*—'the Others'—are the true experts." The victim studies "European cultural practices" with an aim to subvert this "Other's" hegemony (*Frontiers*, 69, 266). "Are you girls doing some sorta anthropological study of these Indians?" a white male tourist asks three mature Indian women note-taking at New York's National Museum of the American Indian. "We *are* Indians . . . , and we're doing an anthropological study of white tourists" (Hilden and Huhndorf, "Performing," 163). This is the more reason why the cawing imposes obliteration, refusing "openness of mind and . . . readiness to accept another way of looking at reality" (Achebe, *Conversations*, 64). For the voice it seeks to gag, "once filled with rage and pain that corroborated the reality of the jailer, is addressing another reality, in other tongues. The people who think of themselves as White have the choice of becoming human or irrelevant." Which we become depends on whether or not we can begin to learn different tongues, stretch to know something of different realities, give up that singular regard for Power and Plunder on which "that identity which calls itself White has always seemed to depend." As we begin so to learn, we will also make a richer identity, for you dehumanize others only by dehumanizing yourself (Baldwin, *Notes*, xv; cf. 25).

Even the most superficial awareness of elements taken to ground the concept and practice of "literature" (and any number of other intellectual and material practices that one might wish to interrogate) suggests that these, and its, universalizing views have *always* been untenable, even in the culture that supports them. What follows attempts to show not only why this is so from within that European culture—trying to grasp the development, reason, and action of a series of cultural instruments and their operation *against* (and *with*) alternatives—but also why it is so from without: suggesting (here) just a few cases where counterclaim, reuse, and deliberate "antiuse" mark the grounds of different homes. While for these last I focus mostly on Africa and, especially, the Caribbean (which Achebe has described as for its size "perhaps the most dynamic literary environment in the world in our time"; *Conversations*, 173; where Ngũgĩ finds "the most exciting literary outbursts in the world today"; *Homecoming* 81; and which Kamau Brathwaite characterizes as having "produced more brilliant word-skattering literature per head of population . . . than perhaps anywhere else in the world"; Editor's note, 4), I sometimes knock on other doors, I hope with suitably wary gentleness and readiness to listen—which is why, too, I quote many voices. I do so because, as what follows often notes, one great peril is that of reducing endlessly diverse cultures to a single Other of one Same, the West's "non-West" (Nandy, *Intimate*, 73).

For we must beware of the homogenizing stew. It may be the case that instruments of a conquering culture mix with cultural forms of a conquered to compose, as Michael Taussig avers, "a chamber of mirrors reflecting each stream's perception of the other" (*Shamanism*, 218), but the general kind of sense his phrase makes hides the perils of its imprecision (if clear enough in the single case he was exploring). Nandy is perspicuous in showing how the mutuality comes from a certain shared "social consciousness" whose "codes" "alter the original cultural priorities on both sides and bring to the center of the colonial culture subcultures previously recessive or subordinate in the two confronting cultures" (*Intimate*, 2). For we cannot forget that each victim's chambers differ, that material organization and spiritual and conceptual structures are total homes that are never the same as one another; a conqueror's technique is to make them all one. Nor must we forget that the first violence and continuing power are still the conqueror's. Cultures differ not only in their own traditions, organizations, and institutions, but (therefore) in the ways and whats of their appropriations—varied even in one culture, according for example as they occur "not only in familiar disciplinary institutions such as the school or the family or the court of law, but in a host of other arenas such as religion, politics, and art" (Chatterjee, "Disciplines," 25). By from time to time proposing varieties of differences (not pretending to be able to approach them in detail—and certainly not from within), I hope to help undermine the constant contrary temptation of a conquering West.

I add that the criticisms and analyses to follow do not constitute some mea culpa for being born to a European culture that has historically dominated others in often cruel and violent ways. Besides the (here irrelevant) fact that no culture has ever been free of such violences, the idea of such a mea culpa makes no sense to me. Indeed it smacks of overreaching self-indulgence. Guilt and atonement are due from those who use cultural instruments for harm—those who did so in the past or compound them in the present. Those born to a culture are not *guilty* of its past—but we are *responsible* to it and must be *responsive* to it. To recognize "one's own place in a community" is to accept, as Aryeh Neier puts it, "that this imposes certain political obligations" ("Watching Rights"). As we live in a mutual exchange of benefits and duties in a community, so are we responsible and accountable for that community's behavior to others. To belong to a culture is to be willy-nilly responsible for all deeds done by its means and in its name—a responsibility that increases the more we share and fully enjoy our culture. All who have suffered and do suffer from that culture's uses justly demand accountability and expect the responsibility that goes with belonging to a community. Indeed, where cultural dominance and oppression are concerned, its victims are especially right to hold those who still natively benefit by them to such responsibility. Beneficiaries have an obligation to counter present and future hostile consequences and to change conditions that enable—make—their continuance. But responsibility and responsiveness *to* the past are not the same as responsibility *for* it. To say otherwise is a perilous exercise in cant, confusing circumstance with agency and cultural life with some uses of cultural instruments. It is perilous because it incites the facile demagoguery of dismissing all responsibility ("I can't help where I was born") and of defending a culture as universal (by its longevity and living force).

I have noted that we see daily the insensate ends of this demagoguery in claims making beneficiaries victims, privilege deprivation, deprivation equality, advantage disadvantage, white black. This is "*adversative* action," a world upside-down: how can one not recall Thucydides' argument that the Peloponnesian Wars began in just these misuses of language? "Words have no words for words that are not true," Philip quotes W. H. Auden, "hiding the body dying behind the words," she adds (*Frontiers*, 254). So in the United States, we ever more often see white men claim to be "victims" of affirmative action—and laws passed or erased accordingly. Contrariwise, of a sudden they claim to be the Indian who is to benefit from such action: "How," asks Jamaica Kincaid of such, "do you get to be the sort of victor who can claim to be the vanquished also?" (*Lucy*, 41). How is it that "the *ability* to use the voice of the Other," Philip wonders, "has for the most part realized itself in the oppressor using the voice of the oppressed, and not the other way around" (*Frontiers*, 274)? Blind champions of hegemonic culture forget—deny—that past cultural oppressions and injustices inhabit the present. The welfare of societies, their very existence, exact this recognition and the necessary redress it entails. Certainly, there *is* guilt *now*, as Philip puts it too gently (not for her, but for us of the hegemonic culture): "by virtue of living in the West, and partaking, however unwillingly, in some of the advantages that come from living here I, too, am implicated and share in the responsibility the West must take for the plight of many of these [developing] countries. My morning cup of cappuccino is closely linked to the skewing of these cash-crop economies to the consumption habits of the West." This coffee, "our cheap clothes, the computers we use," the food we eat, the communications we enjoy are privileges "bought at the expense of others" by which "*all* our hands are soiled" (*Frontiers*, 61, 259). The *New York Times* pieces mentioned earlier are all accidentally crystal clear on this.

These blind champions kill both knowledge and compassion—not the kind that takes a Cambodian war orphan to an alien culture to display the compassion and forget her. That kind thrives. Harder is the sort which strains to know the past that its knower may be responsible to the present. Such a one, says Jan Carew, "must penetrate into the unfathomable silences where a part of the . . . past is entombed, he must gnaw at the bones of universal griefs, and the reservoir of compassion in his heart must be limitless" (*Fulcrums*, 108). Perhaps only victims of past violences and their continuance may fully know these many silences, that imposed by conquerors who, like god of the first word and then Babel, enforce their "words and more words," those worn by victims as resistance or from knowing that everything's and everyone's "sound, speech, or language" are silences to their oppressors (Philip, *Looking*, 12, 35). These are the victims' legacies: silences that imbue their present as vast loss. For the perpetrators, these silences were/are a means among many. *Their* descendants and opponents must try to hear across and through them, "listen and allow [themselves] time to feel" (Mphahlele, *Down*, 218). Like the voices of ancient Chinese poetry of which Stephen Owen writes, echoing Achebe, Coomaraswamy, Baldwin, Mphahlele, or Philip, we of the present West "cannot expect them to speak to the concerns of [our] world; it is we who must be changed to hear them" (*Traditional*, 6). Compassion needs memory. Responsibility demands history, histor*ies*—the sounds of silences. To mock one is to comply with denial of the others. All, where cultural differences are at issue, require attention, willingness to listen, readiness to hear. To defend a culture by sealing it from others, fitting it between straitened gates of sameness, marks a fearful despair, an insecurity of origins.

To defend a culture in these last ways implies denigrating others—as if there must be one universal culture—even though to denigrate *any* culture is meaningless. Cultures exist in history. They are places, events, and experiences in which we are born and from which we spring. In themselves and in relations with different cultures, they are both "good" and "bad." The place and meaning of such judgments require explanation and detail, for they immediately seem to suppose some site outside any particular culture. Yet their where, what, how, and why certainly first need teasing out from a specific cultural context. To some degree, some elements of this are what my earlier chapters essay. At the same time, as cross-cultural judgments, at the very least when concerned with relations between cultures, they clearly must be unfolded from some sort of cultural interweaving. At the twenty-first century's turn, cultures anyway globally engage with one another in new and unfamiliar ways. All the chapters of this book try to offer differing ways, degrees, and examples of interweaving cultures. They are linked, too, by recurrent explanatory and illustrative motifs: Venice as emblematic but equivocal city of a conquering West; Descartes and cartesianism as ambiguous imposing "source" of one kind of reason; the Spanish so-called Generation of '98 (scarred by last loss of empire in the Spanish-American war) whose ambivalent nostalgia for imperial grandeur exacted new versions of Spanish and European history and of the invasion of the Americas, 1492 and 1898, violently opening and closing one (version of) history; Don Quijote as model "frontier" figure between geographies and varieties of history; sparrows, spiders, and bees, webs and honey as signals of different *rationes*, kinds of writing, dilemmas of pleasure and knowledge, modes of tradition. . . . While two of these also have chapters devoted to them, their recurrence intends to mark how cultural instruments, their making, their processes, and their effects, however separable, are at the same time interwoven. These efforts seem to me to return to an earlier point, part of our cultural responsibility in this time and place.

I happen to have been born, bred, and mostly formally educated in Europe. My culture is *per necessitatem* European. Further, it is in large degree remnant of a culture that has in late centuries been thought more or less its quintessence—that of German and central European Jewry. In our case, it came through the textile community of nineteenth- and early twentieth-century Manchester—home of Engels and Herzl, and of close aunts, one of whom, Erna Reiss, the second Englishwoman to be admitted to the Inns of Court as a barrister, was Chaim Weizmann's assistant at times during the post—World War I debates before becoming a Northern Circuit judge, while another, Lily, was among the first to help build and run mass public housing. Our father began World War I with Edmund de Rothschild, David Ben-Gurion, and Itzhak Ben Zwi (whom he promoted to sergeant), disliked T. E. Lawrence in the mess, was friends with Jacob Epstein (after being on his court-martial), chatted with David Lloyd George at the Armenonville in 1919, played bridge with Sun Yat Sen in Shanghai in 1921: we were not from a culturally deprived or underprivileged community. But as often, later conditions modified the past in oddly displacing ways. For three of us raised and first educated in Hardy's Dorset, social and financial circumstance made most of our youthful acquaintance members of a varyingly "ancient" Catholic and Protestant gentry, the West Dorset "County." A northerner and Jew whose height and mien were Sephardic, our father (who with his family thought our name from Portuguese *Reis* and our ancestors part of the sixteenth—seventeenth century exodus to northern Europe, settling in Palatine Heidelberg and later moving to Manchester—where they lived, laughably enough, at the end of another Palatine in Didsbury, called by the bus conductors "Yidsbury" and the "Palestine Road") was twice foreign. So, I suppose, were we. Certainly at boarding school, my brother and I were "Yids." Our diminutive grandmother (who never lost her strong German accent), aunts, and father were as unfailing a source of other boys' mirth as they had been earlier for our cousins: "Look out! Reiss' aunts are coming under the door!"

Perhaps such things and the countless minor slights which mostly only hindsight explains (and as often only hindsight sees) are why all three of us now live as émigrés—although my sister recalls no very evident contempt. I write this not to appropriate or lay claim to kinds of violent exclusion that so many have endured in this century—among them one of the dedicatees of this book. Such rancid me-too-ism repels not just by its appropriation, but by its claim of instant empathy and untroubled grasp of experiential and cultural diversity. No one tortured us, took our names and language, forced us to various slaveries, or made us suffer even less urgent nastiness.[9] We were neither "islanded in the midst of marginal tides of sorrow, despair, hope, whirlpools of anxiety, cataracts of rage" (Carew, *Fulcrums*, 102) nor set in Philip's "geography of exile" (*Frontiers*, 10). But this past marks the place from whence I must speak and the ordinariness of these kinds of not-too-uneasy dislocations. For first, our culture is not a choice, Césaire reminds us, but birth and belonging (Baldwin, *Nobody*, 53); we are "immersed in it like the drop of water in the passing cloud" (Ortega, *Meditations*, 103). Second, these dislocations should make us more, not less, aware of the need to know our own culture even as we venture on the seas of others', trying not to take but to stretch toward and feel for other peoples' homes, to interweave cultures—to realize Harris' mutualities, even at the risk that before these silences, "Words strain,/Crack and sometimes break, under the burden,/Under the tension, slip, slide, perish" (Eliot, "Burnt Norton," *Four Quartets*, 8). Perhaps too these dislocations and the fact that our family, like so many in this century's first half, was deeply involved in war and political argument are not alien to what I see as an ongoing effort to understand the origins of our Euro-American modernity.

My earlier *Discourse of Modernism* and *The Meaning of Literature*, like *Tragedy and Truth* and even *Toward Dramatic Illusion* before them and *Knowledge, Discovery and Imagination* and *Mirages of the Selfe* more recently and now, are efforts to understand how particular forms of cultural analysis and practice *grew into* our modernity and to grasp something of the consequences they inevitably had. At the same time, successfully or not (the thing is hard), they try to show how tied to particular historical event and social conjuncture these discursive practices were. The "other end" of the instauration these works explored was the topic of *The Uncertainty of Analysis*, examining how European efforts in this century to reuse and restructure older forms of its discourse led at best to ambivalent results, at worst to repetitious aporias. Taken together, these works conclude that the practices (epistemes? classes of discourse? regimes of meaning?) into which they delve cannot themselves, as such, be directly turned to renewal. This is not to say that emergent practices are not now available or that even seemingly defunct or residual ones may not be. It is to say that they can be used only in quite new configurations dependent on and related to a whole environment that includes the many cultures that European culture of the preceding five hundred years exploited and oppressed precisely by ignoring the specificity of *their* historical environments, *silencing* them.

Here, too, the initial object is to analyze the nature and origins of some modern European culs de sac. But it is not enough just to look at their present aporias, nor just to condemn those who blindly defend them, however virulently they do so. In a contemporary world ever and ever more marked by conflict, barriers, and dissonance, we need to envisage new departures. And that cannot occur without continuing efforts to understand reusings that reinstate such same old processes as have only too well shown their wrecking capacities. It also cannot occur without attempting new weavings in which these old processes necessarily have their place—as many of this book's chapters try to show. This is not to make gigantic claims but to participate in change and *being* changed. As they stand, these are a small contribution to what may one day become new forms of cultural production and new practices of political association.

In many ways, then, this book follows directly on *The Meaning of Literature*. It pursues in a general way issues raised in that book's epilogue, as a subsequent one will do so in the context of the particular contemporary situation of Europe. At the same time, as I have just suggested, they have become personalized for me in unfamiliar ways (in part because polemics force one to take stock of an intellectual trajectory). But if this thinking and research engage much in my own life, they also try to intervene particularly in some of the major cultural debates and developments of our time. They wish to do so by arguing that cultural production (in a "narrow" sense of that phrase: referring to the fictive imagination, not to the putative objects of sad anthropology and ethnography) not only can affect social life more broadly understood but is inevitably caught up in and with all the other human practices that compose such life. This book makes the case mostly for literary work—or, rather, since it does not limit the case to post-Renaissance western Europe, to work of the "fictive imagination" (of which, as I say, *literature*—like *orature*—would have been one historical form and practice; see, for example, Reiss, *Knowledge*, xiv–xvi).

More vitally, this research and thinking make one see that the relative freedoms of such cultural creation and the particular forms of exchange that occur in its realm can *change* other practices: the point of my earlier quotations from Haidu, Ngũgĩ, Philip, Richards, and Soyinka. This proposition has been doubted, in recent years most steadily by Marxist or *marxisant* critics, but C. L. R. James made it a main tenet of his important *History of Negro Revolt*, published in 1938 and reprinted four times as a *History of Pan-African Revolt*. The very rule of the *négritude* writers, Léopold Sédar Senghor held, was that "independence of the spirit, *cultural independence*, is the necessary prerequisite of other independences: political, economic, and social" ("African Road," 69). And if against these Ngũgĩ urges that claims for *precedence* of cultural over political and economic practices are clearly false (*Homecoming*, 11) he agrees that they are intricately and unshakably tied, changing of forms being many-directional (*Homecoming*, 26). In this dialectical complex, the *imaginary island* of this book's epigraph from Saramago (*Stone Raft*, 48) *is* created. The issue will recur, but doubts over such relations and exchanges between discourses and practices took hold even before the European eighteenth century, due to assumptions about the autonomy of all human praxes and spheres of attention. Soyinka calls this "a recognisable Western cast of mind, a compartmentalising habit of thought which periodically selects aspects of human emotion, phenomenal observations, metaphysical intuitions and even scientific deductions and turns them into separatist myths (or 'truths') sustained by a proliferating superstructure of presentation idioms, analogies and analytical modes." At their clearest, these are the disciplinary practices of the West's regime of knowledge and power. Soyinka amusingly imagines them as the freight of "a steam-engine which shunts itself between closely-spaced suburban stations," picked up and dropped off as so many wagonloads of "truths" (*Myth*, 37).

My first chapter gives most of its scrutiny to the claims made about such autonomy, their aims, consequences, and wider cultural patterns into which fit both the claims and the supposed autonomy. Most generally, it shows them essential to the kinds of canting denials, demagogic refusals, and irresponsibility we saw earlier, disculpating an oppressive use of cultural instruments on grounds of their "universality." So, for example, claims about the equality and freedom of individuals rely on ways of understanding that take such "individuals" from complex real-life contexts, split the contexts into separate activities and experiences treated by different knowledge "disciplines," and make manifold strangers of people who are not. Philosophy, psychology, economics, sociology, and whatnot are unable to put poor broken Humpty Dumpty together again as an unequal, unfree member of a collectivity. This chapter discusses such "autonomization," especially in its manifestation in the aesthetic realm along with specific kinds of memory and nostalgia, making not a little of *négritude* as a form of "othering" such western "autonomy." Subsequent chapters build on divers elements and consequences of this first chapter's arguments as they relate to the fictive imagination, its place in European culture, and its role in present and future cultural interweavings. For if claims of "autonomy" are a response to one particular cultural category or instrument, they and others are buttressed to similar effect and purpose by others. Subsequent chapters thus discuss a series of such instruments, from the idea of otherness to the *ratio* of tragedy, from uses of mimesis and representation to essays of universalist self independence, from history and memory (or their difficulties) to claims about individualism and the making of fictions, from the titles of science, analysis, and aesthetics to the demands of locality.

The second chapter discusses the very notion of "other" as it has been too much used in contemporary western criticism—returning here as well to *négritude* and debates around it. The third chapter examines tragedy as a literary mode that archetypically utters otherness and the experience of culture as a succession of divides whose depiction in tragedy is also strictly and uniquely western—but that has nonetheless been ascribed to or turned by different cultures. This then takes me, in Chapter 4, onto the equally archetypal western aesthetic notions of mimesis and representation. This chapter suggests that efforts to claim some sort of monolithic universalist value for western literature, one based in a particular idea of *mimetic* art, are actually rendered footless from within and without. From within, they are sapped by a tradition about the meaning of such concepts and practices as mimesis and metaphor that may have taken a largely reductive form during and after the European Renaissance but that was far more fluid and complex before. From without they are queried by experiences and ideas of the fictive imagination's relation to its sociocultural embedding that cannot be rendered in any ready way by familiar mimetic supposals. This chapter, too, discusses notions of mimesis as they have been used to seize different cultures' notions of how the fictive imagination works and looks at what they do with them or against them.

In ways the reading makes clear, this leads directly to Chapter 5's discussion of "cartesian rationalism" (a favorite figure of different cultures' readings and usings of the West) and, again, history and othering. Now too—and through Descartes—it moves to consideration of subject and self as western cultural instruments—or *rationes*; hence the following Chapter 6 focusing on the Freudian notion of the self as an instrumental product of the same cultural history and on its questioning elsewhere. Grounded in matters raised in the preceding chapters, these two thus now add the issue of the historical making and present construct of western experiences of the self, issues that will crop up continually in later chapters around this charged and problematic instrument. And they lead directly to Chapter 7, querying the very idea of a self-conducted, subjectively constructed, and constructivist rational scientific discourse (one form of what Édouard

Glissant calls "totalitarian monolingualism")—more precisely, trying to show rapidly its production from a particular history and the kinds of questions raised against it from elsewhere. Here I use Witold Gombrowicz as a central figure, because his questioning is partly from within a European tradition but partly from without: coming both from what he and his colleagues saw as an "edge" of Europe and from Latin America, where he spent more than twenty years—the most productive of his writing life. He thus also makes a direct bridge to the next chapters.

From here, I pass more directly into discussion of what other fictive imaginings have done with some of these variously central instruments of western culture—dealing chiefly, now, with the Caribbean and Latin America (although, I recall, every chapter considers such "turning" to a greater or lesser extent). Chapter 8 focuses on Brathwaite and the creating of a Caribbean culture and a "nation language" by taking over and turning various western notions of the aesthetic in general and the poetic in particular. Chapters 9 and 10 discuss the uses of mimesis, history, and geography in Caribbean writing. Chapter 9 does so finally by following the fortunes of a particular trope, that of flowers—or flora more generally—as a way to "escape" an imposed history by grasping a local geography: subverting, fictively at least, continuing western aspirations to economic and political domination, what J. J. Thomas in 1889 called "the dark outlines of a scheme to thwart political aspiration in the Antilles," "thinly draped" behind Froude's "rhetorical flowers" (*Froudacity*, 5). Chapter 10 uses the figure of Don Quijote to trace actual confrontation of such an imposed history by different histories. Thus do both turn western discourses. Chapter 11 compares the uses of (what I call) geography and history in Caribbean and Latin American writing to suggest how both are writing back in different ways against western instruments.

The Meaning of Literature argued that what has been called "literature" in Euro-American parlance was created and consolidated roughly from the first quarter of the seventeenth century, chiefly then in France and England, somewhat later in the German lands and elsewhere. It was part of a broader response to a widespread sense of social dissolution. Its constitution was overtly political, however structurally and functionally imbricated that aim may have been with others—principally those I called ethical, aesthetic, and epistemological. I believe that this literature lost its "organic" social role, that of "mutual action and reaction," as Ngũgĩ has it (*Moving*, 27), in the course of the nineteenth century, although various inertias—

willful and not—have sustained it. Much of what I argue in the last chapters of this book shows a renewed organic role (that the book on contemporary Europe will try to apply specifically to *its* cultural arena): showing how many of these instruments and categories can in fact be turned back for other uses, how different times and places do make, for instance, not just new geographies and histories but new ideas and *practices* of what those things may even be. This renewed organic role will be—is—different in context, analogous in function. In this regard, we may fruitfully distinguish between "literature" as one historically punctual manifestation of the fictive imagination and the wider human capacity of the fictive imagination itself, such that in its changed organic role, we may need to find another name for its functioning.

The risks of foolishness and utopianism in some aspects of this project are clear: for you have, Günter Grass remarked, "no distance." "But sometimes," as he went on, "literature has the possibility to reflect fear in the mind, and perhaps if you write it first, you can stop bad results from happening" (quoted in Fein, "Günter Grass"). In the present age, it is not hard to be convinced that economic, commercial, legal, and political forces have any way to be countered by others—no less powerful, if more fluid and less definite. I call them "cultural." It is not hard to be convinced, either, that old forms of business as usual in the Euro-American cultural context that sees the appearance of a book like this one are no longer viable, even in their increasingly polarized homelands, let alone globally. Discussion of these issues that questions the instruments of that culture has to set them in a far wider topography and finally give them no more than equal play with those of different cultures. And it has to counter the autonomies—and antimonies—mentioned in ways of which Ngũgĩ sees Brathwaite an ideal teacher, finding "no barriers between geography, history and literature. [For him, w]hat form[s] the African and the Caribbean sensibility [can]not be divorced from the landscape and the historical experience" (*Writers*, 134). That is where this book will end, but all these things are what it is about.

1

Uses of Autonomy: Nostalgias, Prescriptions, and the Fictive Imagination

Notions that human practices occupy separate compartments and are in some fundamental way autonomous of one another seem recently to have reached a paroxysm in the West (spread, too, to all other events and phenomena in so far as they are held to be conceivable). Supported and legitimized by some centuries of claim, they are now the very ground of a "postmodernism" that makes fragmentation and juxtaposition of separates its life principle. They produce and are balanced by nostalgias for wholeness whose pedigree is rather newer but whose dream of enchanted plenitude has its own distracting and misdirecting effects, or aims. Literary practice and its criticism, as well as ideas of the aesthetic more generally, have played and continue to play their role in giving weight to such notions, which lie at the end of a cultural development in the West that began at least four centuries ago. What that same West since, and elsewhere more recently, has known as *literature* took a major role in this development (a centering of certain claims and practices, marking "consolidation of a dominant discourse," and soon given the name of "progress"). This suggests that the fictive imagination may now be able once again to play a part as, but differently, renewing.

So it is germane to approach the terms of this chapter's title through a fictional conversation between two historical notables, one of whom regales the other each evening by describing a city through which he has passed on his travels . . . or might have passed . . . or imagines he could have passed . . . or imagines might have been there to pass through . . . or to imagine passing through. . . .

Such syntactic jollities can clearly be endless, and I would not be first to have them trace an autonomous path. Although "*clear*" may not be how best to describe them, their illimitable "indecidability" is why the traveler's repertory, says the teller in Italo Calvino's *Invisible Cities*, "could be called inexhaustible." The conditional—or optative—is vital, however. It signals that such self-reproducing autonomy must come to an end (contrary wishes notwithstanding), and that if it in fact fails to do so, then that very failure *has* an end—one perhaps of hiding a fundamentally ideological claim. Indeed, autonomy comes to its end with and on the divulging of such claim—when the real in which the text is embedded becomes visible. For now the traveler, we are told,

was the one who had to give in. Dawn had broken when he said: "Sire, now I have told you about all the cities I know."

"There is still one of which you never speak."

Marco Polo bowed his head.

"Venice," the Khan said.

Marco smiled. "What else do you believe I have been talking to you about."

The emperor did not turn a hair. "And yet I have never heard you mention that name."

And Polo said: "Every time I describe a city I am saying something about Venice."

"When I ask you about other cities, I want to hear about them. And about Venice, when I ask you about Venice."

"To distinguish the other cities' qualities, I must speak of a first city that remains implicit. For me it is Venice."

"You should then begin each tale of your travels from the departure, describing Venice as it is, all of it, not omitting anything you remember of it."

The lake's surface was barely wrinkled; the copper reflection of the ancient palace of the Sung was shattered into sparkling glints like floating leaves.

"Memory's images, once they are fixed in words, are erased," Polo said. "Perhaps I am afraid of losing Venice all at once, if I speak of it. Or perhaps, speaking of other cities, I have already lost it, little by little." (86–87)

This colloquy on memory and imagination, nostalgia and loss, representation and reality, home and alienation, colonizing center and its "others" (the last being but versions of the first), origin and difference, occurs more or less at the midpoint of Italo Calvino's *Invisible Cities*. My set of oppositional terms intends mildly ironic attention to present fashion, to signal that *ideology* is, after all, in question. Emphasis on the exchange's centrality means to underscore western norms of aesthetic judgment, here the significance of the written artwork's midpoint—if the work follows prescriptions of coherence. Linking them tries to suggest at the outset that even the most apparently autonomous and self-contained of texts is grounded in an ineluctable sociopolitical reality. For, as the arguments of this chapter and of this book progress, such norms and prescriptions will themselves be seen to be aspects of what I am calling "cultural instruments." For now I just add that the Kahn is right: Venice, or indeed any other actually known city, has not been named before.

Still, Polo and Kublai Khan are visiting the city of Kinsai, with its

> bridges arching over the canals, the princely palaces whose marble doorsteps were immersed in the water, the bustle of light craft zigzagging, driven by long oars, the boats unloading baskets of vegetables at the market squares, the balconies, platforms, domes, campaniles, island gardens glowing green in the lagoon's grayness. (85)

Polo's own description of Kinsai had shown it much like Venice (one manuscript even saying so), down to its many bridges and the boats poling their way over the city's great lake.[1] He had, indeed, given the "City of Heaven," as its name translated, more space than any other (*Travels*, 213–29), a fact not indifferent to Calvino's tale, given its inspiration in *The Travels*, whose prologue tells how the Khan especially prized the Venetian for his ability to relate the "remarkable things he had seen" (41). The exchange just quoted had indeed been launched by Kublai's question, "Did you ever see a city resembling this one?" and Marco's answer: "No, sire, . . . I should never have imagined a city like this one could exist" (85).

Kublai's skepticism and the ensuing daylong silence are small wonder. Although the narrator may name a "palace of the Sung," he reveals a place more than akin to the almost mythical Adriatic city of northern Italy: yearly marrying the sea, jumping-off point for repeated Crusades against the infidel, origin—or something near—of modern financial and commercial styles and goals, founder of the "institution of permanent embassies" (Veyne, 26; Pemble, 75), inventor (perhaps) of the government archive as a basis for the subsequent writing of history (Pemble, 73–81), creator of the first germs of a modern press, greatest early center of printing,[2] menaced exemplar of a Renaissance whose glories founded the modern era of Europe and its avatars, symbol of a tolerant republican liberalism taken as the storied font of modern democracy, and, with its university of Padua, home of the origins of modern scientific method and reason, and so the earliest, Girolamo Cardano tells us, to forbid rewarded accusations of witchcraft (Weyer, 207: III.xiv). Small wonder, perhaps, that even the displaced Russian Joseph Brodsky might lay claim to Venice as "possibly one's own birthplace" (*Watermark*, 8).[3] And this, despite its being the builder, one should add, of the first ghetto: "the stones of Venice are cold," writes Kamau Brathwaite from a Caribbean homeland of which we will see much more, "gondolas of king arthur's nights bring the jews in at evening" ("Salt I," *X/Self,* 5). As capital city of the European imagination and of non-Europeans' imaginings of Europe, Venice holds a place of its own. Not for nothing did Moderata Fonte write in her 1581 romance, *Floridoro* (whose eighty-nine-stanza twelfth canto was an encomium of the city) that "Europe and the whole world" were under obligation to Venice and that the city "embraces a universal contract with the whole world ("abbraccia/Impresa universal con tutto il mondo") (*Tredici*, 199: xii.23; 207: xii.63).

Earlier medieval Venetian annals and ritual had embedded the city in a series of grounding European myths. Claiming the city to be ancient Aquileia, supposedly founded by the Trojan hero Antenor, they made it New Troy. Aquileia having been reputedly visited by the apostle Mark and his remains moved to Venice in the eighth century, the town was set in the foundational myth of Christian tradition and a cult established making Venice a New Jerusalem. It was also the direct successor of Imperial Rome, not only as its Trojan competitor but by the claim that survivors from ruined Rome had settled and created the city on the lagoon (Muir, 23–25; Tafuri, 14). These bonds of myth and history, church and state, Troy, Jerusalem, and Rome, eastern and western Mediterranean, were not all. Venice was seen—or saw itself—as a "second Constantinople." Here, too, sovereign title was supported by sacred device: the presence in the Church of San Salvador, fabled to have been founded at the urging of Christ, of the relics of the supposed Byzantine martyr Saint Theodore (Tafuri, 15–19). The city's basilica copied Constantinople's Apostoleion and was ornamented with Byzantine spoils (on these myths, see Brown, *Venice*). At the fall of the eastern empire's capital in 1453, Venice could thus be site of a *translatio Imperii* that made it rival not just ancient but also modern Rome, center of the Christian Mediterranean and western world. So it was that the Venetian Girolamo Muzio held in his 1571 *Lettere catholiche* that Venice was center of the real "new world," not through worldly treasures of the "Indies" but divine ones of "the supracelestial world." In this sense, as in that of material wealth, writes Federica Ambrosini, people could "say that the new world was wholly contained and as if epitomized in Venice." So Luigi Groto declaimed in 1556: "Wherefore one cannot tell whether Venice is in the world or the world in Venice. Here [are] the fortunate isles with their birds, . . . the new world with its riches and its varieties of species" (Ambrosini, *Paesi*, 185–86)—the whole great world in little.

This Venice exemplifies one Europe, the imperial, military, diplomatic, economic, cultural, political, and epistemological mastery which that continent exercised in historical fact and for which its name still stands in the lingering wish of many and the often ambivalent, not to say self-serving, opposition of many more (no more self-serving the one than the other). That is why two mid-sixteenth-century humanists, Girolamo Fracastoro and the ideologue architect Alvise Cornaro, imagined and planned recreating Venice as Tenochtitlán (Tafuri, 152–53). Just to have destroyed the by-then legendary lake-bound capital of Aztec civilization was not enough. It had to be absorbed, removed from its home, taken over, appropriated, made into a literally contained "other" of our "same"—ghettoized, one might say. It is no surprise to find Ambrosini describing "the Venetian public" as adhering closely, for at least the first decades of the sixteenth century, "to the Spanish point of view on the conquest" of the Americas (*Paesi*, 53). Seeing the same connection, Leopold Ranke, "discovering" the Venetian archives for modern historiography, described himself as "the Columbus of the *relazioni*" (Pemble, 77). Cultural memories lie deep; they and the claims they permit and conceal are curious in their surfacings and expressions. They are also why Alejo Carpentier, more equivocally than Brathwaite, had his noble Mexican *criollo* of *Concierto barroco*, seeking paternal Europe, leave cheerless Madrid to relish the virtues of electric Venice in its "splendid human energy," as John Ruskin had once insisted ("Traffic," 237), or indeed as had Petrarch not long after the historical Polo, half a millennium before, calling Venice "the most powerful and most magnificent city in our world" (*Letters of Old Age*, 1.115: IV.1—to Luchino dal Verme), and elsewhere "the most miraculous city of all those that I have seen—, and I have seen almost all those of which Europe is most proud" (*Le familiari*, 2.172: VIII.5—to "Olimpio" [Luca Cristiani]). Fonte's later encomium echoed multitudes.

Here, in Calvino's novel, the city of Shakespeare's merchant, Otway's preservation, Ruskin's stones, and Thomas Mann's death, of Galileo's thriving (his mistake was to leave), Bellini's majesty, Tintoretto's drama, Titian's grandeur, and Veronese's harmony—the last two of whom painted famed versions of that *Rape,* or *Abduction, of Europa* whose myth of divine election and violence remain foundational to imaginings of Europe—here, this exemplary city figures only by its "absence": in Polo's assertion that its very existence is "unimaginable" (*Invisible Cities,* 85).[4] Or rather it figures because one looking to describe, understand, explain, or imagine another place has to have a starting point, a place against which difference can be measured, "a first city that remains implicit." So it is said. But Polo is reserved, suitably relativist, one might say: "For *me* it is Venice." For you, it will be wherever you call home. If so, of course, the measure of comprehensible difference is limited and in good part unknowable, trammeled as it always is in one's own place, whose memory may be diluted as its image is absorbed into the images one has of other places, but which, by doing just that, simultaneously makes those latter images into versions of home: "Every time I describe a city I am saying something about Venice." So, too, in a sense I will be clarifying, are Brathwaite, Carpentier, and myriad others, still fighting, as they are, against the topography of a European-forged map, against the clamor of a voice made in Europe.

For the difficulty is not that speaking from such a home "devours" those of others, as Walter D. Mignolo remarks, but that "it banishes them from the view of those who belong to the" speaker's home (*Darker Side,* 5). "To make the alien familiar, it has to be translated into the categories of one's own culture." And this suppresses "alternative organizations of knowledge" (*Darker Side,* 199). Thus only things easily recognized by that home are accredited, such as in *the New York Times'* characterization of Rushdie's *Midnight's Children* as "a continent finding a voice," as if, Ahmad remarks, "one has no voice if one does not speak in English," as if millennia of poetry and prose, written and oral did not exist, as if only a text able to be defined in "metropolitan" norms could be "a 'true' narrative" (*In Theory,* 98, 105). We must hope, of course, that this cecity is an inevitable tendency rather than an absolute, laziness of attention rather than impossibility of knowledge. This is why decolonizing the mind (that of the colonizer, no less than that of the colonized) is at once so hard and so necessary. It means not making the alien familiar but the familiar alien.

Interest asserts this Venice's absence to be a hidden trace of ideological grip on the "other," of the mastery which Venice once and Europe later made their historic due. Interest may be right. It is surely true that ways of knowing, titles to authority, claims of possession, and patterns of right order characterizing the "Europe" it symbolizes have been made into a universal mold able rightly to shape or justly to exclude. In response, some interests may have to be manichean, simplifying complexities for *their* own ends. But just because we have no choice in having to speak from home, from some familiar place, so we have to sort out the complex legitimacies of history and memory from the reductive—and *se*ductive—simplicities of dogmatic interest. Like Kublai, we first need the generosity, sympathetic or not, to recognize their existence, then the patience to explore their complexities, and, yes, the interest to undertake the kinds of exchange with others' histories and memories as will go around or between efforts to impose monotonous claim. Like Saramago, we need to learn to tap the "data and minutiae" of "memory" to undermine and change the systems of dogmatic histor(iograph)y (*History*, 221).

It is most surely not enough to rant, with so many minatory contemporaries, about being snared in "the site whence one speaks," and to fancy—or pretend—one eludes it by wandering in such autonomous verbal indecidabilities as those that I proposed at the start of this chapter. Constructing identity, *knowing* identity (one's own or others'), at least partly requires notions of "home" and "elsewhere," whose actuality, Edward Said observes, "is always subject to the continuous interpretation and reinterpretation of their differences." These processes are ongoing, but ever anchored in some notion of home. To recognize them matters deeply. For they "are not mental exercises but urgent social contests involving such concrete political issues as immigration laws, the legislation of personal conduct, the constitution of orthodoxy, the legitimization of violence and/or insurrection, the character and content of education, and the direction of foreign policy" ("East," 3). To transform one home into another or to reclaim the first always involves a "redistribution of power relations" played out on the ground (Mignolo, 260). That is why, too, more useful than ranting about mental snares, are Brathwaite's "tact and selfless grace" attending to places, tones, and feel of elsewhere, letting play of contrast and difference focus in home as a necessary dwelling, not as a source of predatory will (*Contradictory Omens*, 61). These are not just correct pieties echoing as well Achebe, Baldwin, Coomaraswamy, or Owen, and will return.

"So then, yours is truly a journey through memory!" later protests "the Great Khan." "'It was to slough off a burden of nostalgia that you went so far away!' he exclaimed, or else: 'You return from your voyages with a cargo of regrets!' And he added, sarcastically: 'Meager purchases, to tell the truth, for a merchant of the Serenissima!' " (Calvino, 98). Memory and nostalgia are ineluctable elements in discovery and in all efforts to understand otherwise—to know different things in other ways. Not only is this because a home starting point is always in and on the mind, nor even because all knowing is already "theory-laden." It is also, Polo suggests, because knowing *demands* a point of departure: *e nihilo nihil*, as the old tag has it. And this is so even if one stresses, as Polo does, that the point in question is particular "to me." A Venice, I have sought to suggest, could in any case never be a "particular," myth-laden focal point, as it is of the European imagination. Its very stones, Ruskin told, encapsulated and embodied a story of Europe which will reecho throughout these chapters. Home and ideological interest are ineluctably bound together. That is why so much care is needed to disentangle them and tease out their complicated but at least partly distinguishable expectations and demands.

This brings me back to this chapter's title and the questions it addresses. For they bedevil our modernity, inertially, as it were—residues of that past to which I have been referring through Calvino. Who? "Our"? You ask. "What do you mean 'we,' whiteman?"—Well, all who live willy-nilly under the sway of the hegemonies of western aspirations; even those who, escaping them or removing them from the "center," are nevertheless obliged to engage them. These questions—here, and as already I have been suggesting—have to do with "autonomies" of discourse and practice, the function of literature, ideas of the aesthetic, exchanges of cultures, issues of ideology, history, and spirit of place—to say nothing of those concrete political actualities of which Said writes and variants of which I recalled in the Introduction: a tall order.

With growing frequency, critics and others assert, in Said's words, that "it has been the practice in the west since Immanuel Kant to isolate cultural and aesthetic realms from the worldly domain." With others, he proposes that "it has been the essence of experience in the west at least since the late eighteenth century not only to acquire distant domination and reinforce hegemony, but also to divide the realm of culture and experience into apparently separate spheres" (*Culture*, 58). Such autonomization of realms of understanding and practice is here offered as the very ground of empire and the ideology subtending it. This demands analysis, but before attempting it, I should say that however much separation of the aesthetic and the worldly has become a mantra of contemporary critical talk, these divisions of discourses and practices often put under the rubric of "autonomy" were always less a matter of *experience* than of *claim*—although no doubt from claim they could readily become something like "experience." And, by the twentieth century, they assuredly did become reified into the way systems of knowledge were understood to work: "such autistic undertakings," Jürgen Habermas has called them (*Past as Future*, 116).

Others do not stop at Kant. Anthony Cascardi has caught the cliché well even as he traces it to an origin in what is taken as the very place and time when modernity had its start. His *Subject of Modernity* makes two chief claims. One says that after the early seventeenth century in Europe, human praxis was held to derive from and be "legitimated" by an individual subject's will—a predatory will, source of distant domination. The other sees modernity as an arena of fractured and autonomous discourses whose real interaction that subject strives in vain to achieve through the operation of a disenchanted reason—a reason itself uprooted from its embedding in the world.[5] These autonomies supposedly create mutually destructive antinomies.

But to suppose divisions between areas of action and analysis also enables certain kinds of hegemony and legitimation: splitting, for example, the sphere of scientific procedure from that of value judgments, or the arena of political praxis from the philosophical argument of rights. They are held to work in parallel rather than in mutual engagement. Thus claims of equality and freedom typical of liberal morality were founded on practices of inequality and unfreedom in law (regarding women, slaves, and all nonowners); arguments of common rights in political theory faced distinctions of property and ownership in economic actuality; assertions of universal reason in philosophy confronted varieties of exclusionary justifications elsewhere. In our own moment, the selection of "the hundred best English-language novels" is supposed to have been made in an aesthetic discourse quite distinct from the political discourse of worldwide cultural relations and the economic discourse of the global marketplace (see Introduction, n. 8)—or indeed from local ones of education, government art funding, language politics, and ethnic cultures. If the last case seems bathetic, it is surely because autonomies separate these exercises from their wider implications.

Discourses associated for one purpose were divided again for another. Thus although the "liberal theory of power, namely the freedom of the members of civil society, could declare itself the enabling condition for rational knowledge, namely, the condition of freedom of speech and unhindered access to discourse" (an association Chatterjee calls "the founding moment of modernity"), they were redivided in a colonial arena, so that rational knowledge deployed by colonized thinkers could be held *not* to depend on political freedom. In Bengal, this meant a "split" in "the domain of civil society" itself, its two sides occupied separately by colonizer and colonized, "with the rights of the latter being regarded by the colonial state as inferior to those of the former" (Chatterjee, "Disciplines," 14). In certain colonized arenas, Frank argues, western economic analysis translated this putative split (corresponding to "spirit" versus "reason" and so on) into one between feudalism and capitalism. Once this was understood, it was said, the generous purveyors of the last merely had to make their wares available to the victims of the first for its pernicious effects to be overcome, Chatterjee's "political liberalism" here tied less to rational knowledge than to "the doctrine of free trade" (Frank, *Capitalism*, 67).[6] This analysis of "dual societies" usefully gave quite different cases the name and nature of European feudalism. Doing so, it hid the fact that the underdevelopment it associated with "feudalism" far from being defeated by capitalism was in fact *produced* by it as a necessary, integral component of capitalism's functioning. Analytical divisions served to hide actual interconnections (Frank, *Capitalism*, 145–46, 221–77; Frank, *Latin America*, 4, 221–47, 318–32, 350–61 for the dualism argument, the entire works for its rejection).

These examples begin to make clear that the idea of autonomy itself serves what one may well call ideological purposes and must anyway acknowledge as particular interests. To give contradictions separate spheres hides many of their implications even as it allows them to feed off one another. John Locke's argument, that property is so basic to being human that possession precedes the social contract, legitimates later inequalities by making nonowners not only less than human, but themselves responsible for being so: qua humans, they must either have failed fully to act as such (in not acquiring property) or have made a rational choice not to own. This justified many things, from limiting suffrage to property owners to the savage treatment of slaves and genocide of indigenous peoples. So it is no "paradox" that Locke had "no difficulty accepting that [human] freedoms could not and should not extend to African slaves" (Philip, *Frontiers*, 271). This case will return toward the end of Chapter 2. But such examples begin to make clear how the idea of autonomy was rooted in Enlightenment's own self-understanding and surely had (has), as I said, as much to do with claim as with experience, both on the part of formative actors of the Enlightenment and on that of later critics.

It seems clear enough that the arguments of these last have to do with what has been termed the "legitimacy of the modern age"—a notion which itself presupposes "a post-Hegelian or post-Marxist teleological view of history, for what, otherwise, can it *mean* to speak of an 'illegitimate development of human history?' " (Reiss, *Meaning*, 4). They concern, that is to say, an essentially European debate set both in long-term philosophical and political argument and claim, and in a specific historical context. They came together in discussions of Oswald Spengler, Ferdinand Tönnies, Weber, and others at least partly in reaction to revolution in Russia, World War I, the fall of Austria-Hungary, and the quite ubiquitous sense of endings. The debate continued in Edmund Husserl's questionings of the 1930s, in the work and unambiguous political activities of his pupil Martin Heidegger, and in the elucubrations of Walter Benjamin and members of the Frankfurt School.

The collapse of Weimar and establishment of the Third Reich highlighted the urgency of the debate's issues. World War II and the Holocaust made them anguishing. German thinkers, especially but not only, asked whether their recent history was unique, or whether Nazism and all its works were the natural outcome of Enlightened reason. This debate about "legitimacy" thus arose from a precise historical situation and the dilemmas it created. So Cascardi is entirely right to locate notions of autonomy and their intellectual history in the work of such as G. W. F. Hegel and György Lukács, Weber, Max Horkheimer, Theodor Adorno, and Habermas. They were and are engaging agonizingly immediate issues of guilt, responsibility, and legitimacy less of modernity than of a particular modern state and society. But then to add Richard Rorty, François Lyotard, and John Rawls, as Cascardi (not alone) does, both widens the case to that of "universal" Enlightened modernity and risks hiding a real history in idealist obfuscation, just as the *Historikerstreit* of 1980s Germany showed that to emphasize a "natural outcome" of Enlightenment could become an alibi, a means to evade specific responsibility. One thus abrogates the need to respond to the past of one's own.

The tactic once more showed the uses of Enlightenment self-understanding—which many trace from Miguel de Cervantes, Thomas Hobbes, René Descartes, and others, a historical claim that Chapters 5 and

6 contest directly. For this, too, may be to accept a self-evaluation whose ideological utility is becoming clear and that surely owes much to later interest. Maybe a bit unfairly, I will show two cases from Cascardi, both because
our quarrel is already public and because I can embed them in research of
my own. He insists that Descartes and Hobbes make "reason" set "history"
aside. Their "self-legitimizing project," he says, clearly "cannot fully com-
prehend the process of its own historical origination. Thus, rather than say
categorically that history is absent from the *cogito*, it would be more accurate to say that history is rendered unreadable by it" (*Subject*, 32). They
claim, he asserts, an "absolute" origin: a time out of, and that remains out
of and separate from, anything of history. There are real difficulties in this.

Firstly, history (understood both as actual events and as the narration
of them), whether personal or political, is certainly not absent from those
texts in which the *cogito* was first embedded. One could argue over its presence in the *Meditations*, but the *Discourse* is imbued with, and to a great extent grounded in, historical argument (Reiss, "Descartes"). Secondly, if history was indeed "rendered unreadable" (assuming one accepts the phrase),
then it was made so only by a deliberate act of the subject of the *cogito*.
Descartes' deliberations on memory were elaborated over many years. They
were intimately linked with the *cogito* and culminated in the making of a
subject who deliberately avoids particular kinds of prejudiced remembering; but the very fact of deliberation also, of course, leaves history as an actually present issue. This deliberate act of will, then (the terms are not accidental), allows the subject of the *cogito* to be generalized, but it only
displaces "history." It does not exorcise it or make it "unreadable." So far
was it from being unreadable, indeed, that a *morale par provision* was
needed to enable action in the world at all, a "provisional morality" that enabled worldly life and action until such time as a newly ordered reason
made it possible to analyze and order history rationally. The *Principia* and
the *Passions* make interesting reading in this light (see Chapter 5, which
proposes that Descartes was knowingly working through two very different
ideas of "history").

Thirdly,—*pace* Cascardi—Francis Bacon, Descartes, Hobbes, Galileo,
and others did indeed "explain" "where" reason was and why it needed to
make another beginning: it was without guide or misguided, as a particular history now showed. All said this quite specifically. They did *not* claim
"an absolute beginning" but argued for a *new* one: New Instauration, new-
found Method, new euclidean science of politics (whose nonoriginating

claim is transparent—a new application, not a start). In this way, they *did* give reason a history. If "subjective reason" did come to be "an instrument through which the transformations of historical experience could be legitimized and grasped," yet it was only ever partly—and partially—itself removed from that history. I can make a similar point from Cascardi's analysis of Blaise Pascal's supposed separation of the rational and scientific realm from that of the grounding of faith (*Subject*, 33, 70, 129). For contrary to what Cascardi claims to be Alasdair MacIntyre's view, Pascal was not just dividing powers of reason from the realm of faith but giving *rational* grounds why the rational gambler should choose to place him- or herself so that faith might absorb him or her. In fact, MacIntyre argues something very similar: Pascal's was a rational argument about the limits of reason and the spheres in which it could be applied. Science assuredly occupied a different discursive realm from faith, but it was needed to make a space for faith's operation (MacIntyre, *After Virtue*, 40, 54).

I am of course suggesting that philosophy, science, religion, and history—in these instances—are not so readily differentiated as Cascardi and others argue. The claim that they are has purposes we must seek elsewhere, some of which I have already suggested. One of the major ones, these last cases show no less than the earlier *Historikerstreit* reference, is to remove analysis and understanding from a particular history—to universalize it. Such universalizing can and has been put to justifying hegemonic grip on other times, places and cultures—not, of course, without help from other forceful practices.[7] We can easily see this in the singular instance to which I now come: the aesthetic, and more specifically, literature. Here, Kant's third *Critique* and its thesis of disinterested detachment are emblematic: the aesthetic as the very model of autonomy. That this may be a flawed evaluation of Kant's work matters less here than that so many commentators have found the evaluation useful.[8] Such is the view of literature since about his time, although according still to most western pedagogy and cultural claim, we recognize a work as "literary" by its place in a canon, however derived, that binds humans across ages and places, from Gilgamesh to Gordimer, Homer to Yourcenar, Solomon to Shakespeare, Valmiki to Mishima—although our magnanimous generosity alone admits some of these to the kraal.

Those who think this a dead horse are simply wrong. We do not need the Bennetts, Allan Blooms, and Kimballs to suggest otherwise, nor another Bloom—Harold—melodramatically expostulating similar notions in a *New York Times Magazine* feature (September 25, 1994), and now in *The Western Canon*. We need only recall a renowned text first printed forty-five years ago and still standard inside and outside the academy. The work sought to give a systematic compendium, wrote its authors, of literature and of "literary scholarship, conceived as a super-personal tradition, as a growing body of knowledge, insights, and judgements": as, that is to say, a particular Enlightened discourse and practice. "Literary criticism," they explained, "and literary theory both attempt to characterize the individuality of a work, of an author, of a period, or of a national literature. But this characterization can be accomplished only in universal terms, on the basis of a literary theory. Literary theory, an *organon* of methods, is the great need of literary scholarship today." So wrote René Wellek and Austin Warren in 1949 in *Theory of Literature* (19), a book that has been continuously in print ever since and translated into many languages—which suggests that they did indeed provide something like that missing *organon* to most people's satisfaction.

But just what was this seemingly autonomous theory *about*? Such was the question Wellek tried to answer, curiously, in the *second* chapter, "the nature of literature," and Warren in the third, "the function of literature." Wellek rejected any idea of literature as identifiable with a broad "history of civilisation" or as the study of the "great books." He urged limiting the word "literature" to "the art of literature, that is, to imaginative literature." Admitting the clumsiness of the terms (22), he decided that they would by and large leave us "Homer, Dante, Shakespeare, Balzac, Keats rather than . . . Cicero or Montaigne, Bossuet, or Emerson" (26). Deliberately or not, the list acknowledged that it articulated no fundamental questions and that traditionally familiar assumptions grounded its justifying terms. These meant emphasizing *Wortkunst*, isolating literary language from purely referential scientific language and the negligent verbiage of everyday language, focusing on "organization, personal expression [of the *subject*], realization and exploitation of the medium, lack of practical purpose, and, of course, fictionality" (27). Of course.

This is "Kantianism" with a vengeance: literature defined into autonomy—or autism, as Habermas has it, self-regarding internal virtuosity, as we shall soon see Gloria Anzaldúa propose. It gives a pretty problem: what, then, can its "function" be? Resorting to the Horatian *utile/dulce* pair, Warren first gets the bonus of a tradition whose claim, being unspoken, he need not justify. Then he declares the "higher pleasure" of literature as one of "non-acquisitive contemplation." Lastly, he asserts its use as "a pleasurable seriousness, i.e. not the seriousness of a duty which must be done or of a lesson to be learned but an aesthetic seriousness, a seriousness of perception" (31). Ignoring both the solipsistic and tautological nature of such descriptions and his reference to Kant's three *Critiques* for his varieties of the serious, Warren asserts that this specificity dates at least from an age when Plato could "speak of the quarrel between the poets and the philosophers as an ancient quarrel and mean by it something intelligible to us" (29). He could do so because we, too, Warren suggests, recognize the same distinction between different forms of presenting different kinds of "truths" (35–36). He ignores the possibility (surely, rather, a certainty?) that "recognition" and "intelligibility" may depend on misreading, on inserting texts into the readers', not the writers', contexts.

It is clear that for these mid-twentieth-century critics, at least, the rule of autonomy is absolute. Precisely for that reason, no doubt, one has some difficulty establishing just what is being said, beyond the assertion of the validity of a certain kind of discourse, assured by a particular tradition whose own universal and ubiquitous claims to reliability we are expected to take on faith. For all this begs the principal question. Whatever questions are raised, the authors in fact take for granted what *literature* is and that it has "an objective existence in itself" (Soyinka, *Myth*, 62). They assume that Plato's poets are our producers of literature; that Horace's pair is Scaliger's or Boileau's, Pope's, Goethe's, Calvino's—or Achebe's, Anzaldúa's, Baldwin's, Brathwaite's, Carpentier's; that something particular falls between science and the everyday, engaging a specifiable verbal attention and formality; and that something such has always and everywhere come between the transparently cognitive and the lax imprecision of quotidian verbal exchange. They suppose that those authors and that something are literature and its writers, doing and being enough alike wherever found as to be "*universal*," and to be treated in the equally "universal terms" of a discourse of theoretical knowledge called "literary theory."[9]

The assumptions and defining claims are clichés. Indeed, although changes may be rung, to call oneself a "literary critic" still by and large obliges one to engage them. The pleasures of disinterested fictions are to be found in Roland Barthes' *jouissance* and Terry Eagleton's "reflections and refractions," in Kenneth Burke's grammar and Paul de Man's rhetoric, in estrangement, undecidability, and exchanges of formal hybridities. Reading literature, Harold Bloom sighs, has no aim outside itself; to lose the capacity for such reading is—and I quote him—"a tragedy." For it is to understand literature as *essentially* engaged in other processes—and so to bewray (they cry) the very virtues that define the literary. Literature is thus taken to "have no social origins, no social context, no consequences in the real world; and if it [thus] exists in an autonomous, self-contained realm of its own, it becomes easy to insist that you exclude from it such annoying, unorthodox and perhaps embarrassing questions as are raised" by understandings moved by "political and social matters which would sully the purity of literature" (Chinweizu, *Decolonising*, 238). But naturally "autonomy" itself poses a further problem. To the very extent that this and other discourses and practices assume the guiding subject mentioned earlier, its engagement with autonomies (and antinomies) supposes a fracturing at another level of attention: of that subject as it moves from one to another. This yields the fragmented subject (and object) that has so often also been held to characterize modernity, whether in "fiction" (over whose "endless and corrosive self-concern" Geoffrey H. Hartman worried: *Fate*, 314) or in "fact": the "poor me, poor me" of contemporary complacent alienation and self-indulgent irresponsibility, to quote Patricia Penn Hilden's ironic apostrophe.[10] But it has had variously familiar forms from the late nineteenth century on.

I still speak, of course, of a western modernity that, however nonhomogeneous, is ever eager to identify all elsewheres with itself (Venice's others visited or imagined by its representative citizen) and of the uses of a literature that was no more autonomous in function and actual experience than were those other practices we have seen. I will not repeat here just how embroiled were its political, epistemological, ethical, and aesthetic goals and actions with the elaboration of particular forms of state and society from the European seventeenth to nineteenth centuries (Reiss, *Meaning* and *Discourse*). Rather, my interest now is uses of claims to autonomy, some of which I have already proposed. And since these uses involve concealment of ideological interest, it is no surprise that we find them occurring with special clarity of form and purpose in colonized situations. There, writers readily repeat this view of "the purely spiritual character of poetic activity, which in its essence is autonomous, independent of intellectuality, utility, or morality," as S. K. De writes approvingly of "the Sanskrit theorists" (*Sanskrit*, 65), virtually parroting Wellek and Warren.[11] For fuller implications of this sort of adoption and its western original, I will turn for a moment to a writing by one of the now older "literary" members of the

African diaspora, to an almost thirty-year-old essay drawing together many of these issues. Here Mphahlele asked a familiar question: "what is poetry?" what its role? what, especially, its place in contemporary African exigencies?

He began by opposing to the idea that poetry had any such place the view just seen, one expressed notably often in western Europe and North America in the 1960s and 1970s, when books like Erich Kahler's *Disintegration of Form in the Arts* and *Inward Turn of Narrative* bewailed efforts to splinter subjective consciousness and produce incoherence (Reiss, *Meaning*, 342–43). Kahler was writing variants on the by then commonplace thought that literature was indelibly marked by "the disinherited mind" of western writers, by "intellectual frivolity" and "clever meaninglessness," and by a broader "dissociation of sensibility" supposed to have split a once-whole mind into "scientific" and "poetic."[12] These views of literature were the aesthetic face of a dismay with the Enlightenment expressed early in the century by theorists such as Weber and Husserl and with larger fury by others later. Disinheritance, frivolity, meaninglessness, and dissociation were so many versions of autonomy and a wider "disenchantment" brought about, *dixit* Tönnies, by the passage from *Gemeinschaft* to *Gesellschaft*, from Émile Durkheim's organic to mechanistic society, feudal to capitalist relations of production, whole community to competitive conflict among alienated puppets at the mercy of master capital, from an integrated culture of mutual exchange and recognition to a fragmented society of individual rights and drives.

But the fraudulence of this kind of nostalgia—false and kitsch memory—is manifest now, if not then, when the pressures to escape from and respond to the outcomes of events explained—and may have necessitated—the flight from the realities of anything like "memory's curious salvage operations," as Primo Levi described the recall of pieces of a later catastrophe, operations made curious and first opaque by their very concreteness ("Mystery," 67), Saramago's minutiae of memory sapping hegemonic histories. For this European nostalgia derived not from an effort accurately to assemble the complicated actualities of the past but from an idealist description of the present, or maybe rather from setting such an idealist description in tandem with the murkier actualities. "Idealist" it was in that it took its details from the rational speculation of autonomous explanatory argument, making ideas *about* phenomena and events *into* events and phenomena.

Thus the seeming lack of fit between an idea of a "democracy" of "separate but equally free individuals" on one hand and on another political pressures, economic inequalities, voting rules and exclusions, realities of electioneering, funding, fraudulence, and so on could readily be translated into a failure of the first. An idealized, efficient, and "decent" division of labor could be set against real anomic workers divided from products and others' labors (Ruskin saw here a basic sign of the brutality of modern so-called civilization). Setting ideal against actuality, imagined perfection against concrete event and experience that could never be clearer than Levi's curious memories, gave parts for a fractured conflictual dystopia, its existence predicated on imagined perfection. Its piece-by-piece opposite was by definition an enchanted utopia, whole and concordant—reversed other of its fragmented dystopic version. (All efforts to historicize the enchantment, as we shall see further in Chapter 5, emphasize the fraudulence of a nostalgia made from a desire to idealize perfectibility in the face of its "failure.")

This was perhaps understandable as a first try to face, if not criticize, the disasters of a certain history. Yet to return to Mphahlele, the flaws of the response and its hegemonic source could readily be seen in its African diasporic counterpart—however complicatedly, we shall see, since here it replied directly to "aggressive, expansionist, colonial" power (Philip, *Frontiers*, 94). The wish to replace colonized alienation with enchantment gave "a derivative kind of *négritude*," a nostalgic longing for an "intellectual and emotional projection into pastoral Africa"—a view that some had had of the negritude idea almost from its beginnings in the early 1930s. "The poetry of *négritude* origin," Mphahlele wrote in "African Literature: What Tradition?", "may also falsify the image of Africa by representing it as a symbol of innocence, purity, naked beauty, human decency" (*Voices*, 15 and 15n, 137; cf. "Remarks," 249). "Emotion is black," Senghor insisted, "reason is Greek" (*Négritude*, 24). To the same purpose, Soyinka cited "a Ghanaian poet":

> Come and restore
> Again to us
> The dignity
> Of our ancestral past
> The charity of heart
> And benevolence of soul
> Regard for age . . .
> And readiness to use
> Our strength
> To animate the weak.

As René Depestre dismissed what he called Senghor's "absurd assertion" ("Jean Price-Mars," 63), so Soyinka did his poet's, naming it "pure
fiction" and citing a play to quite opposite effect (*Art*, 13). A contemporary
analog may be Molefi Kete Asante's Afrocentrism—nostalgia for a mythic
and innocent wholeness that strikes out against the disinheritance that
Mphahlele was addressing. But Mphahlele saw that that derivative *négritude* "never addressed itself to power," so that even its (perfectly genuine)
address to real human suffering had a veil of unreality (*Voices*, 16). This was
so "because the tools of political power—western education, a money
economy, a western language, etc.—needed a suspension of negritude at
its most basic level" ("Negritude," 85). Depestre earlier made the same
point, remarking that Senghor's opposition of "'african spirituality,' considered as an emotional block, to 'white rationality' also considered as a
global, monolithic fact," meant that "all class contradictions are diluted in
negritude's abstraction, and the black bourgeois of Africa and America
can, in full safety, with neocolonialism's benediction, exploit black workers in the name of a shared spirituality" ("Jean Price-Mars," 63).

Derived, like the *Gemeinschaft* idea which it in many ways repeated,
from speculation made autonomous of the actuality it sought first to address, negritude became, said Mphahlele, only a taunting of white authority and values, turning its own past, now in Soyinka's 1967 words, into "a
fleshpot for escapist indulgence," creating a myth "of irrational nobility, of
a racial essence that must come to the rescue of white depravity" (*Art*, 19).
Further, not only did it echo the form and content of the western discourse
it derided, but its iteration of the very autonomies it was battling was mark
of its refusal to address power and fully identifiable interests. In just this
sense, Soyinka referred to it in 1982 and 1985 as the "Cartesian response,"
replying directly to "I think therefore I am" with "I feel therefore I am"; its
writers choosing "Descartes as the scapegoat of their own complementary
rejection" and giving birth "in Paris" to "a new round of ecstatic man" (*Art*,
125, 171; cf. *Myth*, 138). Even replying to critics, Senghor did insist that the
African answer to the *cogito* was "I feel, I dance the Other; I am" ("African
Road," 73). Not for nothing does Chinweizu, a contemporary urger of
something like this *négritude*, unwittingly see literature itself in terms that
he could have drawn directly from the second part of Descartes' *Discours de
la méthode*, whose author likened rational method to house- and city-
building. Thus Chinweizu envisages a "nation" as "a creative enterprise,
much like rebuilding, according to some new design, an old city going to

ruin" (*Decolonising*, 217). So too had Cheikh Hamidou Kane adopted these
terms to describe the building of the colonizers' schools and their teaching
"how to construct dwelling houses that resist the weather," to join "wood
to wood" in ways making the colonized "forget" their own culture and
"eternalizing conquest." For "the cannon compels bodies, the school be-
witches souls" (*Aventure*, 21, 44, 60; *Adventure*, 11, 34, 49).[13] African emotion would thus have been crushed by a cartesian rationalism whose opposed Other it was.

Chapter 5 follows implications of this naming of the argument, tying
it to a supposed cartesian tradition. Here I continue to explore workings of
other instruments. For turning to an imaginary Africa that largely just inverted the West's self-description *and* adopted main elements of ethnography's description of its Other (de Certeau, *Écriture*, 11, 215—and see note 6
above), urgers of this *négritude* partly turned away from actuality. Asante
runs this risk in drawing from an African American culture of resistance
(*Afrocentric*, 83–156) a set of a priori opposites read back into Africa: circu-
larity/linearity, mother/father, reason/emotion, "prediction and control" vs.
"interpretation and understanding" (18), community/individual, territori-
ality/openness, boundaries/transcendence (62–63), observer/participant,
confrontation and dissonance/harmony and coherence (64–65), dis-
tance/inclusion (69–70). Whatever the initial political weight of such a
gesture, Henry Louis Gates Jr. notes how the "belief in an essence called
blackness" was limited to "think[ing] of oneself as free simply because one
can claim—one can utter—the negation of an assertion." Worse yet, he repeats Kane, Mphahlele, and Soyinka: "it is to take the terms of one's assertion from a discourse whose universe has been determined by an Other"—
the European white (*Figures*, 53).[14]

Mphahlele argues that the loss of concreteness involved in any case
characterizes those who have been colonized, just as it may do those who
have been culturally displaced or who have suffered other kinds of historical change. Like Kane, he gives the example of Africans who have been educated to a European tradition, receiving an overlay of Christianity, and so
who have lost immediate personal immersion in a surrounding culture
binding them to a land and life-world (*Voices*, 123–24). In such a condition,
négritude could easily become an internalization of cultural displacement
by which an innocent imagined "Africa" was abstracted into a romanticized
pastoralism and substituted for a real world "alienated" for others' use, a
land both stolen and made foreign. In a case like that of apartheid South

Africa, where whites justified "bantustans" precisely on the claim of cultural difference, the idea was potently dangerous (Mphahlele, "Remarks," 247). A like point was made at length by Okot p'Bitek:

The preachers of the false doctrine of Negritude, where feeling, but not logic is the essence of African-ness, and by extension of all Black people . . . would not fail to be false. The Negritudists came to such absurd conclusions because they did not begin to understand the culture of the African tradition. This is why, speaking in French or English or Portuguese or Spanish or German or any of the languages of their foreign enslavers, they cry "Hurray! To those who have invented nothing"! Those words cannot be translated into any African language, because they are meaningless. African languages themselves are the epitomes of African inventiveness. And each word, each expression, each exclamation, each pose in speech; the softness and loudness, the tone with which a word is spoken is pregnant with meaning. Negritudism is a creation of the alienated Black man. What else could you expect of the Black man in exile, in the *diaspora*, whether in the Caribbeans or in Paris, torn from home, either by the "rape of Africa" called the slave trade; or by the alienating process at home miscalled education? The Negritudist is as ignorant of the culture of the African of tradition as is the missionary. But if he was not as conceited or contemptuous, (this he could not be, because, root-less as he was, he wished to cling to some branch of Africanness), both the negritudist and the missionary sang empty *songs*. Neither one nor the other spoke meaningfully to the African of tradition. And like those *authenticists*, the Negritudists have not addressed the masses in Africa. Their throats croak to the winds and their voices are, sometimes, accidentally and faintly heard in the capitals of imperialdom. (*Artist*, 63)

Césaire, one of the founders of *négritude*, put the case against cultural imposition and prescription with equal vehemence, but drew opposite conclusions. He pointed out that ex-slaves above all (and especially in the diaspora of a Middle Passage whose perpetrators had deliberately destroyed their victims' cultures) had no choice but to use their oppressors' tools to dismantle his power and his victims' alienation. His Christophe exclaims:

All humans have the same rights. I agree. But among common peoples some have more duties than others. There is the inequality. An inequality of obligations, you understand? Whom will you have believe that all humans, all I say, without exception, without particular reason, have gone through deportation, slave trade, slavery, collective reduction to bestiality, total violation, utter insult, that all have received, spattered on body and face, all-denying sputum! Only us, madame, do you hear? only us niggers! (*Tragédie*, 59)

That is why one has to "succeed in the impossible" in fighting "against History," while using tools from that History (62). One way of doing so is to introduce new, different, or reworked memory into it, to repeat the thought drawn from Saramago. This may be why in *Une saison au Congo*, Césaire's Patrice Lumumba, knowing he is likely soon to die, also recalls the architectural terms in which Descartes had spoken in the *Discourse* of the new construction of knowledge (and, we shall see in Chapter 5, of history, identity, and the *polis*). He is speaking, precisely, of the creation of a new state from a postcolonial zero point, and he is speaking to colonial power:

I regret nothing, Mpolo. Doesn't the architect go directly to the goal, projecting the whole house at once? When the sky was black and the horizon blocked, it was my job to set out the sweeping path with one magic stroke. (*Saison*, III.1: 87)

Fanon noted that to counter western colonizers in their own terms was an inevitable first step in rejecting their cultural impositions (*Wretched*, 209–13). Such temporariness of race consciousness has also been Depestre's argument (*Bonjour*, and Reiss, "History and Language"). Even Soyinka has echoed this historical argument about the uses of negritude, noting its aims and dangers (*Myth*, 126–39), terms Mphahlele also adopts: "It is initially a healthy thing to create a myth for the furtherance of an ideology," although "a desperate necessity" forced by circumstance (*African Image*, rev. ed., 70, 39). Achebe made the same point, negritude being among "props we have fashioned at different times to help us get on our feet again. Once we are up we shan't need any of them anymore" (*Morning*, 59). Jean-Marie Abanda Ndengue adds that *négritude* should be seen as "gift, acceptance and refusal": "refusal of political, economic and cultural annexation, of the politics of forced assimilation; acceptance of and search for a past unknown, distant and scorned, but real; gift of oneself, contribution to human civilization" (*De la négritude*, 51). Even so, and however liberating, it was an "attitude, a stand of the colonized or independent black against power, against political or intellectual imperialism" rather than a constructive project aimed at a new future (54). Abanda Ndengue quotes Senghor as at least once sharing such a view, appealing to a different project for change (101). *Négritude* should be understood as recovering "the state of the entirety of black African cultural values before the whites' arrival in Africa," deep and necessary reaction to "the anxiety of no longer being oneself" ("l'inquiétude de n'être plus soi"; 133, 137). For him, too, it was a transitory prop.

To know that its use was as risky as Césaire's Christophe's last—equivocal—failure was perhaps then integral to the idea of *négritude*. Ultimately, to rid oneself of western subjective indulgences was *also* to rid oneself of such dangerously fraudulent nostalgias: of both, as well as "in so many areas," wrote Mphahlele in 1964, the African "wants to decolonize his mind."[15] Ngũgĩ, after Fanon, has been equally explicit on the consequences and the need, noting how cultural impositions make a people's own past a "wasteland" and annihilates their deepest beliefs—"the intended results are despair, despondency and a collective death-wish" (*Decolonising*, 3)—and how "colonisation systematically tried to kill the African individual and collective image of self. Get at their self-hood, fervidly urged the governor and the settler" (*Writers*, 117).[16] *Négritude* was responding precisely to the consequent "inquiétude de n'être plus soi." As Prakash remarks of late nineteenth- and early twentieth-century nationalist essentialism in India, perhaps thinking of critics of a colonized Indian historiography like Thapar and Chandra, "it is important to bear this contestatory aspect in mind" and not "overemphasize epistemological complicity at the expense of the contest between colonialism and nationalism" ("Writing," 361). Reacting in 1966 to the negritude debate, Ali Mazrui urged that the exact instrument of resistance hardly mattered: "in regard to negritude there prevails a deep conviction that there is dignity in cultural defiance itself." Like so many others, he saw it as a form of "cultural defensiveness" that would "wane" once other forms of assertiveness better took its place (*Ancient*, 7, 24).

Yet the problem was that both in form and effect the idea of *négritude* could be used, sponsored, and adopted by the colonizers and further, as Depestre vehemently observed, by the neocolonizers. It gave a wonderfully pleasant version of *otherness*. Indeed, it was offered as the very embodiment of the white's "Other," a recognition to which Achebe gave sardonic voice in commenting on Senghor's idea that Africa might "irrigate" "the Cartesian rationalism of Europe with black sensitivity through the gift of emotion" (*Morning*, 31). To abduct Europa was perilous. No doubt there was, Mphahlele agrees, an original *négritude*, Césaire's, that in expressing a positive total of black values at the same time attacked white colonialism and western culture as its agent. Césaire's *Cahier d'un retour au pays natal*, written on the eve of World War II, was such an expression (*Voices*, 16–18), although Cheikh Anta Diop expressed doubts even about this (*African Origin*, 26). Soyinka echoes Mphahlele with regard to Léon Damas, Césaire's and Senghor's original companion (*Art*, 176). Fanon and Achebe also saw matters as more complex, recalling a first need for Jean-Paul Sartre's "anti-racist racism" (*Black Skin*, 132–40; *Morning*, 59), although absolutely *not*, said Fanon, just as a moment in someone else's dialectic. Philip, we saw, also argues the *political* need for the oppressed to take the voice of the oppressor (*Frontiers*, 274).

This recognitition is why Asante, too, aims to avoid these ready opposites, aware that to adopt a "concept of Africa" is in part "to speak the same language as the oppressor" (*Afrocentric Idea*, 115) and to adopt "a discourse of frustration" (147). His purpose, like that of Ngũgĩ and others, has been to turn this *Gemeinschaft* myth to new account, to oppose and escape discourses and practices of "universal hegemony" and claims to set "standards for the rest of the world" (4, 62). He seeks "an expansion of cultural perspectives" (55) through analysis and actual practice of home, so to speak—the hard understanding of local complexities. The risk is lest basing analysis on abstract alterities lead to the peril noted by Diop, Mphahlele, Ngũgĩ, Okot, and Soyinka—not Fanon's praxis but Senghor's aestheticism.[17] For however necessary, this manichean view of the world readily slid into rehearsing—not even very differently—the poles already simplified in the *Gemeinschaft/Gesellschaft* pair, wholeness and division, harmony and discord, stability and rout. It projected every non-European place as "'the other world' . . . where man's vaunted intelligence and refinement are finally mocked by triumphant bestiality," as Achebe began his analysis of Conrad's *Heart of Darkness* (*Hopes*, 3). It invested the peoples of these places with an inhuman humanity, a slightly higher animality, made their reason wild frenzy, their order disorder, their language babble, their human varieties a dehumanized mass (*Hopes*, 5–9, 12).

Just so does Édouard Glissant fear that to adopt a counter-manicheism was mere mimicry of western protocols, objectively only furthering the Caribbean's self-alienation and anomie. Thus he wrote of the "insidious violence," even "perhaps, the most extreme form of violence," of this "mimetic impulse," of its "trap" (*Caribbean Discourse*, 18; 46; 38 n. 1). Patrick Chamoiseau and Raphaël Confiant, for whom Césaire and Glissant are decisive predecessors, repeat the point, reaffirming its general grounds: "[*Négritude*'s] resistence, its battle, is fought with weapons which come from Europe, from elsewhere, and which, while they raise consciousness at first, alienate in the long run" (*Lettres*, 128). Its time is past, had agreed Mphahlele, "the historical factors that gave rise to negritude in the first place do not exist any more," quoting Depestre's 1968 view, mentioned above, that it "had become a dangerous doctrine, a new form of alienation which only promoted the interests of neo-colonialism in Africa and

America," aesthetically hiding "the economic and political factors that had led to" and maintained oppressed and underdeveloped conditions ("Negritude," 81, 89).

Mphahlele and others may long have resisted such manichean poles and the cruel meetings they hide (even as they justify them), but these simplicities and their avatars have become the currency of much popular modern and contemporary political and critical assertion. Soyinka's laughter is small wonder, echoing Mphahlele's wariness: "the duiker (a small African antelope) does not proclaim its duikritude. You know it by its elegant leap." His later and better known tigritude and tiger's pounce catch the confusion of fantasy with fact more savagely if less humorously (Chamberlin, *Come Back*, 52; 278 n. 34; and see Biodun Jeyifo's introduction to Soyinka, *Art*, xiii).[18] Arnold Krupat observes ("Ideology," 560) that Anthony Appiah has made the same point in commenting on Yambo Ouologuem's *Bound to Violence*, a novel that among other things captures the collusion between European nostalgias and African copies of them (whether ironically intended or not). Ouologuem's savage story ends with a reminder (also quoted by Appiah) that nostalgic wish spoken through some autonomous *Gemeinschaft* myth serves only to hide real interest and suffering in the present: "Often, it is true, the soul desires to dream the echo of happiness, an echo that has no past. But projected into the world, one cannot help recalling that Saif, mourned three million times, is forever reborn to history beneath the hot ashes of more than thirty African republics" (Ouologuem, 181–82; Appiah, "Is the Post-," 353).[19] Is it enough, then, even for an initial prop, to reply to Soyinka, as Senghor did, that "a tiger does not talk" and that at least the manicheism gives Africans a voice, shows that "the Negro talks! And talking is a measure of his humanity" (Achebe, *Hopes*, 24)? What he says is presumably of as much matter and the fruitful turn of the manichean cultural instrument is Achebe's and others' reminder that "the negritude/tigritude argument" was just a start, "a source that could" help start a "momentum" for recovery and advancement of culture (Achebe, *Conversations*, 151).

To resist manicheism can itself, however, be a problem. To do so necessarily demands and rests on finding meetings, overlappings, and connections that may seem actual collusion, not just commentary on it. Achebe noted that European admiration for Ouologuem's novel might not be innocent. Showing violence endemic in Africa, it let those readers off many hooks of responsibility and responsiveness. The Africanist Philip M. Allen had praised Ouologuem as "cured of the pathetic obsession with racial and cultural confrontation and freed from invidious tradition-mongering," for depicting not the particularity of an African society but a "Hobbesian universe." How, asks Achebe, was Ouologuem "able to accomplish that Herculean feat of forcing moral universality on Africa?" (*Morning*, 13)—to say nothing of freeing Africa of its traditions—an odd reading of a novel relying on their deployment. What let the European claim universality for his? Whether or not Achebe was holding Ouologuem responsible for Allen's views (he did elsewhere: 67–68), the point lies in the ease of such readings (compare Soyinka's analysis of the novel: *Myth*, 98–106; but see, too, Miller on Ouologuem's contestatory "refusals": *Blank*, 216–38). When a culture has been and stays dominant (for whatever economic, political, and military reasons and by whatever of these means), do attempts to defeat mere confrontation inevitably play into its greedy hands? Is "collusion" inevitably one not of commentary on the use of cultural instruments but of novelist and critic who, wilfully or not, reinforce and benefit from the dominance?

If the answers are forever affirmative, matters are hopeless. But we begin to see the wider consequences and implications of the claims of autonomy and the nostalgias they allow—indeed authorize. To tell endlessly how the modern world has been divided evilly or beneficially into Enlightenment autonomies of discipline, practices and experience, is not innocent—whether involuntarily or deliberately. As I have said, it is more a matter of claim than experience, and it is as claim that it serves. Of this we shall see more in several later chapters, but it is worth recalling here Achebe's and Fanon's argument that *négritude*, for example, only countered colonizers' prior dualisms. Hegel's claim that Africa marked an absence of history is notorious. Chinweizu (like Diop and Chancellor Williams) recalls that this myth fully served the colonizers (*Decolonising*, 111). For them, the native "represents not only the absence of values, but also the negation of values . . . the absolute evil" and at the same time "the deforming element, disfiguring all that has to do with beauty or morality" (Fanon, *Wretched*, 41). Guha-Thakurta points out with others that from the eighteenth century, European thinkers took their choice of such native places, whether China, Egypt, or India, each in turn the "instance of the early history of art [for example], trapped in antiquity, outside the pale of history and progress" ("Recovering," 67). For Saint-John Perse, the issue was just this exile of *all* others from a self-designated center:

Étranger, sur toutes grèves de ce monde, sans audience ni
témoin, porte à l'oreille du Ponant une conque sans mémoire:
    Hôte précaire à la lisière de nos villes, tu ne franchiras
point le seuil des Lloyds, où ta parole n'a point cours et
ton or est sans titre . . .
    «J'habiterai mon nom», fut ta réponse aux questionnaires
du port.

Stranger, on all shores of this world, without audience or
witness, lift to the ear of the West a conch without memory:
    Precarious guest at the edge of our cities, you shall not
cross the threshold of Lloyd's, where your word has no currency and
your gold has no title . . .
    "I shall dwell in my name," was your answer to the port authority's
questionnaire.

(Exil, in Collected Poems, 166)

A major difficulty was and always is that of avoiding simply being set
in the place of *one* "Other" of *one* "Same." For the colonial world, Fanon
wrote, is one of "reciprocal exclusivity," "a world cut in two," "a
Manichean world" (*Wretched*, 39–41). "By its very structure, colonialism
is separatist and regionalist" (94). It is so not only in concept, but mapped
onto the ground: "The colonial world is a world divided into compartments . . . native quarters and European quarters . . . schools for natives
and schools for Europeans . . . apartheid" (37–38).[20] And as it forged
divided "realities" on the ground, so, intellectually, it forced colonized
thinkers into disciplinary autonomies (50). We saw Frank and Chatterjee
ground analogous observations in arguments drawn not so much from
local actualities as from the implications of European autonomous discourses (38 above). Fanon's countryman Glissant shows sectorial labor
divisions to be signs of the same imposition. Here are vividly clear
instances of how claim is turned into experience. They echo on the ground
the sort of western "compartmentalization" and division of which we earlier saw Soyinka write and which is that autonomizing of thought and
practice typifying European thought and practice since at least the eighteenth century.

Pickwickian talk of the "end of history," confusing hegelian and post-
hegelian speculation with real agency in the world, is a most recent version
of the same sort of assertion. "History" is not some master operator's inexorably determined plan but the turbid vitality and measureless variety of

peoples, experiences, events, actions, memory. History is in the bone. Ignazio Silone had *Bread and Wine*'s Pietro Spina reject "abstract and inhuman symbols" that removed people from "practical life."[21] Eduardo Galeano has written of the "ideologues specialized in raising walls and digging ditches" to compartmentalize creative activity (*We Say No,* 151). Endlessly indeed we learn how literature became and must stay divided from the real world. Endlessly we are hammered with the claims— nonetheless—that literature, for all it echoes a dominant ideology and is made for and by that ideology's elite, somehow *in spite of* itself "reflects and refracts" along with the dominances also the "faultlines" that show the strains and tensions that will finally break these dominances.[22]

No doubt. But literature does not do so by accident or by constraint, contrary to what is implied by the oft-stated unease of Marxist critics at dealing with literature instead of the actual "struggles of men and women to free themselves from . . . exploitation and oppression" (Eagleton, *Marxism,* vii). Aesthetic work is and always was trammeled in the world. "How do you judge poetry separately from the ideology that makes it?" asks Mphahlele, echoing such as those named in my Introduction. "How do you separate the value of a poem from the value of its content, its tone, its intention, its emotion," conditioned as all are by their being in the social and ideological world? ("Negritude," 83). To start by assuming division is to avoid understanding the nature and functions of intricate engagement. Aesthetic work could only always be utterly imbricated in complexities specific to a historical context. One should not confuse the heuristic uses of autonomization with actuality, false nostalgia with real memory.

A main point has to do not with difference or autonomy (which at some level, in a coherent culture, cannot be the case), but with the nature of overlappings, interplays, and specific ways in which any practice and/or discourse identifies its own role and realm of operation—provided we understand that such specification relies on all discourses and practices of a culture. Arguing for autonomies and antinomies permits us to ignore the greater complexities (and, certainly, contradictions) of these interactions, to say nothing of the real suffering and actual violence they overlay—as I proposed of Locke's analysis of property and the human and, of course, as Fanon argued of colonialist techniques throughout his *Wretched of the Earth.* That is how and why current discussion of Enlightenment often sees it as sickened in some basic way, making a fragmentation of action and analysis that—it is said with a certain dose of self-indulgence—makes the modern western age "illegitimate." It is self-indulgent because instead of engaging the long, difficult, and often dull analysis of resistant complexities, it urges a leap into some other "place," the adoption of some other culture's successes (whatever that might be): a hardly more sophisticated version of New Age essentialist imaginings.

One does not solve local harms and hindrances by trailing one's coat into someone else's home, violently knocking down doors, trying to repair the imagined miseries of one's western place by taking over the equally imagined glories and spiritualities of victimized Others, whose actual oppression leaves space to suppose them nostalgic bearers of a wise *Gemeinschaft.* One does not solve these miseries and these harms simply by imagining what Taussig calls fetishized antiselves, those of which Achebe wrote in his essay on Conrad, mere opposites produced by civilizing histories of what made dismay in the first place (Taussig, *Shamanism,* 215), or which Derek Walcott portrays toward the end of his *Dream on Monkey Mountain,* with the "African" Monkey King and his acolytes betraying a dream of freedom by adopting a fetishized other of the white oppressors' "law" and violence—echoing, with like ambivalence, Césaire's vision of Christophe's court as a "perfect replica in black of what old Europe did best where courts are concerned" and that comes to "resemble something awfully like what we once experienced and fought against" (*Tragédie,* 31, 80). Indeed, that imagining falsifies the actuality in which we live, for however practices and discourses may be speculatively separable from one another, they are yet caught up with one another and in the whole culture which surrounds them, which they create, which is the sum of their parts (and which is the other side of Christophe's vision, as it is of Walcott's Makak). To think culture in terms of opposites is indeed to leave the many questions I have been asking bereft of reply, as Mazrui suggested in *The Trial of Christopher Okigbo.*

In this novel, the poet is put on trial in "After-Africa" for betraying his artistic obligation by putting himself in a position to be killed fighting as a Biafran major in the Nigerian civil war. The prosecutor, "Counsel for Damnation," first sets his case by arguing that "a great artist was first of all an individualist, secondly a universalist, and only thirdly a social collectivist" (67). As such, the artist's first duty is to what he or she alone can produce by their "experience [of] the depths of individualism." Such "lives are more sacred than others": "the inner creativity of the artist requires a doctrine of the primacy of the self. The aesthetic meaning of the artist requires a supporting doctrine of aesthetic universalism." Only in the service of that universal should the artist "be expected to serve his own society" (68–69). Kwame Apolo-Gyamfi, the Counsel, might well have been reading Wellek and Warren. Hamisi Salim, the defense counsel, argues that it is not "universally true" that "creativity derives from individualism." "Much of Africa's art," he says, is "a collective experience . . . shared moments of being." Europe's great art "may have been at best a mode of communication; great art in Africa had always been a flow of interaction." The "description of the artist as being ultimately a person loyal to himself as an individual must therefore be dismissed as an alien idiosyncrasy imported from the principles of European aesthetics" and could not be used to understand African artists or their art, which depended on "meaningful interaction," on "the power of sound and the excitement of listening," on "*Making harmony among the branches*," as one of Okigbo's verses had it (77–79). Put in terms of such oppositions, the jury concludes at the end of the novel, the case must be held "Not Proven" (143–44).

That the novel elides differences of African cultures and is ever tempted by a simplistic "individualist"/"communitarian" opposition certainly weakens its effect (and its principal question as to whether the artist has the "right" to sacrifice his artistic duty to the community, which he or she alone can fulfill, to a different duty—here, that of fighting—which any citizen can fulfill). But, contrary to what Eldred D. Jones asserts (along with too many others; "Price," 61–62), the jury's decision rejects such simplifications. The complexities of cultures have no "opposite," no "other," at one (logical) level simply because they are not singular. Complexity is where one must start, knowing that if aesthetic work is in an "organic" relation with its surrounding culture of mutual "action and reaction," with all other practices and the *place* in which it thus belongs, as Ngũgĩ has put it, then we have first to grasp that concrete setting (*Moving*, 27). When literature or any artifact loses that relation, becoming object of distanced and disinterested contemplation, separated from and autonomous of its originating life-world, a displacement has occurred whose grasp may be of interest, but which makes it no more part of, inside, the culture.

"Even when I was far away," says Pietro Spina, "the reality I lived in was my native air. But with the distance it slowly became an abstraction to me and an incubus. I really needed to feel my feet on the ground once more" (Silone, *Bread and Wine*, rev. ed., 40). Looking at church artifacts in

Spanish provincial museums, Cees Nooteboom wonders, "How does a thing which to some extent was an object of everyday use become transformed into an art-object?"—statues that explained aspects of faith, paintings that told stories to those who could not read, meanings that have become mere forms (*Désir*, 75–76). Like Soyinka, Anzaldúa, naming this separated art an "aesthetic of virtuosity," calls it "typical of Western European cultures," an art turning on its "own internal system," "dedicated to the validation of itself": "its task is to move humans by means of achieving mastery in content, technique, feeling. . . . It is individual (not communal). It is 'psychological' in that it spins its energies between itself and its witness." Such art is housed apart and protected in museums and galleries. Others' art "is transposed into an alien aesthetic system" and valorized in its terms. Different cultures ("tribal," for instance, in her word) "keep art works in honored and sacred places in the home and elsewhere." Parts of everyday life, their "'witness' is a participant in the enactment of the work in a ritual" (*Borderlands*, 67–68).

This embedding in the real, of which Anzalduá, Nooteboom, and Silone write here, is what Mphahlele and so many others address more generally. Paule Marshall talks of it when she tells of learning about language from her mother and friends in the childhood kitchen: language as physical relief, as site of creative energy, a way of taking control. "They made of it an art form that—in keeping with the African tradition in which art and life are one—was an integral part of their lives" (*Merle*, 6). When she emphasizes an "African tradition," she reflects modern claims about the western case—that of autonomization—and alternatives. As Anzaldúa puts it, in words whose typicality and familiarity resonate through this book and whose precise assertion I shall be exploring and questioning in greater detail and depth most especially from Chapter 5 on: "Let's all stop importing Greek myths and the Western Cartesian split point of view and root ourselves in the mythological soil and soul of this [American] continent" (*Borderlands*, 68).

These modern claims assert that cultural artifacts, events, phenomena are transformed into "art" objects by being somehow or other displaced from their general cultural setting so as to emphasize only one of their sensuous aspects—visual, auditive, tactile, or whatever, a dimension western art culture then terms "aesthetic." What would be taken from it is the authenticity obtained from its embedding in a tradition whose past, present, and future remain vital within it because it shares a material and spiritual culture peopled not just by its creators, but by its users. Those characterizing the art of nonwestern cultures typically assert how they keep this embedding, avoiding disunion. "A national [African] culture," wrote Fanon, "is the whole body of efforts made by a people in the sphere of thought to describe, justify, and praise the action through which that people has created itself and keeps itself in existence" (*Wretched*, 233). Achebe comments similarly on the *mbari* ceremony of the Owerri Igbo, with its "profound affirmation of the people's belief in the indivisibility of art and society" (*Morning*, 28). The ceremony's "artists," making its artifacts over two years, are "ordinary members of society." No rigid or permanent distinction exists between makers and consumers of such artifacts (29). The case will come back in Chapter 4, as one that Achebe himself revisited later and at greater length.

Basil Davidson also emphasizes the totality of the cultural event and its entanglement in communal actions, needs and everyday life, frequently expressive of "unities between the known and the unknown," "art for life's sake, but also art for pleasure's sake," recreational, social, political, religious in no way that suggests these refer to separable activities (*African Genius*, 160–67). Baldwin recorded Senghor's comparison of western to African art: "more present and pervasive . . . infinitely less special . . . 'done by all, for all' ." "European art attempts to imitate nature. African art is concerned with reaching beyond and beneath nature, to contact, and itself become a part of *la force vitale*. The artistic image is not intended to represent the thing itself, but, rather, the reality of the force the thing contains. Thus, the moon is fecundity, the elephant is force" (*Nobody*, 24). Even if one ignores so dubious a characterization of western art, one must wonder just what this "different" representation is (the issue of Chapter 4). Baldwin takes it to found a fundamentally diverse practice of art, similar again to that of Achebe, Anzaldúa, Davidson, Fanon: "the idea that the work of art expresses, contains, and is itself part of the energy which is life." It is communal and dependent "on the actual presence of other human beings," embedded in a "past, which had been lived where art was naturally and spontaneously social, where artistic creation did not presuppose divorce" (26).

The last sentence is especially revealing. For once again the clear dilemma is to give a meaningful and precise idea of what the differences might be. Baldwin declares them to lie in the opposite of what western art is taken to be. The pervasive typicality of the idea is shown by analogous efforts to adumbrate artistic life in cultures quite different from either of these environments. Ranging from the offensive to the complex, these judgments mostly cluster around the same basic themes. Characteristic of the first sort are early views of what jazz brought to "mainstream" music. "We [sic] needed the roar of the lion," wrote George Antheil in the 1920s, "the stalwart shoulders of a younger race. . . . The [American] Negro taught us to put our noses to the ground, to follow the scent, to come back to the elementary principles of self-preservation." Jazz "is fundamental," said Serge Koussevitzky. It "comes from the soil" with "new vigor, . . . new vitality." And, of course, connected with this soil, as Antheil noted, was the fact that "the Negro has a rhythmic sense second to none." Most remarkable were rhythmic and tonic patterns so intricate that "one can scarcely believe that one has not to do with a highly civilized race." What one actually had to do with are memories bound up with the intricacies of animal and vegetable life in and from which these sounds were born (Locke, *Negro and His Music*, 89, 95, 137).[23]

That the first two of those judgments were made by white men in the 1920s about black artistic endeavor explains the difference of tone from those I quoted earlier, chiefly from black writers considering African activities. But the point has not only to do with questions of tone that can only be judged racist (as Achebe observes in his Conrad analysis; *Hopes*, 1–20), views not inevitably connected with the difficulties I am circling here. For again quite different in tone and import is what the Pueblo Indian poet Simon Ortiz says of his culture's art: "One lived and expressed an artful life, whether it was in ceremonial architecture, painting, speaking, or in the way one's social life was structured" (quoted in Hilden, *When Nickels*, 45). The issue is the striking affinity of all these assessments. To be sure, they are rapid efforts to define deeply complicated wholes. But the problem is not one of simplification. It is that the starting terms matter. The suspicious likeness of judgments that supposedly refer to wholly different societies and cultures cannot but give pause. Furthermore, they do not concern "only" African, African American, Caribbean, and Pueblo, but, in the first case, all the diversities of African cultures across their continent and, in the last, of Indian ones across theirs.

Ortiz is clear that he is addressing just Pueblo circumstance, but what does it mean, too, that so many of those quoted on African circumstance (Achebe, Mphahlele, and Ngũgĩ excepted—and Soyinka occasionally) deem it not useful, far less necessary, in this context of art culture to consider how many historically distinct cultures are elided under that single adjective? (Fanon asserted that it was, at a certain historical moment, inevitable; *Wretched*, 212–13.) Africa as a whole confronts a globalized Europe: the West. Are these evaluations not again all predicated on an "opposite" of western art's supposed separation from communal life? Do they not again ignore that one complex system of measureless multiplicity is not the "opposite" of another? Are they not largely caught in that trap of sounding board and lens to which I referred earlier (note 14)?[24] And what does that separation mean? It surely remains in some way part of some "lived" reality? How could it not? In the western case alone, then, must not different concepts and practices of "separation" be at issue? The ones would involve long-lived processes in some way fundamental to the practices and self-conception of the culture(s). These would themselves be one aspect of that culture's complexities and so one way in which "art" (for example) was embedded in its life. Other practices of separation might be more punctual, perhaps signaling a critical moment. The first will be the concern of later chapters (especially 2 through 6). It may be that the second marks a particular paroxysm in the historical movement of the first, and we may already have seen this suggested.

Achebe's, Anzaldúa's, Hilden's, Kane's, Marshall's, Mazrui's, Mphahlele's, Ngũgĩ's, Nooteboom's, Ortiz's, Ouologuem's, Okot's, Silone's, and Soyinka's similar points imply that the division of any practice, aesthetic, or other, from the concreteness of historical context, signals elements of drastic cultural change. Just talking of this cannot—and cannot want—to stop it, but it may help offer directions. Such separation may also aim to prevent participation: creating confusion, Galeano observes, of "democracy with elections," economic theory and statistics with real practices and consequences for life, or of a notion of development with "the ultimate goal of all societies" (*We Say No*, 165). Here, talking of it can indeed change it, for it makes one see what is happening (as we saw Grass remark). In both cases, it must act from within—part, not patron. To fancy we are where we are not may have uses. To want to transfer ourself literally to that imaginary place smacks of escapism or illness. To divide our practices of attention may simplify knowing, but it removes us from the living muddle of the everyday in our own home. To imagine we are in a dream, fooled by our senses or tricked by a demon, may be useful devices to understand where we are and the limits of that understanding, but they cannot replace dwelling in and knowing the actual.

This last sentence closely paraphrases the Calvino with which this chapter began (*Invisible Cities*, 103–4). Other than to most of the preceding, it refers to Descartes' *Meditations*, emphasizing their usual consideration as an originating text of modern Europe and western thought (even if the claim is as flawed as Chapter 5 proposes). They, and the style and content of their imaginings and the demands of their self-reflection, are also part of our home. Their later explication underlies many of the arguments this chapter has been addressing, as Achebe's irony on Senghor's "irrigation" of cartesian rationalism or Kane's and Soyinka's doubt about "cartesian" negritude indicated. Like theirs, Anzaldúa's point was precisely that the rationalism supposedly represented by the *Meditations* was not part of *her* home, although willy-nilly it *is*. Whatever one's view of them and their consequences, one cannot pretend otherwise, clambering to reach some "pure" high ground elsewhere. Descartes spent much time trying to defeat biases of memory and custom. But their importance is insistently to remind us of the concrete and particular. Only an accurate grasp of history, a recognition that it is *not* first to be gripped simply as an "Other" to our "now," enables us to avoid such false nostalgias as those observed. That is why Philip adds "that even the mere determination to remember can, at times, be a revolutionary act—like the slave who refused to forget his or her rituals, or music, or whose body refused to forget the dance." Such memory is refusal to accept another's impositions as if they were "ours"—in this case, those of displaced African peoples. It is to remember that such seemingly shared cultural institutions "are really tombstones erected on the graves of African customs, culture and languages." So "not to remember" these last "is simply to collude in our own erasure, our own obliteration" (*Frontiers*, 56, 19). In that sense, memory and nostalgia are not only needed to understand our own home, but—as I said at the outset—"are ineluctable elements in discovery and all efforts to understand otherwise" (36 above).

By this I mean simply that cultural exchanges and interplays must be as wholes and with full grasp of what I have been calling "home." This *in*cludes, and does not *ex*clude, those dominant modes of thought we habitually call "ideologies." It is when we think we have eluded them that we are most captured. False and imaginary nostalgias, "aesthetic" divisions of practice, supposed autonomies of discourse and knowledge, are all parts of our home. We need to take account of them if all exchange and interaction of cultures is not to be reduced again to competition, conflict, and seizure. To abstract ourselves from them, to alienate ourselves from their actual embedding, is to lose our own culture, as Silone's Spina put it, as it simultaneously prevents our contact with different ones—for they, too, become abstract fantasies of desire. But we have to avoid being taken in by the autonomies, divisions, and nostalgias.

I recall a touching passage in Goethe's *Italian Journey*, as he first wends his way southward down the valley of the Adige:

> As evening draws near, and in the still air a few clouds can be seen resting on the mountains, standing on the sky rather than drifting across it, or when, immediately after sunset, the loud shrill of crickets is heard, I feel at home in the world, neither a stranger nor an exile. I enjoy everything as if I had been born and bred here and had just returned from a whaling expedition to Greenland.[25]

". . . doch einmal in der Welt zu Hause"—"yet altogether at home in the world." "Aha!" will say so many moderns—Goethe imposing his superior imperialism on the nearby other, adopting it for his own pleasure and as image of his own desire. We saw Venetian humanists proposing already to appropriate Tenochtitlán to their city in just this way. But Goethe was not "German" in any modern nation or state sense, and wrote of a network of small cultures. It was one where, suspected of spying by locals in the Veneto, he could call himself "citizen of a republic which, though it cannot compare in power and greatness with the illustrious state of Venice, nevertheless also governs itself and, in its commercial activity, its wealth and the wisdom of its councillors, is inferior to no city in Germany. I am, that is to say, a native of Frankfurt-am-Main" (46; September 14, [1786]).[26]

"I cast about," remarks Habermas, "sometimes here, sometimes there, for traces of a reason that writes without effacing separation, that binds without unnaming difference, that points out the common and the shared among strangers, without depriving the other of otherness" (*Past as Future*, 119–20). It will be a reason free of appropriative will, aware of others' homes and *being* in difference, with, George Lamming wrote, "a felt recognition of my capacity for experience, my particular way of seeing" (*Pleasures*, 74). It will be a reason accompanied by a "natural discretion . . . quite incapable of forcing the doors of another's privacy," to quote Saramago once again (*History*, 228). One needs such reason both to deny false nostalgias of our own pasts forged from abstracted autonomies and to avoid what Ouologuem calls the "Shrobeniusology" that constructs different cultures into our (or their own) "other" (cf. Appiah, "Is the Post-," 354). No simple map is available for the reworking of cultures and for new and quite unfamiliar forgings of exchange. We only know that they must first engage our home localities, which Goethe here, like Kublai, Polo, and Calvino five fictive centuries earlier and two actual centuries later, all measure against Venice.

"If I tell you," says Polo, "that the city toward which my journey tends is discontinuous in space and time, now scattered, now more condensed, you must not believe the search for it can stop." The Great Kahn, like many of our contemporaries (of whom the next chapter will discuss a number), wants a simple design and a ready map, be it joy of utopia or terror of dystopic inferno. Marco Polo responds once again:

The inferno of the living is not something that will be; if there is one, it is what is already here, the inferno where we live every day, that we form by being together. There are two ways to escape suffering it. The first is easy for many: accept the inferno and become such a part of it that you no longer see it. The second is risky and demands constant vigilance and apprehension: seek and learn to recognize who and what, in the midst of the inferno, are not inferno, then make them endure, give them space. (164–65)[27]

"Occidental rationalism," Habermas agrees once again, "must go back into itself and overcome its own blindnesses in order to open up dialogically what it can learn from the traditions of other cultures. An intercultural encounter worthy of the name would also demand that the submerged elements of our own tradition be brought to light" (*Past as Future*, 96). No doubt not just the West must do this, as Ouologuem makes clear. But just because the West *has* in recent centuries sought to impose itself as universal, so it has the greatest debt to pay, the hardest self-criticism to undertake. At the same time, the discovery of such blindnesses cannot suffice. For even so, we must acknowledge "the inexorably mysterious and dangerous relationships between ways of life, which are also ways of thought." Even knowing our own blindnesses (at best only some), barring lifetimes one could hope to see others' homes only "through chinks and cracks and keyholes" (Baldwin, *Nobody*, 187). So further peril lies in the belief that one has somehow seen all walls, from all openings, into all corners, that knowing homes, experience, and ways of seeing can be complete.

The same seeking and recognizing as that intended by Polo and urged by Habermas and Lamming led Carpentier's *criollo*, in another Venetian tale fusing four centuries, to Scarlatti and Handel and Vivaldi and a wild jam session to which his own servant/companion brought a contemporary Caribbean rhythm. This baroque concerto wove a fantastic intricate tracery, each player binding without undoing his difference, incorporating without obscuring his way of seeing, sharing without effacing other experience.[28] In turn, the concerto showed, says the protagonist to his now no-longer servant, of just what Venice was the home, triply emphasizing its difference of *place* (an emphasis lost in the published English translation and indeed awkward to render in English, as my own efforts in the following passage show):

> "And all at once, I felt out of position, foreign in this spot, out of place, far from myself and what is really mine . . . [*me sentí como fuera de situación, exótico en esta lugar, fuera de sitio, lejos de mí mismo y de cuanto es realmente mío . . .*] *It is sometimes necessary to distance yourself from things*, to put an ocean in between, *in order to get a close look at them*." At that moment, the *mori* of the Orologio Tower began to hammer, as they had been doing for centuries.
>
> "This city sticks in my craw, with its canals and gondoliers. . . . enough is enough! I'm returning to my own, this very night. The air I need is of a different kind that as it enfolds me sculpts me and gives me shape [*Para mí es otro el aire que, al envolverme, me esculpe y me da forma*]." (*Concierto barroco*, 76–77; *Baroque Concerto*, 110–11)

For Brathwaite, too, the city was harmfully lacking, flawed beauty, ambivalent imposition—surely not Goethe's home away from home. The ghetto at its oppressed heart haunted like menacing death of sinking or flood. Byron, Henry James, Thomas Mann, Ruskin all felt the "ghastly death's head" at the core of "the general romance and the general glory" of Venice's imperial reason (James, *Aspern Papers*, 483, 497). Its enclosing *locus amoenus* threatened always to shrink to the space of a grave, casting its appropriating net over Tenochtitlán and mourning pall over Carpentier's and Brathwaite's open oceans or Glissant's "patient landscapes": "not saturated with a single History but effervescent with intermingled histories, spread around, rushing to fuse without destroying or reducing each other" (*Caribbean Discourse*, 154). *This* Venice did not allow such intermingling, so not for nothing, too, has Carpentier noted a neocolonial Barbados as the island "where Haendel's music has been heard most and, especially, Haendel's *Messiah*, whose famous *Alleluia* chorus is the theme song of one of the local radio stations" ("La cultura," 179). No jam session here, but an echo of Brathwaite's story of how his first efforts to broadcast jazz and blues in the Barbados of his teenage years was swiftly halted before an onslaught of vehement objection (*Barabajan Poems*,

36–42)—echo, too, of the numbing neocolonialist thought expressed by Christophe's secretary Vastey: "Sometimes History has only one path for its passage. And everyone takes it!" (Césaire, *Tragédie*, 80). But these bring matter for later chapters.

Knowing where and what "home" is and striving to know just how and where varied times and places are others' homes are parts of a *process* that itself makes for Polo's endurance and space. We cannot remove ourselves from a present that willy-nilly holds all the consequences of its past. It "can't just be peeled off like a dirty shirt. It's in our skin" (Habermas, *Past as Future*, 94). But we most certainly can sap its nostalgias and undermine its false memories. We certainly can refuse claims of autonomy used to assert crippling universalism and singular rectitude of reason and knowledge. We can deny an aesthetic that purports a ubiquitous standard of judgment floating somehow above, before, and outside history, society, and the environment of everyday event. We can, too, accept the limits that must come from seeing always through chinks and cracks and keyholes. None of this has anything to do with that foolish red herring of "relativism," of "anything goes," supposed denial of values composing the favored clamorous outcry of those who think their culture in jeopardy. It means accepting the ancient challenge of knowing oneself *with* others, of making the immense effort to *know* others in their own embeddedness, not as objects of one's own unique gaze. Truly universal values cannot be that sort of self-legitimated imposition. They must surely lie in what one might call a process of embedded exchange, interweaving cultural experiences and ways of seeing, an effervescence of intermingled histories, a knowing of homes from home.

2

Mapping Identities, Othering Cultures

The tangled matters now broached, then, concerning ideas of the "aesthetic"; history and memory; home and spirit of place; art, culture, and fictive imagination; and interweavings and frictions of wider cultural environments, collect around and focus on a kernel of practice and concept that the term "autonomy" adequately captures. More precisely, western treatment of these matters has depended and still depends on an assumption of autonomy. And that European culture has framed instruments presupposing confrontation and separateness, isolation, independence, and particularity creates clear difficulty of understanding. For how then are Baldwin's "gaps," "chinks," "crannies," and "spaces between" cultural places, units, and individuals to be bridged? If separateness is a norm, how can one understand homes, places, times in their own real differences?

The obvious immediate answer is that one does so in that very difference, as *other*. The dilemma here, we have just been seeing, is made by turning equally immediately to that same culture to define what the *otherness* of that other can be. It provides the conceptual instruments determining "recognition" of alterity: "The other," Michel de Certeau writes, for example, "is the phantasm of historiography" (*Écriture*, 8).[1] This, at least, has historically been so in a first phase of felt need of such "recognition" (prior to which not recognition but exploitative use was at issue)—negritude and east or American Indian spirituality being evident examples. The reverse of this is the (consequent) critical thought that if this is so then "we" (in one culture) have no genuine access to those in another; that the "other," de

Certeau again observes, is either merely produced within "our text" or wholly inaccessible (*Heterologies*, 69). In saying this, one must, however, avoid another irresponsibility. That such instruments develop within cultures and so deploy, as it were, the constraining parameters for action does not make cultures their agents. It is actual users who employ them, in particular ways and to particular ends. And, of course, in the end, it is users who make and change them. That is why, to explore efforts to recognize differences beyond one's culture (and sometimes even to bridge gaps), this and other chapters must show how a number of such actual users in fact employ those instruments. That is why, too, to avoid the reverse thought that differences are inaccessible, they must also try to make contact with different cultures and listen with care and tact to their voices and to their silences.

Among other matters, the first chapter already began to show that for those who publicly consider relations between literature and nation, between poetics and imperialism and associated issues, the temptation to adopt a high ground of rectitude is matched only by the peril of binary extremism. To have been born and raised in a European metropolitan culture is to wear a mantle of guilt or carry a torch of civilization. Not to have been is to wear an aureole of glory or carry a duty to acquire universal values. Those carrying torches or duties believe they argue for the good of common humanity. Those mantled in guilt or crowned in glory claim to argue actual pluralism of humanity that their antagonists deny and crush under self-serving oppression. For them, to dwell in the centers of high capitalism is to have to find a way to go "all the way through" its foundational practices "and out the other side," as Terry Eagleton puts the case (*Nationalism*, 23). To be sure, we born in evil must traverse "the very metaphysical [and social] categories" we hope "finally to abolish" and cannot "live sheer irreducible difference *now*" (23–24). Still, although "we have as yet no proper names" (24) for what that "other" may be, its existence as the bright future of changed humanity is a fulfillable dream. It may not be "*now*," but it definitely has a when.

Half a century ago, Jean-Paul Sartre was arguing a thesis not so very dissimilar, although his view—that the "other" was already showing metropolitans the limits of their categories and putatively making some Hegelian sublation historically inevitable—was different from a later view that not seldom supposes that those who have "progressed ahead" have a duty (guilty or not) to show the way. At the time, Fanon took Sartre to task bitterly and with a potency to which I will return later in this chapter. Fanon's bitterness was appropriate. Sartre supported *négritude* in his celebrated preface to Senghor's *Anthologie de la nouvelle poésie nègre et malgache de langue française* by asserting the glories of "otherness." Further, he did so by arguing that black poets did not use the semantic values of language, its words' meanings, but instead its as-it-were concrete sound and feel as a kind of hammer—not reason but emotion, or what Senghor called a "reasoning . . . intuitive by participation" ("African Road," 74). Here, meaning came from the *meeting* of poet and reader. Whether or not Sartre so intended, it was easy to understand him as asserting that black poets needed white readers in order to be meaningful.

Sartre had argued in general that the most effective poetry worked not through prosaic meaningfulness but by conflict between poet and reader from which meanings burst. Its principal meaning lay in the conflict. The black poet chose poetry because prose was the ordering language of white oppression. In the black writer's poem, white readers saw their situation in history flung upside down. The poet used the *sense* of language, its function as "outdated signs," in such a way that for white readers language became *other*. Alienated from their language, white readers were forced into the same relation to the poetry as its poets held to the idiom of their white oppressor. Sartre proposed that such poetry spoke the sociopolitical conditions of an African diasporic time and place as the antithesis to the thesis of white Enlightenment. These would be *aufgehoben* in a hegelian synthesis, final *meaning* of the writer/reader conflict ("Orphée noir").[2] Soyinka opined that in the context of a *négritude* often tending to adopt old European racist views that "Africans neither think nor construct, but it doesn't matter because—voilà!—they intuit" (*Myth*, 129), simply adopting the "other" of the cartesian *cogito* (135, 139), Sartre's evaluation was not inexact: the *négritude* poets *had* fallen into the European trap of self/other (127–29, 134–39). But Sartre came to praise and Fanon accused him of a familiar colonizing tactic. As Achebe was to say, "we were taken out of our history and dumped into somebody else's history" (*Conversations*, 58) on the pretense that the latter was universal. Mphahlele agreed that the Hegel/Sartre path was just a "philosophical" version of politico-military banditry: "It all started when Africa was shanghaied into the history of the west in the late nineteenth century" (*Voices*, 121). Fanon saw this as one more appropriation of black life and struggles to benefit white vision, one more way to silence black voices, "to open and lift," wrote one of

Ngũgĩ's colonizers, "a dark country onto the stage of history" ("Goodbye Africa," *Secret*, 75). "With friends like this . . . ," Fanon inclined to lament, before turning Sartre's argument to bountiful use. But that story is for the end of this chapter.

Sartre's argument beautifully illustrates Homi Bhabha's remark that

the site of cultural difference can become the mere phantom of a dire disciplinary struggle in which it has no space or power. Montesquieu's Turkish despot, Barthes's Japan, Kristeva's China, Derrida's Nambikwara Indians, Lyotard's Cashinahua pagans are part of this strategy of containment where the Other text is forever the exegetical horizon of difference, never the active agent of articulation. (*Location*, 31; cf. 261 n. 5)

So do José Piedra's and Fernando Coronil's showing how work like Tzvetan Todorov's *Conquest of America* rewrites "under a new guise, the old ontological distinction between self and other which western colonialism has posited in the process of subjecting nonwestern peoples" (Coronil, "Discovering," 325; cf. Piedra, "Game," 39–41, 44–46).[3] To think cultural difference as the other of metropolitan practices has united writers on these topics—and not just western ones we see. Integral to a still colonial condition, this way of thinking remains a problem for all commentators, whatever resolution is essayed. And resolution there must be. Otherwise, the colonizing gesture is forever replicated. Partly, Eagleton notes, that is because the critical tools have mostly been shaped "on a terrain already mapped out by [these] antagonists" (*Nationalism*, 24).[4] This is so whether the commentator is of "metropolitan" origin or not: for Bhabha, Sylvia Molloy, Edward Said, Gayatri Spivak, or Gregory Jusdanis (who claims for modern Greece a "marginal" status), no less than for Eric Cheyfetz, Eagleton, Fredric Jameson, Todorov, and most of the authors in a collective work like Bhabha's *Nation and Narration* that is especially conscious of its "postcolonial" status. Some negotiate the problem better than others (Ahmad has been notably critical of Jameson and Said). I take these only as representative of many.

For metropolitan writers, at least, a further complexity is at issue: one to which some are blinder than others. It has to do with learning to listen, precisely, to differences; with trying to understand them on their own terms as wholes rather than absorb them as "our" "other"; with knowing that diverse cultural processes *do* exist, binding people in different kinds of relations and understandings of being (for example), and that these must change our ideas of literature and criticism just because they query the claim of any culture to centrality or universality. "To be incapable of seeing that Nature has more than one face, that humans have a variety of ideas and interests," wrote José Enrique Rodó a century ago, "is to live in a shadowy dreamworld penetrated by a single ray of light" (*Ariel*, 42). It is to be willingly and wilfully blinkered, Achebe repeats, into refusing "the validity of sensibilities other than [one's] own," it is to "lack enough imagination to recreate in ourselves the thoughts that must go on in the minds of others, especially those we dispossess" (*Hopes*, 89, 149). This is a further complexity for metropolitan critics if it is true that a critical craft developed under western skies offers only endlessly self-repetitive devices of entrapment. Those who come from different cultures would benefit from already inhabiting different cultural processes from those that made the craft. But I say "at least" about those metropolitan critics at the start of this paragraph because although many claim this gain from "nonmetropolitan" status, real practice rather suggests that the status often derives from simple negation of metropolitan claim, *négritude* from whiteness, subalternity from dominance. The craft's very force may be disabling—although Bhabha, for one, argues that, if anything, this location of theory makes its commitment the *more* essential (*Location*, 19–39). We have seen much of this dilemma, whose complexity will bring it time and again to our attention.

This is not to belittle achievements of metropolitan cultures (a self-flagellating gesture that but obfuscates or blocks efforts of real exchange). It is to open them up to others, to "jolt all the familiar landmarks of thought," voice, and action (Foucault, *Mots*, 7). It is, with Kane, to open others and refuse to let "the most strident voices . . . cover the others." It is to try and understand how cultures together build "an architecture of responses" that are all equally necessary (*Aventure*, 81; *Adventure*, 69). To do this involves many tasks. The history of the invention of metropolitan cultures needs exploring, to understand both their own mechanisms and their relation with other cultures. The ways in which different cultural arenas function and can take up processes found elsewhere is a subject demanding attention. Fanon's reply to Sartre will be observed later as in this respect exemplary. Too, the manner of such relations needs explaining. Most who address the issue assume cultural antagonisms that take the form of oppressor and oppressed, of colonizer and colonized. It matters to know the mechanisms of dispossession, of internalized oppression, of identity bereft, and of how cultural territory is mapped (a much-worked concept). But the similarities of explanation and vocabulary among so many tend to be dispiriting. Further, seen through such spectacles, cultural territories inevitably fall into here and there, self and other. As an explanatory tool, the device may not be unhelpful. As an instrument of the changes rightly sought by most writers in this arena it is less so. Conflictual divisions, neat explanatory boxes, correspond neither to the reality of cultural meetings nor to the complexity of their creation. They repeat the confrontations and oppositions of the last chapter.

Said argues in "Yeats and Decolonization" that imperialism means a loss of the colonized place by its natives as colonizers "map" it, "chart" it for themselves. The place acquires a "second nature." Once so mapped, it no longer seems a colonial creation. To recover the place, the "anti-imperialist nationalist" must "remap" it, people it with myths and religion, as well as find a language, by "an almost magically inspired, quasi-alchemical redevelopment of the native language" (Eagleton et al., *Nationalism*, 77–79; the essay is now in Said's *Culture*). Such finding, remapping, has to use the "second nature" made by previous mappers, at the same time as it draws on other cultural memories. What is so made has much to do with conflict, nothing with simple polarities. Walcott's Shabine similarly cried at the end of his sea- and self-search of "The Schooner Flight": "make these islands fresh. . . . Open the map" (*Collected Poems*, 360).

Cultural categories mingle and float. "Borders" are more than just porous. Cultures are mutually defining. The fault of European culture was to believe they are not; that the burden of definition lay wholly on it— Rodó's "single ray of light." The challenge for contemporary critics working from within that arena is to avoid the trap of that belief. As de Certeau pointed out, all everyday living entails in some way the establishment of "a geography," a space in which stories are told to "mark out boundaries," to organize meaningful spaces of life, "the determination of frontiers." Here, Ortega y Gasset suggested, the *actual* we experience is in fact "a certain manner of happening that is familiar to us." Where such stories disappear, "the group or the individual regresses toward the disquieting, fatalistic experience of a formless, indistinct, and nocturnal totality" (de Certeau, *Practice*, 122–23; Ortega, *Meditations*, 132). But these mappings, frontiers, and boundaries are endlessly complex in their interrelations. Simplified binarisms will not do—nor, I think, will notions of living in interstices, as if margins, peripheries, or limina were themselves other than inventions of some putative "center." Even in all their endless complexities and ongoing makings, what are mapped remain *homes*, places where people *belong*, knots in the net of world cultures. To be in the interstices is precisely not to be home. It is to be making a passage *between* homes—and to know that one is, however perplexedly (which seems part of Bhabha's point in *Location*, 9–18; see, too, note 17 to Chapter 3 below).

"Tell me, Askar," asks that protagonist's uncle Hilaal in Nuruddin Farah's novel, *Maps*, "do you find truth in the maps you draw?" Answered by silence, Hilaal clarifies his question: "Do you carve out of your soul the invented truth of the maps you draw? Or does the daily truth match, for you, the reality you draw and the maps others draw?" A pause ensues before Askar replies "with the confidence of one who's regained possession of a mislaid identity":

"sometimes," I began to say, "I identify *a* truth in the maps which I draw. When I identify *this* truth, I label it as such, pickle it as though I were to share it with you, and Salaado. I hope, as dreamers do, that the dreamt dream will match the dreamt reality—that is the invented truth of one's imagination. My maps invent nothing. They copy a given reality, they map out the roads a dreamer has walked, they identify a notional truth." (216)

In fact, Askar was mapping a Somalia that included the Ogaden region and the lands for which the Western Somali Liberation Front was fighting against Ethiopia. His "notional truth" could become a "third nature," no less real than the present one. The creation of such national territory depends on people identifying it as such—and no less does their identity depend on it. As Ngũgĩ puts it with force: "When a people's land is taken away, the basis of their being is removed" (*Writers*, 108). To retake the land is to reestablish being. The maps with which Askar has to start, whether Mercator or decimal, are European in origin. But in turn these overlay earlier ones.

Farah writes of a quest for national and personal identity, recovery of things of which one has been dispossessed. But his narrator, a voice always switching between second, first, and third persons, traverses frontiers that move, gazes on seas that acquire changing meanings, delves into divers tales of his and others' pasts, explores the varieties of culture—why, for example, a long-lived written culture has no "single . . . genius of a poet," whereas one that has had a script for less than a century has "many hundreds of major poets"—and wonders whether these varieties let one rank cultures (201).[5] These questions, including the last ethnocentric one (as Hilaal accuses), are among those of this chapter. For Farah, writing in 1986 from an unsettled place of strife, they could only be matter for telling and retelling: "in the process he became the defendant. He was, at one and the same time, the plaintiff and the juror. Finally, allowing for his different personae to act as judge, as audience and as witness, Askar told it to himself" (246). These tellings, says this last sentence of the novel, can never escape forensic inquiry. No judgment is at hand. The teller never gets beyond queries, however they and he cry for resolution. He has nowhere to fix the bounds of an answer, nowhere from whence to project the lines of an ordered cartography, no "self" to give a source for the survey: "no one has ever explained how to read maps, you see, and I have difficulty deciphering all the messages" (111).

Most critics rarely admit to such perplexities. Evidently, if you see cultures as oppressors and victims, as sites of historical conflict between takers and producers, as neatly bounded spaces of difference, matters are simpler. In itself, that neither invalidates the arguments nor makes them not worth repeating. It may though limit their import. Introducing the anthology from which I quoted Said, Seamus Deane (like two of his three authors) thus takes a rather uncomplicated view of Irish culture and its relation to British nationalism. He notes how revisionist Irish history, by seeing Irish–English relations in localized terms, too complex for systematic explanation, tends to play the game of the conqueror by occluding the effects of conquest and denying they can be at all analyzed. A whole analysis, he insists, must bind the localisms and account for Britain's imperialist role. Not to do so is to repeat universalist claims that give imperialist culture title over the localisms of Irish culture (introduction to Eagleton et al., *Nationalism*). We earlier saw Fanon propose that "separatism and regionalism" were in fact deliberately deployed by colonialism (*Wretched*, 94). Deane's problem is that nothing goes beyond terms of conflict.

Like everyone reviewed here, Deane rejects claims that any particular art is universal: it is a "specific activity indeed, but one in which the whole history of a culture is deeply inscribed. The interpretation of culture is not predicated on the notion that there is some universal quality or essence that culture alone can successfully pursue and capture. That is itself a political idea that has played a crucial role in Irish experience" (7). Universalist claims let one national culture be imposed on another: the second inevitably then modeled on the imposing culture (7–8). "At its most powerful, colonialism is a process of racial dispossession. A colonized people is without a specific history and even, as in Ireland and other cases, without a specific language" (10). As we saw Said remark, a first step will thus be to regain a language of culture. The process is perforce communal, however it is lived in individual cases, and "often begins with the demolition of the false stereotypes within which it has been entrapped. This is an intricate process, since the stereotypes are successful precisely because they have been interiorized" (12).[6] It is how a hegemonic system "continues to exert," avers Eagleton here, "an implacable political force" (24).

For Eagleton also agrees that the victim is forced to struggle in terms supplied by the oppressor (not so simple, Farah suggests). The fight, therefore, "will demand a difficult, perhaps ultimately impossible double optic, at once fighting on terrain already mapped out by its antagonists and seeking even now to prefigure within that mundane strategy styles of being and identity for which we have as yet no proper names" (24). Eagleton calls this double optic "irony." *Ulysses* and *Finnigan's Wake* both perform it, rendering a sardonic "aesthetic totalization" of the Enlightenment "opposition" between aesthetic particularity and abstract understanding. Dublin becomes at once an iteration of imperial centers and "an expression of the rootless conditions of an international monopoly capitalism" (35). James Joyce gives Ireland a center that is none (34–37). Like Said's Yeats, Eagleton's Joyce reaches a threshold he cannot cross, for colonialism "is a *relation*" and a "nation cannot live on as some corporate self-identical entity once those political relations have been dismantled" (28).

One takes the point, but the trouble, always and always, lies in the implacable conflictual critical model. Neither Deane nor Eagleton escapes the thought of opposed bounded entities, so matters come there to an end. They do, too, in Jameson's piece in this collection, analyzing "varieties of imperialism" in works by writers such as Forster and, again, Joyce. He takes *Howard's End* to show imperialism as "bad" infinity: an endless effort of motion that is "the bad opposite of place itself"—"cosmopolitanism, London, the nomadic, the stench of motorcars, antibilious pills, all begin to coalesce as a single historical tendency" (57). In Forster, this is named "Empire," a place of finally meaningless and continuous motion. To Jameson, this lack of meaning marks the disunion between a metropolis and the colonies that enable its life, while staying invisible to it. The very working of Empire is hidden from its metropolitan beneficiaries (50–51). In Dublin, however, Joyce finds place: enclosed, always already "told," repeating in minor key the habitation of an older imperial dispensation—

where meetings and conversations evince "an older urban life," a totalizing map that turns "the great imperial space of the Mediterranean" into a closed "space of the colonial city" (60–64). Jameson's view—this opposition—echoes Eagleton's and Deane's, ignoring Ahmad's potent 1987 critique of Jameson's influential essay, "Third World Literature in the Era of Multinational Capitalism," on just this ground of reifying nonwestern literatures into his "civilizational Other" (Ahmad, *In Theory*, 96; see also 95–122). Although Jameson there acknowledges the deep problem of what he calls this "strategy of otherness," he finds it unavoidable for the "first-world intellectual" if she or he is not to fall "back into some general liberal and humanistic universalism" ("Third World," 77). So years later (1998), he still ends his introduction to an anthology ostensibly moving beyond this familiar paradigm by praising its address to "the West and its Others" (Jameson, preface to *The Cultures of Globalization*, xvi).

This view and this opposition is also that of the authors of many of the essays in Bhabha's collection—which are indeed so many and varied as rather to impede commentary; I surely belittle many subtleties of argument in reducing them to a place in my present one. They include efforts to suggest that (even) in the West's past, forms of patriotism have existed that offered a civic arena of debate akin to Habermas's public sphere, quite different from post-eighteenth-century nationalisms, and opening ways to "otherness" blocked by these later developments (Simon During, John Barrell). Such views may have shared much with Jean-Jacques Rousseau's offering narration as escape from nation as nature and its violence and a rediscovery of nature before violence: true nation (Geoffrey Bennington). Such claims about historical binarisms are echoed with more or less nuance of nineteenth-century North American writing (David Simpson, Rachel Bowlby), twentieth-century English writing and criticism (Francis Mulhern, Gillian Beer), and current criticism in Australia, where it is argued that hegemonic tendencies can be and are countered by formation of a supposedly "counter–public sphere" (Sneja Gunew).

Although I am being reductively unjust to some of the authors, binary claims overwhelm the reader. They point to flaws widespread in this writing. These have to do with neglecting the complications of history, with taking parts for wholes and so thinking narrow argument to be broadly validated, with confusing words and things—allowing for a certain ease of dogmatic assertion. Something of all these practices has already been at least suggested. Let me quickly take three cases—probably unfair to the overall arguments advanced by their authors, but suitably indicative of current discussions of literature, colonialism, nationalism, and such other vast bogeys of contemporary academic (and political) debate as multiculturalism, pluralism, and the canon.

For the first—skimming historical complexity—I take issue with a claim made in Timothy Brennan's essay in Bhabha's anthology, not because it is central to his argument but because it has become an article of faith in discussion about the relation between metropolitan literature and nationalism/colonialism (Brennan offers such names with which to conjure as those of Mikhail Bakhtin, Eric Hobsbawm, and Benedict Anderson; Said has reiterated the claim in *Culture*, 70, and *passim*). It is that the novel is most especially tied to the creation of the myth of the nation and divers secondary(?) myths sustaining it. Since the novel is thought a creation of the European eighteenth century, the tie knots happily with asserted implications of a dialectic of Enlightenment and a destruction of Reason. The claim merrily fits those of Bennington, Burrell, During, and others about a generosity of debate having been lost in the eighteenth century. But the force of the tie depends wholly, Brennan rightly sees, on the claim of novelty (the overall assertion seeks to bind capitalism, nationalism, imperialism, and colonialism to new European cultural forms—so many eighteenth-century "deviations").

So, Brennan holds, the novel's ancestor, the epic, was (unlike the novel) never addressed "to or for one's contemporaries" (Bhabha, ed., 50). This is patently false, whether of the *Aeneid*, the *Divine Comedy*, the *Lusiades*, *Orlando furioso*, the *Franciade*, *Gerusalemme liberata*, the *Faerie Queene*, the *Pucelle*, or even *Paradise Lost*; all addressed contemporaries in very particular ways, and most meant specifically to elaborate myths of national origin or achievement (cf., for example, Helgerson, *Forms*; Quint, *Epic*). At least as far as literature is the issue, the story *has* to be complicated. Bhabha and his contributors, Deane and his colleagues, Jusdanis, Gourgouris, and many others (after Horkheimer, Adorno, and Lukács) want to fix nation-making basically in the European nineteenth century, when it would have been consolidated as a main "imaginary form" of Enlightenment (Gourgouris, 15; but cf. 51–52, where he seeks to extend Enlightenment backward). History will not allow: not with regard to the cultural narrations that develop the idea (nor to wider activities, including, I have urged in *The Meaning of Literature*, the making of "literature" itself). Epics were not just "ritualistic reaffirmations of a people." They may not have sought to "*create* a people"; they most assuredly sought regularly to establish a dynastic legitimacy *for* a people. Some sense of "national identity," of a localizable, differentiated community with which one could and did identify, with its myths and tales, long preexisted the European nineteenth century—as did its modern understanding of literature.[7] (This is not even to start addressing the old chestnut of the novel as descendent of epic, a myth dating from Fénelon's *Télémaque* and its early eighteenth-century consecration as *the* archetypal novel—as if the genre had not existed at least since Hellenistic Greece.)

How much does this matter? For one thing, it queries the many blindnesses hidden behind Bruce Robbins' recalling, in the same collection, a question put to Raymond Williams by the editors of the *New Left Review* and which have to do with my second issue: about narrow parts confused for broad wholes. The editors noted that (Williams') literary criticism did not cope with the Irish famine or the 1848 revolutions, thus showing that there was indeed no way of getting from texts to structures of feeling, to real experience and thence to social structures (the editors' main reference for their bizarre positivism must be Williams' *Marxism and Literature*) (Bhabha, ed., 213). Williams replied with the case of Charles Dickens. Robbins does not question this reply. Both are emblematic. For while *New Left Review may* be able to make the assertion apropos of *a* novel, it cannot be meaningful to make it of *the* novel: from Edgeworth and Austen to Balzac and Sue, from La Roche and the Brontës to Turgenyev and Tolstoy, from Sand and George Eliot to Melville and Hawthorne, from Mazzini and Galdos to Chernychevsky, Dickens, and others treated in Bhabha's collection—not to mention their many seventeenth- and eighteenth-century ancestors. The failure—by everyone—is again of the historical imagination (or worse). Somehow too, unselfconsciously, all take a pretended English case as not just exemplary but all-embracing. Long ago, I noted the odd reinscription in Eagleton's *Criticism and Ideology* of familiar but excoriated Great Tradition categories in its explanation of nineteenth-century (English) novels (now in *Uncertainty*, 192–94). Jusdanis finds a like blindness in Eagleton's *Function of Criticism*, which "assumes the existence of a homogenous criticism and deems it unnecessary to mention that its real subject is English criticism" (*Belated*, 6). One recalls Achebe's remark about the weight of a cultural psychology that seems to trap an ever-anxious West in a position where it defines itself and is at ease only as a citadel resisting otherness (*Hopes*, 17).

The blindness of critics to their own historical situation, and to the historical determinants of their chosen cultural object, is not accidental. It is a factor of the very nationalism wherein they operate—at least if we are to believe Ernest Renan, translated in Bhabha's collection: "Forgetting, I would even go so far as to say historical error, is a crucial factor in the creation of a nation, which is why progress in historical studies often constitutes a danger for [the principle of] nationality" (Bhabha, ed., 11). For Renan, of course, nation was a good thing (indeed, a foundation for ranking peoples; 12–14). That the national idea is the result of a particular *story* must therefore be forgotten (18–19). So, too, in an exactly similar way, must that by which the nation as colonizer violates its victim, naturalizing their pasts into two sides of one same, in a shared "forgetfulness." For the colonizer, forgetfulness creates the idea of historically inevitable progress, springing from a "timeless and perpetual" nation, "an ontological presence that has, somehow or other, always already existed" (Gourgouris, 18). For the colonized, it means "our people losing grip on their history, being swept out of the current of their history into somebody else's history, becoming a footnote"—or becoming negritude to whiteness, spirituality to materialism. That the "history of Africa became the history of alien races in Africa, and the real history . . . was virtually forgotten" were necessary consequences of the retelling (Achebe, *Conversations*, 157). Only by forgetting can nations and their oppressions come to seem natural (the "second nature" of which Said writes). The forgetting of the story of origins at the same time makes a space *and* lays a base for forging "a rich legacy of memories," a storied tradition that allows present consent to the heritage (19), such as the invention of "literature" I mentioned in Chapter 1. Clearly, the question is not just nationalism, but the functioning of the cultural environment as a whole.

This is why, I think, a certain obfuscation is needed on the part of dogmatic metropolitan critics. Claims undermining our "rich legacy," our Great Tradition, and arguments suggesting that our metropolis is established simultaneously with the forgetting of that establishment are to be denied. Our comprehension of other cultural traditions requires somehow a stability of cultural distinctness (at the very least to enable an apprehension of contrast). My third issue about binary claims has to do with this. For it is, I think, to save the possibility of such claims, even as Eagleton seeks to discuss abstractly their sociopolitical establishment, that he continues, in *Ideology: An Introduction*, his attacks on Michel Foucault and others. The overt aim of this work is to analyze the meanings of the word and idea of "ideology" and to pursue its history from the eighteenth century to the twentieth. Implicitly, Eagleton also explores the arguments enabling the establishment of his own cultural space (my immediate interest here). Indeed, his focus of debate, setting aside the establishment of "ideology," is almost wholly within the contemporary British left.

That Eagleton should virtually start by attacking Foucault's arguments about the ubiquity of power on the grounds that the claim is so broad as to be useless as an analytical tool is distinctly revealing (*Nationalism*, 7). For there is much difference between saying that all signifying practices involve relations of power and then specifying the nature of the relations. The first is an axiom to ground projects exploring the second. "Foucault and his followers" do not "effectively abandon the concept of ideology altogether" (8). Rather do they suggest a way to understand what enables *all* social relations of any kind, at the same time as they make us aware of what lies within them. The clue to what is behind Eagleton's criticism is his Popperian claim that this view of "power" is too capacious: "For a term to have meaning, it must be possible to specify what, in particular circumstances, would count as the other of it" (7). He believes he is qualifying his assertion by acknowledging that that "other" need not, however, be "*always and everywhere* the other of" the term (7).

Foucault's point is precisely to qualify that very notion of "other." Societies, the ordered and meaningful relations composing them, do not, he says, *have* such an "other." The idea of ordered signifying practices is the *ground* of any and all understanding. So it is of societies, which are to be understood in the intermeshing organization of their multiple signifying practices, *not* in any putative contrast to other societies. "Nature," for example, is always "nurture" in some way—the problem is to understand, as Said and Farah propose, different mappings of nature. As I said before, there can be no "other" as the "opposite" of such kinds of complex processes and entities. So "ideology" can be a way of understanding different *functionings* of power: it deals not with whether power is present or not, but with its "how." In this regard, the very idea of *otherness* is an element *within* the functionings of power particular to western culture(s). It is the inevitable supplement of the self-consciousness taken to be the necessary agent of such power.

So Eagleton's argument is not unlike Joan Scott's odd assertion, which I have discussed elsewhere, that if consciousness is always part and parcel of a changing social environment (just as different functionings of power will be), it means that "political differences among women cannot be explained as false consciousness" (*Gender*, 4). Of course it means nothing of the sort. Consciousness, experience, and identity may change, but in given times and places, they are constrained by specifiable conditions. It is, I observed, in relation to such *conditions* that we speak of "false consciousness," thereby signifying the internalization of a self-understanding that actually betrays the subject's own interests, whether of gender, class, race, or whatever ("History, Criticism," 149–50). This is what Chinweizu means when he describes a colonized population as one "with false historical and cultural consciousness" (*Decolonising*, 219). This *includes* issues of identity per se only as *aspects* of that displacement from one history into another of which I wrote earlier. It is nonsense to *oppose* false consciousness to consciousness as self-identity, whether fixed or in flux; the one is a part of the other. This is, indeed, one of Eagleton's understandings of ideology. In both cases, two different levels of analysis have been conflated. Like "false consciousness," "ideology" signals diverse orders of power and diverse relations of power in an overall social environment usefully understood in terms of signifying practices. These last impose such instrumental guides to activity as we have already seen. Their immense variety of form and nature from society to society is just what causes the dilemmas and predicaments addressed here.

Human consciousness may have been different in ancient Greece from its "counterpart" in modern Europe, among the Hopi or in contemporary China, but within each environment, no analytical difficulty is involved in grasping oppositional functions and practices. One understands, for instance, that in most or all American Indian cultures, autobiography (as a continuous story of a contained and possessive self) has not been possible. This is because individual consciousness did not precede community or make a possession of its "self"—it has not been a bounded and enclosed place or entity. Achebe makes the same point about his Igbo culture, in which the singular human is "in a very real sense subordinate to his community":

But even more important, he is subordinate to the sway of non-human forces in the universe, call them God, Fate, Chance or what you will. I call them sometimes the Powers of Event, the repositories of causes and wisdoms that are as yet, and perhaps will always be, inaccessible to us. (*Hopes*, 57)

But in neither of these cases does this mean there could be no process internal to such cultures playing on that "communal" comprehension in conflictual ways, maybe organizing it in terms of some dominant (or subordinate) interest. Of this, Jomo Kenyatta gave a fine example when observing the material actuality of communal relations among the Agīkūyū of Kenya analogous to those of which Achebe was to speak.

Analyzing land tenure, Kenyatta described how Gīkūyū "communion with the ancestral spirits is perpetuated through contact with the soil in which the ancestors of the tribe lie buried" (*Facing*, 21—hence, among other things, that huge importance of land to being to which Ngūgī alludes). He noted that communal socialization by parents, family, and other traditional groupings did not mean no "individualist" existed, but that she or he was abnormal, with "no name or reputation," "looked upon with suspicion and . . . given a nickname of *mwebongia*, one who works only for himself and is likely to end up as a wizard." Religious practice and belief shared the material actuality of a "communal life . . . regulated by customs and traditions handed down from generation to generation," absent "the individualistic aspects embodied in Christian religion (*Facing*, 119, and see also 99–129; 271, and see also 241–68). "According to Gikuyu ways of thinking," Kenyatta ends, "nobody is an isolated individual. Or rather, his uniqueness is a secondary fact about him: first and foremost he is several people's relative and several people's contemporary." Spiritually, economically, and biologically, a person's life "is founded on this fact," daily work "is determined by it, and it is the basis of his sense of moral responsibility and social obligation. His personal needs, physical and psychological, are satisfied incidentally while he plays his part as member of a" variety of communities. Individualism is associated with evil (309–10). This is not to say that persons cannot be separated from others, but that under normal conditions, that is neither a principal nor a centrally interesting fact about them.

One needs, that is to say, to feel for such conflictual processes as these within unfamiliar parameters (unfamiliar to those in cultures different from these Indian, Igbo, or Gīkūyū ones), but that is quite different from arguing that these conflicts either cannot be analyzed if all are taken as matters of power relations or are not in question if consciousness is a social construct. Since all social order necessarily involves inclusions and exclusions, there is no doubt that such processes exist. Foucault's point is that we need first to try and grasp wholes in their own particular forms of functioning. Where societies and cultures are concerned, we can best do so by seeing them as ways of organizing events, meanings, and activities—ways always imbricated in specific and local relations of power and titles of interest. Eagleton wants, rather, to know them first from *here, as* "our" other. Then what "second" is possible? One could hardly find a clearer instance of the western dilemma with which I began this chapter: using instruments presupposing confrontation, separateness, and isolation, how are the spaces between cultural places to be bridged? How can one even envision homes, places, and times in their own particularities?

Eagleton's repeated attack on Foucault's reminder of Marxism's embedding in nineteenth-century argument (*Nationalism*, 27) also has a kind of ironic poignancy. Elsewhere, too, I have noted that the reminder itself, if its import is to be thoroughly understood and put to work, needs grasping in its own political context ("History, Criticism," 141). Foucault, as what I have just been saying must make clear, always accepted this need to work through the "presentness" of one's own discursive practice (quoted by Jusdanis, xv). Eagleton himself notes, we saw, that hegemonies have to be lived and worked through—one cannot grope around them—although the peculiarly abstract language of his "coming out on the other side," as though ideology and hegemony were reified places, rooms through which one can pass, gives pause. For the fact seems to be that Eagleton, like others here, suffers from a particular blind spot: an inability to do that working through, fixed in an opposition of self and other. That is surely why he reestablishes categories of a familiar (English) Great Tradition and why, as Jusdanis again observes, when he writes an essay on "Literature's Romantic Era," the titular universalism turns out to lie wholly within "the boundaries of England" (6). In his *Function of Criticism* (123), his eye lighting on Habermas, Eagleton calls for an idea of criticism as "a counter-public sphere." The thought is used by Gunew in her contribution to *Nation and Narration*, although she also admits that it has been criticized as meaningless in Habermas' terms: the "counter" is already in his public sphere. The point is that the public sphere is, precisely, *not* a place but rather a practice; once again Eagleton is caught in the trap—trope—of his "other."

Eagleton's repeated criticisms of Foucault's reminder may be thought of as his scratching at a symptomatic itch. Foucault's not very hidden intent (his taking aim at the analyses behind Stalinist excesses of the French Communist Party aside) was at least twofold. First, that Karl Marx had analyzed a particular socioeconomic order at a particular moment of development. Second, that it was nonetheless taken (by Marx and his successors) as universally valid. The first means that new analyses are continually needed and that they are themselves an aspect of the issues they analyze and a part of the solution of their impasses: we analyze our own practices from within—as Cheyfetz carefully observes in his introduction to *The Poetics of Imperialism*. Such analyses are among and made from the signifying practices which compose our cultural home.

The second should act as a warning: to beware of belief, not in totalizing analyses (which do not per se exclude difference) but in the universal validity of any one topical analysis. Historical materialism rested on analysis of a specific moment in a particular industrial society. In *Marxism and Literature*, Williams explored the processes of its foundation and some ways of extending and adjusting them to understanding cultural practices in various times and places. The inevitable fluidity and even vagueness that result are consequences Eagleton and others resist (Reiss, *Uncertainty*, 179–203). His bent is for more foursquare analysis: he knows where he is, and he wants clarity of outcome. He may have doubts as to what exactly he may find when he opens the door on the other side of the room that we (Europeans) now, and everyone will, occupy. He has no doubts of the room, or that it has familiar-looking doors, or that when he finally steps through the *right* one (that with the "proper name"), there will be another room probably not *so very* different—its form already predicated by the analysis and the material of the room which *had* to precede it in the narrow house-trailer of time. You speak, as many have said, from where you live, but that is a far cry from saying everyone else should—or should want to—live there too (which is what *Ideology* is ostensibly all about—entirely, polemically so).

This may be ever so slightly parodic and less than just. But Eagleton's figure, and his figuring, are so ubiquitous in these debates (not least because of the ready analysis and answer he is taken to provide) as to require some observation of their danger. And it is real. For these blindnesses reinscribe the processes they claim to question. What is the function of criticism? To query the dominant claims of cultural hegemonies? Or to maintain them? To make a "counter"-public sphere? Or rest in the same? The questions and choices are not unfamiliar ground. That is not the point. The irascible inability to question the ground is. Eagleton stands in here as the figuring of danger just because his work has proven so seductive. To use his name so would be ungracious and gratuitous were the peril not, I have tried to show, general: that of making one culture central, deriving as it were all cultures from that one, valorizing universally one standard of taste, analysis of worth, and imperative of order, without adequately determining the grounds and sources of the valorization, or marking the limits not necessarily of application but of the grounds of application. The danger is not that one speaks from within "the formative places of Enlightenment"—those born there have no choice in *that*. Rather, is it that without knowing the grounds of the practices from within which we speak, we may do so without being able, as Günter Grass has put it, to tell the "old story . . . altogether differently" (Reiss, *Meaning*, 346–47).

The object, really, of all those examined here, is to try and find ways of carrying out Grass' suggestion, to tell an old story differently, rework ways of seeing, open up a western enclosure. I put it that way because most analyze cultural relations of power in that enclosure and want to change them, although they perforce do so from a position, as it were, "on top." Most of the authors work, like myself, in metropolitan universities and publish with metropolitan presses (Cambridge, Oxford, Verso, Routledge, Minnesota, to name the presses that publish the work of the authors discussed in this chapter) for a principally academic audience. That, again, is why I have used Eagleton as an emblem of the dangers of enclosure. For to speak of the "other" is *not*, is *never*, to step outside. "The other," Antonio Machado's Abel Martín insisted, "does not exist." The self's identity in western culture as always "one and the same" is its lived reality. What it experiences as a persistent and ineliminable *other* is "'la esencial Heterogeneidad del ser,' como si dijéramos . . . la incurable *otredad* que padece lo *uno*" ("the essential Heterogeneity of being", . . . what we might call the incurable *otherness* which *oneness* suffers"; *Juan de Mairena*, 1:85). It is no surprise that Octavio Paz used this passage as the epigraph to his exploration of what he perceived as Mexico's double reality in his *Labyrinth of Solitude*, its Indianness *inside and "against"* its Hispanicity, where "mask" and "true visage" are part and parcel of the same, as he added later (*Other Mexico*, 216). Ortega y Gasset observed how the "*other*" (*alter*) that the self projects on the outside world as a way to "master" it is just means to overcome the *alteración* that is the self's permanent state of internal agitation—playing on Spanish *alteración*, signifying "alteration," "making other" (etymologically), *and* "commotion" or "tumult" ("Self," 169, 165). The western self *also and simultaneously* always contains and projects its other.

So one of the major ways to start telling the tale differently must start by examining the construction of the enclosure. That is what Jusdanis seeks to do in *Belated Modernity*. The case of modern Greece that he takes is an especially interesting one. Having been marginalized from a western European sphere more or less after Hellenistic times, Greek culture had a quite separate development throughout the Byzantine period and was absorbed, after 1453, into the Ottoman Empire. Earlier western indifference became something akin to willful ignorance (15). At the same time, western European cultures were busy making old Greece into one of their two founding pillars. By the late eighteenth century, many Greek intellectuals were aware of this, and as they began to imagine "the idea of a national community distinguished by language" (25), they turned to this West for cultural aid, unabashedly using its nostalgia for the grandeur of antiquity. By the time of the 1821 revolts (33), a westernizing intellectual establishment was already publishing both newspapers and literary works abroad, mostly in the German-speaking lands.

Jusdanis argues that modern Greek literature sought to constitute itself a bulwark—indeed, seal and guarantor—of a nation-state being established in the struggle against the Ottoman Empire by deliberately modeling itself on the metropolitan cultures of which I have been speaking. Already complicated by argument over the several varieties of Greek language, however, relations with western models were further confused by the fact that whereas in western cases it could be argued that modern literature was associated with "bourgeois individualism," in Greece, the association of literary culture with the 1821 revolts against the Ottoman Empire made it a buttress of Greek "feudalism," however different "clientelistic" relations between "the oligarchy of landlords and military men" and the peasants may have been from an older western European dispensation (32–33). In modern times, Jusdanis suggests, this has given a cast to Greek literature quite different from that of its western European counterparts: not some "compensatory" practice offering "a space of deliverance from the consequences of social fragmentation" (103), but a cultural product resisting "autonomization" until very late in the twentieth century and, in its efforts to remain part of "social and political life," offering a critique of "modernity" (113–21). Here, Gourgouris sees "Greece's ever-receding position in the race toward modern civilization, its irredeemable belatedness in the formation and function of modern institutions, its ever more breathless anxiety for the international prestige of bourgeois regularity" (*Dream*, 70–71).

With regard to how a national literature—and indeed a nation—may be established, the case is a fascinating one, and Jusdanis (and Gourgouris, very differently) seems quite right to believe it holds lessons for many other cultural centers: not least in the play of metropolis and "margin," of how the last may change the first in using it and of how unfamiliar forms of analysis may be needed to interpret texts and understand their functioning. In this regard, Jusdanis seems to avoid (perhaps better than Gourgouris) the danger observed by Prakash that the story of an "aborted or failed modernity defers the conclusion of the modernization narrative but does not eliminate the [western] teleological vision" ("Writing," 367). Making his story one of "belated" modernity, Jusdanis is able to show how Greece diverted and changed the instruments it took over, once they were inserted into a different cultural arena and a different history. Even so, the question of how the occupants of any cultural place could conceivably envisage themselves as "marginal" is one that evidently requires asking, and it will return later.

Other dilemmas exist. One concerns a kind of ethnocentrism. For a good century and a half, with geographic reason, the German lands were the major cultural reference for Greek intellectuals. So Jusdanis takes their development of literary culture as exemplary. From Gotthold Ephraim Lessing and Friedrich von Schiller, Goethe and Hegel, it is easy to develop a thought that literature in western modernity has been a cultural practice compensating for "social fragmentation." This does not require "western modernity" to be homogeneous—a view this book counters. The German case (differently from, but no less than, the Greek) was also one of "belated modernity." For various reasons, so were the Russian, Spanish, and Italian. However much the last two had been originators of concepts of literary modernism in the sixteenth and early seventeenth centuries, there was a kind of later dispersal: occasional peaks, but little sustained depth of "organic" production until much later—probably as late as the Greek ("organic" referring to an essential originary bond with social processes in toto). Perhaps the nation-state has a constitutional relation with "literature" as a whole, rather than with the novel alone. In any case, the problematic tie of the very idea of "modernity," with its divers exclusivities and Europeanist claims, to the ideas raised in my Introduction and first chapter, is among the issues treated here and throughout this volume.

Whatever may have occurred with the Italian and Spanish cases, quite other were those of the models taken by the eighteenth-century German-speaking writers: those of England and France. Here (and they after all did become models, indirectly or directly, angel or demon, for a multitude of later establishments), literature was emphatically not com-pensatory. It was one way of overcoming a sense of disaster and justifying establishment of new social and political sureties. In its first establishment, modern literature was so far from compensating for society's incapacities as to assure its stabilizing benefits. When German thinkers took over these claims a century later, they did so (at first, anyway) in terms enabling es-tablishment, not those compensatory of its failures. To misread German es-tablishment, therefore, may also be to misread Greek. For it, literature *al-ways* played an establishing role in "social and political life." How then are we to understand its differences? The issue, again, and as Gourgouris ex-plores through his *Dream Nation*, has to do with Renan's (and Eagleton's) forgetting, with the instruments, as Levi and others remind us, that not only enable such forgetting but go far to forge it. We have to make every effort to know the details of history, which are necessarily always those of *specific* histories, tied to places and times, to particular homes.

We must also avoid confusing words and things. That the word *na-tion* was not used in its modern sense until the nineteenth century does *not* mean its referent was not yet at issue; that the word *literature* did not ob-tain its modern nuances until Johnson's *Dictionary* does *not* mean that its familiar practice did not exist. Part of the problem in Jusdanis' work is that although he deals extensively with critics, there is virtually no study of "lit-erary" works: one needs some sense of a fit between what is said and what is done. This is a flaw I want to try to avoid here, in this book. Sometimes a problem also arises from using secondary sources: *pace* Habermas (185 n. 8), the term *public* was used in England and France in a quite modern sense well before the middle or late seventeenth century.[8] This matters because it is rightly taken to be at issue in the establishment of literary culture.

The case Jusdanis probes is of special interest, just because it raises is-sues of the relation between metropolis and "margin," literature and na-tional identity, possession and variety, of a kind that most of these critics should find especially fruitful. Modern Greece confronted and adopted western European cultural forms. Too, Greece is a bridge for those forms and their practitioners both to *their* adopted past and to wholly unfamiliar cultures. With Césaire, one must insist

that it is a good thing to place different civilizations in contact with each other; that it is an excellent thing to blend different worlds; that whatever its own par-ticular genius may be, a civilization that withdraws into itself atrophies; that for civilizations, exchange is oxygen. (*Discourse*, 11; cf. Ngũgĩ, *Writers*, 23)

As Baldwin specified the U.S. case: "our dehumanization of the Negro then is indivisible from our dehumanization of ourselves: the loss of our own identity is the price we pay for our annulment of his. . . . Hatred," he added, "which could destroy so much, never failed to destroy the man who hated and this was an immutable law" (*Notes*, 25, 113). For metropolitan critics, the Greek case offers a special sort of unfamiliar familiarity.[9]

There is another way to tell different stories. Simply by starting with the knowledge that one is in a place with its own interests and concerns, or even in a place somehow relieved of local entanglement, one can avoid catching oneself in traps of self and other. In the modern world, one may be caught in the webs of powerful cultural hegemonies, but one's adoption of elements from another (metropolitan) culture remain just that: an adoption. Jusdanis tries to show how a developing Greek aesthetic culture played ambivalently off western Europe to elaborate its own national cultural character. Molloy, astutely using centrally problematic tales of personal identity, shows how autobiographical stories can be ambiguous establishments of *political* actuality.

I earlier mentioned that the very idea of autobiography is no easy one for some cultures (there, American Indian and Igbo). This has been much less an issue for Latin American writers, at least insofar as personal identity is concerned. However, what is matter for arduous debate is the tie between person and political role, individual and community. It is not accidental that most of the autobiographers discussed by Molloy in *At Face Value* are more or less considerable political or cultural figures in various (mostly Argentinian) new sociopolitical establishments. Ambivalent as particular writers may be, individual identity is always constituted by way of political institution. This so differs from the "norms" of western European establishments of identity as hardly to need comment. At least from the seventeenth century, such identity was based in some idea of a self whose independent rights were owed entirely to the individual. It would be hard to find a modern European autobiography that did not make such an assumption, even when seeking to muddy the waters (André Malraux, for instance).

Molloy's persons, even when not major political figures, can think themselves only in the communal political arena. This is no less true of Argentina's founding paternal figure, Domingo Faustino Sarmiento, than it is of the Cuban slave Juan Francisco Manzano; the Argentinian journalist (and more) Victoria Ocampo; the Cuban exile, the Condesa de Merlin;

the Venezuelan Mariano Picón Salas; the Argentinians Norah Lange and Lucio Victorio Mansilla; or the Mexican José Vasconselos. Almost all make a kind of genealogy for their (written) identities by alluding to their reading of European books. But all without exception establish their current sense of stable identity by embedding it, however often tentatively and ambivalently, in a national story—one they have actually created or helped create (Sarmiento or Vasconselos) or one they see as defining the persona worthy of autobiography. Making identity by catching it in books of Europe and places of Latin America, identity at once personal and national, nicely enacts the treachery and fluidity of the frontier between metropolitan artifact and elsewhere. Such identities match Said's establishments of different "natures." Like Farah, they use known maps in a territory whose nature and boundaries will be made by someone other than their first makers.

The very idea of personal identity, as created, for example, in western autobiography, is thus altered, once taken within different cultures, thoughts that Molloy has also explored in fiction. Just as the mostly public figures of her scholarly work fix their being by binding it in recorded political annals, so the more private characters of *Certificate of Absence* seek to grasp a sense of themselves in small acts of mutual violence. Only in such communal antagonisms, grand political confrontation reduced to a minor key, can a protagonist find being: "What she writes does not constitute, and will never constitute, an autobiography: rather, it tries to reproduce a disjointed series of acts of violence that befell her, that also befell others" (Molloy, *Certificate*, 49). The historical figures explored in *At Face Value* had to fuse the artifacts of metropolitan cultures with the constitutions of their own history in order to establish their identity. The persons of *Certificate of Absence*, displaced as they are from the arena of that constitution, trace something like the failure of such an establishment. They remain "ill at ease in [their] skin" (5, 70), simulacra of containment showing themselves as tired efforts to fit one's "own order on what [one] transcribes" (8), fitful bids "to correct the image, or perhaps to restore some kind of order. . . . Order is what she wants to impose whenever she feels the threat of a shared vagueness, of an emptiness invading her emptiness" (10).

Like Farah, Molloy tracks the attempt to establish a sort of cartography of identity. Here too it can be sifted only in fugitive tellings: "Her words, herself: broken up, pieced together. . . . Her body and her phrase will tear again, but not at the old scars: they will split open in a different way, revealing new fractures. She accepts this future violence as something not necessarily negative, as a sign, perhaps, of a secret order." Yet words that "imply an order . . . also lead astray" (*Certificate*, 48). One is caught between need for maps and tales that may always, somehow, belong already to others and need for one's own place of customary habit. For one requires "the support of others" in familiarity (76). Whatever the small local violences, it is they who help "define [one's] existence" (95): "I wanted all of you—mother, sister, lovers—to be here, I live only in you" (116): perhaps in something like Machado's self/other, always producing, separating, and refusing "one another." The unending need to write is an effort somehow to make oneself into the safely continuous place of history. But "how to bring forth violence, how to write it down?" (86). As words escape, so does continuity: in the present ("she feels divided, wavering, suspended before a choice she does not control"; 71); of the past ("How can one return to what one has already seen, what one thought one already knew, and look at it afresh?"; 70).

I am reminded of no novel so much as of Witold Gombrowicz's *Cosmos*, which also tracks something like a dissolution of identity and of telling, not seldom in language almost identical. *Cosmos*, also written by an exile (spending years in Molloy's own homeland of Argentina before coming, like her, to France), ends in banality (see Chapter 7). *Certificate of Absence* ends in an airport: "she is alone: she is very frightened" (125). But I am reminded, too, of a novel some of our commentators have seen as addressing—rather more from the metropolitan side—these hard issues of national culture, colonialism, order, and identity: Rudyard Kipling's *Kim*. So far from being blunt, the novel approaches these puzzles with haunted wariness, avoiding simplistic snares of self and other in its careful wrestling with fluidities of frontiers and identity.

In the essay I commented on before, Jameson, opposing *Howard's End* to *Passage to India*, makes a useful point about the different ways the "colonizer" inhabits a home world and a colonized one. Introducing *Kim* (an essay reworked in *Culture*), Said echoes the point by comparing Dorothea Brooke's "reawakening" to the world at the end of George Eliot's *Middlemarch* and Kim's at the end of his story (introduction, 20). Where Dorothea feels part of an "involuntary, palpitating life," Kim's "wheels" of being "lock up anew on the world without": "roads were meant to be walked upon, houses to be lived in, cattle to be driven, fields to be tilled, and men and women to be talked to. They were all real and true—solidly planted upon the feet—perfectly comprehensible—clay of his clay, neither more nor less" (*Kim*, 331).

"For the European or American women in Europe," writes Said in his introduction (where he has spoken too of James' *Portrait of a Lady*), "the world is to be discovered anew; it requires no one in particular to direct it, or to exert sovereignty over it. [Molloy might well adjust this idea.] This is not the case in India, which would pass into chaos or insurrection unless roads were walked upon properly, houses lived in the right way, men and women talked to in correct tones" (21). But it is Said who adds "properly," "the right way," and "in correct tones," and that surely, as far as *Kim* is concerned, puts him in the wrong. It reduces the tale, as so often, to a mere opposition of Empire and victim. Firstly, to accept Said's own terms, Kim's reawakening is no more voluntary than Dorothea Brooke's or Isabel Archer's: "He *did not want to* cry—*had never felt less like* crying in his life—but of a sudden *easy, stupid* tears trickled down his nose, and with an almost audible click *he felt* the wheels of his being lock up anew on the world without" (331; my italics).

In fact, Kim, contrary to what Said asserts, is, *was always, both* native and nonnative: far more the first than the last. Furthermore, his place in Empire would be ambivalent even were that not so: his father, after all, was Irish, his own name is "Kimball O'Hara." Not by chance does a turning point in Kim's Bildungsroman occur in the high Himalayas in the company of his Tibetan spiritual guide, near and at the very Irish-sounding "shamlegh-midden" (chapter 14). Kim's wilfulness always regards, we learn at the start (51), the pleasures of the game, not the interests of politics. That is why it is *not* ludicrous for him to combine the (Buddhist) Way and the Great Game of imperial intelligence: both are forms of mapping. One has the lama's chart; the other has a surveyor's mensuration. This may be, as Said opines, "ahistorical" (22), but one can hardly bypass that difficulty in the novel by changing Kim. If we read him as a sign of a moment when "India was already well into the dynamic of outright opposition to British rule" (10), his ambivalence may be the more revealing: he embodies the struggle called "ironic" by Eagleton, the struggle neither Joyce nor Yeats, according to Said and Jameson, ever got out of. In many ways, *Kim* was clearly autobiographical of a Kipling who always felt closer ties with India and Indians where and with whom he was born and first raised than with England and the English, where he felt outcast not only because his sensibility set him apart from the sportingly virile ideal of public school manhood, but because his dark skin made him look "noticeably a non-white" (Nandy, *Intimate Enemy*, 67).

An elaborate reading of *Kim* here is probably otiose, but a few comments may at least highlight elements suggesting that even writers from "the formative places of Enlightenment" may begin to tell the tale otherwise, to touch hands, as it were, with Farah, Calvino, Carpentier, Molloy, and so many others. This matters because it already, whatever Said, Ahmad (*In Theory*, 168), and even Nandy (*Intimate Enemy*, 85, 98, 100) opine of Kipling's triumphalism, disables the choice of unambiguous opposition. For *Kim* too deals with maps of identity. Traveling the Great Trunk Road with the Buddhist abbot, Kim finds himself part of the teeming colors of India, not, *pace* Said, potential chaos, but ordered "left and right," composed of villagers purposefully dispersing "by twos and threes across the level plain. Kim felt these things, though he could not give tongue to his feelings" (Kipling, *Kim*, 111). "Who is Kim?" is a constantly reiterated question, from the time he feels himself as one "insignificant person in all this roaring whirl of India" (166). And he is, it is true, caught here between the uncharted free places of his native life (and land—for he *is* native)—unmade no doubt by colonization—and something else. Those places were, for him, a game until *threatened*, and it is indeed so presented in the novel, by its heavy-handed opposite: imperialist militarism, religion, and education at their most brutally oppressive. But Kim slides away from that opposition, toward some new making.

His chosen heroes are precisely those who reject simplicities. Neither Mahbub Ali nor Colonel Creighton is quite Pathan or Sahib. Each plays a wholly ambiguous role in the "confrontation" between oppressor and oppressed. Mahbub works for imperial order (inasmuch as divers imperial powers confront one another on Indian soil), but his dealing lies in the life and welfare of the bazaar. Creighton works for imperial order, but he is utterly absorbed in the life of India. The ("correct") Pathans' insurgent nationalism (Said, introduction to *Kim*, 26) has an exact counter in the brutal colonization of the regiment of Mavericks and its Red Bull ensign. Mahbub and Creighton play quite different roles, something approaching Kim's eventual "middle way," which is why Kim and Mahbub can exchange the "oppositional" terms, "sahib," "black man," "Pathan," as mockingly affectionate "insults." In irony, the very words lose their colonizing bite. Like the words Molloy's protagonists use or the maps put in Askar's hands, the colonizers' epithets get the sort of recast meaning that comes, as we saw

Nandy suggest in my Introduction, from altering "cultural priorities on both sides," remaking "subcultures previously recessive or subordinate," and sapping those "previously salient" (Nandy, *Intimate Enemy*, 2). Kim rejects the hypermasculinity and paternalism represented by the Mavericks and Raj bureaucrats for a "softer side" emphasizing "speculation, intellection and *caritas*" (*Intimate Enemy*, 32). To be sure, much of Kim's instruction will now be in how to measure, map, and order place on behalf of the rulers of the Great Game—so much so that Kim's search for personal identity *does* become caught up in mapping territory.

Likewise, the lama's quest for Enlightenment requires he draw in "clearest, severest outline" a chart of the "Great Wheel" (Kipling, *Kim*, 240). The angry tearing of this chart by the Russian agent results in the "collapse of their Great Game," brought about not by any "craft" or "contrivance" of their opponents, but "simply, beautifully, and inevitably" (297)—words earlier ascribed to India itself: "it was beautiful to behold" (111). There is an obvious lesson in this. As there is, too, in the abbot's discovery that he no longer needs his chart, when he can tell "fantastic piled narrative of bewitchment and miracles that set Shamlegh a-gasping" (307) and ultimately find that he "has reached Knowledge" (333). There is a lesson, too, in the fact that Kim now hears tales of the Sahibs from the Indians' viewpoint, "every detail lighted from behind" (306), and has thrown the fine surveyor's instruments that would have been so useful for him over the two-thousand-foot cliff of Shamlegh-midden; as if this backlighting had indeed overturned "all the familiar landmarks of thought—ours: that which has our age and our geography—, unsettling all the ordered surfaces and all the planes that temper the profusion of beings, disturbing and upsetting for a long time our millennial practice of the Same and the Other" (Foucault, *Mots*, 7). Kim has listened so well to the abbot's culture that he has to cast away the instruments that exactly represent the carefully vehement measuring priorities of European culture.

We may adopt Said's proposal that the museum-keeper's gift of spectacles to the lama to help him see better at the beginning of the novel (60) symbolizes "Britain's benevolent sway" (Said, introduction to *Kim*, 15)—not to mention an arrogant assumption that their eye problem is the same!—but we must then attend to what follows at the end: "even his spectacles do not make my eyes see" (320). Similarly, Said avers that the lama's living on Kim's "strength as an old tree lives on the lime of a new wall" (321) signals his dependence on Empire. He neglects not only Kim's ambiguous role but his answer that "Thou leanest on me in the body, Holy One, but I lean on thee for some other things" (321): spiritual growth and maybe the very changes we are tracing. To adopt a turned proverb Nandy uses somewhere to describe how the colonized may reassert cultural control in the face of the colonizer's force, this gives a new and more powerful twist to the maxim about the spirit being strong but the flesh weak. "Weakness" can itself become means to reassert a cultural home (*Intimate Enemy*, 64–113). It is no cause for surprise that the lama closes the novel: "he crossed his hands on his lap and smiled, as a man may who has won salvation for himself and his beloved" (338). This is the abbot's victory, not the Raj's. The "colonial system" may have "acquired the status of a fact of nature," from whose colonizing side Kipling inevitably wrote (Said, introduction to *Kim*, 10), but its interests are finally the lesser.

In some sense, of course that makes no difference on the ground really mapped out by and for those interests. In objective economic and political terms, the lama's gesture may be one of withdrawal: power, wealth, and advantage are the colonizers'. To see all that as "illusion" is to yield any alternative hold on it. Kim's own quest, you might say, now additionally buttressed by the lama's assurance, remains that of colonial adventurism, a game of "glory" which has, in some sense beyond ambivalence, coopted the way of the other. (What does it *mean* that Kim awakes to spiritual renewal, not unlike the Buddha, from a sleep under "a young banyan tree"?; 332). Still, of his Way, the Teshoo Lama is certainly not dispossessed, even if he symbolizes all other dispossession: his chart destroyed and his body beaten, with no worldly belongings—religion as satisfying opiate. But *that* interpretation turns the novel into a critique of everything British India stood for. So does Kim's wending a path between the Game and the Way, West and East, reason and spirit. And may not the destruction of Russia's part in the Great Game prefigure that of Britain's? The lama's mapping in his head can be India's of itself.

For one may interpret in quite different terms the fact that *Kim* ends with the abbot's contentment. His smiling wisdom seems to reflect Chatterjee's argument about the "strategies one encounters in the emergence of the disciplines in colonial society. The claim is not that the field of knowledge is marked out into separate domains by the fact of cultural difference," or that one is excluded from knowledge. It is "a claim for an alternative science [way of knowing] directed at the same objects of knowledge" ("Disciplines," 18–19). It happens that Chatterjee is writing of work in Calcutta exactly contemporary with Kipling's experience in India, as is Nandy in making virtually the identical point about figures like Sri Aurobindo (*Intimate Enemy*, 85–100), Mahatma Gandhi (*Intimate Enemy*, 48–63, 100–107), and certain scientists (*Alternative Sciences*). Such alternative ways work cumulatively, not exclusively, eventually leading to new cultural configurations. That, too, *Kim* indicates less than surreptitiously. Whatever others may do, Kim himself idolizes Lurgan (no European), Creighton, Mahbub, the Babu, and above all the lama. The first four inhabit a twilight world of ambivalent mappings. The last we have seen. For the reader, it is Kim's judgment, eponymous hero as he is, that must finally set interpretation.

A novel cannot change the objective realities of economic and political relations. It can elaborate their patterns. It may not only make us aware of differences of life, custom, culture, and language, but provide—require, it may be—some sort of access to them. Indeed, it is surely products of the fictive imagination that as much as any other practice change over time cultural instruments and the way they work and are used. An admired eighteenth-century predecessor of Kipling, Edward Gibbon, had long since, and no less ambiguously, proposed something similar:

An Iroquois work, even were it full of absurdities, would be an invaluable treasure; it would offer an unique specimen of the workings of the human mind, when placed in circumstances which we have never experienced, and influenced by manners and religious opinions entirely contrary to our own. We should be sometimes astonished and instructed by the contrariety of ideas thus produced; we should investigate the causes of their existence; and should trace the progress of the mind from one error to another. Sometimes, also, we should be delighted at recognizing our own principles recurring, but discovered in other ways, and almost always modified and altered. We should there learn not only to own, but also to feel the power of prejudices, not to be astonished at what appears most absurd, and often to distrust what seems best established. (*Essay*, 654)

In such commentary, to be sure, there may be much of Kipling's own "What do they know of England, / Who only England know?": the thought that even unfamiliar customs, practices, and artifacts exist to be turned to the service of metropolitan culture, to make "the site of cultural difference" into that "mere phantom of ['our'] dire disciplinary struggle," to repeat Bhabha. "Prospero," as Lamming once opined of the extent to which white western culture could accept crossings and interweavings, "doesn't mind re-marking these frontiers provided Caliban doesn't play the ass with further intrusion; provided, in other words, he doesn't ask for a new map altogether," demanding belief when he says to the old imperialist, "it has happened that Shakespeare and I have more in common than you and I or you and Shakespeare" (*Pleasures*, 202). Whether or not this is a new map, and how, are of course serious questions that will return. Exclusion, appropriation, interweaving are, so to speak, scales on a very wide spectrum indeed. To judge distances from one to the other is simple enough, but to attempt to evaluate intentions where one begins to pass into another is fruitless.

For whatever someone like Gibbon may have come to think in later and more conservative work, here, at least, in this youthful *Essay on the Study of Literature* (first written and published in French in 1761), he surely suggests that real contact with other cultures must change our views of our own, must make us "distrust" many of our clearest certainties. The "absurdities," "prejudices," and "error" are as much our own as the Iroquois': "what we learn in one bound, what, by means of a fable, is shown as the exotic charm of another system of thought, is the limit of our own: the stark impossibility of thinking *that*" (Foucault, *Mots*, 7). This is a challenge we *have* to take up, to strive and open ourselves to thinking *that*. We learn "the power of prejudices" precisely by not remaining in our "monologue," as Césaire (after Rodó) put it. The self/other opposition is a form of that monologue, a continuation of the "colonial enterprise." "The truth is," Césaire went on,

that this policy *cannot but bring about the ruin of Europe itself,* and that Europe, if it is not careful, will perish from the void it has created around itself. They thought they were only slaughtering Indians, or Hindus, or South Sea Islanders, or Africans. They have in fact overthrown, one after another, the ramparts behind which European civilization could have developed freely. (*Discourse*, 57–58)

Gibbon's astonishment, delight, and instruction, his demand that we investigate "contrarieties," modifications, alterations, and differences, should not be belittled, any more than the new patterns woven in *Kim*. The lama refuses to be trapped in "limits set by" his "rulers," to lose his "soul" to "internalization of [his] victor," forced to fight "according to the victor's values, within his model of dissent" (Nandy, *Intimate Enemy*, 3, 111). But Kim, too, shares in a mutual reweaving.

Cultural meetings produce as much a questioning of familiar traditions as an exploration of different ones. Or they may produce some quite new hybrid, a second, a third nature. Of course, such hybrids may signal some cultural imposition, as Cheyfetz argues they were and are in the official documents of English and American imperialisms, incapable of the effort of understanding indigenous peoples "as integral, different entities" (*Poetics*, 11). But these sorts of document have their own imaginative interest. Their imperial work demands reduction. Indeed, it may do so just because it recognizes that difference is irreducible. You make blank silhouettes or demons of those whose place you wish to occupy because you know they have rights like yours, because they must not be granted the right to do unto you the same, and because to make the effort to apprehend difference in detail would be to acknowledge the first and deny your wish: "in dealing with this subject, the commonest curse is to be the dupe in good faith of a collective hypocrisy that clearly misrepresents problems, the better to legitimize the hateful solutions provided for them" (Césaire, *Discourse*, 10).

Cheyfetz's imperial documents are instruments that come after the actions they justify. For colonization is not

evangelization, nor a philanthropic enterprise, nor a desire to push back the frontiers of ignorance, disease, and tyranny, nor an attempt to extend the rule of law. . . . The decisive actors here are the adventurer and the pirate, the wholesale grocer and the ship owner, the gold digger and the merchant. . . . I find that hypocrisy is of recent date; that neither Cortez discovering Mexico from the top of the great teocalli, nor Pizarro before Cusco (much less Marco Polo before Cambaluc), claims that he is the harbinger of a superior order; that they kill; that they plunder; that they have helmets, lances, cupidities; that the slavering apologists come later. (Césaire, *Discourse*, 10–11)

Frank is equally clear, as he is on the fact that such brutal instruments take a variety of forms: "The instruments [of colonial expansion in Brazil] were then, as they have been since, conquest, pillage, plantations, slavery, investment, unequal trade, and the use of armed force and political pressure" (*Capitalism*, 151). These brutalities are obfuscated, forgotten, and concealed by being moved, as we saw in Chapter 1 through various examples, from one autonomous discourse to another, translated into different orders of argument.

The documents justifying imperialness still show an awareness that the critics of otherness find a way to obfuscate (not altogether innocently, no doubt). The documents make no secret of their denial or of the denial's reasons. The critics seek to assimilate difference to their own perception of legitimacy. But a Gĩkũyũ or a Nez Perce is not some opposite "other" of simple European claim, constitutents of a benign *Gemeinschaft* "alternative" to malignant *Gesellschaft*, an ecohuman reply to the stripped reason of Enlightenment.

In 1971, Roberto Fernández Retamar published his now classic essay, "Caliban: Notes toward a Discussion of Culture in Our America." Like others already (Brathwaite, Fanon, Lamming), he insisted on home cultures before accepting the need to adjust to imposition, as Rodó had done in *Ariel*—a pattern also adopted in Césaire's 1969 contrast between collaborating Ariel and resisting Caliban in *A Tempest*. They urged the necessity, if you will, of seeking and finding the lineaments of an earlier map before using its overlay. For all intents and purposes, naming Retamar but once, Cheyfetz dilated these notes into a book. I do not mean to demean his long, in many ways profitable, gloss on "Caliban," from Shakespeare, *Tarzan*, and colonialism to Montaigne, cannibals, and the force of translation. Expanding on Retamar's hints, Cheyfetz's *Poetics* is an exploration, with *The Tempest* as sounding board, of how European literature made the "different" of imperial expansion (foretold in Gibbon?) into the "other" of aesthetic and political imagining. The first is brute imposition. (Kipling's perception of *that* may be what makes *Kim* a poor object for critical othering.) The second, whether in *Tarzan*, Fenimore Cooper's *The Pioneers*, or *The Tempest*, means "to rationalize the policy of dispossession" (*Poetics*, 14).

To this end, it has at least two philosophical instruments. One involves ideas of translation and metaphor brought from antiquity, founded on *translatio* as making the familiar foreign and as working (*specifically* since Aristotle and subsequent western tradition) on the play between them. The figurative is the foreign, the proper is the national and the normal (*Poetics*, 36; cf. Eagleton). Throughout the tradition Cheyfetz examines, translation was seen and explained as "an act of violence" by the explanatory texts themselves (37). Not for nothing were those whose language one did not know called barbarians. The theory and politics of translation were those of deprivation. So, for example, "this process of translation . . . prepares the way for and is forever involved in the dispossession by which Native American land was *translated* (the term is used in English common law to refer to transfers of real estate) into the European identity of *property*" (43; some of this will recur in Chapter 4). Such "translation," I have suggested, also functions between autonomous discourses to move one kind of action or condition into a new context, alienating it from one circumstance and argument, familiarizing it to others.

The second tool was of later vintage but directly tied to this last aspect. Making property the mark of political citizenship as of civilized humanity itself, as Locke did in the *Second Treatise of Government* (55), made those who had no such concept of alienable property (as all Native Americans), or those who were deprived of it (European lower classes), automatically not just precivilized but indeed not yet wholly human—for to be that one had to have gone through the civil contract, to have passed from the monstrous state of nature into the rational order of civil society. The terms of the Lockean guarantee of property—even before the contract, we saw in Chapter 1—served the needs of a domestic social hierarchy and justified *pari passu* the hierarchical relations of colonialism. "The failure of dialogue, figured as a genetic inability in the other, rather than as a problem of cultural difference" (16), was thus given a dual explanation and alibi. The one, concerned with property, justified a claim of ontological inferiority as well as of political disablement. The other, concerned with language, legitimized a violent imposition of right speech (but never so simply or one-dimensionally as the "correct talking" of Said's *Kim*).

These tools still lie behind the happy binarisms of critical seizures of cultural difference. In some complexity of detail, Cheyfetz displays throughout his work, but especially at the end, how *The Tempest* used or predicted these strategies of property and dispossession (*Poetics*, 157–72). He also suggests, in a pretty discussion of Montaigne's "Des cannibales," how these very terms could be made equivocal. Bereft of its violence, translation became problematic. Talking with Indians, Montaigne found he needed "a translator to translate between himself and the translator" (153). Yet he somehow "understands" the Indians to whom he "speaks" as occupying a culture and language in some way essentially "democratic," where property, possession, and exploitation are literally inexpressible (155–56). By some curious leap of imagination, Cheyfetz implies, Montaigne grasped not simply the violence *translatio* did to its victims but the very difference it sought to conceal: "Indian people," writes Paula Gunn Allen in a passage Cheyfetz uses as a chapter epigraph (22), "don't believe in metaphor. Very few of us even understand what that term means." The claim is odd; the reasons for it are not (an issue of Chapter 4). Montaigne would somehow have instantly intuited them.

Metaphor, *translatio*, is the absorbing of the other in the one. Somehow Montaigne would have grasped that multiplying places and levels of translation denies such possession, although Cheyfetz's elision of the meaning of that dispersion with a critique of later colonialisms is at the very least anachronistic, and one suspects elements of *Gemeinschaft* in this reading of Montaigne. Certainly there is something of such a myth in Montaigne's own understanding of the Indians, precisely because he had no (translated) access to the different culture at issue. He could write only from "common opinion," analogy of "ancient sources," or second- or third-hand translated "contemporary information" (de Certeau, *Heterologies*, 69; cf. 70–73). None of these are a different culture's own voice; all reproduce their own Other. This is so even though Montaigne, relating his meeting with the Indians, assured the reader that his "own man" was present, who had lived long among Americans and who, being "simple and crude" and so not given to interpretation, was bearer of "true witness" (*Oeuvres*, 200, 202: I.31). The perfection and contentment of these Indians' life and culture was supposedly both discussed by them through an interpreter, although elsewhere, Montaigne wrote that their language was incomprehensible to any French person there (II.12: 445–46) and experienced at first hand by his man. The language problem suggests that when Montaigne relates their criticisms of France at the end of his essay (I.31: 212–13), it has more to do with otherness than with any reality on the ground.

Still, ambiguities are many. What is interesting about Gibbon's putative "Iroquois work" is that it would have been the actual voice of the different culture. And just because it would not be "inaccessible" is why its mere idea provoked such ambivalence and instability in Gibbon's writing. Absurdities, errors, prejudices, and doubts work in both directions. Potentially, at least, Gibbon was hearing the Iroquois' voice, accepting the interference it would introduce into his own no-longer-mastered (or master) discourse. Montaigne's "man," with his physical experience of the Americans, their culture, and their land, was intended to give similarly direct access. While he clearly did not, the skeptical Montaigne had enough to *imagine* Americans' speech and set its own difference against his own French sufficiently to perturb the sureties of his own discourse, if not to know the realities of theirs.[10] In his essay in *Nation and Narration*, James Snead makes a similar point regarding contemporary African and African American writers by speaking of "a certain linguistic and cultural eclecticism or *miscegenation*," of something "hybrid" (232, 234). Cheyfetz cites Walter Benjamin (133–36), explaining how languages "supplement" one another by voicing different "intentions." In a "Letter to the author" before Gibbon's *Essay*, Matthew Maty denied "the unsociable genius of different languages" and argued that while "every language, when complete within itself, is limited," yet they are all "enriched" by "admixtures": "Like those lakes whose waters grow purer and clearer by mixture and agitation with those they receive from neighbouring rivers, so modern tongues can only live by intercommunication, and I might venture to say, by their reciprocal clashings" (629–30). This view of language was already tending toward those such as Baldwin, Césaire, and Kane were to hold of cultures more broadly.

A century further on, Augustin Cournot said more, lamenting our inability "to arrange all spoken languages to suit . . . the need of the moment." To this, Victoria Welby soon added that "what we do want is a really plastic language," one somehow able to "store up all our precious means of mutual speaking" and let us "master the many dialects of thought" (cited in Reiss, *Uncertainty*, 34; see, too, "Significs"). These are perhaps closer to Snead's idea. In the same collection, Brennan recalls Salman Rushdie's case about how the English language has been deeply altered and adjusted by "those whom it once colonized" (Bhabha, ed., 48). From Martinique, Glissant adds his Caribbean voice to this swelling chorus, calling for a "multilingualism" to counter "the arrogant imperialism of monolingualism." He means by this less an "ability to speak several languages" than a "passionate desire to accept and understand our neighbor's language and to confront the massive leveling force of language continuously imposed by the West . . . with a multiplicity of languages and their mutual comprehension" (*Caribbean Discourse*, 249; he has explored the matter further in *Poétique*; see Chapter 4). Brathwaite's search for and use of "nation language" echoes the point (see, for example, *History*). Ngũgĩ's efforts to create as many different language centers as there are cultures using them and to forge multiple bonds among them on the basis of the surety of their *home* language furthers it. Perhaps Paul Ricoeur's thought of "a plurality of spheres of discourse and of the fecundity of the intersection of their semantic aims" joins these preoccupations (*Métaphore*, 336).

These hopes, visions, questings, reflect the desperate need to escape imposing ideas of otherness—and not only to make terms with difference (if in self-protective guise), but to welcome the hybrid(s). Carlos Fuentes adds his voice: "One of the wonders of our menaced globe is the variety of its experiences, its memories, and its desire. Any attempt to impose a uniform politics on this diversity is like a prelude to death" ("Harvard Commencement," 199). A minor issue here may be that *hybridity* implies a fusion of differences whose result (if not aim) would be a flattening, homogenization, or entropy of the very political diversities to which Fuentes refers. One needs to remember that there are many different kinds, arrangements, and forgings of such hybrids. *Interweavings*, Fuentes' own *alternativities* or Wilson Harris' *mutualities*, are thus better terms for processes that seem to have to involve recognition and maintenance of diversities, even as they rub against and off one another.

One thinks of Ngũgĩ's bid to make a Gĩkũyũ literature in the language of and from the store of his own culture's tales, bringing to it elements and processes from many cultures and languages. Or one thinks of Brathwaite's efforts to make an identity (*X/Self*) within a history of the voice that recognizes its colonized and its autonomous past, as well as its multiple present. This may not always be welcomed: "the fifth world had become entangled with European names: the names of the rivers, the hills, the names of the animals and the plants—all of creation suddenly had two names: an Indian name and a white name" (Silko, *Ceremony*, 68). Only rather recently have instabilities of the sort come to matter to those of us who write from within so-called metropolitan spaces. Only too many readily fall back on familiar sources of response, on sureties of habitual ideas of frontier, on known schemas of conflict. For Farah, for Molloy, for Leslie Marmon Silko, for so many others in a world whose order was (once thought to be) constructed by outsiders, things have fallen, are falling, apart, have no ready means of repair. The local models are no longer at hand, only second natures that exist on someone else's maps (in an outsider's dream). Indeed, they who would repair them have yet fully to identify themselves. Questions of power remain unresolved where you have neither identity nor a way of knowing what "identity" might be.

The issues of who mapped whom, of avoiding absorption as some second nature, of negotiating one's own home were those on which Fanon took Sartre to task for his "Orphée noir" preface. Sartre, we saw, took *négritude* as the antithesis, the fundamental *other*, of western culture's thesis in a confrontation that would be sublated in a later synthesis. "I felt that I had been robbed of my last chance," wrote Fanon in the hurt surprise of his initial reaction:

Help had been sought from a friend of the colored peoples, and that friend had found no better response than to point out the relativity of what they were doing. For once, that born Hegelian had forgotten that consciousness has to lose itself in the night of the absolute, the only condition to attain the consciousness of self. In opposition to rationalism, he summoned up the negative side, but he forgot that this negativity draws its worth from an almost substantive absoluteness. A consciousness committed to experience is ignorant, has to be ignorant, of the essences and the determination of its being. (*Black Skin*, 133–34)

Sartre was stealing actual event, real memory, felt experience, to make them the abstracted other of western meaning and "History." In that way, Fanon went on, the living and lived urgency of the poetry presented became an ineluctable moment in someone else's history: "And so it is not I who make meaning for myself, but it is the meaning that was already there, pre-existing, waiting for me" (*Black Skin*, 134).

But Fanon was far from being simply "outraged," as Lewis R. Gordon has it (*Fanon*, 32). He went on to make clear that the gap between himself and Sartre was the gap between colonized and colonizer, between black and white. Sartre could *only* speak from outside an experience he would not know. The alternative would be for him not to have written "Orphée noir," a choice that would have been a worse and more cowardly refusal. Sartre was in fact putting his white and western meaning and morality on the line. Meaning, as Fanon showed, is *simultaneously* in history—or, rather, histories—and made by oneself (cultural instruments surround us, but it is we who use them). He was not yet possessor of any authoritative discourse whose perturbance should (or could) be sought: "I *needed* not to know" (*Black Skin*, 135). He needed to be able to *live* the experience "in ignorance" of any prescribed meaning. He needed to be able to make his own meaning. But—and the "but" is a mighty one—*négritude*'s meaning and event was inevitably and always caught up (from the very history of colonization alone) in white exegesis. As Achebe once spoke for African writers with respect to western critics: "we have brought home ant-ridden faggots and must be ready for the visit of lizards." Nor are lizards all bad. They stop ants from filling your home as the faggots burn (*Morning Yet*, 62, 81).

Sartre's dialectical reading and other western reactions were always part of its experience, itself always partly ignorant partly knowing: Levi's "curious salvage operations" of memory. Sartre saw *négritude* poetry from his outside, inside the colonizers' dwelling, where he was also making an acerbic response to Hegel's notorious contention about Africa and prehistory, such that African cultures were now included in a hegelian dialectic of History in Hegel's own terms. Lest this seem a pointless exercise in intellectualism, we should not forget that in 1948, African liberation movements had not got very far (even where they existed), and colonialism in

Africa remained much as it had been for far longer than the sixty years since Fashoda. Sartre's argument was aimed more at western claims than at African interests—could he do otherwise? Fanon resisted such appropriation to others' purposes, even (perhaps especially) when its author's heart was in the right place; it was no less an appropriation.

This working out of experience, meaning, interpretation, and life is what we watch Fanon work through in his remarkable reading of Sartre, making Sartre's exegesis itself part of ignorant lived experience, working through and beyond western interpretation to absorb it into political *négritude*. For Sartre had not forgotten that white and black "suffer in [their] body quite differently," and Fanon knew he had not: he quotes *La putain respectueuse* to show it (138–39), comparing its black to Richard Wright's Bigger Thomas (of *Native Son*). Quite simply, they inevitably speak from different places. Fanon's argument with Sartre is essential for that reason. White meaning has to be incorporated, appropriated by black life into its own meanings. At the time Fanon wrote *Peau noire, masques blancs* (1952), an essential element of that latter "meaning" had to be to make white exegeses an aspect of the colonization rejected, but used in that rejection, incorporated into a *political* response and responsibility:

I feel in myself a soul as immense as the world, truly a soul as deep as the deepest of rivers, my chest has the power to expand without limit. . . . Yesterday, awakening to the world, I saw the sky turn upon itself utterly and wholly. I wanted to rise, but the disemboweled silence fell back upon me, its wings paralyzed. Without responsibility, straddling Nothingness and Infinity, I began to weep. (140)

"Orphée noir" was to be made part of yesterday's weeping. *Black Skin* was the awakening from western universals to realities of South Africa's segregation and violence, the destruction of Bantu society, Parisian racism . . . (186). It was "a mirror . . . in which it [would] be possible to discuss the Negro on the road to disalienation" (184), to replace and absorb others' abstractions and "ideals" with and into one's own experiences.

Complexities of exchange create numberless levels of anxiety and fear of the other, no less real in one culture than in another. "They are afraid, Tayo," says the Mexican dancer in *Ceremony*. "They feel something happening, they can see something happening around them, and it scares them. Indians or Mexicans or whites—most people are afraid of change. . . . They are fools. They blame us, the ones who look different. That way they don't have to think about what has happened inside themselves" (Silko,

Ceremony, 99–100). The ones who look different are, need one say? those who are already "hybrid," crossblood, already interwoven. But they are not, never have been, never will be "our" others. Of them, perhaps something of a model is found in works like Silko's own *Storyteller*, Anzaldúa's *Borderlands*, or Hilden's *When Nickels*, whose speakers themselves seem already elsewhere, frontiers down. They mingle east/west, north/south borders, white/Native American, male/female, or other bounds. They weave a web knowing no such different places, elaborating some new space of action. Proper metropolitan critics could do some learning here.

No doubt, just as in the case of *Kim* or Carpentier's *Concierto barroco*, to do this in fiction is somewhat different from doing it on the ground. But when Abraham Lincoln "greeted [Harriet Beecher] Stowe in 1863 as 'the little lady who made this big war,' " (Douglas, introduction to *Uncle Tom's Cabin*, 19), whatever his irony, he was quite serious as to the important added focus and sentiment her novel had brought to already moving passions, an enigmatic consequence of fictive imagining of which Mark McWatt exclaims,

> To right
> the historical wrongs
> of all traffic in tongues
> is beyond the power
> of sentence, story,
> novel-writing—and yet . . .
> Olive reading *Summer Lightning*!
> And yet . . . Bob Marley's songs!
>   ("Enigma," *Language*, 62)

The next chapters argue how cultural instruments, generally, affect and change ways of thought, starting with one that is a particular way both to create the *othering* and the *other* we have just examined and to put them to use, at once inside western culture and outside, in its relations with different cultures.

3

The Law, the Tragic, and Cultures of Dissonance

The notion of the other is one among innumerable instruments that function by disunion. Inasmuch as it is given as the opposite of some version of self-ness, it may be the one instrument most characteristic, indeed defining, of a solipsistic cultural order. It is the self's negative pole, Machado's unsettling "heterogeneity," Ortega's *alteración* within the self. That is why self can see its other's action only in terms mirroring its own and why, too, it imagines the other elsewhere, casting it outside, in the world, where it is to be acted upon and dominated (Ortega, "Self," 172). Self then imposes its understanding as a system it calls "History," universally the same for all, enabling the self and its avatars to make the other part of a single historical process whose comprehension, and so manipulation, lie with that self. This history is another cultural instrument (whose operation Glissant has partly examined in *Caribbean Discourse*, 61–95). It is a constant theme in all these chapters, as well as the focus of two. One may presume the number of such instruments to be more or less measureless. Here, I can obviously note only some of the most exemplary—limited by space, the bounds of my own study, and their relation to the fictive imagination. The point is anyway not to be exhaustive but to show the existence and working of a few instruments drawn centrally from the culture's tradition. Although a culture cannot itself see such practices as instruments, purposeful devices, it may dwell on them with enough insistence to imply they have special weight. This chapter's topic is one such. I use it to explore the determining nature of these cultural tools as well as critics' use and making of them.

With some notable exceptions, western commentators happily emphasize how special is tragedy, how unique in and to its culture, how inaccessible to others.[1] It offers a standard of judgment, a scale of comparison, even a way to possession (never innocent, but perhaps unaware)—naming "tragic," for example, the victims of some impersonally noble "tragedy" of cultural clash. To such effect, Borges has a story of Averroes' bafflement by "a problem of philological nature related to . . . his commentary on Aristotle . . . , two doubtful words had halted him at the beginning of the *Poetics*. These words were *tragedy* and *comedy*." The lacuna disabled interpretation. Nor was he helped when an associate recounted a dramatic performance seen in an unspecified East. Averroes, "closed within the orb of Islam, could never know the meaning of the terms *tragedy* and *comedy*" ("Averroes' Search," *Labyrinths*, 181, 187). He was not alone. Lacking the tragedies and Aristotle's *Poetics* based on them (not rediscovered for the West until around 1490), analysis was skewed. In Toledo in 1256, Hermann the German latinized Averroes' gloss on the *Poetics*: poetry was a species of logic and a rhetoric that moved imagination to moral purpose. Tragedy was praise, *laudatio*, teaching virtue by painting people better than they were; comedy was blame, *vituperatio*, discouraging vice by showing them worse (Reiss, "Renaissance Theatre," 10; Minnis and Scott, 289–91).

This is as strange to western critics as the Greeks were to Averroes, and asks for explanation. So I want to look at the cultural specificity of tragedy and its ramifications (although performance will be of no concern), to examine tragedy as a category of western thought and ground of practice, to look briefly at what occurs when it is applied outside that western arena, and to get a quick sense of the goals of such application. The overall effort is to analyze and understand one principal category of thought enabling in this "metropolitan" culture, the "colonization" of others, to find the ways in which certain kinds of cultural instruments function within and without that culture. My interest, here, is the theoretical, critical, and philosophical machine that has grown around tragedy; what it tells us of a culture in which humans are characterized as essentially separated from and opposed to some other realm of being and action; and how it captures relations with different cultures. To these ends, the first half of this chapter rapidly discusses the historical establishment of tragedy (and the tragic) as just such a cultural category and instrument—*ratio*. The second half seeks to offer a glimpse of its use on and by different cultures and to mark what deconstructive criticism might call effects of *differance*, although I hesitate to use this term here, because while instabilities within the instrument and discourse of tragedy are an issue, far more important are concern with discursive forms belonging to different cultures, how they work in themselves, how they play with western instabilities, how they write back and write against them.

Two special issues need addressing before getting to these arguments. The first concerns the "absence" of tragedy from cultures different from that of the West. This is an issue that raises several associated matters. That the truth of this claim may not be absolute matters less to me here than that it has been so widely made. I take the fact of this claim, that is, to be part of what this western cultural instrument *is*. So the existence of possible exceptions does not actually matter very much for my argument here. Whether and how, for example, Noh theater may be considered tragedy involves many questions, almost all of them extraneous to those with which I am concerned in this (or other) chapters. Three questions that are not would be: by whom is it so considered? for what purpose? and how does such a classification help understand Noh in its own cultural specificity? I would answer the third by saying that it doesn't, simply because "tragedy" has not been a *Japanese* cultural category. Perhaps it has not been such a category because concepts of scission, it seems, have not been central and fundamental to that culture (Ohnuki-Tierney). This interesting proposal is one I'm not qualified to pursue. The other two questions are directly addressed in what follows.

Another associated matter involves the actual contemporary use of "tragedies" in different cultures, such as John Pepper Clark's *Song of a Goat* and *Masquerade*, Soyinka's *The Bacchae of Euripides*, Césaire's *Tragédie du roi Christophe*, *Et les chiens se taisaient*, or *Une saison au Congo*, perhaps Efua Sutherland's *Edufa*, ·Zulu Ṣofọla's *Old Wines Are Tasty* and *Wedlock of the Gods*, and others. I shall argue that the changes rung in such cases confirm my argument as they also show how cultures adopt and transform another's instruments (although Soyinka argues that there *is* Yoruba tragedy; *Myth*, 140–60). The last matter associated with this issue of the absence of tragedy is the question of how one can hope to speak *to* (not *of*) it. How, that is to say, can one speak through this "absence" about *differences* that within these cultures are of course not "differences" at all, but simply processes indigenous and natural to them? From inside, tragedy's absence is evidently no incompletion; this last can *only* be a western perception. The second half of this chapter tries to respond, not altogether mischievously, to this matter.

The second issue concerns the fact that tragedy is no very "strong or eloquent example of 'colonization' given the brutal history of this imperial practice" (the words are Lambropoulos'; personal communication, November 16, 1997). In some sense, one must agree with the observation, although it would hardly give a reason for ignoring the role cultural practices have played and do play in cultural impositions and oppressions. One need only refer to the many ex-colonized writers who comment endlessly on the manifold ways in which colonizing cultural forms are imposed on their victims to replace those of indigenous cultures and, precisely, to colonize minds. These forms, we begin to see, become instruments through which the colonizing culture seeks to grasp (in that word's several meanings) those different cultures, to organize *their* forms and *their* ways of meaning and understanding in *its* terms. As Mphahlele wrote of a culture's very language, in his case of being forced to use Afrikaans: "I was caught up in a situation where a language had been thrust upon us which was the instrument of our oppression and the source of our humiliation" (*Down*, 167). This does not mean one must agree with Piedra's claim that "the historical implications of [Spanish] intervention [in the Americas] are negligible compared to the linguistic ones" ("Monkey Tales," 122). That language may be "co-conspirator in the process of enslavement" and colonization cannot make it paramount (Gomez, 171). Only the euphemism, "intervention," used to name conquest and destruction explains how genocide and its aftermath can be called negligible compared with stealing, changing, and imposing language—unless, of course, Piedra is ironically deploying an illustration of his own argument as he begins it.[2]

That issues of "linguistic self-affirmation and separation" repeatedly recur (Soyinka, *Art*, 82–83) does not make them all-important. But perhaps Piedra is taking language as a synecdoche for the wider cultural deprivation to which Ngũgĩ and others give powerful weight. As Philip angrily makes her way through this minefield of cultural and physical violence:

There have been times when I have thought the unthinkable—that it is a less cruel act to kill a people, leaving their culture and respect for it intact, than to denude them of their culture and by various means deride and destroy it, leaving them to howl their pain and anger on down through the centuries. (*Frontiers*, 14)

Still, cultural *rationes* are not political, economic, or military ones. We must not confuse, I recall Césaire, adventurer and pirate with slavering apologist. Nor need we have them compete for honors in harm. Cultural instruments accompany political, economic, and military praxes. They explain and warrant them. Just so did Hernán Cortés insist on always razing Mexican "idols" and replacing them right away with a cross and a statue of the Virgin. In another place and time, Thomas Macaulay's notorious 1835 educational project for India may have followed military and economic oppressions, but it was also the end point and last shape of a longer cultural project that had accompanied the first. Of course, these things are never, finally, one-way processes, and among the questions this chapter and this book ask are what does it mean when these cultures take up these instruments for their own ends (as in Soyinka's *Bacchae*, Ola Rotimi's *The Gods Are Not to Blame*, or Sutherland's *Edufa*, the last two, respectively, reworkings of *Oedipus rex* and *Alcestis*)? what happens when they join them to processes of their own? how do they turn them back on the culture(s) from whence they came? how does this affect each and both cultures?—although the last question must mostly be left for a different book. This is just one set of questions; it orients the second half of this book. Another principal set involves the historical building, organizing, and functioning of these cultural forms or categories, instruments or *rationes*.

In this last regard, here, in this chapter, I may perhaps best start by recalling Athena's establishment of the new law toward the end of Aeschylus' *Eumenides*, a moment known to most western readers:

> And now
> if you would hear my law, you men of Greece,
> you who will judge the first trial of bloodshed.
> Now and forever more, for Aegeus' people
> this will be the council of judges. . . .
> Here from the heights, terror and reverence,
> my people's kindred powers
> will hold them from injustice through the day
> and through the mild night. Never pollute
> our laws with innovations . . .
> Neither anarchy nor tyranny is the rule I advise
> my people to maintain with reverence, and never
> to banish fear from the walls, not altogether.
> Where is the righteous man who knows no fear?

The stronger your fear, your reverence for the just,
the stronger your country's wall and city's safety . . .
Untouched by lust for spoil, this court of law
majestic, swift to fury, ever wakeful, watching
above you as you sleep—I found it here and now.

Thus did the earliest and only extant Greek trilogy narrate the establishment of human law and the well-walled city, whose further rampart it was against panic fear and disorder: δίκας, δικαστῶν . . . βουλευτήριον, ἀδικεῖν, νόμους, ἔνδικος, ἐνδίκως.³

To say that my Greek is weak is to understate the case, and I dare give this sequence only because I think it essential not to lose the play's emphasis here as much on terms of justice and right as on its expression of the city's enclosure. It was enclosed not against that dose of fear needed to keep human justice alive, but against the deeper anguish of a difference from a fundamentally inexplicable nonhuman world. In later Greek tragedy, the city's law, even with its flaws exposed as they often were by Euripides, offered a rational bulwark against the unknown and sufficient explanation of an ordered human world. (It may be usefully added that at the Dionysia tragedy also evinced Athens' sense of its own power and its imperial separation from the other Greek cities; before days of performance, the stage was the setting for the display of the year's booty and tribute.) The protagonist of tragedy somehow exposed the fragility of that wall, revealing not simply a conflict but some irreducible disjunction. "Greek tragedy," Bernard Williams opines, "precisely refuses to present human beings who are ideally in harmony with their world, and has no room for a world that, if it were understood well enough, could instruct us how to be in harmony with it" (*Shame and Necessity*, 164).

In Aeschylus and Sophocles, actually, matters are far less clear. We need to remember, after all, that the Erinyes did become the Eumenides, incorporated in some hopefully auspicious way in a world of the younger gods and human law. We need remember that to read *Antigone* as a conflict between individual conscience and the state is a post-Renaissance and, even more, a posthegelian interpretation that is more curious than Heidegger's later vision of the play as performing a conflict between the powers of earth and the violent laws of humans.⁴ This may well be closer to the original moment of the play. Antigone was clear that the rule to be obeyed was Zeus', not Creon's; that of Δίκη, dwelling beside the infernal gods, not a Theban king's. None could think a mortal's orders so strong as to "over-run the gods' unwritten and unfailing laws [θεῶν νόμιμα]."[5] Antigone's memory of an ancient harmony at peril might be singular, but was assuredly not individual. Ismene's rallying to her sister, Haemon's accusing his father, Tiresias' augury, the Chorus' fears, told us so long before the final catastrophe. The Chorus' last strophe on wisdom and divine duty ratified a hope of restoring some fuller harmony. Elsewhere, I have suggested that Antigone performs a harmony of the *oikos* in the world set over and against the new authority of the *polis* as represented in the increasingly tyrannical Creon (*Mirages*, chapter 3). One could readily interpret the *Oedipus* plays along such lines.

Still, that neither Aeschylus nor Sophocles seems to justify unambiguous later claim that tragedy shows lasting deep disjunction between humans and the world is not the point. And one can credibly hold that *Oedipus rex* (with its vocabulary of *knowing, discovering, clarifying, making visible*) set reason against opening dissonance—plague and decay—and final fragmentation—fall of royal family and self-wounding of its head—to depict mortal disablement. To George Steiner, tragedy always figures human existence so: "there are no temporal remedies . . . Tragedy speaks not of secular dilemmas which may be resolved by rational innovation, but of the unalterable drift toward inhumanity and destruction in the drift of the world" (*Death*, 8, 291). Orotund echo of Heidegger, Unamuno, Friedrich Nietzsche, and Arthur Schopenhauer, the claim was habitual in western tradition. It tells us as much about that tradition and its precepts as about tragedy.

For whatever tragedy may have done in fifth-century Greece (and exiguity of surviving traces forbids unwary generalization), the point is that Bernard Williams' and Steiner's assertions typify one of two later styles of claim: that tragedy performs a permanent and awesome abyss between humans and the world. Details of discordance vary greatly, but that is one broad paradigm indicated by the terms "tragedy" and its later derivation, "the tragic." The second claim takes tragedy to show "the limits of meaning and knowledge. . . . This showing presupposes a human capacity for order" (Reiss, *Tragedy and Truth*, 12). It confronts what Bernard Williams and Steiner show as inhuman, meaningless, disordered (or ordered on grounds that humans cannot know), with knowledge and order given as their "solution" and polar opposite. Raymond Williams says, "The tragic action, in its deepest sense, is not the confirmation of disorder, but its experience, its comprehension and its solution." It solves what it *first*—but *only* first—shows as "a terrifying loss of connection" (*Modern Tragedy*, 83, 13). Positing "a formed world," Friedrich Dürrenmatt writes, it presumes "guilt, despair, moderation, lucidity, vision, a sense of responsibility," human reactions to the knowledge form implies ("Problems," 30–31). But, we shall finally have to ask, whose guilt and despair? whose moderation, lucidity, vision? whose responsibility? and for what?

Both claims take tragedy to depict disunion between world and humans. But I would say that while Steiner and his predecessors see tragedy by its writers' and critics' own self-evaluation since the European Renaissance, the other view wants rather to understand the interplay of tragedy and its cultural tradition—to know not what many call the *nature* of tragedy but its cultural meaning. The first begets divers solemnly sonorous pronouncements, supposals of some humanity's grave import. Even in Raymond Williams, I admit to not knowing what the phrase "its deepest sense" means. It is clear, too, that disorder and loss of connection are not the same. We have no sense in Aeschylus that the terrors and disasters endured by the House of Atreus are disordered—on the contrary, they are all too ordered. So is the catastrophe suffered by Oedipus and the conflict ruling *Antigone*. They assuredly do show, though, the loss of connection that Raymond Williams points out, whether or not they show how it may be overcome. Either way they would be taken to show dissonance and disconnection to be essential factors in human life and being.

For my present purposes, all this is to say that it matters not whether one follows a hegelian or a nietzschean path, whether one asserts that tragedy momentarily ends disjunction—for the space of the close of a performance, or whether one claims it is left agape. An analogous Christian and Greek opposition may echo this: whether the former be understood to put an eschatological term to suffering and unknowing or to provide an interpretive law. This does not have importance here either. What matters is the permanent underlying assumption of "some deep and fragmenting chasms" between humans and a realm of otherness differing from them.[6]

Instauration of the law and enclosure of human space, I wish to argue, have always been the fundamental terms of *all* discussion of tragedy in the western tradition. I have mentioned the cliché that no other culture *has* tragedy—a fact itself requiring explanation. I am going to suggest that both the practice of and the critical terms surrounding tragedy tell us something essential about western culture. For it is not accidental, either, that western criticism has been and stays so preoccupied with its form and its idea. I want to spend the first part of this chapter in showing that the idea of a basic separation between a finite arena given as human and a limitless space given as something else, and the idea of rational law applied to—applying in—the first so as to combat or protect against such dissonance have been essential to the idea of tragedy, no matter what other great differences may lie between exegeses. I want at least to suggest that it has been so throughout the entire tradition—basic, indeed, to the notion that it *is one* tradition. I want then to give some idea of why some other cultures cannot use the notion (or practice), and of what happens when the concept and the term are nonetheless applied to them. Doing this, I mean to say nothing about such other cultures, much about the West's.

In this regard, two historical facts may be set down. One is that however rare the appearances of tragedy, they have always occurred at times of reorganization of the political and social order. The heyday of Greek tragedy fell between the Persian and the Peloponnesian wars. The first war signaled a passage from archaic Greek society toward consolidation of the city-states, whereas the second marked the decay of those conflict-prone states before consolidation of Macedonian hegemony and the building of the "Hellenistic world." In early modern Europe, the age of tragedy was also one of war and social dissolution that saw the slow making of modern nations from religious strife, revolts against Spain and Empire, civil broil in France, the Thirty Years' War, English civil war, and the Frondes. In Germany, the time between the mid-eighteenth century and the nineteenth, from Lessing to Friedrich Hölderlin and Franz Grillparzer, likewise showed the start of a change from feuding principalities to Customs Union (1830), and then wider unity under Bismarck. In *every case* the appearance of tragedy was followed by the consolidation of an enormously powerful political-philosophical theory: Plato and Aristotle; Hobbes and Locke; Hegel and Marx.

It was as if tragedy had discovered in a confused environment "some new conceptual and discursive process enabling certain doubts to be overcome, clearing up incomprehensions inherent in earlier social and political decay and dissolution, and facilitating the establishment of a new order of rationality" (Reiss, "Tragedy," 1299; cf. *Tragedy and Truth*, 282–83). Thereby it enabled (established?) the argument that a "new" civic reason was being set against an old incomprehension—an incomprehension that could be understood to refer to anything conceived as "outside" or "beyond" customary human life. That writers of tragedy so marked a transition was no doubt why Plato banished them from the lawful city and Aristotle rehabilitated them. For it was simultaneously with debate about a new civic reason in Greece that tragedy found in him its best-known analyst, one whose explanations would be repetitively taken up and elaborated at later reappearances of the genre.

This first of my two facts, historical and political, will hover on my discussion's horizon (Peter Euben has dwelt on it with regard at least to Greek tragedy). The second, aesthetic and critical, leads directly to my gloss on the tradition it established.

Later criticism quite unanimously took Greek tragedy to mark a historical moment of disjunction, given many analogs—Dionysos against Apollo, *Gemeinschaft* against *Gesellschaft*, Eden versus a fallen world, Astraea's Golden Age versus the savagery of an Iron, Arcadia versus Rome, or even, in Marx's telling, ignorance versus the first childish glimmerings of reason. These oppositions were readily grounded in Aristotle's implication not only that tragedy signaled such a moment of disjunction, but that it depicted it. Apart from matters peculiar to dramatic performance, the Stagirite specified three elements essential to tragedy, each involving assumptions and *being techniques* of disjunction. (Which is not to suggest that *he* argued for any "abyss" between human and other realms, Aristotle being the least "abysmal" of philosophers.)

One was the primacy of plot: human action in the world that showed humans *against* the world and its divers constraints, death, the gods, Fate, Justice, or whatever. The other two were structural devices that became the most controversial and vehemently contested of cruxes in the *Poetics* despite, or because of, the imprecision and rarity of their formulation. I mean *hamartia* and *catharsis*, the last term used but twice in the *Poetics* (1449b28; 1455b14). *Hamartia* named disjunction directly: an unbridgeable cut between action and its comprehension, phenomenon and understanding, event and explanation. Whether called ignorance, unwittingness, overweening pride, willful disregard, or, later, moral error, the "flaw" of tragedy's protagonist signaled a gap between experience and however reason might grasp it, between world and human action. *Catharsis*, whether you interpreted it as a factor within the play (like Goethe, "On Interpreting," 197–98; Gerald F. Else; *Aristotle's Poetics*, 437–38; and Harvey Goldstein, "Mimesis," 572–76), or as "purgation" or curing of spectator and audience without (like all Renaissance commentators and the vast mass since), was either an actual overcoming of such disjunction "through pity and fear" or a numbing of its effect, reducing it to levels no longer grievous—so Lodovico Castelvetro in 1570 and Daniel Heinsius in 1611.

Aristotle offered two less controversial major technical tools specific to tragedy: *anagnōrisis* and *peripeteia*. Formulas of abrupt transition, both unequivocally mark a lack of fixity and fixedness in the relation between human experience, the world, and its—their—comprehension. But I am not going to explore what happened to all these in detail through the European Renaissance and beyond. Many others—I too—have done it elsewhere (see Works Cited). I want, rather, to come to the far more general claims and considerations—revealingly so—that have been made for tragedy since the European Enlightenment, on the basis of such details as these. By then, the medical and legal interpretations of Aristotle (anchored in notions of purgation and reparation), which saw in tragedy a means to a *mise en ordre* of mental and emotional health and a guiding of spiritual law, setting a late Renaissance neo-Stoic ethic to rational ordering of society, culminated in an idea of "poetic justice" through such as Pierre Corneille, John Dryden, Thomas Rymer, and G. W. Leibniz that eventually connected rational law and ethical legitimacy in a Schillerian "aesthetic education" (Reiss, *Meaning*, 87, 170–72, 176, 323–24). Tragedy could be a principal tool in an aesthetico-political ordering of the *civitas* against the ever-present threat of an increasingly immoderate nature.

By then, too, civil society was imperatively seen as built on and from separate and willful individuals. Tragedy was taken to set them, their desires, and their society either against others' desire or against some ineluctable obstacle in the world. "Ancient tragedy," Goethe insisted,

is based on an inescapable moral obligation [to the gods and society] which can only intensify and gain momentum if it clashes with an opposing desire. . . . there are many variants of obligation, but it is always despotic, no matter whether it is embodied by reason, as in moral code or civil law, or by nature, as in the laws of birth, growth and decay, of life and death. We recoil from all these laws, without realizing that they serve the welfare of the whole. Desire, on the other hand, is free, is perceived as free and favors the individual. . . . Desire is the god of modern times. ("Shakespeare," 170)

Tragedy's always confrontational and disjunctive understanding was expressed as a series of divides between individual desire, civic and moral obligation, and natural law. The idea and its expression grew to a paroxysm in the course of the next century. "The moral law," Goethe's colleague

Schiller had already written, "manifest[s] its entire power when it is shown contending with all the other forces of nature, and all of them lose their power over a human heart beside it. . . . The more terrible the antagonists, the more glorious the victory; *resistance* alone can render the power visible." Tragedy is the poetic form affording most "moral delight," for "its domain comprehends all possible cases where some natural purpose is *sacrificed* to a moral one, or one moral adaptation to purpose to another of a higher order" ("Nature of Tragedy," 222–23; my italics). Hegel's exploration of tragedy in the *Aesthetics* grew straight from such assertions as these.

Their admirer Benjamin Constant, admitting that he had not ad-justed Schiller's *Wallenstein* to right French taste, wanted the disjunctive confrontation even purer: "By depicting just one passion [as Jean Racine had done in *Andromaque*] instead of embracing an entire individual person [as Schiller had], you obtain more continually tragic effects, because indi-vidual characters, always mixed, spoil the unity of effect. . . . There is," he said, "far less variety in passions appropriate to tragedy than in individual people as nature has made them." Tragic poets, he wrote twenty years later in 1829, "need clearcut characters." Nature's indecision, uncertainty, lack of consistency, mixture, and incoherence was useless (*Oeuvres*, 869, 908). Agreeing on the ideal but not with Schiller, Dürrenmatt thought that he did offer "a world that the eye can take in" ("Problems," 29). Tragedy sim-plified the actual, Constant held, by reducing "wholeness" of being to one emotion, unique drive: Alexander Pope's "lurking principle of death . . . the Mind's disease, its ruling Passion" (*Essay on Man*, II.134, 138). This ruling passion, innate unfathomed absurdity of nature, became one with an inborn ache of death marking an essential disunion of world and human reason, though compact with that very reason. From Schopenhauer to Nietzsche and Unamuno, "tragedy" named an ever more fraught disso-nance peaking at last in nothing less than a tragedy of Europe itself, twi-light of the gods, "decline of the West."

Oddly, then, it may be Pope who linked—or even enabled—the modern coexistence of the two interpretive strands earlier called hegelian and nietzschean. The subject now *contained* the abyss of the world in both senses of the verb: it embraced it, it limited it. Half a century later, a figure of greater shadow less surprisingly offered a similar juncture. For Goethe's, Schiller's, and Constant's desiring subject had its philosophical counterpart in the rational subject of Kant's first *Critique*, which, critically or not, had its most radical extension in Schopenhauer's *World as Will and Representa-*

tion: "That which knows all things and is known by none is the *subject*. It is accordingly the supporter of the world, the universal condition of all that appears, of all objects, and it is always presupposed; for whatever exists, exists only for the subject" (1:5). *Will*, ultimately just inexhaustible "will to live," necessarily grounds representation, for without it the world itself no longer is. The effective being of the world and the subject are coextensive. The nonhuman world threatening the human in old Greek tragedy becomes the negative antihuman at the core of self, the *other* of which we have already seen so much.

But then tragedy becomes "the summit of poetic art" because it shows "the antagonism of the will with itself," its pain in living, its fear of and attraction to death. The opposition of world and human becomes internal conflict of the will, but on which rides the world's very being (1:252–53). The loss "of the whole will-to-live" that tragedy shows us in "the noblest men, after a long conflict and suffering," reveals a dying of the world itself (1:253). The finest kind of dramatic tragedy, Schopenhauer thus wrote, is that which shows how the entanglements leading to the protagonist's loss of will are those "whose essence could be assumed even by our own fate" (1:255); it shows us how the general condition of humans comes home to ourselves. Schopenhauer's "reading" of Kant finds in will's internal conflict a death-of-the-world at the very core of the rational individual subject.

Because death is by definition the loss of the will-to-live and of the world, "the life of every individual, viewed as a whole and in general . . . is really a tragedy" (1:322). Tragedy as a form shows this "terrible side of life . . . , the wailing and lamentation of mankind, the dominion of chance and error [that combats all hope of rational order], the fall of the righteous, the triumph of the wicked; and so that aspect of the world is brought before our eyes which directly opposes our will" (2:433). Tragedy's aim then is for the spectator to achieve a "resigned exaltation of the mind," which "turn[s] . . . willing away from life" toward "an existence of a different kind," with the sense "that life is a bad dream from which we have to awake" (2:435, 433). The world is matter for tragedy because it is "the battleground of tormented and agonized beings who continue to exist only by each devouring the other" (2:581). The world exists for us only as representation, which itself survives only by a will-to-live in *that* world. The radical fixing of such a subject signals something like a final disjunction; there *is* no world but that of my representation and will.

I have been a bit long on Schopenhauer because he is avowedly a principal source beneath the two thinkers who may be considered the last actually to appropriate this tradition of tragedy while seeking to further it or take it in new directions—as opposed, I mean, to commenting on it: Nietzsche and Unamuno. The first did of course begin with a Borgesian philological problem: trying to grasp a history of Greek philosophers that he saw as leading from "one homogeneous company [*einer zusammenge-hörigen Gesellschaft*]" to a case in which "with Plato, philosophers became exiles, conspiring against their fatherland" (*Philosophy*, 34–35; *Philosophie*, 303–4). The first philosophers, especially Heraclitus, saw things whole, noting that "injustice" in the world could exist "only for the limited human mind, which sees things apart and not together" (*Philosophy*, 61; *Philosophie*, 324). This passage from the thinkers of unity and continuity to those of "exile," along with the notion of the rational mind as divisive, gave Nietzsche the theme and the organization of *The Birth of Tragedy*, both as an effort to analyze the historical invention of tragedy and as a post-Schopenhauerian critique of his own era.

Like his predecessor, he thought "the Greeks . . . keenly aware of the terrors and horrors of existence" (*Birth*, 29). These essentially came from our separation from the world. Tragedy represented a last effort to "identify with the original Oneness of being" (the Dionysiac) even as reason (the Apollonian) was elaborating its divisions. That is why all "true tragedy" provided "metaphysical solace"—something like Schopenhauer's exaltation (38, 50). It was a moment before a later fallen state, when a "chasm of oblivion separates the quotidian reality from the Dionysiac," revealing all "the ghastly absurdity of existence" (51). Thus were Sophocles' persons "Apollonian masks" producing "a deep look into the horror of nature; luminous spots, as it were, designed to cure an eye hurt by the ghastly night" (59–60). In tragedy, the human world of split appearances "denies itself and seeks to escape back into the world of primordial reality" (132). The "contrast between this truth of nature and the pretentious lie of civilization is quite similar to that between the eternal core of things and the entire phenomenal world." So tragedy "points to the eternity of true being surviving even phenomenal change" (53). Such being was "the most *venerable* exemplar of the species man," superior and just, dwelling in inevitable solitude and "tragically consumed by an impossible virtue" ("On the Uses," 88). It scarcely surprises, in view of what we saw in Chapter 1, that Nietzsche took a familiar western place as his city of these supermen: "a hundred deep solitudes taken together form the city of Venice—that is her charm. An image for the men of the future" (cited in Tafuri, *Venice*, xi).[7] But more of that later in this chapter, and others.

It is commonplace to assert that the last age of connectedness between reason and nature had been succeeded in Nietzsche's view by long but ever quicker decay: dissonance, disjunction, fragmentation were now endemic—at least in Europe. This view, and these previous thinkers, to a considerable extent, came together in Unamuno, where a disconnection of memory, self, intellect, will, and reason found their only hope in "Divine Consciousness" (*Tragic Sense*, 255), a movement out of the world altogether. This was counterpointed by pseudohistorical arguments of Tönnies, Weber, and Spengler, by philosophical claims of Husserl and Heidegger, by critical analyses of Horkheimer, Adorno, and Lukács, and most recently by clamorings about the end of history in Fukuyama and François Furet. These are not, I propose, as disparate a group as may appear.

Long before he wrote *Del sentimiento trágico de la vida* (1937), Unamuno had extended a feeler in his *Vida de Don Quijote y Sancho* (1905). Here the human being was "the divine idea of which you are a manifestation in time and in space. And your longing impulse toward the one you want to be is no more than nostalgia drawing you toward your divine home. A man is fully a man only when he wants to be more than a man" (*Our Lord*, 51; *Vida*, 190). One sees the effect of Schopenhauer and Nietzsche, the last especially as Unamuno stresses the yearning toward the *sobre-hombre*, "superman" (53; 193). Too, disjunction and dissonance are fundamental, as they are in another echo of Schopenhauer: "the world is what it seems to each of us, and wisdom consists in making it into the image of our will, as we rave without reason, filled with faith in the absurd" (112; 264). Unlike Schopenhauer, Unamuno holds will to be endlessly diverse, just as it seems to each. For "if my neighbor is merely another me, what good is he to me? For myself, I am enough and more than enough" (130; 284). Absurdity and divided willfulness characterize a world where the communal seems possible only out of it.

Like Nietzsche and Schopenhauer, Unamuno posits an ineluctable contradiction between "necessities of the heart and will" and those of the intellect, between "living" and "knowing," the "vital" and the "rational" (*Tragic Sense*, 15, 34; *Sentimiento*, 20, 33). At the same time, he posits an absolute primacy of the self and its desire to live—elsewhere: "I am the centre of my universe, the centre of the universe." "I love my neighbour because he lives in me and is part of my consciousness, because he is like me, because he is mine." "I want to be myself, and yet without ceasing to be myself to be others as well, to merge myself into the totality of things visible and invisible, to extend myself into the illimitable of space and to prolong myself into the infinite of time" (*Tragic Sense*, 45–46, 38–39; *Sentimiento*, 41–42, 36). The disjunction here has become so great that the only possible universe is a "tragic" self, torn between willful imposition and rational knowing, straining, as he so often says, toward some kind of eternal life, away from a terror of dying utterly that "corrodes the marrow of the soul" (43; 40). That is why we have "not just to accept, but to found life upon an ethic of battle [*una moral de batalla*]" (108; 87), against the world, against our internal contradictions, against death, and against others.

Human intellect, this "terrible thing" (90; 73), in itself creates dissonance. "Consciousness is a disease" that cuts us from the world, life, and others (18; 21). So he asks, "May not disease itself possibly be the essential condition of what we call progress and progress itself a disease?" (19; 23). Again something deathly watches at reason's core. One recalls Pope's "lurking principle of death," Claude Lévi-Strauss' idea of western culture as a virus in civilization, Horkheimer and Adorno's thought of instrumental reason as a cancer in the mind. T. S. Eliot joins the chorus:

> Our only health is the disease
> If we obey the dying nurse
> Whose constant care is not to please
> But to remind of our, and Adam's curse,
> And that, to be restored, our sickness must grow worse.
> ("East Coker," *Four Quartets*, 18)

Still today, Saramago echoes Pope and these many successors:

We are all ill, with one malaise or another, a deep-rooted malaise that is inseparable from what we are and that somehow makes us what we are, you might even say that each of us is his own illness, we are so little because of it, and yet we succeed in being so much because of it. (*Year*, 106)

In different but analogous ways, these mark a sense of the negative at a center of being. We find it, as well, in Freud's death drive at the nub of the psyche, in the Nothingness essential to Being in Sartre, and no doubt, too, in Derrida's erasures, *ratures*, that negate positive concepts even as they are voiced (or written). We find it too in those various "deviations" indexed in Chapter 2 (78 above). The West, Achebe observes, "seems to suffer deep anxieties about the precariousness of its civilization" (explaining thereby its commentators' "need for constant reassurance by comparison with Africa"—or any other cultures; *Hopes*, 17).

Giorgio Agamben has traced this negativity as it emerged in Hegel's "faculty for death" characterizing human consciousness, and in Heidegger's *Nichtigkeit*, knowing of death, grounding in negation essential to *Dasein*. In varied form, he shows how such thought came from Aristotle through the European Middle Ages more or less to now (the "tragedy of Europe" "decline of the West" mentioned before). By negation, "the model" was elaborated "according to which western culture construes one of its own supreme problems: the relation and passage between nature and culture, between *phusis* and *logos*" (85). Predictably, he adds, "It is here that the western philosophical tradition shows its originary link with tragic experience." Here, he repeats so many, "the experience of the human as both *living and speaking*, a natural being and a logical being . . . has appeared in the tragic spectacle divided by an unresolvable conflict" (88)—one more version of civilization and its other. This is the "disease" breeding Unamuno's anguish, "abyss of the feeling of our mortality," from which we may hope to "emerge into the light of another heaven" (*Tragic Sense*, 41–42; *Sentimiento*, 39). The hope was literal, founded on lasting despair of division: "Le silence éternel de ces espaces infinis m'effraient," Unamuno could well say with Pascal. After World War I, to interpret life and (European) culture as tragedy was the ubiquitous norm.

"Men have always had to choose between their subjection to nature or the subjection of nature to the Self," wrote Horkheimer and Adorno a few years and hideous catastrophes later (in 1944). But "social domination of nature" is an "inescapable compulsion" (like Schopenhauer's or Unamuno's "will") and "the principle of self" is "the evolutionary law of society" (*Dialectic*, 32–36). This echoes in a different key Unamuno's more melodramatic mystical assertions about self and "progress." All could equally have drawn the idea from Georg Simmel's 1911 essay, "The Concept and Tragedy of Culture," which reiterated this opposition of life and reason, the notion that what made culture possible also destroyed its vitality (Connerton, 120). Luigi Pirandello's first major interpreter, Adriano Tilgher, saw in Simmel's contrast if not the source at least a contemporary echo of what he described as Pirandello's tragic conflict between "Life" and "Form" (Sciascia, *Pirandello*, 141–42, 161–64). Indeed, during the 1920s and 1930s, Pirandello's exegetes invariably saw his theater as one in and about "tragic" crisis.

Agreeing that his theater was one of tragic conflict, Pirandello wrote to the drama critic Silvio d'Amico in November 1927 that Tilgher had nonetheless misdescribed it. The conflict was not between "life" and "form" but between "motion" and "form":

> For me life is tragic because it must obey two contrary necessities, motion and form: fatal necessities. Conflict is born from these two necessities. If life obeyed just one of them, and was only motion, it would never gain consistency. To gain consistency, it must obey the other necessity, acquire form. Form imprisons motion. Motion saps and slays forms. Whence the perpetual, fatal series of motions and forms in continual conflict, that is, precisely, life. (Sciascia, *Pirandello*, 201)

Such Life defeated Enlightened Reason's order, and Leonardo Sciascia rightly recalls Lukács' critique of fascism as a "destruction of reason" in favor of what it claimed as a "philosophy of life," nostalgia for some supposed wholeness of being and world. He likens Pirandello to Quijote, caught unavailing between reality and illusion, masks of "agony" (*Pirandello*, 158, 179; in a later chapter, we shall see just how a different cultural sphere turns this European reading and image of Quijote on its head, making the knight not a marker of division but a fount of joinings and rejoinings). Pirandello's falling into "life," caught between motion and form but claiming this lost wholeness of being as its source, may thus justly be thought one with his public adherence to the fascists after Giacomo Matteotti's murder in 1924, whatever his later ambivalence.[8] A like urge had Unamuno back the Falange until the epiphany caused by Millán Astray's encomium of death. These links catch well one extreme form of dissonance and stress how politics and aesthetics, epistemology and ethics, metaphysics and ideology are of a piece.

This tradition and set of ideas underpinned Tönnies' familiar poles of *Gemeinschaft* and *Gesellschaft* and the German and French sociological debates that followed (the split echoing in Durkheim's *organic/mechanistic* opposition). It underlay Husserl's analysis of western science and Heidegger's contrast of technological reason and embedded nature, holy soil of the *Provinz*. It begot Spengler's rejection of a rational socialist world system in favor of a sinister idea of western "high tradition and an ambition of strong families that finds its satisfaction . . . in the tasks of true rulership . . . by blood" (*Decline*, 2:506–7), awarding itself responsibility to rebuild the inferior civilizations whose destruction the West's wrongheaded rationalism had caused. Ramiro de Maeztu, member of the same '98 generation as Machado and Unamuno (and maybe the slightly younger Ortega), analyzed Spengler as expressing a nostalgia not for some "primitive" time but for a (Rousseauesque?) culture before "civilization." This they saw as decayed from a preceding whole culture and bound to reach a final stage of utter decay. Maeztu agreed that in "culture" people believed in war and transcendent gods, dwelt in the country untouched by what he calls "the fact of the human sterility of great cities," and rejoiced in the vigor of a nietzschean (or other) self set against the universe:

The countryman is fecund because he is alone facing the mystery of the world and of immense space, and his sole defense consists in perpetuating himself and defeating with the infinity of time the infinity of space. But in the great cities he loses the dread of death and has no need of children/sons. ("Decadencia," 123)

One cannot help recalling *Eumenides*, optimistically setting the city against a nonhuman world, human civilization against a culture of untamed gods in a division Nietzsche condemned; remembering Unamuno's "moral de batalla"; or thinking of Heidegger's nostalgia for the country *Provinz* against the technologized city and his view of *Antigone* as baring the conflict between violent human law and embracing chthonic powers. Maeztu quotes Spengler's comparison of city decadence to the childlessness of an American debutante because she can't miss the "*season*," of a Parisienne because she fears losing her lover, of an Ibsen heroine because she "belongs to herself." All "belong to themselves and all are infecund" ("Decadencia," 123–24). Decadence is thus feminization of civilization—or, rather, of culture *into* civilization and beyond. *Gemeinschaft* is manly, warlike, qualitative, dwells in time, admits unreason, recognizes divine mystery, creates; *Gesellschaft* is feminine, pacifist, quantitative, abstractly rational, secular, makes nothing. (This curiouly seems opposite to what would now be the sexualized characterization of these poles; do men simply valorize as "feminine" whatever we dislike?) For many of the Generation of '98, this decadence was precisely signaled by a loss of warlike ability that had resulted in the loss of empire in 1898, when the United States grabbed its last remnants in Cuba and the Philippines. Reading Spengler right after World War I, Maeztu found in Germany's loss of empire a parallel and in *The Decline of the West* an exegesis of both.

As we shall see in Chapter 10, Maeztu's generation depicted Don

Quijote as figuring both a past storied "hora de España," as Azorín had it, and the bewilderment of a time of passage. Just so did Azorín portray himself leaving the city of anomie that Madrid had become to find Quijote in a more vital countryside, but even so in perilous flux, riven with nostalgia for a lost Spain (*Ruta*). Quijote was used to query certain views of history—or views of certain History. For Maeztu, after Spengler, decadence was also removal of peoples from History—less into nonbellicose peace than into submission to another nation as through a Pax Romana or consequences of 1898 and 1918 for Spain and Germany ("Decadencia," 122). Regret for loss of a conquering history (correlated with the time of the countryside) climaxed in an enumeration of the causes of a depopulation—notably of those "capable of culture"—to which Europe was now condemned (as Rome and Spain had been in their eras of greatest glory), and from which it could be saved only by a new "imperialism or caesarism (maybe a fascism!), which will be a return of the old powers of the sword and cross, aristocracy and priesthood, against the present powers of the plutocracy and intellectuals": a last resurgence before final decay ("Decadencia," 124; see also 124–29). Even this was desperately unsure, for city civilization also dated from this conquering time and imperial Spain always already contained (like the rest of Europe) the civilizing seeds of its own destruction.

Maeztu did not aim such criticisms as he had of Spengler's argument at his eurocentric systematic model but at the idea that Europe was at this critical stage; Italian fascism and Spanish military rule in 1923, he found, were not "manifestations of decadence, but expression of a will to [social] *convivencia* that is superposed on desires for dissolution" ("Decadencia," 134). Will and *convivencia*, like "beauty," "truth," "goodness," and "love," came from a realm of "*values*," a "third" realm of "*spirit*" that Spengler had omitted in his insistence on "body and soul" alone. For an ascendent, not decadent, society one had only to turn to this *convivencia*, love of God and one's group (136–45)—a finale tellingly like Unamuno's and critical to points raised later, because Latin American thinkers such as Vasconselos, Zea, and Hector Murena saw in this "spirit" how a new Latin American vanguard could reverse the West's rationalistic decline by reinserting lost values into its history, spiritual synthesis ("cosmic," for Vasconselos) following material or barbarian or primitive and rational or civilized or urban phases. Doing this, Zea argued (it is the overall theme of his 1957 *América en la historia*), Latin America would enable Europe to overcome its internal conflict and make its "highest values, as these relate to the dignity of the person," no longer contradictory because no longer exclusive to Europeans, but universal (*Role*, 100). Their hegelian arguments *may* fit the divisive instrument of tragedy into a different conceptual network. We shall have to see. Maeztu's and Spengler's certainly did not, and their assertions about the forms of scission and how to use them amply confirm the political and ideological thrust that we have seen the instrument increasingly given.

Arturo Labriola's sharp rebuttal of Spengler's mystical denial of economic socialism and his new "enslavement of non-white races" deserved (and deserves) to be better known. His basic point, naively put, was that Europe was not the vital end point of a single legitimate progress of culture. There are many cultures: the "life of all peoples is a civilization." To the idea of one "legitimate" process, Labriola in 1936 opposed that of a heterogeneity of possibilities (*Crépuscule*, 181). The West's instrumental need for expansion and ever more consumption, embedded in its economism and its disjunctive ethic, could only lead to "permanent war" (333), the logical conclusion indeed of much else that we have been seeing, and programatically called for, in a sense, by Spengler, Unamuno, and Maeztu. But Fukuyama's argument, and indeed those of all who reject what is too readily called a "third way," are as much continuations of the same debate as are queries about "the legitimacy of the modern age." What do they express? other than a belief in one right kind of cultural motion, building in an endless incomprehension of cultures? or declaring others worthless?

Too, hallowed schisms between self and other, individual and community, divided reason and enveloping nature, as clear in Horkheimer and Adorno's remark as in Unamuno's poles of living and knowing, Simmel's of life and reason (even as altered in Horkheimer's *Eclipse*), Maeztu's and others' of country and city, Pirandello's of motion and form, or Agamben's of nature and logic, and basic to all exegeses of tragedy, remain dogma of western debate and its assumptions about the world. Unamuno found a possible bridge in memory: "basis of individual personality, just as tradition is the basis of the collective personality of a people." Momentarily it quelled division. All that "conspires to break the unity and continuity of my life conspires to destroy me and consequently to destroy itself. Every individual in a people who conspires to break the spiritual unity and continuity of that people tends to destroy it and to destroy himself as a part of that people" (*Tragic Sense*, 8–9, 11; *Sentimiento*, 15, 16). But division comes fast: our vehement life-wish produces a "tremendous struggle to singularize ourselves, to survive in some way in the memory of others and of posterity." Memory is rapidly no longer collective, but a claim of self: "a tremendous passion is this longing that our memory may be rescued, if it is possible, from the oblivion that overtakes others" (52, 55; 46, 48). Such singularity of memory matches the self-desired singularity of western history itself—a matter to which I will return at length.

In no very different terms, this struggle with the tie between individual and rational community, assuming some idea of the self's "authenticity"—its wholeness, self-possession, containedness, and originary nature— is still the core of western liberal social and political thinking, setting autonomous authenticity against formal order, desirous self against civilization, existential Right versus rational civic Obligation, Categorical Duty. So, writing of "being true to oneself," Charles Taylor virtually echo Unamuno: "If I am not, I miss the point of my life; I miss what being human is for *me*" (*Multiculturalism*, 30). But this incurs the hard "problem" of "recognizing" the "other" in his or her authentic difference, in the point of *their* life, so that what is "full humanity" "for them" may be part of the "dialogical" relationship that is society (33). Such arguments require familiar assumptions, and in the same volume of essays, Habermas reflects our many commentators by noting how Taylor supposes a conflict between "collective identities" and "the right to equal individual [*subjektive*] liberties" (110).

His retort that our acquiescence in, and indeed understanding of, ourselves as "authors" of the laws enabling judicial solution of such conflict make "private and public autonomy equiprimordial" (112–13) is not a convincing argument that liberal society thus sees people as "individualized only through a process of socialization," so that a properly "understood theory of rights requires a politics of recognition that protects the integrity of the individual in the life contexts in which his or her identity is formed." Again one catches echoes of the strife between knowing and living, form and movement, reason and emotion, logic and experience. One might as well claim as much of Athena's institution of the law in *Eumenides*, as if Orestes and Apollo, Athena and the Erinyes, chosen judges and Athenian population had consulted with one another to agree on the nature and establishment of society, rational dispute, and lawful—or even simply judicious—disagreement. Neither an ancient Orestes nor a modern Hamlet could so conceive his individual integrity or his relation to others—any more than could those others.[9]

Habermas acknowledges his abstraction's unreality and distance from actual practice and assumption, adding that such recognition, with its hoped-for results, would never occur in real life "without social movements and political struggles," often requiring violence (113). This is to acknowledge the very divisions the debate sought to deny, or at least to offer ways to overcome. They seem insuperable as long as people are seen as elements of mixtures rather than of compound organisms. We remain fast in Unamuno's "abyss [where] the scepticism of reason encounters the despair of the heart" (*Tragic Sense*, 105; *Sentimiento*, 84), where the tragic self asks, "Is it possible to contemplate the all with a serene soul . . . while thinking that a time must come when this all will no longer be reflected in any human consciousness?" (102; 82)—my own above all. And why may it not be? It only requires a collective concept and practice of "social movement." Of course, that "only" begs a sea of questions. I mean it to indicate how much lies at stake under such categories of thought as that or those of "tragedy" and "the tragic." How, as I said before, the aesthetic and political, the ethical and metaphysical are organized according to a particular cultural *ratio* that takes form, is manifest in such instruments as tragedy.

Tragedy would have been the aesthetic manifestation of an idea and experience of human life fundamental to many (all?) areas of western praxis, expressing something fundamental in the western imagination. For in Habermas' acknowledgment that violence alone may solve the principal dilemma of western liberalism, we yet again glimpse Dürrenmatt's and others' vision of "the tragic . . . as a frightening moment, as an abyss that opens suddenly"—between self and others, reason and motion, ordered society and muddled life ("Problems," 32). In an extraordinary passage in the central chapter of his *Stones of Venice* ("Nature of Gothic"), John Ruskin imagined this dissonance, this abyss, geographically and meteorologically patterned onto Europe's very surface. Picturing a bird looking down upon a Venetian Mediterranean—"for the most part a great peacefulness of light, Syria and Greece, Italy and Spain, laid like pieces of a golden pavement into the sea-blue, chased . . . with bossy beaten work of mountain chains, and glowing softly with terraced gardens, and flowers heavy with frankincense"—he fancied following its flight northward, finally to the "hill ravines" of "irregular and grisly islands," where "the hunger of the north wind bites their peaks into barrenness; and, at last, the wall of ice, durable like iron, sets, deathlike, its white teeth against us out of the polar twilight" (*Unto*, 81). But if the "zoned iris" of the earth revealed a gilded

Mediterranean distantly bounded by an iron wall of ice, it was an eye whose pupil was a Venice that itself had a negative at its core.

Ruskin saw this manifest in the gap between a Gothic architecture rising from "a state of pure national faith, and of domestic virtue" and a Renaissance architecture showing "a state of concealed national infidelity, and of domestic corruption," "a religion of Pleasure in which all Europe gave itself to luxury, ending in death. First, *bals masqués* in every salon, and then guillotines in every square" ("Traffic," 239, 242). "Death and Venice go together," asserts James Morris (*World*, 163–69). The grandeur of Venice was always taken to mask death and decadence at its heart. Even that had its ambiguity, for if it could be marked as the very ground of the city, "the floating muck" on which it was erected, to quote Walcott (*Omeros*, 204), it could also be marked as the presence of that fearful Other, a deadly menace from within: the Jews locked away at sunset in a ghetto "windowless on its outside walls . . . , cut off entirely from the rest of the city" (Morris, *World*, 106).[10] Here was the internal counterpart to Ruskin's distant iron wall against the external. And if Ruskin set purity against decay, Herman Melville preferred to set nature against culture, the little "worm" of the coral sea "With Pantheist energy of will" building "his marvellous gallery/ And long arcade," while Pan's "prouder agent," man, "laborious in a shallower wave" raised Venice's "reefs of palaces" ("Venice," *Selected Poems*, 144). Tony Tanner saw the latter as proof of Pan's power to raise beauty (*Venice*, 8–9), but the poem actually stresses men's weak laboriousness in the shallows against the energetic will of nature's tiny agent. Anyone who reads *Typee* knows how fiercely Melville indicted the "polluting examples" of colonizing Europeans and Americans, those men who built Venice, "vipers whose sting is destined to poison all the [natives'] joys (*Typee*, 25, 37). Small wonder that another Venice poem, "In a Bye-Canal," has the poet flee the "sirens, waylayers in the sea," as noon turns to night and a "basilisk glance" transfixes him.

Melville and Ruskin see the city on the Adriatic with as much fascinated horror as all the others we have seen. Venice is again taken as both symbol and concrete evidence of a culture defining itself in dissonance and negation, peopled, if we believe Nietzsche, by supermen joined only in their deep singularity. Of this symbol "in peril" of drowning, Saramago still writes, "By restoring Venice, a solution will be found for the rest of Europe" (*Stone Raft*, 53, 125)—a Latin American one perhaps? Montezuma getting a different kind of revenge as Saramago's floating Iberian island drops south to a spot in the Atlantic "between Africa and Central America" (257)? Grand, beautiful Venice, whether with Ruskin's or Melville's symbolic darkness or the ghetto's real darkness at its heart, *also* incarnated the sense of a reason with madness or death at its core.

As the preceding arguments proposed, we see how it—and they—depict a dilemma both inside western society and outside it, between its idea of order, let us say for example, and societies, cultures, that yield only with difficulty—and violence—to *that* idea of order. "Lowering Venice" marks "the weight of cities that I found so hard to bear," Walcott continues; "in them was the terror of Time," whose history sought to impose a "place that was not mine" (*Omeros*, 204). We have seen this view recorded by African and Asian writers, and we shall see it again in Latin American and other Caribbean ones. The dilemma lies, as well, in notions of separation between world and humans endemic to western culture, of reason as bearing within it its own death, of knowing as defying the motion without which life is not, and of the universality of these and other essentials of the tragic vision. And they *are* specific. These sunderings, I observed at the start of this chapter apropos of Japanese culture, do seem particular to the foundations of western culture. Just so does Owen remark of Chinese poetry that it may well reveal "a world in which there is misfortune, but no tragedy—no irreconcilable conflict between human will and mortal contingency, or between a merely human morality and some transcendent law that undoes the human ethical order" (*Traditional*, 192). This is why "we" must be especially careful in listening to differences not to "hear" them as "absences," whether of tragedy or any cultural product. This would be to ignore a prime tenet noted by Mignolo, for example: that "it is unfair to ask members of a culture different from ours ['ours' just indicating the speaker's cultural location] how they do something we do. It is unfair because it assumes that whatever we do has a universal value and, as such, every culture on earth has to do it, one way or another, if they pretend to be human" (*Darker*, 332). Beyond "unfairness," it is in fact one element of oppression: Venice preserved, Tenochtitlán captured and appropriated.

All this, with Labriola's argument about variety, brings me back to Nietzsche and the last part of this chapter, to efforts, firstly, both to understand how the instrument of tragedy has been used to order intercultural relations and to indicate how different culture may "turn" it, and secondly, to speak *through* the supposed place of tragedy's "absence" to *different* ways of taking back cultural space. In some sense, as I said earlier, there *is* no such place of absence seen from within any different cultures, and this last effort may seem hardly necessary. On the other hand, my argument here starts from the formation and use of western cultural instruments, and there is, I think, a somewhat mischievous way in which some cultures have responded—and do respond—fairly precisely to the *West's* perception of such an absence and, more importantly, to its imposition of the "tragic" as a means to mark violent destructions as "inevitable" and "destined" and so no matter of guilt and responsibility, and as a means to lay claim to that absence. Briefer than the brisk "trot through the tradition" that my case has needed, these efforts start with two remarks in *The Birth of Tragedy* ignored by commentators.[11]

To mark the transition hallowed by tragedy, Nietzsche took the satyr, whom the Greeks "did not confound . . . with the monkey. Quite the contrary, the satyr was man's true prototype, an expression of his highest and strongest aspirations"—Dionysos *with* Apollo, one might say (*Birth*, 52; *Geburt*, 54). But the contrast is ambiguous and unstable. The satyr, as Nietzsche said, was among other things intimately associated with the flute. Many stories tell us that the satyr Marsyas was first to play the instrument, obtained from Athena when he observed that playing it deformed her face inhumanly (Vernant, *Mort*, 55–63). This may be why Nietzsche added his rider about *dem Affen*, for the two were not otherwise associated. Playing the flute gave the satyr a frightening mask not unlike the visage frequently associated with the monkey, often considered lecherous, evil, foolish, vain, and the rest—characteristics that would come down to the European Middle Ages and Renaissance (Janson). For Nietzsche, man's prototype the satyr, while other than the monkey, was at the very least monkeylike. Yet why, save possibly for the music associated with the implicit flute, did Nietzsche associate either with tragedy and the transition he took it to represent between Dionysos and Apollo, the last moment of their union? It is certainly possible that the German philosopher was cued by a couple of remarks Aristotle made toward the end of the *Poetics* when talking about the degenerate performance of tragedies and more particularly of actors overacting, like "flute players whirling about" exaggeratedly or the player Callipides whom his older contemporary Mynniscus "dubbed an 'ape' [πίθηκον]" (1461b30–35).

This may well have provoked Nietzsche's second remark, which also concerns an ape. It comes a few pages later, after Nietzsche has written of "the Heraclean power of music, which reached its highest form in tragedy" (*Birth*, 68). He accuses Euripides of having killed tragedy, adding, "you could easily put in its place an imitation, masked myth, that, like Heracles' ape [*der Affe des Herakles*] would trick itself out in old pomp" (*Birth*, 69; *Geburt*, 70–71). Here, too, ambiguity reigns. For Marsyas' face when playing the flute was often compared to a player's mask, and perhaps not so very different from that *maskirten Mythus* which Nietzsche now identifies with Heracles' ape. The reference was to Lucian's *Piscator*, whose accuser of false philosophers (but also, ironically, of "true" ones), first remarked to Plato and the others that the former were "as if some actor in tragedy . . . should act the part of Achilles or Theseus, or even Heracles himself . . . showing off airs and graces in a mask of such dignity." They "made bold," he added, "though but apes [εἰ πίθηκοι ὄντες], to wear heroic masks." He ended with the apostrophe: "Have their sort anything to do with you, or have they displayed any similarity or kinship in their mode of life? Aye, 'Heracles and the monkey,' as the proverb has it!" ("Dead," 47–49, 55–57).[12]

Later on, the ape became for Nietzsche more clearly something other than a masked imitator, more clearly the sign of a passage from a world of wholeness to one of separation and abyss. It became the very symbol of what would be left behind when humans progressed to a new stage: "What is the ape to me? A laughing-stock or a painful embarrassment. And just so shall man be to the Super-man: a laughing stock or a painful embarrassment" (*Zarathustra*, 42: prologue, §3). But perhaps this simply explained why the ape could *only* be a masked imitator of the human? Like tragedy itself, the ape marked steps in a tragic disjunction of humans from the world. Just the same image and view lay behind Thomas Jefferson's sourly pejorative opinion of Phillis Wheatley, the first published African American poet: "The heroes of the *Dunciad* are to her, as Hercules to the author of the poem" (Gates, *Figures*, 6). Here were emphasized a series of disjunctions identical to those Nietzsche was to assert. Examples abound. Like tragedy, this meaning of the ape figure seems all but unique to western culture.[13] Unlike tragedy, the figure itself is not. But elsewhere it always has radically different meanings, meanings unrecognizable to disjunctive claim, meanings that use ambivalence, as Piedra writes, "not to create a traumatic split but a balancing act of cultural defense" ("Monkey Tales," 125)—although not just "defense" is at issue, since different cultures are not constituted only against a western colonizing one. But that is why it matters that Nietzsche brought the figure into his discussion of tragedy.

So, too, from a different angle but presumably silently recalling Nietzsche (as we shall see of another argument in Chapter 10), does Walcott. He speaks of the difficulties faced in the 1950s and 1960s by those wishing to create a Caribbean theater, one, he thought, that had to be "not only nostalgia for innocence, but the enactment of remorse for the genocides of civilization, a search for the wellspring of tragic joy in ritual . . . gropings for the outline of pure tragedy, rituals of washing in the first darkness." A good reader of Nietzsche, he adds that for actors and director, this "darkness which yawns before them is terrifying. It is the journey back from man to ape" ("Twilight," 5–6). In this essay, Walcott sees the Caribbean as living a massive series of dislocations, represented in such forms as the "tragic bulk" of Christophe's Haitian citadel, as tragic as the man himself, who "believed then that the moral of tragedy could only be Christian" and who lived in a "tragic anguish" that was the deep consequence of "divisions" (12) imposed by European mappings. Although Walcott is fraught with an ambivalence that often leads to fathomless contradiction, here he observes that this passage from tragic division back to the prior moment of the ape would thence institute a delivery "from servitude" by beginning to forge "a language that went beyond mimicry" (17). The Calibanlike "ape" would be the one to forge this newly "revelatory" language.

Walcott returned to this in reply to V. S. Naipaul's rejection of Caribbean culture as but the lowest mimicry, noting that despite destructions, what "Americans" (of all the Americas) have from Europe, Asia, and Africa is language (he surely ought to have added the Americas), and that if this is to be "condemned as mimicry, then the condition is hopeless and men are no more than jackdaws, parrots, myna birds, apes." The thought quickens: "The idea of the American as ape is heartening, however, for in the imitation of apes there is something more ancient than the first human effort" ("Caribbean," 7). If ape is prior to human, who or what is imitating? You then have an "image of the first ape applauding the gestures of the first man," the one repeating the other. Did this ape, seeing "his reflection in the mirror of a pond," utter a sound of "astonishment or terror," and so "become man" in inventing language (7)? You cannot capture the moment when ape becomes human, any more than you can separate "the old ape of Old World" from that of the New, who, after crossing (or not), might see the future as a parody of the past. All fictive imagination is mimicry, but mimicry of its own creativity, always making anew. Carnival and its calypsos, for instance, "originated in imitation if you want"; they "ended in invention" (9). These name one process. Mimicry is the chameleon, the butterfly or the tiger adapting hues and designs to environment, geography (10): "what is called mimicry is the painful, new, laborious uttering that comes out of belief, not out of doubt" (13) and builds communities "according to the topography of where you live" (10). A far cry, this, from Nietzsche's scorn, if not, we shall see in the next chapter, from what Aristotle really meant by *mimesis*. Walcott knows he is poking at a particularly European story: "We continue far enough and we arrive at Voltaire confronting Nietzsche: 'It is necessary to invent God,' and 'God is dead.' Join both, and that is our twentieth-century credo. 'It is necessary to invent a God who is dead'" (11–12).[14]

In ancient Egypt, the ape was "the holy animal of Thoth," the trickster god. William McDermott sees it as having "embodied the principle of balance and equanimity" (*Ape in Antiquity*, 7–8). The same figure seems to have accompanied the virtually pan-sub-Saharan trickster god, Esu-Elegbara or Legba, who represents an imagining of the world that Robert Pelton catches well while speaking more generally of the Fon pantheon in which Legba is a main figure and of whose signification he is the interpreter and mediator:

Its meaning is not so much rooted in the coincidence of opposites or in the mere passage between structure and antistructure as it is in a perception of life as a rounded wholeness whose faces both mask and disclose each other. These faces are simultaneously present, but this is a simultaneity of process, a turning by which one face not only succeeds but is transformed into the other. (*Trickster*, 104)

For such a worldview, Pelton remarks that even myths relating taboo or fearsome acts do not take on an "aura of tragedy." They are "*overcome*," to ground a "conviction that reality is always moving in a spiral of growth drawing even rebellion, incestuous desire, paternal rage, murderous jealousy, and death into the service of life" (214). It leaves no place for a tragic sense of "discrepancy" (270).

When Soyinka reworked Euripides' *Bacchae*, he demanded that it be staged as "a communal feast, a tumultuous celebration of life" (xix). The play in fact becomes not just a playing out (among other things) of the fraught dilemmas of decolonization, of confrontations between "collaborators" and "refusers" (to put it altogether too blunt-mindedly), between Primo Levi's drowned and saved, but also, precisely—and *through* that very playing out—a celebration of reestablishing a culture that somehow unites death and life, divine and secular, human society and natural world. The disaster and banishment which conclude Euripides' play are transformed. In Soyinka's play, something like a hegelian *Aufhebung* is performed whereby dissension and dissonance are sublated, by means of their very interplay, into the communal feast of which the playwright speaks in his foreword. Pentheus' bleeding head becomes a fountain of joyous wine, parody of the Eucharist marking a deeper wholeness of culture and history and geography (and assimilating fragments of another western tradition). Depestre had set an identical affirmation in political terms when celebrating a journey to Berlin in 1951:

> Je vais à Berlin dans le sillage du printemps
> Pour que les lendemains de tous les hommes
> Soient ruisselants de lumière
> Et que jaillisse la paix
> Du vin le plus rouge de la fraternité.

> I go to Berlin in springtime's wake
> So that the futures of all men
> Will be streaming with light
> And so that peace may spurt forth
> With the reddest wine of brotherhood.
>   ("Au rendez-vous de la vie," *Minerai noir*, 31)

Elsewhere, Soyinka writes of the "tragedy" of "man . . . grieved by a consciousness of the loss of the eternal essence of his being" that is portrayed in "Yoruba traditional drama": a "severance, . . . fragmentation of essence from self." At the same time, he proposes that the drama performs "symbolic transactions to recover his totality of being" (*Myth*, 144–45). That "totality" effaces what the West would call "tragedy." The performance takes its protagonist—its "votary"—"through areas of terror and blind energies into a ritual empathy with the gods, the eternal presence, who once preceded him in parallel awareness of their own incompletion" (146). Performance conjoins; no lasting blind Oedipus or finally blasted Pentheus here. In a way, the point is emphasized by Clark's dramatic duo, *Song of a Goat* and *Masquerade*, which adopt a very Greek tone of divine implacability to the story of a family suffering under a curse which has made an elder son, Zifa, impotent to conceive more children (he who as "a dutiful son" had "brought back home among his people" for proper burial his father's body cast out by his village for having died of "the white taint"—leprosy; *Song of a Goat*, 9). After finding out that his brother Tonye has lain with his, Zifa's, wife, Zifa first humiliates him in a scene heavy with symbolism by forcing him to break a cooking pot by stuffing into it the head of a freshly and ritually slaughtered goat, then pursues him with a cutlass, only to have Tonye hang himself first, so, Zifa laments, "again perform[ing his, the elder son's] part" (32). Zifa drowns himself in the ocean. *Masquerade* continues this Oedipal-style story, with Tufa, son of Tonye and Ebiere, Zifa's wife (but not knowing his incestuous origins), going to another village and courting Titi. His past is revealed just before they are due to be married, but Titi refuses to give Tufa up, on the grounds that he is not responsible for or to this ancestry. Her furious father shoots her dead and, in the course of a fight a little later, Tufa as well.

Apart from the Greek-tradition elements of the story itself, both plays' titles seem to refer to that tradition. The word "tragedy" reputedly derives from *trágos*, meaning "goat." Tragic actors always performed in mask. Both plays include groups functioning as choruses. More importantly, as Gerald Moore points out, what these plays omit is any deep sense of communal engagement across time or place. "It is always hazardous," Moore agrees, "to generalize about African traditional religions, but it is certainly true of most of them that they offer means by which contamination can be explained or cleansed. These means may involve the death or expulsion of a single person," but Clark's two plays do not in fact seem to expiate anything, and the second ends with what appears an announcement of more disaster to come, "full of danger/And portent for all of us" (*Masquerade*, 69). Moore further adds that a creation myth of the Ijaw (Clark's people; his father was Ijaw, his mother Urhobo) does tell how a child at birth makes an unrescindable choice of attributes to be borne through life, but without any suggestion "that the consequences of choice endure beyond the life-span of the person making it" (*Chosen*, 149–50). Perhaps one could argue that Clark used tragedy to show how colonial impositions had broken traditional bonds, set individualistic values against communal ones, but unlike Ṣofọla's plays or, say, Soyinka's *Death and the King's Horseman* (where that issue is central), nothing in the plays suggests such an interpretation—except the tragic form itself. And then it will, precisely, be tragedy that guides the reader or spectator to how that history and its deformations are "properly" to be understood, western *ratio* imposing its "explanation" on a quite different culture. Ezenwa-Ohaeto has been concerned, precisely, to argue that disaster ensues exactly when "the individual refuses to accept the dictates of his society" (9), when he splits from community.

Césaire achieves an analogous sublation, I think, to that traced in Soyinka's *Bacchae* in his *Tragédie du roi Christophe*, whose protagonist also walks narrowly between using western History and fighting it. He has no choice. The oppressors have disjoined colonized Haiti, remade it in their own disjunctive image:

> Stone, I'm looking for stone!
> Cement! I'm looking for cement!
> Everything is disjoined, oh! to get all that upright!
> Upright and in the world's face, and solid!
>
> (*Tragédie*, 45)

His citadel becomes the image of this demand and duty. Like Pentheus, Christophe dies in the trap forged by this disjointed History. But at the end, as his last followers carry his body through the mountains toward the citadel, he becomes increasingly "weighty." They set him down, stand him "upright," "facing south," to make his own journey, his own "stature," remaking Africa in and bringing Shango to Haiti; "upright King" standing in newly affirmed liberty. They leave him standing there, joined to those mountains and forests of Haiti whose praises he earlier sang (23), affirming a history within, and particular to, a Caribbean geography (matter of the last chapters of this book). Césaire writes that *Une saison au Congo* enacted a similar rejoining. Lumumba, "both victim and hero," was also "conqueror. Breaking himself against the bars of the cage, but also making a breach in them. Through this man . . . the whole history of a continent and of a people is played out in an exemplary and symbolic manner." So that the Sanza player is right to conclude the play with a reference back to Lumumba's architecture (see Chapter 1) about not doing things "by halves," "growing straight," and, finally, to the humorous banter of his own chattering (*Saison*, III.8: 116). These surely turn tragedy on its head.[15]

The Swahili dramatist Penina Muhando makes a remark that is suggestive in indicating why a different cultural tradition may do this:

There is still much more to be done with the African tradition. To give this simple example, I have noticed the way the African audience laughs, even when the play is tragic. The point is that Africans are not callous people, it doesn't mean they enjoy seeing people murdered, it means they have a different perception. Maybe they are laughing at the perfection of the acting, seeing that the actor has managed to imitate the action so well. I don't know, but these are things that need to be researched. (James, *In Their Own Voices*, 88)

Perhaps, too, they laugh because the action is somehow incomplete and falsifies life's ultimate jointure. So Mphahlele says of the Christian biblical version of such "tragic" scission, particularly of its slavering apologetical use to back and justify savage oppression: "Man's first disobedience—that can be a mighty big joke in Africa" (*Afrika*, 16). This nears what one finds in Clark's two tragedies (if not in others of his plays), uttering decisive and very western incomprehension and rupture: "Who/The gods love they visit with calamity" (*Masquerade*, 69). Differently, Soyinka's compatriot, the dramatist Ṣofọla, speaking of the violence resulting from "traditionally" immoral behavior that ends her play *Wedlock of the Gods*, says that what matters is that "those violent deaths are going to affect the families because of re-incarnation" (James, 148–49). They disrupt life immediately, but more importantly, they unbalance the long-term course of the community and humanity. The end of the play, therefore, is not the mark of scission and death but that of the continuities and interlockings which they interrupt and which, Ṣofọla is saying, must be seen to be there. This is very similar to the point Soyinka was urging about Yoruba drama.

An analogous view of the world is captured by ape figures in Asian lore, and we cannot be surprised to learn that when ancient writers of Greece and Rome mention the Indian ape, they "seem to be wholly unaware that the animal was sacred" (McDermott, 73). The secularization signals the same loss of connection between a divine and a whole natural world as did tragedy, a new sense of dissonance replacing one "of balance and equanimity." That was Nietzsche's meaning as well—and Walcott's point against him. Here was no place for the god Hanuman of the Hindu *Ramayana*, the transformative ape who rode winds and crossed at will and whim over the divine and human, the natural and social; nor for the divine trickster monkey Sun Wu Kong of the Chinese *Journey to the West*; nor for the mediating sacred monkey of medieval Japan; nor for the African monkey accompanying Esu, for Legba of Brazil, Haiti, or Barbados, where god and monkey are often elided, for *Mono, Mo-Edun, Mono Sabio, Coco Macaco* of Cuba, for the signifying monkey of African America—all connections and reconnections, like Octavio Paz's Hanuman meditations of *The Monkey Grammarian*.[16] None of these cultures had or have tragedy.

The varied wealth of roles occupied by the monkey figure may then be used positively to bolster the silent argument of tragedy's absence. For its difference says vital things about tragedy and the tragic to which Nietzsche, Lucian, Walcott, and others have tied it. These things concern categories and instruments of understanding that have been means to describe and pigeonhole peoples, actions, and realities otherwise unable to be situated and grasped. And I use this last verb because control is indeed at issue. I direct the ending of this chapter, then, not at specific cultural conflict (and assuredly not any East–West one; my examples are much nearer home) or at the ways in which any of the cases suggested themselves order their cultural categories. I mean to indicate how the categories of tragedy and tragic just explored do—have—become tools for a culture to order others. They are clearly not the only such tools, nor the only ones for which a usefully simple use of polarized concepts is endemic: parts/wholes, us/them, same/different, linear/circular, self/other. These tell us of the way these categorizing instruments work, but nothing of real cultural differences or possible interweavings.[17]

The force of their working has, however, been prodigious, and their users' cruel impact huge on lives, places, and societies. Not tragedy as such, but its sidekick in Nietzsche's ape thus had its small but telling moment in Octave Mannoni's *Psychologie de la colonisation* (*Caliban and Prospero*) of 1950. Writing of colonizers' fears, he described the European's "urge to identify the anthropoid apes, Caliban, the Negroes, even the Jews with the mythological figures of the satyrs" as sexual predators on (white) women and agents of subhuman or bestial violence (Mannoni, *Caliban*, 111). The justice of the notoriety Mannoni's book acquired, largely from Fanon's 1952 attack in *Peau noire, masques blancs*, is emphasized by the fact that Mannoni did not (as I have him doing) write of "the European," but of "man," as if the word meant only white European men and as if none of those enumerated could be qualified as "man." The force of the ape figure reduces them to objects of the "man" facing them, and we can equate Mannoni's enumeration with Jefferson's, which let him relate the poet Wheatley to Pope's dunces as the crippled ape, Pope himself, to Hercules. For Mannoni was certainly right about a *European* tradition that led Charles Darwin, for example, to include a peculiar Latin note in *The Descent of Man* about anthropoid apes' attraction to women (397n; Reiss, *Meaning*, 220 n. 77).[18]

And it is Pope again who links it for us to a tragic tradition placing death at the core of mind, disjoining life and reason. He and his friends wrote the *Memoirs of Martinus Scriblerus*. Visiting a freak show, whose Siamese twins he will wed, the eponymous hero comes across an ape. This "Manteger was a true descendant of the celebrated Hanniman the Magnificent" (Arbuthnot, *Memoirs*, 144).[19] One of the "dog-fac'd men," Plutarch's "Cynocephali," the baboons of Egyptian lore, his name is held "a corruption of the Mantichore of the Ancients, the most noxious creature that ever infested the earth; who had a Sting above a cubit long, and would attack a rank of armed men at once, flinging his poisonous darts several miles around him" (145). This surely recalls the *Ramayana*, whose Hanuman was just such a fighter. But the unusual genital endowment prepares us for the lesser ape met here. As Martin's beloveds escape through a window, they get stuck with their clothes "up to the navel." This excites the manteger, loose in the house, who "rushed upon Indamore like a barbarous ravisher." Battling "the hairy son of Hanniman," Martin kills him in good colonial fashion, one might say, with "the pointed *Horn* of an *Antelope*." He is indeed now characterized in a way that would be typical of colonialist discourse as "the grinning Offspring of Hanniman" (152–53): sex, violence, and inarticulate subhumanity. Here, the bonds between ancient European commentary on other cultures, western categories of thought and discourse of dominion are transparent. They answer Katha Pollitt's question as to why, in Disney's 1994 film *The Lion King*, "did the wise old shaman, the only character with an African accent, *have* to be a baboon?" (9).

Less than a century after Pope and his friends, Goethe used Hanuman equally exactly to emphasize both the particularity of *his* literary tradition and that of the idea of civilizational progress it supposedly embodied. Understanding the growth of his own mind as ontogenetically manifesting the phylogenesis of western humanity, he observed the importance for his creative imagination of its absorption of elements from different cultures— the northern sagas, the Edda, Ossian, the "Indian fables." Remarking how, in his own retelling of the *Ramayana*, "despite the many persons in this tale, the ape Hanuman remained the favorite of my public," he added that "these unformed and over-formed monsters could not satisfy me really poetically [*unförmlichen und überförmlichen Ungehauer konnten mich nicht eigentlich poetisch befriedigen*]: they lay too far from the truth toward which my mind unceasingly strove." Shades of Faust. Goethe explained how the cavalry of western literary tradition rode to his defense: "But against all these specters hostile to art [*Doch gegen alle diese kunstwidrigen Gespenster*],

my feeling for the beautiful was to be protected by the noblest power"—
none other than Homer, akin in force to "Holy Scriptures" (*Autobiography*,
2:162; *Dichtung*, 9:537).[20] This is the aesthetic and literary counterpart to
Pope's cultural and perhaps political dismissal of the processes enacted via
the figure of Hanuman. It is one which spiritualizing nationalist writers
like Coomaraswamy, reversing earlier writers' exact adoption of Goethe's
view, we saw in the Introduction, ardently rejected by showing that for the
Other, aesthetic "specters" were beautiful (see, for example, "Indian Images
with Many Arms," *Dance*, 67–71, but also longer works recovering Asian
artworks from European condemnation).

   In light of all this, we need not be surprised if efforts to respond to a
dominant western—and nietzschean—tragic world picture increasingly
draw on these monkey figures, seeking to resolve what has been called, in
regard to the African American author Jean Toomer, a "tragic" sense of "the
soul's transit through an unsoulful world" (Mackey, 269), a phrase I cite to
signal again this picture's ubiquity. For if, in Naipaul's *A House for Mr.
Biswas*, the symbol of Hanuman marks breakdowns caused by western
hegemony,[21] in so many others, Timothy Mo's *The Monkey King*, Maxine
Hong Kingston's *Tripmaster Monkey*, Walcott's *Dream*, Robert Antoni's
Divina Trace, he and Sun Wu Kong articulate rejoinings with memory and
tradition, connections and junctions between cultures, efforts to recapture
harmonies rather than to dwell in dissonance. In the Luso-Chinese Wallace
Nolasco, the Chinese American Wittman Ah Sing, and Antoni's
Trinidadian Hanuman, the trickster monkey is a figure of thought to ex-
orcise and overcome the tragic sense of life. Too, it establishes and reestab-
lishes weavings and reweavings. Piedra shows several other cases: from
Borges, Ishmael Reed, and Paz to Miguel Barnet, Teófilo Radillo, Nicolás
Guillén ("Monkey Tales"), and Carpentier ("Return").

   Of course, to repeat a point made at the end of the last chapter, no
more than Habermas' desperate abstraction can the fictive imagination directly cure worldly practice. But they certainly change habits of mind—just
as, I have been suggesting, tragedy itself did. Sciascia has remarked that
Unamuno saw Don Quijote as Spain itself, not metaphor or allegory, but
true depiction of Spanish reality (*Heures*, 40–44). Maeztu felt the same,
calling Quijote "una figura única, símbolo de realidad histórica," embodiment of historical reality ("Don Quijote," 67). Borges urged a similar point
about how imagination forges cultural figures and categories in "Pierre
Menard, Author of the *Quixote*" (*Labyrinths*, 62–71). Just so, the compre-

hension of life as "tragic," and all it has been held to mean, derived from tragedy. That Averroes could not conceive the meaning of tragedy was precisely because no such derivation existed in his world. This fact tells nothing else of Islamic culture, but Sciascia, too, has taken it to say much of the West's, using the same Borges tale to distinguish a "humorous" and dialectical style of life in once Arab-occupied Sicily from a divisive one in parts colonized by Greeks and left unoccupied by Arabs (*Pirandello*, 24–26). Just so, victims of such figures of thought internalize their dominion, "enslaved," Lamming agrees, "by a particular way of learning, a particular way of receiving" (*Pleasures*, 15).

For once a category is fundamental to a cultural imagination, it is a way to analyze and classify actuality. As Hilden observes, "Cherokees, still quite numerous and highly literate, soon became a symbol of tragic bravery, painted, celebrated in song and poem, marching along and dying, albeit of those things acceptable to readers of the national history: disease, cold, hunger, exhaustion." Just so, "this symbol of tragic Cherokee nobility became the means by which all the other genocidal acts of the invasion and conquest could be overlooked" ("What Happens," 13). To set the story and stories of Native America into tragedy and the tragic is to use cultural power to remove peoples from their present. Tragedy and the tragic make things destined, personally irresponsible, fated by greater nonhuman forces. Glissant has also written illuminatingly of how these categories let western culture place or, it says, "understand," conquered and colonized peoples: "tragedy, in the western sense, is discriminatory. It reconstructs the legitimacy of a culture's emergence, it does not offer the infinite variations of cultural synthesis." Because the very idea denotes divergence, he infers that there could be no "tragedy of the cross-cultural imagination." For tragedy *always* implies "Us," "Me" and "the unifying force of History, another trap. . . ." Against this, Caribbean folktales are always offered as "antitragic," precisely in "their disruption of history and the rejection of any form of transcendental legitimacy" (*Caribbean Discourse*, 86–87). Wilson Harris, too, suggests that breaking scission and forging a "complex mutuality of cultures . . . offers . . . the only doorway into a conception of genuine breakthrough from tragedy." Otherwise, "tragedy lives, and within our carnival age . . . it accepts the ultimate inversion of all by a structured and tamed nature that becomes, in stages, a decadent and fatally diseased or exploited muse" (*Womb*, 18). To make "others" into a tragic story is to hold different peoples hostage to the West's tale no less than does writing them into any version of western history.

Fanon's reply to Mannoni and others had made similar points (often with practical and less utopian intention and consequence). In this sense, Baldwin recounted a moment in a speech by Césaire in Paris in 1956 recounting just this removal and alienation. "The situation . . . in the colonial countries," he said, "is tragic." It is so because "the indigenous culture begins to rot" from the pressure of an uncomprehended foreign culture and its scission from the lifeblood of its own peoples. It becomes a "subculture" created to "exist on the margin allowed it by European culture" (Baldwin, *Nobody*, 34). It is "tragic" in that it has been made a separated dependency of European culture. Observing Césaire, Baldwin deepens the implications by recording his own uneasy sense that the speaker himself had been rendered unable to catch his own actual situation, to realize his own now ineluctable relation to European culture. A principal aspect of the "tragedy," therefore, is that disunion from one's own culture is augmented by "tragic" blind scission from any other.

To denominate a culture and its members as tragic, its deeds and experiences as tragedy, replaces the local ambiguities of life and the realities of particular place and time, with someone else's overlaying transparency. This transparency tries literally to translate the overlaid culture into some other place. As Baldwin put it in regard to Césaire, such translated culture is "deprived of any revivifying contact with the masses of the people" (*Nobody*, 34). That is why defeated and devastated peoples are described as "tragic" by the winners: they are understood as tragically disjointed from the necessary progress and "legitimate" direction of human history. But also as already constituted into another's story of separateness, as Marshall tells of Bourne Island: "it's every man for his damn self. That's the reality and the tragedy of us on this island" (*Chosen*, 211; a rather more sour version of Nietzsche's glories). So, Glissant, Harris and others propose, to resist this tragic setting problematizes the "metropolitan" claim. Making experience and its stories unilinear, *effects* of someone else's history, that claim disjoins. Ambivalence and ongoing wealth of experience are reduced to a tale told by an idiot, engraved with the *hamartia* of overweening ignorance. It adds to the ruin of those it seizes as part of its story, making them a tragic Other forever disconnected from the sound and fury of its own history, at whose emptiness of meaning Macbeth may grieve, but not Malcolm, the finally victorious remaker of sovereign dynasties. For however tragic, that Other is made into Pope's, Goethe's, Nietzsche's, or Mannoni's grinning and misformed ape, gazed at, categorized, possessed, and used by "man."

The responsibilities of authentic experience in, in this case, all their violence and horror are thus distanced into a sentimental glow of false sympathy. For as these categorizations split peoples from their actual cultural lives, they turn lives and peoples into abstract fantasies. Hilden quotes another instance of both from Henry William Elson's 1904 *History of the United States*, where the historian, "safe inside the conqueror's heroic myth," explains the "serious, almost sad expression" of the "characteristic Indian countenance" not as mirroring conquest, genocide, ongoing violence, and victimization but as showing "the Indian's" deep sorrowful disjunction from an inexplicable otherworld: "his unceasing fear of [the myriads of invisible spirits] for ages has probably set his stamp indelibly upon his face" (*Nickels*, 75). Tragic victim of some impersonal tragedy, "the Indian" becomes the inferior objectivized "Other" of "Our" gaze, explained and categorized as the inevitable victim of technological progress, fixed forever in the otherness of ancient superstitions.

Baldwin accused William Faulkner in 1956 of opposing immediate desegregation in the American South on like grounds, replacing the violence and combat of sociopolitical actuality with the mystical spirituality of a tortured Southern soul. "And it is, I suppose, impertinent to ask just what Negroes are supposed to do while the South works out what, in Faulkner's rhetoric, becomes something very closely resembling a high and noble tragedy" (*Nobody*, 119).[22] Deprived of history, indeed, placed outside history in some tragic eternity, "the Indian" or "the Black" is unable to understand or be in harmony with the world, taken in the unalterable drift toward inhumanity and destruction, caught in the conflict between human will or morality and mortal contingency or transcendent law (recalling words of Bernard Williams, Steiner, and Owen) for which only inexplicable destiny or fate is responsible—or irresponsible.

For those questions of "guilt, despair, moderation, lucidity, vision, a sense of responsibility," raised before by Dürrenmatt, here come back and back. Now "we" know to whom despair and guilt belong—if to anyone: the "Other," who has not managed to come to terms with "his" disunion from the spiritual world. Just as vision and lucidity belong to those who *know*. Just as Lockean property makes one human and its rejection shows one non- or subhuman. And responsibility? Not for violence or terror or deprivation or genocide (as Walcott notes in "Caribbean," 13). That belongs to those who have let disjunction drown them. "Our" fated destiny and burden now turn responsibility into spiritual charity and sympathetic understanding for the victim protagonist of high and noble tragedy. This is how one so easily gets caught in such handy ideas as those of conflict between "East" and "West," of civilizational clashes or, even better, the flattening euphemisms of "cultural encounters." Abstraction reduces all confrontations to one set of constants, actual struggles to just so many variants. Egyptian, Yoruba, Hindu, Chinese, Japanese, or African, Caribbean, Arab, American Indian, African American cultures, endlessly plural, are readily equated with one another. Cultural practices and ideas like tragedy and the tragic, ineluctably one with the actions of *their* culture, may be used to make all alike *others* of the culture whose categorial instruments they are.

So one must distinguish the false nostalgia—kitsch memory, as I called it in Chapter 1—that enables such seizures, from real memory and experience. The first makes others, antiselves, from an idealist, abstract version of one's own present caught by habitual cultural categories. The second essays the hard mining of past experiences in their inner ambiguity and diversity, which have been and are no less manifold than the peoples to whom they belong—as Labriola argued. Tragedy and the tragic are categories that capture other cultures in just such false nostalgia and kitsch memory. In 1595, the heyday of that English Renaissance that also saw Shakespeare's beginnings, Sir Philip Sidney had already more than glimpsed this instrumental potency:

And do they not know that tragedy is tied to the laws of poesy, and not of history; not bound to follow the story, but having liberty either to feign a quite new matter or to frame the history to the most tragical conveniency? (*Defence*, 66)

Like all poetry, tragedy made its own imagined realities, just as it also turned history to its own purposes.

By nature and in deed, Sidney suggested, it was a tool to bend culture "to the most tragical conveniency." The sixteenth-century soldier-courtier doubtless did not have in mind the implications of less innocent employment one day to be advanced by Borges' story and Sciascia's analysis, or those of predatory association with a long western tradition of tragical apes. He was assuredly far from Baldwin's, Césaire's, Glissant's, Hilden's, Harris', Marshall's, or Walcott's suggestions as to just how the thought categories of tragedy and the tragic can be and are used as means of cultural dominion, making real history into disjunctive conveniency wrought on antiselves. They disconnect lives from the varieties of their own experience and reduce them to "opposites" of what is taken as the common(sense) experience of western civilization. Scission and dissonance repeat the nature of the culture for which tragedy and the tragic have been such vital categories—which, despite its many doomsayers and like all other cultures, is not a priori good or bad, but must be understood in its own "odd customs and superstitions," as Achebe has it (*Hopes*, 2), in its own difference and particularity, before teasing out whatever may be generalizable, and certainly before turning that to dominating abstractions deemed universally beneficial.

Others reject the cultural, political, and economic divisions marking a dissonant culture. So Makak, in Walcott's *Dream on Monkey Mountain*, signing himself as monkey, king, lion—and healer of deep wounds (249, 289, 291)—seeks a particular identity, and more:

> I have live all my life
> Like a wild beast in hiding . . .
> And this old man walking, ugly as sin,
> In a confusion of vapour
> Till I feel I was God self, walking through cloud.
>   (*Dream*, 226–27)

Divers intercultural antitragic bits combine: Hanuman's power; Sun Wu Kong trapped—hidden—in his mountain, before his release to travel toward enlightenment; the touted "ugliness" of now familiar apes; who yet know, like the Monkey King and monkey general, how to tread vaporous clouds to knowledge. Walcott and so many others do not accidentally reweave these shards. They seek healing by exchanges that recognize differences between cultural homes at the same time as the *mestizaje* or "*mutuality*" (Harris, *Womb*, 13) on which they depend if any are to perdure, as Césaire insisted years ago in his *Discourse on Colonialism* (11) and Sciascia implied in seeing once Arab-occupied Sicily as living a "humorous" mingling of comedy and tragedy (*Pirandello*, 25). These needs are performed by Wittman Ah Sing, a contemporary trickster living a mix of cultures in an arena of social, economic, and racial conflict. He ends with a monologue warning the audience at his play of mingled Chinese and American traditions against being taken in by the hiding of such conflict, against being caught in others' stories, against disablement from understanding, crossing between and interweaving one's own and others' homes: "In the tradition of stand-up comics—I'm a stand-up tragic—I want to pass on to you a true story" (Kingston, *Tripmaster Monkey*, 317). This truth is the contrastive and equivocal weaving just told, disfiguring familiar western categories of knowing and explaining.

4

Disjunctive Culture, Representation, and Mimetic Ends

This rapid trot through one (western) tradition may suggest that the overwhelming sense of scission and dissonance is actually of rather recent vintage. The Greeks may have found the gods difficult to understand and the meaning of Fate and Justice obscure, yet there was no question but that, as persons and as communities, they were wholly imbricated in them, trammeled up with them (Reiss, *Mirages*). We have seen western ideas of literature and history as characterized by ideas of conflict and a tragic agon. For I have been arguing that tragedy, the tragic, and what I call dissonance or disjunction together composed one coherent, if complex, aspect of western culture. I also suggested that in an era of colonialism and imperialism, they became cultural instruments to turn different cultures toward the one "universal" one, using a "western model," Jenine Abboushi Dallal observes, "to preclude and devalue other aesthetic standards and modes" ("Perils," 8).[1] Doing so, these *rationes* fix different cultures as definitively and irreducibly "other." Tragedy and the tragic are seen to be categories of thought or activity corresponding to a deep emotional sense of disconnection and an equally strong philosophical concept of disjointure that they implied to be a far more general ground of western culture.

It has been objected to me that tragedy is by definition a mimetic practice, all art being representation, and that it therefore *depends* on separation and division simply *as* art. However artistic representation is defined, it always assumes, this argument went—goes—that the work itself lies across, as it were, from what is being represented. The objection further runs that such "artistic" representation is common to *all* known human societies, and so one could always show such works to *require* what I was calling "disjunction." Earlier chapters (especially Chapter 3) have already begun to query this universalizing claim. Indeed, as I remarked in the Introduction and later, it is actually a rather odd one, rationally speaking (involving less reason, perhaps, than what Achebe calls the psychological needs of western culture; *Hopes*, 1–20). For even a not very deep acquaintance with elements understood to ground what has been called (for three centuries) "literature" shows that this idea of artistic representation is hardly tenable as a defining necessity even in the culture from whence it springs. As a practice (and indeed as a concept), "literature" has been anything but disjoined. So my immediate response to the objection was simply that the objection seemed to make my points, both about disjunction and about the claim to universality, simply stating both as axioms.

A look at the essential concept of *mimesis* helps understand why. At least in the West, people have argued since the ancient Greeks that mimesis is the essential mechanism in making what can be called by the general term *art*, humans' ordered *makings*. Indeed, for Aristotle, mimesis defined art—*technē*—in general (*Physics*, 194a21), and when he came to talk about "poetry in itself" (*peri poiētikēs autēs*) in the first two sentences of the *Poetics*, its particular defining attribute was "*mimesis*" (1447a10–16). Two questions are what this hard word *mimesis* may have meant and what it has been taken to mean. We have already seen Walcott make "mimicry" into a simultaneous invention and imitation that queries both the particularity of the categories these terms frame and the priority and universality of those doing the framing. I noted then (Chapter 3, note 14) that Aristotle may be similarly understood, although the standard interpretation has not done so. We shall see more of the complications this implies for the practices devolving from the fictive imagination. But it is certain that since the European Renaissance, at least, *mimesis* has generally been held to denote a "representation" of what is different from the forms and techniques of the art itself by means whose central term would doubtless be *metaphor*—a statement that does not predetermine the status of that difference. (That historically the word μεταφορά as a defining term for a particular linguistic turn came *after* the use of *mimesis* to signify a specific human praxis—the first not found in Plato, but in Isocrates and then Aristotle—and was then given so large a place, suggests both its need and its subordination; Stanford, 3–4.)

Since the Renaissance, artistic representation was supposed recogniz-
able to all as "being" what it "imitated" and subject to a common "taste" as
to accuracy and moral and aesthetic value. At the same time, it was taken
to "stand across from," "opposed to," "cut off from" a real world of which
it nonetheless gave "true" (or verisimilar) knowledge. True art, it was said,
was thus by definition, *qua* art, separated and different from the real world.
Art, critics, theorists, and connoisseurs agreed, was of necessity divided
from what it represented. So, for example, if African or Asian or American
art forms were to be valued in the West (as we have been seeing), they had
to be moved to its terms, divorced from specific contexts and seen to be
"universal" as well and in the same ways, subject to the *same* aesthetic criteria as western forms, settled into *their* museums and art fora, if sometimes
slightly differently adjudged (this is why Saul Bellow supported Allan
Bloom by asking, notoriously and now proverbially, to be shown "the
Tolstoy of the Zulus, the Proust of the Papuans").[2] Literature developed,
Owen offers, "in a melancholy competition between determining representation and a determining but hidden 'original' content" (*Traditional*,
21). Even in the West, though, there was also a very different idea of what
might be meant by *mimesis* and by *metaphor*—so, too, of what "art" might
be and of what the "fictive imagination" might do.

But Christopher Prendergast, who made the objection noted (and
who has himself written importantly on mimesis), is not alone in taking
the experience and concept of division as essential to the very notion and
experience both of "art" in general and of "literature" in particular. Sandro
Briosi, for example, author of important books on metaphor and symbol,
asks the same thing: "does not scission always characterize literature [and is
this not simply] to declare the symbolic nature of literature?" (personal letter, June 1996). Its primary figure would then indeed be that of metaphor,
defined in one ancient and probably most widespread view as the transfer,
tra[ns]latio, of meaning from one image to another, of a "tenor" from its
usual "vehicle" to another—unusual—vehicle (Cicero, *Orator*, xxiv.81). So
Cicero praised Demetrius of Phalerum for "lighting up" his oratory with
"the stars, as it were, of transferred and transformed words [*tra(ns)lata verba
atque mutata*]." By transferred words, he wrote, he meant "those which are
transferred by resemblance from another thing for the purpose of pleasing
effect or for lack of a good word [*quae per similitudinem ab alia re aut suavi-
tatis aut inopiae causa transferuntur*]." Transformed words referred to those
cases where "for a proper word [*pro verbo proprio*] was substituted another

that meant the same but was drawn from some other thing [*ex re aliqua*]" (*Orator*, xxvii.92). In this understanding, metaphor works, Max Black remarks, by "substitution" or "comparison" ("Metaphor," 30–37).

Unsurprisingly, Desiderius Erasmus echoed the definition: "Another method of varying comes from metaphor, which is called *translatio* (transference) in Latin because it transfers a word from its real and proper meaning to one not its own" (*On Copia*, 28: I.xvi). The *Oxford English Dictionary* keeps this definition: "The figure of speech in which a name or descriptive term is transferred to some object different from, but analogous to, that to which it is properly applicable." In his popular *Handlist of Rhetorical Terms*, Richard Lanham expands the idea to end his entry on metaphor: "to appreciate the metaphoricality of a metaphor we must posit a nonmetaphorical, normative 'reality' against which to project the metaphorical transformation" (101). It is not clear *why* such a reality needs positing or just *what* it would be, but the fact remains that for these views, both literature as symbolic form (and "art" more generally) and its principal figure, fundamentally dependent on relations of division, answer exactly to forms of practice noted in previous chapters and echoed in the wider aesthetic and sociopolitical assertions of such as those named caustically in my Introduction. In just this sense, Ortega thought contemporary poetry characterized in its essence by an aesthetic of increasingly divisive distance, having "become the higher algebra of metaphors" (*Dehumanization*, 30). Metaphor required division, functioned by its means ("Las dos," 246, 255; this is the whole essay's point). Emerson Marks finds such views to exemplify *right* ideas of art's work and of "poetic imitation" since Samuel Taylor Coleridge, for whom "the reconciliation of opposites effected by the creative imagination is anything but peaceful." Art's reconciliations needed "polarities" in lasting "tension." Philosopher critics like Nelson Goodman asserting that "wherever there is metaphor there is conflict" or Philip Wheelwright finding "the essence of metaphor in . . . 'semantic tension' " confirm this view that the "basic act of imagination" lies in "the apprehension of polarity" typified in metaphor and basic to mimesis (Marks, 152–53).

The view offers a powerful case. Certainly, in the *Sophist*, Plato was harsh on *mimesis* as freighted by the false over the true, the fictional over the actual, essentially marking our distance from the real (*Sophist*, 234a–235b). In *Republic* (373, 596–98, etc.), just the fact that art played on that disjunction from the real was reason for its dismissal. Although Plato was not always so negative about mimetic practice (*Cratylus*, 423a–424c, 431a–

434b), he always understood it as based on disjunctive premises. This is so even though many see some opposition between a Platonic tradition and an Aristotelian one. Plato is supposed fraught with ambiguity, torn between the *Republic*'s understanding of mimesis as a distant copy of a copy already itself distant from any substantial reality and *Phaedrus*' understanding of it as a creative play ultimately allowing the soul at least some access, be it only by imagination, to that reality (Melberg, *Theories*, 10–50; cf. Gebauer and Wulf, 31–52; Prendergast, 9–12), and then endlessly expansive to an echo of the universal (McKeon, "Literary Criticism," 149–59). Aristotle, partly responding to his teacher, is taken to have fixed a potentially less ambiguous meaning of the word. He defined tragedy, for example, as the *mimesis* of an "action," "*praxis*," which used "plot," "*muthos*," as its precise means of imitating such action (*Poetics*, 1449b24, 1450a4). *Muthos* was a particular narrative "structure of events" that Aristotle called "the soul of tragic art" (1450a38–39). *Praxis* was one structured action, "complete and whole and of a certain magnitude"—"whole" meaning that it had an ordered beginning, middle, and end (1450b24–27). Mimesis showed the order underlying human action in the world. It was *made* (the verb *poieîn*) by the rational mimetic faculty that especially characterized humans (see, too, Aristotle, *Rhetoric*, III.x.7–xi.16: 1410b7–1413b1; Briosi, *Senso*, 15–19; McKeon, "Literary Criticism," 160–68). Whatever it or its status might be, this exegesis said, *something* over and across from literature was being represented, mimicked, imitated.

Other accounts of metaphor were available. But this interpretation of what was supposed to have been Aristotle's view has dominated western understanding of mimesis. This or analogous interpretations may have been "a serious misinterpretation [*un grave contresens*]," as Paul Ricoeur has put it (*Métaphore*, 56), and they raise an issue which will return at some length. But whether or not "Platonic reminiscences" (Melberg, 44) may have surfaced along the way, and whether or not they introduce ambivalences, both views established distance and difference as essential characteristics of art, an activity divided from a world of which it gave some kind of depiction, manifestation, or presentation—however that "world" might be separately defined and regardless of the status given to it. Discussing Plato and dismissing any idea that art could reproduce the real or the true as "similarity," Heidegger also rejected any association of mimesis with what he called "primitive" imitation. Rather was it a "doing-after: production that comes afterwards. The *mimesis* is in its essence situated and defined through distance."[3] In the same years that saw Heidegger echoing such an understanding, Erich Auerbach, in exile, was writing what was surely the most influential modern work on the subject: *Mimesis*. There he sought to show how (western) literary writings represented what he termed the totality of the real at the particular moment of their production. They did so, and *could* do so, precisely because they *translated* it in particular ways, because they metaphorized it, because they operated a particular kind of *transference*.

Such ideas of artwork, mimesis, and metaphor are held to have come down to us from Aristotle via Cicero, Quintilian, and the debates on mimesis and representation that preoccupied critics and others during the European sixteenth and seventeenth centuries. It was also then held, certainly, to characterize art and what the West has since called literature and is deeply familiar at least to western ears. Indeed, speaking of the Renaissance as the "era of the image of the world," Heidegger sought to historicize the idea. In *Holzwege*, he asserted that the Renaissance could "be considered as the moment in modern history of *repraesentatio*," "an era in which man carries before him simple presence like a contrary thing," an otherness that a new sort of human "subject" had to form to its—or his—intent (Tafuri, *Venice*, x). Of course, one needs to ask just whose "modern history" is in question, and Cheyfetz is surely correct to observe how concepts of *translatio* and metaphor could serve to make the victim of imperial expansion into the *other* of aesthetic and political imagining. The proper is there the national and the normal—even the universal; what is figured is foreign. This is not too much of a stretch, for the texts explaining metaphor, *translatio*, and such often saw them as "an act of violence." To good effect, we saw in Chapter 2, Cheyfetz notes how these concepts were "forever involved in the dispossession by which Native American land was *translated* (the term is used in English common law to refer to transfers of real estate) into the European identity of *property*" (*Poetics*, 36–37, 43). *Translatio means* metaphor, and one can, again, readily understand Paula Gunn Allen's claim that Native American thought neither knew nor practiced metaphor. The claim is otherwise, I suggested before, somewhat odd (surely inaccurate as to linguistic usage in general)—and beside the point: it's not its use but its dominance that matters, the manner of its conceptualizing, the centrality it is granted, and the uses to which it is put.

Not only, then, is this view of art and literature associated with a particular history, but it can also become a particular, and I hope now relatively transparent, way of negotiating and grasping different histories, turning the figured toward the proper. Ortega noted how "metaphor disposes of an object by having it masquerade as something else," something familiar to its user who thus avoids "certain realities." He agreed with Heinz Werner, who argued that metaphor was born in "the spirit of taboo," enabling things forbidden, threatening or wholly unfamiliar to be known, controlled and used (*Ursprünge*; see Ortega, *Dehumanization*, 31–32). From the side of a Caribbean culture figured by the proper culture of the West, Édouard Glissant remarks in this regard, revealingly if unknowingly echoing Lanham's terms:

All mimesis presupposes that what is represented is the "only true reality." When it involves two realities of which one is destined to reproduce the other, inevitably those who are part of the process see themselves living in a permanent state of the unreal. That is the case with us.

"Mimesis," he comments a bit later, "operates like an earthquake. There is something in us that struggles against it, and we remain bewildered by it" (*Caribbean Discourse*, 242, 244). Mimesis (in its most common interpretation), he is observing, imposes a particular view of the world.

Pauline Yu, comparing western to Chinese traditions, makes not dissimilar observations, less the colonial earthquake: "The most fundamental disjunction posited and bridged by western metaphor is more than verbal—it is that existing between two ontologically distinct realms, one concrete and the other abstract, one sensible and the other inaccessible to the senses" (*Reading*, 17). In this, metaphor is a synecdoche for mimesis as a whole, which is "predicated on a fundamental ontological dualism—the assumption that there is a truer reality transcendent to the concrete, historical realm in which we live, and that the relationship between the two is replicated in the creative art and artifact" (*Reading*, 5). Yu then seeks to show the immense difference of the Chinese tradition from any western one, and she is precise about the extent and nature of one fundamental difference—one that is quite total:

Indigenous Chinese philosophical traditions agree on a fundamentally monistic view of the universe; the cosmic principle or Tao may transcend any individual phenomenon, but it is totally immanent in this world, and there is no suprasensory realm that lies beyond, is superior to, or is different in kind from the level of physical beings. True reality is not supernal but in the here and now, and this is a world, furthermore, in which fundamental correspondences exist between and among cosmic patterns . . . and operations and those of human culture. (*Reading*, 32)

Above all, these correspondences exist because they are at the same "here and now" level. No anguishing division of experience or sentiment requires or refuses healing. From earliest times, discussion of the written "artwork" did not center "on developing a notion of poetry as fictive artifact," but rather on exploring the assumption that poetry invoked "a network of pre-existing correspondences—between poet and world and among clusters of images" (32).

We have seen Owen make altogether similar comments. And to this precise point, he writes of the T'ang poet, Tu Fu, that for the reader his poetry "is not fiction: it is a unique, factual account of an experience in historical time." In a given poem, Tu Fu creates a pattern (*wen*) whose "correlatives echo in the poet's life, in the order of the universe, in the moral order, in the social order, in the order of literature (also *wen*; *Traditional*, 15, 17). The Chinese word usually translated as "image," *xiang*, can, says Yu, be translated as "representation" or, better, "reproduction," but, far from indicating any "fundamental disjunction," it points to "a seamless connection, if not virtual identity, between an object, its perception, and its representation, aided by the semantic polyvalence of the term *xiang*." Further, not only is there no "disjunction between image as object and image as representation," but one cannot separate image and meaning (*Reading*, 39–40), for, as another commentator puts it, image is "saturated with a much greater and many-sided content than a representation abstracted from observation."[4] An image's meaning is grounded in "categorical correspondences" (*lei*) and is indivisible from image simply because it lies in "the fact that objects and situations were believed traditionally to belong to one or more non–mutually exclusive, a priori, and natural classes" (41, 42). "Each thing and event of the world," Owen adds, "is the fragment of a coherent whole and knowledge of the whole unfolds out of the fragment. To see a single leaf is to know autumn; to know autumn is to know its correlatives in the cycle of human life, in the dynastic cycle, in all domains of reference" (*Traditional*, 23).

Concrete polyvalence is essential to an image's meaning(s), whose precise flow and spread depend on their expression in *that* image. Yu explores in detail how these founding views developed from earliest times up to the T'ang dynasty and even as late as the eighteenth century, arguing that however they may have changed, never would anyone "have denied the validity of cosmic correspondences presumed to link all things in a network of associations to be elicited by the poet, however elusively" (*Reading*, 217). Too, although the images eliciting these correspondences were taken ultimately to refer "to the poet's historical world and not some fictional construct," at the same time, they were "felt to belong to a culturally shared lexicon within which correspondences of meaning were pre-established." Indeed, just because of this network of correspondences, the poem was "viewed as a record of the poet's actual experience" (218). Simultaneously, it *is* that experience. No suspension of disbelief is needed, nor any recollection in tranquility. Owen offers a number of carefully delicate readings of poems to show how they "enact" poets' and readers' factual experiences not of "the manifest state of the world's inherent order" but, in the poems' movement, "the process of that order *becoming* manifest" (*Traditional*, 25).[5] One might say, in addition to all the rest, that the poem *presents* rather than *re*presents, produces rather than reproduces. "Words with pattern [*wen*]," wrote the celebrated critic Liu Hsieh—"literature," that is to say, the verbal product of the fictive imagination, "indeed express the mind of the universe" (*Literary Mind*, 10).[6] These polyvalent patterns are why western translators have such difficulty translating classical Chinese poetry and prose, different versions yielding drastically different meanings: western desires for denotational precision and distinctness fail to cope with writings where *all* these meanings are simultaneously present. Western culture is sure that there must be distinct monads of meaning, distinguishable as the true from the false. (None of which is of course to suggest that any culture is without fictions.)

Arguments and comparisons of the sort proposed by Yu, Owen, and Glissant show how the idea that literature or art as defined through differences is itself tied to a particular place and, no doubt, a particular time; that it is neither essential to what societies understand "art" to be nor a *necessary* definition; that it may have served purposes specific to a particular cultural time and place, both within and without. We shall see much more of analogous objections from different cultures. If I have been a bit long, here, on the Chinese case—later chapters expand much more on the Caribbean—the reason is that I wish from time to time to try and detail differences, not expatiate some putative "otherness" to western rectitude. This very multiplicity in difference shows that Jean-Pierre Vernant has always been right to argue apropos of the ancient Greeks that "the notion of figurative representation does not go without saying; neither univocal nor permanent, it constitutes what one can call a historical category. It is a construction worked out, and worked out with difficulty and along very varied paths in different cultures" ("Présentification," 360). He has argued often that while "imitation of appearance" *eventually* became one strand of the fictive imagination; not only did it derive from experiences of "mimesis" as efforts to "figure the invisible" (the divine), but it stayed in many ways subordinate to them. Whatever fourth-century thinkers may have worked out with regard to a representational "mimesis," it was for long just one strand of art, *technē*, among others (see, e.g., "Présentification," "Figuration," and "Naissance").

For setting aside for a moment what one may find in different cultures, I would like to focus on another definition of art and the artist even from that very Greco-Roman antiquity taken to be the source of this western idea, one using *mimesis*, and so *metaphor* as well, in what at least seem radically different ways. This definition may well start with Aristotle himself, of whom Goldstein argues that by poetic *mimesis*, Aristotle meant the actual human *process making* the work through the rational, internal organizing principles enabling it. Pierre Gravel likewise notes that *poiētikē* and *poiēsis* named first of all a "mode of production" assuming a particular "know-how" on the producer's part whose core was *mimesis* (*Accompagnements*, 24, 27). Goldstein also points out that if interpreters had looked beyond the *Poetics*, they would have seen that Aristotle never ascribed any sort of autonomy to the mimetic work of art. The *Politics* concludes with a long discussion of music and theater "as efficient causes in relation to good citizenship," the *Metaphysics* refers "to poems as sources of our knowledge of the gods," the *Ethics* mention them "for the ethical doctrines" they contain, the *Rhetoric* analyzes "the nature of thoughts" they communicate, and so on ("Mimesis," 567–68). Aristotle's concern in the *Poetics* was not to cut poetry from its multifold contexts but simply to analyze what made it *poetry* and not something else. About this Aristotle was clear: *mimesis*. Goldstein shows that several times Aristotle distinguishes mimesis from copying (568–69). Thus the synthesizing making of plots is distinguished from just copying what actually happened (1451b12–19), as is the mimesis that is the poet's art from the objects that may be used for such mimetic ends: an incorrect copy does not matter to the art *qua* art, but an incorrect mimesis most certainly does (1460b15–30). This does not, however, tell us what mimesis *is*, save only in saying that it always involves a *making*, a *bringing of something into existence*—which is the meaning of *technē*, the word rendered as *art* here and in my next paragraph.

Goldstein then turns to the *Physics* and Aristotle's careful comparisons of art and nature as *makers*, art being "like" nature precisely in its
ruled processes of *making* (193a31–b2; 199a10–b30): "if a house," Aristotle
writes in the second case here, "had been a thing made by nature, it would
have been made in the same way as it is now by art; and if things made by
nature were made not only by nature but also by art, they would come to
be in the same way as by nature" (translated by R. P. Hardie and R. K.
Gaye, *Complete Works*, 1:340). The same comparisons are found in the
Metaphysics, where Aristotle talks of art as "the art of making" things which
cannot make themselves and of its doing so just as nature produces *its*
things: "For the seed produces [natural things] as the artist produces the
works of art" (1034a19–b1; translated by W. D. Ross, *Complete Works*,
2:1633). In the *Nicomachean Ethics*, Aristotle exactly remarks that an art

is essentially a reasoned state of capacity to make, and there is neither any art that
is not such a state nor any such state that is not an art, *art* is identical with a state
of capacity to make, involving a true course of reasoning. All art is concerned with
coming into being, i.e. with contriving and considering how something may come
into being which is capable of either being or not being, and whose origin is in the
maker and not in the thing made; for art is concerned neither with things that are,
or come into being, by necessity, nor with things that do so in accordance with nature (since these have their origins in themselves). (1140a6–15; translated by W. D.
Ross, revised by J. O. Urmson, *Complete Works*, 2:1799–1800)

If we tie such remarks to the *Poetics*, treating "the poetic art" (=*poiētikē*),
which like all art is mimesis, producing things *in the same way* that nature
does, then its object is to show the means specific to poetry's mimesis—notably, in the case of tragedy, that of the forging of plots distilling the actuality of human action (Goldstein, "Mimesis," 570–72; cf. Gravel, *Accompagnements*, 23–32).

The important point here is, of course, that this understanding of
mimesis not only does not presuppose division but assumes that ruled
making is *common* to nature and to humans. They are mutually imbricated. If the poetic art has roles to play in every sphere of human activity,
it is because its ruled production is also inherent in them and in nature as
a whole. That is surely why Aristotle began the *Poetics* by saying that humans were by nature the "most mimetic" animal. This potentially different
idea of art and artist, mimesis and metaphor is readily drawn from
Aristotle. Further, he also defined metaphor as an "*epiphora*," a "contribution" or a "crediting" (the word used in classical Greek for paying taxes or

tribute) of "a name belonging to another" to some thing that has its own proper name. This proposes an economy not of substitution, but of accumulation.[7] Its idea of mimesis has to be separated from what Aristotle often says of metaphor as well as face other difficulties (not the least being the standard tradition), but it has a later fulfillment.

I am thinking of Seneca's known but much-scanted adoption of Plato's image of the artist as a bee (never mentioned by any of the important writers on mimesis whom I have named or to whom I have referred—although Seneca was named, fundamentally, in a tradition involving what became a quite other idea of *imitatio*, related to the copying of previous writers).[8] In Plato's *Ion*, the image was so slight as scarcely to tell us very much: "For the poets tell us, I believe, that the songs they bring us are the sweets they cull from honey-dropping founts in certain gardens and glades of the Muses—like the bees, and winging the air as these do."[9] But Seneca took it to show how the artist absorbed elements from many different "flowers" to create a quite different amalgam and compound, perhaps reflecting Aristotle's cumulative *epiphora*. Writing became a weaving of ideas:

We must imitate, as they say, the bees [*Apes, ut aiunt, debemus imitari*], who flit about and cull the flowers most suitable for making honey, then, whatever they have gathered, they arrange and dispose it in their combs. (*Ep*, lxxxiv.3:II.276/7)

"It is not certain," he went on, "whether the juice which they obtain from the flowers forms at once into honey, or whether they change what they have gathered into this flavor through some mixture and property of their breath [*spiritus*]" (278/9).

It is assuredly the case—as endless later writers observed, from Macrobius through Petrarch, to Erasmus, Juan Luis Vives, Pierre de Ronsard, and Nicolas Boileau, that Seneca was writing—as well—about how one might "imitate" those whom one read.[10] There is no doubt that these later writers understood *this* Senecan *imitatio* to mean a quite different idea of copying—following, imitating, emulating—previous writers.[11] In this sense and in that of making a single fine representation from the "best" pieces drawn from several models (real or themselves copies), this understanding of mimesis had always had a place in the most familiar Platonic–Aristotelian tradition. This was exactly how Xenophon had had Socrates describe the painter's and sculptor's reproduction of "things seen" (*Memorabilia*, III.x.1–7) and how Isocrates had talked about students imitating their teacher (McKeon, "Literary Criticism," 168–72). As such, it certainly had to do with *imitatio/mimesis*, but in a disjunctive (and far more simplified) way that had little to do with the complex process of the fictive imagination's working that Seneca sought to describe. I propose that this later normative interpretation of Seneca, diverting his thought into different streams, was itself a form of cultural forgetting under the pressure of these other dominant forms and categories. It effected a cancellation, as it were, of his own more complex notion of *mimesis*.

For, as he began his argument, Seneca chose to quote Vergil describing how Aeneas looked out over Carthage and marveled at its builders, lawmakers, and artists:

> qualis apes aestate nova per florea rura
> exercet sub sole labor, cum gentis adultos
> educunt fetus, aut cum liquentia mella
> stipant et dulci distendunt nectare cellas . . .

> As bees in early summer do their work
> across the flowering land beneath the sun,
> when they lead out their race's grown-up young,
> or pack the flowing honey and push their cells
> to bursting with sweet nectar. . . .
> (*Aeneid*, 1:430–33)

Here, the bees were not conceivably an image of imitating others. They denoted human creativity in all its forms and at its most originary level. Vergil had been at pains to indicate its varieties. His bees were makers, fictive imaginers in the most essential ways: they created new forms and experiences.[12]

In the post-Senecan tradition, this side of the argument was lost or, we shall see in Hobbes, for example, rejected as the sharply threatening "other" of language rightly used. From Macrobius to the later Middle Ages into the European Renaissance and the tradition's modern commentators, even those arguing that Seneca was making a strong case about the transformative power of imitation have asserted that this power related not to creation but to artists' relation to their predecessors. Petrarch is a good instance, who more than once used Seneca's image to laud those who knew how to join different thoughts and styles in a new creation and condemn those who just copied (like Macrobius, he wrote in a long letter on the subject to Tommaso da Messina; *Familiari*, 1:84–95: I.8). He took the Vergil passage just cited to mean only that, ignoring, like everyone else, the context in which Vergil used it (*Familiari*, 1:92). He repeated this view at least twice to Giovanni Boccaccio (*Familiari*, 4:106: XXII.2; 4:206: XXIII.19), as well as to others. No doubt Seneca *was* writing of that kind of imitation. Equally clearly, however, it was just one aspect of a mimetic process whose creative functioning involved broader, subtler, and more complex arguments about the fictive imagination and cultural creation. That imitation of authors and this process of creation are not, of course, mutually exclusive, although they have been made so. Even in his long letter to Tommaso, before narrowing his talk to imitation of authors, Petrarch had seemed less clear: "[Seneca's] loftiest advice about invention is to imitate the bees which through an astonishing process produce wax and honey from the flowers they leave behind" (*Familiari*, 1:85; *Letters on Familiar Matters*, 1:41, for translation).

For Seneca, both the idea of mimesis and the metaphor he was using to express it took on different dimensions from a Platonic–Aristotelian tradition. Aristotle had insisted that similes and metaphors were merely different forms of one another (see, for example, *Rhetoric*, 1405b, 1406b, 1412b–1413a): both worked by a transference of traits in some way shared. In Seneca, here, the status of any "similitude" became unclear: the mind and the art it produced were not *like* a bee and a comb: they *were* them. As John T. Hamilton observes, Greek dispenses with need for transportive metaphorical understanding of their interchange. The language offers a play on the *méli-* of honey and the *mélê-* of verses and music: melipoiesis and melopoiesis. Pindar wove them to an imbricated manifestation of the fictive imagination's very act of creativity, of making (not representation of, comparison with, or substitution for some other actuality; "Soliciting," chapter 3). They were them because both "blended these various flavors into one savor, in such a way that even as it showed whence it came, yet it appear[ed] as other than whence it came" (Seneca, *Ep*, lxxxiv.3.II.278/9). We shall see in a moment that Seneca may have had in mind a specific moment that went back perhaps as far as the "Homeric" poems. These too, like Pindar, may well signal a more complex mimetic and metaphorical process.

Indeed, referring to familiar post-Renaissance European ideas of imitation and metaphor, Phillip Damon began an analysis of the use of "metaphor" in the Homeric poems themselves by remarking on the "tenuousness of the logical connection between the imagery and the point of likeness in many of Homer's long similes"—such that likeness, resemblance (substitution or comparison) were surely not at issue. This might not, he suggested, be a matter of "incoherence" but of a different "understanding of the category of relation" (*Modes*, 265). Homer's use of metaphors that do some fictive work other than comparing or substituting becomes, here, problematic: as in the seagull that changes from mark of effortless flight into battle against "the waves for its dinner" (271; referring to *Odyssey*, 5.51). Damon cites a passage from *Iliad* 12.278, "in which the stones the Greeks and Trojans throw at each other are compared to falling snow":

And as snowflakes fall thick on a winter day when Zeus the counsellor launches a snowstorm, showing those arrows of his to men; and he stills the winds and continues to shed down snowflakes until he has covered the peaks of the high mountains and the steep headlands and the grassy plains and the rich fields tilled by men; and it drifts on the harbors and the beaches of the grey sea, though the wave breaks against it and keeps it off, but all other things it enwraps from above when the storm of Zeus drives it on; so their stones fell thick from both sides. (Damon, *Modes*, 262)

Glossing the Greek, Damon observes how its first lines "suggest suddenness . . . and martial violence," evoke "the rattle and heavy fall of the stones," connote heavy noises and clashings, before they modulate into "a soft sound pattern," imaging "snow drifting over a broad landscape," emphasizing quietness and "inertia." Too, he remarks that commentators have seen the passage as superficial, contradictory, or, worse, incoherent. He himself urges that the "inappropriateness" is a fundamental addition to the "epic style" (262–63, 271).

But there is more here than a difference in "the category of relation." At issue is a sense of how the fictive imagination mingles possibilities of those relations we call meaning and understanding. If you take all the "difficult" similes and metaphors Damon explores in Homer, you find them admirably suited to the description Seneca offered in Epistle 84. They *accumulate* elements into something new. They function not to contract (or contrast) likenesses but to elaborate variations.[13] More, they depict the fictive imagination itself at work, making, as Sidney put it in his *Defence*, "another nature" by means of the poet's particular "skill" to weave it from "that *Idea* or fore-conceit of the work" (Ulreich, "Poets Only Deliver," 137). They manifest an idea of poetic mimesis, John Ulreich argues in reading Sidney, "as an internal reproducing of those vital energies which have engendered nature" (141). These "new" relations are made because the fictive imagination reproduces the organizing of nature itself: not a representing but a like making (Gravel, *Aristote*, 24: 1448b4–11 n. 17; Ricoeur, 61). The argument echoes the "alternative" reading of Aristotle. Where Sidney is

concerned, the view seems clearly to fall on the side of *difference*, of making, exactly, "another nature." Such is not at all evidently the Homeric case,
which seems to come closer to the simultaneity and polyvalence of image
and meaning that Owen and Yu explore in the Chinese tradition.[14]

In Homer, here, and the Seneca I am suggesting as recalling such
processes as these, *mimesis* and metaphor were not characterized by difference and distance, but were actual absorption and mingling of new powers of mind and expression, so that its true "image" would "impress its own
form on all the things which it has drawn from what we may call its exemplar, so that they join in a unity" (Seneca, *Ep*, lxxxiv.280/1): tradition coming from the cave of Montesinos to mix and be made afresh. For Seneca,
mimesis was this composing of many into some new compound, a turning
of potentially "discordant voices," as he said, into a single harmonious soul
(280–83). Furthermore, as he wrote elsewhere, for the human fictive imagination, "*imitatio*" was not a representation or a copy; it was an actual carrying out of the powers of a divine reason of which it was part and which
it embodied. It iterated in little the very process by which divine reason ordered the universe and life as a whole (*Ep*, lxv.3, 12–14: 1.444–46, 450–52).
In this regard, we would do well to recall that the word *spiritus*, translated
before as the "breath" of the bees by means of which they absorb and mingle powers of expression, mind, and concrete world (*Ep*, lxxxiv.278/9), was
the Stoic term for the actually present life force in living creatures, in the
world and throughout the entire universe. So Seneca was not simply writing—as later tradition most thoroughly had it—of imitating other writers.
He was emphasizing the working of the "fictive imagination," humans'
imagining of new orderings, possible worlds. In this regard, the ontological or epistemological status of what was being "imitated" hardly mattered.
What did matter was the imaginative process that made it afresh.

Of course, I am not suggesting that Seneca made this sort of analysis
of the Homeric poems themselves. But in these sorts of comments, he may
well have been remembering what was certainly a far older text than Plato's
Ion, one taken as contemporary with Homer. I mean the *Homeric Hymn to
Hermes*, the end of which has Apollo giving to Hermes the three prophet
bee-sisters of Mount Parnassus:

> From there flying now here, now there,
> they feed on honeycomb and bring each thing to pass.
> And after they eat the yellow honey, they are seized
> with mantic frenzy and are eager to speak the truth.

> But if they are robbed of the sweet food of the gods,
> then they do buzz about in confusion and lie.
>
> (*Homeric Hymns*, 558–63)

I don't think I'm being an antiquarian pedant in recalling these lines (see Nagy, 24; Scheinberg). What Apollo gave Hermes was not his own all-embracing and universal powers of prophecy. He gave local powers, the ability to express truths attached to a particular place, attached concretely to a specific topography and geography. The arguments expressed through the image would always involve a balance between the local, its incorporation into something wider, and its readiness to disincorporate, as it were, into other localities. Art—and more precisely, the written art of which Seneca was speaking in the bee letter—was thus an incorporation, a process of growing a new creation by bringing together what were once parts of different growths. It did so not by depriving that other growth of its necessities but by using exchanges, mutualities that were in fact necessary for those other growths to flourish as well. Of such a process, we have already seen Césaire say

that it is a good thing to place different civilizations in contact with each other; that it is an excellent thing to blend different worlds; that whatever its own particular genius may be, a civilization that withdraws into itself atrophies; that for civilizations, exchange is oxygen. (*Discourse*, 11)

In 1970, Amilcar Cabral, even in the midst of the violent struggle in Portuguese Guinea that would see him assassinated three years later, also remarked that while free peoples had to "return to the upwards paths of their own culture," which "is nourished by the living reality of the [local] environment," "national liberation [being] necessarily an *act of culture*," they also needed to incorporate "positive contributions from the oppressor's culture and other cultures" ("National Liberation," 143).[15] It is surely not chance that Cabral, who understood a people's rebuilding of a "national culture" as a way to its own history, that "inalienable right of every people" (143), also called such culture the "flower" on the "plant" of history (142).

Ngũgĩ is similarly exemplary here. In *Moving the Centre*, his main theme concerns what we might call networks of cultures, exchanging or "interweaving" with one another without passing through what are still thought of as "centers." Each knot of culture is strong in its sense of identity but at the same time depends on all the other knots for survival and its differentiation. He agrees with Césaire that we depend on the surroundings and interminglings of different cultures, of others' homes, for the survival of our own. So very different a writer as T. S. Eliot made the same point (*Notes*, 57, 62).[16] Like these, Seneca's image of the bees is not that of a transfer of one object *from* its "proper" place *to* another, but more like an exchange of vital nourishment, incorporating one thing *into* another while giving something vital back to the whole of which that thing is a part. Here, too, metaphor itself does not mark any sort of separation of vehicles and tenors, for its full meaning as an imbricated process of exchange and mutual growth is only evident if continuous attention is paid to all its sides.[17] It is no surprise that Petrarch did just this—Petrarch who, despite his narrow exegesis of Seneca's bee, saw human life as constant growth and as *always* lived as an exchange of person in a community, not Goethe's Faustian progress, whose singular "divine" worth (says God) is its striving ever "forward" and "upward," "error" and sin notwithstanding (Goethe, *Faust*, 1, prologue 3, ll. 315–17), but a vital process of ongoing adjustment to persons and places and times whose constant movement was defining of what the person was, no less than it was of culture as a whole (Reiss, *Mirages*).

It may not be altogether just to assert that this "mutuality" view of mimesis and metaphor disappeared wholly from western tradition. Not very much later, we find the curious eccentric Robert Burton picking up directly on Seneca in his *Anatomy of Melancholy* (1636):

As a good housewife out of divers fleeces weaves one piece of cloth, a bee gathers wax and honey out of many flowers, and makes a new bundle of all, *Floriferis ut apes in saltibus omnia libant* [as bees in flowery glades sip from all; Lucretius], I have laboriously collected this cento out of divers writers. . . . The matter is theirs most part, and yet mine, *apparet unde sumptum sit* [it is plain whence it is taken] (which Seneca approves), *aliud tamen quam unde sumptum sit apparet* [yet it becomes different from whence it is taken]; which nature doth with the aliment of our bodies, incorporate, digest, assimilate, I do *conquoquere quod hausi* [digest what I have swallowed], dispose of what I take. (*Anatomy*, 24–25)

Burton was writing of mimicry and copying but chose to stress not just that copying authors could be per se creative but that in doing so original matter, its absorption, and whatever was made both from it and from one's own body and mind made something new, yet all somehow coexisting in mutual relation.[18] We have seen Sidney seem to reach for something not dissimilar, if ambiguously so. The English metaphysicals, too, may be thought to have practiced a view at least approaching this (which may

partly explain Eliot's particular affection for them), while Emanuale
Tesauro's *Cannocchiale aristotelico* (1654) could well be interpreted as a dis-
quisition on an analogous idea of both mimesis and metaphor (as, with
others, I once suggested; *Discourse*, 26–27).

It matters, though, that the metaphysical poets were scorned by the
tradition until Eliot rediscovered them in the 1920s and 1930s. It matters
that Burton has always been looked on as eccentric to the tradition. And it
matters that Tesauro's work virtually disappeared from western view until
the 1950s (Benedetto Croce's writings on it from 1899 being an exception).

These are forms of cultural forgetting, cancellations made by dominant forms and categories, akin to those evident in Aristotle's case and
those of which I spoke earlier apropos of Seneca himself. So, this different
view surfaces, *when* it does so at all, as the *other* of right discourse, as one
clearly sees in Hobbes' objection regarding right "Reason, and Science" (his
terms):

> The Light of humane minds is Perspicuous Words, but by exact definitions first
> snuffed, and purged from ambiguity; *Reason* is the *pace*; Encrease of *Science*, the
> *way*; and the Benefit of man-kind, the *end*. And on the contrary, Metaphors, and
> senslesse and ambiguous words, are like *ignes fatui*; and reasoning upon them, is
> wandering amongst innumerable absurdities; and their end, contention, and sedi-
> tion, or contempt. (*Leviathan*, I.5, 36)

Certainly Hobbes had immediate vital reason to fear contention—and that
misuse of words that Thucydides criticized in the history whose translation
was Hobbes' first avowed published work. And if *Leviathan*'s first concern
was to avoid misuse of words, insisting that explicit and clear definitions
would altogether banish metaphor, the later *Behemoth* made such misuse
the very cause of the English civil wars. Indeed, Robert E. Stillman and
Gordon Hull rightly view Hobbes' political philosophy as "haunted" by the
"possibility of impure and 'metaphoric' meanings" (Hull, 174). Social chaos,
epistemological confusion, and verbal misuse were of a kind, thought
Hobbes. Metaphor was the type and often the cause of all. And whatever
the results of this kind of thinking in the realm of philosophy and political
thought may have been, this rejection of metaphor precisely serves to erase
other practices of mimesis and metaphor that do—or could have—come
down from Seneca, and to a much lesser degree from Aristotle.

For if, we have seen, Aristotle's idea of mimesis *may* have approached
this "mutuality" practice, it nonetheless comes up against his explication of

metaphor. Flattened out by Cicero, the Stagirite's definition had been that "a metaphor is the application of a word that belongs to another thing: either from genus to species, species to genus, species to species or by analogy" (1457b6–9). In premising "categorial transgressions" (Ricoeur, 31) as moves of thought forging new analogies and knowledge (32), this coheres with the alternative understanding of mimesis. The idea is akin to Damon's earlier thought about a different "understanding of the category of relation." I proposed, though, that the thought falls short of what was at stake. Indeed, Ricoeur's use of the word "transgressions" underscores the huge distance between this and anything like Yu's "categorical correspondences." Metaphor here (and a fortiori the mimesis of which it is a mainstay) depends, both in Aristotle and these commentators, on categorical differences. Pierre Aubenque adds that if Aristotle urges—in his frequent expression—that "art imitates nature," he also urges that it does so by "completing what [nature] was unable to" (Aristotle, *Physics*, II.8: 199a15–17; Aubenque, *Problème*, 498): Sidney's idea, as well, although again it is not as clear in Aristotle as this would have it. Art fills the gaps in nature's activity, or as Aubenque remarkably puts it, "strains to fill the scission that separates nature from itself, from its proper essence or idea" (*Problème*, 498–99). This is remarkable because it suggests that "art" strives to overcome the division that it has itself created. Here again is Marks' understanding of Coleridge's art as an unpeaceful tension between opposites, Ortega's, Wheelwright's, and Goodman's metaphor as division, tension, and conflict. What is clear is that whatever potential ambiguities Aristotle may have left, the principal western tradition has cut through them with small dissent.

Imitative art, Aubenque proposes—at least for Aristotle—would be a huge creative effort to overcome a division between the human, the material, and the divine (*Problème*, 501). I. A. Richards' "interactions" (*Philosophy*, 107) between words and concepts seem an effort to recapture that kind of creativity. All, however, prescribe a "gap," "*écart*," fissure that mimesis and metaphor act to overcome or fill (Ricoeur, 384, 394–95). Thereby, in a familiar western tradition, metaphor and mimesis would have created the conditions for their own practice: a series of scissions— very foundation in division—that would be the ground of all understanding, knowledge, and being. This may be the readiest way to follow Jacques Derrida's argument that western philosophy itself is but a twist of metaphorical argument into a claim of universal truth, willfully forgetting its origins in a mimesis straining to defeat the abyss between humans and whatever the "world" is ("Mythologie")—curious recall in philosophy's name of Werner's and Ortega's idea of metaphor as rooted in taboo, naming and so erasing what is forbidden, menacing, or unknown.[19] Language, in Hölderlin's thought, may be the "world's flowers," but these "words as flowers" (Ricoeur, 361) still presumed their growing from a deep divided ditch, as Césaire has it (*Tragédie*, 59). These notions of mimesis and metaphor as grounded, still and always, in division remain quite different from the lost—or discarded—Senecan tradition.[20]

For metaphor, in Seneca's bees, becomes not a movement from/to, involving properness and, if we believe many, property, but exchanges of/in, involving Wilson Harris' "complex mutuality of cultures," creating a new *mestizaje* of relations between different cultural homes, overcoming what he calls the egoistic evils "in which cultures are enmeshed in codes to invert or overturn each other" (*Womb*, 13, 18). Okot p'Bitek's simple image from cooking of the absorbent gourd versus the excluding glass catches the same idea of absorbing and giving back, as well as the difference between the experience of being pervious to the world and that of being impermeable to and divided from it: "the half-gourd/And the earthen dishes" breathe to the earth below them and the food on them, quite differently from "The white man's [porcelain] plates/[that] Look beautiful" but make warm food wet and cold:

> On my return home
> Give me water
> In a large half-gourd
> Water from the glass
> Is no use.
> It reaches nowhere.
>   (*Song of Lawina*, 61).

For it is evident that not all cultures understand art works in a post-Renaissance and Enlightenment western sense, or that artifacts and activities that give what westerners may understand as aesthetic pleasure (perhaps with other effects) are "defined" (itself a potentially problematic word) in terms of what they call mimesis or representation. It is not clear that *any* others do or have done. Many issues require teasing out here. But we might also wish to come back for a moment to the broader issue, not so much of *mimesis* as of the very idea of art, of bodying forth the imaginary, of what I now prefer to call the "fictive imagination." For as Aristotle put it in a passage we saw before but that is worth quoting again:

All art [*technē*] is concerned with coming into being, i.e. with contriving and considering how something may come into being which is capable of either being or not being, and whose origin is in the maker and not in the thing made; for art is concerned neither with things that are, or come into being, by necessity, nor with things that do so in accordance with nature (since these have their origin in themselves). Making and acting being different, art must be a matter of making, not of acting. (*Nicomachean Ethics*, 1140a10–15)

Art made possible worlds interacting with a "real" world whose idea, perception, and experience depended on those possible worlds. They obeyed a rationality wider than any local or singular reason, a rationality on which the maker of the *technē* drew. The later Greek writer, Philostratus, had much to say on this point in his biography of Apollonius.

In the course of their travels, Apollonius and his companion, Damis, were moved by their admiration of an especially striking mosaic to discuss the nature of painting (the words used are *gramma*, *graphein*, and their cognates) and mimesis. Damis' (or Philostratus') view is extremely interesting because he argues that mimesis as simile or direct imitation means little. It depends, he says, on the fact not that humans somehow reproduce chance-occurring and meaningless natural phenomena (his terms), but that "we who by nature are prone to imitation rearrange and create them in these regular figures" that are designs and pictures made up of lines, colors, light, and shade distributed according to certain rules (174/5). Humans' "mimetic faculty" (176/7) is a mental capacity to be kept separate from, for example, painting (τὴν γραφικὴν) as an art (*technē*; 176/7) and is enjoyed by all humans: "those who look at works of painting and drawing require a mimetic faculty; for no one could appreciate or admire a picture of a horse or of a bull, unless he had formed an idea of the creature represented" (179). This doubtless referred back to Platonic ideas present in the human mind through memory as much as to Aristotle's definitions of the mimetic faculty and his thought of the bond between human and natural mimetic making. At the same time it surely recalled Seneca's view of human creative reason's iteration of the divine.

Philostratus' idea corresponds not simply to our artistlike image of such creatures in the natural world—a matter of *technē*—but, more, to mental understanding of the rule-defined forms which we accept as representing them. Indeed, one needs knowledge quite different from a mere sense of the real, as Apollonius continued immediately: "Nor again could one admire a picture of Ajax, by the painter Timomachus, which represents him in a state of madness, unless one had conceived in one's mind's eye first an idea or notion of Ajax, and had entertained the probability that after killing the flocks in Troy he would sit down exhausted and even meditate suicide" (179: II.xxii–1.172–9 for the whole discussion). All this assumes that mimesis carried no sense of some sort of direct representation of otherness or difference, held here to be a meaningless idea.[21] Rather was it a socially—or communally—driven "agreement" as to what kind of ruled forms and feelings, lines and colors, figures and contrasts were to be identified as meaningful images of the real. But this *real* itself appeared as just the most commonly accepted of a culture's possible worlds or, rather, as what corresponded to the totality of habits of knowing, doing, and feeling embodied in what Kendall Walton calls "the whole body of a culture's discourse" (*Mimesis*, 102). Here, too, there is no simple "representation," but a complex intermingling of pollens, one forged for, even by, a specific community in a specific place.

I am struck here by what seems to me an extraordinary conjunction between the terms of this sort of argument and one coming from the American cultures of which I have already made much. Although this may be, in some sense at least, happenstance, it clearly is not in the wider scheme I am trying to follow, since arguments are made against one another. Nor should it surprise one that contestatory modes occasionally meet (although here "contestatory" may be the wrong word—since, historically, the Senecan trajectory just traced seems the older tradition). But startling is the verbal similarity of argument. I refer to Paz's Hanuman, who stands as a weaver of significations within and across cultures, maker of mutualities, opposer of impositions and who, precisely, forges new actualities out of cultures' possibilities. Can it then be mere accident that almost as if he had just surfaced from Philostratus, Paz offers Hanuman as

a *gramma* of language, of its dynamism and its endless production of phonetic and semantic creations[?], an ideogram of the poet, the master/servant of universal metamorphosis: an imitative simian, an artist of repetitions, he is the Aristotelian animal that copies from nature but at the same time he is the semantic seed, the bomb-seed that is buried in the verbal subsoil and that will never turn into the plant that its sower anticipates, but into another, one forever different. (*Monkey Grammarian*, 131)

Shades too, here, of Walcott's mimetic monkey, creator of new—or rather, of first—stories.

Analogous ideas to those of the Senecan trail just followed are thus to be found in African and Caribbean cultures, as well as in Asian ones and others. Reading the Syrian poet Adonis (Ali Ahmed Said), for instance, one may well find striking such sentences as the following:

Metaphor in Arabic is more than an expressional device; it is in the structure of the language itself, an indication of a spiritual need to transcend reality, that is the immediate and the given. . . . [M]etaphor releases reality from its familiar context, while releasing the words used to discuss it from theirs, changing the meaning of both words and subject matter, and in the process constructing new relationships between one word and another, and between the word and reality . . . , the relationships which it establishes between words and reality are potential relationships; many meanings are possible within them, and this produces divergences in understanding, leading to divergences of opinion and evaluation. Metaphor does not allow a final and definitive answer, because it is itself a battleground of semantic contradictions. It remains a begetter of questions. (*Introduction*, 70–71)

Arabic, Adonis adds, "is a language which arouses a desire to search, to know the unknown and to attain perfection . . . : there is a dimension of infinity to its powers of expression, which corresponds to the non-finite aspects of knowledge" (72).

He agrees with the celebrated eleventh-century critic 'Abd al-Qāhir al-Jurjānī (d. 471 A.H./A.D. 1078) that this central metaphorical element is the constant renewal of poetic speech: "It gives you an abundance of meanings in the simplest of words"; "it shows you 'subtle meanings—secrets of the mind—as if they had been made flesh,' and refines 'physical characteristics until they become spiritual and can only be grasped by intuition' ." It brings us into "a world of 'strangeness' . . . where poetic images cannot be grasped quickly by the mind and do not take shape in the imagination at a mere glance" (Adonis, *Introduction*, 46–47; cf. Abu Deeb, 61, 64–65). They require a sort of (neo-Platonic?) remaking of the mind's powers. The language-bound work of art, poetry, wrote al-Jurjānī, has an "alchemical" power that creates "inventions of transcendental value," and as it does so, it also obliges the listener to echo the poet's new creation of meanings (Ajami, 55, 65; cf. Abu Deeb, 67–68). Dallal remarks that such a notion of language creation has nothing conceivable to do with any imitational notion of mimesis, depending entirely on an interplay of *meanings* that establish new—in al-Jurjānī's term—transcendental meanings, but which are at the same time "unstable," always suggesting motion, as Adonis implies, toward something else, but always also retaining their earlier meanings.[22]

It is the case that many have interpreted al-Jurjānī in much more—or entirely—in terms of the "Renaissance Aristotle" (see, for example, Heinrichs, *Hand*). Indeed, Kamal Abu Deeb quotes one critic who deems his works to be but "commentaries on Aristotle's views" (75). In this connection, it is worth noting that before the great eleventh-century critic forged a consensus, there had long been disputes (that had nothing to do with Aristotle) over what was called "natural" and "artificial" poetry, the one taken to stay close to common understanding, the other to rely on forging elaborate metaphorical structures. Critics fought over which was the best kind of poetry. One is tempted to see in this opposition something like that between Hobbes and the metaphysicals indicated before, although in this case the outcome would have been different. Al-Jurjānī "depolarized" this debate and forged a view of language creation that combined "fine craftsmanship" with "natural aptitude" (Ajami, 51). He did so by emphasizing the creative process itself, stressing how the poet *made* meanings: "speech consists of concepts, or meanings which are created by the composer in his psyche [*anima*? soul?—*al-nafs*], and which he considers in his mind, and whispers to his heart" (quoted in Abu Deeb, 59 n. 1). It may be, then, that in forging this consensus, al-Jurjānī may well be considered to have simply absorbed—sublated, even—Aristotelian ideas of transference into a different synthesis. He would thus have exemplified a view Adonis repeats with so many others: "no culture exists in isolation from other cultures—they give and take from each other." And "the first condition for this process of interaction is that it should be characterized by creativity and particularity at the same time" (Adonis, 89; cf. 90–91).

Like Seneca's (or Hermes') bees, they exchange local particularities, making them into different wholes, even while retaining the particulars. I do not suggest that the Arab tradition is the *same* as this lost Senecan one, any more than I did the Chinese. On the contrary, if I have tried to be a bit detailed about them, that is precisely to indicate as well their diversities, how they *cannot* and *must* not be garbled into one Other of a western Same. For the diverse understandings of verbal fictive imagining that we have so far glimpsed make for very different ideas of what "art" and its various forms—"literature," for example—are and do. One observes, too, for instance, the Gikũyũ concept and practice of *kĩrĩra*, word-focused "imaginative" work as totalizing cultural expression. Of this, Ngũgĩ writes that it expresses an "orature" as a "total aesthetic system" integrated in the whole world and social system that is that of Agĩkũyũ society, to which it corresponds and which it supports as that world system supports it. *Kĩrĩra* denotes everything involving language "that enhances human spiritual, moral, and aesthetic strivings" (Ngũgĩ, *Penpoints*, 119).[23] Except that it *always* involves language, it seems close to some understandings of what in the West is called "art." It is no less hard to specify its "functions." Here, of course, lies one of the outsider's particular problems. Properly to understand *kĩrĩra*, one needs to have a deep sense of the kind of social organization producing it and with which it necessarily engages. One needs to know something of political practice, ethical demand, and religious belief in which it is also imbricated. Even then it will always remain an outsider's understanding, for lacking in such knowledge will be the simple fact of having been born and reared to it. This is not to say that one cannot hear and understand voices of different cultures, but it does mean that one always does so with a great tentativeness, with Brathwaite's "tact and selfless grace." One thing that *is* clear about *kĩrĩra* is that it names a process to which notions of division and conflict are foreign, both within and without the culture.

Even to say this needs care, however, for simply opposing ideas of a mimetic western art (taking "mimetic," here, as *repraesentatio*) to embedded African, Caribbean, or Asian ones all too readily repeats familiar oppositional views: indeed, critics' comments on fictive imaginings in these very different cultures too often look curiously alike—several versions of the West's supposed "other" return to some nostalgic negritude. The effort to avoid cultural hegemony and its effects then merely repeats it in another form, reducing all differences to a single mark of *otherness*: Jameson's ever-persistent "West and its Others" that we saw before (Chapter 2). Still, at least where African cultures are concerned, such broad embedding of the fictive imagination in the totality of culture does seem to correspond to widespread and common experience. In Chapter 1, we saw Marshall speak of it when writing of how she learned of language from her mother and friends in her childhood kitchen: "They made of it an art form that—in keeping with the African tradition in which art and life are one—was an integral part of their lives" (*Merle*, 6). This is, of course, set against that western dissociated and autonomized artistic tradition of which Anzaldúa and Nooteboom, among others, were taken as representative commentators. Like Fanon, too, Cabral argued that a people's culture was the totality of their efforts in thought to understand and practice their particularity, and what one might think of as the aesthetic realm was merely one cast upon that wholeness (e.g., "National Liberation," 150). Ngũgĩ has consistently made the same point (notably in *Decolonising* and *Moving*).

Achebe again takes the Igbo *mbari* tradition to show something of the difference between a western divisive idea of the aesthetic realm and an altogether more inclusive one. "*Mbari* is an artistic 'spectacular' demanded of the community by one or other of its primary divinities, usually the Earth goddess." To this end, the community selects a small group who, while they erect "a befitting 'home of images' filled to overflowing with sculptures and paintings," are "secluded for months or even years" (*Hopes*, 48; cf. *Conversations*, 165–66). As we saw in Chapter 1, these people take no personal credit of any sort for the sculptures and paintings they make, being just "vessels" of the gods and the community. They are a part of what Achebe elsewhere calls the "dynamic world of movement and of flux" which characterizes the Igbo sense of their place and, above all, of its communal and public nature (*Hopes*, 62, 64). Achebe opposes this to western notions of individualism and separation from others, most especially as they are taken to define "the artist" (*Hopes*, 49), which he sees as essentially dangerous, in that the very idea is a threat to community. Like others, we have seen and shall see more, he once again ascribes the division to poor old Descartes. Quoting the protagonist of Kane's *L'aventure ambiguë*, he agrees:

It has seemed to me that this history has suffered an accident which has turned it aside and, finally, removed it from its plan [*projet*]. Do you understand me? At bottom, Socrates' plan does not seem to me different from that of Saint Augustine, though there was Christ between them. The plan is the same, as far as Pascal. It is still the plan of all non-occidental thought. . . . But don't you feel how the philosophical plan is already no longer quite the same in Pascal and in Descartes? Not that they were preoccupied with different problems, but that they were preoccupied with them differently. It is not the mystery which has changed, but the questions which are asked of it, and the revelations which are expected from it. Descartes is more parsimonious in his quest; if, thanks to this contraction and also his method, he gets more replies, what he brings also matters less to us, and is of little help to us. (*Aventure*, 126; *Adventure*, 113–14; Achebe, *Hopes*, 50)[24]

Achebe gives Augustine's "African communalism" as "more congenial than western individualism," expressed in the effort to "acquire mastery over nature" and in the "triumphant, breathtaking egocentrism" of the "*Cogito ergo sum*," an exclamation repeating Kwame Nkrumah's twenty-years-earlier analysis of Descartes' "specious solipsism" (Achebe, *Hopes*, 51; Nkrumah, *Consciencism*, 16–18). Achebe, like others, quite ignores such complexities as Descartes' debt to Augustine, insisting on an abyss between them. For Achebe, Kane's Samba Diallo returns home to Africa from his European education quite unable to participate any longer in any communal sense of being: "Poor fellow; the West has got him!" (*Hopes*, 52). This particular issue of selfhood will come back principally in my next two chapters; my point here is more precisely concerned with the relation between the fictive imagination and the totality of culture, with different understandings of "mimesis," with the disparity between dissociation and association, "difference" and "correspondence" (although these various instruments are of course all tightly conjoined). A basic heterogeneity lies between a culture of individualized "collecting," as it were, and a tradition, as was said in Chapter 1, whose past, present, and future remain vital within it because it shares a material and spiritual culture peopled not just by its creators, but also by its users. Those characterizing the art of nonwestern cultures typically assert how they keep this embedding, avoiding disunion. We saw Baldwin (and others) refer such a thought to a fundamentally different idea and practice of art, one that was communal, dependent "on the actual presence of other human beings" and embedded in a "past, which had been lived where art was naturally and spontaneously social, where artistic creation did not presuppose divorce" (*Nobody*, 26). Here, Seneca and Philostratus seem not to have expressed fundamentally different views. But to associate all these is to risk mixing them all into a single stew of representational culture's "Other." Perhaps they can each only truly be told from within.

Here, I have suggested, Baldwin's last sentence is especially revealing. Confronting the problem of giving a detailed idea of what might be specific to an African "aesthetic" arena, he just asserts that they can be characterized as the opposite of a western "cartesian" art. How habitual this "solution" is can be seen in the endless attempts to understand the place of the fictive imagination and cultural creation in cultures different from either European or African ones. The danger is that of defining one culture by its differences from another: from one in particular. That is why it would be useful first to focus on specific localities, in themselves, not as differences. And that is why I quoted Owen and Yu at some length in an effort to capture at least *some* idea of what is particular *within* Chinese poetry, what it is, to use a phrase from before, in its own home, beyond some simplistic idea of its just being an other to the West. That is also why I referred to debates among Arab writers about verbal creation in Arab culture and why I mentioned the experiences called *mbari* and *kīrīra*. But it is not easy to get at such particulars. Micere Githae Mugo, from the same Gikūyū culture as Ngũgĩ, has tried to express *kīrīra*'s basic aesthetic and ethical values as

> rhythm, harmony, non-antagonistic antithesis in rhetoric, balance, order, contact, dialogue, wit, roundedness or circularness or curvedness (as opposed to linear progression), energy, cohesiveness, communication, demonstrativeness, performance, articulateness, motion, openness, colour, debate, feeling, participation, involvement and many others. (*African Orature*, 26)

The difficulty of capturing differences in themselves is apparent here, in these nouns that sound much like those through which Asante defines Afrocentricity.

This, no doubt, marks one of those instances where learning how to listen and what to listen for is of principal importance, since to echo Asante is clearly *not* what Mugo intends. The hard issue is to know just what she is translating. For I do not think it impossible to hold onto differences, even though, as Haun Saussy observes, to do so surely does involve retranslation from both (or more) cultural homes involved (*Problem*, 14–17). One thinks, for example—to come back to another place—of the many ways in which Caribbean artists join certain forms, rhythms, and what western critics would call "images" into writing that itself becomes what Brathwaite calls "nation language," capturing the very being of cultures and societies making themselves—a demotic, Philip adds, we shall see especially in Chapter 8, that alone utters the "i-mages" expressive of such deep being. These i-mages can have many sources. Even Venice—again—may become such a one, now turned "against" its originating culture, reused, recombined.

Just so, writing of "Salt," originally the prologue to *X/Self* and so of that whole sequence of poems and indeed of its trilogy, Brathwaite describes how he tries to make the haunting presence of Venice a fused experience of the ambiguous and complex material, cultural, and sociopolitical effects of empire, from Rome to Tennyson, all the terms and contexts in which it is, by which it is surrounded: memories of Othello the Moor and Galileo the Italian, of a Mediterranean from Jewish Herod to Greek Herodotus, African Severus to Cypriot Makarios, from the multimillennial depot of Alexandria to a Bosporus storied with Crimea and English light brigades, from a Dardanelles of World War I disaster to biblical memories of Sodom, tied to

England and Gaul, America and India, myths of all places, Carthage and Christ. Venice's imperial "vultures . . . wheel high over the desert, over tripoli and tunis over/the head waters of the nile over/chad over timbuctu over lagos, over ile ife over ibadan and the/fat markets of abomey" (*X/Self,* 8–9). Venice becomes a kind of "*disclosure*" of meanings, it "acquires unto itself a whole burden of meaning and connectivity and as you probe into the experience which is the poem; as you become increasingly aware of its world, so do the word/name: images: begin to disclose the history of them/selves," being experience of actual, real connections—between Americas, Caribbean, East and West Africa, Europe—"so that the connections are there, and not only in metaphor, the metaphors, in fact, seek out the natural and ancient connections within the time-continuum" ("Metaphors," 465–67). Not just metaphors at all, they disclose or *become* experience.

Brathwaite shows how what began as *X/Self*'s next poem, "Mont Blanc"—now set later in the sequence—with first lines repeating those of "Salt" ("Rome burns/and our slavery begins"), similarly makes a "geological monument" demarcating "equilibrium and disequilibrium," placing against Kilimanjaro a universalist claim to empire, experienced not just as geopolitical violence against different cultures but as production of imbalance in actual geographical forces and relations ("Metaphors," 467–72). This is far from Percy Bysshe Shelley's sense of the mountain as a direct metaphor for such universalism. *His* "Mont Blanc" stood foursquare to mark Reason's firm grasp of its world. It epitomized how "The everlasting universe of things/Flows through the mind, and rolls its rapid waves" (ll. 1–2). "[P]iercing the infinite sky . . . ,—still, snowy, and serene" (60–61), this Mont Blanc typified the self-image of European Reason as deep yet clear, gentle yet not dull, fair yet decisive, wide-knowing yet forceful: "Mont Blanc yet gleams on high:—the power is there,/The still and solemn power of many sights,/And many sounds, and much of life and death" (127–29). Brathwaite puts *this* european Mont Blanc, "their holy mountain," into a "cultural equilibrium," making it "flow down rhine down rhone down po down dan down/tiber," across Asia and Africa, making the reader *feel* each mountain, Mont Blanc and Kilimanjaro, "affect" each other "as in a psychic mood or mirror" and affect, too, the world about them ("Metaphors," 467–69; *X/Self,* 31). The movement of the poem's language is to make the reader not *see* as metaphor but understand as experience.

The bees do indeed express mutualities, make new stories:

I must be given words so that the bees
in my blood's buzzing brain of memory

will make flowers, will make flocks of birds,
will make sky, will make heaven,
the heaven open to the thunder-stone and the volcano and the un-
    folding land.

(Brathwaite, "Negus," *Islands, Arrivants*, 224)

For many Caribbean artists, webs of mangrove, motions of tides, tactile savors of endlessly different flowers seem to take on a force beyond image, uttering precise relations between land and people, people and their own histories very much in the way all this tries to describe. Indeed, in much Caribbean writing, flowers themselves become a way to write back, turning a European tradition against another: "When I first got to England in 1951," writes Stuart Hall,

I looked out and there were Wordsworth's daffodils. Of course, what else would you expect to find? That's what I knew about. That is what trees and flowers meant. I didn't know the names of the flowers I'd just left behind in Jamaica. ("Local," 24)

Hall was contrasting his moment of arrival with Britain's later condition as an ever more "decentered" ex-colonial power, whose daffodils would be absorbed into an endlessly richer, more variegated flora. Many anglophone Caribbean (and African) writers, Ngũgĩ reminds us apropos of Brathwaite (*Writers*, 132), have taken Wordsworth's daffodils as a signal of colonization—not least perhaps because they were actually imported into a foreign geography. For Kincaid's Lucy, they become the stuff of a recurrent nightmare of "being chased down a narrow cobbled street by bunches and bunches of those same daffodils that I had vowed to forget," finally burying her "deep underneath them . . . never [to be] seen again" (*Lucy*, 18). Surely, Philip asks sarcastically, "that same child whose childhood boundaries were constant sunshine, black skins and mangoes could understand about Wordsworth's field of daffodils. Why the hell didn't she?" They were, she agrees, forced on the minds of these British Empire subjects, whose "entire livelihood and future . . . often depended on understanding daffodils, nightingales, fogs and winter, while living with constant sunshine, hummingbirds and poinsettias" (*Frontiers*, 100, 164). One interest is how so many contemporary Caribbean writers have retaken their flowers to signal their own culture in their own geography, turning Seneca back against the universalizing side of his tradition. Chapters 9 and 11 explore this, and we shall see how these flowers become images in something like the Chinese sense cited earlier, manifesting correspondences of expression, sensuous grasp of place, communal history, and more, that in some sense go beyond "meaning" to become a performance of cultural creation set concretely in a particular home.

Heberto Padilla envisions Walter Raleigh in his prison reflecting on the narrowness of his "blood-sweating tower" contrasted with "el vuelo azul sin viento/y la humedad sin lluvia" ("the blue windless flight/and the rainless damp") of the wild flowing Orinoco, flooding the trees, covered everywhere with birds, the "beautiful" and "wondrous" open places of the tropical Caribbean lands. We might, he writes, see this opposition or the granite building stones of the Tower as metaphors of something, but that is simply a way of comfortingly ordering our world:

> *La gente se oculta o alivia con metáforas.*
> *Para mí son simplemente piedras bajo la lluvia.*
> *Sólo las cosas brillan por sí mismas,*
> *los hombres necesitan su bufón y su espejo.*

> People take refuge in, comfort themselves with metaphors.
> For me, they are simply stones under the rain.
> Things shine in themselves alone.
> It is men who need their jester and their mirror.
> ("Los últimos recuerdos de Sir Walter Raleigh en la
> Torre de Londres," *Legacies*, 76/7; his italics)

For Brathwaite, too, in the idea of a Barbados whose life water wells up not from rivers but from within the limestone of its coral base, there is an other than metaphorical relation with the experience of discovering remnants of hidden African cultures, memories, and experiences deep in everyday actions and knowings (e.g., *Barabajan Poems, passim*). The magic force of flowers, of colors, rhythms, webs, and the rest are not metaphors "plagiadas," copied, from those who would "let" them be reused (Padilla, "Nota," *Legacies*, 124/5) but a setting of "simple stones under the rain." They are also ways "to educate, or rather to de-educate ourselves into the meaning of these names/words," ways to "acculturate," "creolize," forge "the fusion and erosion of cultures" (Brathwaite, "Metaphors," 464–65). This has to refer to explorations elsewhere (e.g., Brathwaite, *Love Axe/l*) and later (Chapters 8 to 11), but may well be what Caribbean writers are putting to work. For, as Césaire again puts it, using the same "imagery," the need for a locally founded "State," one with its own history and culture, is ineluctable, "grâce à quoi ce peuple de transplantés s'enracine, boutonne, s'épanouisse, lançant à la face du monde les parfums, les fruits de la floraison [thanks to which this people of transplants may root itself, bud, blossom forth, casting in the world's face the perfumes, the fruits of its flowering]" (*Tragédie*, 23). The flowers of culture are ultimately people themselves, poet makers of their own culture. They are Cabral's flower on the plant of history ("National Liberation," 142).

None of this is to say, of course, that these many traditions do not know metaphor—as Paula Gunn Allen has of American Indian ones. Rather, is it to say that what the West has named "metaphor" does not *define* a "mimetic" functioning of the fictive imagination, but is merely one among its attributes. It is to say that the kind of transference between differences and divisions presupposed in metaphor and in almost every familiar western notion of mimesis is not central to these traditions but at most just one possible aspect of them. As V. K. Chari writes of Sanskrit traditions, for example, however wide the currency of the—chiefly theatrical—term *anukarana*, translated as "mimetic reproduction," "it can safely be concluded that mimesis was not a seminal principal" of the "literary work," never as important as "symbolic representations of certain concepts," for instance, or as central as presentation of "emotive meaning" as universalized emotion (*Sanskrit*, 33–34, 39). Further, in many cultural cases, any such mimetic operation appears to go against the very grain of what fictive imagination and cultural creation are understood to do and to be.

For the moment, these matters and more must needs remain questions, seekings whose difficulty, incompletion, and awkwardness are manifest. But beyond mere utility, it is essential to explore these differences of culture and tradition, both in themselves and as they mingle with processes from different cultures, as incorporated, for example, into contemporary writing in English and other languages, coming from the old centers of "literature" and from the Caribbean, Africa, and almost everywhere else, where expressions of the fictive imagination historically had very different shapes. These offset views bruited by such as Huntington or Bellow focused on and buried in their nostalgia for a particular conquering European tradition and overcome the impoverishment they presuppose (even in that tradition's own terms), as Césaire long ago argued in his *Discourse on Colonialism*. Allied with aesthetic and political thinking voiced by such as

Adonis, Brathwaite, Césaire, Cabral, Harris, Mugo, Ngũgĩ, and others, these make for a necessary new idea and practice not so much of "literature" as of what I am naming by the broader term of the "fictive imagination" (not "fictional," of course, but *making*).

The last chapters of this book make an effort to work toward an understanding of some such new idea and practice in one place, and especially as they take over and use for their own purposes "instruments" that once "belonged" to an earlier imposition. But before we can get to that, we need to explore more closely some of the more powerful of the instruments whose terms and elements have already repeatedly appeared. Among these, prominent are those having to do with the very idea of identity, more especially of *personal* identity, and those involving history (or, even, History). Most immediately, I will be interested in a union between changing experiences of identity and history, recorded most notably by, but not the responsibility of, Descartes: from "history" as somehow possessed *in* and possessive *of* one's present being in the world to History as a "plan" that one can, as it were, view from afar; from personal identity as bound in that "possession" to personal identity as distanced actor (the terms are awkward and only partly accurate). I shall also, of course, be interested in what has been made of these.

5

Denying Body, Making Self?
Histories and Identities

In her 1959 novel, *Brown Girl, Brownstones*, the Barbadian/American novelist Paule Marshall described her autobiographical protagonist, Selina Boyce, present at a conversation between her mother and friends in their kitchen. In its course, she comes to understand language as expressing the basic life of her culture, just as it does for all those others we have been exploring: "The words were living things to her. She sensed them bestriding the air and charging the room with strong colors" (*Brown Girl*, 71). Twenty-four years later, in an essay first published in the *New York Review of Books* in January 1983 touching her apprenticeship as a writer, Marshall again described such long afternoon conversations through which her mother and friends relaxed in the family kitchen. Marshall recalled their language as a cultural "homeland" in which they saw things made of opposites, yet not torn; rather, things were completed and made whole by them, joining seeming "contradictions [to] make up the whole": "Theirs was not a Manichean brand of dualism that sees matter, flesh, the body, as inherently evil, because they constantly addressed each other as 'soully-gal'—soul: spirit; gal: the body, flesh, the visible self. And it was clear from their tone that they gave one as much weight and importance as the other. They had never heard of the mind/body split" ("From the Poets in the Kitchen," *Merle*, 7, 9). Language would give their home a fullness quite different from the dissonant autonomies of western practice. But the closing claim is not self-evident. Whether or not the women had *heard* of the mind/body split depends on the meaning given the verb "hear." The "cartesian" division was surely embedded in their language, however much the phrase "soully-gal" might recombine its parts.

It was embedded in their language willy-nilly and in just the same way as the many other contraries and binarisms we have seen. We cannot easily avoid them, although we may sap them with vigilance and hope to weave them into different figures. So, reading the fictional case just cited, we should avoid the simplistic temptation to set a "woman's" space of the kitchen against a different "man's" space, nourishment against reason, wholeness against fragmentation. In this novel, relations are more complex. It is, for example, Selina's father Boyce, a dreamer indifferent to material goods, who is most deeply attached to his Barbadian home—and who will die when deprived of it. It is her mother Silla who bears the "realist" burden of survival in the western city. These only begin the complications. But I am reminded of such reductive interpretations by de Certeau's use of some of Saint-John Perse's poetry to set the inaccessible "savage in the kitchen" against his western "master" in the parlor, Friday against Crusoe, as signals of the oppressions and exclusions of western discourse (*Heterologies*, 36, 46). In justice to de Certeau, he uses the passage in passing, as a brief invocation to the muse of his chosen subject: the savage in the kitchen as a mark of western discourse's otherings, exclusions, and inaccessibilities. But in these poems, both Crusoe and Friday are sufferers, equally deprived of their island home, without its sun, its clear light, its greens and reds and yellows and blues, its crickets and birdsong, salt and spice, equally exiled from its geography and from its local (hi)stories. Crusoe may be in the parlor, but his armchair is as greasy as the taste of European sauces on his gums, hardly better off than Friday in the oily kitchen smelly with fish, where his laughter can be condemned as vicious— much as Montaigne's Indians found themselves and their vital culture dismissed because "they did not wear britches" (*Oeuvres complètes*, I.31: 213).

Since Crusoe and his poet both inhabit—by race, by class, and by gender—the hegemonic discourse, they certainly occupy the parlor and can say but little about Friday, save briefly that he shares Crusoe's loss of home, his dismay of Europe, and Europe's exclusion of him. Yet the opposition of Europe's kitchen and parlor, one entirely *inside* its discourse, only emphasizes the *different* cultural reality that all three share, somehow excluded because they know better a discourse of mutuality (Saint-John Perse, "Images à Crusoé," *Éloges, Collected Poems*, 58–69). This of course simplifies again. That is the point. These easy opposites are themselves—we have amply seen—a product of a discourse dependent on binary "otherings," claiming autonomous spaces and distinct arenas of order where *tertium non datur*. They were not at all so readily present, I propose in this chapter, in their supposedly principal source. To read Descartes as if they were, as if he were, to use John Sutton's phrase, "the demonic source of modern alienation" (*Philosophy*, 24), is to impose later claim on his thinking—again, for purposes having to do with particular argument and interest. Opening up the complications of that thinking and so the torsions of its putative avatars, perhaps we help defeat the latter's simplifications and purposes and start enabling the former's figures to be rewoven.

Besides Marshall, we have seen Achebe and Soyinka, Nkrumah, Kane and Senghor, Césaire and Anzaldúa take Descartes' name and reason as auguries of western individualism versus African, Caribbean, or Indian American/Chicano communalism, marker—if not maker—of a long set of divisions. Philip too "take[s] liberties with Descartes' maxim," putting "We bleed, therefore we are" against the "white male"'s idea that "thinking proves our existence" in the real world. The maxim works, she says, to hide power realities (*Frontiers*, 66–67). So ubiquitous is the usage that it is expedient, even essential, to scrutinize Descartes to get at what I style the cultural instrument/*ratio* of individualist identity. This *ratio* is *essentially* tied to the mind/body split, the second as property and tool of the first, the subject agent "inhabiting" it. (The property is another's—or others'—body if the agent gets power over it or them.) For Descartes' reason, misapprehendedly central to western claim, has become a chief stalking horse for cultures oppressed by the West. My exploration is dual. This chapter explores the usage and Descartes, who tied the matter complexly to an argument about history and historical understanding, the role of memory and the place of forgetting—thus letting us tie "selfness" to concepts of history that we have begun to see. So the *ratio*/instrument of personal identity is far less clear-cut than claim holds. At least in Descartes it leaves room for correspondences as well as differences. We shall see Kane and Nkrumah agree. The next chapter explores aspects of the "other end" of this subjective individualism, marked (here) by Sigmund Freud. There we shall see more of the normative view of the subjective individual. Here I try and introduce ambiguities of Harris' mutualities into Crusoe's parlor.

In light of preceding chapters, it is, though, inevitable to ask whether the so-called mind/body split came from Descartes and early European debates, linguistically colonizing all who came into its sphere—Nigerians,

Senegalese, Barbadians, Brooklynites. Whether it came from a Christian heritage, with its haggling over bodily mortality and immortality of soul. Or indeed, whether it came from an even older Greek tradition, dating at least from Plato, which saw the body as container (or "prison") of the soul, establishing, as Fuentes has it (echoing many), an "old manicheism which since Plato has led us by the nose, forcing us to divide, to choose, to see things in black-and-white" (*Cambio*, 241; translated by Van Delden, 105). The last three chapters, at least, suggest it to be of a piece with the sorts of divisions we have been looking at and so grounded in the older of these three. Christian or Greek could explain how Sidney, again, would assign a split in being and appearance, in body and mind or just within the soul to a tragedy of love: "Then thinke my deare, that you in me do reed/Of Lovers ruine some sad Tragedie:/I am not I; pitie the tale of me" (*Astrophel and Stella*, Sonnet 45, ll. 12–14); or how Shakespeare's Iago could at the start of his tragedy set out the story's many divisions—moor and white, man and woman, Europe and Africa, Othello and Iago, "the Ottoman" and Venice—in the short phrase: "I am not what I am" (*Othello*, I.i.65).

The philosopher Adriana Cavarero, furthering arguments advanced by Hannah Arendt, agrees that the split comes from the Greeks, especially Plato, establishing "an ancient mind–body dichotomy, with its strong hostility to the body, [that] persists along the entire history of Western philosophy." Philosophy's goal became that of "untying" itself from body— thought preparing for death (*In Spite*, 25–28). But perhaps the origin of the split matters little. A first point is that the mind/body division *is* still *everyday* western experience, deeply buried in language and so in ideas, feelings, and meanings. A second point is that the "postcartesian" debates—grossly to simplify for a moment—were and are but a variant in much longer received wisdom. The simple fact of the matter is, though, that such wisdom is now tied to that variant, which, willy-nilly, gives one set of parameters to a common experience—at least, to that of those of us who dwell under western hegemonies. It gives them also, we have begun to see, to many who live within these hegemonies at once less clearly and more contentiously.

I would like to offer a further powerful instance, if but to emphasize what and how much is at stake in these questions. It occurs in a writing by the Guyanese novelist Wilson Harris, his *Palace of the Peacock*. First in a tetralogy, this novel recounts something like a journey away from a life of colonial and postcolonial violence and oppression toward a hoped-for rebirth in "fulfilment and understanding" (*Palace*, 116). Early on, the harsh protagonist, Donne, mocks the narrator, his mysterious "double" and "brother," Dreamer, who has remarked their distance from "the folk." "Is it a mystery of language and address?" asks Donne. Slightly bewildered, Dreamer struggles to suggest that the obstacle is less of language than of a deeper disjunction:

"it's an inapprehension of substance," I blurted out, "an actual fear of the substance of life, fear of the substance of the folk, a cannibal blind fear in oneself. Put it how you like," I cried, "it's a fear of acknowledging the true substance of life. Yes, fear I tell you, the fear that breeds bitterness in our mouth, the haunting sense of fear that poisons us and hangs us and murders us. And somebody," I declared, "must demonstrate the unity of being, and *show* . . ." I had grown violent and emphatic . . ."that fear is nothing but a dream and an appearance." (*Palace*, 52)

Recovery of "unity" might become a way to defeat political and historical violences. In the next novel in the sequence, one of two self-indulgently whining characters, accused of pining for a woman who has run away to seek education, explodes: "I don't believe you can begin to see how some *body* like they born seeking for *mind*" (*Far Journey*, 174). For peoples of the colonized Americas, imbued with "the great civilization of the American Indian," this urge, Harris then wrote in a critical essay echoing many elements we have been seeing, was simply the personal form of a social and political necessity to recover still-living elements of a culture for which "matter truly bore the imprint of genius," refusing "the dead stamp of industrialization or the taboo of spirituality removed from sensuous direction." Human presence to the physical world was quite different from "diminutive man of the cities of the world today and the tragic ancestry of his gods which failed him with the rising tide of individualism which exploited these gods." Through disillusionment with this divided civilization, "the real rhythms of the human being are innately strengthened and discovered, the complexity of value is shown to be—flesh and blood, not spirit and stone" (Harris, *Tradition*, 17). Some of our divisive instruments are clearly depicted here, set in the context of the division of spirit/mind and body/senses. Recently, Harris has worried this anew, relating conquest and "Cartesian dualism," pitting the "biased ego" of "the Cartesian dictum . . . *I think therefore I am*" against "a brooding solitariness of Soul": a phrase that fights to express a "steep[ing of] oneself in a theatre . . . of plural masks that bear on the travail of humanity," some "epic" wholeness countering "the Cartesian ego that underpins the mind-set of Europe" ("Quetzalcoatl," 30).

The many such moments in contemporary writers from many different cultural traditions imply how central are forms of the mind/body split to the global imagination, how closely they are bound to ideas of a specifically European individualism and of European oppression and colonialism, how overcoming or replacing them may conduce to new understandings, behaviors, and conditions, and how even overcome or replaced they still leave indelible traces.

Again, it matters, therefore, to understand the origins and devices that set these forms. Indeed, the issue of the guiding traces left by coercive prejudices was itself fundamental to early modern thinking about mind and body. How to defeat them was a principal question in debate. It has been useful in subsequent hegemonies to forget, even to conceal, that issue, just as it was useful to conceal different "mimetic" traditions or to exclude nonwestern figures and modes of understanding. It may therefore be equally useful, here, to return the issue of coercive prejudices to the fore. But we need also understand the origins and devices of these forms of the mind/body division because their wisdom is grounded in a series of simplifying misunderstandings. Further, they are sustained as much by philosophical commentary as by "popular" claim—indeed, Anglo-American "analytical" philosophy has largely relied on the belief that these forms of mind/body split defined cartesian thinking.[1] Descartes' work was itself far more complicated, and others do not hesitate to note that most such views are little more than "caricatures." Such commentators argue that Descartes sought to conceive of an "interaction" that yet avoided the idea of some impossible "union" between "two *different* sorts of things" (Mattern, 221, 218, 220). Others note that Descartes did in fact argue for a union and that to lay the split at his door has been just "mythology."[2] He, no less than Marshall's guides and Harris' characters, was fully aware that whether or not mind and body were different, even contradictory (it is not clear what that could mean—one is again caught in binary otherings), they nonetheless "make up the whole" (Marshall, "From the Poets," *Merle*, 9). The issue was how, meaningfully, to conceive such a whole and its consequences for reason and questions of common life.

Still, Descartes' responsibility for the philosophical arguments that hold mind and body separate is a commonplace: mind identified by its chief attribute of thought, body by that of extension. Like most of its kind, the commonplace is partly correct; but the issues behind it are so much more complicated as to make it a bludgeon, if used for anything beyond entry into those complexities—a criticism I do not aim at the imprecisions of everyday assumption or of the fictive imagination. Descartes did of course find the process of thinking to be the ground of being. This in itself did not separate thinking from body. Indeed, no more than others did he consider extended thought possible without information garnered by and through the body, whatever the primary importance of innate ideas. Besides, no one ever doubted that the seat of thought was physically situated in the human body, focused, wrote Descartes, in the pineal gland, although he also came to assert that it was "really joined to the whole body" and was not able to be conceived clearly in terms of any limiting dimension. There is actually much justification for seeing the 1649 *Passions de l'âme*, whence come these last remarks, as showing how mind and body work together through those passions.[3] Descartes himself said as much in a letter to Henry More (April 15, 1649; AT, 5:347; CSM, 3:375). But he had long since made the point in the *Meditations* themselves, the very text taken to found the mind/body division.

In the sixth and final Meditation, he wrote, "I am not merely present in my body as a sailor is present in a ship, but . . . I am very closely joined and, as it were, intermingled with it, so that I and my body form a unit." However different in nature mind and body might be, the mind was nonetheless "united to the whole body" (AT, 7:81, 86; CSM, 2:56, 59). It was united to a *particular* body, rooted in a here and now that he had to *begin* by setting aside but to end by bringing back in all its material actuality. Had he not been able to do so, the *Meditations* would have failed, for their whole point was to find and show how humans could have true knowledge of god and world. Contrary to what too many people assert, then, in the *Meditations*, Descartes did not "cease to see the world," as Gordon claims, contrasting him to Fanon. The *Meditations* were *not* "a flight from the world" but, as Gordon allows for some twentieth-century thinkers, "a bracketing or suspension of certain kinds of judgment *about* the world for the purpose, ultimately, of returning to an originary or primordial reflection *on* the world," and of seeing, then, what it is possible to know at all (*Fanon*, 10, 15). The first Meditation takes the thinker and reader *through* the steps of that bracketing, removing one by one the sources of prejudice—prejudgment; the sixth returns both to a material world where mind and matter are reunited as only together enabling life and practice in that world. All the accusatory criticisms *may* be exact of postcartesian claim. They are most inexact of Descartes. This chapter suggests that the distinction and its implications matter to the issues discussed in the book as a whole.

Nonetheless, at least one aspect of taking mind and thinking to be foundational posed a problem of a different order. To speak of "good sense" or "reason" as being "naturally equal in all men" and so able to be led into "the right path," given only a correct method of how to think (*Discours de la méthode*, AT, 6:2; CSM, 1:111), presumed a universal nature that was surely not evidenced in physical differences among humans, corresponding, precisely, to the material particularity of body. On the contrary, most people held humans—at least where mind and passions were concerned, if not soul—to be of infinite variety. One of Montaigne's major sources, Juan Huarte de San Juan, famously argued so. In Descartes, the seeming contradiction was the more problematic in that the universality of thought and reason was held not just to be of here and now, but of all time. Socrates' reason, *qua* reason, was as like Descartes' as his was like that of those scientists who would, no doubt "several centuries" in the future discover "all the truths that can be deduced from" his new principles (preface to *Principes de philosophie*, AT, 9B:20; CSM, 1:189).

Reason, mind, that was to say, had no history. Bodies, on the other hand, only too clearly did. They were subject to all kinds of ills and changes, as were the societies they composed and which defined them (good Aristotelians that they were). One substance might have diverse appearances. Water might become ice, cloud, or steam; wax might be hard or supple, or it might flow away. Human bodies decayed, in disconcerting and discomfiting ways, as Montaigne had recently described of his own. They died. Human societies, present evidence proved all too well, decomposed. Of mind, only content changed. Its nature stayed the same. So either mind had to be divided from body, or body had to be placed somehow outside history. Descartes tried the second as well as the first. To think of bodies as automata—clockwork, hydraulic, or whatever—was to free them of *organic* change.[4] Parts might wear out. But the body did not have within it that "lurking principle of death," of which we saw Pope write in his *Essay on Man*: "The young disease, that must subdue at length,/Grows with his growth, and strengthens with his strength/ . . . cast and mingled with his very frame" (*Poems*, II.134–37). Of course (we saw in Chapter 4), *this* "disease" was mostly not the body's organicism. It was that immortal soul was set in decaying body—Descartes' issue of conscious mind in body, "Adam's curse," as Eliot was to put it ("East Coker," *Four Quartets*, 18). For

such automata, a geometry was possible. And geometry, too, was not subject to the vagaries of embodied history. Far from it: its clear figures, especially the triangle, made it the age-old exemplum of innate common and
universal truths.

But the same difficulty lay upon mind, which was after all firmly located in body. And minds had memory, which was itself fundamentally
physical. Yet reason *depended* on memory. A good part of Descartes'
story—his several "*fables*," as he called them—was that of constant tension
between memory and forgetting, between history and "science," between,
if you like, organism—body—and mathematical method. Here, he echoed
a major aspect of the beginnings of our varied western modernities. In
these, toward the turn of the sixteenth century, we can identify a struggle
between two sorts of knowledge and analysis. One, founded in historical
understanding, was typical among many of those we think of as "late humanists." They held that it led to wisdom, *sapientia*. The other was
grounded in mathematical method, derived *more geometrico* from the ordered operation of reason on the world. It gave science, *scientia*, and eventually an instrumental technique for operating on the world, for *using* the
world. (In different form, the *sapientia/scientia* opposition of course had a
far longer history.) Such universalizing, mathematical, and instrumental
science, if it could be found, would be bound to a particular notion of rational agency (we shall see Kane, again, make the point).

We all know how this last was victorious. The mind/body commonplace nowadays gives motive for blame, as we saw it do gently in Marshall's
recounting, meditatively in Kane's, sardonically in Achebe's and Philip's, vehemently in Harris'. But it has widely come to allow a kind of fetishized
nostalgia among many dissenting moderns—those, I mean, who fear that
not only is something frightfully wrong with the present western world view
and the thinking and practices it engages and enables, but that its foundations in Enlightenment and cartesianism were a priori flawed. Those who
think so, I have suggested, run a gamut from Marxian-inflected Frankfurters
like Horkheimer or Adorno, to structuralist entrepreneurs like Lévi-Strauss
(calling Enlightenment a "virus" on civilization's body), to virtually apoliti-
cal deconstructors like Derrida. They include promoters of a *philosophia
perennis* like Carl Gustav Jung or Coomaraswamy, the latter arguing, for example, that modern western art is a sad degeneration from the deeper and
quasiuniversal "art" forms of "traditional societies" as represented in Persia,
India, ancient Greece, China, Japan, medieval Christian Europe. . . .[5] We

have seen an analogous view adopted by Achebe and Kane, whose cartesian "accident" separated a new, divisive "occidental" thought from one that was "non-occidental" (*Aventure*, 126: shades of negritude again). The spectrum is vast, and these names do not catch its many hues.

For most of these contemporaries, the sixteenth century was a last moment of "wholeness" in European history, a time when *homines euro-peani* were still one with each other and the world, when body and soul were yet unbroken. Albrecht Dürer's perspectivized and exhaustively phys-ical bodies and Pieter Bruegel's people-crowded world joined in François Rabelais' laughter as it rumbled through bodies and tuned souls. Erasmus rejoiced in warm inns and amity as he anatomized the Bible anew and thought a politics of friendly exchange rather than of imposed sovereignty. Huarte, even more than Vives, so linked mind to physiology as to argue that different *ciencias* were natural to different people, however sure all were of having equal powers of *ingenio* (*Examen*, 428–33, 447–51, 412). Montaigne, who echoed the idea, aligned cited memories of Latin and Greek culture in endless quest for thought's motion by rooting them in physical presence of his body and its functions. Luisa Oliva Sabuco found the soul and its powers—understanding, memory, reason, and will, as well as its passions—to be firmly set in the cerebrum and compact with the senses (*Obras*, 8, 41–42, 49). Indeed, the crucially *human* rational soul was in body alive before taking on a mental thinking and feeling nature thanks to the senses. Eliot perceived in George Chapman and John Donne no dis-sociation of mind and body but "a direct sensuous apprehension of thought," poets feeling "their thought as immediately as the odour of a rose" ("Metaphysical," 29, 30). Equally far into the seventeenth century, Robert Burton's *Anatomy of Melancholy* still explored the world's decay as one of body itself, and the doctor could hope to heal the world and rem-edy its history just as one could nurse a body back to health.

All these certainly did live—with their analyses, and hopes, and thoughts, and projects. They offer fake nostalgia and kitsch memory for moderns when we fetishize them and their ideas as some enchanted world whose elements—whose ecohuman holism, as these yearners see it—can be reinstituted. For this image of the past requires falsification. The enchanted whole never was. Many have had past golden ages as others present Eldorados. This is one. We usefully forget how tiny and singularly privileged was the elite to which belonged such as I have named. We also forget that the body in which they dwelt was that of the 98 percent of laboring people, peasant and artisan, the vast majority illiterate, poor, short of life, doomed to spend their days at or below subsistence. There was no beneficent whole community that in some elusive way collapsed into the brutish competitive strife of economistic society, *Gemeinschaft* yielding to *Gesellschaft*, as early twentieth-century German sociology and political economy had it. There were, to be sure, very different ways of understanding the world and humans' place in it. But let us not fetishize those differences into some lost, but recoverable, perfection. For we also forget that the modern West's brokenness is also less a matter of fact—or even experience—than it is, as Bruno Latour argues, merely a way of sorting "out elements belonging to different times" and places, no less coexistent than they were in those times of supposed "wholeness." It is, he adds, *"the sorting that makes the times, not the times that make the sorting"* (*We Have*, 76).

What I wish to get from these—here, now—is that sense of the human body as bearer of memory, as *essentially* engaged in, marked by, and presentative of history. That, I think was what gave Descartes many of his dilemmas. Picture Dürer's heavily *present* architecture, his weightily *physical* humans and their body parts; not to mention the materiality of his fantastic figures. Remember Bruegel's frighteningly active crowds, almost overly physically combative, in explosions of pleasure that surely provoke a sense of unease in the modern spectator. Corporeal anomalies suggest too much body. His crowds appear at the threshold of angry chaos and antisocial rage. His "gay, robust" figures, as I have seen them described, strike one more as rather sinister in their straining contortions: a "gaiety" that belies the grim reality of lives made clear in physical excess and distortion, latent fury within the everyday. Perhaps these are already those hybrids whose proliferation Latour sees as one characteristic of modernity (*We Have*, 1–3, 30, 131). I am reminded of Lear's cry in Shakespeare, "O let me not be mad, not mad!" as he reacts to what seems to him a unique and quite new corruption in the world's order—his realization that Regan's behavior is new and unnatural: "But yet thou art my flesh, my blood, my daughter;/Or rather a disease that's in my flesh,/Which I must needs call mine: thou art a boil,/A plague-sore, or embossed carbuncle/In my corrupted blood" (*King Lear*, II.iv.220–24). Here something seems to be passing away, something new and deadly arising—reminiscent of Pope's future disease, Venice's ghetto at its core. Such tensions were freighted with far-flung actual violence, from minor and major intolerances to physical oppression, from intellectual censorship to witchhunting, from rebellion and banditry to civil and foreign wars (the point is much reinforced in Sullivan, *Bruegel's Peasants*, especially 25, 48–55).

My point here is the insistence, in Dürer, Erasmus, Rabelais, Huarte, and in Bruegel, Montaigne, Shakespeare, and Burton, on the human body as bearer of history, mark of memory, and site of thought. It is Sabuco's or Chapman's bodily soul available for sensuous knowledge, Donne as a "voluptuary of thought" (Eliot, *Varieties*, 158). It is history as present encroachment on the body, so to speak. For—nostalgia or no nostalgia, fetish or no fetish—it is clear that during the century and beyond indicated by these names, something surely did change. I do not take Descartes as the cause or origin of that change. I take him to typify it—in the kind of analysis that will now be sought; and to exemplify it—in the subtlety and strength of details of his version of such analysis. At least the last five of those mentioned put before us another aspect of the age's sense of itself (if I may be allowed momentarily to make an agent of an era): the widespread, overwhelming feeling of dissolution and decay, issuing in *personal* anger and grief, wrote Sabuco. Ubiquitous war, famine, disease, and seemingly endless economic pressures were the real ground of such feeling. It explains both the sense of urgency behind the work begun by Descartes and his contemporaries and the way in which history weighs on them, particularly, I shall try to show in the wake of Chapter 1, on Descartes himself. The point is that the elaboration of a particular sense and kind of identity (which I explore more in "Revising") was thoroughly joined to a particular understanding of history.

Descartes' first published work was the 1637 *Discours de la méthode*. It famously began with a history of his own mind and its training, and, a bit less famously, with that of his travels—corporeal, these—in Europe at the time of the outbreak of what was to become the Thirty Years' War; in which he participated, the latest and culminating in a string of catastrophic disasters. Interestingly enough, the goal of this personal history was to deny history's utility: "one who is too curious about the practices of past ages usually remains quite ignorant of those of the present. . . . Even the most accurate histories . . . almost always omit the baser and less notable events[, and so make] the other events appear in a false light" (AT, 6:7; CSM, 1:114). Yet the very purpose of the *Discourse* was incomprehensible without such history. It aimed to do nothing less than furnish the foundations for a new construction of knowledge (and all that went with it—eventually, and despite his overt claim, in philosophy, science, education, ethics, and politics), precisely and exactly because the old no longer worked. In the *Discourse's* Parts 2 and 3, Descartes used that (highly politicized) architectural explanation we saw taken up critically by Césaire and Kane (and uncritically by Chinweizu) to present this new construction, comparing it historically with Lycurgus' Spartan laws and theologically with God's laws of the universe.[6] The house not built to one architect's plan was liable to fall, the city not built to one map became a meandering riot. Subject to the vicissitudes of unordered history, both failed.

Well, only history could speak of that failure. At the same time, its very failure meant its encroachment upon the present had to be resisted: the worm in Bruegel's pleasure. The body bore the mark of that history. It had somehow to be hidden, its importance denied—or maybe the very conception and form of history had to be changed—to be not history as encroachment (be it divine or secular) but history as "rational" order, methodical construction of the actuality of events. This last could be a history watched as a sequence running "unilinearly" through "the past, the present, and the future," ignoring, for example, as Hamisi Salim observes in Mazrui's novel, *The Trial of Christopher Okigbo*, "the simple and obvious principle of simultaneity" (79). It may be that Hamisi's idea has to do with an experience involving the simultaneous presence of the living, the dead and the yet unborn different from any experience available to any of the westerners I have just mentioned, but most of these still had a very profound experience of dwelling simultaneously with thinkers and writers of their own "past." The conflict between attention to body and the need to release it—as container of universal mind—from *that* history is everywhere to be found in Descartes' work. In that, too, it exemplifies this modernity so many now wish somehow to forget, in its and their turn.[7] But, as I proposed, not only the body bore the mark of history. So, too, did the mind. Indeed, it bore it precisely inasmuch as it dwelt in the body. One "entered the world in ignorance," wrote Descartes in the *Recherche de la vérité*, "and the knowledge of one's childhood being based solely on the senses' weakness and teachers' authority, it is almost impossible for one's imagination not to be filled with innumerable false thoughts, until reason can take on its conduct" (AT, 10:496; CSM, 2:400).

Let me return to the *Discourse* whose opening I mentioned. The first part's end is scarcely less well known, with its instruction to forget everything earlier read and learned: "as soon as I was old enough to emerge from the control of my teachers, I entirely abandoned the study of letters."

Instead he went off to study "the great book of the world" (AT, 6:9; CSM, 1:115). Since this other volume finally gave knowledge no more useful, he quit its study in turn, so as "to undertake studies within myself." This "had much more success" than either of the others (AT, 6:10; CSM, 1:116).

To acquire true knowledge, one had first to forget every book, every kind of history, every notice of history, every experience of body in the world. In the *Recherche*, Epistémon compared a child's imagination to a tabula rasa on which senses and authority had laid out a picture. "Understanding," he went on, "is like an excellent painter hired to put the last touches to a bad picture sketched by young apprentices . . . from the start design was poorly understood, figures ill placed, proportions badly observed." Eudoxe offered a more radical correction: "your painter would do far better to start the picture again from scratch, first taking a sponge to wipe away all the marks there, rather than wasting time correcting them. Just so, as soon as a man reaches what we call the age of discretion, he should resolve once and for all to wipe from his imagination all the imperfect ideas marked there up till then, and begin in earnest to form new ones" (AT, 10:507–8; CSM, 2:406–7). This reiterated the *Discourse*. Descartes started, that is to say, with what one might call a deliberate *will to forget* or, more exactly, we shall see, to avoid a particular prejudiced remembering. What was to be "forgotten" was a particular—even physical—imposition of history, unwanted and prejudged encroachment on mind. And it is as we ask what such an amnesia can have meant to Descartes and his contemporaries that we get to the problem of the body, even supposing such willful forgetting to be possible.[8] For how, in actuality, could one hope to carry out such a project?

The authors of the *Objections* to the 1641 *Meditations* did not fail to put the question. "You assume *that the mind can be freed of all prejudices*," wrote Pierre Gassendi, "but that seems impossible. Chiefly because memory, the treasury of judgments previously made and deposited within it, cannot be erased at will. Everyone learns this by inner experience, and he best knew it who wanted less an art of remembering than of forgetting. It is certain that formed judgments so persist in our *habitus*, and stick so like the imprint of a seal, that it is not in our power to get rid of them or erase them at will."[9]

As was his wont with Gassendi, Descartes was scornful. Indeed, the reminder of their school reading in Cicero's *De oratore*, where Themistocles was twice recalled as the one who would rather be able "to forget what he wanted than to remember," contradicted the requirement advanced in the *Discourse* to rid oneself of one's school learning and emphasized the gap between the two thinkers.[10] Descartes replied that Gassendi had simply misread him and that he had never claimed that one could empty one's memory. He had merely insisted that "it is an act of will to judge or not to judge." Saying this, he was further confirming the argument of the fourth Meditation, where, after establishing the existence of God as the perfect thinking process (in the third Meditation), he deduced from it that the power of divine will accompanying that perfect process was, *qua* power of decision (of acquiescing or denying), echoed in the human will accompanying its *imperfect* thinking process (the argument is detailed in my "Revising"). Understood simply as a power of decision, the will's power was absolute. Will was the mark of human agency. Error resulted from the discrepancy between the uncertainties of human reason and senses and the certainty of will. That was why (fourth Meditation) one should make no decision concerning things of which one had inadequate knowledge. As he said in the precise instance that concerns us here, "for in the end, to rid oneself of every kind of prejudice, one need do nothing more than resolve to assert or deny nothing that one has asserted or denied previously, save only after having first examined it, although one does not fail, for all that, to retain the same notions in one's memory" (Gassendi, *Disquisitio*, 634; AT, 9:204 [letter to Clerselier, January 12, 1646]). Memory was physically stamped upon and into the matter of the brain, but will could decide how to use such memory or, even perhaps, what such memory was. . . . For it was surely nothing so straightforward as a representational image.

The issue was fundamental: nothing less than to find a way to prevent the senses (essential for our knowing and being as humans but fundamentally marking, and marked by, our presence in the historical world) from obstructing true knowledge and the right life that could be derived only from such knowledge: one that could be termed "generous"—responsible, loyal, faithful, honest, aware of communal duties and obligations. These particular, individual senses were no less essential to knowledge than was memory: perilous, necessary, and anyway ineluctable. History, memory, sense, body—all were bound in the particular and local, and so (as the wholly private implies what is noncommunicable) something nonuniversal and irrational. Where could a seeker for universal reason even begin? Descartes' thinking is fraught with these conflicts between different histories and identities, between universality and particularity, between needing history and escaping its weight, between necessity of mind and attention to body.

Like his contemporaries, Descartes drew his thinking about memory chiefly from Aristotle. Through his Jesuit teachers, he drew from the *De memoria* an idea of memory as impress stamped in wax, notions of seals, traces, painted "figures," but also the thought that memory came both from the external and the internal world, from the senses and from "the recovery of knowledge which is one's own, from within oneself."[11] Descartes picked up this distinction in what he called "intellectual memory" and "material memory." The first dealt with innate, "pure" ideas, the other with objects "imprinted" on the brain. But how could one distinguish them? Even if one could, how could one avoid in either case being trapped by prejudice, all that has been "pre-judged," *imposed, impressed,* from well before any moment of personal judgment? Replies to these questions could answer Gassendi. They could also answer the universal/particular, the mind/body, problems.

So I start again, this time with a simple-seeming query. What is or was memory? Was it not quite like history physically imprinted on and in the body? Descartes held three rather different ideas of the physiology of just such memory. I do not think the differences had any great impact on Descartes' thinking about mental creation, but we must record them. For if the differences matter little, his insistent view that they were none of them metaphors, but all real effects in the brain, surely did/does matter a lot. For, firstly, it is hard to see how all three could be simultaneously correct. Secondly, if memory were a permanent physical mark or scar, it is equally hard to see how Gassendi's objection could be met. Thirdly, such "prejudicial" impress would surely mean that any new conception and form of history was, by definition, impossible?

From the *Regulae* on, Descartes urged that the relation, external objects/sensations/ideas, was that of a seal leaving its impression in wax. First, he wrote, our "external senses" operate "strictly speaking . . . by a passion [possibly], in the same way as wax takes on its shape from the seal. Nor must we think that a mere analogy is in question here: we must think of the external shape of the sentient body [the brain] as being really changed by the object in exactly the same way as the shape of the surface of the wax is altered by the seal" (*Regula,* 12; AT, 10:412; CSM, 1:40). Second, the imprint "is conveyed" instantaneously, "to another part of the body known as the 'common' sense, without any entity really passing from the one to the other. In exactly the same way," he added, "I understand that while I am writing, at the very moment when individual letters are traced on the paper, not only does the point of the pen move, but the slightest motion of this part cannot but be transmitted simultaneously to the whole pen" (AT, 10:414; CSM, 1:41).

One may note, here, that the movement is identical to the way in which Descartes would later describe the action of nerves in general (in the *Traité de l'homme*, for example, or the *Description du corps humain*), and, in the *Passions de l'âme*, of the particular nervous reactions provoking all those passions on which reason and will must be brought to bear. From the start, memory was a mental operation essentially trammeled and embroiled in the body. For the moment, in the twelfth *Regula* from which I have been quoting, the philosopher chose to deepen his pit. Between the senses receiving impressions from without and the common sense organizing them, the play went on: "thirdly, the 'common' sense functions like a seal, fashioning in the phantasy or imagination, as if in wax, the same figures or ideas which come, pure and bodiless, from the external senses. Phantasy is a genuine part of the body, and is large enough to let the different parts of it take on many different figures and generally to retain them for some time; in which case it is to be identified with what we call 'memory' " (AT, 10:415; CSM, 1:41–42).

This idea of sensation and memory as wax impressions was not replaced by others.[12] Rather, a kind of steady accretion occurred. In the *Traité de l'homme* (AT, 11:177–79; CSM, 1:106–7 [partial]) and the *Description du corps humain* (AT, 11:127; CSM, 1:316), Descartes added the idea of memory as consisting of holes opened between the fibers of a woven cloth by the body's animal spirits. These spirits being moved in similar ways by similar experiences, they gradually loosened up, as it were, well-trodden paths as holes in the brain's cloth. Such holes remained afterward able to be reopened to new passages of the same effects as opened them originally. Descartes explained the process at length in the *Traité de l'homme*. There, he depicted the brain as "a thick and close-crowded network or lacework whose meshes are so many tubes through which the animal spirits can enter" from the pineal gland, their source, moved by the senses whose effects the gland receives. These tubes run through myriad fibers which can be "folded in all sorts of ways" and among which, too, the tubes run like pores able to be "enlarged or narrowed by the force of the spirits entering them" (AT, 11. 170–71). After a long description of how the spirits move and how they carry "l'impression de quelque idée [the impress of some idea]" (AT, II. 177), he explains how the spirits create these memory channels:

they have the force to enlarge somewhat these intervals [pores between the fibers], and to fold and arrange differently the small fibres they encounter on their paths [*de plier et disposer diversement les petits filets qu'ils rencontrent en leurs chemins*], according to the various ways in which they move, and the various openings of the tubes through which they pass: such that they also trace figures there which relate to [*se rapporter à*] those of the objects; not so easily or so perfectly however on the first occasion as on the [pineal] gland, but gradually better and better according as their action is stronger, and lasts longer, or is repeated more times. That is why these figures do not disappear so easily either [*ne s'effacent pas non plus si aisément*], but remain there in such a way [*s'y conservent en telle sorte*] that by their means the ideas, which were previously on this gland, can form themselves there [*s'y peuvent former*] again long afterward, without requiring the presence of the objects to which they relate [*auxquels elles se rapportent*]. And it is in this that *memory* consists. (AT, II:177–78)

Descartes equated this process to carding a cloth, the metal teeth of the card eventually leaving a permanent pattern (AT, II:178). One question, of course, is just what sort of *figures* (Descartes' word) were at issue. First of all, Descartes did *not* write that they "correspond" to the figures of the objects, as most English translations have it. He was less precise: they "relate" to them. Nor did he write, as English translations seemed constrained to have it, that the figures "are not effaced" or "are preserved" or "can be formed." With the reflexive, Descartes implies that they do this themselves, once the animal spirits move through the pores and affect the holes and folds in the same way as they did before. Sutton argues that this passage shows that the "figures" (or "patterns," as he rather tendentiously translates the word the second time) "are not *stored* faithfully" but only "'in such a way that' they play a part in the (re-)creation of the idea on the surface of the gland" (*Philosophy*, 58). But, firstly, it is not clear whether the last *y* refers to the pineal gland or the pore opened by continual passage of animal spirits. The syntax clearly *says* the pore (both the previous *y* and the positioning of commas), although in a sense naming both, since the figure in the pore must appear on the gland in order to be used as a memory. Secondly, the reflexive verbs certainly do indicate that "figures" have been stored faithfully enough to bring themselves back into view as iterated memories. They may not be "resembling images of dubious ontological status," as Sutton protests (*Philosophy*, 63), but they do "preserve themselves" in the brain's woof and pores. (For his argument about the superpositionality of memories in Descartes, Sutton insists that the *process* of animal spirits far outweighs in importance the *storage* of figures; *Philosophy*, 64 and *passim*. I find this claim less necessary to his point than he does and mildly unfaithful to Descartes' several different ideas about the nature of memory.)

Perhaps we need to take *figures* more literally—indeed, not as resembling images but as something like the *contours* of the perceptual *ideas* recorded through the senses in the pineal gland, projected thence into the brain's pores and folds via the animal spirits and that redevelop themselves (to use a photographic image unavailable to Descartes) upon successive movements of the spirits. In a way, they are the outlined "signs" of ideas, just as our perceptions are outlines of natural signs (in the world) standing for objects whose ultimate nature we can never know: those "*signs*" of light, of heat and such, with which he began *Le Monde* (AT, 11:3–10; on this, see Reiss, "*Concevoir*," especially 211–14). And as the ones are *really there* in nature, so the others are *really there* in the brain, as Descartes made quite clear when further explaining the process in the *Passions*:

> when the soul wants to remember something, this volition makes the gland lean first to one side and then to another, thus driving the spirits towards different regions of the brain until they come upon the one containing traces left by the object we want to remember. These traces consist simply in the fact that the pores of the brain through which the spirits previously made their way owing to the presence of this object have thereby become more apt than the others to be opened in the same way when the spirits again flow towards them. And so the spirits enter into these pores more easily when they come upon them, thereby producing in the gland that special movement which represents the same object to the soul, and makes it recognize the object as the one it wanted to remember. (§42; AT, 11:360; CSM, 1:343–44)

(These nervous "spirits" may have had aspects of what we would now describe as neuroelectrical impulses, although Sutton rightly advises care here; *Philosophy*, 50–51. He has now offered the subtlest reading of animal spirits for this period; *Philosophy*, 25–49, 102–6, 119–28.)

Impressions in wax, openings that readily yield to future passages. . . . To these, Descartes added, we have begun to see, an equally constant third view of the physiology of memory: that of the fold. Writing to Lazare Meyssonier on January 29, 1640, he said: "as for the species preserved in the memory, I imagine they are not unlike the folds which remain in this paper after it has once been folded; and so I think that they are for the most part in the whole substance of the brain." But they are in the body as well: "some of the species which serve the memory can be in various other parts of the body, for instance the skill of a lute player is not only in his head, but also partly in the muscles of his hands, and so on" (AT, 3:20; CSM, 3:143–44). He repeated these thoughts to Marin Mersenne on April 1, 1640, embroidering a bit on the last: "all the nerves and muscles can also be so utilized, so that a lute player, for instance, has a part of his memory in his hands: for the ease of bending and positioning his fingers in various ways, which he has acquired by practice, helps him to remember the passages which need these positions when they are played"—folds in the very fingers. Here he added the thought of an "intellectual" memory "dependent on the soul alone" but whose operation he did (or could) not explain (AT, 3:48; CSM, 3:146).

Himself a player of the lute, Descartes was here expressing a sense of his own body, his very feel of memory under the skin, as it were, on the sinews of the body. From the *Studium bonae mentis* of his youth, of which Adrien Baillet wrote in his biography (*Vie*, 2:66), to letters to Mersenne in 1640 and to Denis Mesland in 1644, this idea of folds in the brain's matter, as in paper or stiff cloth, stayed ever-present. And as I noted the importance of motion in nerves, I would remark here how the idea of folds permanently engraved, for example, on muscles could readily involve the frictional or other wear and tear to which clockwork, hydraulic, or wind-driven automata were heir. At the same time, we have now seen, it could ambiguously be altogether more organic.

This implied, too, that folds were actually the most complex of the body's memory devices. As he wrote to Mersenne on June 11, 1640, "There is no doubt that memory's folds get in each other's way [*s'empêchent les uns les autres*], and that there cannot be an infinite number of such folds in the brain; but the fact remains that there are quite a number of them there." He added, again, that "intellectual memory has its own separate species [*ses espèces à part*], which in no way depend on these folds, whose number I judge need not be very great" (AT, 3:84–85; CSM, 3:148). Two months later, he told Mersenne that this small number did not affect the extent of memory (and we must also recall that other kinds of brain paths functioned as well): "I do not think there has to be a very large number of these folds to serve for all our memories, in that a single fold relates to [*se rapporte à*] all the things which resemble each other, and that besides the corporeal memory, whose impressions can be explained by the folds of the brain, I judge there is also in our understanding another sort of memory, which is altogether spiritual and is not found in animals, and it is this that we mainly use" (AT, 3:143; CSM, 3:151). This intellectual memory was never to have its operation explained; while the folds' storage of like images seems to solve the previous letter's worry about their getting "in each other's way."[13]

Whatever the exact form of the trace or physiological vestige, one thing was sure. Whether imprint, pore, or fold, the impressed mark was permanent, whatever exactly the "figure" or "species" may have been. It was *there*, once and for all. And as Gassendi observed, it could not be "erased at will." This explains, too, why Descartes constantly returned to the question of what a child "in its mother's womb" could know. When mind and body were yet scarcely separable, thought nonetheless existed—but thought imprinted on a mind still soft and inapt to take permanent imprints. Indeed, as Henri Gouhier interprets the argument: "the union of soul and body is so tight that the soul, as it were, thinks through the body and for the body. Of course, it is a thinking thing, but it has no other thoughts than those through which it feels/senses whatever affects the body" (*Pensée*, 57).

For clearly, the issue of innate ideas readily coincided with that of memory. Imprinted on the brain, as both were, how could one hope to find any *originary* truths? truths, that is, that one could know as due to some initiating act of thinking? that could create the new? that were not just the prejudice of a literally corporeal history? Literal mark of history as encroachment, memory was always firstly an obstacle—hence the first part of the *Discourse*. But memory was also "weak and unstable" and had to "be refreshed and strengthened through this continuous and repeated movement of thought" (*Regula*, 11; AT, 10:408; CSM, 1:38). This is not the contradiction Sutton suggests (*Philosophy*, 99). The permanence of the figures and species and the fact that they and no others are available to develop does not mean that motion is not needed for them to suscitate themselves in those impresses, pores, and folds. Repeated movement was by definition errant and so liable to error. It was this that made necessary both that clear and distinct intuition able, so to speak, to leap memory impressions and the efforts to elude the need of memory:

We must in general bear in mind never to commit anything to memory that does not require constant attention if we can set it down on paper: indeed, we must not allow a needless effort of memory to distract a part of our mind from its knowledge of the object before it.

In this respect, we must try to find means, ordinarily those of writing, to apply ourselves "to the particular subject we are dealing with, *without any recourse to memory*" (*Regula*, 16; AT, 10:458; CSM, 1:69).

Memory was thus deeply ambiguous. At once useful and biased, usable history and idolatrous prejudice, tool and trap, it was clearly most perilous. There we fasten ourselves to words, "to certain terms" (as Descartes put it), to whole series of received ideas. These ideas result from the sequences of "figures" of past events and perceptions. Singly, they are so tiny and scattered as to elude separate estimate and measure (another reason for memory's "weakness and instability"). Together, they establish a sum of knowledge that seems inescapably *right*. An aspect of universal reason impressed upon the particular body, memory was the place of opinion, authority, our teachers: the site of physical and unchangeable impressions, sealed in mind as prejudged history ineluctably charging the meaning of the present. And we had no way to erase this encroached history, these physically impressed, bored, enfolded figures—so how could we hope to change anything?

To get around memory and to find new ways to jump over it were therefore essential tasks; hence the *Discourse*, its will to "forget," and its presentation of universal method. Method had nothing to do with memory. On the contrary, it provided something like the rules for writing. It acted by the strict organization of good sense, and entirely on its own. Its operation was always the same, ever true, general, rational, and universal (hence, for example, Port-Royal's later linking of its *Logique* and *Grammaire générale et raisonnée*). Method operated not by reiterating discrete terms, not by thinking the variables of locally specific instances, but by repeating the course of reasoning itself, the constants that enabled thinking at all—only afterward to be applied to the objects that it could seek to know and manipulate. Method was the opposite of memory. Perhaps even it was the unexplained "intellectual memory." It required that memory of books be rejected. It required the establishment both of what might be called a "practice of intuition"—leap to clear and distinct primary ideas, opening to "that pure, sudden illumination which characterizes truth . . . at the moment of discovery" (Ortega, *Meditations*, 67)—and of a repeated course along the very process of that discovery, continuous reiteration of the steps of reasoning. It could hope to enlighten the dark of what the Irish poet Eavan Boland has called the place "of fixities and resistances where the inscriptions of a tradition meet the intentions of an individual poet . . . a place of change," with Descartes in the poet's role ("Making," 14a).

Memory, then, was to be avoided in favor of a methodic reason that was always primary. It was to be avoided also by replacing it with (a new sort of) writing. For memory, wrote Descartes,

is often unreliable, and in order not to have to squander one jot of our attention on refreshing it while engaged with other thoughts, human ingenuity has given us that happy invention—the practice of writing. Relying on this as an aid, we shall leave absolutely nothing to memory but put down on paper what we have to retain, thus allowing the imagination to devote itself freely and completely to the ideas immediately before it. (*Regula*, 16; AT, 10:454–5; CSM, 1:67)

Above all, memory had to be avoided because it was the site of false imprints (*Regula*, 16; AT, 10:458; CSM, 1:69).

Descartes' notion of *intuition* was thus essential. So, too, was the methodical course along the stages of reason that followed such intuition. They took one over and then past the entrapments of memory. What Gassendi and others failed to understand, I think, was this precise project of avoiding prejudices, those many divers traces always already imprinted on, bored through, folded into the brain, the project of avoiding the impress of encroached history, history in the bone. They did not grasp that it was never a question of making these vestiges disappear. Descartes agreed that such a project would have been time wasted, because impossible. The body's marks were indelible. What he sought, rather, was to render this physical history inoperative. These opponents did not gather the objective of working through previously known things as if they were *all* categorial prejudices (first Meditation). This, too, was just what we saw familiar mimetic metaphor unable to do, quite differently from a Chinese tradition of convertible categorical correspondences.[14] These opponents did not understand the tactic of jumping over and bypassing imprinted prejudice in order to find some indubitable ground of truth. Still less did they grasp the tactic of setting one prejudice, one seemingly solid memory impression, against its contrary. In all these regards, a sense of history's hold was fundamental—and, thence, of ultimately needing to make some new experience of "history." But the incomprehension led Gassendi to an astonishing and revealing remark: "I add that the idea of making the mind more capable of true perception by turning it towards a false seems to me like that of requiring that one who wished to become white should first be made an Æthiop."[15]

Descartes might have accepted the criticism if Gassendi had written, rather, that it was like requiring people, *in order to perceive themselves* as white, to see themselves first—by contrast—as black. Descartes' tactic aimed at nullifying a prejudice by demanding that one strive to see oneself in a contrary case, that one make the effort to imprint an opposing prejudice in the brain, that one come to *live* it as one has always lived its too readily accepted opposing prejudices. Three hundred years later, Senghor used similar words to describe John Howard Griffin's taking the instance literally, a "white man who, to understand the situation of Negro Americans, blackened his skin with a chemical product," living and working as an African American the better to understand both blackness and his own whiteness, hoping ultimately to help find a third way between such "opposites" ("African Road," 71; his unnamed reference is Griffin's *Black Like Me*). Gassendi did not grasp the intellectual tactic because he refused any concept of a divided idea of concrete being (whence the "become white," *dealbetur*, and the *Æthiopem*).[16] For Descartes, because one could not erase a memory trace long since imprinted, one had to imprint another. That would establish a balance (*æquilibrum faciat*) such that "the mind suspended in this kind of balance could no longer be distracted from a right perception of things."[17] Or as he put it in the *Passions* (I.50), "although nature seems to have joined every movement of the gland [through which the soul acts] to certain of our thoughts from the beginning of our life, yet we may join them to others through habit" (AT, 11:368; CSM, 1:348).

The mind was not thereby freed of prejudices—contrary to what Gassendi thought should be the result—because, as we have already much seen, their marks could not be erased. About these imprints, pores, folds, whatever they might be, everyone agreed. They were permanent. But by inventing "opposition," by creating a new mark to "balance" the old, one might hope to pass between them, drawn neither to Scylla nor to Charybdis. "I have been thrown into such serious doubts by yesterday's Meditation," Descartes thus began the second, "that *I am quite unable to forget them* nor do I see any way of resolving them."[18] Doubts have been pressed, bored, or folded in memory to counter old certainties.

We should see the opening sentence of the second Meditation as voicing a *positive* step on the way to full understanding. Inability to forget doubts balanced indelible prejudices. With the scale set, as it were, Descartes could now start to look for "resolution."

Memory was not erased, and that was not at all how Descartes sought to reply. But having established opposites, he could now use his cartesian "pen" to pass between them, writing those letters so often opposed to physical memory. This gave a different "history," abstract no doubt, more in thought than on the brain—and that much the more certain, rather like the black marks of a pen on the white page, produced at the end of the movement transmitted down the body of the quill, but *not* permanently present in it. Those marks, and their contrast with the white paper, expressed an intuition before, or, rather, between and apart from any imprinted memory. Those "written" marks could write a new identity and a new history, ones that passed between the Scylla and Charybdis of old prejudices and their counters, creating a *third* path. One hundred sixty years later, Goethe exactly iterated Descartes' enabling maneuver for originary thinking as he described efforts to express ideas with clarity and precision. He did so in the context of arguing that misunderstanding occurred because of one's own and one's interlocutor's prior expectations, prejudices about the probable and true, imprinted memories: "since we cannot express precisely what we feel, our mind tries to work with contrasts, to answer the question from two sides, and then tries to grasp the matter in the middle, so to speak" ("On Realism," 75). This new clarity and precision could produce the written letters of a new history: ordered, methodical construction of the actuality of events, recounting them as a unilinear causal sequence running through "the past, the present, and the future," one that could tell the story of humans organizing the objects—"tools"—now set between them and the world, as Rodolfo Kusch has it of a western history whose invention he asserts to have occurred more or less simultaneously with the West's invention of *its* America and to be coincident as well with the growing importance of *la ciudad*, the city—contrasted with the *anti-ciudad* of myth (*América*, 135–42).[19] This last aspect will be important in Chapter 11.

With the possibility of this new written and methodical history confirming a new sense of identity, one understands why Descartes tried to turn body itself into a kind of abstract, an automaton that might also no longer bear the imprint of history as involuntary encroachment—or rather, whose history would not interfere with the operation of universal reason:

I suppose the body to be nothing but a statue or machine made of earth, which God forms with the explicit intention of making it as much as possible like us. Thus God not only gives it externally the colours and shapes of all the parts of our bodies, but also places inside it all the parts required to make it walk, eat, breathe, and indeed to imitate all those of our functions which can be imagined to proceed from matter and to depend solely on the disposition of our organs.

We see clocks, artificial fountains, mills, and other such machines which, although only man-made, have the power to move of their own accord in many different ways. But I am supposing this machine to be made by the hands of God, and so I think you may reasonably think it capable of a greater variety of movements than I could possibly imagine in it, and of exhibiting more artistry than I could possibly ascribe to it. (*Traité de l'homme*; AT, II:120; CSM, 1:99)[20]

For automata were also endlessly repeatable, and by definition not particular, not the subjects of a specific history. They were just the "marvels of mathematics" of which the Jesuit Étienne Binet wrote in 1621 (*Essay*, 481–85). This is not to say that Descartes ever thought humans (or animals) *were* such automata, as Sutton could rightly object (*Philosophy*, 95). It is to say that such automata offered a limit-case of living creatures outside history. Descartes' final achievement would have been to bring back the particular body with its specific passions, produced by particular perceptions, and controlled by a reason and a will, local yet common to all humanity, to put a momentarily estranged mind back into its concrete history and into its physical place in a social whole where one could then dwell in "concord," as he wrote in the preface to the French translation of the *Principes de la philosophie* (AT, 9B:18; CSM, 1:188). He began this in his last completed and published text, the *Passions de l'âme*, and would have pursued it in whatever was to come after—whose remnants are in the correspondence and whose loss More and Gabriel Naudé so bemoaned.[21]

But before he got to this attempt, we may well understand, in view of what I have been saying, why Descartes went so far as to claim to remove himself, as it were, from history—from one particular sort of history, at least. Commenting in his replies to Antoine Arnauld's fourth Objections on the reasons he gave in the sixth Meditation about "the distinction between the mind and the body," but also about how they are "substantially united," Descartes added that he found his own arguments "as strong as any I can remember ever having read."[22] By the next year, 1642, his claim to precedence had become more intractable. Replying to the Jesuit Pierre Bourdin's seventh Objections, he asserted of his proving "the existence of

God and the immortality of the human mind," that "this is something that, so far as I know, has been done by no one before me [*a nemine ante me*]" (AT, 7:549; CSM, 2:375). In 1648, in the *Notae in programma*, he more or less repeated these terms in respect to the primacy of the faculty of thinking for any understanding and definition of the human (AT, 8B:347; CSM, 1:296). There, he named himself the very mark of forgetting: "no one before me [*nemo ante me*]."

Descartes thus situated himself *as* the start of a new history in 1648, the very year of that Treaty of Westphalia so often taken by historians as signaling a new beginning in European political order. One recalls earlier widespread feelings of social decay, *his* deliberate setting of the *Discourse* in the wars leading to this new beginning, the hard problem of discarding history in the very body—under the skin, in the bone—and his profession to deal with matters of science, education, and ethics, not of state. Now, he situated himself anew, too, as he published the psychological analyses of the *Passions de l'âme* and was preparing more elaborate work on ethics and politics—to which his premature death in early 1650 put an untimely end. This pattern of thinking corresponds to techniques exemplified in the *Meditations*. The "degree zero" of radical doubt was repeated in this self-representation, as it had been in the effort to reach the sources and origins of memory by means of a forgetting that he had also radicalized, and then go back even beyond them.

Having reached such points of thought—and there are other examples—Descartes climbed back. In this instance, his justified claim to have shown the unity of mind and body in the sixth Meditation—in metaphysical argument—was put through the probing psychological testing of the *Passions*. There, history and memory were brought back in conjunction with a specially strong claim about universality of reason and particularity of every individual's free will, *libre arbitre*, but common volitions, *volontés*. This is not the place to go into that, but I hope to have shown some aspects of the complexity of the early modern debate about reason and history, will and memory, mind and body; but also what inclined a passage from one sense of history to another, one experience of personal identity to a different one. By the end of this process, perhaps, history having been enabled as the written third path between unexamined and unexaminable prejudices, a different sort or application of memory would be waged. The separation from concrete immediacy of methodical history allows for, indeed appeals to, a use of memory that is not prejudice but the sense of the immediate. This memory is Levi's "curious salvage operations," Saramago's "data and minutiae," which appropriately and *necessarily* put back the local and concrete into ordered history. This immediacy, McWatt writes, creates "an interior space/where memory now blooms/like the smell of time/in long-shut rooms" ("Amakura," *Language*, 14).

Although such memory may be enabled and necessitated by the elaboration of this new history (which Descartes did not make but whose ground he helped typify), that in fact was not the outcome. On the contrary, forgetting this *local* memory's blooming, its data, operations and minutiae, allowed, rather established, as Kusch and others observe, the hegemonic imposition of that history, rationalized as an absolute order separate from the human and world events that fulfill it. That this imposition was as much on the self as on any other was what Fernando Pessoa deplored in *The Keeper of Sheep*: "All this demands serious looking into,/A thorough learning in how to unlearn" (XXIV; *Keeper*, 65), and in even more cartesian terms in a later poem from the same series used as one of this book's epigraphs:

> My thought swims the river only quite slowly,
> Heavily burdened by clothes men have made it wear.
> I try divesting myself of what I've learned,
> I try forgetting the mode of remembering they taught me
> And scrape off the ink they used to paint my senses. . . .
> (Alberto Caeiro, *The Keeper of Sheep*, XLVI;
> "One way or another," Fernando Pessoa, *Poems*, 24–25)

If Descartes never thought you could scrape off *that* ink, he did think you could make a space on which to use a different ink, one inscribing carefully sought data and minutiae. For him, such concrete actualities were essential to knowing how mind was in body, how a person was in the world and how people were to be *concordantly* in society, having found ever "higher" truths and final "perfection in life" in private and public concord (AT, 9B:18, 20; CSM, 1:188, 190).

Yet others did in fact think you could scrape off the ink, that you could forget, that you could create something like an entirely new history. In the previous chapter, we saw Hobbes take verbal definition as a way to escape the chaotic ghosts raised by metaphor. By this process of definition—or redefinition—of the nature and experience of political authority, he intended to destroy precedent historical memory and establish a quite new scientific civic arena. The very *"fiat"* that he named as establishing the covenant that founded civil society was itself a precise rejection of historical memory, a moment whose only analog, Hobbes insisted, was the divine *Fiat* recorded in *Genesis* as establishing the world itself: creating human history "out of" and in opposition to god's eternity (Reiss, *Discourse*, 136, 222; *Meaning*, 147–48; *Uncertainty*, 249, 204–50 *passim*). Gordon Hull has argued convincingly that "modern political philosophy" has been predicated since its founding on its *originary* nature and on the originary nature of the state it depicts. Between Hobbes and Hegel, he shows, western political thought involved a "strenuous art of forgetting" whose dismantling Marx undertook ("Hobbes," 83–84, 163–64; cf., for Hobbes and Hegel, Reiss, *Meaning*, 327–28).

We still live these dilemmas, and I end this chapter with five authors from diverse lands, picking up on where we began. For I want to insist on how alive these issues are in the very forms this exploration has been trying to propose. The first involves a commentary on a closer difficulty of reason and history, in terms Descartes would surely have understood, and whose witty irony he would doubtless have approved and appreciated. Their purport and drift still remain those of Descartes, if not of later so-called cartesians.

In spring 1990, at a cultural congress in Berlin five months after the fall of its wall, the Dutch novelist, essayist, and travel writer Cees Nooteboom contemplated the aristocratic German president Richard von Weizsäcker:

and I meditated upon the tenacity of the human body. The president's seems at once solid and fragile, I find it hard to imagine that this same body already sheltered its soul when both of them were before Leningrad in 1943. Not that I know exactly what his soul is, but it must be what I see radiating through his cold and luminous eyes when I come near him a bit later. Tenacity. I find no better word: I mean the body as bearer of memory, of experience, this body that with its memories of war, of its regiment nineteen of whose officers were put to death after the attempt on Hitler and almost all of whose other ranks perished, has gone on living in a single unbroken line, right up to this present moment that finds him here, in this room destroyed back then, with a glass of champagne in his hand, smiling, chatting, and listening. (*Année*, 200–201)

This is certainly a very different idea of body and soul, of memory and reason, from what was depicted and elaborated by Dürer, Rabelais, Bruegel, Huarte, Montaigne, Sabuco, or Burton. It is not so different from what Descartes was engaging, despite doomsayers of post-Enlightenment nostalgias and those who yearn to "return," they profess, to a simpler time of healthy holism. It is the body as concrete data manifesting, buttressing, and even confirming (here) the actuality of a history whose order the rational "soul" knows. This idea seeks, rather—just so—to "reconcile," as Boland writes, "element to argument," thing to thought ("Water Clock"). When she elsewhere writes of the perplexing wonder of *seeing* "with the body," it is only inside the sensibilities, the structures of feeling created, made, by *this* debate that we can understand her idea.

Like Nooteboom and Pessoa, Boland echoes Descartes—*this* Descartes. And it matters that she links just the same problems. First she recalls how, aging: "I saw [my children] with my body. And the sight of my body was clear and different and intense." Then she observes another level of understanding, aware of that body as itself in history, a process. "What was seen by it was both made clear and more ominous because I knew I could not see it that way forever" ("Making," 16b).[23] Descartes had in fact expressed an issue of memory in just these terms, remarking in a letter to "Hyperaspistes" of August 1641 how the soul/mind was at first so closely joined to the body, so "intermingled with the body" that it could be said actually to "*perceive*" directly or feel "the ideas of pain, pleasure, heat, cold and other similar ideas which arise from its union" (AT, 3:424; CSM, 3:190). It is almost as if Boland were taking Descartes' sense of the child growing into a (male?) adult and *away from* a particular sort of memory to understand her experience as a mother growing away from her child in terms drawing directly on that earlier recounting. I, it, mind, body, history and heritage, change and stability, tradition, memory, and reason remain the imbricated terms of sense and understanding. So they are in Harris' early novels and recent commentary, in Marshall's story, and in the working of so many others.

The body and the wisdom of history did not disappear, as if some immune system had disfunctioned to let in Lévi-Strauss's and others' "virus." They had been reconfigured. A vital "adventure in perception" had occurred (Boland, "Making," 16b). I stress "vital." For while Descartes assuredly did divide mind and body, I have been arguing that he did so only as one of what I elsewhere call his "passage techniques," interim strategies enabling him to get from the known to the new (in my "Descartes," "Neo-Aristotle," and "Revising," for example). The adventure was vital because it aimed to reset mind in body, so that a different kind of analysis and new sense of the human in the world would be enabled. It aimed first to get beyond a history that *held* us within its "accumulation of past events[, its] sum total of elements so small that they could no longer be measured," as Nooteboom has put it elsewhere, using thoughts again strikingly like those we have seen in Descartes (*Désir*, 138). It sought, second, to get by memory, to reinvent an origin that might then use memory and its now-measured sums to create something new. Distancing history into reason, it could make memory into Levi's and Saramago's concrete minutiae, McWatt's blooming, and Philip's particular cultural recall eventually usable to sap such history's universality of embrace and imposition. Doing so, third, it could rebuild and reform what it had temporarily divided.

Descartes died before completing the adventure. Cartesianism thought it closed and adopted the provisions of this incomplete philosophical project as if it were finished. Other subsequent practice and thinking assumed so too. Cartesianism's Enlightened descendents and avatars fell into the "imaginative poverty" that "consists in learning codes by heart," as Unamuno somewhere has it (Carpentier, prologue to *Kingdom*, x–xi). Kane's *L'aventure ambiguë* is, to a degree, about that identity-making system set up as a "parsimonious" science that is "a triumph of the surface, a proliferation of the surface. It makes you masters of the external, but at the same time it exiles you there, more and more" (90; *Ambiguous*, 78). The West, Diallo's father continues, "sets up science against this invading chaos, sets it up like a barricade" (*Aventure*, 91; *Ambiguous*, 79; cf. Mazrui, *Trial*, 69). This startlingly resembles Kusch's idea of history as instrumentalized objects lying between humans and the world. It is one more mark of scission, accumulating, it is said, surface "accidents." Indeed, the "accident" that was the supposed cartesian twist in the West's trajectory was itself product of a break with the world that marked a fundamental difference from Diallobé culture, whose simplest peasant could not believe in such an "accidental" world (126, 87; 113, 75) Those this "science" colonizes, we saw Harris decry, it either "turns into hybrids . . . filled with shame" (125; 113) or it makes them an actual colonized mind, cloned into a western image. What, wonders Samba Diallo in Paris on receiving a letter from his father recalling his communal obligations, have the problems of his people, the Diallobé, to do with him? "After all, I am only myself. I have only me" (138; 126). Separated from his embedding in a community and in those powers of which we earlier saw Achebe speak, "[h]ere, now," says Diallo, "the world is silent, and I no longer resonate. I am like a broken balafong, a dead musical instrument" (163; 150). In the end, he is killed exactly because he has become a stranger to his own world.

Kane's novel recounts the agony of an imposed conflict between cultures, one that is destructive precisely because the oppressor does not want—or is unable—to listen to the voices of the oppressed, refuses to hear them not as the phantom of his struggles but as an authentic home of their own. But the "adventure" is also "ambiguous." Kane, too, recognizes that whatever system Descartes may have been seeking, this reductive travesty was surely not it (and even that, we saw Césaire imply in *Saison*, was not necessarily wholly deforming, reworked by its victim). Here, it may be, the victim listens (we saw Baldwin and Mphahlele observe in my Introduction) as the victimizer does not. Meditating one night before he has left for Europe, Diallo contemplates the nature of one's absorption in community and wider powers:

> To believe . . . is to recognize one's will as a fragment of divine will. Therefore, activity, creature of the will, is creature of God. At this moment, his thought brought back to memory another recollection, a page from Descartes. Where had he read that? In the *Méditations métaphysiques*, perhaps. He no longer remembered. He only recalled the French thinker's thought: the relation between God and man is first of all a relation between will and will. Can there be a more intimate relation?
>
> So, he said to himself, the thinkers are in agreement. Descartes, like the teacher of the Diallobé, like my father, have all experienced the irreducible force of this idea. (*Aventure*, 116; *Ambiguous*, 103–4)

The relation between god and human is also a fortiori a relation between human and human. An analogous case is made more directly philosophically by Nkrumah who, even while criticizing Descartes' solipsism and "duality" (*Consciencism*, 16–18, 85–87), yet affirms that aspects of these very flaws are available to different cultures for different ends. Because in Descartes' philosophy "we all share public objective truths, and pursue them," so "support is given to co-operative socialism." Indeed, not only did ascertaining of truths have to be cooperative, but ignorance demanded no less collective attention to "supporting the stability and order of society." What Nkrumah calls the "*social contention*" of Descartes' philosophy was its "most radical break in a social sense from the hegemony of the Church and her aristocratic allies," by creating an "egalitarian philosophy . . . with its removal of the region of truth from mystic revelation to mathematical and public demonstration." This created a conflict which led, Nkrumah asserts, to the Revolution (*Consciencism*, 52–53). One may disagree with details of this analysis, but seeing Descartes in *his* own history lets Nkrumah emphasize some of the real ambiguities of Descartes' analyses and use them for the actual purposes of a different historical place and time. And Descartes *did* indeed urge that his entire science and philosophy aimed to enable people to live *together* concordantly. To be sure, to return to Kane, once Diallo is in modern "cartesian" Paris, the full force of colonizing culture overwhelms such ambiguities (even though, I have suggested, Diallo's analysis was in fact a most accurate echo of what Descartes wrote). Perhaps its violence demanded their excision. Perhaps instrumentality required that complex thought be reduced to parody.

But perhaps, too, the trajectory of a conquering western history required that Descartes' remnants be read according to that *history's* legitimating needs, not according to those remnants' own internal logic and elaboration. So the patterns of these last were disfigured into just *one* of the forms of history they propounded. No matter. The codes so made fixed the evermore widespread terms of future understanding. Identity was established not as a fragment of God or community, but as the subject possessor of instrumental agency. Nor was it embedded in history felt as a difficult *presence* to be constantly negotiated. That agent subject was itself turned into a maker of history, of a *lettered, written*, and methodical history that ran from simple to complex (the "primitive" to the "civilized"), as the Method set out, from cause through effects, from maker to made. That these establishments were not Descartes' (not, at least, his final word) is in some sense indifferent. Practically and historically, we can do nothing about it. Waters have long since flowed under myriad bridges. Yet the misunderstanding matters because we may now be returning to the point where the adventure was left. We are doing so under the pressure of vital political, social, and historical conflicts and tensions which call for "a contestatory practice [that] demands the disfiguration of those patterns of history that have served the relations of dominance" (Prakash, 382). Fanon, responding to this pressure sees a solution exactly in these terms of identity and history, both being transformed by the weight of a *different* history—even a different *kind* of history.

He writes of how the colonized indigenous intellectual, accepting the "cogency" of "the essential qualities of the West"—especially the centrality of the individualism we have just been seeing—became "a vigilant sentinel ready to defend the Greco-Roman pedestal" (like Diallo, no doubt). But Fanon adds how, "during the struggle for liberation, at the moment that the native intellectual comes into touch again with his people, this artificial sentinel is turned to dust. All the Mediterranean values—the triumph of the human individual, of clarity, and of beauty—become lifeless, colorless knickknacks. . . . Individualism is the first to disappear," because when the native intellectual returns to the people, "the idea of a society of individuals where each person shuts himself up in his own subjectivity, and whose only wealth is individual thought" can only be seen to be inactual, a fragment of a different story. The intellectual then learns "a different vocabulary," one that comes from discovering "the substance of village assemblies, the cohesion of people's committees, and the extraordinary fruitfulness of local meetings and groupments. Henceforward, the interests of one will be the interests of all, for in concrete fact *everyone* will be discovered by the troops, *everyone* will be massacred—or *everyone* will be saved" (Fanon, *Wretched*, 46–47).

Fanon's point is not simply that individualist values erode under the pressure of the violent crisis of liberation. Like Cabral, he argues that westernized, mind-colonized intellectuals are thereby put permanently back in touch with different values and the vocabularies that express them: among others the experience, idea, and vocabulary of a communal sense of personhood, one in which subjective individualism—if it plays any part at all—is just one aspect of person-in-community (see too the introduction to my *Mirages*). Nkrumah dug this very thought out of Descartes himself. This occurs, too, because these intellectuals are forcibly set in a different history, one that comes under new—or renewed—pressures from local tradition. The weight of these pressures is why I have wanted to show some of the elements behind and within the earlier European reconfiguration, whose result all these writers take principally to characterize particular elements of the oppressing, colonizing culture and the specific forms of suffering and victimization they produced. The vital political, social, and historical conflicts and tensions that necessitated this reconfiguration, and their contexts, are now much forgotten, but they were central to debates and practices that gave our (western) modernity. To recover these (beyond so-called cartesianism or a thinking that runs from Hobbes through Hegel and perhaps beyond) may be, as I say, to have a hope of recovering the adventure where it was left.

That forgetfulness (unlike Descartes' or that inherent in "ahistorical" cultures, according to Nandy, coming surely not from art but utility) allows or produces other simplifications. Not the least of them is the belief in a nostalgic return. Only those same reified codes permit such belief, providing the "other" or "Other" of so much western indulgence. Harris' "folk" and Fanon's "people"—or rather the relations and conditions in which they engage and are engaged—are not one with Bruegel's crowds, nor is Harris' "solitariness of Soul" and spirituality-with-sensuous-direction or Fanon's indigenous intellectual. They belong in quite different situations and circumstances. Recalling the elements, contexts, and stakes of the early modern debate replaces lost threads on a loom whose shuttle is now ours to handle. It may also enable us to change the patterns. But efforts to elaborate on *that* hope must await later chapters. What I wish to do in the next is take a closer look at some aspects of that (noncartesian) individual subject which for so many thinkers from a wide variety of different cultures has indeed been one of the major ways of colonizing their cultures and their minds. Above all, I want to show how that subject and its "science" are related and indebted to particular Enlightened science and philosophy and woven into a specific polity, one contained in the psychoanalysis I will be examining, Nandy observes, as "the Enlightenment vision of a desirable society," whatever Freud's own "insecurities and ambivalences" in this regard (*Savage*, 136).

6

Dreams of Science, Science of Dreams:
Selves and Reasons

In autumn 1895, Freud for the first time wrote out his idea for a psychology able to claim a place among the *natural sciences*: "The intention is to furnish a psychology that shall be a natural science: that is, to represent psychical processes as quantitatively determinate states of specifiable material particles, thus making those processes perspicuous and free from contradiction" ("Project for a Scientific Psychology," *Standard Edition* [hereafter SE], 1:295). Here he asserted two principles: firstly, that a psychology desiring to be scientific had to adopt the experimental, "objective," and instrumental methods of the "hard" natural sciences familiar now for some two centuries or more; and secondly, that such a science "represents" what he called "psychical processes," those of the "psyche" making itself and its way in a world, as composed of elements able to be studied "quantitatively" and *as if* they were "states," stable moments in psychical processes that were actually never *not* in motion. Freud clearly said then that a psychological science was *a way of understanding* these processes, ultimately so that one could intervene in them. He was not proposing that psychology give "transparent" knowledge of objects whose existence was separable from and precedent to the science taking them over. That the states explored by such a science were "perspicuous and free from contradiction" would be proven only by that science's ability to change and direct them into other paths—that is, to develop a technique, a *practice*. This has been standard from Galileo and Bacon to Louis Althusser :

If psychoanalysis is certainly a science, since it is the science of a specific object, it is also a science according to the structure of every science; possessing a *theory* and a *technique* (method) which allows knowledge and transformation of its object via a specific *practice*. As in every authentic established science, practice is not its absolute, but a theoretically subordinate moment: the one when theory turned method (technique) makes theoretical (knowledge) or practical (the cure) contact with its specific object (the unconscious). (Althusser, "Freud et Lacan," *Positions*, 15)

Every science is first of all the establishing of a certain conceptual order. While this order can subsequently be readjusted to make room for new information, it can never fundamentally challenge its underlying ground without giving notice of its limits and so showing its *constructed* nature and casting out all claim to transparency and "objectivity." The aim of this chapter is to offer elements basic to the "scientific" ground of psychoanalysis—the science of the self—and to suggest its limits, whether or not the "Project" itself was "abandoned" as an "unfortunate attempt" (Bouveresse, *Wittgenstein*, 88). For it is of course the case that even excluding some of Freud's own writings, people have written tirelessly on the scientific status of psychoanalysis and still do. The bibliography is vast. But although the epistemological status of psychoanalysis is certainly at issue in what follows, it is so only as an aspect of its place in the "epistemic" whole of modern western culture. *That* interests me not only because unpacking this "place" can tell us a lot about the nature of western "scientific" discourse in general (partly *because* of its marginal scientific status) and about matters of subject, self, identity, history, and more that earlier chapters have been exploring, but also because psychoanalysis wants to be, as Ricoeur observes, a global "interpretation of culture" (*Freud*, xii). No doubt in part for this reason, literary and cultural critics of the past half century have made and continue to make massive use of psychoanalytical concepts and categories, from Mannoni and Fanon to Nandy and Antonio Benítez-Rojo. I name them because I argue that psychoanalysis is in fact part of and belongs in a particular western history and that to transport its categories elsewhere, into cultural realities different in place and/or time, at best requires that they first be problematized, at worst twists those realities into shapes found (perhaps) only in and anyway determined by the West.[1]

Following a path frayed by Foucault, I have proposed that during the 150 years separating Machiavelli and Hobbes, a particular "discursive practice" was established in the West that became dominant by the mid-seventeenth century and stays largely so still today, although it began to be seriously questioned by the end of the nineteenth (Reiss, *Discourse* and *Meaning*). I have called this discursive practice by the descriptive if ugly name of *analytico-referential*. On the one hand, its order (when *properly* used) was supposed that of right reason *and* of the mechanics of the material world. On the other, the elements (signs) composing it were taken to express an adequate *grasp* of real objects "external" to it (languages besides English show that the conceptual *grasping* is taken literally: French con*cevoir*, Latin con*cipere←capere*, German be*greifen←greifen*, all meaning to seize, grip, capture). So a well-written text and a well-ordered reasoning provided an exact and correct representation *and* analysis of what they referred to. The *cogito-ergo-sum* could easily be seen as the exemplary formal statement of this claim: reason—mediating semiotic system—material world. Its principal metaphors were that of the telescope: eye—instrument—world; and the voyage: port of departure—sea journey—land claimed as the explorer's legitimate possession (for more on this, see my *Discourse*, 25, 31, "Cartesian Discourse," and "Espaces").

The telescope metaphor, dramatically presented in 1610 in Galileo's *Sidereus nuncius* with its powerful instrumental praxis, preceded Descartes' publication of its formal pendant by a generation. And in another generation, in his baroque poetics entitled *Il cannocchiale aristotelico* (1654), Tesauro could invert the meaning of Galileo's telescope to assert not that it was an exact metaphor of the only "legitimate" human reason but that metaphor as an "aristotelian telescope" *was* reason: such reason did not grasp the real; it "played" it by way especially of two processes, *perspicacia* and *versibilità*. The first of these allowed reason, starting from one place or element, to grasp all kinds of details and events, "penetrat[ing] the farthest and most minute circumstances of every subject"; the second united, composed, bound, and disbound one process with/from others: comparing "all these circumstances among themselves and with the subject, it connects and separates them, increases or diminishes them, derives one from another, outlines one with another or with marvellous dexterity puts one in place of another as the juggler does his stones" (*Cannocchiale aristotelico*, edited by Buck, 51). The first, allowing one element to display a whole complex network, worked by *condensation* or synecdoche, the second, permitting relays from process to process, acted as a *displacement* of events/circumstances subject to reason (which *were*, here, reason). So only fifty years later, the telescope metaphor was powerful enough to withstand being stood on its head. No doubt for that reason, this poetic treatise, as I mentioned in Chapter 4, was rapidly relegated to the ranks of the unread—for three centuries. Its disappearance corresponded to the hegemony of the analytico-referential (*Discourse*, 26–27). Not by chance do "condensation" and "displacement" become principal interpretive devices in psychoanalysis—no directly conscious historical reference or connection but result of the analytico-referential way of thinking.

Two and a half centuries later, in 1892, wanting to set a wavering science on surer logical and semiotic ground, Gottlob Frege returned to the telescope metaphor, at once demystifying and reviving it. He quite exactly repeated its earlier establishment, emphasizing now that meaning, communication, and epistemological reason were in question:

The meaning [*Bedeutung*] of a proper name is the object itself which we designate by using it; the idea [*Vorstellung*] which we have in that case is wholly subjective; in between lies the sense [*Sinn*], which is indeed no longer subjective like the idea, but is yet not the object itself. The following analogy will perhaps clarify these relationships. Somebody observes the Moon through a telescope. I compare the Moon itself to the meaning; it is the object of the observation, mediated by the real image projected by the object glass in the interior of the telescope, and by the retinal image of the observer. The former I compare to the sense, the latter is like the idea or experience. The optical image in the telescope is indeed one-sided and dependent upon the standpoint of observation; but it is still objective, inasmuch as it can be used by several observers. ("On Sense," 60)

In this sense, the image inside the instrument "lasts." Whoever looks at the image sees it in the same way and with the same form as long as the mediating instrument is present to retain it, so to say, as a trace, a "memory." Frege made explicit here that the metaphor names a certain mode of signifying, "regime of meaning," or discursive order even as he sought to reaffirm its force (an effort, with whose limits, I have explored at greater length in *Uncertainty*, 19–55).

Eight years later, five years after the "Project" had announced the need for a scientific psychology, Freud published what has come to be considered a scientific classic and foundation text of psychoanalysis, *The Interpretation of Dreams* (1900–1901). Here he used the telescope not only to explain the psychology of dreams but to make his reader *know* how the mind is tied to the external world. The metaphor, I am evidently urging, is not anodyne; it asserts a set of claims about supposedly universal forms of human knowledge and thought, and, we shall see, of moral and political claim. Ernst Kris, observing the unique influence of a single researcher in this one science (of psychoanalysis), noted a peculiar consequence: "terminology and constructs reflect ideas and connotations dominant in Freud's formative years, i.e. in the 1870s and 1880s." In fact—as is surely always the case?—one needs to go much further back than his formative years to account for elements of Freud's science, but Kris and others nonetheless find that its being bound to a certain scientific tradition is irrelevant, because its framework, terminology, and development occurred in an entirely new context ("Nature," 240–41; cf. Assoun, *Introduction*). Even were this the case, the argument would be invalid. The context is itself perforce grounded in a long past. And because psychoanalysis became for our age a scientific practice and theory in many ways exemplary, and stays so even if its *scientific* nature is now doubted, it is useful to know how far its founding texts repeated the particular history of the dominant analytico-referential. At the same time, by adopting and questioning previously "occulted" elements, these texts reveal certain limits of wider praxes and thought. Doing this, they sap their own and other claims to the *human* universality of their object (the self), taking "too quickly for a reality of history," as de Certeau says, "what is only the coherence of historiographical discourse, and for an order in the sequence of facts what is only the order postulated or set down by his thought" (*Écriture*, 299–300).

In 1892, Frege had used the telescope metaphor to clarify how a given regime of meaning worked. In 1900, Freud recomposed it to represent the real relation between the mind (or psyche) and the world, the former being a "reflex apparatus." At least in part, the telescope explained a concrete reality, those "quantitatively determinate states of specifiable material particles" of which he wrote in the "Project" and which could be understood as "places" in the instrument called the "psyche." This psyche was a concrete reality not as a fixed and singular reality but insofar as it could be understood as a real, actualized "psychical process," a true functioning of the mind:

Accordingly, we will picture the mental apparatus as a compound instrument, to the components of which we will give the name of "agencies" [*Instanzen*], or (for the sake of greater clarity) "systems" [*Systeme*]. It is to be anticipated, in the next place, that these systems may perhaps stand in a regular spatial relation to one another, in the same kind of way in which the various systems of lenses in a telescope are arranged behind one another [*etwa wie die verschiedenen Linsensysteme des Fernrohres hintereinanderstehen*]. Strictly speaking, there is no need for the hypothesis that the psychical systems are actually arranged in a *spatial* order. It would be sufficient if a fixed order were established by the fact that in a given psychical process the excitation passes through the systems in a particular temporal sequence. (SE, 5:536–37; *Traumdeutung*, 2:513)

Freud's metaphor was precise. The verb *hintereinanderstehen* indicated the determinate temporal order in exact spatial terms: the several lens systems stood one behind another. It is revealing that Freud immediately added that it was not essential that the spatial order be "true": this "ambiguity" of space–time relation would intervene constantly between his use of visual image (telescope, microscope, mirror) and that of writing. Many recent writers have argued that there was a "passage" in Freud's work from the visual to the linguistic (thus placing Lacan, for example, in a linear history that would be Freud's own). I find this incorrect; rather do the two constantly play against one another, just as they did already in Descartes. This play lets Freud articulate temporal process and spatial instrument on one another—or, as he wrote a little earlier, set his hypothesis simultaneously "upon the structure of the apparatus of the mind and upon the play of forces operating in it" (SE, 5:511). Here Freud's science reacts to, or at least repeats, a problem, even a contradiction, that worried the analytico-referential from its inception, with its model in science as an expansive process in constant movement but its *final* goal in complete and static knowledge. Descartes offered a method whose efficacity depended on its expansive linear repetitivity but which would give complete knowledge, he said, in a few centuries (AT, 9B:20; CSM, 1:189). Bacon did the same when he remarked that "the investigation of nature and of all sciences will be the work of a few years" (*Description*, 356). Analytico-referential discourse and the science that became its model was thus presented as a *process* denied by the static ideal that was its goal. In this regard, it is worth emphasizing that it was thermodynamics, in particular its model articulating process and entropy together, that led thinkers in the nineteenth century to question the classical model of science, just as a bit later, tellings of light as undular and particulate would allow newly efficacious "complementary" descriptions of material actuality and a new articulation of space–time would hold out hopes for a new ordering of signs (of world and mind).

This effort to overcome what Freud and the tradition saw as opposition between stasis and process partly justifies what many have noted as Freud's "difficulty in constructing a stable and satisfying representation of the nature of the mind," due to what Jacques Bouveresse explains as "the frequent oscillation and constant tension between two analogies or paradigms, one of which, the mechanical, seems to correspond to what must be an impersonal, scientific approach to the phenomena in question, while the other, the anthropomorphic, regularly leads him into the realm of what [Ludwig] Wittgenstein calls mythology" (*Wittgenstein*, 38). The difficulty was not Freud's alone, and one might rather say that the oscillation signaled in fact his readiness to grapple with the divisions endemic to the western mind of which we have already seen so much: process and stasis, time and space would be more such. Then one might ask with Maryse Condé (or André Breton or Césaire) whether the "stunning image is born not from a comparison but from bringing together two remote realities" (Condé, "Tracés," 149). Constantly reused, the telescope was always there for just that: image, producer of images, commentary on the making of images.

The psychical apparatus Freud proposed in the above-cited passage of the *Traumdeutung* was set in action by a "perception" (stimulus) whose effects ran through a series of systems, on some of which "memory traces" were deposited, to arrive at a motor stage where a psychical or mental action resulted:

All our psychical activity starts from stimuli (whether internal or external) and ends in innervations.[2] Accordingly we shall ascribe a sensory and a motor end to the apparatus. At the sensory end there lies a system which receives perceptions; at the motor end there lies another, which opens the gateway to motor activity. Psychical processes advance in general from the perceptual end to the motor end. (SE, 5:537)

The force of the telescope metaphor can easily be seen, although the presence of "memory traces" implies complications (explored especially by Derrida and Lacan and already at issue in Frege's signifying model) that tie this metaphor to the widespread one of the mind as a camera. They also of course tie it further to a tradition going back to the Descartes explored in Chapter 5.

Freud's first actual use of the metaphor seems to be the one quoted before. But the notion of the "dream image" (*Traumbild* as *reflection* of experience retained in memory) resulting from this apparatus always implied something like it. In 1894, Freud's collaborator Josef Breuer had offered such a model in a note to which Freud still referred a quarter century later. In their joint *Studies on Hysteria*, again facing issues central to Descartes' deliberations, Breuer specified:

This perceptual apparatus, including the sensory areas of the cortex, must be different from the organ which stores up and reproduces sense-impressions in the form of mnemic images. For the basic essential of the function of the perceptual apparatus is that its *status quo ante* should be capable of being restored with the greatest possible rapidity; otherwise no proper further perception could take place. The essential of memory, on the other hand, is that no restoration should occur but that every perception should create images that are permanent. It is impossible for one and the same organ to fulfil these two contradictory conditions. The mirror of a reflecting telescope cannot at the same time be a photographic plate. (SE, 2:188–89 n. 1)

One notes here that Breuer's clear separation of movement and fixity as contradictory echoed the opposition between process and stasis (the problem that Descartes sought to resolve). Freud took it up in the second and third parts of his 1895 "Project," proposing the existence of two different types of material particles that he called "neurons": ones that let perceptual excitations pass and others that blocked them and held a memory trace (SE, 1:297–302). He developed the distinction a year later in a letter to Wilhelm Fliess (SE, 1:233–37, December 6, 1896). In 1920, in the fourth part of *Beyond the Pleasure Principle*, he still stressed that he grounded his theory of memory traces on Breuer's ideas (SE, 18:25 ff.). Nonetheless, from the time of the *Interpretation of Dreams* the metaphors of telescope (or microscope) and camera were fused, articulated as a single process.

Establishment of the visual metaphor was accompanied, even preceded, by use of a more general mechanistic model to describe the same "mental" or "psychical" apparatus (*seelischer* or *psychischer Apparat*). In the "Project," Freud wrote: "In the first place there is no question but that the external world is the origin of all major quantities of energy, since, according to the discoveries of physics, it consists of powerful masses which are in violent motion and which transmit their motion" (SE, 1:304). It goes without saying that this motion is transmitted to and through the psychical receptor system: the telescope of 1900. The system then continues the transmission of energy, sometimes with interruptions (caused by "contact barriers" corresponding to the lenses), sometimes more easily. At the time of the instauration marked by the names of Galileo, Bacon, and Descartes, Hobbes had also equated mass and motion in the material world both with the functioning of the individual and with the organization of humans into society; the continual war of the state of nature matching the "conflictual" motion of substances in nature, civil society matching a falling into stability and stasis. This proximity of hobbesian and freudian concepts is neither idle nor, we shall see, coincidence.

Freud never dropped the optical model for thinking his new science. The telescope is less metaphor than identification of an ordered system permitting "psychology to take its place as a natural science like any other" and producing a phenomenal knowledge entirely like that achieved "by chemistry or physics" (SE, 23:158). This remark comes not from an early work but from the penultimate writing of his life, the 1938 *Outline of Psychoanalysis*. He asserts:

We know two kinds of things about what we call our psyche (or mental life): firstly, its bodily organ and scene of action, the brain (or nervous system) and, on the other hand, our acts of consciousness, which are immediate data and cannot be further explained by any sort of description. Everything that lies between is unknown to us, and the data do not include any direct relation between these two terminal points of our knowledge. If it existed, it would at most afford an exact localization of the process of consciousness and would give us no help toward understanding them.

These sentences lead to a restatement of what Freud calls his two fundamental hypotheses. One perceives the psyche or mental life in terms of "localization," as "the function of an apparatus to which we ascribe the characteristics of being extended in space and of being made up of several portions—which we imagine, that is, as resembling a telescope or microscope or something of the kind." The model is more than an "imaginary" conceptual aid: "the consistent working-out of a conception such as this is a scientific novelty" (SE, 23:144–45). It isn't, of course. The working-out and instauration of exactly this model was the very foundation of the analytico-referential, whether in Galileo or Descartes as a mechanistic conceptualization or in Frege as a semiotic one.

Freud's other hypothesis, naturally enough, concerns not stable localization but psychical dynamism: this apparatus and its functioning are just what are to be called the "unconscious." It is this very view, he insists, that enables psychology to become "a natural science like any other." For consciousness as one experiences it could only consist of "broken sequences," whereas the psychology of the unconscious aims at the "laws" beneath these sequences and so "obeyed" by the apparatus itself. So this psychology is able to "follow [the] mutual relations and interdependences [of unconscious processes] over long stretches—in short, to arrive at what is described as an 'understanding' of the field of natural phenomena in question." The only difficulty then is that while "every science is based on observations and experiences arrived at through the medium of our psychical apparatus ... *our* science has as its subject that apparatus itself" (SE, 23:158–59). This does not prevent him from asserting in *The Future of an Illusion* that psychoanalysis is "an impartial instrument, like the infinitesimal calculus, as it were," a comparison also not without interest, since calculus developed strictly within the analytico-referential (SE, 21:36).

The dilemma that Freud emphasized in the relation between the analyzing psyche and the analyzed remained:

A further difficulty results from the fact that psychoanalytic theory has to deal with the relation between observer and observed in the analytic situation. . . . The field of observation includes not only the patient, but also the observer who interacts with the former. . . . The interactions of analyst and analysand are accounted for in theories of transference and countertransference. (Hartmann, 22–23)

Heinz Hartmann goes on to assert that this is a source of error which nonetheless is known and defeated. But the difficulty is hardly so simple, because at issue is not just the scientific status of psychoanalytic theory and practice but the very experience of the "cure" (more important for an Anglo-American–type psychology of the self than for, say, a lacanian one), which becomes by definition "double"—and what then can be the analyst's privileged status? The series of lacanian splits (from more traditional practitioners) occurred in part over this issue of the "play" between a process involving at once instrument and "object"—at once the analyst's and the analysand's "selves" *and* the psychoanalytic session itself—and the problem of the "paternal" status of the scientific speaking subject represented by the analyst (Turkle, 12, 120–21, 128–29, 154, 210–24).[3] An analogous problem had been raised almost simultaneously in quantum mechanical enquiry. Werner Heisenberg and Niels Bohr in particular were exploring the philosophical and scientific consequences of the input of the experimental instrument of knowledge into the observation, experiment, and knowledge it enabled (cf. Reiss, *Uncertainty*, 114– 27).

Cesare Cremonini had refused to look through Galileo's telescope, not because he did not want to believe what his friend claimed to see but because he did not see how one could measure the instrument's distortions. He did not understand how to adjust to one another the instrument's action, the truth value of the observation it produced, and the object observed (a difficulty Galileo often acknowledged). Considerably nearer to

Freud, Hegel had raised the issue in terms to which one has to wonder whether Frege—and then Freud, whatever he may have said—was not directly responding. Writing precisely of the *limits* of philosophy and specifically of its tool of cognition [*Erkennen*], in the introduction to the *Phenomenology of Spirit* (1807), Hegel commented:

For, if cognition is the instrument for getting hold of absolute being, it is obvious that the use of an instrument [*eines Werkzeugs*] on a thing does not let it be what it is for itself, but rather sets out to reshape and alter it. If, on the other hand, cognition is not an instrument of our activity but a more or less passive medium through which the light of truth reaches us, then again we do not receive the truth as it is in itself, but only as it exists through and in this medium. (46; *Phänomenologie*, 53)

Hegel observed that in both cases cognition falsified its aim, since it gave not the truth but the instrument's alteration of it. One would think, he continued, that "this evil could be remedied through an acquaintance with the way in which the *instrument* works," enabling one to eliminate whatever was "due to the instrument, and thus get the truth in its purity." But if we removed the reshaping, we could only have whatever we had before the instrument's intervention—Cremonini's aristotelian moon, for example.

On the other hand, if some kind of instrumental transparency were taken to hold, so that "the Absolute is supposed merely to be brought nearer to us through this instrument . . . , it would surely laugh our little ruse to scorn, if it were not with us in and for itself, all along, of its own volition." Our ruse would be that of pretending to make a cognitive effort which was "something quite different from creating a merely immediate and therefore effortless relationship." Lastly, he adds, setting aside correction of the instrument or suppositions of its transparency, if we think that "by testing cognition, which we conceive of as a *medium*, we get to know the law of its refraction, it is again useless to subtract this from the end result. For it is not the refraction of the ray, but the ray itself whereby the truth reaches us, that is cognition; and if this were removed, all that would be indicated would be a pure direction or a blank space" (46–47; *Phänomenologie*, 53–54). Hegel seems here to be wholly questioning the efficacy of the telescope metaphor, asserting that at least as far as knowledge of "*des absoluten Wesens*," of the Absolute, is concerned, it must be an immediate apprehension. Since the Absolute was the ground of all right knowing and doing, this may be no small reason why Freud criticized Hegel (much as Wittgenstein would him) in *New Introductory Lectures on*

Psycho-analysis as having given birth to practice not of a scientific political order but of a new religion and to theory as merely "a precipitate of the obscure Hegelian philosophy" (SE, 21:180, 177). Nonetheless, Hegel's use of the telescope to explore how the mind functions (here, as to its processes of knowing) quite clearly shares both its terminology and its dilemmas with Freud's later adoption of it.

Fliess raised Cremonini's and Hegel's dilemma at the start of his friend's psychoanalytical researches, apropos, exactly, of *The Interpretation of Dreams*. In a note to that work's Chapter 6, Freud remarked,

The first reader and critic of this book—and his successors are likely to follow his example—protested that "the dreamer seems to be too ingenious and amusing." This is quite true so long as it refers only to the dreamer; it would only be an objection if it were to be extended to the dream-interpreter. (SE, 4:297–98 n. 1)

Since interpretation is always involved, this was hardly an answer, and Freud had admitted as much in an only slightly earlier letter to Fliess :

The fact that the dreamer seems too ingenious, too amusing, is certainly correct, but that has nothing to do with me and I deserve no reproach. All dreamers are, just so, incorrigible jokers, and of necessity, because they are in difficulties and the direct path is closed to them. (*Naissance*, 264, September 11, 1899)

But that was just Fliess' question: how to verify that *this* way of grasping the turn in the direct path was the right one? how to validate *this* interpretation? how to eliminate the possibility that what we take as the truth of the dreamwork (the moon) is simply a product of our interpretation (of our telescope)? how to eliminate the possibility that it is merely the result of a particular refraction of its ray? or that more may be reflected back up the telescope than passes down it? Every science rests on a theory of meaning and can even be understood as a system ordered according to parameters specified so as to produce meaning. Hartmann, among others, has thus seen "psychoanalytic method as a method of interpretation" of the multiplicity of "signs" ("Psychoanalysis," 28; this is a leitmotiv in Weber, *Legend*; see especially 84–117).

The issue is fraught with consequence. From the basis of the interpretation of dreams, the very concepts of the unconscious and of the self are at stake. Not only then may a particular western idea of a scientific discourse of knowledge be put in question but also the self/subject that is its supposed origin, ground, and, in this instance, its object. It is indeed startling that Freud rejects the question more or less by a founding fiat, simply asserting in reply to Hegel that one *can* know the telescope's structure and how it works and that one *can* know just how "rays," the psychical processes, pass down the system from the perceptual to the motor end. Doing this, we effectively make both the instrument and our knowledge of it transparent. So he insists.

But although Freud maintained that it was no issue, the dilemma remained to be resolved. In the so-called "Autobiographical Study," written in 1925 and revised in 1935, he agreed that "the work of analysis" functioned by means and in the form of "an *art of interpretation*." He even insisted on it, since the italics were his (SE, 20:41). But he went on to argue that this in no way shook the objective certainty of the objective reality interpreted, adapting to his own case the rejection of Cremonini's gesture, disdaining those who saw "psycho-analysis as a product of [his] own speculative imagination" having "nothing to do with observation or experience" and ending: "Others again, who did not feel so strongly convinced of this, repeated in their resistance the classical manoeuvre of not looking through the microscope so as to avoid seeing what they had denied" (SE, 20:50). Freud was adopting the very terms Jung had used twenty years before. In the preface to his *Psychology of Dementia Praecox*, dated July 1906, Jung enthusiastically defended Freud's work, insisting that anyone who had never used his method, and over many years, neither could nor should "pronounce judgment on Freud, else he acts like those notorious men of science who disdained to look through Galileo's telescope" (*Collected Works*, 3:3–4). Jung no doubt mainly had in mind Gustav Aschaffenburg, a vehement opponent of psychoanalysis who was often mentioned in the earliest letters between Freud and Jung. On October 5, 1906, for instance, it was apropos of Aschaffenburg that the Swiss insisted on the necessary distinction between the "psychological realm" as Freud's "essential" contribution and "externals" which were to take or leave, repeating a distinction already made in the sentences following the above-quoted passage from the preface to the *Dementia Praecox*, published in December 1906 (Freud and Jung, *Freud/Jung Letters*, 4–5).

According to Jung, externals are such things as the precise methods of interpretation and cure, "merest trifles compared with the psychological principles" Freud has discovered (Jung, *Collected Works*, 3:4); "essentials" are those elements depending on the concepts of psychical structure and process, thus corresponding as well to the telescope through which one must dare to look. How was one to distinguish between the "object" of science and the basic axioms of scientific method aimed at that object? It was to be expected that in a letter of April 7, 1907, Freud should see himself as oppressed by that church of despotic "pundits" whom Jung had seen applauding Aschaffenburg (Freud and Jung, *Freud/Jung Letters*, 4) just as Galileo had been before him: "We are being asked neither more nor less than to abjure our belief in the sexual drive" (Freud and Jung, *Freud/Jung Letters*, 28). *Eppur si muove*. It is not unimportant that Freud, answering what he calls Jung's efforts "to sweeten the sour apple" in choosing to stress the sexual drive, picked the element not only that his opponents found the most provocative but also that would be a principal cause of his eventual break with Jung. But what matters here is the further evidence that they saw the issue of natural science's status in the exact terms of its origins. The issue and its "solution" thus opened and sought would stay as a kind of wound in the body of psychoanalysis—and other western sciences.

One may indeed assert that the very concept of the psyche as in its essence the functioning of unconscious processes derived from the telescope as Freud used it. The instrument gives us, he says right away, "the idea of *psychical locality*," yet lets one describe the mental apparatus while avoiding "the temptation to determine physical locality in any anatomical fashion." In this regard, the identification of the optical instrument with mental processes is extremely precise and, as for Galileo, provides a description of the (psychical) "apparatus" as well as a metaphor for its processes—hence the many ambiguities (and Jung's assertions): "I shall remain," writes Freud, "upon psychological ground, and I propose simply to follow the suggestion that we should picture the instrument which carries out our mental functions as resembling a compound microscope or a photographic apparatus, or something of the kind": memory or passage, impress or motion. Shades of Descartes. The metaphor offers a way of grasping "psychical locality" as corresponding "to a point inside the apparatus at which one of the preliminary stages of an image comes into being. In the microscope or telescope, as we know, these occur in part at ideal points, regions in which no tangible component of the apparatus is situated" (SE, 5:536). The unconscious is the process independent of these tangible components. The ideal points of which the entire apparatus is composed as far as its functioning between the two "terminal points" is concerned *are* the unconscious, likewise indirectly accessible. Freud's telescope echoes Galileo's earlier use of it to establish classical science. It is his reply to Fliess' question. The ideal points guaranteed the telescope's trustworthy functioning as an instrument allowing a correct interpretation of the world and practical understanding of it—one producing foreseeable and useful effects. These *effects* respond to Cremonini's hesitations and Hegel's questions: the pudding's proof. The telescope's success thus guarantees its representation of the unconscious.

Freud's precautions against a too-literal understanding of the telescope "metaphor" suggest the very "defense mechanisms" he will also study. His accumulation of negatives and "hedges" is striking: "*I see no necessity to apologize for the imperfections . . . Analogies of this kind are only intended to assist us in our attempt . . . So far as I know . . . and I can see no harm in it . . . all that we need is the assistance of provisional ideas . . . these systems may perhaps . . . Strictly speaking there is no need for the hypothesis . . . It would be sufficient*" (SE, 5:536–37). Further, these precautions are in fact denied by the very detailed manner in which the "image" *does* serve "to make the complications of mental functioning intelligible by dissecting the function and assigning its different constituents to different component parts of the apparatus" (SE, 5:536). One is tempted to say that rather than making psychical functioning intelligible, it makes psychical functioning. The stunning image of the telescope produces the western self, makes the freudian psyche.

The structure Freud sets as the ground of all psychical activity belies the precautions still more essentially: "All our psychical activity starts from stimuli (whether internal or external) and ends in innervations" (SE, 5:537). Now whether any instance of the process can be viewed as wholly external or a combination of external/internal stimuli, the mechanistic model first indicated in the 1895 "Project" and the division world/"subject" (stimuli/innervations, perception/judgment) are both a priori and are so even if the concept of "subject" needs some redefining. The dual hypotheses of unconscious psychical functioning and of psyche as telescopic apparatus themselves correspond to the division at issue here; insofar as they are a way to conceptualize the psyche, they correspond to the dualisms external/internal, process/stasis, and so on. So they correspond as well, therefore, to all the many scissions we have already been looking at.

These divisive a prioris hold so strongly that they remain even when the process is grasped as solely internal. The "Project" stresses that Freud is seeking the *mechanism* of *identification*: "The aim and end of all thought-processes is thus to bring about a state of identity." In the case of *cognition*, this is with something perceived as "outside" the psyche; in the case of "*reproductive* thought," it is with the psyche itself, a *self*-identity (SE, 1:332–33). Freud repeats here the analysis of the very problem whose resolution was basic to the instauration of analytico-referentiality: the need to "discover" and explain the adequacy of the internal/external relation, to articulate inside on outside such that true thought and right practice of mental subject on *separate* material or conceptual object would be possible at all. The telescope is not just a metaphor. The psychical apparatus merges with it, Freud claiming to "fulfil a requirement with which we have long been familiar, namely that the psychical apparatus must be constructed like a reflex apparatus. Reflex processes remain the model [*Vorbild*] of every psychical function" (SE, 5:538; *Traumdeutung*, 514). *Vorbild* opens, *Traumbild* *closes*, as reality becomes concept or event-in-the-mind; or as fiction of the material telescope becomes reality of psychical process. This movement is identical to Descartes' fabulous passage in *Le monde*, as he proceeds from modeling "story" (*fable*) of the material world to its concrete reality. *Vorbild* is neither "model" nor "reality." Like the baconian *writing* I have analyzed elsewhere (*Discourse*, 198–225), it *precedes* and enables the discourse that can (then) make such a distinction. The same goes for Descartes' *fable*. Once the discourse has been created, however, it redefines *Vorbild* as model or reality according to need. In the first case, it is just an explanatory device whose arbitrary and conventional tie to reality is emphasized—a saving of appearances. In the second, it involves the "illusion," Wittgenstein remarked, "that the so-called laws of nature are the explanations of natural phenomena," the illusion of functional identity between laws, phenomena and human mental operation (*Tractatus*, §6.371).

Since this psychoanalytical process repeats the inception of the analytico-referential in the European sixteenth and seventeenth centuries, it is relevant to observe that when Freud writes of the operation of blocking mechanisms, as which the apparatus' "ideal points" also function (especially in the forgetting of dreams), he elects to refer to just that era. The reference is in the same chapter of the *Interpretation of Dreams* as the introduction of Galileo's telescope. In the chapter's previous section, Freud compares "the forgetting of dreams" resulting from a psychical "proscription" or "resistance" to "the state of things . . . after some sweeping revolution in one of the republics of antiquity or the Renaissance." With regard to the latter, he pursues the analogy at length, thinking perhaps particularly of Machiavelli, since he emphasizes the proscription of nobles left over from a previously dominant state power structure (SE, 5:516).

Freud had pursued this political analogy in discussing dream distortion (and its systematic interpretation), a phenomenon closely bound to dream forgetting. There he used the analogy of *political* censorship. Again it is question of identity rather than analogy or metaphor: "The fact that the phenomenon of [political] censorship and of dream-distortion correspond down to their smallest details justifies us in presuming that they are similarly determined" (SE, 4:142–43). The implications of later texts like *Civilization and Its Discontents* (1929–1930) and *Group Psychology and the Analysis of the Ego* (1921) are similar. In *The Discourse of Modernism*, I showed to what extent Bacon, Hobbes, and others made political reference an essential means of developing and consolidating the analytico-referential. Machiavelli's analysis of a particular political practice had given basic elements for establishment of its final dominance. I have already mentioned Hobbes in relation to Freud. But it further matters that in 1914 Freud added a footnote to his definition of the dream process as a regression (a kind of traveling backward up the telescope), referring not just to Albertus Magnus but, more to my purpose, to Hobbes' discussion of dream regression in *Leviathan* (SE, V.542; *Leviathan*, 17–19, part 1, chapter 2).

Jean Roy shows the link to be yet tighter. I suggest it is a necessary *condition* of Freud's science, like the visual "metaphor" with which I began. Writing of the connection between reason and passion (one not distant from that between conscious/unconscious or even drives/superego), Roy remarks of the seventeenth-century philosopher and the twentieth-century psychologist:

In their minds, however, their anthropology assumes such universality as to defy any invalidation for being culture-bound and any eschatological illusion: across the diversity of time, humanity remains fundamentally the same, a being of desire. Freudian *libido* corresponds to hobbesian *conatus*. The dramas of universal history are lit up with the blaze of individual and collective passions: "for the Passions of men, are commonly more potent than their reason." (Roy, 11; Hobbes, *Leviathan*, 131: 2.19)

So it is that the only truly unambiguous drive for Freud is precisely the one that for Hobbes requires creation of civil society, faced with the permanent threat of individualist aggression. "If Freud feels torn between the claims of sexuality and those of civilized life," writes Paul Roazen, "he feels no such ambivalence here about the aggressive drives. 'In consequence of . . . [the] primary mutual hostility of human beings, civilized society is perpetually threatened with disintegration' " (Roazen, 271; Freud, SE, 21:112). As Freud emphasizes in this same section of *Civilization and Its Discontents* just quoted:

As a rule this cruel aggressiveness waits for some provocation or puts itself at the service of some other purpose, whose goal might also have been reached by milder measures. In circumstances that are favourable to it, when the mental counter-forces which ordinarily inhibit it are out of action, it also manifests itself sponta-neously and reveals man as a savage beast to whom consideration towards his own kind is something alien. (SE, 21:111–12)

This hobbesian view leads, Roazen comments, to the corollary that "Freud explicitly rejects Marxian hopes for the melioristic consequences of alter-ation in property rights. 'Aggressiveness was not created by property'" (*Freud*, 271; SE, 21:113): a reply, too, to Rousseau's earlier thought that prop-erty and aggression began simultaneously with the cry, "Ceci est à moi."

It follows that Freud would translate the contract itself into exact psy-chological terms. For a society in which these aggressive individualities sub-sisted could not survive. This was the very problem faced by political phi-losophy after Machiavelli's observation that the State could well go along as an uninterrupted series of coups d'état. Society would then be unlivable:

Human life in common is only made possible when a majority comes together which is stronger than any separate individual and which remains united against all separate individuals. The power of this community is then set up as "right" in opposition to the power of the individual, which is condemned as "brute force." This replacement of the power of the individual by the power of a community constitutes the decisive step of civilization. The essence of it lies in the fact that the members of the community restrict themselves in their possibilities of satisfaction, whereas the individual knew no such restrictions. (SE, 21:95)

Commenting this passage, Roazen warns us against seeing it "as a kind of social contract gimmick. . . . The parallel in Freud's mind is the way a child is socialized, through countless instinctual restrictions, into adulthood" (*Freud*, 270–71). Philip Rieff foreshadowed this view in his analysis of the earlier *Group Psychology* (*Massenpsychologie*) as the tale of how individuals are "suggested," or rather "fascinated," via the erotic drive, Eros, into their place in group relations, society ("Origins"; cf. "Psychology"), making so-ciety the phylogenetic follower of a development whose model and source is ontogenetic—which is, to be sure, an inevitable analysis in a discourse for which (and of which) the individual subject is origin.

Yet Roazen's warning is surely misplaced, and we do better to view this idea of infantile psychology as hypostatizing political contract theory, essential element of analytico-referential discursive history. We shall see, here and in Chapter 7, how important is this paradigm to western thinking, relating progress from chaos to order, unknown to known, doubt to certainty, insecure outside to stable inside, as growth to enlightened maturity led by a secure agent subject. Nor does Freud doubt that agency. His "unconscious" is little other, Yuri Lotman remarks, than "masked consciousness" which diverse symbols explicate and ultimately "account for adequately." Similarly, "the child receives its first cultural rules from the adult world. . . . Erotic drives develop spontaneously in the child but it is from [the adult world] that it gets the language necessary to become conscious of them, the language which precedes and stimulates its interior development" ("Réduction," 47, 50–51). Consciousness to unconscious is as maturity to immaturity, the difference between passionate savage or unsocialized child and rational individual (socializable in civil society)—hence Freud's identification of ontogeny and phylogeny.

So there is nothing unexpected about "Freud's early disciples who went out to 'primitive' societies to pursue the homology between primitivism and infantility. They, too [like Marx with his very kantian idea that cultures went through stages of growth from childhood (primitive forms of economic relations) to maturity (feudalism via capitalism to socialism)], were working out the cultural and psychological implications of the biological principle 'ontogeny recapitulates phylogeny,' and that of the ideology of 'normal,' fully socialized, male adulthood" (Nandy, *Intimate*, 13). Roazen is surprised that "Freud gave a new twist to the rationalistic tradition by locating the state of nature in childhood" (*Freud*, 164). But this was not new. The state of nature, from its equivocal historicizing in Locke (or indeed from the innocent noble primitives of much sixteenth-century fantasy), was ever imagined as humanity's childhood and explicitly linked to ontogeny at least from Rousseau's *Émile*, whose eponymous hero is precisely educated away from childhood *as* the state of nature. When Freud stresses in *Group Psychology* that creation of the group from individuals (formation *wholly* repeating the individual's internal socialization) produces a higher form of consciousness, he adopts an old equivalence between individual body and social body: it is a matter of being able "to procure for the group precisely those features which were characteristic of the individual and which are extinguished in him by the formation of the group" (SE, 18:86). Freud made the individual not just contractual originator of society but origin and epitome of its very nature.

As I have just suggested, it is not only in Hobbes, Locke, and Rousseau (to say nothing of Marx) that we can show the continuity of this thinking's dominance. Kant set out the same argument in his 1784 *Idee zu einer algemeinen Geschichte in weltbürgerlicher Absicht*. In this brief work's fourth proposition, he explained how nature used a social "antagonism" to develop the innate capacities of human reason, "*in so far as this antagonism becomes in the long run the cause of a law-governed social order*" (*Political Writings*, 44). The idea of progress in reason was central to Kant's thinking—taken up by Hegel and in materialist form by Marx. Roazen is surely mistaken about the relation between Freud and Marx. *The Future of an Illusion* seems to hold an implicit argument supporting such development (despite Freud's claims in *New Introductory Lectures*, for example, to be rejecting Marx's and Hegel's social diagnoses; SE, 21:67, 176–81). This makes it yet more interesting that Kant's argument manifestly prefigures that of *Civilization and Its Discontents*. Kant's "antagonism" lay between the individual's desires and its consciousness of social demands (another way to express the conflictual articulation of Rousseau's individual and general wills):

By antagonism, I mean in this context the *unsocial sociability* of men, that is, their tendency to come together in society, coupled, however, with a continual resistance which constantly threatens to break this society up. This propensity is obviously rooted in human nature. Man has an inclination to *live in society*, since he feels in this state more like a man, that is, he feels able to develop his natural capacities. But he also has a great tendency to *live as an individual*, to isolate himself, since he also encounters in himself the unsocial characteristic of wanting to direct everything in accordance with his own ideas.

The passage discusses, among other things, the individual and mutual "resistances" and "a *pathologically* enforced social union [which] is transformed into a *moral* whole" (*Political Writings*, 44–45). Our discursive paradigm could hardly be more clearly shown.

I think too, then, that de Certeau may be pushing things a bit when he asserts that Freud was "reversing" Kant. Referring to the philosopher's short text, "What Is Enlightenment?", and after noting the individual to be "the central epistemological and historical figure of the modern western world, the foundation of capitalist economy and democratic politics [or their creation]," he argues that this figure is "undone" in Freud's work that, "though born of the *Aufklärung*, reverses the act that founded enlightened consciousness—Kant's assertion of the rights and obligations of that consciousness: 'freedom' and full responsibility, autonomous knowledge, and the possibility for a man to progress at a 'steady pace' and escape his 'tutelage.' The response of psychoanalysis to Kant was to send the adult back to its infantile 'tutelage,' to send knowledge back to the instinctual mechanisms determining it, freedom back to the law of the unconscious, and progress back to originating events" (*Heterologies*, 15; cf. 24). What Freud actually did is turn these discursive foundations into the ground of individual being and then argue that the former, transformed into social "reality," were themselves forged out of the very nature of that human individual. For this is the *same* history—just as the use of capitalism or the nation-state to "counter" negritude, spirituality, or whatever as *their* other also are.

In continuing this discourse on the fraught relations between immature individual desire and the mature moral unity of the social, Freud had another ancestor in Schiller, Kant's younger contemporary. For my discussion, his terms were remarkable. Avowedly indebted to Kant, Schiller began his *Aesthetic Education* (1795) by exploring at length the "disequilibrium" of the human individual due to disagreement with the whole community as manifested in the modern State. He concluded this part of his argument:

So when Reason introduces her moral unity into any actually existing society, she must not damage the multiplicity of Nature. And when Nature strives to maintain her multiplicity within the moral framework of society, there must be no rupture in its moral unity; the triumphant form rests equidistant from uniformity and confusion. Wholeness of character must therefore be present in any people capable and worthy of exchanging the State of compulsion [*Not*: need or necessity] for a State of freedom. (*Aesthetic*, translated by Snell, 34; corrected from translation by Wilkinson and Willoughby, 20–23)

It was the task of "aesthetic education" to enable this individual/social balance. Given what we have seen, it can be no surprise that Hegel opened his 1820s lectures on aesthetics (published in 1835) by praising Schiller as his most important predecessor in these matters, "breaking through the Kantian subjectivity and abstraction of thinking" and correctly grasping "scientifically as the principle and essence of art . . . [the] *unity* of universal and particular, freedom and necessity, spirit and nature" which would ultimately enable a reconciliation of self and world (*Aesthetics*, 1:61–62). Put this way, and coming from a view of the divided German states and warring Europe of the end of the eighteenth century and of the lack of individual role within them, Schiller's influence on all Hegel's thinking is clear.

Schiller sought a synthesis before Hegel, trying to rejoin art and political society, reason and morality, individual and community. So it matters that he now took up Galileo's telescope as at once the model of Enlightened reason *and* the mark of a dismemberment of reason, of an individualism of discovery itself emblematic of the breakdown of a previously whole and unified culture (Greece offered as the exemplary nostalgic case). At the same time, he argued that such a breakdown was historically and conceptually necessary, since that culture had reached some kind of end point. He offered the telescope as reason creating rational community by enabling the individual to share in, understand, and be united in and through the universality of that reason, a reason that, as it were, lets the individual sublate its very individuality:

One-sidedness in the exercise of powers must, it is true, inevitably lead the individual into error; but the species as a whole to truth [reason and truth as a system of laissez-faire!]. Only by concentrating the whole energy of our mind into a single focal point [*Brennpunkt*], contracting our whole being into one single power, do we, as it were, lend wings to this individual power and lead it, by artificial means, far beyond the limits which Nature seems to have assigned to it. Even as it is certain that all individuals taken together would never, with the powers of vision granted them by Nature alone, have managed to detect a satellite of Jupiter which the telescope reveals to the astronomer, so it is beyond question that human powers of reflection would never have produced an analysis of the Infinite or a Critique of Pure Reason, unless, in the individuals called to perform such feats [*wenn nicht in einzelnen dazu berufnen Subjekten*], Reason had separated itself off, disentangled itself, as it were, from all matter, and by the most intense effort of abstraction armed their eyes with a glass for peering into the Absolute [*ihren Blick ins Unbedingte bewaffnet hätte*]. (*Aesthetic*, translated by Wilkinson and Willoughby, 40–43)[4]

The telescope to the abstract would enable the "state of freedom" in which individual and community would overcome their felt divisions. The aim of subsequent letters of the *Aesthetic Education* was to defeat the historically necessary dismemberment of reason—and of self or psyche accompanying it—by baring a new road to wholeness. This was the challenge that Hegel took up, that Schopenhauer responded to with pessimism and Marx with optimism. It involved the human in a whole sociopolitical, natural, and rational order. Freud's systematization of the human psyche does not seem a response to this challenge but a return to an earlier set of problems. And if Hegel's declaration of the end of effective—socially organic—art was confirmed by a European art lost in ever-more pessimistic and corrosive exploration of the self as opponent of socialization (Reiss, *Meaning*, 334–46), it may be that freudian psychoanalysis expressed something similar. Its assumptions and its practice served to assert not the possibility of social wholeness but the need to confirm the psyche in its privacy and to allow that privacy to be maintained without disturbing or being disturbed by a social community conceived as outside it—Schiller's one-sidedness of error. The psyche may be adjusted to "live with" society without being troubled by its exigencies and certainly without having to be in any way responsible for them or its relation to them.

So for Freud, the contract has a ready-made *internal* explanation, since social organization supposes the ego identification of each to one and the same object. Once the "ego ideal" has been able to identify with this single object, he wrote in *Group Psychology*, all members of the society are by definition equal: "*A primary group of this kind is a number of individuals who have put one and the same object in the place of their ego ideal and have consequently identified themselves with one another in their ego*" (SE, 18:116; see too on this Vološinov, *Freudianism*, 61). This equalizing of the individuals depends by definition on one exception: "The primal father is the group ideal, which governs the ego in the place of the ego ideal" (SE, 18:127). So the "contract" is natural for every social formation and necessarily takes the shape of equality of all before their leader—the sovereign authority of the liberal philosophical tradition (Reiss, *Meaning*, 93–96, 167–68, 275–76). When this ends in the father's ritual murder and the establishment of a fraternal group, is this not the lockean transformation?—that moment when the contract becomes a permanent function and sign of the operation of a "general will" rather than one establishing the power of one. But the end of this state remains entirely hobbesian, and the absence of civilization will put the individual back into a "state of nature" exactly of the sort Hobbes envisaged (*Future of an Illusion*, SE, 21:15–16).

The similarity is the greater when Freud compares this return to the state of nature to the states of panic that follow the loss of the leader/father in *Group Psychology*:

[I]t is of the very essence of panic that it bears no relation to the danger that threatens, and often breaks out on the most trivial occasions. . . . The loss of the leader in some sense or other, the birth of misgivings about him, brings on the outbreak of panic, though the danger remains the same; the mutual ties between the members of the group disappear, as a rule, at the same time as the tie with their leader. The group vanishes in dust. . . . (SE, 18:96–97)

The group breaks up in a kind of generalized schizophrenia: "The collapse of the group releases the hostility which had been bound up in the libidinal ties; instinctual defusion occurs" (Roazen, 142).[5] Writing precisely of this disappearance of the sovereign, Hobbes had written, for example: "If a Monarch shall relinquish the Soveraignty, both for himself, and for his heires; His Subjects returne to the absolute Libertie of Nature" (*Leviathan*, 154: 2:21). The importance of collapsing ontogeny and phylogeny is clear. As Roy puts it a little differently: the "meeting of the spontaneity of desire and the objectivity of a culture determines the most exemplary libidinal destiny, the Oedipus complex that is the freudian match for Hobbes' social contract: it is the moment of culture's coming into authority" (*Hobbes*, 81). And that was exactly what Schiller had rejected as the society of compulsion or necessity, *den Staat der Not*.

So Lotman may be wrong in thinking that he was correcting Freud when he pointed out the child's dependency on the adult world for the rules producing maturation into both self-consciousness and socialization. Lacan and Foucault, too, insisted on this, while others have observed certain practical political consequences. But one may say that Freud had already said so. And one may add that the western analytico-referential tradition contained these suppositions about self and "progress," individual and society, and that classical science grounded them in a particular grasp of an internal conceptual ordering of the external world. Cultural demands may change, like the forms taken by the contract or the components of the Oedipus complex, but the structural presuppositions remain in one paradigm, where common sense guides action, where sovereign authority directs power, where the eye at the telescope organizes knowledge, where the individual self asserts will; paradigm of a linear reason that determines and is determined by "exemplary cultural goals: human fraternity and reduction of suffering" (Roy, 36), a project which *The Future of an Illusion* represents superbly, seen as "a passionate reformulation of the ideals of reason and progress inherited from the Enlightenment" (Roazen, 103). So when Lotman asserts that "Freud's unconscious is a masked consciousness" and above all, when he "replies" to the question about the scientific status of psychoanalysis by saying of this "unconscious" that it "is *reconstructed* from the researcher's meta-models and quite naturally is translated in their terms," we cannot but agree ("Réduction," 47). But we add that these metamodels are directly given by a dominant analytico-referential practice and were there from the start. This is not to condemn. It simply observes the existence of a specific cultural space, defined by the dominance of a discursive network of which thinkers like Galileo, Hobbes, Descartes, and Bacon set one of the borders, while those like Frege and Freud set the other.

So elements like the epistemological/psychological form established by the telescope and like the social/individual organization figured by the contract and its analogs affirm that not only psychical processes taken as a whole (the telescope, for example, that represents the psychical apparatus at the same time as expressing its activity *and* the play of forces underway inside) but also such particular functions as regression, forgetting, resistance, repression, association, and so on, are hypostatizations of analytico-referential discursive history, hypostatizations of a particular western cultural practice: psychical realities created out of discursive elements that give this history its paradigmatic shape. They imply that freudian psychoanalysis *re*formulates the (same) analytico-referential concept of individual self, its internal organization, and its relation to others. Thus the "work of displacement" and the "work of condensation" that permit "representation" in dreams (*Interpretation*, SE, 4:277–338) seem to reproduce rather exactly Tesauro's *versabilità* and *perspicacia*, respectively. In their day, we saw in Chapter 4, they had been opposed to the "right" forms of analysis and reference as in some sense their "other" and so quite irrecuperable; Freud makes them processes internalized as unconscious functionings, the inverse of conscious ones. Thus hypostatized into psychical realities they can be reincorporated into a history that had had to occult them as processes of reason. It is then the analyst's job to *right* their deformations, to enable the analysand, if not to live in, at least to live with society as a whole.

So far, these things are all aspects of the *way in which* dreams and the unconscious were held to function. No less revealing is the *purpose* ascribed (for example) to dreams. Dreams, said Freud, are wish fulfillments. Their manner of functioning is by regression: "In regression the fabric of the dream-thoughts is resolved into its raw material" (SE, 5:543). Both Bacon and Galileo had rejected "raw material" as unusable for knowledge. In their view, raw material ("brute experience," said Galileo, unordered and chaotic) was useless. Only already ordered experience (experiment, Bacon's *experientia literata*—or even perhaps *Vorbild*) had any epistemological—

and practical—use. Nonetheless, the ideal of analytico-referential discourse was eventually direct access to such immediate concrete reality. The fulfillment of *its* most ardent wish would have been immediate knowledge of nature's raw material. Again a major problem attending the inception and progress of the discourse of analysis and reference is absorbed into the psychical mechanism. The *use* of raw material in dreams corresponded to the *wish* for scientific knowledge of such material (for utility and knowledge are one, said Bacon). Such "*a wish from the unconscious*," Freud wrote, was "invariably and indisputably" the "*capitalist*" in the service of an "*entrepreneur*" who "can do nothing without capital" and who must therefore resort to someone "who can afford the outlay, . . . who provides the psychical outlay for the dream" (SE, 5:561).

Once again, one is constrained to note that this "analogy" is not innocent, that it corresponds to the fact that this telescope, the unconscious, is completely at the service of the *I*, which in turn corresponds to capitalist desire: "Dreams are completely egoistic" (SE, 4:322, a view slightly modified in 1925). This legitimates Foucault's otherwise curious remark: "consciousness is a form of knowledge; and consciousness as the basis of subjectivity is a prerogative of the bourgeoisie" (*Language*, 208). One recalls Fanon's comment, quoted earlier, about the western "idea of a society of individuals where each person shuts himself up in his own subjectivity, and whose only wealth is individual thought," a society whose grounding in the individual as self-possessed capital was simply inactual elsewhere—or "actual" as a forcefully imposed overlay (*Wretched*, 47). Freud would not see the latter, supposing the psyche common to the human *qua* species, but had essentially said nothing else; *this* consciousness is the prerogative of a western culture for which the bourgeoisie is the typical and exemplary figure of what it is to be human at all.

We have already seen that such hypostatizations hold constantly for the unconscious itself. But the centrality of the concept (to understate the case) makes it bear repeating. The unconscious corresponds precisely, Freud proposes, to the intangible system of places inside a particular type of optical apparatus. Cremonini (and his antifreudian successors, according to Freud) refused to look through the telescope, claiming (so it is said) that his acceptance of the accuracy and truth of what he would see depended on prior acceptance of a conceptual order extrapolated from the functioning of the instrument as such. It depended, that is, on acceptance of implications of baconian "writing," galilean "mathematical language," cartesian "method," hobbesian (or spinozan) "geometrical" thought—or freudian *Vorbild*. For similarly, "access" to the unconscious results from extrapolating from what is taken as the functioning of the entire apparatus. Freud's equation of ontogenesis with phylogenesis, of individual development and functioning with those of "the human race" (SE, 5:548; and see especially *Totem and Taboo*) should best be seen as the theoretical hypostatization of a historically situatable discursive "birth" into the form of permanent human psychical and mental processes, just as the psychoanalytical theory that contains it may be viewed as the hypostatization of that discursive history itself.

It goes without saying that the telescope is not alone an entirely accurate or self-sufficient model. At each ideal stage of the apparatus, we saw, is left an imprint described "as a 'memory trace' [*Erinnerungsspur*]" (SE, 5:538; *Traumdeutung*, 514)—hence the fact that Freud adds to the telescope the metaphor of the camera. This too was destined to a great future, not just in Freud's own work but in that of many of his most recent successors and commentators. Once again, one could of course lay this at the door of the Descartes we saw in Chapter 5. For this involves psychical processes as *writing*, or at least as the production of meaning in a manner strictly analogous to the functioning of natural languages. Some contemporary writers have sought to ascribe a special importance to a *passage* in Freud's writing from the "optical" to the "linguistic." These writers can then play down the "positivistic" side of psychoanalytic theory and practice so as to offer that science as an *other* way of knowing, a praxis leading to an "*athesis*," (anti-) knowledge quite different from traditional experimentalist knowledge, as if, far from marking limits of western (scientific) discourse, it were already in some new space of thinking and doing.

Thus Derrida asserts that the metaphor of text precedes that of machine, though he in fact shows the former developing between the time of the "Project" and that of the *Interpretation of Dreams* (in the correspondence with Fliess). We have already seen Freud working out the "mechanistic" metaphor of the telescope at least at the same time—present as it was since Breuer's note to the *Studies on Hysteria*, with Freud then developing it in the "Project." Similarly, Derrida asserts that "all the mechanical models will be tested and discarded until the discovery of the *Wunderblock*, a writing machine of wonderful complexity into which the entire psychical apparatus will be projected," despite the telescope's still being essential in 1938, although one can no doubt say that the telescope is not "mechanical."

Indeed, Derrida tries to downplay the kind of significance I am here drawing from the optical metaphor by asserting that in any case, Freud's telescope is not to be understood as "a simple homogeneous structure"—a fact indicated, he writes, "by the diverse refractions of light (excitations) as it passes through the lens system (ideal points) and by the changes in medium contained in the system" ("Freud," 206, 200, 215).[6] This last point is exact. But it had never been otherwise. That was just why Galileo, for example, remarked that to change the length of the telescope was to change both the "object" observed and the observation—or again, that the star seen through the telescope was not the same as that seen with the naked eye. Perhaps that was why Cremonini refused to look through it. It was why Schiller's telescopic reason was universal, yet dependent on fragmented gaze. It certainly gave the triple terms of Hegel's criticism of telescopic cognition, aimed at the instrument's structure, its internal medium, and the diversity of refraction characterizing the light coming from its object.

Echoing the "linguistic turn" of so many western disciplines in the 1950s and 1960s, writers like Lacan, Derrida, and others (whatever their differences) thus sought it in psychoanalysis by taking up Freud's other favorite "metaphor." Here the issue of interpretation prevails over what is to be interpreted. They stress a different reading of the *Traumdeutung*, along with that of such texts as *Jokes and Their Relation to the Unconscious*, *The Psychopathology of Everyday Life*, *Beyond the Pleasure Principle*, "The Uncanny," and the "Note upon the 'Mystic Writing Pad.'" The notion that such an interpretation of psychoanalysis is the path to a new discursive future has been widespread—however diverse the specific interpretation. But Freud figured no such "radical break" (Foucault, "Confession," 212). Here, as we have seen, the optical metaphor and that of the *trace* were in fact simultaneous, aspects of *one* description. They evolve as simultaneously as they had at the inception of analytico-referential thinking. Terms of writing and ordered language use were essential to Bacon's Instauration, to his identification of humans' capacity for knowing and doing and his characterization of coherent social *being*. Galileo figured the *same* instauration via the telescope. In his 1678 *Defence of the Royal Society*, John Wallis named these two as cofounders of modern science and knowledge.

Derrida calls the images "apparently contradictory" ("Freud," 216).[7] If so, the contradiction inheres in the entire tradition, and we earlier saw Descartes adopt an idea of memory reliant at once on ideal points that filtered perceptions, on "written" traces and then on writing as process, constantly articulating motion on stasis. His psychological writings always linked them. In the *Passions de l'âme*, he suggests that one's first perception of an object is due to a sort of mental vacuum, a total lack of previous experience. The first passion, unique to Descartes, is visual—*admiration*, a looking with wonder (*ad-mirari*), letting the mind fill the emptiness, passing from ignorance to knowledge:

When our first encounter with some object surprises us and we find it new or very different from what we knew before or from what we supposed it ought to be, this makes us look at it with wonder [*que nous l'admirons*] and be astonished by it. And because this can happen before we know at all whether or not this object is useful to us, I regard wonder [*admiration*] as the first of all the passions. And it has no opposite, for if the object before us [*qui se présente*] has nothing that surprises us we are not at all moved by it and look at it [*le considérons*] without passion. (§53, AT, 11:373; CSM, 1:350)

This "visual" passion, the first of the passions and unique (every other has its opposite), is purely intellectual—and is alone in being so: "having neither good nor evil as its object, but only knowledge of the thing that we wonder at [*qu'on admire*], it has no relation with the heart and blood, on which depend all the body's wellbeing, but only with the brain, where are located the organs of the senses used for this knowledge" (§71; AT, 1:381; CSM, 1:353). One recalls Freud's telescope, *not* physical yet working and having its physical site in the brain. For Descartes, this knowledge, insofar as it allows action, exists because *admiration* enables first perception then *memory*: by it, "we learn and retain in our memory things of which we were previously ignorant" (§75; AT, 11:384; CSM, 1:354). We saw how an aspect of memory for Descartes was composed of "*traces*" left in the brain, traces that were just openings in "the pores of the brain," kinds of empty spaces making it easier to repeat already-recognized motions, traces whose first cause was *admiration*, enabling habitual experience and knowledge (see above, especially 200–202). He went further, describing how all particular passions (secondary in respect of *admiration*), love, hate, joy, grief, desire, were enabled by the single fact that a certain "motion" was *imprinted* in our "being" at birth when soul and body were joined, and how our organism, habituated to this motion, always recalled it in like circumstance and acted according to the same habit (*Passions*, §§107–11; AT, 11:407–11; CSM, 1. The trace left by visual wonder thus explains all the soul's functions after its first setting in motion (as *imaginary* as the telescope or the *Wunderblock*).

In the *Traumdeutung*, Freud first links optical instrument to written "trace" when broaching the idea of *association*. It is not just a joke to note that association is enabled by the *simultaneous* functioning of telescopic perceptual apparatus and "writing" coupled with it: "Our perceptions are linked with one another in our memory. . . . We speak of this fact as 'association' " (SE, 5:539). The association of the two functions is as essential to Freud's analysis as it was to the inception of the discursive history of which it is part. This is why the term "metaphor" is inappropriate; these really are "discursive functions," units essential to the elaboration and function of particular thinking and practice. Freud never dropped either, though he seems to insist on the visual one. Even so, I recall that Frege (not to mention Galileo, Descartes, Tesauro, Schiller, and Hegel) shows how visuality is *also* a particular elaboration of the signifying process, at the same time as it *is* the process. Both the apparatus and the play of forces are hypostatizations from *the same singular discursive history*. Derrida sees the two as contradictory, arguing that the "conflict" was at last erased in the 1924 writing machine. But one wonders if "oppositions" like unconscious *process*/memory *trace* (as fixed imprint) and telescope/writing, which are so permanent in Freud, and "contraries" like the "readable" trace/"deferral" combination in Derrida are not again efforts to overcome the process/entropy, motion/stasis opposition central in analytico-referential discourse, which Bacon, for instance, had already "resolved" in his own way (Reiss, *Discourse*, 213–18). The very notion of the psyche as at once "apparatus" and "process" exemplifies the same opposition, internalizing it in the very psyche, the western self.

The same duality is played out and provided with a certain stability in a more significant way in various of Freud's writings from the early 1920s. One sees it in such texts as *Beyond the Pleasure Principle* (1920), which introduces two fundamental instinctual urges: not just the familiar sexual impulses (drives to life and conservation), but the new drive toward death (the "death wish," impulse to dissolution and inertia). Now life itself, and not only the organization of the unconscious, becomes the place where the process/stasis conflict is played out. In *The Ego and the Id* of 1923, Freud makes this explicit:

The emergence of life would thus be the cause of the continuance of life and also at the same time of the striving towards death; and life itself would be a conflict and compromise between these two trends. The problem of the origin of life would remain a cosmological one; and the problem of the goal and purpose of life would be answered dualistically. (SE, 19:40–41)

Here the central conflict of a particular discursive history is hypostatized into the principle of all human life, whenever and wherever it be found. The discursive elaboration is analogous to what we have seen, although we are here concerned with later texts more or less contemporary with that of the writing machine, of which too much should thus surely not be made. The life/death duality is not yet found, for instance, in the 1917 *Metapsychology* (which offers only the urges to life). So the *ongoing* discursive elaboration exactly follows the set terms of a particular discursive history, without changing them. Its basic functions are the same and develop quite predictably.

Further, as to this junction of life and death drives, one recalls writings seen in earlier chapters to fit exactly this development. Let me just repeat Pope's 1733–1734 *Essay on Man*:

> As Man, perhaps, the moment of his breath,
> Receives the lurking principle of death;
> The young disease, that must subdue at length,
> Grows with his growth, and strengthens with his strength:
> So, cast and mingled with his very frame,
> The Mind's disease, its ruling Passion came.
>
> (Pope, II.133–38)

Pope's concepts may not be Freud's, although those of some with whom I associated these lines before—Unamuno, Horkheimer and Adorno, Lévi-Strauss, Eliot, Saramago—surely are. Nor are these just thematic resemblances. Pope's debt to Locke and his predecessors is also Freud's, and even if the terms may differ a bit, they live in a common conceptual framework. So this dualistic "division" at the heart of the psyche returns us by another route to issues explored especially in Chapters 1 and 3. Now the scission, fragmentation, has been internalized in the very self, that articulate subject long ago explored to quite different ends by Descartes—but then by Locke to essentially "modern" ones.

This internalized fragmenting is a modern western phenomenon, says Mphahlele (Chapter 1 above). An early exemplar was Søren Kierkegaard, not just writing under so many diverse egos but seeing in that fragmentation a critique of totalizing analyses and practices—after Denis Diderot's *Neveu de Rameau*, adds MacIntyre (*After Virtue*, 40). Kierkegaard's contemporary Matthew Arnold, usually figured as a pillar of the imperialist bourgeois British establishment, early experienced what Nicholas Jenkins calls "a terrible dissolution of the self." To write poetry, he wrote as a young poet, demanded "not merely an effort and a labour, but an actual tearing of oneself to pieces." This was not a momentary but an enduring experience: "my poems are fragments" because "I am fragments" ("Story," 12).[8] In our century, Machado and his alter egos Juan de Mairena and Abel Martín relay that sense of heterogeneity of being and self we saw in Chapter 2. Fernando Pessoa's "heteronyms" wrote radically diverse poems founded on quite different ways of being. At the start of *The Year of the Death of Ricardo Reis*, fiction of one of these heteronyms after Pessoa's death, Saramago quotes Reis and sets this sense of fragmentation in "cartesian" terms—appropriately, because it can only come *after* establishment of self, although Freud and Lacan are clearly contributors here:

Innumerable people live within us. If I think and feel, I know not who is thinking and feeling. I am only the place where there is thinking and feeling, and, though they [the verses] do not end here, it is as if everything ends, for beyond thinking and feeling there is nothing. If I am this, muses Ricardo Reis as he stops reading, who will be thinking at this moment what I am thinking, or think that I am thinking in the place where I am, because of thinking. Who will be feeling what I am feeling, or feel what I am feeling in the place where I am, because of feeling. Who is using me in order to think and feel, and among the innumerable people who live within me, who I am, Who, Quem, Quain, what thoughts and feelings are the ones I do not share because they are mine alone. Who am I that others are not nor have been nor will come to be. (13)

For such as Machado and Pessoa, their experience may have been reactions to empire—in one case to its loss, in the other to its weight and wrongs, in both to its assurance of a conquering ego's possessive centrality (an issue revisited differently in Chapter 8 briefly, at greater length in Chapter 10, regarding both poets). For the loss of a sense of firm self replies more generally to the virile Renaissance man of Jacob Burckhardt's imagination (cf. Chapter 1, note 4 above) by fracturing, in the event, the *male* subject. Just so is Franz Kafka's K unable to make whole the broken episodes whose unintelligibility reflect an incapacity both to situate himself as a single identity and to distinguish the identities of his persecutors or of the institutions they putatively compose. Joyce could only make *Ulysses* the tale of fragmented memories and events composing a day in the life of Leopold Bloom's identities. Although all these pursue a path in this modern discourse endemic from the beginning and climaxing theoretically in Freud's version of it, this is *not* freudian—who had no such doubts as to the place of self and its solidity, however hard it might have been on occasion to track down.

Indeed, Joyce's, Kafka's, and Pessoa's coeval Machado, recasting echoes of a cartesian past, limned this sense of a heterogeneous self *and* attacked Freud's mystification of the subject, his continuing a lost notion of stable agent self even as he occulted that agency. In Machado's "Cancionero apocrifo," Abel Martín insists on "being . . . as active consciousness," a "subject, never the passive object of external energies." It is ever-moving activity consciously making self. So

"the mechanical conception of the world—added Martín—is being thought of as pure inertia, being which is not for itself, *immutable and in constant movement*, a whirlwind of cinders that the hand of God moves, we know not why or how." When this hand, evident even in the cartesian *chiquenaude*, is not held in account, being is already thought of as that which absolutely is not. (286)

Martín offers a Descartes knowing the deficiencies of the mechanical concept but leading to a Spinoza for whom "the attributes of substance are already . . . the attributes of pure nothingness," consciousness "thinking itself as total object, thinking itself as it is not" (286). At issue is not the accuracy of Martín's view of Descartes (for whom being was filled with god as perfect thinking process, manifestation indeed of god's thinking, and who may have *led* to Spinoza but who was *trying* to *re*build something from the past) but the thought of being as conscious making of self. Martín answers Freud directly on the ground of sexuality, as also lying in conscious self-making: "sexual disorders, according to Abel Martín, did not originate—as modern psychiatry supposes—in the obscure zones of the unconscious, but, on the contrary in the brightest workshop of the conscious. The erotic object, the ultimate case of objectivity, is also, on the lower plane of love, a subjective projection" (280–81). The unconscious is deliberate self-delusion, an effort to ignore, says Martín (like Mairena), that the subject is composed of conscious self-creating fragments.

In a similar way, I think, Foucault remarked against freudian dream analysis that "if the dream is the bearer of the deepest human meanings, this is not insofar as it betrays their hidden mechanisms or shows their inhuman cogs and wheels, but on the contrary, insofar as it brings to light the freedom of man in its most original form" ("Dream," 53): dream as clearest evidence of human self-creation. Freud saw this self-creation in the psychical mechanism's function in relation to vagaries of individual experience on the one hand and in its refusal of or adjustment to social demand on the other. One could say that Freud's establishment of psychoanalysis was such an assertion of the self. For Machado and his others, Freud was simply occulting the fact that his psychoanalysis was best seen as an entertaining translation of the discourse and discursive history of a particular moment in western culture, translating the course of analytico-referential thinking into universal processes of the human psyche. Just so did Witold Gombrowicz, of whom we will soon see more, take Freud as translating the self's fully conscious awareness of conflict between willed "kantian" maturity in relations with others and immaturity in our "confidential, intimate life" into a story of "freudian instinct and unconscious" (*Entretiens*, 86). Foucault came close to a similar view, if with less assurance. The dream, he wrote, was "that movement of the mind which, of its own accord [?], goes into the world and finds its unity with the world." Doing this, "it explains . . . that waking knowledge of the world is opposition, for the receptivity of the senses and the possibility of being affected by objects are nothing but opposition to the world." For Foucault, dream was the mind undercutting and *explaining* a western tradition based in those oppositions and scissions we have been seeing—though it did so by "immersion . . . in the night of the unconscious." Yet even yielding this, Foucault turned Freud's psychical telescope back to its rational and conscious predecessors, adding that "the dream experience would be a *Fernsehen* like that 'farsighted vision' which is limited only by the horizons of the world" ("Dream," 48–49).

So where dream was concerned, Foucault echoed Gombrowicz's view that immaturity was to maturity as wisdom to division and rupture—repeating, he wrote, Plato of *The Republic* (571d–572a), for whom dream was "that absolute disclosure of the ethical content, the heart shown naked" ("Dream," 52). This view of Freud's work is why one of Gombrowicz's Argentine friends assured him that "Freud is useless to South Americans. 'Because Freud is European knowledge and this is America' " (*Diary*, 2:135)—this in the midst of constant assertions that America needed to forge its own different thinking. "We are not Europeans," said another, "European thought, the European spirit, are something alien that invades us, as the Spaniards once did. It is our misfortune that we have the culture of that 'Western world' of yours which we have soaked up like paint," losing an original "Indo-American one." Gombrowicz recounts as a constant Argentine refrain the idea that "We live by the borrowed light of Europe . . . we have to break with Europe, and find within ourselves the slumbering Indian of four centuries ago" (*Diary*, 2:93, 128). Equally often, we shall see, the opposition takes the form of maturity versus immaturity.

In this regard, Gombrowicz was doing nothing more unexpected or surprising than did those early freudian disciples on whom Nandy commented, for whom the paradigm of *passing* from immaturity to immaturity became in Gombrowicz's case the establishment of immaturity *against* maturity as a way to undermine Enlightenment (see, e.g., Lipinska-Illakowicz, 113–17, and my next chapter).

We have seen that functions like displacement and condensation, regression, forgetting, and association, factors like the *I* of the unconscious, purposes like wish fulfillment, processes like the unconscious itself, and indeed the very concept of life provide a complete repetition of the discursive means by which analytico-referentiality was installed. So it is small wonder if even Freud often translated these into terms of scientific experimentalism, economic possessivism, or political individualism. These terms offer access to another set of complex relationships that briefly need to be indicated.

Locke's dictum that a human may suspend action until desire is elevated above baseness, "till he *hungers or thirsts after righteousness*" (*Essay*, 253, book II.xxi.35), is not far structurally from Freud's concept of sublimation, although the process is obviously a conscious one for Locke. Nonetheless, human freedom (here to elevate or sublimate base desires) as a manifestation of some absolute notion of moral inclination is close to the operational function ascribed to the superego. Since it is "human freedom," Locke could not present it as constraint, but he does give it as avoidance of "unpleasantness." Inspecting this notion, we see immediately that we are not far from the hobbesian argument concerning the free cession of individual power (possessed in the state of nature) to the singular authority of the state. For both Hobbes and Locke, society functioned as a result of an individual's urge to find the best way to do good for oneself in a context of others' requirement to do good for *them*selves. Both held that individual freedom implied an individual's self-restraint on behalf of oneself and one's good; self-restraint and social authority acted as one. Laissez-faire economics (and Schiller's laissez-faire reason) depends on no other assumption, Freud's capitalist and entrepreneur made foundational in society as in the self.

Pushing Kant's later "resistances" further, Freud inverts this process, arguing that the urge is in fact an internalization of restraints imposed by society—society of a certain kind, one may add. It is indeed just this mechanism that allows the theoretical assumption of individual equality to conceal a practice of inequality, as we saw in Chapter 1. In one sense, Freud's

analysis shows how it does so. The association of rational and moral freedom with a particular concept of social constraint (called "civil liberty" by
the liberal philosophers and made into an aspect of psychical functioning
by Freud) was available from the outset. In 1707, Shaftesbury could write
that what essentially raised humans above beasts were "Freedom of Reason
in the Learned World, and good Government and Liberty *in the Civil World"*
(*Several Letters*, 8, May 10). Through the eighteenth century, people argued
that rational and moral freedom in the individual coincided with civil liberty as a certain social order and constraint and that the conjunction was
the essential human characteristic. At the start of George I's reign, eight
years after Shaftesbury's proposition, that excellent Whig, Joseph Addison,
unambiguously reinforced it: *"For such is the nature of our happy Constitution, that the Bulk of the People virtually give their Approbation to every thing
they are bound to obey, and prescribe to themselves those Rules by which they are
to walk"* (*Freeholder*, 50, no. 1, December 23, 1715). Rousseau, too, praised
Geneva's constitution in 1754: "I would have liked to live and die free, that
is, so obedient to the laws that neither I nor anyone could shake off their
honorable yoke, that soft and beneficial yoke which the proudest heads
wear the more compliantly for being cut out to wear no other. . . .
Peoples," he went on, "once accustomed to masters are no longer in condition to do without them" without losing entirely "the beneficial air of liberty. . . . The sublimest reason" and "wise laws" agreed in assuring us that
"this precious liberty . . . costs . . . nothing to preserve." He ended by ex-
claiming, "so what else need you do than carry out with a good will and
justified trust what you would always be obliged to do out of true interest,
duty and reason?" ("Discours," 26–27, 29–30).

The relation between laws and freedom is a commonplace of every
political philosophy based on a theory of the Rights of Man. In question
here, simply, is its internalization. Freud demystifies this conception by reversing it: the liberal concept of individual freedom is the consequence of
a particular order of society (but did Addison, Rousseau, or Kant actually
say anything else?). The difference is that Freud asserts that that order of society is itself founded on the true nature of the individual human psyche or
self. The limits of a particular class of discourse, regime of meaning, may
have been reached and *shown* to have been reached. But even if Freud were
reversing one among its (principal) conceptions, this would not be to sur-
pass or change the order. As it is, he sets the self even more firmly as its
foundation.

Derrida asserts that "the freudian concept of trace must be radicalized and extracted from the metaphysics of presence" ("Freud," 229). In view of what I have been arguing here, one wonders if that is possible, if the attempt is not bound to end up in the same discursive "space." Both of our central "images," the optical instrument and writing, had been of first importance in Descartes (where visuality is not, however, really assimilated to an *instrument*), as in Galileo and Bacon, and are primary in Locke's analysis of human understanding (and psychoanalysis, said Freud, was first of all an art of interpretation). Locke supposed the mind "a white Paper, void of all Characters, without any *Ideas.*" Experience wrote on this paper by observation of "*external, sensible Objects*" and by consideration of "*internal operations of the Mind*" (*Essay*, 104: II.i.2). Freud was to remark that all "major quantities of energy" proceed from "the external world" into the mind. Simultaneously, psychoanalysis took on understanding the mind's internal operations, that mind being obscure and unconscious in its functioning. Just so did Locke view the mind not just as a white paper where experience would write its traces but at the same time as a kind of camera obscura, illumined only by "external and internal Sensation":

These alone, as far as I can discover, are the Windows by which light is let into this *dark Room*. For, methinks, the *Understanding* is not much unlike a Closet wholly shut from light, with only some little openings left, to let in external visible Resemblances, or *Ideas* of things without; would the Pictures coming into such a dark Room but stay there, and lie so orderly as to be found upon occasion, it would very much resemble the Understanding of a Man, in reference to all Objects of sight, and the *Ideas* of them. (*Essay*, 162–63: II.xi.17)

On the *Essay*'s publication, John Norris had criticized Locke for refusing the possibility of unconscious elements in the mind, objecting that "If there be Impressions made on the Mind, whereof we are not conscious, or which we do not perceive, then . . . the not perception of them is no Argument against such Original Impressions" (*Christian*, 4). Locke indeed rejected such criticism; he denied unconscious ideas, not unused ones. In his view, individual will and judgment ordered ideas in a perfectly comprehensible way, however complex it might often be. Nothing in the mind was hidden. Certainly Norris was also thinking of "*Innate Principles*, . . . Reasons drawn from the inward, and to us unknown contexture of our Minds" (11–12) that, he wrote elsewhere, were the "not conscious" presence of a sort of "platonic" foreknowledge lost to the soul's conscious life, ideas lost to the soul at birth and hidden until some impe-

tus caused recall and recuperation (*Essay*). This was not Freud's unconscious either. But kinship is not wholly wanting, for awareness of such lost
knowledge was blocked by the soul's being born into the body and into
conscious human life, which life in many ways depended on the soul's forgetting of its former essence even as it was grounded in it. So when the
"German psychologist Karl Fortlage, in his *System of Psychology* (1855),
went so far as to interpret consciousness as a product of the inhibited
unconscious" (Kahler, *Disintegration*, 32), was he looking to an older (pre-
cartesian?) culture or prefiguring Freud? Freud brought back or created the
occulted subject and simultaneously thrust it deeper beyond reach: one
could only know its functioning via manifestations analysis brought to the
"surface." Yet if "cure" was "interminable," as only ever bringing to light
the past of the unconscious, not its ongoing present, the very possibility
of analysis and explanation is lockean. The subject might be occulted but
it was no less solidly *there*, available to and made by the speaker of psychoanalysis as analytico-referential scientist. As such, it revealed the limits
of a certain discourse—as a Machado seems to confirm.

So Freud was right to assert the importance of his science: "*The interpretation of dreams is the royal road to a knowledge of the unconscious activities of the mind*" (SE, 5:608). He was even justified in proclaiming it a
"science" in an analytico-referential sense, its being not just "the investigation of dreams or of any other mental function taken *in isolation* . . . [but]
a comparative study of a whole series of such functions" (SE, 5:511), one
grounded in a systematic theory. He was right to claim of this dream science
in the preface to its third English-language edition that it "contains, even
according to my present-day [1931] judgement, the most valuable of all the
discoveries it has been my good fortune to make. Insight such as this falls
to one's lot but once in a lifetime" (SE, 4.xxxii). Yet the insight in question
did not concern new objects but the discourse organizing objects, reworking a way of thinking. Psychoanalysis would affirm that my partial analysis
only indicates the world-historical validity of its model—at least for the past
three hundred years. I assert the reverse: that it merely hypostatizes—into
the psyche—that history. That achievement and its internalization can only
be seen as an ideological effort to maintain the discourse in question:
"human thought never reflects merely the object under scrutiny. It also
reflects, along with the object, the being of the scrutinizing subject, his concrete social existence. Thought is a two-sided mirror, and both its sides can
and should be clear and unobscured" (Vološinov, *Freudianism*, 26).

Ignoring this history must lead into further traps: principally, no doubt, repetitions of the same process, mistaking known ways of thinking and doing for the new and unfamiliar, deluding ourselves that we work in a new logic, a new "spirituality," a "reenchanted" praxis. Psychoanalytic science may be taken to illumine a certain historical place and time—once we grasp, as Jameson observes in *The Political Unconscious*, that it can only be situated in a *specific* history:

To come to some ultimate reckoning with psychoanalysis would require us radically to historicize Freudianism itself, and to reach a reflexive vantage point from which the historical and social conditions of possibility both of Freudian method and of its objects of study come into view. . . . The conditions of possibility of psychoanalysis become visible, one would imagine, only when you begin to appreciate the extent of psychic fragmentation since the beginnings of capitalism, with its systematic quantification and rationalization of experience, its instrumental reorganization of the subject just as much as of the outside world. That the structure of the psyche is historical, and has a history, is, however, as difficult for us to grasp as that the senses are not themselves natural organs but rather the results of a long process of differentiation even within human history. (62)

Freud himself commented at the start of *The Future of an Illusion* (1927) that "the less a man knows about the past and the present the more insecure must prove his judgement of the future" (SE, 21:5). Maybe psychoanalysis will have been the science which shows us not only that every western science creates its own objects (the issue of "status" with which this chapter began), but also that every science makes its own history—or rather opens and marks out its own place in the historical arena and culture containing the discursive and conceptual means for it to exist. Freud's science sought to become established at a moment when the dominance of a certain (so-called) mechanistic model was becoming ever more insecure. This was perhaps its privilege as much as its peril. Within that insecurity, psychoanalysis reaffirmed the subject as the ground of the social, ontogenetic originator of right community, retelling an old tale of selfness. A science of frontiers (in the several connotations of the word), psychoanalysis will have been a dreamwork doomed to vanish with the disappearance of the western discursive apparatus that furnished its means of existence.

7

Disordering Narrative Grasp

Beyond such narratives as we have been seeing—*of* a particular history and also *telling* (if unawares) that history—what I now trace are questions posed to these normative narratives of universalized western reason, to their structures, hopes of meaning and grasp of "reality." I shall do so by looking through a novel of exile from these narratives, one written *from* the periphery of Enlightened Europe but written *in* the Americas and completed at the very center of European culture, on a postwar Berlin/Paris axis. But much contemporary European and North American fictive writing, showing its awareness that a supposed universal *ratio* is a local language—or conceptual—game stretched beyond bounds, works as a thought experiment practiced on discourse at the end of its tether, its bond lost with familiar norms of meaning and truth and reference to customary environment. For some such writing, the resultant seeming loss of coherence is as problematic as Bacon found the thinking and writing of certain predecessors to have been without the guide of his new right idea of knowledge and practice: "Yet what spiders' webs they wove for us, wonderful for their texture and the fineness of their thread, but useless for any practical purpose!" ("Refutation," 118). Verbal coherence that "spin[s] out . . . laborious webs of learning" was nothing without attachment to external reference, some correspondence in the world:

For the wit and mind of man, if it work upon matter, which is the contemplation of the creatures of God, worketh according to the stuff, and is limited thereby; but if it work upon itself, as the spider worketh his web, then it is endless, and brings forth indeed cobwebs of learning, admirable for the fineness of thread and work but of no substance or profit. (*Advancement*, 202)

Bacon was dismissing the medieval schoolmen. But that dismissal was part of a broader one of all forms of knowing, *scientia*, that preceded his own arguments for renewal, emphasizing the instrumental utility ("fruit") of action ("experiment") based in true knowledge ("light").

His beloved spider story could be embroidered to serve this more embracing dismissal and wider search for right knowledge and action:

Those who have handled the sciences have been either men of experiment or men of dogmas. The men of experiment are like the ant; they only collect and use; the reasoners resemble spiders, who make cobwebs out of their own substance. The bee takes a middle course; it gathers its material from the flowers of the garden and of the field, but transforms and digests it by a power of its own. Not unlike this is the true business of philosophy, for it neither relies solely or chiefly on the powers of the mind, nor does it take the matter which it gathers from natural history and mechanical experiments and lay it up in the memory whole, as it finds it, but lays it up in the understanding altered and digested. (*Magna Instauratio*, 313: I.xcv)

Bacon's dismissal of scholastic spiders in favor of senecan bees matched the so-called cartesian change explored in Chapter 5. Many have echoed him, worried by loss of coherence and of commonsensical truth in worldly reference. Thus Wittgenstein opposed "the cobwebs of metaphysics" of a nonscientific psychology to real "scientific activity" (Wittgenstein, MS 165: 150–51, in Sutton, *Philosophy*, 25). Less grandly, the fictional detective seeks his truths: "All gossamer and spiders' webs; nothing tangible. What I want," Agatha Christie's Inspector Grange grumbles to Hercule Poirot, "is a good solid *fact!*" (*Murder after Hours*, 223)—worthy shade of Dickens' Gradgrind; although we cannot ignore the experimental/rational play insistently basic to Bacon's argument (and Poirot's) or Wittgenstein's assent that the psychology's nonscientificity does not mean that it "isn't interesting"—just that it isn't rational scientific knowledge. A *move*, like Descartes', is not always as clear-cut as its later perception as *change* would have it.

Some writing accepts the loss and the conflict as a prospectively joyous release, although the terms remain those of binary dissension. Just so did Jonathan Swift delightedly adopt Bacon's tale, making the bee the truth-telling other of the spider's weaving. The bee, snarls Swift, is "a Free-

booter over Fields and Gardens" who "will rob a Nettle as readily as a Vio-
let," menacing the spider whose "large Castle (to show [his] Improvements
in the Mathematicks) is all built with [his] own hands, and the Materials extracted altogether out of [his] own Person." The bee naturally replies in
kind, drawing too on senecan tradition, that his visits to "all the Flowers and
Blossoms of the Field and the Garden" enrich him "without the least Injury
to their Beauty, their Smell, or their Taste," whereas the spider's web has
come near killing him. Too, whatever "Labor and Method" may have gone
into the web, it is, as the bee's breaking of it shows, merely ephemeral, not
something whose "spinning out all from [him]self" should be boasted of: "if
we may judge of the Liquor in the Vessel by what issues out, You possess a
good plentiful Store of Dirt and Poison in your Breast." So which is better?
asks the bee: "That . . . which feeding and engendering on it self, turns all
into Excrement and Venom; producing nothing at last, but Fly-bane and a
Cobweb: Or That, which, by an universal Range, with long Search, much
Study, true Judgment, and Distinction of Things, brings home Honey and
Wax." The point is rammed home by Aesop, concluding that not the spider's solipsistic weaving, but the bee's "infinite Labor, and search, and ranging thro' every Corner of Nature" provide "the two Noblest of Things,
which are Sweetness and Light" (Swift, *Battel*, 382–85).

So with *this* bee's labor, search, and ranging, we end not only in
Bacon's fruit and light of deed and truth but in a familiar *utile/dulce* western tradition, used unquestioningly by Warren in assuming that literature
expressed "the higher pleasure" (which is also an active effect) of "disinterested knowledge" (*Theory*, 31; Chapter 1). *The bond between truth and
instrumental action and literary use and pleasure is fundamental.* Western
theorists and critics have long supposed that *literature* since Horace
(though the word meant something far different to him) joined or had at
least to be defined by "opposites" of emotion and reason, delight and instruction, action and knowing. Poets, he wrote, "Aut prodesse volunt aut
delectare . . . /aut simul et iucunda et idonea dicere vitae" [wish to benefit
or to please . . . /or to speak matter at once pleasing and useful to life]
(Horace, *Ars poetica*, ll. 333–34). Some such view *may* have lain in Seneca's
idea of the bee forging delightfully new understanding from known but
diverse local sources, even as it involved for him a different concept and
practice of "mimesis." Something akin to *this* concept may lie in other
contemporary fictive writings of a kind that strives to find a way to new
sorts of relation:

The word he chose to express "fragile" was filled with the intricacies of a continuing process, and with a strength inherent in spiders' webs woven across paths through sand hills where early in the morning the sun becomes entangled in each filament of web. It took a long time to explain the fragility and intricacy because no word exists alone, and the reason for choosing each word had to be explained with a story about why it must be said this certain way. (Silko, *Ceremony*, 35)

I choose expressions of these different views that nonetheless all share images of spiders' webs (and bees) partly because differences in the same better catch nuances of what this chapter addresses, partly because differences in usage reflect some of the diversities spoken of in earlier chapters (especially Chapter 4, such that the last example is scarcely a *metaphor* at all), and partly because we shall see in later chapters how spiders and their webs are used in different cultures (as again in the last example here) to voice different relations of reason and language to the world, ones which find small delight in Bacon's or Poirot's demands. For Bacon, Swift, Wittgenstein, and Poirot, spiders' webs sternly or merrily criticize ways of understanding asserted to contradict or contravene in some way methodical rationality. For Silko, it names a hope of knitting up a painfully unraveled world. In this chapter, I use Gombrowicz's *Cosmos* to analyze something like the aspiration for a passage between these instances or, more exactly, the voicing of western reason's insufficiency: that its narrow local reach cannot be universalized, cannot manage even the sapience and praxis it has claimed to manage, and provides no means to get past its own limitations. It expresses from a European side an inevitable failure to knit up *its* unraveled world, doing so in ways that specifically undermine the self and rational knowing—the subject with its methodical history-telling—that previous chapters have explored.

But *Cosmos* is not told just from a "European side." Gombrowicz had sailed to Argentina in 1939, the recipient of a paid trip on a new liner; as a literary correspondent, he was to represent Poland's new writing and culture to its émigrés in Buenos Aires (Rita Gombrowicz, *Gombrowicz*, 19; Baranzcak, introduction, x). Arriving on August 21, he felt trapped by the immediate outbreak of war. At the same time, he said later, exile gave occasion to revise the forms of European thought and praxis "from an extra-European position," to "launch an open criticism of modern culture"—so much so that when he went to live in France in 1963, this "return told me: you've reached the end of the road, you're done" (*Entretiens*, 82, 164, 207). For meanwhile he had written a startling novel, *Trans-Atlantyk*, derisively trashing European ideals in their Polish guise and using Argentina or, better, his cultural dislocation there, as means to do so; further, he had been writing his *Diary*, which among other things is an unsystematic assault on one Enlightenment ideal after another.[1] Around 1960, he had written a series of talks for Radio Free Europe that are a dialectic between Argentina and the Americas, Poland and Europe, play and apprehension of each against and with the other (*Pérégrinations*). *Cosmos* appeared in Paris in 1965. It too is embedded in Argentina. Gombrowicz apparently shaped it as a shortish tale as early as 1951. He had made it a novel by 1961, written much of it during stays in Uruguay between then and 1963, and thought it all but done in February 1963, well before he left for Europe (R. Gombrowicz, *Gombrowicz*, 112, 161, 219, 226; *Diary*, 3:17, 67). He wrote it as a critique from outside Europe, from his "23 years and 226 days of Argentina" (*Entretiens*, 191).

This chapter closely sifts the critique that *Cosmos* is. I hope not to fatigue, but to be as "instructive" as only "criticism . . . enter[ing] into minutiae" can—to quote an author who will return to greater effect (Coleridge, *Notebooks*, 3:3970), by analyzing in small detail just how the novel disables a dominant mode of western discourse, the narratives it permits, and the claims made for it and them. Because of the minuteness of this analysis, however, for greater clarity, I start with a rapid overview of my wider argument.

From its start, *Cosmos* struggles with that difficulty of knowing which began this chapter. Its speaker battles what he experiences as a meaninglessness of habitual "analytico-referential" knowledge and discourse, those assuming, since the European seventeenth century, that concepts *analyze* the world as they *refer* and *correspond* to it, giving true knowledge and right means of action (Reiss, *Discourse*, 21–54, 351–85; *Uncertainty*, 1–11, 19–55). We cannot call this speaking subject a "narrator" precisely because the experience prevents the coherent, reasoned *telling* named by the word *narrator* and its cognates. Too, this errant speaker abruptly faces something like a fregean "unmediated image," a sudden physical event whose alien nature eludes all pattern of discovery. A sparrow inexplicably hanged by a wire in the shrubbery forces the speaker to try to grasp and speak it as, to use Frege's terminology, a *Vorstellung* (an immediate perceptual image) whose strict privacy is foreign to the public intelligibility of *Sinn*, meaning: unordered perception offers access to no familiar meanings. This unmediated, unpatterned image intrudes in habitual forms of understanding. They cannot hold it. It demands a different discourse, language-game, or logical world. It *need* not do so maybe (Poirot could explain it), but in *Cosmos*, it destroys analytico-referentiality. Language is unsettled. Theoretical and practical distinctions like signified, signifier, and referent (Ferdinand de Saussure's triplet) or form and substance of expression and of content (Louis Hjelmslev's quartet) are upset and made inoperative. Internal truth-telling (analytical coherence) dissolves. External truth-telling in the adequacy of sign to thing or event (referential correspondence) is rent.

As the power and possibility of standard narratives collapse, *Cosmos* becomes a quest for new understanding and way of speaking it, marked by what Gombrowicz praised as "immaturity," youth, and "incompleteness" sapping Kant's *mature* European Enlightenment with its venerable, totalizing "reason" and "Mastery" and opposing "younger cultures," Argentina with its "slumbering Indian" thought and Poland at the edge of Enlightened Europe, to "France and England" and a "European spirit" (*Diary*, 1:135; 2:93, 128, 205; 3:96, 104). Just so did Gombrowicz experience Berlin as a quintessentially *European* center, bathed in a history whose meaning and consequence it did not wish to explore: "I, a person from Argentina, rather ahistorical and inexperienced, kept having the feeling that Berlin, like Lady Macbeth, was endlessly washing its hands . . ." (*Diary*, 3:116). But Europeans cannot be self-righteous about Berlin. Paris, too, is ever on the "rockier and rockier road to Mastery. Never even once look[ing] back," likewise ignoring the history it embodies (*Diary*, 3:104). Paris, too, in its "old age" (3:96), epitomizes Europe with its "proud nose of maturity," its adulthood. It is "the maximal expression of European aesthetics," where

beauty becomes civilized, that is, organized, and what's more it is subject to a division of functions: some exist to make beauty, others to consume it. The beauty of man, humanity, seems to be fragmenting more and more into the writing of poems and reciting of poems, into the painting of pictures and looking at pictures, into producing lipstick and applying it, into dancing in a ballet and watching it. (*Diary*, 3:149)

Other fragmentations match the scissions of act and thought we have seen vital to the European "spirit" Gombrowicz scorns and undermines, including the "aesthetic" ones of use and pleasure, instruction and delight, reason and action.[2] *Cosmos* explores the ground of that spirit, sapping the baconian, "cartesian," Enlightenment work of analysis, reference, and instrumental action.

The novel offers several paths. Each fails. (1) The search for a coherent series of signs able to be *interpreted*, given one or more specific and limited meanings according to familiar habit, peters out and collapses. (2) The speaking subject's will to impose itself *as* ordering subject on objects leads to discursive isolation, comprehensible to others but giving a wholly subjective and "perspectival" ordering of what seems beyond discourse; this "will" becomes impotent or only autotelic and solipsistic. (3) Discursive transparency becomes impossible as discourse itself shows that there is no correspondence between its order and that of things or of experience. (4) The speaking subject takes responsibility for the creation of events, construction of the experienced world, until it again faces an event whose creation it cannot claim, once more incomprehensible (the sense of "comprehension" already having changed, since at the very least it no longer means a collective communication of universally accepted truths). (5) The only possible meaning finally becomes that of the very process of producing signification, of only and always inscribing one's own signature (as speaking subject) in and on discourse. The novel spells out these failures in technically detailed ways, as, for example, undermining "natural" language in the first instance after specific linguistic models and disarming ways of knowing in the others according to specific epistemological models— which is to say not that Gombrowicz knows these or *intends* using them, but that his subversion of language and discourse is exact enough to be explicated via the "scientific" models that Enlightenment discourse applies to its own self-understanding, implicitly and simultaneously limiting them as it sets bounds on the discourse and practices they analyze. I shall propose just some of these models as representative in analyzing these subversions.

With approach 5, the subject enfolds itself in a private language that makes any relation with others impossible, withholds community, and indeed frustrates any and all social activity. At the end of *Cosmos*, that failure is marked by a return to familiar ways of discourse, now unable to express anything but meaningless banalities. The novel's experiment on discourse will have undermined all the basic elements of analytico-referentiality (and its accompaniments) and shown the need for different forms of discourse. At the same time, it will have implied that the willful subject of speech (or any subject) is unable to generate these other forms or even to think them, that Wittgenstein was right (before so many later arguers) to claim that one cannot escape the rules of a language game from within, the *episteme* in which one *is*. The willful hobbesian *fiat* only repeats itself. And even Wittgenstein could imply (at least in 1931) a more universalizing claim for one such game when asserting of a perceived similarity between ancient Greek and modern European thought and experience that however different in size and kind "even the hugest telescope has to have an eye-piece no larger than the human eye," as if human differences were ever but superstructures laid on a single infrastructure and one rationality ruled, or should rule, ubiquitously (*Culture*, 17e).

But here, there is perhaps also a sense that even when reasons (tele-scopes) differ there has to be a way for everyone to have at least *some* view of and into them. For different modes of reason and experience cannot be *totally* closed to our perception and understanding of them. This conclu-sion that they could be is inadmissible in real life. It would testify to the *es-sential* impossibility of any prospective thought and action other than mere repetition of the past, impossibility of ever forging Saramago's imaginary is-land. It would say that hegemonic change cannot only not be achieved but cannot even be thought. So *Cosmos* also shows why the fictive imagination and its products are embedded in all a culture's practices and not somehow to be thought autonomous of them. Operations of language and mind, with the activity of the "subject," cannot be isolated from their whole en-vironment. Language and the consciousness it expresses, we have much seen, are parts of social praxis. This means not that the fictive imagination is secondary or subordinate but that it is in a dialectic with all a culture's practices. *Cosmos* thus undermines a usual western claim, "change the way we speak/write/think and we change the social order," and its denial, that language and thought have *no* direct impact on that order. *Cosmos* shows the futility of the idea of autonomy at the same time as it ridicules that of too readily transforming a *particular* mode of making sense, of thinking, into something universal.

I begin with a passage that encapsulates the novel's "agenda"— or, rather, its praxis. It concerns the process and stability of writing, Gombrowicz's own and that of western literary discourse:

Extraordinary. A hanged bird. A hanged sparrow. This shrieking eccentricity indi-cated that a human hand had penetrated this fastness. Who on earth could have done such a thing, what could be the reason? (P8; E10; F15)[3]

This brief passage marks the willful subject's *intention* to *discover* meaning and the prospective absence of this meaning (the *extra*ordinariness and *ex*-centricity of the hanged sparrow). Meaning may become just a mark of what is not expressed and of what will perforce remain inexpressible in language. Indeed, the only "meaning" of discourse may well become that of the *im*possibility of finding and applying meaning. The passage continues:

> I thought in confusion, standing in the midst of this chaos, this proliferating vegetation with its endless complications, [my head full of] the rattle and clatter of the night-long train journey, insufficient sleep, the air [and] the sun [and] the tramp through the heat with this [man] Fuchs, [and] Jesia [and] my mother, the row about the letter, [and] my rudeness to the old man, [and Julius] Roman, and also Fuchs' troubles with his chief at the office [about which he had told me], and the bad road, [and] the ruts and lumps of earth [and] heels, trouser-legs, stones, [and] all this vegetation, all culminating like a crowd genuflecting before this hanged sparrow—reigning triumphantly and eccentric over this outlandish spot. (P8; E10; F15)

What happens, though, is that the hanged sparrow will stay neither outlandish nor eccentric. It becomes central to any putatively meaningful discourse. Doing so, it strips habitual discourse of familiar sense.

The words *eccentric* and *eccentricity* designate something taken as outside a center, away from a mean. But what is such a center? Clearly, any ordering of material, social and personal worlds (marked here by the jumbled association of memories, feelings, events, observations—a jumble that the translator seeks to soften and even remove) into which the hanged sparrow will not and cannot enter. What is taken as central are the classifications that make "ordinary," "familiar," and "habitual" the entire domain of things, events, observations, and so forth that is *conceived* as "outside" whatever enables such classifications (i.e., discourse and thought). This *outside* is itself a prior reduction dependent on one such classification—hence the need to write of the phenomenal domain as *conceived* in such a way. But the extraordinariness signaled by the hanged sparrow is not due just to its exteriority to such classification or, rather, not *simply* to it. It is, after all, not a natural phenomenon kept out of the codifying process only because the code (system enabling application of meaning) is not adaptable to its inclusion.[4] On the contrary, the extraordinariness comes from the very codifying process: sign "that a human hand had penetrated this fastness." The difficulty comes from the fact that the sparrow's presence is not usual, defies expectation. Its presence will uncover the classifying/codifying process just because it is *there*, amid the "ordinary." Perhaps even it marks another possible process or system whose order will have to be grasped, or created, and will show the limitations, irrelevance, and/or particularity of "our" discourse and companion practice. Or else it will have to be reduced to our expectations by ascription of a meaning such as its being the act of a madman or a delinquent.

Most familiar now in the West as a possibly different discursive process is what has been called *myth*. Myth, as a total discursive practice, is not at all mere content, as once imagined. Since Ernst Cassirer and even more Lévi-Strauss (whether or not one accepts their understanding of it), myth has been seen as *a way of composing contents*, a specific kind of classifying process, that is to say. From his unabashedly western perspective, applying his argument to American indigenous peoples, Lévi-Strauss described myth as the manufacture from "bits and pieces" of an observed world of a structure, letting members of a given culture grasp a set of relations between themselves, their culture, and nature or the world (see *La pensée sauvage* and, more extensively, *Mythologiques*). Writing of eastern Indian ways of understanding, Nandy has described as *myth* a process of making historical event conceptually active in the present (see Chapter 5, note 8). *Myth* spells to western ears a lack of epistemological seriousness, "a flawed, irrational fairy-tale produced by 'unconscious' history, meant for savages and children" (Nandy, *Intimate*, 60). This is telling. For precisely at issue are differences of logics, language-games, regimes of meaning, as well as western claims to universality. Michael A. Gomez gets at a narrative process relating past to present seemingly akin to that of Nandy's observation without resorting to the awkward term of *myth*. He notes that the job of the West African *griot* was/is analogously "to re-create the past, or whatever the subject of his dissertation, in such a way as to make the past present, to make it palpable, to place the listener within the framework of the text" (*Exchanging*, 280).[5] Again at issue are varied logics of knowing humans' situation in the world and relation to each other.

Such discursive processes, like others, could be serially recurrent, or always potential practices even where another process dominates. Were this last the case, how would they work with respect to the dominance of the different order of discourse? In *The Discourse of Modernism*, I argued that "instauration" of analytico-referential discourse occurred with gradual disappearance of a "patterning discourse" and progressive occultation of elements that would otherwise have prevented this instauration. For a main aspect of patterning involved what "postcartesians" would think of as a "nondifferentiation" of elements they separate as words, concepts, material objects, events, numbers, and more—a nondifferentiation that would shatter a process functioning in terms of identity and difference, presence and absence, sameness and alterity (on patterning, see *Discourse*, 21–107, especially 46–48). Chapter 5 explored an analogous setting of one sort of historical relation to the world against another, consummated as an actual break sometime after Descartes, who himself, I suggested, was willing to live with ambivalences. Indeed, a fundamental uncertainty should be created whenever western analytico-referentiality—or any of its subcategories (science, history, literature . . .)—meet different discursive processes and their accompanying practices.

Cosmos seems in just this way to confront us from the first with the mark of a potentially different practice of meaning. What directly follows the textual mark of an unexplained piece of the world (the sparrow) is first an effort to insert this possibly different practice in the "normal," next dissolution of the language of that effort and last confrontation of the difficulty thus posed of expressing any meaning at all—not least that of *this* composition called *Cosmos*. The attempt to insert a wholly unfamiliar element provokes the breakup of our (western) normal discourse. From the start, the initially indicated "presence" remains an absence for discourse. It occurs as an "immediate perception," a *Vorstellung*, as what Gaston Bachelard, to take another instance, called a "material intuition." Discourse can do no more than mark the presence. It cannot explain it, make it meaningful. For that, a new sort of ordering process seems required. Yet such a new process, it will be suggested, erases habitual discourse and its consecrated knowledge. At best, it is made wholly equivocal and perplexed. The point of departure that the sparrow marks in the text is of some kind of experimental nexus, setting as around some central point a heap of experiences with no apparent link. They can be reduced to no clear series that would in and of itself produce meaning. The narrator can only align a series of "thoughts in confusion" that accumulate almost *against* any analytical ordering. These "pieces," which could be explained (which the English version does try to "explain" by reforming the discourse), might "normally" work to contain the eccentric hanged sparrow by inserting it in the (cartesian?) order of memory that we expect them to provide. What actually happens is close to the opposite: they yield to the "triumphant reign" of the outlandish presence.

Gombrowicz wrote that *Cosmos* is somewhat a "detective novel," a narrative form realized as "an attempt at organizing chaos," predicated on a "search for an explanatory, ordering idea" answering the "demand [for] sense." It wants to impose "Form" on a whirlwind of "excessive fact" (*Diary*, 3:160–61). Such fact even precedes the *Vorstellung* as a first, private, conceptual reduction; as a result, "Form," Gombrowicz said, must also be seen "in its autonomy, its perpetual openness [*disponibilité*], its creative fury, in its whims and perversities, its accumulations and dissolutions, its constant tangles and untanglings" (*Entretiens*, 193–94). One confronts chaos both where Form tries to make meaning and on the site of *Dasein*, being-in-the-world. So *Cosmos* is "a novel about a reality that is creating itself" in *both* these places: "In light of our building our worlds through associating phenomena, I would not be surprised if at the primal beginning of all time, there was a *double association*. It indicates direction in chaos and is the beginning of order" (*Diary*, 3:160, 162)—whence the novel's title. It queries analytico-referential discourse's claim to make absolute what should be seen as a specific local way of understanding and form of action.

Since the seventeenth century, Enlightened Reason has accorded itself such universalizing privileges. John Stuart Mill's view of the right method of history is an exemplary transfer of this "scientific" model into another domain, where it

consists in attempting, by a study and analysis of the general facts of history to discover . . . the law of progress; which law, once ascertained, must . . . enable us to predict future events, *just as after a few terms of an infinite series in algebra we are able to detect the principle of regularity in their formation, and to predict the rest of the series to any number of terms we please.* (*Philosophy*, 344–46: *Logic*, VI.x.§3)

Mill, to be sure, argued that where society and history are predicated this could not be more than an "empirical law" without the rigid uniformity of a mathematical series. But Karl Popper rightly observed that this assumed no less that such a series matched some naturally sequential "progress" of societies sufficiently rigorously as to provide full understanding of them (*Poverty*, 117–18).

We have little difficulty in seeing Mill's view (*intended* as a critique of Auguste Comte's stricter mechanistic materialism) as transposing into social history the marquis de Laplace's claim that if one knew the present position and motion of every atom, one could predict the future of the universe to all eternity. Bernard Le Bovier de Fontenelle and others had long advanced the same idea about history; poets and critics like Dryden and Rymer had said right literature to be as exact as Euclid's geometry; in 1803, Samuel Taylor Coleridge professed to be drafting a theory of human morality and psychology guided by just this predictability (Reiss, *Meaning*, 179–80, 309–10). All expressed the Enlightened rationality that Virginia Woolf debunked with ironic glee in *To the Lighthouse* when describing how the young painter Lily Briscoe imagined Mr. Ramsay's alphabetically linear work, progressing inexorably and authoritatively from one letter to the next:

she always saw clearly before her a large kitchen table. It was Andrew's doing. She asked him what his father's books were about. "Subject and object and the nature of reality," Andrew had said. And when she said Heavens, she had no notion what that meant, "Think of a kitchen table then," he told her, "when you're not there."

So now she always saw, when she thought of Mr. Ramsay's work, a scrubbed kitchen table. It lodged now in the fork of a pear tree, for they had reached the orchard. . . . Naturally, if one's days were passed in this seeing of angular essences, this reducing of lovely evenings, with all their flamingo clouds and blue and silver to a white deal four-legged table (and it was a mark of the finest minds so to do), naturally one could not be judged like an ordinary person. (38)

What Lily Briscoe knows as virile analytical discourse is as outlandishly alien to her as is whatever might be manifested by the sparrow in the chaotic undergrowth for *Cosmos'* speaker. Both cases, in often similar terms, offer oppositions between what seem incommensurable orders and show the impositions and dominances that occur—or try to—as a result. In *To the Lighthouse*, for example, the imposition is in place from the start, in the form of the patriarchal analytical discourse. The novel recounts Mrs. Ramsay's sardonic acceptance of its dominance as she plays the role set for her by her husband as representative of familiar forms of societal control: giving men "chivalry and valour" and all power in the public domain, receiving for herself "something trustful, childlike, reverential," aspects of an attitude, remarks the narrator with biting irony, "which no woman could fail to feel or to find agreeable." In the meantime, Lily Briscoe rejects the imposition and seeks a personal vision able to withstand constant interference of that dominance; even if, under present social conditions, it means exclusion from them. Her picture "would be hung in the attics . . . ; it would be destroyed. But what did that matter? she asked herself," adding the last essential stroke to the canvas. For after all she had "had [her] vision" and so established her identity outside others' narratives (*Lighthouse*, 13, 309–10). No doubt in the attic spiders would gather about her painting and hang it with their cobwebs.

In *Cosmos*, the ordering process shown in *To the Lighthouse* through Ramsay or Charles Tansley is not so much subject to acceptance (however ironic) or rejection as simply put off. Any meaning that might have accrued to any narrative ordering is continually deferred. *Cosmos* offers such order as itself a deflection, a falsification: "How is it that, born as we are out of chaos, we can never get up against it? No sooner do we look at it than order, pattern, shape is born under our eyes (P28; E31; F41). The hanged sparrow demands a new order *after* a first constitution from chaos has become habitual. It queries whatever order we *already* have, positing a need for something different, more complete but also always recognizing and speaking its incompleteness. *Cosmos* sets before the reader the threat of a total decay of meaning. It cannot actually achieve it because, as the speaker says, we *always* make order, pattern, shape, adding the reductions all meaning requires in order to be cut out of chaos. Thus the novel's opening sentence insists on the mark of history, on an intentional narrative origin that ought to have controlled the entire story: "I will tell you another, more curious adventure" (P7; E19; F13). But the narrative falls apart almost instantly. Only falteringly is an ordered syntax produced and after feeling about amid mere accumulation of nouns (again changed in the published English version):

Sweat, Fuchs walks, I behind him, trouser-legs, heels, sand, on we walked, on we walked heavily, earth, ruts, vile road, gleams from shiny pebbles, air shimmering, buzzing with heat, everything black with sunlight, houses, fences, fields, woods, this road, this walk, why and how, it would be a long story, to tell the truth I was sick and tired of my father and mother, and the whole family, also I wanted to pass at least one exam and get a bit of a change, escape, stay somewhere afar. (P7; E9; F13)

The heap of nouns is gradually gathered in a linear syntax, forged, one may say, by three phrases toward the end: "a long story," "to tell the truth," "I wanted." These depict the essence of Enlightened discourse: elaboration of an analytical logical system (establishing an internally coherent truth of narrative), relation of reality (establishing a truth of external correspondence to real events, etc.), the speaking subject's intentional role in these establishments. These three elements were fundamental to the scientific model of analysis and reference. Its exemplary and simplest literary version may well have been the very detective story Gombrowicz urges us to recall in *Cosmos*, a kind of *Endpunkt* of literary writing as euclidian system that Jean-François Marmontel modeled in the Enlightenment

Encyclopédie, writing under "Invention": "A poem is a machine in which everything must be combined to produce a mutually coherent movement" (*Encyclopédie*, 18:968). For at least since Edgar Allan Poe, the detective novel (indeed, from long before, perhaps, the novel in general) has been marked by a desire to tell truth, give facts, and wilfully organize the enigma's solution, which is always offered as the conclusion of an analytical series of reasonings as coherent as Marmontel's machine of poetry, as clear-cut as an expansive "history that never stands still, that presses on, swallowing up those civilizations for whom time has stopped still" (Calvino, "Montezuma," *Numbers*, 193)—no doubt those using such logics as Gomez and Nandy name. Nor does it matter who actually declares the solution, whether the narrator is the detective or a third person.

Truth results from the will of the encoder, the one who enacts the system along its double track: firstly, a logical train of cause and finality climbing back from its own conclusion, murder, theft, or whatever; secondly, a chain that is the represented/related objectification of the first, the association of the logic's constants with the variable events—"facts"—in the world concretizing them. The relation of the two gives our history of truth. Poirot never tired of explaining how to reach this sort of truth:

> "Not so. *Voyons*! One fact leads to another—so we continue. Does the next fit in with that? *À merveille*! Good! We can proceed. The next little fact—no! Ah, that is curious! There is something missing—a link in the chain that is not there. We examine. We search. And that little curious fact, that possibly paltry little detail that will not tally, we put it here!" He made an extravagant gesture with his hand. "It is significant! It is tremendous!"
>
> "Y-es—" [from Hastings].
>
> "Ah!" Poirot shook his finger so fiercely at me that I quailed before it. "Beware! Peril to the detective who says: 'It is so small—it does not matter. It will not agree. I will forget it.' That way lies confusion! Everything matters!" (Christie, *Mysterious Affair*, 34–35)

The stuttering form, the exaggerated use of exclamation (the questing, ordering mind at work: Oedipus' "I *will* know!"; Archimedes' "Eureka"!), the detective narrator's aggressive stance would repay further exploration. The difficulty, as Gombrowicz observes, is that if *all* the facts matter, then what criterion can we use to grasp the beginning of the chain? what chain do we select? what detail can be made to tally with what other detail? how can we find the "right" order? "You have given me the facts faithfully," says Poirot to Hastings. "Of the order in which you present them, I say nothing—truly, it is deplorable!" (35).

As we know, narratives are actually open to varied solutions. In real life, the detective often invents facts needed to complete a story. Courts adopt "legal fictions" to enable narratives to work their truth. A fact, Philip's Traveller accuses Livingstone, "is whatever anyone, having the power to enforce it, says is a fact. Power—that is the distinguishing mark of a fact" (*Looking*, 67). A language user *has* to select what she calls facts. Facts are facts-for-us inasmuch as they are held in a story whose legitimation is that of the habitual logic in which it is told. That habit and its acceptance are its and *all* its speakers' power. But some speakers have the different sort of power over and in language of which Philip speaks: power to impose or exclude, knowledge/power of the scientist, force/power of the colonizer . . . , coming from what Nandy calls "a culture of hyper-masculinity, adulthood, historicism, objectivism, and hypernormality" (*Intimate*, 100). Does one tiredly need to add that this is not to say there are not observer or speaker independent events-in-the-world? It is to say that once they enter a pattern of observation and a system of speaking, they are *also* relative to pattern and system—and perhaps, as many have observed, we have no access to them except under their aspect as given to us by "the whole body of [our] culture's discourse" (Walton, 102). *Cosmos* proposes that there can be no such thing as an absolutely *right* order: among the chaos of things, any choice is only *not* arbitrary to the extent it fits that body of discourse. The problem is that such truth-telling is ineluctably tied to forms of action. What is needed to solve crimes, says Poirot elsewhere, is "a passion for the truth." That, replies Henrietta Savernake, begs a major question: "would knowledge be enough? Would you have to go a step further and translate knowledge into action?" (Christie, *Murder*, 153).

The detective story, narrative history, like any other *rationes*, need sortings of events in the world (what are at any rate given as such) to disclose those susceptible of entering the linear discourse of analysis and reference. Events that will not go in ("red herrings," those outside the willed order, beyond the pale) are set aside. The conclusion or result to be explained must be sufficiently "normal" to adopt a code shared by reader and narrator; one that *is* our "horizon of expectation," "communal competence." There must be familiar context and syntax: Wittgenstein's chessboard and the moves allowed on it. Outside them are spiders' webs. As he put it,

Augustine, we might say, does describe a system of communication; only not everything that we call language is this system. And one has to say this in many cases where the question arises "Is this an appropriate description or not?" The answer is "Yes, it is appropriate, but only for this narrowly circumscribed region, not for the whole of what you are claiming to describe." (*Philosophical*, 11ᵉ: I.§23)

Heisenberg reached an analogous concept with his *abgeschlossene Theorien* (Heelan, *Quantum*, 142 ff.). Grounding this idea is the principle that a given theory holds for one applicable area, laws governing the theory (not laws of nature but of observation of nature) holding true within the limits of the logical space they describe—the area of applicability referred to as a "closed system." So newtonian mechanics holds for macroscopic events greater than intra-atomic ones (wherever Planck's constant h can be ignored) at "one end" of its applicability and, at the "other," where movement is negligible in proportion to the speed of light. Our "commonsense reality" is simply *that* closed system. Heisenberg designated four such closed physical systems: newtonian mechanics, electromagnetic theory and relativity, theory of heat, and quantum mechanics. The search for a unified field theory is an effort to find a system of laws enveloping them all.

These are varieties of positivistic analysis and reference, of western scientific narrative, versions of what *Cosmos* questions. Especially is the last in eliciting some *magna realitas* to be explained in one nomothetical system of *the* one complete "law of nature." Not dissimilar is the idea that beneath the varieties of biological life, whether revealed in the patterns of flowers, seashells, or animal markings, are mathematically organized "deep rules." This idea of basic logics of the physical and biological world *corresponding* exactly to the laws of human explicative reason carries into popular dicta about human intelligence and its fancied machine analog the computer: in the thought that intelligence is just "a matter of getting the right formulas in the right combination and then applying them over and over . . . 're-cursively,' until [its] problem is solved," as John R. Searle critically expounds one writer. This writer, Ray Kurzweil, is sure "we" will soon find "the complete set of unifying formulas that underlie intelligence." Bettering Descartes, who proposed, we saw, that complete scientific knowledge would take a few centuries (but then we've already had their benefit), Kurzweil is sure "we are likely to finish the job in a few more decades" (Searle, 34).[6] The exactly describable mechanical processes of this mental equivalent of a unified field theory are taken accurately to depict *all* processes of intelligence and what it knows. Like Fontenelle's, Rymer's, and

Coleridge's hopes for history, literature, and ethics, these have their illustrious precursor in Descartes' compeer, Galileo, whose celebrated adage in his 1623 *Saggiatore* about the founding mathematical language of nature set their stage. Mathematics was "the key to" knowing nature because it mirrored the rules of human reason. Yet as God's written rule in nature it was "universal and not man-made" and so "the perfect instrument," taken to express those aspects of what was to be known that were "humanly understandable without imposing a limiting human vision on it" (Bezzola Lambert, 54).

One question *Cosmos* asks is how to mark and grasp a system's limits, justify such limits, make them useful—and then trace its exclusions, their implications, their nature and effect on discourse and action. The sparrow is the catalyst. It signals a departure from the board. Leaving open the question "Departure into where?", it asks, "How can the novel or any narrative descriptive system deal with this eccentric departure from the habitual?" Heisenberg's *potentia* offered an approach—an objective tendency with subject and object essentially interactive (implying that a universal closed descriptive system was impossible). A system and its producing, the sense it composed when "read" and whatever referent it was taken to have, formed a kind of triadic process: the system accounting for a set of observations, series of narrative elements (syntax), and body of narrated facts (truths). *Potentia* was the process joining them, giving them meaning. Heisenberg proposed *potentia* as explaining the generation of speech performance in specifically scientific areas. Perhaps, though, social communication and interaction *always* so functioned:

This is the order that the actual generative process of language follows: *social intercourse is generated* (stemming from the basis); *in it verbal communication and interaction are generated and in the latter, forms of speech performances are generated; finally, this generative process is reflected in the change of language forms.*

So writes Vološinov (*Marxism*, 96). These processes are *potentia* in another area. They hang over all activity stemming from them—already always making meanings. *Cosmos'* sparrow forces speaker and reader to know them to be inevitable and ever limited in appropriateness and applicability.

For a commonsense attempt to narrate, describe, and explain, the hanged sparrow is monstrous in at least three ways. Firstly, in the "syntax" of everyday life, one does not hang sparrows. A hanged sparrow is unusual, a fact without expected meaning, senseless, save by its ascription to an act of madness or delinquency. But this makes it no more meaningful. Since fact and madness are mutually defining, the ascription only acknowledges meaninglessness. The explanation is the tautology of a given logic. This factual level, I add, is that of reference in analytico-referential discourse, "telling the truth." For such discourse, second, order lies at the level of the signified, the concept: in the description of proliferating vegetation, monstrosity is in the presence of death amid life, of the human hand's "technicity" amid nature: "hanging by a bit of wire attached to a branch of a tree" (P8; E10; F15). Thirdly, in the told imprecision and confusion of the thicket, in the asyntactic accumulation of nouns, sits a named "something peculiar and strange," different, "other" (P8; E10; F14: *cośsterczało*, something that "projected out"—of the habitual, precisely), "peculiar" *because* it is, with respect to the signified and referential levels, different and strange, because it is not readily adaptable to the vegetal and verbal confusion. It does not fit, yet at the level of the signifier, now, it is far and away the most exact element: "It was a sparrow. A sparrow hanging from a bit of wire. Hanged. Its little head bent and its mouth wide open. It was hanging by a bit of wire attached to a branch of a tree" (P8; E10; F15).

The economy of this passage contrasts sharply with the confused piling up in evidence in the two passages on either side of it. I have already cited the one that follows (265–66 above). Here is the one that precedes:

He plunged deeper into the thicket where there were nooks, crannies shaded by the mingling hazel-trees and branches of pine. I gazed into the maze of leaves, little branches, speckled light, thickenings, gaps, turns, thrustings, windings, openings, heaven knows what besides, in this dappled space which came forward and receded, calmed down, pushed, I don't know what, jostled, made way. . . . Lost, covered in sweat, I felt the bare, black earth under my feet. (P8; E10; F14)

The mentioned reversal indicates the thing's monstrosity. What one might expect to be easily and "automatically" described escapes clear syntax, replaced by accumulating verbs and nouns (which the English-language version again readjusts). Too, at other levels of language, these parts of speech designate and refer to actions, events, and situations in a nature that would generally be indifferent in the detective novel. What defies explanation is held in a usual and even rigid syntax. How this initial presentation of the sparrow's material presence works serves to signal a first, quite familiar, possibility of "fix[ing] a direction in chaos and install[ing] an order": just that of "commonsense" discourse. But it is achieved at the cost of isolating that presence altogether. (It does not matter whether or not one accepts Saussure's analysis of language followed here, the point is that the text undermines in exact ways "mature" analytico-referential discourse, however described.)

The reader will understand that the thicket's told (signified) disorder, becoming a disorder of discourse (at the level of signifier), is nothing other than the remnant, as it were, of the usual social systematizations with which we come to terms, into which we habitually seek to insert our individual "will" (as enunciating subjects), intending rationally to *understand* and instrumentally to *use*. The hanged sparrow evades such efforts. Doing so, it puts in doubt the normal model of discourse, as well as all the notions of use, understanding, rational method, individual knowledge, and the rest that characterize it—not to mention ultimately the very function of such concepts as individual, will, subject, intention. The sparrow's presence is from the start incomprehensible. It occurs in forms of language rendering meaning only in the vaguest and most confused ways. Wittgenstein remarked that "the *speaking* of language is part of an activity, or of a form of life" (*Philosophical*, 11ᵉ: I.§23). Heisenberg analogously urged that a set of physical theorems (e.g., those composing "newtonian mechanics") presented us with a "world." Such a world or form of life gives a frame for what we take as the *objective reality* given by its corresponding discourse but it is perceived as the *whole* of such reality. It follows that if the known discourse is disabled the world it produces breaks up: here, referential truth, analytical understanding, objective reality lose anchorage. A manipulatory technique is lost: "To understand a sentence means to understand a language. To understand a language means to be a master of a technique" (Wittgenstein, *Philosophical*, 188ᵉ: I.§199). In *Cosmos*, the hand's technical manipulation undoes the linguistic technique supposed to match it: for Gombrowicz, like Husserl, his pupil Heidegger, and others, *technique, technology*, and *science* are shorthand for flaws of Kant's mature Enlightenment (e.g., *Diary*, 3:119)—maturity, we saw, marking a destructive hegemony, technology being "the god that rules the world with a savage unforgivingness" (Philip, *Frontiers*, 250).

So the difficulty raised is not just for the potential narrator/detective of *Cosmos* (or of any novel, come to that), or even for the reader/decoder of the coherent world it might have been showing if that world could be placed in any way "parallel to ours" (as the imagined world of a utopia or of science fiction, for example). The difficulty is that of any kind of understanding once touch is lost with usual techniques. *Cosmos* starts by showing how everyday commonsensical language is composed of such, however unaware of this most speakers may be—or unaware of it as a constraint, at least. *Cosmos* starts by throwing in doubt ordinary western discourse as a way of knowing and acting. As we have been amply seeing, a given society, culture, place, and era is governed by one most familiar "dominant" discourse, governed by a particular set of use criteria (although other, less habitual discourses are doubtless available). For western discourse of analysis and reference, the truth or falsity of an interpretation, for instance, is judged by the degree to which the interpretation or "reading" in question fits the horizon of users for whom a proposition is defined by its agreement with the criteria of truth-functionality: "to say that a proposition is whatever can be true or false amounts to saying: we call something a proposition when *in our language* we apply the calculus of truth functions to it" (Wittgenstein, *Philosophical*, 52ᵉ: I.§136). An interpretation is meaningful for us when it uses and accords with such criteria. What we call "intention" in this context has been that application and then its inscription: "when we grasp a single point on a map we are quite well aware that others elude us" (*Cosmos*, P17; E20; F27). But not everyone *is* so aware. Incommensurabilities existing within and between cultural spheres wherever different stories, histories, and understandings meet usually clash more or less violently when users of one try to impose it on others: "Fact— Livingstone discovered Victoria Falls . . . *That* is a lie, *and* a fact" because the colonizers had the power to make it so (Philip, *Looking*, 68). Is *anything* a fact in the three words of the sentence "Columbus discovered America"?

For in a different discourse, *that* grasp might not be meaningful at all, or it would possess a different meaning, or indeed the very idea of meaning—of the will to mean—might be altogether absent (surely Rousseau imagined his noble savages' cries quite differently—as perhaps Gibbon did his Iroquois writing). To users of *this* discourse, the ways and claims of European histories simply do not *fit* their reality; force may impose them for domination and exploitation, but what they *say* has no truth, fact, or perhaps even meaning. In another logic, interpretation in terms of fiction/fact, true/false, good/bad, beautiful/ugly may be meaningless. Nor need we go this far: "Not all cultures," Walton avers, "are as constantly preoccupied with truth and falsity as ours is" (95–96). To use such terms is to try to grasp difference in alien criteria taken from our discourse (see note 5). That is always a difficulty: "And the worst of it was that it was impossible to place the sparrow on the same map as the mouth, it belonged to an entirely different one, a different area altogether, a fortuitous and entirely absurd and irrelevant area . . ." (P18; E21; F28). *Cosmos'* speaker starts with this dilemma, for he appears precisely as the (potential) *narrator* of a *novel*. To try to express the unfamiliar must be, in a familiar discourse, to mark the individual *will* to speak. And *here*, the dilemma is of the will to mean as a refusal of habitual meaning. The speaker can only attain that in already given discourse, because it is *its* production of meaning that he refuses: "I looked around at what was to be seen, though I had no desire to see it, because I had seen it so often already: pines and hedges, firs and houses, grass and weeds, a ditch, footpaths and flower-beds, fields and a chimney" (P7–8; E9; F14). Humans' order, their ordering of nature, is well composed and relatively cultivated. Even the thicket's confusion owes something to human hand, like the hanged sparrow's incomprehensible presence. It is set in white—"The air was shimmering with sunlight"—and black: "but black, the trees were black, the earth was grey, the vegetation at ground-level was green, but everything was pretty black" (P8; E8–9; F14).

This is a passage that the French translation exaggerates: "mais en noir, le noir des arbres, le noir de la terre, le noir des plantes, le tout était plutôt noir" ("but in black, black of the trees, black of the earth, black of the plants, everything was pretty much black"). Did Gombrowicz have a hand in this? In his 1968 *Entretiens*, he certainly took the thought to epitomize the entire novel:

For me, *Cosmos* is black, first of all black, a kind of black stream, boiling, full of vortices, stops, stagnant waters, a black water full of a thousand residues that man fixes by trying to decode it, understand, tie what he sees in a certain totality . . . Blackness, terror and night. Night crossed with a violent passion, unnatural love. Whatever . . . I think this dramatic aspect of *Cosmos* will only be fully legible after some time. (*Entretiens*, 192)

May we take the contrast in *Cosmos* as the black and white of printed signs? so many figures in relief against the whiteness of bright air (more "young" Argentine than old European)? blank page lying open to be filled with the order of clear and distinct discourse? "normal" knowledge? echo of the "silence" of habitual meaning as it awaits insertion of "shrieking eccentricity"? "By using black print on white paper, we make each letter stand out sharply against the background. Thus a printed page consists of a set of discrete and easily classified shapes, and is in consequence a logician's paradise. But he must not delude himself into thinking that the world outside looks equally charming": so Bertrand Russell (*Inquiry*, 23), tacitly reproving too-easy oppositions (as black/white, young/old), chiding ideas like Mill's method of history and mildly echoing Woolf's mockery. But if the charm fails outside writing, expression of our logical discourse, if nature and society are not charmed into order, how can this language-use function at all? We always assume it does, even finding analogous symbols outside writing itself.

Amid all the uncertainty and ambiguity of existence and human relations expressed in *To the Lighthouse*, for example, the lighthouse itself mirrors this lust for certitude: "There it loomed up, stark and straight, glaring white and black, and one could see the waves breaking in white splinters like smashed glass upon the rocks" (301). Woolf naturally treats the moment with irony. It is the self-centered Ramsay, paternalist controller of wife and children, finally taking two of his near-grown offspring to the lighthouse, for whom this erect construction becomes the oppressive symbol of legitimacy (twice ambiguous, since it also saves lives). Tying the black/white contrast to a masculinist order is something to which Russell could well have given thought when writing of a logician as "he" and "himself": at the turn of the century, his close friend C. K. Ogden had apprenticed himself to the logician Victoria Welby. This issue, too, is ever present in *Cosmos*, whose male narrator remains as unable to "understand" women as to explain the hanged sparrow. To be overwhelmed by the blackness or the whiteness of which Gombrowicz writes would be to lose contrastive relations, the *divisions* that make European reason work. It must set them "stark and straight," sharply delineated against one another. Not Gombrowicz or Russell or Woolf can move into a space such as that where Philip writes of loving equally the many colors of silence, "the absolute silence of black, or the distilled silence of white . . ." (*Looking*, 55), creating a different response to masculinist dominance and, no less here, to a racist colonial one where, remarks Gomez, "white was associated with power and control; black, blackness, black was the equivalent of subordination," a contrast buttressed by "the moral attributes of good and evil" (*Exchanging*, 169). These connotations are not just free associations. They are embedded deep in the language, discourse, thought, and action *in extremis* in Gombrowicz's novel.

Later in *Cosmos*, most of the characters take a trip to the mountains in a carriage. It, too, becomes a version of writing, an attempt to make the "silence, an incomprehensible, motionless, universal silence" clamorous, an effort to inscribe dark figures against a sunlight again more southern American than northern European—Gombrowicz saying elsewhere that he had become "Argentinian . . . saturated with its sun and sky" while European "shapes and lights [had] been lost in" him (*Diary*, 3:110), a remark whose weight is already clear—youth over age, immaturity over maturity, hesitancy over mastery, incompleteness over completeness:

> Excess, turbulence, confusion. . . . Too much, too much, too much, mass, movement, crush, pilings up, overturnings, general shambles, huge mastodons that swelled up and a moment later vanished into a thousand details, sets, heaps, clashes, in unruly chaos. . . . I seized on the ever new combinations that our little carriage joltingly extracted from the bosom of the mountains. But nothing, nothing. A bird appeared—high in the sky, very high and motionless—a vulture, a hawk, an eagle? No, it was not a sparrow, but by not being a sparrow it was a non-sparrow, and as a non-sparrow it was slightly sparrowish. . . . By what miracle did this little dot in the distance rule like the discharge of a gun, scattering the turbulence and confusion? (P92–3; E98–99; F128–29)

The punctuation of this single dark point imposes order where the effort at linear speech fails. It recalls the sparrow whose "shriek" was also a potentiality to order, needing explanation just because it had been met in the familiar alternation of black and white, escaping it on the one hand by its initially not being either, on the other by its pointed singularity. The initial lack of definition within black and white clarity was, if you will, an additional mark of monstrosity, eccentricity, at the level of the signifier. At the level of the signified, meanwhile, its abrupt singularity stood out against the vegetation's confused combinations.

The first, referential, sign of monstrosity was further emphasized at the sparrow's first discovery, by the very failure of a first attempt to explain its presence:

> "Who could have hanged it?"
> "Some boy or other."
> "No, it's too high."
> "Let's go." (P8–9; E11; F15)

The issue is to assimilate something like a "material intuition" not resulting from an analytical calculus to the logical sequence of meaningful "ordinary language." In fact, this primary image will itself come to "explain," fix in its terms the mental and practical reactions it provokes. We have seen how it starts by aborting any ordering by analysis and reference. Discourse adjusts to the sparrow's terms rather than the contrary (intuition given sense by familiar discourse). Rather as Lévi-Strauss depicts mythical discourse as working or as patterning discourse disposes its heterogeneities (as they seem to modern westerners), things compose themselves around the sparrow. Familiar syntax snaps, concepts change their usual logical bounds and act as unmediated *Vorstellungen*:

But he didn't budge. The sparrow went on hanging. Except for some grassy patches, the earth was bare. A lot of things were lying about: a strip of galvanized iron, a twig, another twig, a torn cardboard box, a twiglet, there were also a beetle, an ant, a second ant, an unknown worm, a log, and so forth, all the way to the undergrowth at the foot of the trees. (P9; E11; F15)

The speaker is quickly unable to utter linear motion, analytical transition: nouns again pile up, verbs accumulate, ending in the abortive "Let's go." Even that aborts. He and his companion cannot leave: "perhaps because we had already stayed there too long and had missed the right moment for going . . ." (P9; E11; F16). The protagonists are as if suspended outside a narrative time of story and history ordered by sequential elaboration of things and events. That ordering, also that of our notion of "time," no longer works: "the right moment" cannot be found. In this respect, myth and patterning appear to those used to a narrative of analysis and reference to be in some profound way "atemporal." "Past," "present," and "future" are not divided terms of a linear narrative. And western historical time is no less monstrous or eccentric when set in those ways of thinking and acting than is a primary intuition's presence in the analytico-referential. They are incompatibles. As American Montezuma says in Calvino's parable, "What is this thing you call history? Perhaps all you mean is the absence of equilibrium. Whereas when men live together in such a way as to establish a lasting equilibrium you say history has stopped" (*Numbers*, 193). In *Cosmos*, something like this occurs: "I had the hallucinatory impression of a sort of proportion askew, a lack of tact or unmannerliness on our part." The will to ordered narrative then fails: "I was sleepy" (P9; E11; F16). One might liken this inability to control meaning to the exactly similar failure of Woolf's Orlando: "And so bewildered as usual by the multitude of things which call for explanation and imprint their message without leaving any hint as to their meaning, she threw her cheroot out of the window and went to bed" (*Orlando*, 111). Woolf's point may be that now as a woman Orlando cares less about such systems. Her "bewilderment" is without anxiety, whereas for Ramsay in *To the Light-house*, the call to order is an unremitting source of strained discomfort, and for the speaker of *Cosmos*, it is constant cause of struggling effort.

With the remark "I was sleepy," the potential detective novel that Gombrowicz proposed *Cosmos* to be reaches what we may call the end of its first sequence. Only with difficulty do the two protagonists succeed in getting underway again: "But plodding on down that road in the heat of the sun made us sweat again, it was too much, after going a short way we stopped, exhausted and miserable" (P9; E11; F16). The difficulty is expressed, signified. This time, at this level of signifying, the syntax is successfully familiar—more so than at the novel's beginning. But from now on, the text will bear the mark of uncertainty, a kind of gap between the form of utterance and what is uttered, the trace of the sparrow suspended over the text, suspense and suspension in it, always on edge. For the time being, though, the novel continues its narration as if regardless of this gap, and the next "sequence" syntactically repeats the first. Content differs, but form is the same: a long paragraph characterized by amassing of words (adjectives now), gradually but at last ordered into a usual system, concluding with a brief dialogue. However normal this may be, a "monstrous" or "eccentric" mark again breaks into its familiarity—the maid Katasia's mouth:

I was startled by a strange deformity on her decent blue-eyed maid's mouth: it was as though her mouth was too much split on one side, and thus infinitesimally prolonged, by about a millimetre, her upper lip acquired a darting or sliding motion, almost reptilian, and this lateral slipping, fleeting, had a repellent coldness, like that of a snake or frog, but still it warmed me, immediately excited me, for it was like some obscure transition leading to her bed, to some genital, slippery, mucous sin. (P10; E12; F17)

We might *interpret* this, if we willed, as a fragment of an obsession, particular evidence of a narrator's desire. And this would henceforth be repeated through the whole story, sign of reality ordered by *desire*. . . . Were it not for the sparrow, countering, evading such an exegesis. Even so, we could doubtless read "back" from here to analyze the sparrow's presence in terms of an obsession like this. For it is clear that critic, reader—and translator—have many ways to put order into the text, interpret it, read *into* it. Gombrowicz more than once remarked that criticism is "one more obstacle on the path that leads to the reader," that it necessarily "catalogues, classifies, levels," reduces to familiar terms (*Entretiens*,

156–57). The provocation of *Cosmos* is not that it denies the propriety of such orderings within the a prioris of analytico-referential discourse. It just evidences how *arbitrary* are such interpretations. Even a polysemous interpretation merely aligns several "different" readings, each ascribing signifieds by light of the linear analytical and referential signifying process of the same dominant discourse: one subgenre, the literary-critical, appealing to others, psychoanalytic, sociological, biographical, or whatever. Thus do we seal in a series of "truths" providing anchors in "rational knowledge."

Here, one could conceive a sociological gloss relating to the political situation in Poland and Argentina, World War II, and the author's exile, marxism, and literary writing. One could imagine a biological/historical version—overlapping the last. One could suggest a psychoanalysis, maybe most directly tempting (and titillating). The Polish word for "bird" is indicative: *ptak. Tak* means "yes"; inverted to *kat* it means "executioner," one who lops heads, for example—perhaps cognate with English "cut."[7] Simply invoke a castration complex and the many erotic overtones—Katasia's slithery mouth, from about the same time the landlady's daughter Lena's leg against a bare bed wire, later a play of her and her husband Louis' hands, fingers in his and a priest's mouths, "stabbings" of objects in Katasia's room—easily obtain psychoanalytic meaning. They tie to the speaker's later potential "berging" of Lena (a made-up verb variably interpretable) and the constant play on dispersion, loss, dissemination. One could further this exegesis by recalling that one of the speaker's goals is to elude his parents, while that of his companion Fuchs is to escape his office manager. The analysis makes the oft-noted textual "dispersion" just a signified result of a familiar complex originating a causal linear chain. It is indeed a usual reading of Gombrowicz's novels (whether freudian or lacanian), easy because of its analytico-referential nature: assume a (freudian) psyche as origin and the rest follows as a wittgensteinian tautology in an intensional logic. Such readings suffer flaws of analytico-referential meaning, for example, that the discursive origin of meaning (the mere act of utterance) is hypostatized as an extradiscursive event (here, a psyche) to be explained by the very discourse originating it; or that "mastery" of a discursive "discipline" is just the speaker's control of utterance reified, such control also being transformed into the mark of the knower's "objectivity": the detective whose analysis produces the one correct solution. *Cosmos* thus also questions the very act of analysis that the critic wishes to apply to it.

Further sanctioning this reading of *Cosmos* is the fact that we "know" that the traces of obsession *have* to be reduced by another's analysis before its sufferer can know it. These traces *have to* seem inexplicable compared to directly accessible habitual discourse; that is what justifies psychoanalysis, the application of Freud's (but not, I think, Wittgenstein's) telescope. This only emphasizes the habits: the premise of Enlightened analytico-referential order is that it *explain*. Failing to do so, it becomes suspect. These readings are plausible because they follow normative relations of European Reason. Unintentionally, MacIntyre points the same lesson, arguing that narratives serve to make potentially unintelligible things intelligible by giving a familiar context. Since "stories are lived before they are told," such contexts are reliable gauges of a narrative's truth. Those who say that "stories are told not lived" just ignore that in life we cannot "live what story we please" and not be "under certain constraints" (*After Virtue*, 209–14). While this is clearly the case, MacIntyre has already given up too much in agreeing that "we live a story." The constraints under which we do so are among issues to be resolved, issues of how we know what it is we are living, what events and understandings we take to matter, and how, therefore, we act and react, and to what purpose. One might better say that stories are lived *as* they are told, told *as* they are lived. "Factual" contexts are *themselves* already in a story, and "constraints" are elements of a narrative. The issue is to know what and whose story.

So here, in the proffered "psychoanalytic" reading of *Cosmos*, *we* give meaning to the speaker's confusion, one fitting neatly into a settled explicative schema. And we can dismiss the discursive difficulties posed in the text as resulting from an unfortunate but common obsession. They are no longer problematic for *us*. The speaker is a narrator, after all, but one whose story *we* have to straighten out by giving it a suitably intelligible context. But if we take the hanged sparrow as a point of departure, problematizing the *development*, the very *generation* of discourse (and thought and action), rather than merely as an element already reducible to the norms of a habitual language-game (if in that game's terms we see if from the victim's, not the analyst's, spot), then the sparrow is immediately a barrier to familiarity. It opens a gap in normal systematizing, and any explanation becomes less sure when one looks first at what *happens* to discourse, before trying to explain it. For if linear analytical thinking is itself the issue, then a psychoanalytical exegesis, for example, is clearly no more than a desperate grasping at straws, an effort to fill gaps in an elementary table.

The split of Katasia's mouth with the sexual innuendoes of the last passage from *Cosmos* meet discourse's undoing: *what* is said with *how* it is said. Here the maid's voice surprises in its ordinariness (P10; E12; F17). A gap has opened in meaning: a slippage of personality and its understanding. For as Vološinov (or Mikhail Bakhtin) has written, "*consciousness itself can arise and become a viable fact only in the material embodiment of signs. The understanding of a sign is, after all, an act of reference between the sign apprehended and other, already known, signs*" (*Marxism*, 11). Signs unusable or unknown are not or no longer signs at all, just marks that are not discourse or knowing. Decay of habitual meaning leads to dissipation of "self" and then to uncertainty about the very nature and possibility of social intercourse at all.[8] In such a case, some new order is needed or society would be abandoned to anarchy (a return to Hobbes' unordered state of nature). That is what *Cosmos* is about. The space opened by the sparrow makes an entire loss of meaning, exactly what Johnson had feared of a first "abyss of unideal vacancy" opened by Dryden's treading "on the brink of absurdity" (*Lives*, 194)—a fear in the domain of thinking identical to Pope's or Eliot's "disease" in that of being. Starting from the possibility of analytical ordering (so-called textuality), everything begins to slip away, including the very fact of primary observation—assuming a knowable, external objective reality as sure confirmation of discursive truth. The speaker is no longer sure, for instance, that the strangeness of Katasia's mouth is not a phantasm or delusion brought on by the sparrow's suspended presence. The flaw in her mouth *can* readily be explained as resulting from a bus accident, not a deformity but a scar. Unfortunately, the explanation comes as a last gasp too late and has the same force as that proposed for the sparrow: a parenthesis from an already lost discursive space or language game.

Like the hanged sparrow, Katasia's mouth halts elaboration of any utterance willed by an independent subject: "I was getting more and more tired of his [Fuchs'] fish-face. To sleep . . . To sleep. . . . I flung myself on the bed, fall, dizziness, went to sleep, a mouth emerging from a mouth, lips with more lips, lips which were all the more like lips because they were less . . ." (P11; E13–14; F19). In dream, primary intuition is supreme, composed maybe wholly of fregean *Vorstellungen* such that the material image orders "thinking" rather than the reverse (although we must not forget that here it is *told*). The mouth surpasses and defeats possibilities of explanation, ordering familiar reason, as does the sparrow. Subsequent efforts to establish familiar novelistic discourse are not caught in the indescribable or the unsayable (*indicible*), save insofar as the last signals any discourse's bounds of sense. They are mined by the senseless: sleep, going to dinner, "eloquence of Mr Wojtys" (P12; E14; F19) marked by a florid and ludicrous banality matching the trivial meaninglessness of those minor, everyday events that alone seem able to be told. Yet Leo Wojtys' eloquence does suggest an effort to impress individual will-to-mean on otherwise banal socialized discourse—which will become one main way to place personal "signature" in language and action—one (false) solution to the dilemma of meaning. Here, will removes "eloquence" from the habitual rationality of everyday discourse, yet keeps some tie of meaningfulness with it. Wojtys' speaking is a kind of gloss in the margin of familiar sense.

Still, besides inscribing a personal and private signature, Leo's eloquence plays with the potentiality of meaning. His bizarre utterances make an ambiguous field where sense is as it were *being generated*. This practice will culminate in a word to which the speaker Witold will finally also give a meaning, but one always hidden from everyone else, including the reader. Witold will *make* a meaning for it, precisely, that signals secrecy, waste, loss, but also centrality. "Berg!" points to the hidden and unspeakable, under the mass—even so—of the mountainous, to something hard and obstructing even as it recalls the sparrow, Katasia's mouth, and Witold's earlier thought of some "mucous sin," but all of this quite alone. The word traces a delirium in the text, or, to play with a French invention, a *dé-lire*, an un- or nonreading: "Bamberging of bambergers in the berg" (P159; E165; F220). Between this final unreadable delirium (cut abruptly by a last sentence, "Today we had chicken and rice for lunch," that returns us to earlier banalities; P159; E166; F221) and the hanged sparrow and flawed mouth of the beginning, the reader follows the collapse of analytico-referential discourse.

Firstly, there ensues a search for signs that might have meaning. But the search never concludes. "Meaning it," said Wittgenstein, "is not a process which accompanies a word. For no *process* could have the consequence of meaning" (*Philosophical*, 218ᵉ: II.xi). Meaning is the seal of systematic space, closure of a language game. In the realm of language and concepts, it is what Charles Sanders Peirce called a "final interpretant." The sparrow's and the mouth's eccentricities set of a *process* that *mines* meaning: "I have chosen," writes Tobagonian Philip, "to 'mine' a language—both in the sense of making it mine, as well as plumbing its depths and, if necessary, exploding it" (*Genealogy*, 70). *Cosmos'* European speaker finds that the second two lead to a first that is so much "mine" as to be incomprehensible to anyone else. Secondly, the search for meaningful signs, *by* plumbing and exploding discursive familiarities, produces a will to impose oneself on people and objects that is found trivially impotent or wholly solipsistic. These failures of signified and signifier match that of referent in growing awareness that "transparent" mediation is impossible. It is soon clear that no "correspondence" is to be found between discursive order and that of things or experience—at least not in the object-terms of true/false logic. Experienced events and phenomena become meaningless, "except that one was 'related' to the other—like on a map, like one town on a map in relation to another—the idea of maps would not leave my head, map of the sky, ordinary geographical maps with towns, etc." (P17; E20; F27).

The will to mean of a map ordering signs no longer touches a goal, nor do projects for working a program for finding truth—or narrating a detective novel. Purposive "calculation," however "difficult and complicated," will still be a "system" even if its producer knows it for "a piece of foolishness, a crackpot enterprise" to which he devotes energy only because he has "nothing, nothing better to do" (P18; E21; F28–29). Such projects do not end, serving only to keep him apparently busy amid the emptiness and habitual banality that "reality" has become now that it is irreducible: "Our return along the gravel path was like that of two detectives. Working out our plans in the greatest detail would enable me to hold out honorably till next day" (P49; E53; F71). These efforts have already yielded to the whiteness of the blank page, to sleep, to the impossibility of discourse. Language no longer concludes: "every now and then Fuchs said something in a pale, white, phlegmatic voice . . ." (P12; E15; F20–21). It is increasingly hard, even impossible, to organize an exterior (whether supposed "true" or otherwise) through discourse: "in reality this 'link' was not one" (P17; E20; F27). To try and play the detective, seek out truth, actuality, is to risk provoking unspecifiable harm: "Fuchs! Where was he, what was he doing? 'Playing the sleuth?' As long as it did not end in scandal" (P17; E20; F27).

The scandal is not just the effect their nocturnal wanderings may have, not just the social or more exactly familial disturbance (*powud* implies a family or local, restricted scandal) that the reader may infer the speaker to mean. It is the scandal of mining familiarities, and so the scandal too in the very idea of seeking an "objective truth" to legitimate its enunciator's subsequent action—as Henrietta Savernake implied to Poirot (in a story where they keep a final retribution secret precisely because it *was* scandalous). The sparrow's presence was scandalous because its hanging implied commission of a quite arbitrary, gratuitous, and so inexplicable harm. As it took charge of discourse, so it asserted that one similarly *commits* meaning: imposing arbitrary and gratuitous order for purposes that are not always clear but never disinterested. That "special providence in the fall of a sparrow" of which Shakespeare's Dane spoke (*Hamlet*, V.ii.209) has acquired a new meaning, one that saps the whole tradition to which it referred. That the human (let alone a particular humanity) has any special value is not at all evident once the idea has been shown the solipsistic creation of a particular discourse. For matters in *Cosmos* do indeed end in two scandals of just this kind. First is the discursive creation of actual events: the hanging of a cat that results directly from Witold's detecting and that in turn leads equally directly, perhaps (though we never find out), to Louis' hanging. Second is the final scandal of "Berg."

But long before either, the "cerebral" space of analysis (P16; E19; F26) had begun to collapse into the irrecoverable space of the sparrow:

in front of me the garden, shrubs, paths that ended in a place with a pile of bricks right up to an astonishingly white wall, the whole scene struck me as a visible sign of what I didn't see: the other side of the house where there was also a bit of garden, then the fence, the road, and beyond the thicket . . . and the tension of the stellar world fused in me with that of the hanged sparrow. (P17–18; E20; F27)

This very collapse will give hope, not of an explanation but of a provision of sense. Thus the nonsparrow seen on the trip into the mountains

had revived my spirits, perhaps (I thought) because, being a bird, it was related to the sparrow, but also, and chiefly perhaps, because it had remained suspended in the sky thus associating sparrow and hanging and permitting the association, through this idea of hanging, the hanged cat and the hanged sparrow, yes, yes (I saw it more and more clearly), it conferred on this idea of hanging a primordial quality, hanging over everything, regal . . . (P95; E101; F131)

Actually, this will help little. By now, a collapse has occurred of anything able to furnish object for experience and familiar discourse: language does not communicate, the human body dissolves in unaccountable shapes and fusings, the countryside produces endless profusion, speech falls into nonsense. We are, muses Witold, in "a bottomless pit of distraction, of dispersion" (P22; E25; F34): "Oh, I felt so scattered about!" (P45; E48; F65). One is in an empty, expectant space where meaning is only potential, lost and irretrievable as a system: "The unpleasant thing about it was that the emptiness of our boredom, in this isolated spot came together with the emptiness of these so-called signs, these indices which were not indices, all this idiocy: two emptinesses, and us in between. I yawned" (P47; E51; F69).

There is no longer a place to anchor signs and their significance. The possibility of fixing meaning dissipates in this "between"; between we may say the emptiness of being (cartesian *sum* or heideggerian *Dasein*) and the emptiness of conception (*cogito*). They are empty because once the *ergo* of discourse has decayed, no operation is available to "link" them (we saw Witold say). *Cosmos* sets us in this between, depriving us of sure habitual use of signs. How, then, is speaking possible at all? *about* anything? or even just to make comprehensible contact with interlocutors? "I was absent," says Witold later. "Moreover (I thought) we are almost always absent, or at least not entirely present, because of our fragmentary, chaotic and superficial, feeble and shabby contact with our surroundings" (P89; E94–5; F123–24). Discourse had given humans some control over the world: "Fear ye not therefore, ye are of more value than many sparrows," asserted King James' Gospel writer, quoting Jesus' counsel to the Apostles (Matthew 10:31). Once upon a time, maybe. Now things are reversed and the sparrow has become overwhelmingly more important. The old order and tradition have been inverted. The unrational has defeated rational explanation, disorder order, youth age, immaturity maturity. No wonder Gombrowicz wrote of his "science"-loving Berlin hosts in 1964 (while he was putting the finishing touches to *Cosmos*) that "sparrows" were creatures "no German ever chase[d]" (*Diary*, 3:112)!

Reason, speaking, discourse are all ex post facto. Understanding requires the continuity of what has already been (said) before. Comprehension is subjected to an order already fixed and therefore unable to grasp the *process* of present being:

How can one avoid telling a story *ex post facto*? We must then suppose that nothing will ever be expressed in its reality, reconstituted in its anonymous process of becoming, that no one will ever be able to reproduce the incoherence of the moment as it is born; born as we are out of chaos, how is it that we can never get up against it? No sooner do we look at it than order, pattern, shape is born under our eyes. (P28; E13; F41)

Such process and the very idea of meaning, Wittgenstein remarked, are utterly incompatible. The distance described in Enlightened discourse is a fixation entirely comforting (to its subjects, not its objects). Once recognized, though, it becomes ambiguous and a source of unease. It seals its speaker safely away from the incoherence of the actual and is only the worse for its essential artifice: "the idea of this outing [to the mountains] was disastrous, they could have thought of nothing worse; distance wiped out nothing, on the contrary, it froze somehow and reinforced, to such an extent that one felt as if one had spent years there being with the sparrow, with the cat, that we had come here years afterwards" (P102; E109; F142).

To this difficulty, Witold had already essayed the response that one may compose a system in full awareness of its conceptual and other consequences:

How many sentences can be composed with the twenty-six letters of the alphabet? Now many meanings can be deduced from these hundreds of weeds, clumps of earth, and other details? The wall and the boards of the hut were similarly pouring out innumerable combinations. I got bored. I stood up to look at the house and garden. The big synthetic shapes, huge mastodons of the world of things were re-establishing order, and I rested. To go back. I was going to say so to Fuchs, but his face stopped me, directed fixedly at a precise point. (P33; E36–37; F48–49)

Gradually, reader and speaker follow elaboration of a reality that does end in its own creation: the hanging of the cat (P64; E68–69; F90–91). In some way the "exterior" is *forced* by discourse. It gets a sort of significant direction, a line of meaningfulness. "The speaking of language," we saw Wittgenstein assert, "is part of an activity, or a form of life" (*Philosophical*, 11ᵉ: I.§23). Witold goes one better: speaking is the *entire* activity. Language's meaning, here, can only be its use, what it actually *produces* as a result of that use. Beyond actual discursive use, language, thought, concept, and the rest are so many abstractions. "Real" meaning, discoverable authorial intention, generative grammar, or semiotic square, the subject (stable or unstable) as anchor, at least for the last two, are all revealed as a priori reductions, produced by reading back from what is a posteriori. Their case goes as follows: since "we" all seem to use the same words in recognizably similar configurations, since the actual number of words and possible configurations are finite (however immense), but since the possible number of meanings and/or uses is seemingly unlimited and unlimitable, there must be some fundamental underlying system allowing such extension. This is to place a saussurian or chomskyan cart before a bakhtinian horse, the idea (and need) of a rational system before the heteroglossia of social generation.

Following Wittgenstein's analysis, the forms and moves of a language are intelligible only insofar as it and they are *used* and as the user *already* knows use. For example, "only someone who already knows how to do something with it can significantly ask a name" (*Philosophical*, 15ᵉ: I.§31). Discovery is always already patterned (even if the patterns have to be found in unfamiliar places). *Cosmos'* initial move was to show the ludic nature of these processes but then the utter seriousness of the game: as it *made* sense, it made and imposed reality. If uneasily, Witold seemed to keep some control of discursive activity. Indeed, a process of trying to forge sense and of reading things for a possible order goes on until Louis is hanged. Witold's activity is then again displaced into a "space" whose elements are unknown. By now we are already well into the delirium of "berg." What might be the meaningfulness of experiences, events, or relations is no longer that of a sense produced from the order of discourse. It lies only in the *process* of signifying, generation of meaning—proliferating into senselessness: "she was lying. No, she was not lying! It was truth and lie at the same time. Truth, because it corresponded with reality. And lie because the import of her words (as I already knew) did not come from their truth, but from the fact that they came from her, like her gaze, like her perfume" (P71; E77; F102). In a manner of speaking, all discourse lies, makes its own activity—and the lie is the greater, we saw Philip suggest of its imposition as "fact," when its speaker refuses to see or hear its limits or its imposition. Adopting just this thought, Witold achieves his rapport with Lena by knowing these. What could she say, when asked, about his having knocked on her bedroom door prior to killing the cat? To avoid being compromised, she affirmed that she had knocked. Witold rejoins: "Oh happiness, triumph, my lie had caught hers and we were united in a common lie, and by my lie I implanted myself in hers" (P73; E79; F104).

Human relations are thus as exactly part of a self-inventive discursive process as the very self, made up from fragments composing the only "subject" possible, faced with its analytical discursive dissolution: a self whose ordered identity can only always be fixed as a *past*. "I" is composed of moments coming into being, always told after the event, like stories and histories, ex post facto. Consciousness is created in exchange of discourses and in the discourses it (then) enacts. As Leo asks: "What am I? I am a certain number of seconds—that have fled. The result: nothing. Nothing" (P111; E117; F155). To produce discourse is to compose that fleeting self, but as a past "belonging" to someone else: "stiff, he kept his hand outstretched, and he looked mechanically at 'his' hand, just as the priest played with 'his' finger, as Jadeczka found pleasure in 'her' love . . . and . . . and . . . and as I had corrupted 'mine' . . ." (P116; E123; F162). The remains cannot be said—mere surplus of possible meaning: "You rest in broad daylight among ordinary, everyday things, familiar since childhood, grass, shrubs, a dog (a cat), a chair, but only so long as you have not realized that each object is a huge army, an inexhaustible host" (P124; E131; F172–73). This remarkably echoes Maurice Merleau-Ponty's phenomenology of knowledge, whose "world of teeming things" in which one is "swimming" is first a chaotic mass without determinate points, then "crystallizes" into an ordered perspective whereby things lose "their aggressiveness" (revealing word in this context) and "order their interior lines according to the common law" of a familiar structure, so that "the whole scene is in the past, in the order of completion and eternity" (*Prose*, 53).

In Witold's echo of this, finally one is oneself (one's speech) just a black dot against the empty whiteness marking a disappearance, a vacuum: "a great solar void, a kind of sunny emptiness signaled by the tension of the brilliance striking from behind the mountains, as from a hidden source" (P128; E135; F179). This is again the sunlit brilliance of a certain vision of "youthful" Latin America rather than the gray age of European Warsaw (or Paris or Berlin). Momentarily absorbed in it as he is, it is perhaps no longer that contrastive one. After such dissolution, all that remains is to generate not meaning but discursive relations with others:

If he alone had said "berg," it would have done nothing. But I, too, had said "berg." And my berg, joining itself with his, deprived his berg of its privacy. It was no longer the personal little word of a crackpot. It was now something real . . . something that existed! Before us, right here! And immediately it dominated over, pushed towards, overcame. (P144; E151; F200)

This was prefigured in Witold's potential relationship with Lena after the cat's hanging, in the linking of lies. Could it be a conclusion? Not at all. Firstly, it produces a private language shared only most tenuously (do Lena and Leo understand these associations at all similarly to Witold? We cannot know, they have no contact about them). Secondly, it turns in circles. At the end of *Cosmos*, this private fabrication of discursive "relations" is all we have. If it is the case, as Sophie Janik argues, that others "berg" in their own way—Fuchs vainly calculating a winning system for roulette, the priest always toying with his fingers, Kulka (Mrs. Wojtys) losing herself in her culinary and other activities ("Gombrowicz," 269 n. 33)—then replacing a discourse of analytical meaning with one merely (and falsely) generating relations is worse than inadequate.

Totally removed from each other, they do not communicate. All are resolutely separate, marked by utter division (even the culinary, as a form of "berging"). Leo had placed his signature on a private discourse, ultimately not communicable either. His generation of signs stays set by the analytico-referential which it has fleetingly disoriented. Bathetically, the analytico-referential ends the novel: "Today we had chicken and rice for lunch." No doubt Witold has generated changes "of language forms," "forms of speech performances," "verbal communication and interaction," and "social discourse" (to repeat terms from Vološinov/Bakhtin). They have led nowhere. Indeed, the sparrow has expanded to threaten habitual western discourse and the practices and manners accompanying it: "but here you are my little sweet pea, my little sparrow, my little treasure, oh, how you've grown, you're a man now, alleluia, alleluia" (Gombrowicz, *Marriage*, 32).

Matthew's and Luke's sparrows were kept in their place: two for a farthing or five for two farthings, following the careful calculations of the King James version (Matthew 10:29–31; Luke 12:6–7). Shakespeare's Hamlet similarly took the sparrow to allegorize small things. By Pope's time, sparrows and humans attained a certain equality, even if only before an absolute outsider's gaze: "Who sees with equal eye, as God of all,/A hero perish, or a sparrow fall" (*Essay on Man*, I.87–88). In *Cosmos*, the sparrow has taken over, disabling settled discourse and leading in this European side to an impasse of sound and fury. The immature speaker has undone the instrument of mature Enlightenment, but like the hare pursued by hounds who escapes only by staying absent or unseen in a furrow, as Gombrowicz depicts such ones in *Trans-Atlantyk* (7, 27, 66), or like the sweet fruit of youth trapped in maturity's excrement, "a plum in dung!" (16; cf. 97), he can go nowhere with it (this novel also ends in carnival "berging" in the cultivated woods of a semitropical estate in Argentina). The sun of youth undoes the "blackness, terror and night" of maturity, but ends in an unfulfilled "great solar void, a kind of sunny emptiness." For Witold finally stays caught in these oppositions and scissions. He cannot "translate the *i-mage*," as Philip calls it—not a familiar or potentially familiar *image*, but something like an unmediated intuition—he cannot create from that sun "new *i-mages* that speak to the essential being of the people among whom and for whom the artist creates" (*Genealogy*, 43; cf. *She Tries*, 12–16). Or perhaps he does, but for the very people who rely on just these old familiarities. Elsewhere, though, in that Caribbean, for example, of which Philip is writing, Gombrowicz's sparrow may be able to become Mighty.[9]

8

Reclaiming the Soul: Poetry, Autobiography, and the Voice of History

Through Kamau Brathwaite's work run three favorite metaphors. The earliest uses the iambic pentameter that had become a norm in English poetry from roughly the seventeenth century. The second represents the Caribbean islands as the result of a child's (or god's) skipping stones in a great curve across the ocean from the coast of Guyana to the tip of Florida. The third transforms the waters buried deep in the porous rock that is Barbados into the welling of a buried culture whose very concealment has made it the more vital to the life above. The first concerns the constitution, practice, and differentiation of a poetic voice; the second holds an individual's sense of a home place, a local geography; the third captures something like a collectivity's living cultural and political consciousness and its historical memory quickened *in* that place.

At the same time, each one works and plays with the other two. More than tropes in language, more than just representation, capture, or comparison, the finest metaphors are alive and manifest vital actualities: the actual process of cultural creation making new experience of place, the "senecan" process we saw in Chapter 4. These are such metaphors. Barbados *is* rock of the sort Brathwaite takes for his i-mage. Beneath and in it *is* the fresh water making life on the island possible. As the poet/historian has also been able to show, Barbados *does* have a hidden culture, living remnant of Igbo consciousness, however much mixed with others, both African and Native American.[1] Too, Barbados is geologically unique among the islands, and the more-than-metaphor grasps that singularity as it simultaneously situates it among its companion islands geographically, historically, and culturally. Lastly, the skipping stones, as well, offer not just an image of place, but a rhythm and the curving shape of an imagination, sung and stamped by a calypso drawn to the measure of their multilingual islands:

> The stone had skidded arc'd and bloomed into islands:
> Cuba and San Domingo
> Jamaica and Puerto Rico
> Grenada Guadeloupe Bonaire
>
> curved stone hissed into reef
> wave teeth fanged into clay
> white splash flashed into spray
> Bathsheba Montego Bay
>
> bloom of the arcing summers . . .
>   ("Calypso," *Rites of Passage, Arrivants*, 48)

These metaphors and rhythms ground a different poetry and a consciousness not best rendered by that iambic pentameter whose exemplar Brathwaite finds in Thomas Gray's eighteenth-century *Elegy*: "The Cúrfew tólls the knéll of párting dáy." He observes that before Chaucer, no such dominant meter was to be found, but that since then, poetic effort in the anglophone world has increasingly kept to its terms. (Walt Whitman tried to overcome it by noise, "a large movement of sound"; e. e. cummings by fragmentation; Marianne Moore "with syllabics": *History*, 10.) Yet it stays. And although Coleridge and Eliot praised "the generic variety its rhythmic pattern could accommodate" (Marks, 300–301) and many have observed how flexibly it modulates, its grounding rhythm remains directive. "It carries with it a certain kind of experience, which is not the experience of a hurricane. A hurricane does not roar in pentameters. And that's the problem: how do you get a rhythm which approximates the *natural* experience, the *environmental* experience?" (Brathwaite, *History*, 9–10). This is not just a matter of speaking nature's most violent dramas. The need, too, is of telling the ritual rhythms of an old woman "sweeping the sand of her yard away from her house . . . her body silhouetting against the sparkling light that hits the Caribbean at that early dawn," seeming as if she were "walking on the water . . . travelling across that middlepassage, constantly coming from where she had come from—in her case Africa— to this spot in North Coast Jamaica" (*ConVERSations*, 30–33). The need is of writing "the sunlight under her feet—she walk on water *and* in light,

the sand between her toes, the ritual discourse of her morning broom"
(35). The need is of "seeing *our* things and trying to express *that* way of seeing—the movement, the glitter, the *kinesis* of it . . . giving ourselves a history that is original and new and ancient—that understands the meadow
of **ancestor** and ancestor(y)" (38–39).

This needed rhythm is grounded and trammeled in the skipping
stones and rock-concealed water, both bearing spirit of place. But that is
not the only problem. With experience of place tied in form goes that bond
of culture of which Brathwaite is speaking here. So Coleridge argued at
length that the poet's language was essentially bound in an experienced
world, meter being "superadded" (in poetry over prose) yet inseparable
from thought, content, emotion, expression, and the poet's mind and particular sense of place (*Biographia*, chapter 18, 2:58–88; cf. Marks, 141–49).
The choice of "a form" and its rhythm, wrote Eliot of Shakespeare's son-
nets, is that of "a precise way of thinking and feeling" (*Sacred*, 57). Like
Brathwaite, Philip applies the thought to a Caribbean case, agreeing that
the choice of language between what he calls "nation language,"
"Caribbean demotic and standard English . . . is a choice which often
affects the choice of subject matter, the rhythms of thought patterns, and
the tension within the work. It is also a choice resonant with historical and
political realities *and* possibilities" (*Frontiers*, 37). One would say it *always*
affects, and indeed *effects*, all these.

In *History of the Voice*, quoted a moment ago, Brathwaite did not
dwell on Gray's celebrated poem, and for good reason: he wanted to get on
to the forms of a new voice. Here, though, we may grant it a bit more attention, and I would like to quote a bit more of its beginning:

> The Cúrfew tólls the knéll of párting dáy,
> The lówing hérd winds slówly ó'er the léa,
> The plówman hómeward plóds his wéary wáy,
> And léaves the wórld to dárkness ánd to mé.
>
> Now fádes the glímmering lándscape ón the síght
> And áll the áir a stíllness hólds,
> Save whére the béetle whéels his dróning flíght,
> And drówsy tínklings lúll the dístant fólds.

If you look at where the accents fall in the first stanza, you see how
the long vowels echo tolling bell and "lowing herd." You see, too, how

these same long vowels combine with the assonance of the labial and nasal consonants (*l* and *r, m* and *n*) to trace the slow rhythmic trudge of animals and men tiredly returning home at day's wane. Fading landscape at dusk, evening quiet of late summer, wheeling beetles, tinkling sheep bells, the later "ivy-mantled tow'r," "mopeing owl," "rugged elms," "yew-tree's shade," and "swallow twitt'ring from the straw-built shed," are stereotypes meant to summon the image of an age-old country England to frame the elegy on humble folk that is the principal weight of the poem: "the short and simple annals of the poor" (l. 32). They frame a nostalgic musing on those who might have been great churchmen, rulers, or musicians, except only that "Knowledge to their eyes her ample pages/Rich with the spoils of time did ne'er unroll" (ll. 49–50). So these remain a gem unknown in ocean cave (53–54), a flower "to blush unseen" and "waste its sweetness on the desert air" (55–56), "a village-Hampden," a "Cromwell guiltless," or "some mute inglorious Milton" (57–60).

The advancing expansive pentameter, Coleridge's "march of the words" (*Biographia*, chapter 15, 2:20), contains a particular history and cultural experience. "The madding crowd's . . . strife" may be called "ignoble" (*Elegy*, l. 73), but the nostalgia grounding the poem's theme depends on the achievements of those who supposedly formed and sprang from that crowd. Those achievements themselves are taken as due in some *essential* way to their embedding in this storied and Edenic countryside. Not for nothing did Froude, a bit more than a century after Gray, fall back on these terms to introduce what J. J. Thomas in response called the "ghastly imaginings" in which he grounded "the dark outlines of [his] scheme to thwart political aspirations in the Antilles" (*Froudacity*, 9, 6). Froude began by recounting the train journey toward his West Indian packet at Southampton away from the "destructive," "dishonest," and self-defeating London debates urging independence and separation for the Caribbean colonies of Britain's empire. As they rode past fields "deep with snow," under a "winter sky . . . soft and blue," frozen "ponds and canals" where "all was brilliant and beautiful," the "air cleared, and my mind also. . . . It was," he wrote, "like escaping out of a nightmare into happy healthy England once more." Against the background of this landscape (now wintry, in contrast to the tropical islands where he was going), and out of it, came not only bullish Froude himself, complacent in his righteous Englishness, but his "several gentlemen" traveling companions, "officers," "planters," and "young sportsmen." These would lay to rest the degenerate debates of the capital and firmly reestablish England's rightful hold on its Caribbean colonies (*English*, 16).

Gray's lowly Hampdens, Miltons, and Cromwells, who, lost in poverty, misery, and illiteracy, never did share this expansive culture, would nonetheless have done so if only they had had the wealth and learning to give them the necessary competitive edge. Gray glories in a "loss" that proves the depth of English culture, with its myriad putative conquerors, preachers, and poets scattered about the countryside. Froude nostalgically embroiders on its and their continuing power. Indeed, the Hampdens, Cromwells, and Miltons raise before us the image of those churchmen, rulers, and artists who were *not* silent or "wasted" in the desert or under the seas; those who *did* "wade through slaughter for a throne" and "shut the gates of mercy on mankind" (67–68), whether at home on those of a different class, abroad on those of a different race, or everywhere on those of a different sex (a shutting, oppression, and exploitation justified, we saw in Chapters 1 and 2, by various cultural instruments). Well might Eliot say that while the language of such as Gray may have become "more refined" than that of his poetic predecessors, "the feeling became more crude" ("Metaphysical," 30).

In Froude, what Thomas called his "flowers of rhetoric" quite deliberately hid the actuality of "a degrading tyranny" (*Froudacity*, 6, 78) and their author's desire to see it extended, while expressing a savage racism that he did not at all try to hide. On one hand was "a strange rhapsody on Negro felicity," as Thomas again ironically put it (82). Here were noble natives under British colonial rule, untrammeled by sin or shame and living in a "happiness" that made them "the supremest specimen" of fortunate humanity, "the most perfectly contented specimens of the human race to be found upon the planet" (*English*, 49–50, 79; cf. 73, 78). Such, he wrote, were those of Barbados and Trinidad, where "a white community" could help lead "blacks" to such "progress as they [were] capable of making" (88), bringing them "along with them into more settled manners and higher forms of civilisation" (90), toward "a peace and order" that could not be "of their own creation" (98), but from which they could benefit because "a negro can be attached to his employer at least as easily as a horse or a dog" (106).

On another hand was the evidence of what happened when colonizers left, when once "docile, good-tempered, excellent and faithful servants . . . peel[ed] off such civilisation as they have learnt as easily and as willingly as their coats and trousers" (286–87). Haiti's "ghastly example" (81) was Froude's constant motif for representing what happened when "the inflammable negro nature" (104) was thus deprived of European guidance: an island of "cannibalism" (112–13), where "children [were] offered to the devil and salted and eaten" (164), where white people were not only excluded "from any share of the administration, but forbid[den from] acquisition or possession of real property in any form" (165–66), where "African Obeah, the worship of serpents and trees and stones . . . , witchcraft and poisoning" were rampant (126), where Port-au-Prince was just "the central ulcer" of disease rampant nationwide (342). No wonder, he intoned, "the better side . . . would welcome back the French" (344; cf. 120, 183–88, 333, 340–48). To be sure, Froude was not writing poetry—but besides "the flowers of rhetoric" for which he was celebrated, he likened English colonial power and expansion to a Homeric epic, asserting that the proper (and propertied) men of his storied English countryside were alone the worthy and legitimate inheritors of "the bow of Ulysses." This phrase and idea gave him both his subtitle and another recurring motif for a book which assumed that "these beautiful West Indian islands were intended to be homes for the overflowing numbers of our own race," an escape from "the lanes and alleys of our choking cities" into a new countryside of their own possession (362)—*rightful* possession since, according to the Homeric metaphor, they were *returning* home. Froude supplied what C. L. R. James later called "the prose-poetry and the flowers" to transmogrify violence, greed, and prejudice (*Black*, 63), the hypocrisy of Césaire's "slavering apologist."

For we may perhaps see how the marching linear pentameter (or its equally normative counterpart of the French alexandrine, whose more or less clearly set caesura and alternating masculine and feminine rhymes beat repetitively onward in what Depestre in an aberrant moment called "the great adventure of the alexandrine and traditional forms"[2]) corresponds to a broader cultural reality, one anchored in political theory and historical actuality. I mean the argument that what makes a "healthy" state, society, and culture is expansion. The idea dated at least from Niccolò Machiavelli's suggestion that the reason a society needed to think constantly of outward expansion was clear in its image as a place composed of endlessly active animals who would turn destructively against each other if not directed elsewhere. So Bacon thought "Forraine Warre" the vital regimen of nations, "like the Heat of *Exercise* [that] serveth to keepe the Body in Health"; so did Hobbes, Locke, and many heirs. Bacon had linked the health of European nations rather precisely to their control of and expansion across the seas and the riches they brought, "because, the Wealth of both *Indies*, seemes in great Part, but an Accessary, to the Command of the *Seas*" ("Of the true Greatnesse of Kingdomes and *Estates*," *Essayes*, 97–98). After Hobbes, the individuals whose threatened warring necessitated the founding covenant of civil society provided the very image and model of the states that those individual societies were to become. Reason, knowledge, will, and power to act became their organizing axioms. The order of reason matched that of the world, the accumulation of material knowledge let such reason instrumentally adjust the world to its own benefit, will urged one to it, and power gave the tools to make intervention sure.

What came to be called "literature" participated in these changes, adopting what I have called "epistemological," "ethical," "aesthetic," and "political" roles—the last being initially the most important. Literature confirmed a (sometimes complicated) politics of singular authority, however embodied; it claimed to be ordered by a syntax that was both that of right language and that of universal reason; it portrayed and asserted an ethics of individual interest whose virtue lay in simultaneously benefitting the community; and it placed beauty in a personal "taste" that echoed general reason (Reiss, especially *Meaning*, but also *Discourse*, chapters 1 and 2). Literature's "guarantee" of political claim and historical practice ultimately helped "universalize" these developments, so that the assertion of a right to intervene in others' histories and cultures became grounded in Europe's claim to being the vanguard of human progress, with no less than an obligation (god- or history-given) to put others in the way of such progress. Such writing, then, echoed the project of those "worthies of England," Froude gloried, "who cleared and tilled her fields, formed her laws, built her colleges and cathedrals, founded her colonies, fought her battles, covered the ocean with commerce, and spread our race over the planet to leave a mark on it which time will not efface" (*English*, 35). To possess "these beautiful West Indian islands," to destroy or control whoever might be their inhabitants and to impose a culture (poetic and other) upon whoever remained or was brought were elements of a god-given right—indeed obligation.

We Euro-Americans do this of course only with deepest regret and a sensitive awareness that something has been lost. Gray's mid-eighteenth-century nostalgia was typical of that of many others: Oliver Goldsmith's, for instance, in *The Deserted Village* or *The Traveller*. And that Samuel Johnson mocked Gray's linguistic archaisms changes not a whit the nostalgia's significance. We have already thrice seen Pope put it perfectly in his *Essay on Man* not long before (1730–1734), writing of the "lurking principle of death" that dwelt in the body as ever-present threat or loss: "The young disease, that must subdue at length,/Grows with his growth, and strengthens with his strength/ . . . cast and mingled with his very frame" (I.134–37). Johnson himself, *dixit* James Boswell, might be able to parry the menacing lions of his mental Colosseum; he could not keep them in their den. This death lurking in the heart of expansive Enlightened Reason has its modern currency, I proposed, among many earlier named in this regard—Horkheimer, Adorno, Husserl, Heidegger, Lukács—who have argued that within this Reason lies a virus destructive not just of the European—western—world and its culture, but of all civilizations. Some think it means the need to find something quite new (or to take over others' "spirituality"); others to complete an unfinished, unperfected Enlightenment; yet others a rediscovery of what came before, of some supposed wholeness with the universe.

Whatever the solution, golden age or Eldorado lost meant golden age or Eldorado had to be found. With or without regret, expansive Europe would have to march out in file and find it. Death could not be allowed its victory. Just so did the degeneracy of Froude's London have its counter first in a glowing English countryside, then in the happy "singing, dancing, and chattering," noble if ignorant "coloured people" of a West Indies "old-fashioned" because its denizens had retained their sense of their places (*English*, 48–49). For the English, there, still knew they had just to rule or let things fall into the decay and death of "Hayti, where they eat the babies, and no white man can own a yard of land" (56). For whatever they might be, right reason and knowledge would first be Europe's. Others, Asian, African, or American, untutored like Gray's inglorious Miltons and guiltless Cromwells, poor like his "rustic moralist" (84) or "hoary-headed Swain" (97), without power and the knowledge of right reason, would justly be put in order by the vanguard—unless they managed to ride the coach out and take power abroad. These were exactly the terms, we have seen, which Froude still used more than a century later. For after all, as James Thomson wrote of these others in the artful pentameters of his rewritten *Summer* of 1744:

Ill-fated race! the softening arts of peace,
Whate'er the humanizing Muses teach,
The godlike wisdom of the tempered breast,
Progressive truth, the patient force of thought,
Investigation calm whose silent powers
Command the world, the light that leads to Heaven,
Kind equal rule, the government of laws,
And all-protecting freedom which alone
Sustains the name and dignity of man—
These are not theirs.

(Seasons, ll. 874–84)

One can but admire these "softening arts of peace" that by teaching us that we alone rightfully possess "the name and dignity of man" so readily justify the manipulation of those who therefore do not. The two iambs of "These are not theirs" readily modulate to beat out their phrase in rhythm prefiguring the opening of a not-yet-born Ludwig van Beethoven's Fifth Symphony, poetically glorifying an imperialism long since in place and due only to become an increasingly competitive race in the era following the expansive extravagancies of the hero for whom Beethoven's bars tolled, Napoleon Bonaparte. Gombrowicz was not eccentric in tying Beethoven's "drama in history" to his music's "Form" as a gracious "evening stroll" through a fresh, "splendidly fertile" land of "forests, groves, stream and pools, flowery meadows and fields rustling with wheat" (*Diary*, 2:183–85), unerringly bringing us back to Gray. Brathwaite analogously links the "Miltonic ode"'s "nobility" to that of the same romantic symphony, simply observing that "the models are important" (*History*, 22–23). Mark McWatt, recalling Bacon, Thomson, and so many others, catches these narrow bonds between poetry, history, expansionist despoliation, and imperial rapine:

the osmotic assault
  of the history-mongering tribes
of Europe, with their penchant
  for names and other subtleties,
fretting about "Indies" amidst the
  righteous bleeding, as the ruddied
occidental light, shipped home in galleons,
  leapt from divine gold and silver.

("Then," Language, 9)

I am not—need I say?—proposing that pentameters or Beethoven create (or in themselves are) a tool of oppression, a title of hegemony. Nor was Brathwaite. Language and style no more make hegemony than revolution. But they do confirm and guarantee them. As Coleridge, Eliot, and so many others have asserted, they are nonetheless the form of a particular pattern of thought, bearer of certain structures of feeling and expression of specific kinds of practice. Formal models do matter. And that is one reason why Eliot could speak of Gray's poem as "a good example of a beautiful poem which is nearly all platitude."[3] In its very rhythm and meter, it manifests patterns of thought, structures of feeling, and kinds of practice crucial to this experience that never had to learn to roar with the notes of a hurricane, catch the damp glint of sunlit sand between the toes, curve with stones skipping across the ocean, limp with the life of Legba, or dance with the rhythm of Shango. In his 1992 "Columbus poem," Brathwaite aims Colón westward into the future as a linear missile whose sure systems become less assured when he looks out over the changed history and geography for which he has been willy-nilly responsible. Not for him the view of Keats' Cortez in Darien. Both the rhythm and the "Sycorax" typography of the poem (a computerized typography using fonts, spacings, word breaks, icons, and other devices to track the voice's rhythms, volume, tones, accents, and cadences) aim to undermine the patterns, structures, and practices which Columbus was to come historically and culturally to embody and exemplify.

Just for these reasons did the Spanish, after the disastrous 1898 defeats (of which we shall see more in Chapter 10), bring back Columbus' bones from Havana for reburial in Spain (Carr, 3). Their return exquisitely symbolized the reversal of all that the Admiral of the Ocean Seas stood for. With his usual soft irony, Saramago manages to catch how the poet's voice willy-nilly confirms these patterns, structures, and practices, offering a similar tale about the '98 Generation's poet, Machado. As the Iberian peninsula separates from Europe in *The Stone Raft*, ready to sail into the Atlantic, an early event is theft of his bones from their grave in Collioure for reburial "somewhere in the fields of Soria, beneath a holm oak, which in Spanish is called *encina*." Wondering if the Portuguese have such a poet in France, Saramago names Pessoa's close friend Mário de Sá Carneiro, but adds that there'd be no point trying to move him, "first of all because he wouldn't have wanted to come, secondly, because the cemeteries in Paris are well protected, thirdly, because so many years have passed since he died" (*Stone*,

55–56). For Sá Carneiro and Pessoa, the Portuguese empire of history and the nation's most renowned poem, Luis Vaz de Camões' *Lusiads*, the empire's celebration, were legacies of profoundly unhappy weight, an egotistical infliction of power and abuse to which a response was flight, either as physical departure or as resistence to the singular egotism that it presupposed and that sustained it. In like manner, the poet Brathwaite has Columbus regain his sight, and with it a different point of vision. Doing so, he recalls a later admiral, directly at imperialist war with Beethoven's Bonaparte, setting a telescope to his blind eye to avoid seeing his commander's signal and decisively winning the battle the signal had ordered him not to engage. Raising this blindness to heroic virtue, Horatio Nelson gave a metaphor for imperialism's deliberate unseeing of difference and colonialism's internal blinding of the cultural mind. Brathwaite's Colón recovers from these blindings.

By seeking different rhythms, using other metaphors, working in "nation language," Brathwaite wants, he once said, "a revolution of consciousness" (Walmsley, 242), different cultural realities. From them he raises a voice that confronts and saps the heroic tradition of Nelson's telescope and rejects its justifying claims while generously pushing away its vices and abuses and striving to include its virtues in a new—yet old—*mestizaje* made from Indio-American, European, and African strands. "*Bajan culture*," he writes in *Barabajan Poems*, "is this shared collective xperience on a rock of coral limestone, half-way from Europe, half-way (?back) to Africa; but like Nelson's statue in both Trafalgar Squares—but I'm talking about *ours* [Barbadian Bridgetown's, that is]—seeing, it see/ms, with only one & outer eye of the plantation; while the other inner eye & world of art & dream&meaning was for too long a time ignored, eroded, submerged; treated not only as if it did not xist, but that it could not: *Carry on Big Inglan, Lil Inglan is behine yuh!*" (21–22). Brathwaite's poetry turns away from that internalizing of oppression to face its history and its causes— *causers*; to forge a *home* culture from a forcibly fragmented language and a naturally fragmented geography. It seeks to get out from under imposed "dischordant skeletones," discarding them for a new—newly refound— body and a new music and rhythm (Brathwaite, "Metaphors," 456).

It turns away as Césaire's does, echoing the *imposure* (in Brathwaite's word) of imperial statuary. For Césaire, it is Bonaparte's empress looking out over the Savane, Fort-de-France's main square as Trafalgar is Bridgetown's, leaning on a medallion of Napoleon in profile: "l'impératrice

Joséphine des Français rêvant très haut au-dessus de la négraille. . . . dreaming way up high above the nigger scum," marking political, military, and cultural oppressions and where the wages of Western economies have been and are still further splinterings (*Cahier*, 34/5; 36/7).[4] For Philip, it is the "heavy, oppressive" architecture by whose means Spanish "history weighs on this country, this island" of Cuba (*Genealogy*, 151). Such monuments are foisted on "ces pays sans stèle, ces chemins sans mémoire, ces vents sans tablette," these lands without a stele, these paths without memory, these winds without a tablet (*Cahier*, 70/1; 48/9). Brathwaite may have been speaking directly to Césaire in writing of how *processive* memorializings replace "colonial ikons," tying "stelai" to people, their cares and deep sense of being, rhythms, and cadences: "the Ja reggae film, *The harder they come* (1972) w/ Jimmy Cliff & a host of real-life Ja ikons. This + the pres of Bob Marley, the Wailers, the I-Trees, Michael Manley, Walter Rodney, Carifesta Guyana, Black Power & the resurgence of Rastafari—to nam(e)/identify a few stelai—all in the 70s—leads to an alterNative iconography . . ." (*ConVERSations*, 49).

Indeed, one way in which Césaire imagined the difficulty of casting off the experience of oppression as internal self-loathing may have led Brathwaite to his skipping stones. For *Cahier* traces onto the islands an anguished dialectic between colonized negation and joyous revolt:

à moi, ces quelques milliers de mortiférés qui tournent en rond dans la calebase d'une île et ce qui est à moi aussi, l'archipel arqué comme le désir inquiet de se nier, on dirait une anxiété maternelle pour protéger la ténuité plus délicate qui sépare l'une de l'autre Amérique, et ses flancs qui sécrètent pour l'Europe la bonne liqueur d'un Gulf Stream

mine, these few thousand deathbearers who mill in the calabash of an island and mine, too, the archipelago arched like aching desire for self-denial, as if in maternal anguish to protect the most delicate tenuity that separates the one from the other America, and its loins secreting for Europe the good liquor of a Gulf Stream (*Cahier*, 64/5; 46/7)

At the same time, the "exaltation féroce de forêts et/montaignes déracinées" (ferocious exaltation of forests and uprooted mountains) on "les îles liées pour mille ans" (islands bound joined for a thousand years) gives rise to the hymn to joy of

voum rooh oh
pour que revienne le temps de promission

et l'oiseau qui savait mon nom
et la femme qui avait mille noms
de fontaine de soleil et de pleurs
et ses cheveux d'alevin
et ses pas mes climats
et ses yeux mes saisons . . .

voum rooh oh
that the promised times may return
and the bird who knew my name
and the woman who had a thousand names
of fountain of sun and of tears
and her hair of minnows
and her steps my climates
and her eyes my seasons . . .
                          (*Cahier*, 80/1; 52/5)

The dialectic runs through the poem, Césaire finally making it even more immediate and agonizing:

Iles cicatrices des eaux
Iles évidences de blessures
Iles miettes
Iles informes

Iles mauvais papier déchiré sur les eaux
Iles tronçons côte à côte fichés sur l'épée flambée du Soleil
Raison rétive tu ne m'empêcheras pas de lancer absurde
        sur les eaux au gré des courants de ma soif
votre forme, îles difformes,
votre fin, mon défi.

Iles annelés, unique carène belle
Et je te caresse de mes mains d'océan. Et je te vire
de mes paroles alizées. Et je te lèche de mes langues d'algue.
Et je te cingle hors-flibuste

O mort ton palud pâteux!
Naufrage ton enfer de débris! J'accepte!

Islands scars of the waters
Islands evidence of wounds
Islands crumbs
Islands unformed

Islands cheap paper torn on the waters
Islands stumps spitted side by side on the Flaming sword of the Sun
obdurate Reason you won't stop me casting absurd on
    the waters at whim of the currents of my thirst
your form, deformed islands
Your end, my defiance

Ringed islands, single lovely hull
And I caress you with my oceanic hands. And I turn you
with my tradewind words. And I lick you with my seaweed tongues.
And I sail you unpirate

O death your spongy swamp!
Shipwreck your hellish debris! I accept!

                             (*Cahier*, 132/5; 74–76)

In Césaire, scars, wounds, formless shards, spitted stumps cast on a death-giving sea are in anguished tension with the islands as a lovely ship on a caressing ocean. They end (here) in a slough of despond, a hell of debris, whose "acceptance" shouts a defiance formally, rhythmically, and assonantly recalling Émile Zola's famous cry of outrage against the anti-Dreyfus French government, military, and church elites: "J'accuse." In *L'Aurore* of January 13, 1898, Zola had talked of France's "rot," of the "master's sword" the "criminal" generals sought to drop on a nation misled, of "their boots on the nation's neck, forcing back down its throat its cry of truth and justice, under the lying and sacrilegious pretext of *raison d'État*." Does *Cahier* not echo this (especially as Alfred Dreyfus was jailed on Devil's Island, in "Caribbean" French Guiana)? recall a shard of metropolitan history? yet charge, too, that the islands might be all too ready to bend the neck. Brathwaite starts by affirming rather the beauty and inherent value—and virtue—of *place*, though he, too, admits ambiguities of colonized and neocolonial minds.

    In both cases, however differently, the moves to change the voice and the cultural patterns it embodies are essential. The issue is not just the language of poetry, of course. John La Rose once commented on that "imprisonment in English, in Spanish, in French, in Dutch which accordingly denies areas of experience which, if made available, would immediately disclose the total specificity of Caribbean life" (Walmsley, 251). Voice, language, forms of expression capture and colonize the mind just as surely as more overt ways of seizure. As Joyce's Stephen Dedalus put it in a famous passage: "His language, so familiar and so foreign, will always be for me an acquired speech. I have not made or accepted its words. My voice holds them at bay. My soul frets in the shadow of his language" (*Portrait*, 189). For Dedalus, this linguistic oppression is never "resolved," Denis Donoghue notwithstanding, who will have it that a "resolution" comes "fifty pages later" when Stephen records in his journal his discovery that the word "tundish," criticized as outlandish by the Jesuit Dean of Studies and to be replaced by "funnel," was in fact "good old blunt English." "Damn the Dean of Studies and his funnel!" he exclaimed: "What did he come here for to teach us his own language or to learn it from us. Damn him one way or the other!" (Donoghue). This is far from any "resolution." On the contrary, Stephen emphasizes the imposition of the colonizer's language as something the victim can never escape, ineluctably oppressed by being deprived of control over its representational possibilities and orders, but even, too, of any "comfort" in its ready availability as weapon, subversion, or strategy of concealment. That the victim may know the language better than the victimizer still cannot put it in the former's control, tied as it is to the patterns and structures of a culture.

Ngũgĩ has put the matter at the center of his creative and critical project. Many others have, of course, spoken of language as "instrument of oppression and source of humiliation," principal tool of culture letting you know that "it was your soul that was imprisoned" (Mphahlele, *Down*, 167, 202). But these and others have a different mother tongue into and in which they can move (despite the difficulty that these often have had no written tradition, so that both a written form and an audience literate in that language need to be created and established—dilemmas that Ngũgĩ has been very conscious of needing to face and overcome). Brathwaite inevitably puts the issue differently: "It was in language that the slave was perhaps most successfully imprisoned by his master, and it was in his (mis-)use of it that he perhaps most effectively rebelled. Within the folk tradition, language was (and is) a creative act in itself" (*Development*, 237). Similarly, Gomez observes how slaves sought to "attenuate" "the meter" of English "so that when spoken, the language would be as deracinated as possible" (*Exchanging*, 172). Brathwaite (like Philip) is looking for something beyond deracination. For language is not and cannot be separated from a whole culture, and the West Indian case was graver still than such a one as the Irish to which Dedalus referred.

The modern peoples of the islands never had a tongue alive in and imbued with the place where they dwell. They were forcibly brought to lands whose own peoples had been largely destroyed. At the same time, the languages whence they came were robbed of their source, shattered, and fragmented. Some argue that speakers of the same language were separated, those of different languages put together, forced finally to use the slave owners' language. As early as 1657, Richard Ligon thought the black slaves of Barbados could not revolt—despite overwhelming numbers—because "[t]hey are fetch'd from severall parts of *Africa*, who speake severall languages, and by that means, one of them understands not another" (*True*, 20). With their bodies, their words would have been "bought, sold, owned and stolen," leaving only a silence of which they were also robbed, forced as they were into an alien language, Philip stresses (*Looking*, 43, 20, 57, 69; cf. *She Tries*, 56). Others argue that there is no "hard evidence" for this and that on the contrary, "there is every reason to believe that [same language users] were kept together," one result of which would have been changes in English traceable to specific idioms, its users being "taught one brand of English but [giving] back another" (Gomez, *Exchanging*, 173, 177). Whichever the case—and no doubt both occurred—the language Dedalus holds at bay is their only option: a language bent to a victimizer's will, interests, and desires. "The place we occupy as poets is one that is unique," writes Philip, "one that forces us to operate in a language that was used to brutalize Africans so that they would come to believe in their own lack of humanity" (*Genealogy*, 63). As one Arwhal tells her narrator elsewhere: "you need the word—whore words—to weave your silence" (*Looking*, 53). Caribbean writers have to use "a language that was not only experientially foreign, but also etymologically hostile and expressive of the non-being of the African" (*She Tries*, 15). Instead of a mother or father tongue, Philip sardonically commented to a group of students, they have an "abusive parent" (seminar, January 27, 2000, University of Oregon).

Brathwaite argued the results in 1963, depicting anglophone Caribbean authors as producing, at home or away, "the same story, expressed in the same rhythms and a similar technique: frustration, bewilderment, lack of a centre, lack of faith in the society into which they were born or in which they find themselves" (*Roots*, 36). Years later, he remained bleak: "we have lyric slavery, romantic violence, rape as survival rhythm, peace as a hollow silence, howl's opposite, so that as writers, supposedly objective perceivers of the probe and problem, we remain trapped in the maelstrom of frustration, trapped and imprisoned within the detonations of our own fragmented worlds" ("Metaphors," 459). These told a story of endless (e)migration—"*nigration*," he later calls it (*ConVERSations*, 38)—of flight from what James called "the cramping West Indies" (*Black*, 397), no matter the flight's direction. In this regard, one reads now, with the surprise a mere generation of altered awareness brings, the pride with which Kenneth Ramchand saw such emigration in 1971: "since 1950 . . . every well-known West Indian novelist has established himself while living [in the English capital]. London is indisputably the West Indian literary capital" (introduction, 5). One recognizes economic and cultural pressures that still drive Caryl Phillips (in *The Final Passage*, for instance) to establish himself in London and repeat this story of exile "frustration, bewilderment, lack of a centre, [and] lack of faith in [their] society" as that which Brathwaite addresses. The point though was the *pride*, regretful and ambivalent as it was, that Ramchand took in such emigration.[5] For after all, Philip observes in a passage this book takes as an epigraph, colonialism and neocolonialism had forced the exile (no longer just toward the old capitals of empire) by first colonizing minds with everything from material goods to imported culture to language: "we not knowing that is exile we smelling when we excited for so, we pressing we noses against the new clothes; we not knowing that the literature and history, even the grammar we learning in school is part of the contour map in we own geography of exile" (*Frontiers*, 10)—too visible clothes of a distant emperor. Generations "grew to maturity knowing, almost simultaneously with awareness of self, that any future lay elsewhere, overseas, abroad, anywhere else but home" (*Genealogy*, 61).

One may characterize Brathwaite's work as historian, storyteller, cultural archivist, educator, essayist, and poet, as a lifelong effort to take up the gauntlet he threw down in his criticism. The effort to find a poetic form that would not just pick at or disrupt the dominant pentameter but use a quite different rhythm, from another place, another environment, another experience, was just the earliest of the shapes that work took. It also led him from the rock of Barbados and the curving stones of its habitat through Europe to Africa and eventually back to the Caribbean. Its aim has been to discover, to invent (in that word's double sense of finding *and* making: *invenire*) that Caribbean—especially his own Barbados—as a *home*, not as a displacement or a surrogate for something else, be it "little England" or robbed Africa. His aim has been to make a written culture and especially a poetry able to write the cultural rhythms, style, sensibility, and language of a particular Caribbean geography much as Velma Pollard calls more re-

cently for the narrower achievement of a "writing system for Jamaican creole" (afterword to *Considering*, 75). His aim has been, as Philip puts it, to
"keep the deep structure, the movement, the kinetic energy, the tone and
pitch, the slides and glissandos of the demotic within a tradition that is primarily page-bound" (*She Tries*, 23), a *poetic* tradition. Without a different
mother tongue, his aim has been so to disrupt forms, rhythms, and structures of the colonizer's language as to make it bear different cultural realities, speak different ways of thinking, manifest changed histories and other
environments. This is surely why Césaire first saw the islands sundered, vile
debris and lovely ship, and why he disjoins French syntax, vocabulary,
punctuation, and rhythm. The aim has had to be to make a "nation language" about which Saint-John Perse's question of an earlier poet would be
entirely apposite: did not Dante, he asks, "place in his Inferno, not far from
the blasphemers, a writer guilty of impiety towards his maternal tongue"
("Pour Dante," *Collected Poems*, 656–57)?

The first part and understanding of Brathwaite's geographical and historical story was told in the Arrivants trilogy. In this trilogy, *Rights of Passage*
"tells the story" of the passage from Africa to the Caribbean as a displacement that remains a displacement, simply the obverse, in a sense, of the coin
that had Europe as center and exile on its other face. Indeed, that particular
passage was evidently part of the same story. Here, Brathwaite echoes
Depestre's gesture of passing through the vast wall of noise erected by a violent European history, to try and find again the sounds of a silenced Africa:

> Dans mon coeur il y a quelque part
>   Un mur du son
> Qui se dresse, géant, nuit et jour
>   Entre le monde et moi.
>
> Est-ce la mer traversée jadis?
> Est-ce mon aïeul enchaîné
> Dans la cale d'un négrier?
> Est-ce toi Afrique qui saigne
>   Dans mes profondeurs?
>
> Est-ce toi que je dois franchir
> Pour être tout à fait moi-même?
>
> In my heart there is somewhere
>   A wall of sound
> That rises, gigantic, night and day
>   Between the world and me.

Is it the sea crossed long ago?
Is it my ancestor chained
In a slave-ship's hold?
Is it you Africa who bleed
       In my deepest parts?

Is it you through whom I must pass
To be altogether myself?
(Depestre, "Le mur du son," *Journal*, 38)

Perhaps this will later be Philip's discovery of the sounds of silence. It was Césaire's vehement sense of the need to break through oppressions of a colonized history in what was nonetheless the native land—Césaire's *Cahier* is a constant presence behind the three parts of the Arrivants trilogy.

   Masks, the next book in the Arrivants trilogy, tells the further tale of a modern poet's return to Africa, less as a search for "roots" than as a way to compose cultural remains into something more "whole," whose masks are successive distancings from a self ultimately able thereby to become part of a collectivity (an "opposite" response to Machado's or Pessoa's in the site of empire: of turning the "self" *into* a collectivity). Again, in a way, this repeats Depestre's search for new—lost—sounds: "Ouvrez la bouche de mes tambours/Et versez-leur à boire" ("Open the mouths of my drums/And pour them something to drink"; "Mes tambours ont soif," *Journal*, 41) . . . drums no less important to Brathwaite, as he describes their making— drawing skin from the death of a goat, barrel from the hard forest trees, sticks from the "stripped tree," accompaniment from the "Gourds and Rattles"—and at the last the "gong-gong" (*Masks*, 94–97) leading into its song:

   Kon kon kon kon
   Kun kun kun kun
   Funtumi Akore
   Tweneboa Akore
   Tweneboa Kodia
   Kodia Tweneduru
   ("Atumpan," *Masks*, 98)

Could these take passage back to the poet's home in the *Islands* whence he came? The third part of *The Arrivants* answers the question with another: can remnants that Africa may "put together" be anything but residual shards in these displaced islands?

Yet it is as shards, pieces fit for recovery, creation, building that they can be fitted into a cultural space that is, precisely, Caribbean—a *home* space.

Brathwaite's poetry has never sought easy answers. There was certainly no hope here for one. This last "conclusion," if it were not to remain a pious wish, required broad cultural work. Already in the late 1950s, Brathwaite had begun writing criticism of Caribbean literary work, and it has always accompanied his poetry and, equally importantly, his work as a historian. That latter work was clearly essential: to understand the place that was and is Barbados and its island companions and the African, European, and American history in which it and they participated. This is not the place to examine the details of that work. What is important here is how it informs the poetry and criticism, infusing it with that very sense of an "environment," a place, of particular historical experience, which is and is not that of Europeans—or Africans, or other Americans (although it may be worth noting that the effort to make anew a culture's voice is seconded by an educative one, where he has made his scholarly work the basis of textbooks for schoolchildren of the Caribbean).

Suffice it to say, as the three metaphors with which I began suggest, that this work has always explored issues similar to that found in the poetry and criticism. One way to get at this, perhaps, and to give it a wider context, is to suggest that the ten years Brathwaite spent in Africa (mainly in Ghana) enabled him to propose, like Depestre in the closing lines of "Mes tambours ont soif," that the ancient drums of a lost African past might themselves at last make the Atlantic passage:

O forêt qui a soif
O tambours haïtiens
Patience, frères,
La rosée est en route

O thirsty forest
O Haitian drums
Patience, brothers,
The dew is on its way
(*Journal*, 42)

The last line's reference to Jacques Roumain's celebrated 1944 novel, *Gouverneurs de la rosée* (*Masters of the Dew*), asserts coming control over one's own political and social destiny, over the geography of one's home. In

El reino de este mundo (1949), Carpentier marks traces of the same passage in the drums throbbing in the hills or Henri Christophe's blood that fore-tell the end of his *ancien régime*, black sun king rule (*Kingdom*, 106–9), whose "syncopated tone in three beats produced . . . by hands against the leather" irrupts into a military tattoo—to Christophe's fury (111–12)—and whose crescendo sounds out his downfall and suicide:

> at that moment the night grew dense with drums. Calling to one another, an-swering from mountain to mountain, rising from the beaches, issuing from the caves, running beneath the trees, descending ravines and riverbeds, the drums of Bouckman, the drums of the Grand Alliances, all the drums of voodoo. A vast en-compassing percussion was advancing on Sans Souci, tightening the circle. A hori-zon of thunder closing in. A storm whose eye at the moment was the throne with-out heralds or mace-bearers. (*Kingdom*, 116–17)

In *The Arrivants*, Brathwaite cannot yet see things so whole, perhaps because coming from fragmented Barbados, *Lil Inglan* still—but this is a hope not clearly fulfilled in Haiti either. Even so, to return from Africa with the drums beating in the poem's rhythm is to make a passage akin to that expressed by Lamming's Trumper, who comes back from the United States having discovered his group identity as a black "Afrosporic" person (to adopt Philip's coinage). Memory, a sense of place, above all a culture-consciousness are embodied for Trumper in this recognition, so that the old "big bad feeling in the pit of the stomach," the dizziness and empti-ness are forgotten: "A man who knows his people won't ever feel like that" (*Castle*, 300–301). Characterizing the anglophone Caribbean novel as frus-trated, bewildered, uncentered, trapped, and fragmented, Brathwaite echoed the first phrases. By the end of *Masks*, and then in *Islands*, he start-ed toward taking up the last. In West Africa, he found both the possibili-ty of a new group belonging and a place to ground many of the fragments he had found and was to find in the Caribbean.

But none of this is to say, as some critics have clamored, that he sim-plistically set Europe aside. "West Indian literature" had to be seen, he wrote in 1967, in its "proper context of an expression both European and African at the same time" ("Jazz and the West Indian Novel," *Roots*, 62–63). It is to say, though, that fragments of the one had to be set against, re-covered from, built into the "imposure" of the other (*Contradictory*, 61, and *passim*). Brathwaite was now prepared to go beyond both those he had once criticized and his own criticism. He would seek the home from a dis-covery of Caribbean geography and its meaning in history (skipped stones and their fall; rock hiding vital waters; windstorms of Africa—Saharan *harmattan*—that are now, after him, understood to affect the December–February droughts that strike the islands and the aforementioned hurricanes), by reconstructing the shards of fragmented cultural memory, by historical recovery, folk recall, and exploration in a poetry that would set out to find not only a Caribbean "content" but its own form of expression, its own rhythms and music. This last he would eventually draw from his work on jazz forms, his sensitivity to local sounds and images, and his deep awareness of the cultural importance of drumming rhythms, refound and remade from more distant rattles, gourds, and drums. But he would also explore the wider more general possibility of "nation language": a language that would itself echo "the environmental experience."

For one—disastrous—way for the colonized mind to face down its colonizer is to do what some did to the normative pentameter: fragment it, take it apart, break it up, even though, as Brathwaite argues, to do so still leaves it as the only hegemonic form. And what the fragmenter risks getting, and indeed gets in the end, is "a frantic impoverished dialect." Here I cite Wilson Harris describing the speech of one of his protagonists, Hassan, in *The Far Journey of Oudin*. He is matched by Kaiser, who had but "a few words of formal English." Neither of them can possibly come close to grasping the "unearthly delicate writing on the sky." And to Hassan's imagined wish to go back to India, Kaiser responds by protesting, "What language had he save the darkest and frailest outline of an ancient style and tongue? Not a blasted thing more." "You have no language," says another, "you have no custom." That is why the Hindus' Indian father feels so distanced from them: "we got to forgive he," says one of them, "for the strict unfathomable way he got of looking at we like if he grieving for a language. In ancient scorn and habit at the hard careless words we does use. But is who fault if the only language we got is a breaking-up or a making-up language?" (*Guyana*, 179–82, 155).

One cannot just "create a language" or "rescue . . . the word" from its possessors, as Galeano writes. No doubt a writer's feel for "his or her people—their roots, their vicissitudes, their destiny—and the ability to perceive the heartbeat, the sound and rhythm of the authentic counterculture" must be intense ("In Defense of the Word," *We Say No*, 141–42, 138). But what and where is such "*another* culture"? How can one recognize its "authenticity"? To say so much leaves yet unsaid the matter of *how* one might create or rescue language and word. One does neither *ex nihilo*: one uses, combines, fuses, and recombines myriad elements from the varied sources that forge everyone's homes or home. These elements already always exist, doing so in cultural experiences and environments whose ramifications may often escape notice. Whatever impoverishment is theirs, they remain remnants of a particular culture, and will do so until we know enough of *that* experience and ours to be able to use them otherwise: "Collective identity is born out of the past and is nourished by it" (Galeano, "Defense," *We Say No*, 138). We must know the working of the elements composing that past and the identities arising from it. To think one can adopt them without preparation as if they were neutral is almost surely to fall back into the patterns customary to the words one supposed one was rescuing—not, perhaps, impoverished, but still colonized.

Brathwaite traced those difficulties—with anger—in *Black + Blues*. There, the angry breaking away from the consequences of colonization and oppression, of cultural "imposure," made use of his gradual uncovering of jazz forms, local sounds and images, the rhythm of the drum, the shards of cultural memory, to rejoin them into something potentially new. Anger, although it is surely the only appropriate response to the theft of a language and a culture, clearly risks rejecting altogether the very elements it must of necessity use: "like a rat/like a rat/like a rat-a-tap tappin // like a rat/like a rat/like a rat-a-tap tappin // an we burnin babylone" ("Conqueror," *Black*, 19, 23). These lines were to be repeated in *Sun Poem* (1982), where they signal even more emphatically Caliban's revolt. *Black + Blues* then takes the reader through a triple sequence of understanding.

The opening anger stresses dismay and disgust of the poet forced to pick through "Fragments" marking the loss of his own culture and the sinister "gift" of the pieces permitted by another only to serve its own interests. Then comes the outrage of "Drought," facing the consequences of oppression: Caliban as "victim of the cities' victory" (30), London or Madrid, Paris or Amsterdam (La Rose's imprisonment in English, Spanish, French, or Dutch); Caliban, too, confronting visions of a place that "is no white man lan/an' yet we have ghetto here" (32), the exile geography of Philip's anger, neocolonial Babylon of the island itself. This yields to the further outrage of being forced to violence to avenge what has been taken (a violence that usually destroys its own), and at the adulteration of African memories: "a forgotten kingdom" (43), a yearning still borne in pain. Yet, at the last, we find the hopefulness of "Flowers": the rediscovery of fragments, African and Caribbean, based in firm geography of place: "the seas drummers // softly softly on sound . . . /it is a beginning" ("Harbour,"

Black, 83); in the symbol and existence of "Crab," who holds memory and geography together; and in the final hope of "Koker," with its "coastline" lying beneath "the sounds of stretched light . . . the don drumming light, against/sky that is their living monument" (90). Such could be a geography no longer of exile, where remnant drums of Africa meet those of North American jazz and blues and Caribbean pan, one taking up the Haitian drums of Depestre and Carpentier.

Black + Blues captured the dismay, frustration, bewilderment, decentering, and grief of Harris' characters in their linguistic and cultural deprivation but found a way to tap new rhythms, a confident history and a solid sense of place(s) to start making something otherwise. In a way, it repeated in concentrated form the movement of *The Arrivants*. We seem to be shifting here from what we may once more call, again after Ngũgĩ and Mphahlele, a decolonizing of the mind, toward something that may be yet harder, something that requires remapping the terrain, reclaiming the soul, allowing that soul no longer to be "lying down," or "*couchée*," as Césaire had protested (*Cahier*, 104/5; 62/3). Brathwaite's second trilogy, Ancestors (as it is now called), consisting of *Mother Poem, Sun Poem*, and *X/Self,* furthered these themes. The first was, so to speak, a discovery of the *place* of Barbados. The poet's quest to know and remember his mother is rediscovery of Barbadian geography, imbued with the Atlantic call of Africa and Europe, but essentially now *itself*, its own, with its own, no longer buried culture. Out of the submerged coral of the island comes its waters of life as out of various cultural practices, now *seen* for the first time, come submerged but ever less fragmented cultural forms, completing the hope expressed at the end of *Black + Blues*. The poet himself gets a grounded (new, but also culturally old) name.

Sun Poem next pursued the poet's paternal "genealogy," confirming his place in the land less "mythically," through the family grounding of grandfather, father, son, and memories of the boy's childhood. The son's name, Adam, symbolized this rooting, discovery, and, no doubt above all, the poet's *invention* of the new. *X/Self* finally explored the poet's now affirmed grounding in past and present, in Europe and Africa, in violence and oppression as well as in tact, grace, and renewal. The islands have become, too, a place of and for their *own* people: "not fe dem/not fe dem/de way caliban/done // but fe we/fe a-we" (*X/Self*, 84–85). This poem was to be reworked, rewritten, and lengthened as "Letter Sycorax" in *Middle Passages*, where the poet himself became and superseded the old Caliban of a past that still depended on fragments tied to a particular hegemonic memory (1992, 76–88; 1993, 93–116). Answering (for example) Galeano's dilemma, this shift may prove as important a one for the Caribbean imagination as was Retamar's replacement of Rodó's Ariel by Caliban himself, following Fanon's acid rejection of Mannoni's oppressive (and repressive) European theme. The negation, aggression, and denial with which Rodó's "Uncle Tom" Ariel was finally rejected yield here to new cultural creation.

Not for nothing did Brathwaite finish the second trilogy by rewriting "shango," a poem that came toward the end of *Black + Blues*. There the poem had started, "huh/there is a new breath here // hah/there is a sound of sparrows" (75). "Xango" begins: "*Hail*/there is new breath here // *huh*/ there is a victory of sparrows" (107). The more European-like "hail" (befitting conquering Rome of the beginning of *X/Self*) was now combined with the thunder-god's "huh"; noncommittal "sound" became the more optimistic "victory"—still perhaps not altogether freed of indecent hegemonies. But if these sparrows remain marked as the New Testament birds whose fall god would heed as much as a human's, we have also seen them become something altogether mightier: victims who turn against the oppressors their own instruments to be free to occupy their own geography and make their own history. Their victory may risk being understood as a version of a central tenet of a text crucial to the European imagination— "and the meek shall inherit the earth." But besides the cases noted in the previous chapter, an extraordinary earlier poem in *Mother Poem* takes this urgent "huh" to figure a break from European imposition.

Listening to a fundamentalist Baptist church service sung by those "meek," the poet overhears an entire shift in culture. First iambic hymns move to the dactylic "praaaze be to," ending in the single syllable, "god," itself lengthening into a kind of guttural sigh ("ggg"). Little by little, the verbal dactyls yield to a simple trainlike rhythm, followed by a long exhaled sigh: "bub-a-dups/bub-a-dups/bub-a-dups/huh/bub-a-dups/bub-a-dups/ bub-a-dups/hah," a sigh stretching to long "shshshshsh" and at last able to be heard as "shaaaaaango." Christian colonization is already ruptured here in *loas* of a different continent and different cultures welling up in language with the rhythms and sounds of Shango, the menacing hiss of the Dahomeyan serpent god of the sky, Yoruba Oshumare or Haitian Damballah breaking through the song of a Baptist hymn in "Angel/Engine" (97–103, a much longer "account"/"version" is in *Barabajan Poems*, 177–202). Césaire, too, had indicted "les sodomies monstrueuses de l'hostie et du victimaire," the monstrous sodomies of host and sacrificing priest of a conquering Christianity, and watched it slide to new forms: "Et ce ne sont pas seulement les bouches qui chantent, mais les mains, mais les pieds, mais les fesses, mais les sexes, et la créature toute entière qui se liquifie en sons, voix et rhythme": "And not only do the mouths sing, but hands, feet, buttocks, genitals, and the whole being that liquifies into sounds, voice and rhythm." Each dancer/singer starts "to pull the nearest devil by the tail, until fear imperceptibly fades"

dans les fines sablures du rêve, et l'on vit comme dans un rêve véritablement, et l'on boit et l'on crie et l'on chante comme dans un rêve, et l'on somnole aussi comme dans un rêve avec des paupières en pétale de rose, et le jour vient velouté comme une sapotille, et l'odeur du purin des cacaoyers, et les dindons qui égrènent leurs pustules rouges au soleil, et l'obsession des cloches, et la pluie . . .

In the fine sandlines of a dream, and you truly live as in a dream, and you drink and you shout and you sing as in a dream, and doze too as in a dream with rose-petal eyelids, and the day comes velvety as a sapodilla, and the manure smell of the cacaos, and the turkeys who tell their red wattle-warts in the sun, and the obsessive bells, and the rain . . . (*Cahier*, 38/9, 48/9; 36/7, 40/1)

Here too, western hymnal slips perhaps into voudou, drifting from a local geography—though more in the poem's sense than its rhythms and voice.

And as at the end of *Cahier*, so at the end of *X/Self*, even if only momentarily, the poet of the second trilogy seemed to have found a moment of that "tact and selfless grace" he found necessary for such peace and balance in the much earlier *Contradictory Omens* (61). It is in light of this that we should read the humorously expressed sense of hope maintained in *Middle Passages* (even after the most catastrophic losses, personal and intellectual): "is a matter of hope.of keep hope alive.to continue the dream/ cause we able.about our rightful place at the table," he wrote in "Duke. Playing Piano at 70" (1992, 27; 1993, 24). Of this collection, Fenella Copplestone observed: "its menace is real, its compassion touches the deepest springs of sadness, and its mythology is potent and frightening. People die in his world" (Review).

But people also live there, and if the world has menace, it is to those whose control is overthrown by it. For here, death is not the lurking disease, at least momentarily endemic to Enlightened reason, recorded, we saw, in seeming unthreatening expansive linear pentameter. Death plays its accepted and unfearful part in the ineluctable rhythm of life, the balanced experience of tact and grace. The "menace" of this poetry (a poor, but revealing, word) is of a site composed from fragments that are no longer just remnants of things lost but rather living crystals recombined and fused into consciousness of a place that does now capture fully "the *natural* experience, the *environmental* experience" of which Brathwaite was writing fifteen years and more ago.

It touches the deepest springs of sadness because the people who die there are vital, crucial to the remaking; their loss—one loss, anyway—is incomprehensible disaster: "without reason," he wrote in the dedication of *X/Self*, "all you hope gone/ev'rything look like it comin out wrong./Why is dat? What it mean?" But these lines come from the last part ("The Return") of *Rights of Passage*, first book of a trilogy whose last word was of hope—"making/with their // rhythms some-/thing torn // and new" (*Arrivants*, 69, 270)—so that the loss itself was now tied to the sense of place. Geography, poetry, self, history come together. The "missile" that was Columbus, that was the whole mighty power of an expansive culture imposed on Africa and the Americas, has yielded to a changed rhythm, a changed voice, the networked circle of Shango hidden in the watered rock beneath the still ongoing destructions of multinational capital, he writes in *Barabajan Poems* (187). Another major impingement of Europe on the Caribbean was of a different missile: a German torpedo sinking the *Cornwallis* in Bridgetown Harbour—but that was fifty years ago. Here, too, marks of European aggression were quickly swallowed by Barbadian waters, becoming a plaything for local boys (153–54, 347–61). This swallowing may also be a harbinger of creation and hope. It is a grieving but vital hope that Brathwaite—and others—have passed along. So Jean "Binta" Breeze puts it:

> lang time we walking, chile
> lang time
> we shapin mountain
> wid we foot
> lang time
> we making waves
> wash rock
>
> an in de walking
> we still
> be doing
> revealing
> wat we is
> ("Caribe," *Spring Cleaning*, 51–52)

Now the older poet returns to the uncle's workshop of his youth, to his limping Bob'ob. In the ruins of the old workshop, he discovers that Bob'ob had carved a forbidden African image. As surprising and mysterious as the carving itself is its survival over the years in the ruins of Bob'ob's home (*Barabajan Poems*, 155). Brathwaite had written in *Islands* of his carpenter uncle and of this "block of wood that would have baffled" those who bought his furniture, carved into shape "within his/shattered/Sunday shop." There, we learned he had angrily shaped the iron god of thunder and creation, Ogun (*Arrivants*, 243). Coming back later, the poet can now recognize the carver. Limping Bob'ob, holding a lost past of Africa and opening it to the poet, is Legba, divine trickster god of Dahomey, once a force of primal energy, now "the limping/crippled African god of the crossroads of beginnings & opening doors—as Bob'ob as Toussaint Louverture—the Liberator or 'Opener' of S Domingue into Haiti—himself a cripple—*fatras baton* they once called him . . . and whose French sobriquet—'Louverture'—was surely a direct translation of the Dahomey Legba (Open/Doorway) & why not?" (172). And what of the poet himself? New "Adam" of *Sun Poem*, inventor of new names, opener of culture, finder of lost presences, joiner of remnants—may he not fill the same role? And why not? He finds too that Bob'ob's ruined workshop has become a Zion meeting hall, a place of worship for a fundamentalist "Christian" group not happily accepted by authorities (166).

Now again, as in *Mother Poem*, listening outside, the poet hears the rhythm of their worship, their singing/chanting, and their movement/ dancing slowly change: "the sound of their voices has gradually gone through an alteration of orbit & pitch . they are into the pull of an alteration of consciousness as if the tides of their lives have paused on the brin(k) of falling onto our beaches & instead have slowly lifted themselves up up up so that the cries that should have been breaking from their crests do not move anymore but glisten in the deep silence of their throats until they begin to sweep slowly backwards like away from our shore from our trees from our hills away from Barbados" (181–82). Rhythm changes, dance moves, cadence slips into the hoarse measured breathing of Shango's visitation. Christian hymnal pentameters give way to a different syncopated drumbeat, that is also the echoed blues and jazz rhythms of the old trains, "sulphur and fire into a sibilant & quiet acceptance of her trans-formation like Aretha coming home in *Pullin*" (196–97; I do not attempt here to capture Brathwaite's typographical play, his Sycorax computer style, echoing visually the changing sounds of voice and rhythm of dance). "Until there is at last what there always was/SHANGO/as she struggles to name almost names him the train comin in/comin in/comin in wid de rain" (200–201; and see again *Mother Poem*, 98–103).

Barabajan Poems culminated for a moment the movement traced here. Bringing together the three metaphors with which we started, it transforms them into the vital essence of a culture. Legba, Shango, the rhythms, voice, and history that together make a whole have come together with other shards of other cultures: steam trains and blues, Christian hymns and jazz, the "rattle and pain" of loss and deprivation (201) with the vivid hope of new names and endless depth of proverbial orality (268–83). Proverbs are another link with a local past still alive in everyday material exchange. They are, Achebe avers, "like citing the precedents in law." They set a present case in ancestral context, give "a certain connectedness" and help "banish the sense of loneliness, the cry of desolation" (*Conversations*, 180). Brathwaite is here far indeed from Pope, Thomson, Gray, and Froude—not to mention the falling snow of his Cambridge youth. He is very far, too, from those bewildered tales of emigration typical of the Caribbean writers of his youth—and still perfectly usual, we saw: both are, we have of course been suggesting, aspects of the *same*, very partial and interested, history—and place (which is not—not just, and not first—Caribbean). *Barabajan Poems* confirms the hopefulness of the lighted living coastline that ended *Black + Blues* and affirms the embedded collective "self" of *X/Self* into what seems a quite new cultural, natural, environmental surety.

This, though, seems a moment of "equilibrium," ambivalent as it was, that the poet has left behind him. On the whole, since 1977, when *Mother Poem* first appeared, his voice has grown bleaker. When he published the complete trilogy in 2001, Brathwaite added and subtracted poems, rewrote all the poems in Sycorax, changed rhythms, cadences, tones, emotions. In particular, perhaps, he added the "bittern poem," "Pixie," deliberately interrupting *Mother Poem*'s flow with the story of a child's flight from horror and consequent prostituting, marking a changing Barbados, a Barbados where the sparrows live in fear and the voice runs hoarse; where the child

> stripped even of her sweat & sweet & sleep & sarrow
> so many serpent esses in this silence where he waits

she watches. a whisper at the corner sounding scared
this scaly voice of sound. dry shak shak shackle pods

scrape scrabble on the ravage concrete brown
                          (*Mother Poem, Ancestors,* 59)

"He" is the policeman who prostitutes the child, the politician who prostitutes his island, the journalist on bended knee to both. The poem joins
newspaper report, letters (from Pixie/Stephanie) and commentary, narrating the corrupting of community and especially of childhood, law and
order's role in that corruption—indeed, the community's making of it.

This story of the loss of innocence is new here, however "traditional,"
even "Wordsworthian," it may be in other regards—a characterization I
dare use only in the spirit in which Brathwaite remarks of the same usage
that it may "make a ?helpful connexion since i/we don't yet have critical references in this area of our ow-(n)" (*ConVERSations,* 54). Particularly damn-
ing is the bleak indifference, even exploitation, that is the story's context
and that overwhelms its atmosphere. "Pixie," with the many other changes
Brathwaite has wrought in the trilogy's first book, tends to subvert the
rural/urban courtesies of *Mother Poem*'s earlier version, marking an erosion
that "Pixie" makes stunningly clear. *Mother Poem* retains its deep compassion and a certain sense of tact and gentleness, but these are now joined by
anger deeper and more evident than before. Not only "Pixie" marks the
change: so, too, do the now more urgent breach of standard written
English, changes in rhythm created by Sycorax, assured handling of unfamiliar word breaks—deliberate sappings of an imposed language—disruption of what had been a certain "evenness" of tone, hugely increased varia-
tion of voice and cadence. Together, they signal a loss of innocence that is
not just the child's but the island's—and surely the poet's as well. It picks
up on the new anger and something often close to despair, apparent in such
other writings of the 1990s as the anguishingly personal *Zea Mexican Diary*
and the painful *Trench Town Rock*, indicting local victim/thug and his colonial creator at one and the same time. Yet the sunken warship turned boys'
plaything now finds its way into the long "Bubbles" of *Sun Poem*. And if a
poem like "Clips," with its "harf-arse" planter father/unfather, uneasy
mixed-blood children, and legacy of desperate stress does convey an atmosphere of decayed racism, sexual violence, it is still deeply compassion-
ate toward a history not altogether lost but the *wrong one*. Despite this
weight of angry mourning in the newly worked trilogy, the sense of *place*

making culture—from histories of its own, among other ways—remains no less overwhelming.[6]

Galeano wrote that "a literature born in the process of crisis and change, and deeply immersed in the risks and events of its time, can indeed help to create the symbols of the new reality, and perhaps . . . throw light on the signs along the road" ("Defense," *We Say No*, 139). Brathwaite, poet, historian, and critic, has brought us—and himself—somewhere else, into a "web," it may be, as Harris puts it, "born of the music of the elements" (*Guyana*, 7). The poet offers a reply of grace and tact to inertias of a European literature whose forms still by and large correspond to needs fixed four centuries ago and query them, sap them, only with a great tentativeness of difficulty, striving against political, economic, and cultural forces whose interests lie in pursuing and retaining a familiar and customary history into the present (pretending its conflicts over; Reiss, *Meaning*, 338–47). This is indeed why Brathwaite argued the need not just to fragment, break up or in some other way "subvert" the pentameter, the King's or Queen's English it measured and the cultural meanings it transported, but to break with these altogether, drumming the rhythms of different histories, singing the marks of a different geography, in sadness, no doubt, but also in hope and in humor. Still another, younger poet has picked up here on Brathwaite's practice and hopes, tying them to Jamaican urban and Rastafarian life. Mervyn Morris reports the dub poet Oku Onuora saying at a public debate in 1986:

Dub poetry simply means to take out and to put in, but more fi put in more than anything else. We take out the little isms, the little English ism and the little highfalutin business and the little penta-metre . . . that is what dub poetry mean. It's dubbing out the little penta-metre and the little highfalutin business and dubbing in the rootsical, yard, basic rhythm that I-an-I know. Using the language, using the body. It also mean to dub out the isms and schisms and to dub consciousness into the people-dem head. That's dub poetry. (Morris, *"Is English,"* 38)

I have suggested that Brathwaite is already followed by a legion of artists and critics questioning and turning imposed or inherited cultural instruments—those practices, reasons, devices, and stories that define a culture's self-understanding. He has, of course, never been alone in doing so either, and it is worth adding one more, older voice to those of his contemporaries already heard: that of Claude McKay, who, like them (and Onuora) spoke, in similar terms of "Babylon" imposing its isms, its doings and beliefs, via the familiar rhythms of its language:

Around me roar and crash the pagan isms
To which most of my life was consecrate,
Betrayed by evil men and torn by schisms
For they were built on nothing more than hate!
(*Selected Poems*, 49; cf. Morris, "*Is English*," 96)

Like these now many others, Brathwaite deeply questions and reworks—replays—the many cultural instruments we have been seeing. He has translated Philip's "*i-mage*," the irreducible intuition of a place and its people, creating "new *i-mages* that speak to [their] essential being," those i-mages whose i utters the essential self expressed by one of the double i's of Rastafarian dread talk, "i-and-i," the other being the i of colonized social being (*Genealogy*, 43; *She Tries*, 12–16). He has done as much as any to confront colonial oppression, decolonize minds, and reclaim a culture's soul. On all of these, finding new i-mages, decolonizing minds, and reclaiming the soul, he wrote wistfully from his Barbadian and Jamaican cultural situations of an advantage he saw in Aubrey Williams' Guyanese one, not so stripped and destroyed as that of the islands:

he could actually *see* the ancient art of the Warraou Indians. Living with them placed him in a significant continuum with it; for high up on the rocks at Tutatumari, at Imbaimadai, people who were perhaps of Mayan origin—the ancestors of the Warraou and others in the area—had made marks, or *timehri*: rock signs, paintings, petroglyphs; glimpses of a language, glitters of a vision of a world, scattered utterals of a remote *Gestalt*; but still there, near, potentially communicative. Sometimes there were sleek brown bodies that could have been antelope or ocelot; there were horns and claws of crabs. There were triangular forms that might have been the mouths of cenotes. But hints only; gateways to intuitions; abstract signals of hieroglyphic art. To confirm that these marks were made by humans, imprints of the etcher's palm were left beside the work; anonymous brands in living stone, imperishable witness from past to conscious present. ("Timehri," 40)

Brathwaite has been in search of his own *timehri*—in Europe, Africa, Amerindia. Certainly, his pictographs are rather more "phonographs": sounds and whispers, cries and rhythms of cultures whose fragments—opposing claims to the contrary—do survive and are part even of cultures where they once seemed to have been lost. They were but submerged: rhythms of Shango in the hounfort; statue of Africa by uncle Bob'ob/Legba in a ruined workshop; hidden fresh streams in the limestone of Barbados—like those imaged cenotes of Guyana or the Yucatan. Brathwaite has been retrieving, present already in his Caribbean world, Harris' "complex mutuality of cultures," breaking across old boundaries, forging new links with different homes, yet staying clearly enlaced in his own—enabling from his *timehri* not some hybrid mush, but new mutualities of distinct vernaculars. He has now explained this at some length, how especially the Sycorax forming and re-forming of his poetry but also the very thought and expression of poetry as "imprint" and record of a *place*'s "enigmatic silence" are *timehri*. His poetry "sign[s] back to life when you see it, say it," the "'silenc-(e)' encoded with that ancient memory—the sound of the fir-rst (forest) trees and rivers, slant of sunlight on the slopes of mountains, anima of dream and nightmare, the voices of all those voiceless generations . . ." (*ConVERSations*, 167, 201). Brathwaite is foremost among those who offer a model and an image of such vital practices—crucial in our time—expressing in his life and in his poetry that "elation" which Walcott once applied, particularly, to two older poets, Saint-John Perse and Césaire, a "staggering elation in possibility" ("Muse," 17).

But this possibility is not just one of elation. These complex mutualities entail other sorts of responsibility, ones calling for the deep pity of a passion without sentiment—to adapt a phrase of Brathwaite's, making history and poetry outcries against violence and oppression, demands for other sorts of attention and justice. Such poetry he has made in the past, such poetry he is writing now, attending to present violences and suffering of desperate, postcolonial catastrophe. He has found and created experience natural to the place that is his, itself made a whole from what had been the blighted fragments he recorded in earlier poetry. This is to go beyond decolonizing the mind, becoming aware of the forms and content of colonization, so as to remove—or at least see past and between—the accretions of alien "imposure." It is to make a culture, as Walcott has put it, "according to the topography where you live" ("Caribbean," 12). It is to remap an environment, a history, a geography, a culture, and an experience. It is to reclaim the soul, to be grounded at last in one's own home.

9

On Languages, Flowers, and Geography:
Outsmarting Sisyphus, Amending Eldorado,
Writing Caribbean

Introducing a recent collection of Caribbean writing to a North American audience, Rhonda Cobham writes as one walking into a room, feeling the conversation stop, then start again, "and yet you have this feeling that it is still quiet." The outsider looks in on the quietness even though, in this instance, she is, has also been, the insider interrupted in this way: we "shift infinitesimally in our seats at moments like these in what looks like a gesture of welcome, even deference, but is really a refusal to let the Other see into your soul" (introduction, 336). Seeing into the soul, I think, is less the question than recognizing that the tension and whatever "answer" or "solution" there is to it all lie in this very counterpoint of exclusion and inclusion, and that they *must* do so. The beginning of understanding between cultures surely lies in knowing, deeply knowing, that we are all some insiders' outsider. The hope is not that the walls may be knocked down, but that one may learn where they are, where the doors and windows are, who the people are who will open them, and when the moment exists to expect such opening. We need, again, Saramago's discretion to be "incapable of forcing the doors of another's privacy" (*History*, 228). To force them is to repeat the violence of the seekers of Eldorado and make those within them into children of Sisyphus. At the same time, to want them opened always and everywhere is to despise the diversities they enclose. One issue is to escape these dualities that always get established.

Many have spoken—not seldom rather despairingly—of these closures and of refusals to accept that those inside must be the ones to open them. The outsider's understanding *starts* from such acceptance, from feeling the walls around the insider's quiet. Just so, in Rosario Castellanos' *The Nine Guardians*, does the seven-year-old Spanish-speaking narrator's Indian "Nana" sit down with a group of other Chiapas Indians, all of them drawing together around a fire, speaking Tzeltal: "They talk, and it's as if a circle had closed around them" (20). The issue is less the language than recognition of people's *space*, of the need for invitations—and above all, of the need first to learn to listen. Responding to a violently appropriative and patronizing attack, Brathwaite likewise remarks on how work between different places requires *active* knowledge that "my work starts from my yard while trying to speak to you in yours." But, he goes on, "this predicates that you will be DOING THE SAME THING: speaking to me from yr yard & LISTENING w/ this understanding to me as I try to be listening w/ understanding to you." Without that, Cobham and Castellanos agree, not understanding, but "the wrong kind of noise" ensues ("Post-Cautionary," 75). Such speaking and listening demand deep care.

For one must remember that these walls, with their doors and windows, with their peoples and their places, are not separated from others by some vast, empty space. The outside of one home is the inside of another. Their geographies and histories open up on one another, into one another. Silences are recognized, to be sure, in response to the talking they interrupt, but necessarily also by reference to that known to the one who did the interrupting. Voice and language, that is to say, like geography and history, are forged in exchanges, Brathwaite's "nation language" neither more nor less than all others. This is perhaps obvious enough in the case of Creoles, but I am reminded of a remark by a once-renowned sixteenth-century European author who thought that his contemporary vernaculars were all hopelessly decayed and unreliable, mixed with bits of old and new languages, but (as he ended an essay on their topic) he noted that their Latin original was itself vernacular to a previous language similarly formed: a regression to which only Adam's and Eve's idiom could put an end—at judgment day (Bovelles, *Liber de differentia*). Yet all these languages, forged from constant borrowings and lendings, from endless mutual decays and growths, do not become some hybrid mess. With all their migrations, they stay distinct.

In their actual functioning, Charles de Bovelles implied, languages *are* a process of emplacement and motion, of history working and geography settling, of reasons various and voices diversifying, of migrations that are also homes. Yet even as they *belong*, they also estrange. They are not the mere image but the actual practice of settling place, moving history, being a culture. In their process, they make a nonsense of now all-too-familiar notions of otherness: versions of difference that reaffirm themselves. Voice, language, is that miracle of tact and grace where migration and distinction forge an equilibrium, *are* a balance. Which is why those who are insecure in place or expansive of desire may demand their destruction.

For the distinctness can be a danger. As the vernaculars whose limitations Bovelles lamented expanded in use, so they competed as to which was best suited to express the single human rationality in which their users increasingly believed and which they soon claimed to represent. Even before Bovelles' lament, the implications of a new vernacular taking over from the older Latin one were made clear in the emblematic year of 1492, when Elio Antonio de Nebrija, dedicating his Castilian grammar book to Queen Isabella, explained its utility by remarking that "language was always companion of empire" as it was also the holder of knowledge and historical memory ("Para nuestra recordación y memoria," *Gramática*, 97).[1] For many years now, this remark, "que siempre la lengua fue compañera del imperio," has been handed down by English-language historians and others in the quite different form of "language is the perfect instrument of empire," a myth that matches the Enlightenment idea of language as nothing but the transparent instrument of reason, as if it did no more than mediate the rule of an authority legitimate because universally *human*. This is to hide the power of language, willfully to conceal how talk is silenced, walls knocked down, and spaces appropriated for different voices.

Nebrija's remark was more interesting, for it made language not the subordinate but the equal of the violences making empire, their "co-conspirator" (Gomez, 171): "For colonization is not evangelization, nor a philanthropic enterprise, nor a desire to push back the frontiers of ignorance, disease, and tyranny, nor an attempt to extend the rule of law," we saw Césaire admonish in this context in Chapter 2:

The decisive actors here are the adventurer and the pirate, the wholesale grocer and the ship owner, the gold digger and the merchant. . . . I find that hypocrisy is of recent date; that neither Cortez discovering Mexico from the top of the great teocalli, nor Pizarro before Cusco (much less Marco Polo before Cambaluc), claims that he is the harbinger of a superior order; that they kill; that they plunder; that they have helmets, lances, cupidities; that the slavering apologists come later. (Césaire, *Discourse*, 10–11)

The point is simply that here one sees what is being done. "Jesus Christ is good, but trade is better," said an old Dutch proverb (Watts, 128). The Spanish invaders of the Americas had been equally clear about imperial violence and greed. "Columbus was of the opinion," Frank recalls, "that 'the best thing in the world is gold. . . . It can even send souls to heaven'; Cortés, on arriving on these shores [Mexico], informed an Indian: 'We, the Spaniards, suffer from a disease of the heart for which there is only one specific remedy: gold'; the Franciscan friars and Bishop Mota y Escobar observed that 'Where there is no silver, the gospel does not enter,' and 'Where there are no Indians, there is no silver' " (Frank, *Latin America*, 233).

Especially interesting in these examples is not only the equation of religious spirituality and mercantile greed but the speakers' overt assertions of it, the fact that they insistently use language to drive the point home. Nebrija saw language as itself a means to dominance. He saw language, and most especially written language, writes Walter Mignolo, as a way to "tame" other voices, other languages (*Darker*, 37–43 *et seq.*). For Nebrija, remarks Eugenio Ascensio, "Language accompanies the organic process of man's supreme creation: the State" ("Lengua," 407). Bovelles, however, called it inept for much of anything, as it needed various aids and supports for competent action. Later users found numerous ways to hold it harmless. The visibility of their equation between place and history, language and memory, power, peoples, and nations was little by little occulted. Appropriations, deprivations, became unquestioned original possession of the appropriator (unquestioned, that is, by him), above all when they were *just* names.

Thus Europe "discovering" the Americas gave them the name of one of those "discoverers": Amerigo Vespucci. Textbook example here of that assault of Europe's "history-mongering tribes" of which we saw McWatt speak, imposing their "names and other subtleties" ("Then," *Language*, 9). This "brutal naming obliterated others" (Philip, *Genealogy*, 9). Naming peoples and their place, we set them in *our* time, we possess them. But in this case, all three acts twist the very memory and history even they claim to confirm. Amerigo was really Alberigo, and he had renovated his name from a people and a mountain range he encountered in what is now Nicaragua, the Amerique. Appropriating another's name, he renamed and remade himself in the image of what he claimed to possess in the name of a thereby altered European story. Telling of this, Jan Carew catches nicely the mixture we have begun to follow:

Robbing peoples and countries of their indigenous names was one of the cruel games that colonizers played with the colonized. Names are like magic markers in the long and labyrinthine streams of racial memory. . . . To rob people of their names is to set in motion a psychic disturbance which can in turn create a permanent crisis of identity. (*Fulcrums*, 98)

Theft of names, Philip agrees, leaves people "fatally ill at ease. In these stranger names. Misshapen. So that nothing, not even our names, ever quite fits" (*Genealogy*, 21).

(A sour historical irony is "America"'s recent return to the area to repeat in reverse Alberigo's earlier appropriation.) But of course names, voices, were not just appropriated. They were also suppressed, obliterated in the many violent ways we know. At the same time, they were overlaid with others—themselves as often as not broken and partly destroyed, or destined to be. Before being made into children of Sisyphus, their speakers were made orphans of their own places and languages. Perhaps the one required the other: the "millions of people made orphans," Jamaica Kincaid writes of England and its colonies, "no motherland, no fatherland, no gods, no mounds of earth for holy ground, no excess of love which might lead to the things that an excess of love sometimes brings, and worst and most painful of all, no tongue" (*Small Place*, 31). This despoliation of names will recur in Chapter 11 in the context of Cortés' invasion of Mexico.

That is why Caribbean writing, by no means alone in this, had first to confront those destructions, appropriations, deprivations. Authors did so by concentrating on and often echoing the dualities that the Enlightenment instituted. Carpentier's "here" and "there," explored by Benítez-Rojo in terms of Law/Father/Europe versus Music/Mother/America might be taken as emblematic, even though one may wonder how much that understanding is from using European Freud and *its* notion of the subject/self as an instrument (which is not to imply that Caribbean peoples don't experience a "subjectivity"—such an argument would be absurd—but to see that *this* instrument is bound to a specific history). Others have seen the same dualism, especially in early writings. Roberto González Echevarría notes how in *El reino de este mundo* (1949) "European history . . . appears as inauthentic in relation to the New World." There, it is opposed not by the later multiplicity of new world "competing histories" of *El siglo de las luces* (1962), but by an African "contrary": European history's "highest representative [is] Pauline Bonaparte, who surrenders to sloth and sensuality in the tropical heat, while African history is represented by the various *loas* who incarnate in the black revolutionaries" ("Socrates," 36, 38). I note the word "represent" here, which itself perhaps signals just this notion of distance and contraries, one to which I will return. In *Reino*, European history's inauthenticity is represented as a product of a theater (via Racine, most notably), the novel (involving such exoticizing gestures as Bernardin de Saint-Pierre's *Paul et Virginie* and René de Chateaubriand's *Atala*), and abstractions projected by Rousseau and others. These are set against the real violence and vivid life of Saint-Domingue and of an Africa represented not just in the *loas* but in the slaves themselves, and indeed, *pace* González Echevarría, in Corsican Pauline Bonaparte, whose native island, activities, and bonds with Solimán are all deliberately and closely associated with Africa, offering us the familiar Dionysos/Apollo, mother/father, sensuality/reason series of oppositions.

That Africa could be "opposed" to Europe as "other" to "same," "absence" to "presence" is of course a familiar idea of which we have already seen much, recycling, in barely updated terms, an older and blunter opposition between black and white, savage and civilized, nonhistory and history, aborigin and origin: Nebrija's imperium, Césaire's piracy. The same duality has characterized much American thought, set out most famously perhaps in Sarmiento's *Facundo*, whose very title opposed European "civilization" to American "barbarism." But the idea has been as much a commonplace in sociohistorical and literary debate in America as it was in Froude's (or still Enoch Powell's) England. Africa, Latin America, and the Caribbean (or almost anywhere beyond the Atlantic and Oder borders of western Europe) are established as "Europe" 's contraries: "Lord, what it is we people do in this world that we have to suffer so? What is it we want that the white people and them find it so hard to give?" asks Sir Galahad in Samuel Selvon's *The Lonely Londoners* (88). The suffering made by the opposition is real; the enabling "opposition" is an abstraction of Césaire's "slavering apologists," whose adoption by its victims is part of its operation as an instrument of cultural domination: "so Galahad talking to the colour Black, as if is a person, telling it that is not *he* who causing botheration in the place, but Black, who is a worthless thing for making trouble all about. 'Black, you see what you did yesterday?' . . . 'Is not we the people don't like,' he tell Moses, 'is the colour Black' " (*Lonely Londoners*, 88–89).

Many Caribbean artists, critics, and others have spoken much on how these instruments make an alienation in the soul, so that it becomes not just a matter of the outsider seeing in, but of the insider having a weight of soul, "solid and complete," out of which to see (Kincaid, *At the Bottom*, 82). Just so did Brathwaite remark in 1957 of Selvon's novel, how "this poverty, this shortage of material on which the spirit is sustained, becomes a famine in the soul of the West Indian artist" ("Sir Galahad," 9). "When the colonizers exterminated the indigenous inhabitants in many regions of the Americas," writes Carew, "they severed connections with a vast network of secret tributaries that led into the mainstream of the memory of humanity" (*Fulcrums*, 103). As a result, the "Caribbean writer today is a creature balanced between limbo and nothingness, exile abroad and homelessness at home, between the people on the one hand and the colonizer on the other" (91). This sense of being caught between two oppressive places and of the inevitable exile that characterized motion between them and absence from them have been the most salient characteristics of Caribbean writing for most of this century. It no longer is, but much has had to happen.

A real history and a place in a particular geography have not infrequently, then, been replaced by snatched names and abstractions, what I earlier called "kitsch memory": one that replaces the complex actualities of the past with a nostalgia forged from an idealized version of the present set in tandem with such murkier actualities, making ideas *about* events and phenomena *into* events and phenomena, creating an etherealized past of New Age beauty and perfection for the spiritual tourist (Chapter 1). José Carlos Mariátegui argued that such "nostalgic relics" always characterized colonial and colonized literature, offering a rosy-tinted, romantic, or traditionalist *pasadismo* that hoped to reproduce *here* the universal values that a universalist and self-aggrandizing imperium claimed for itself in its own *there and* in its supposed other's *here*: a "nostalgic idealization of the past" that satisfied valorizing needs of both colonizer and colonized (*Seven*, 194, 224–25, 274). Nor are these events and phenomena just replaced by kitsch memory. Such idea-forging also aestheticizes real suffering, as Joan Dayan, in "Paul Gilroy's Slaves, Ships, and Routes," thinks Paul Gilroy does in his *Black Atlantic*, etherializing and depoliticizing his black diaspora by removing ongoing pain and violence (cf. Brathwaite's *Dream Haiti* and the shorter version in *DreamStories*). This seems a risk, Silvio Torres-Saillant suggests, in Benítez-Rojo's idea of the Antilles as a "repeating island" which "does not correspond to any of the known Antillean islands. It is an island 'as impossible to reach as the hypothetical *Antillas*' that befuddled the cosmographers in the past . . . like Hellas and the great Malay archipelago, 'the Caribbean is not a common archipelago, but a meta-archipelago'" (Benítez-Rojo,

Repeating, 4; Torres-Saillant, 205). I am reminded of little so much as of Nooteboom's story set in a Netherlands that expands down through the Alps into Northern Italy and toward the Balkans: but *In the Dutch Mountains* overtly makes myths of geography and history to narrate a story of life and death, good and evil, travel and exile, named as a fairy tale.

The Caribbean meta-archipelago is not a real place either. The impulses it imparts relate less to actual suffering and oppression than to the symbolic imagination: "Antilleans . . . tend to roam the entire world in search of the centers of their Caribbeanness, constituting one of our century's most notable migratory flows. The Antilleans' insularity does not impel them toward isolation, but on the contrary toward travel, toward exploration, toward the search for fluvial and marine routes" (Benítez-Rojo, *Repeating*, 25). Torres-Saillant remarks how this "metaphorical logic construes an imperative of self discovery out of what Caribbeanists normally mourn as a bitter drama of uprooting and diasporic dispossession" and draws on Derek Walcott for a "rebuttal": "The Caribbean is not an idyll, not to its natives" (*Antilles* [unpaginated, 36]; Torres-Saillant, 207). At issue here is not native or nonnative, but the relation of the fictive imagination to the actuality in which it is embedded. At issue is not history versus imagination, but their confusing, especially where control over history (we will see in a moment) is a primary dilemma. Dayan's Gilroy courts this danger of aestheticizing reality with false abstractions, making a kitsch Eldorado from, in this instance, elegant diasporic errance into a postmodern future. This may be just a counterpart set in the future of a supposed Eldorado in the past that was never there to be lost and found in the first place, site of an innocence betrayed that was never other than a version of that false nostalgia we already saw as central to western thinking in earlier chapters.

Carew's writer and people risk further deprivation. One cannot amend abstracting instruments by replacing them with others. Certain versions of *Négritude*, of *Créolité* that seek to make identities from contraries or notions of diaspora that turn real migrations and forced exiles to abstract metaphor of good and worthy *communitas*, *Gemeinschaft* set against a greedy and bad *Gesellschaft*, competitive individualism . . . these reestablish sureties of confrontational otherings, repeating the very fragmentation some metropolitan capitals echoed from their colonizing activities: "It divide up in little worlds, and you stay in the world you belong to and you don't know anything about what happening in the other ones except what you read in the papers" (Selvon, 74). The urge to travel and diasporic wandering would supposedly break these down—at the cost of neglecting the realities all around them. Part of the problem comes from the very abstraction of ideas of "otherness" that such devices are supposed to defeat—matching or counteracting those of "ego" and "subject" to which they are a counterpart, from the same European—freudian or lacanian—source. When Benítez-Rojo explores Carpentier's work according to a freudian model of neurosis or Cobham examines Antoni's *Divina Trace* via a version of the same model of subjective identity (although expanded to Lacan), it seems that Torres-Saillant hits the nail on the head in remarking of the former's exploration that then "the Caribbean merely yields a forum wherein to rehearse some of the ideological and intellectual implications suggested to him by certain strands of Western critical theory" (Torres-Saillant, 207): abstracting continuations of familiar impositions—unless perhaps one could see them as instrumental fragments being taken over and "turned" as elements in the establishment of that new language of whose creation we saw aspects in Chapter 8, and like the dominant figures of Caliban—and now Sycorax—themselves. These creations and establishments are principal responses to those hegemonic despoliations of which we have already seen so much.

For if in much of this Caribbean writing and sensibility have not been alone in recording these sorts of experience, where they have been is in their particular history and geography. And this *particular* history is already, it would seem, providing a way from some of these early aporias in Caribbean writing. The many-layered destructions have meant that, for most, what one might call *vernaculars by historical descent* are virtually untraceable save in fragments, and long historical memory has only fractured embedding in place. Glissant sees here a fatal discontinuity between a people's "surroundings (what we would call its nature)" and "its accumulation of experiences (what we would call its culture)." For experience depends crucially on understanding, and forms and facts of understanding imposed from without bend experience away from any embedding in their own home (*Caribbean*, 61). Such discontinuity begs to be filled. And the very thought of "discontinuity" invites a certain *kind* of filling: history as travel between poles or as some version of the establishment of "self" or "otherness" (even to do this in terms of race or class rather than sexuality, as Cobham does of Antoni, is to try to fit it to a certain, new, geography—and history). But adoptions of this sort may already belong to an older mode of Caribbean writing.

Instead of vernaculars by historical descent, one finds (both in current practice and historically) *vernaculars by geography*, Brathwaite's "nation voice," idioms made in synchrony, from the people's oppressors' languages, from each other's languages and in rhythms echoing climates, waterscapes, and landscapes (Brathwaite, *History*) that Wilson Harris' Guyana might be taken to epitomize: "A great magical web born of the music of the elements . . . with its numerous etched rivers, numerous lines and tributaries, interior rivers, coastal rivers, the arteries of God's spider" (*Guyana Quartet*, 7). This sensibility and experience are also, I think, those of Glissant's "*Antillanité*," a cultural "poetics" of *relation*. From *this*, a different "memory" is being forged, from fragments of many histories cemented by a shared geography, "renamings" by place (Walcott, *Antilles*, [12–13]). Too, as Philip shows, from such fragments one forges a personal history that *is* both family story and people's *history-in-place*, an entire and real "genealogy of resistance" (*Genealogy*, 9–30), remapping those bonds explored by Brathwaite, for example, in his two poetic trilogies. Indeed, one may perhaps most properly describe the making of Bovelles' vernaculars as the homing of histories settling into their specific geography. "Anatomy is to history," wrote Bovelles' younger contemporary, the physician Jean Fernel, in the preface to his 1542 *De naturali parte medicinae* (Paris, Simon de Colines; quoted by Sherrington, 64), "as geography is to history, it describes the theatre of events." Through language people forge and tie events to geography, *knowing* them as *their* memory of *their* place.

In the Caribbean, memory, history, and geography are being welded through and across those windows, doors, and walls with which I began this chapter by writers whose problematic situation Lamming in 1960 put squarely at the center of his allegory of confrontation between colonizer's Law and colonized accused:

Another witness arrives claiming extraordinary privileges. He wants to assume Prospero's privilege of magic, while arguing in his evidence that no man has a right to use magic in his dealings with another. On the other hand he sees himself as Caliban while he argues that he is not the Caliban whom Prospero had in mind. This witness claims a double privilege. He thinks he is, in some way, a descendant of Prospero. He knows he is a direct descendent of Caliban. He claims to be the key witness in the trial; but his evidence will only be valid if the others can accept the context in which he will give it. For it is only by accepting this special context that his evidence can reveal its truth. (*Pleasures*, 11)

This catches the befuddlements of loss and imposition, of falsified experience and abrogated history to which all these writers have been speaking.

As Prospero's descendant, Brathwaite tells how only on getting to England did he find, in brutal color sharpness, that he was not English, not the "potential Afro-Saxon" he had thought ("Timehri," 32). Fanon recalls the "black schoolboy in the Antilles, who in his lessons is forever talking about 'our ancestors, the Gauls' " (*Black Skin*, 147; cf. 189, 191–93). Merle Hodge records learning English nursery rhymes from the standard *Caribbean Reader Primer One* (in a series whose influence Brathwaite sought to counter and defeat with his own historical school texts *The People Who Came*), with their utterly incongruous "haystacks" and Miss Muffet "eating her curls away," together with imperial songs and Anglican prayer, discovering "the enviable normality of real Girls and Boys who went a-sleighing and built snowmen . . . called things by their proper names," and learning that over "Natives and Red Indians and things . . . Right prevaileth always just before THE END" (*Crick Crack*, 25–27, 61–62). Really *going* to England was the acme of awesome achievement (109–10). "Have I given you the impression," asks Kincaid, "that the Antigua I grew up in revolved almost completely around England? Well that was so. I met the world through England, and if the world wanted to meet me it would have to do so through England" (*Small Place*, 33). It still does, it would appear, when not only does a *Wall Street Journal* review see fit to praise the author of *Lucy* as "daughter [! Afro-Saxon?] of Brontë and Woolf," but her American publisher uses the phrase as a blurb to recommend the book. These are all products of the history C. L. R. James calls "propaganda for those . . . who administer the old colonial system," inability to "grapple with the national past" (*Black Jacobins*, 408). It was a colonizing history that "aggravated loss and self-defamation," remark Chamoiseau, Confiant, and Jean Bernabé, as "fed the estrangement of the present." It established a "*false memory*," "a pile of obscurities . . . a feeling of flesh discontinued" ("In Praise," 896). This imposed false memory is the counterpart of the false memory of a willful nostalgia, simply its other face.

Not just historical education is at stake. Glissant similarly comments on the vehement oddity of applying Northern European seasons to the Martinican year (*Caribbean*, 56–59). From a different colonial circumstance, Achebe tells of an analogous case of an equally violent dispossession:

Three or four weeks ago, my wife, who teaches English in a boy's school, asked a pupil why he wrote about winter when he meant the harmattan. He said the other boys would call him a bushman if he did such a thing! Now, you wouldn't have thought, would you, that there was something shameful in your weather? But apparently we do. (*Morning Yet,* 58)

I mention this last case because Brathwaite has recorded that it was precisely his discovery of the link between this culturally lost harmattan and hurricanes that enabled him to begin to grasp other links between his Barbados and its own submerged cultural bonds with an Africa that all had claimed to be nonexistent, "Lil Inglan" holding on to its hard-won Prosperity. In this instance, the interplay of geography and history become especially visible, making an eloquent case as to why both sides of the walls must have equal ground, not to hybridize inside and outside (remembering that each is both), but to put their differences in play together. We have seen many African, Asian, and Caribbean writers dismayed by what Fuentes has called "the historical nightmare" of the West's imposition of its history on colonized peoples and lands. We now see that we should more properly speak, as Fuentes does, of "the monolithic impositions of history *and* geography" (*Nueva,* 68, my italics; Van Delden, 112–13).

Lamming, and this matter of different colonial situations, enable us further to complicate the issue. Achebe reacted to the harmattan incident by making it his "job" to teach that "there is nothing disgraceful about the African weather." Fanon answered his "Gaulish ancestry" by participating in the Algerian Revolution. Kincaid's *A Small Place* is an indictment. Glissant responded with irony and the determination to turn from European Enlightenment ideals that his relational *Antillanité* tries to name. Brathwaite replied by looking to African and new Caribbean roots, making new cultural instruments from the fictive imagination. Fuentes proposed that a new kind of novel offered an escape from monolithic impositions. But in another case, the Barbadian Lamming criticizes the North American Baldwin for doing none of these things—indeed for asserting that *he* had no choice but to accept the white traditions into which he was born. Lamming accused Baldwin of seeing himself as "a kind of bastard of the West," situating "the line of [his] past" not "in Europe but in Africa," and so forced both to bring a "special attitude" to the cultural monuments of the West and to confront his knowledge that "[a]t the same time, I had no other heritage which I could possibly hope to use—I had certainly been unfitted for the jungle or the tribe. I would have to appropriate these white centuries. I would have to make them mine" (Baldwin, *Notes,* 6–7; Lamming, *Pleasures,* 31). One might note, in this regard, a distinctly similar remark by C. L. R. James: "we of the Caribbean have not got an African past. We are black in skin, but the African civilisation is not ours. The basis of our civilisation in the Caribbean is an adaptation of Western civilisation" (*Spheres*, 237). In some sense, *no* one has such a pure or unlittered past as these comments propose.

Lamming argues that Baldwin's remark echoes Hegel's denial of African history in the introduction to *The Philosophy of History*, asserting that human history began in the East and had now ended in the West, by-passing Africa altogether (whatever that could possibly "mean"; Lamming, *Pleasures*, 31–34). But both their situations and ideas were quite different. Baldwin was not lamenting any such "embarrassing" absence of history, and surely no "vision of the bush, primitive, intractable, night-black in its inaccessibility" (*Pleasures*, 32–33). "I felt knife blades open within me," Fanon wrote in 1952 (*Black Skin*, 118). Like Fanon's, the "anger" that Baldwin told as a recurrent "blind fever, a pounding in the skull and fire in the bowels" whose snap unpredictability forever made one uncarefree (*Notes*, 94), was not only at the colonizing imperialism also contained in those monuments, but at deprivation of another history—one that would have been his "own," that of Africa—by that colonization, "the utter alienation of himself from his people and his past" (122). To speak of "Mr. Baldwin's terror of the African bush as well as his feeling of impotence before the massive approval of Shakespeare and Rembrandt" (*Pleasures*, 34) is to misapprehend what and whom he is addressing.

In question, rather, is Baldwin's knowledge that the Middle Passage and its aftermath stripped him of a culture properly his own, left him a stranger to the African cultures that could have been his, and at the same time legitimated for him and his only that of white Euro-Americans—even as it deprived them of full access to it—another version or aspect of Philip's language as "abusive parent." For the one, terror is not the word but raging loss; for the other, not impotence but something like its opposite: an equally angry determination to "appropriate" for himself the only culture he finds available to him. Whites and blacks in America are inextricably bound: "bone of their bone, flesh of their flesh; they have loved and hated and obsessed and feared each other and his [the black man's] blood is in their soil. Therefore he cannot deny them, nor can they ever be divorced" (*Notes*, 123). He is simply claiming the "extraordinary privileges" of Lamming's witness. The tension between loss and imposition is what

Baldwin captures in writing: "I imagine that one of the reasons why people cling to their hates so stubbornly is because they sense, once hate is gone, that they will be forced to deal with pain" (101). Here is that ineluctable condition of colonialism that made the slapping of a child in anger a "recoil in the heart [that] reverberated through heaven and became part of the pain of the universe" (106).

Lamming in fact echoes Baldwin's thought in saying that whereas the African "has never been wholly severed from the cradle of a continuous culture," the West Indian has (*Pleasures*, 34). So he echoes, too, this sense of having to appropriate: "Caliban had got hold of Prospero's weapons and decided that he would never again seek his master's permission" (63). Ngũgĩ also adopts the view, observing how writers played their part in the African independence movements of the 1950s: "The Caliban of the colonial world had been given European languages and he was going to use them even to subvert the master" (*Moving*, 61).[2] How different is this from what Baldwin urged to be the task? Well, there is one vast difference between Ngũgĩ's, Achebe's, or Mphahlele's possibilities and those of Baldwin, James, or indeed Lamming. Thus the Barbadian recounts an experience of arriving in Accra and being present when a group of local Boy Scouts greet their arriving English Scoutmaster and then dissolve in a wild, talkative melee that the author finds wholly incomprehensible:

It was at this point that the difference between my childhood and theirs broke wide open. They owed Prospero no debt of vocabulary. English was a way of thinking which they would achieve when the situation required it. But their passions were poured through another rhythm of speed. (*Pleasures*, 162)

The difference is akin to that we saw in the previous chapter, apropos of Joyce, Brathwaite, and Philip. It is Mphahlele thinking first in Sesotho and only then translating his thoughts into English (*African Image*, rev. ed., 244). It is Ngũgĩ remarking that he could only write poetry in Gikũyũ and making it clear that his early English-language novels were also first thought not in English.

The situation for those whose ancestors went through the Middle Passage is quite different. And only quite recently have possibilities different from the overwhelming sense of imposed white European culture been suggested: presences of those "lost" cultures; elements of traditions found that can now be made "articulate," as Baldwin put it (*Notes*, 36). Even so, these are seen and experienced as cumulative—not, I mean, as simply "added on" to "these white centuries," but nonetheless, for those born in them yet always exiled from them, as grounded far within them, patches and traces, palimpsests of cultures, some of whose visible signs lead to riches, buried and present as they are in local geographies. Such was LeRoi Jones' finding of other rhythms and other imaginings in the blues: a protest against slavery, its racist aftermath, and white centuries, but a return to sources in other cultures and places. Such are Brathwaite's streams flowing hidden beneath the surface of Barbados that have become the physical metaphor for the Igbo palimpsest he has shown to lie—actively— not far at all beneath an everyday overlay of "white centuries" that perhaps prove far shallower than the streams (*Barabajan Poems*, 172–205, 228–32; *X/Self*). Such, too, is Henry Louis Gates Jr.'s retrieval of analogous rivers in the figure and practice of the "signifying Monkey," which perhaps responds directly to Baldwin's sense of loss.

Until such retrievals, appropriation seemed an only path. As Lamming himself says, "Caliban cannot be revealed in any relation to himself; for he has no self which is not a reaction to circumstances imposed upon his life. He is not seen as a possibility of spirit which might fertilize and extend the resources of any human vision" (*Pleasures*, 107). V. S. Naipaul's *acceptance* of this state of affairs was what Lamming saw as his "inadequacy" (30). Elsewhere, Lamming notes how Indians' experience in the Caribbean, especially in Trinidad, marginalized them to exclusion and mockery: "it made for an incurable wound in one of their most senior writers" (*Coming*, 40). To a great extent, a poem such as Walcott's *Omeros* powerfully continues appropriation. That this may be misunderstood as acceding to "white authority" may explain why it is easier to award a Nobel Prize to a Walcott than to some others: appropriation by definition works with matter familiar to the culture appropriated. Black Americans, wrote Baldwin in just this sense, "are Americans and their destiny is the country's destiny. They have no other experience besides their experience on this continent and it is an experience which cannot be rejected, which yet remains to be embraced" (*Notes*, 42). He saw clearly that the task was to recapture the lost: "echoes of a past which he has not yet been able to utilize, intimations of a responsibility which he has not yet been able to face." Recovery and appropriation combine: "he is not seeking to forfeit his birthright as a black man, . . . on the contrary, it is precisely this birthright which he is struggling to recognize and make articulate" (122–23).

Doing so, fragments, patches, traces, palimpsests have been and are being recovered, brought to light, cultivated to bear ever more fruit. This is clear in Walcott as it is in Antoni, in Erna Brodber as in Harris: geography is grounding defragmentation of histories, their weaving into something new. And this grounding and weaving are noticeably *collective*, communal. I do not mean, simply, that many people are involved or that many perceive and practice a same sort of undertaking. That is certainly the case, but it is the least of it. What surely matters more is that the processes and practices themselves are *conceived of* as collective. They *occur*, that is to say, collectively. That *ego* or *self* discussed in earlier chapters and several times mentioned earlier in this regard appears as a kind of imposed historical anomaly, an aberration proceeding from a particular history (and source, precisely, of the false *errance* also mentioned before):

The question is—how can one begin to reconcile the broken parts of such an enormous heritage, especially when those broken parts appear very often like a grotesque series of adventures, volcanic in its precipitate effects as well as human in its vulnerable settlement? This distinction is a large, a very large one which obviously has to be broken down into numerous modern tributaries and other immigrant movements and distinctions so that the smallest area one envisages, island or village, prominent ridge or buried valley, flatland or heartland, is charged immediately with the openness of imagination, and the longest chain of sovereign territories one sees is ultimately no stronger than its weakest and most obscure connecting link. (Harris, *Tradition*, 31)

Thus are homes refound that become in some cultural sense not unlike those geographic homelands, "not so very many miles away" to which Baldwin thought the African exile in Paris could return and which "must be given—or must seize—[their] freedom"; as opposed, he thought, to the exiled African American's case. "Colonial" exiles shared a "bitter ambition" to freedom and "a common language" other than the colonizer's (*Notes*, 121). Their American counterparts were forced into and sought isolation; they had but the language of that same colonizer. Not quite so, it would seem, and even less so their Caribbean counterpart. Then already, but even more now, that pain and fury have provided impetus, ground and parts for the weaving of fragments, awareness of

the need for a vision of consciousness. And this vision of consciousness is the peculiar reality of language because the concept of language is one which continuously transforms inner and outer formal categories of experience, earlier and representative modes of speech itself . . . provide a medium to *see* in consciousness' new realities made by the fictive imagination. (Harris, *Tradition*, 32)

So I come back again to the matter of voice and language with which I began and to the ways in which they interweave with and against each other.

I suggested earlier that we can make a distinction (*not* an opposition) between "representing" and "performing." The one may best be suited to certain efforts to show known traditions, settled and familiar histories, unquestioned experiences. The other works all the time on these broken exchanges, these shards and fragments. But *performs* is the word. Voice makes new events from those breakages; hand picks the flowers it needs to set them in new combinations and places; the bee transforms many pollens into new honeys and waxes, so that even Eldorado's violence or Sisyphus' stone may be transformed, as the latter is in Kingston's "Dungle" of Orlando Patterson's *Children of Sisyphus*, the rubbish slum whose pullulating horror comes to represent a vivid life—for all its disasters—that ever pushes back the bland hypocrisies of those who condemn its denizens—a view echoed in the Dungle of Namba Roy's *No Black Sparrows*, where it functions as savior of the "sparrows" from Bangbelly the policeman, archrepresentative of Babylon—until himself finally transformed into a ragged savior. Even the Sisyphian fear- and poverty-ridden "*mornes*" that are the slums of Césaire's Fort-de-France (*Cahier*, 34–37; 36/7) may perhaps be subsumed in the hope the poem itself expresses by its end. This is how appropriated cultural forms take their due place in a process of reweaving that so comes to articulate the tradition expressing "the long and painful experience of [the] people; [coming] out of the battle waged to maintain their integrity or, to put it more simply, out of their struggle to survive" (Baldwin, *Notes*, 36). In this way they do indeed "proceed naturally and organically out of the sensibilities, cultural traditions, moral imperatives, and linguistic styles and resources of the people who are their subject" (Thelwell, 231; Ngũgĩ's *Moving the Centre* is all about this). Sisyphus and Eldorado make not *cultural* opposition, dualism (in Patterson, the first indeed shows a class one), but rather new "mutuality."

Eldorado and the flowers now often mentioned give nice examples of the kinds of performance the fictive imagination voices into being, distinctive migrations, as one might say. Snatched language can be taken back, Froude's appropriative flowers of rhetoric—figures of possessive power—turned against him in joy or in violence. For if so many Caribbean writers have found Europe an ambiguous opponent, they have also turned its instruments in new ways. Indeed, it was just for not doing so that Achebe

(*Hopes*, 27–28), Lamming, Michael Thelwell (in *Duties*), and others have criticized Naipaul. Achebe has lately come back to Naipaul's slamming of Caribbean peoples as "monkeys" and "brutes" and Africans as ignorant savages, whose continent right-minded peoples want to flee "for the bounties of the universal civilization in Europe and North America" (Achebe, *Home*, 88–91). For Naipaul, indeed, Eldorado is a founding myth of the Caribbean as bottomless void, if the idea is not oxymoronic, where no culture, society, or political ground can conceivably be laid or built. "Everything," remarks Walcott, "is made to seem touching and ridiculous. The people he encounters have an antic, desperate pathos." The author seems more eager to make a point than experience place: "It is a case of history versus the aphorist, landscape versus art, compassion versus wit." His writing displays "a chronic dispiritedness" ("History," 18–19). The "savage" and often "racist critique" of his land, Philip agrees, is "a fundamental immorality." For even as he condemns it, he uses "the image of that country or place as Other in the psyches of western and northern countries, to fuel [his] writing and to enrich [himself]" (*Frontiers*, 162, 198), exploiting its people solely to benefit "his writing life" (*She Tries*, 11).

To these writers, not only has Naipaul failed to take language back, but he has wallowed in its having been snatched. Ratifying the oppressors' image and furthering appropriation, he offers the Caribbean as a soup of lands and waters found and destroyed by Europeans pursuing a lie of Eldorado, now doomed to be populated forever by peoples who can only mimic others, fight bootless or fantasy guerilla wars, scrabble desperately against terminal indigence, and strive despairingly to flee to a slough less despondent. Exactly this last point is how Selvon imagines setting the image on its head, England becoming in turn an ironic (and miserable) Eldorado as continental au pairs and West Indians swarm to its capital: "and over there all them girls think like the newspapers say about the Jamaicans that the streets of London paved with gold so they coming by the boatload" (103). The English-based dub poet Benjamin Zephaniah writes equally sardonically of England: "Me love me mudder an me mudder love me/We come so far from over de sea/We hear dat de streets were paved with gold" (quoted in Morris, "*Is English*," 40). Zephaniah almost achieved this reversal in person, as a principal competitor for the Oxford Chair of Poetry in 1989.

Carpentier turns Eldorado into a more ambivalent "revenge of the authentic on the synthetic" (*Lost Steps*, 134). No longer does it figure simple theft, violence, and oppression, but an always ironic mingling of peoples and cultures, occupations, and yearnings. Greeks and Germans, Spaniards and Dutch join with indigenous Amerindians across time and place, taken over by jungle, river, and mountain, whose "immutable rhythms" overwhelm the manic "measuring of time" governing western thoughts of history. "El Dorado" erases—or maybe incorporates—that history, to become an image of place, timeless "wilderness" (102, 128, 156). At the same time, it is they of the "*Discourse of Method*," they who put "themselves in the . . . Cartesian position" and label differences "barbarous," who become children of "Sisyphus," condemned to synthetic history (219, 239). Not for nothing does Carpentier call *Recurso del metodo* his story of a neocolonial dictator who seeks—and for long manages—to impose "colonial" history and "rational" authority on the American state whose reason he controls, both from Paris, where he spends much of his time, and from the two homes cities, his capital and his pleasure dome, whose shape he has remade to his Enlightened desires.

Harris goes yet further. For him, Eldorado was surely a marker of greed and an excuse for cruelty, oppression, and destruction. Echoing Césaire, he comments that the "Spanish Conquistador, . . . the Portuguese, French, Dutch and English" buried a not inconceivably "instructive Idealism" in that greed and exploitation (*Tradition*, 35). But, as McWatt has observed, Harris also saw how the myth of Eldorado could "be used to subvert such a negative vision" ("Two Faces," 37). As in Carpentier, it could give imaginative shape to a new construction of experience, of consciousness, that could hope to be one of a culture and a spirit of place. It is not only that indigenous peoples used the tale to send Europeans on deadly wild-goose chases and so rid themselves of them, but that the myth can also acquire and make new shapes, endowed with "a residual pattern of illuminating correspondences. Eldorado, City of Gold, city of God, grotesque, unique coincidence, another window within, upon the universe, another drunken boat, another dream, another river, changing a flickering past proposing open futures" (*Tradition*, 35–36).

Augustine and Rimbaud, to be sure—the one going to, the other coming from, Africa, both embedded in Europe, are both here, but also Harris' own many rivers of discovery and of place, Walcott's or Brathwaite's or more recently Antoni's and Caryl Phillips' seas and yet more rivers—even McWatt's own *Language of Eldorado* forged afresh. In Harris' astonishing *Resurrection at Sorrow Hill*, El Dorado, through Butterfly, its "frail queen," brought through the Middle Passage, bought by a rich Dutch planter, spouse of Death, mistress of Hope, becomes the very source of "a complex mutuality of cultures," through her—ironic breaker of walls and passer of doors, overcoming the egoistic evils "in which cultures are enmeshed in codes to invert or overturn each other." She achieves "the difficult creation of community" in rich interweaving of times, peoples, and places (*Resurrection*; citations from *Womb*, 13, 18).

Out of the ruins of Eldorado springs a rich mass of flowers, picked by Harris to make the most sumptuous of bouquets. The jungle throbs with them. But others see in the fate of flowers the sign of yet a further betrayal of indigenous experience:

The flowers that grow today are cultivated for export. Sculptured, spotless, striking in precision and quality. But they are heavy also, full, lasting. . . . Arum or anthurium, bunches of which adorn our airport. The porcelain rose, which is so durable. The heliconia, its amazing shaft multiplying infinitely. The King of Kings, or the red ginger lily, whose very heart is festooned with dark red. These flowers delight us. But they have no fragrance. They are nothing but shape and color.

I am struck by the fate of flowers. The shapeless yielding to the shapely. As if the land had rejected its "essence" to concentrate everything in appearance. It can be seen but not smelt. (Glissant, *Caribbean*, 52)

Colonization and its aftermath, writes Glissant, has removed even "the lingering fragrances." The "flowers have disappeared" and the "land has lost its smells." From this Césairean landscape of a land "in breach of fauna and flora," there is no immediate recovery, any more than from other impositions of Enlightenment. They are no longer—and not quite yet again—there for *his* picking. Nor does he seem alone, as Kincaid adds her voice: "No real flowers could be these shades of red, purple, yellow, orange, blue, white; no real lily would bloom only at night and perfume the air with a sweetness so thick it makes you slightly sick" (*Small Place*, 78). Her pessimism has optimism in it, however.

For concealed in this, perhaps, is another current of European writing, the one I discussed at length in Chapter 4: the younger Seneca's familiar analysis of mimesis as imaged in bees gathering juices and flavors from flowers to turn them into a new "savor, in such a way that even as it shows whence it came, yet it appears as other than whence it came." Just so must we mingle the scents and juices of such flowers with our "very powers of mind [*in ingenium*]," and so impress a new, its own, "form on all the things which it has drawn from what we may call its exemplar, so that they join in a unity," the new unity of a new consciousness (*Ep*, lxxxiv: 2.276–85). And we recall how for him as for the earlier poet of the Homeric Hymn to Hermes, what was drawn was a capacity to express truths attached to particular place, concretely grounded in specific topographies and geographies. Yet at the same time, such grounded truth, experience, knowledge were incorporated into wider creations.

These bee and flower images spread through the European tradition. Thus did Petrarch, whom we saw earlier using the image a great deal, write to his friend Boccaccio that one should "write as bees make honey, not by preserving flowers but by turning them into honeycombs, so that from many and varied things one is made, and a thing different and better" (*Familiari*, 4:206; *Letters on Familiar Matters*, 3:302, for translation, XXIII.19). You find it in Erasmus, who echoed Seneca: "They [bees, but thinkers and above all speakers] fashion a liquid with their organs, and after it is made their own, they give that forth in which you do not recognize the taste or the odor of flower or shrub but a product mingled in due proportion from them all" (Erasmus, *Ciceronianus*, 82). That was in 1528. A bit earlier, Dürer told beginning painters that if they wished to assemble a perfect human figure, they would have to gather many things different into one whole, "even as honey is gathered from many flowers" (Dürer, 179). A little less than a century later, Francis Bacon told the traveler to "prick in some Flowers, of that he hath Learned abroad, into the Customes of his owne Country" ("Of Travaile," *Essayes*, 58). This may be a different idea of ornament, company for imperial instruments; yet Bacon, too, for growing a garden, advised making sure to pick such flowers as would give something both natural and cultural: a garden whose blooming would create a "*Ver Perpetuum*," everlasting spring ("Of Gardens," *Essayes*, 140). How can one not see in all this an unsuspecting preparation for the pricking in that J. J. Thomas would achieve to turn the tables on Froude, turning his own rhetorical flowers against him to demolish every step of the Englishman's argument and to construct at the same time a whole new vision of a self-respecting and powerfully capable West Indies? speaking—not for the first time—with the abrasively urgent voice of later Calibans. Depestre and his colleagues in 1945 may have named their activist literary journal *La Ruche*, the beehive, because they thought to sting the then-president of Haiti and his cronies, as the author told Haun Saussy (to whom I'm indebted for the information), but the image accords exactly with this process.

For, as Brathwaite drums out in what perhaps should be read as a train song, "It/it/it/it is not . . . enough . . . to be free of" the symbols, accouterments and dangers of the colonizer's presence, nor is it enough to have access to the various consumer goods with which he's replaced them:

> I
> must be given words to shape my name
> to the syllables of trees
>
> I
> must be given words to refashion futures
> like a healer's hand
>
> I
> must be given words so that the bees
> in my blood's buzzing brain of memory
>
> will make flowers, will make flocks of birds,
> will make sky, will make heaven,
> the heaven open to the thunder-stone and the volcano and the un-
>   folding land.

("Negus," *Islands, Arrivants*, 224)

Unlike Glissant, Kincaid does not turn away from her flowers. Rather does she take them up in perpetual bloom, with yet a catch of ironic ambivalence:

In the night the flowers close up and thicken. The hibiscus flowers, the flamboyant flowers, the bachelor's button, the irises, the marigolds, the whitehead-bush flowers, the lilies, the flowers on the daggerbush, the flowers on the turtleberry bush, the flowers on the soursop tree, the flowers on the sugar-apple tree, the flowers on the mango tree, the flowers on the guava tree, the flowers on the cedar tree, the flowers on the stinking-toe tree, the flowers on the dumps tree, the flowers on the papaw tree, the flowers everywhere close up and thicken. The flowers are vexed. (*At the Bottom*, 10–11)

But *these* flowers stretch open all together in the daylight, and their night is part of natural life. Glissant's artifice is gone. Even in a story of loss and imagination, when the same flowers come to figure that loss, something new happens: "Oh, the fields in which I have walked and gazed and gazed at the small cuplike flowers, in wanton hues of red and gold and blue, swaying in the day breeze, and from which I had no trouble tearing myself away, since their end was unknown to me" (Kincaid, *At the Bottom*, 74). Maybe so, but they become the place of solid memory, enabling the writing that let the speaker "feel myself solid and complete, my name filling up my mouth" (82).

One could say much more of this, of those flowers of speech that through storytelling let Audre Lorde come to wholeness of new being as "Zami"; of the commonplace association in the European Renaissance of the Virgin Mary with flowers and spring; even indeed of Christ and Nazareth with flowers (which would offer almost endless further connections with other writings); or of the most clichéd of all, flowers thematizing young love and life, generalized to *carpe diem*—revealingly rarely used, it would seem, save bleakly, in Caribbean writing. These do not matter here. What does is the turning of so many fragments of different histories to new uses, new unities, and new voices. In Césaire, flowers become the often violent insistence on exactly that: "nous chantons les fleurs vénéneuses/ éclatant dans les prairies furibondes," "we sing of venomous flowers/flaring in fury-filled meadows" (*Cahier*, 82/3; 54/5). The very land responds to its earlier desolation and breach of its nourishing contract with the flowers (see page 358 below):

> les orchidées pousseront leur douce tête violente de torturé à travers
> la claire-voie
> > que deux à deux font les paroles
> les lianes dépêcheront du fond de leurs veilles une claire batterie de
> sangsues dont
> > l'embrassade sera de la force irrésistible des parfums
> de chaque grain de sable naîtra un oiseau
> de chaque fleur simple sortira une scorpion (tout étant recompensé)
> les trompettes des droseras éclateront pour marquer l'heure où
> abdiquer mes épaisses lèvres plantées d'aiguilles en faveur de
> > l'armature flexible
> > > des futurs aloès . . .

> orchids shall push their sweet violent heads of tortured ones
> > through the
> > openwork which words form two by two
> lianas shall dispatch from the depths of their vigils a luminous
> > battery of
> > leeches whose embrace shall have the irresistible force of perfume
> from each grain of sand a bird shall be born

from each simple flower a scorpion shall emerge (everything
   being compound)
the Drosera's trumpets shall blast to mark the hour for
abdicating my thick needle-implanted lips in favor of the
   flexible armature
      of future aloes . . .

(Soleil coup coupé, Collected Poetry, 190/191)

"Elégie," with its "oeil éclaté [burst eye]" of hibiscus, "great black sabre" of the "flamboyants," "Arecas . . . pierced through and through by a pin" (*Corps perdu, Collected Poetry*, 234), tells a similar tale of flowers drawing new violences from old patterns, gathering and forming them to a purpose made explicit in "Mémorial de Louis Delgrès," "last defender of black freedom in Guadeloupe":

je veux la liane qui croît sur le palmier
(c'est sur le tronc du présent notre avenir têtu)
je veux le conquistador à l'armure descellée
se couchant dans une mort de fleurs parfumées
et l'écume encense une épée qui se rouille
dans le pur vol bleuté de lents cactus hagards

I want the liana that grows on the palm tree
(it is on the trunk of the present our obstinate future)
I want the conquistador in unsealed armor
lying down in a death of fragrant flowers
and the foam to cense a sword rusting
in the pure bluish flight of slow haggard cactuses

(Ferrements, Collected Poetry, 331, 334/335)

These flowers are a violence offered *against* European poetic forms, against European History. They are a living weapon against the European culture to whose language and poetic forms Césaire is doing violence here. But they are also a violence remaining in the land from older conquest. Thus, too, against the rich mass of flowers that spring from Eldorado in Harris' *Resurrection at Sorrow Hill*, his protagonist Hope remembers seeing "pictures of the canals of ancient Tetoctitlan in ancient Mexico upon which flowers grew inscribed with dazzling blood and with a slow-motion lightning Milky Way" (91). Out of that violence, the flowers forge a fresh experience of place, one that is anti-European to be sure—here, at least— but which is more importantly and simply *not* European. But that "*not*" is fully aware of *also* being European, of turning a European story in other ways. Meditating on the magic force of flowers, their colors and rhythms, Padilla names Giovanni Pico della Mirandola:

> Como ya no nombraba como al comienzo
> por el mero placer de concretar el aire,
> sino para extraer la corrupción
> del peso de cada cosa, de modo que *flor* decía
> y anulaba de inmediato los tormentos
> de cualquier época . . .

> For now he gave not names as first he did
> for pure pleasure of making the air tangible,
> but to remove corruption
> from each thing's weight, so that he said *flower*
> and immediately wiped out the pains
> of every age . . .
> ("Pico della Mirandola (1463–1494)," *Legacies*, 92/3; my translation)

Reweaving appropriations and fragments of the past—of varied pasts and different memories—to take present into future becomes more than simply "a principle of coherence . . . in so far as it induces in the Caribbean artist a compulsion to sew the pieces together" (Torres-Saillant, 199). Thus do Merle and Harriet, the principal women protagonists of Marshall's *Chosen Place*, one a creator of histories, the other an ambivalent representative of "colonial" disdain, momentarily come together over "the mixed fragrances of the flowers in the garden below and, faintly, the rich odor of the soil that fed them" (72), as Carpentier's hero of *El siglo de la luces*, Esteban, breathes "with delight the delicate fragrance" of endless flowers and fruits (*Explosion*, 161). But of both we shall see more in the last two chapters (of these passages in particular in Chapter 11). Flowers are one mark of a new making, of joining, of setting new histories in their chosen place. Ultimately, for Glissant as well, they define "the patience of landscape . . . not saturated with a single History but effervescent with intermingled histories, spread around, rushing to fuse without destroying or reducing each other" (*Caribbean*, 154).

For Brathwaite, flowers join jazz as two American sources of such making:

> Bassey the bassist
> loves his lady
> plucks her
> chucks her

makes her
bloom
("Bass," *Jah Music*, 59; cf. *Barabajan*, 39)

And when he makes "nation language" out of jazz and Shango, trains and calypso, reggae and Legba, harmattan and hurricane, Caliban and Sycorax, these are not just fragments sewn together. They are webs of a quite new creation woven by Anancy. For

Ban
Ban
Cal-
iban
like to play
pan
at the Car-
nival;
pran-
cing up to the lim-
bo silence
down
down
down
so the god won't drown
him
down
down
down
to the is-
land town
("Calypso," *Islands, Arrivants*, 192)

Carried directly out of Shakespeare—"'Ban, 'Ban, Ca—Caliban/Has a new master; get a new man," as he briefly rejoiced with Trinculo and Stephano at the end of act 2 of *The Tempest* (II.2.178–79)—this Caliban turns Prospero's watery spells. Brought out of the Middle Passage of "long dark deck and the water surrounding me/long dark deck and the silence is over me," this Caliban heeds how "the drummer is calling me . . . /sun coming up/and the drummers are praising me // out of the dark/and the dumb gods are raising me." This Caliban is coming "up/up/up // and the music is saving me" ("Calypso," 194–95). This Caliban makes a "muse" from his computer, writing to and for his mother Sycorax that he's raised and taken over, no longer Prospero's Caliban, but Sycorax's:

> learnin prospero linguage &
>
> ting
> not fe dem/not fe dem
> de way caliban
>
> done
>
> but fe we
> fe a-we
>
> for not one a-we should responsible if prospero get curse
> wid im own
>
> curser
> ("X/Self's Xth Letters from the Thirteen Provinces," *X/Self,* 84–85)

Lamming's Caliban claims his "double privilege," knowing himself "a descendant of Prospero" and "a direct descendent of Caliban" and insisting that those who hear him must "accept the context in which he" speaks. Here and now, in "this special context" his voice "can reveal its truth," a truth of histories and voices in the making of their geography.

The broken vase of which Walcott speaks in his Nobel Prize lecture to be reassembled with a love greater than that "which took its symmetry for granted when it was whole," never did, after all, exist as such. Put together, its "pieces are disparate, ill-fitting, [and] contain more pain than their original sculpture, those icons and sacred vessels taken for granted in their ancestral places," both because of the pain and because it is a whole made of different mutualities. This is another version of Kincaid's, Padilla's, Marshall's, Carpentier's, or Césaire's flowers, assembling noisier or quieter pain into new jointures. The need for Caribbean artists to give themselves to the "restoration of our shattered histories, our shards of vocabulary, our archipelago becoming a synonym for pieces broken off from the original continent," has a coherence greater than that of a mere compulsion (*Antilles*, [10–11]). Building the vase from splinters may alter the forms of a shattered inheritance, but above all, its very process marks and makes the love that every genuinely grounded tradition and culture bodies forth in those who share and partake of it. I recall an exchange between the poets

Alfred Corn and Mark Doty, the first speaking "of a Japanese monk's broken cup that is repaired with a seam of gold solder that gives the object a new, offbeat splendor." Not offbeat but certainly new, these buildings do "fill the seams with beauty" (Kirby, 10).

Perhaps these creations answer Philip's and Kincaid's questions about the pain of the orphans' no tongue. "For isn't it odd that the only language I have in which to speak of this crime is the language of the criminal who committed the crime? And what can that really mean? . . . The language of the criminal can explain and express the deed only from the criminal's point of view" (Kincaid, *Small Place*, 31–32). It may be that she and Brathwaite and Césaire and Carpentier and Philip and so very many others are answering, have already answered those questions, reworking *their* history—perhaps the very notion of "history"—from the geography of "travels in the Gulf of Mexico and the islands of the Caribbean, where words and phrases multipl[y] with surprising fertility," to quote Carpentier again (*Explosion*, 38). This last phrase could itself be a "geographical" reworking of what Quintilian had bemoaned as the Romans' *historical* inability so to invent words, coming as they did after Greeks for whom "the making of names . . . was considered among the highest excellences [*fictio nominis, Graecis inter maximas habita virtutes*]" (Quintilian, 3:318, VIII.vi.32). This may have been just the point on which Bovelles was elaborating in the remarks which began this chapter: seeing, from his dismayed sixteenth century, the historical motion of language as "decay" and "dissolution"—albeit necessary ones from which the new might emerge in another (vernacular) place. In our time, Caribbean writing has indeed been explosively inventive in word-making.

This geographical remaking of history characterizes Brathwaite's two trilogies, as it does Walcott's *Omeros*. And having watched scarlet ibises "cover an islet until it turned into a flowering tree," Walcott uses the flowers of which I have been speaking to translate Quintilian's historical invention of language and culture into Carpentier's geographical one, writing of the "delight and privilege" of "watching a literature—one literature in several imperial languages, French, English, Spanish—bud and open island after island in the early morning of a culture, not timid, not derivative, any more than the hard white petals of the frangipani are derivative and timid . . . this flowering had to come." Natives of the Caribbean have answered its nonidyll by drawing "their working strength from it organically, like trees, like the sea almond or the spice laurel of the heights" (*Antilles*, [9, 17–18, 36–37]).

Just so does Earl Lovelace show revival of a Spiritual Baptist Afro-

Caribbean culture after the oppression and depredations of colonialism in *The Wine of Astonishment*:

> The church was ready too, with its fresh coat of paint and the flowers around it—the zinnias and marigold and croton and Jacob's coat—showing their colours and smelling nice, and the birds come out on the mango tree and among the flowers to hop and whistle and liven the place with their moving and colour and song. (143)

Flowers inside and out prefigure "resurrection." What had been bare "survival" at the end is "resurrection morning," like the recovered shango of the hidden worshippers in Barbados of which Brathwaite writes—Walcott's blossoming of culture or Harris' resurrection of Eldorado. So are remnants retrieved from history through spirit of place, topographical presence, to compose a future. "Cuba," confirms Guillermo Cabrera Infante, was "not discovered for history five centuries ago but for geography. . . . History, that is time, will pass, but always there will remain geography—which is our eternity" (*Mea Cuba*, xiv). The archipelago is indeed home: "De wahter seperatin' you from him," said Lamming's Jamaican many years ago to other islanders in *The Emigrants*, "ain't do nothin' to put distance between de views you got on dis life or de next. Different man, different land, but de same outlook. Dat's de meanin' o' West Indies. De wahter between dem islands doan' separate dem" (62–63). And such is one message of the whole novel.

What gave life to European literatures when they were being made in the seventeenth and eighteenth centuries was that they were then compiling their resources, inventing their traditions, making their bonds between values and being, developing their spirit of place and sense of home. These, too, were fragments of voices and shards of tongues, as my beginning and reference to such central resources as Seneca and Quintilian suggest. But they were quickly neither seen nor felt as such. The process certainly then needed a profound feeling of insecurity and loss. That, too, was soon gone. And over time, the sense of new live creation was absorbed in a new idea not of particular creation but of universal discovery, as if what was good for one place and one people was so for all and every peoples (Reiss, *Meaning*).

By the mid-eighteenth century, Malachi Postlethwayt, "fountain of mid-century British political economic commonplaces" and "the most systematic exponent of contemporary British political economic policy," made this explicit by directly countering Bacon. He urged that Members of Parliament travel but *not* prick in any foreign flowers, *not* "bring back any strange customs, 'lest we infect the people with the itch of novelty, and corrupt their minds with effeminacy; whereby they will be brought to forget the rigid values and plain honesty, with the good manners, wise laws and customs of their ancestors'" (Peter Miller, 163, 113). With acid humor, Hodge has her Trinidadian schoolchildren learn this exact lesson, as they stand in a tropical afternoon listening to their master with his tamarind whip read "stories about exemplary children who quailed not at the call of duty and were loth to tell a lie" (*Crick Crack*, 46). The closing of mind could hardly be more patent, its imposition of strange customs across battered-down walls more visible or its mockery more bitterly poignant and ironic. This is the closing of mind that raises the walls with which this chapter also started. These are the closing walls of which Amboise speaks bleakly to Télumée in Simone Schwarz-Bart's *Pluie et vent sur Télumée Miracle*: "That's how it was, the sky was the roof of the world, the house was vast and various, but the doors did not communicate with one another, for all were closed" (*Pluie*, 218; *Bridge*, 151; my translation). Such are conditions under oppressive colonialism, when the land is—or was—writes Césaire, "embarrassée, rognée, réduite, en rupture de faune et de flore," "encumbered, clipped, reduced, in breach of fauna and flora" (*Cahier*, 32/3; 34/5), when the flowers cannot grow and the land is without its smells.

These are the conditions the writers overcome. Art in particular and culture more widely, one may well think, need "fragments" like those we have seen: building blocks requisite for their very existence. Maybe, even, they atrophy or die when they no longer have the possibility or ability to interweave such findings. So many tales of singers raising cities, poets composing societies, and minstrels forging peaceful intercourse show how widespread these assumptions are. Art makes order from disordered shards and pieces, culture a system from disparities. What differs between cultures is not grounding in fragment, but what fragments they use, how lively they are in weaving, the size, shape, and patterns of the fabric they weave, the suffered and suffering pain they mark, how they turn the fragments taken, how they prick them in. Brathwaite again voiced the reality of *all* cultural creation when he said, "you have to be everything to bring those fragments together because fragments by their very nature are everything. . . . little seeds growing throughout the scattered diaspora, throughout the Caribbean" (lecture quoted in Torres-Saillant, 199). They are tongues weaving together mutualities of culture, not images joining abstract nostalgias, but drawing together the pain and suffering of centuries of separation from unbroken history by violent oppression into a geography of the voice. These tongues, fragments, are drawn from the depths of a culture commonly and deeply felt by those inhabiting the geography whose vernacular they become—however ambivalently Bovelles and others may view such cultural creation. Like Seneca's bees or Depestre's or Brathwaite's, they take their goods from all available flowers, from a local geography and its people, and from their language(s).

From a part of the world to which my final two chapters pay much attention, Mariátegui cited Manuel González Prada reminding "his followers" in his "Lecture at the Ateneo of Lima," Peru, how Plato "said that the populace was an excellent language teacher. Languages are invigorated and refreshed in the fount of popular speech, much more than in the dead rules of the grammarians and in the prehistoric exhumations of the erudite. Original words, graphic expressions, daring constructions spring from the songs and sayings of the common people. In the same way that infusorians change continents, the masses transform languages" (Mariátegui, *Seven*, 205; González Prada, "Conferencia en el Ateneo de Lima," *Pájinas libres*). The zoological/geological comparison is surely not accidental here, although Chapter 11 suggests it better fits a Caribbean than Latin American context. Many have changed Eldorado and Sisyphus, flowers and webs, tragedy and representation, memory and identity, rhythm and meter. So, too, Brathwaite and many others find in Caliban not just a curse(r) but a new language, welling up from European *and* African memories, dance of the Middle Passage (*"limbo/ limbo like me"*: "Caliban," *Islands, Arrivants*, 194, *passim* as a refrain), drums of West Africa *and* the Caribbean, surging waves of the ocean, measured tides on island shores. He and others, from James to Carpentier, Césaire to Depestre similarly see Legba (re)turned in Toussaint L'Ouverture. Yet another of those fragments, of those tongues, we shall now see, is forged from the figure of Don Quijote turned to explore different stories and other histories—and first of all, perhaps, in Mariátegui's and González Prada's land of Peru. Here very early, Don Quijote performs such questions as, "Whose reality? Whose history? In whose name do we open up 'this piece of land'" (Philip, *Genealogy*, 170)? From thence Quijote and his avatars ride out over the hemisphere to create histories and geographies, giving them one of their voices.

10

Caribbean Knights: Quijote, Galahad, and the Telling of History

On February 25, 1605, "Pedro González Refolio presented four crates of books to the Inquisition for its inspection." In one of these, the extant register in Seville's Archivo General de Indias tells us, were "5 Don quixotte de la mancha." The crates were registered to a ship due to sail with the Tierra Firme fleet from Seville to the Americas (Rodríguez Marín, 33). But if González was quickest off the mark—*Don Quijote* had only been published five or six weeks before—he was neither alone nor the heaviest hitter. On March 26, Juan de Sarria, a bookseller of Alcalá de Henares associated with a dealer in Lima, Miguel Méndez, offered sixty-one more crates of books to the Inquisition for its inspection. The registers for the first twenty of these are lost, but the others held another sixty-six copies of Cervantes' novel (Leonard, *Books*, 273). By April 3, a further thirteen copies brought this fleet's known total to eighty-four (Rodríguez Marín, 33–34). This was only the beginning. In the Nueva España fleet that sailed in July of the same year, one shipment alone, to Clemente de Valdés of Mexico City, contained 262 copies of *Don Quijote*, while another, to Antonio de Toro in Cartagena, included 100 copies of the novel (Rodríguez Marín, 35; Leonard, *Books*, 270). Francisco Rodríguez Marín has observed that since fewer than a third of the ships' registers still exist, one may well need to multiply these totals by as much as four to have anything close to an accurate estimate of numbers actually shipped.

The novel and its protagonists were thus rather more successful in their transatlantic travel than their creator, who at least twice—in 1582 and

1590—applied unsuccessfully to the Council of the Indies for an American post (de Armas Wilson, 234, 250 n. 1). His unrequited desire may have its place in understanding Don Quijote. Too, this huge dispatch of *Don Quijote* to the Americas suggests why copies of its first edition are so rare in Spain (Rodríguez Marín, 36–40). Perhaps, too, it implies that if, in its first years, the novel and its main characters were understood in Spain essentially as parodic comedy and figures of burlesque, they had more and different weight on the other side of the Atlantic—or the dealers thought they would. That, anyway, is what I will argue in this chapter, taking Don Quijote as a figure of the mingling of cultures but, more importantly, as an allegory of debates about history, about seizures of and conflicts between cultures by varied tellings of history, about the different ways in which cultures can and do tell their stories, and about the ways in which cultures may establish their homes by such tellings.

Don Quijote, Cervantes' novel and its eponymous protagonist, passing between Europe and the Americas—more particularly here, between Europe and the Caribbean—helped weave these debates, seizures, conflicts, stories, and establishments. They (with other named and unnamed knights) figure the usually unnamed errant exile or semiexile fighting accepted tales and reasons, on a quest for those meaningful to different times, peoples, and places. I do not arbitrarily choose Quijote. His name has been used to clarify or complicate issues in debates about cultural histories in philosophical argument, in fictions of various kinds and as their allegory. It is in, and because of, those guises that he, others, and their avatars, wander in and out of the following effort to describe one version of the complicated passage of the telling of history from seizure through conflict to new establishment. They are meant not just to clarify this passage but to concretize it through one of the images most widely used by all parties to this European and American, European and Caribbean, instance. But it is of course the debate and the passage that matter.

The tale of *Don Quijote*'s travels across the Atlantic does not end with the shipments to the Atlantic's western shores and their dispersal north to Mexico City, south to Lima, and to divers provincial or capital colonies between. Lima was a viceregal capital, and it was there on June 5, 1606, after months of travel across the Isthmus and down the Pacific coast, that Sarria's son, also named Juan, signed over forty-five crates of his father's shipment to their associate (Leonard, "*Don Quixote*," 293–304; *Books*, 284). A day later, he signed contracts to take two consignments of books into the interior, to the high-mountain Inca capital of Cuzco and more remote villages and mining camps. The journey's first leg could take up to two months, ending at what was then "rated the finest city in the great viceroyalty of Peru after Lima." In Sarria's new consignments, a large one of 438 volumes for company profit and a small one of 82 volumes, fifty percent for him, were nine copies of *Don Quijote*, plays by Lope de Vega, other novels, romances, and philosophical and religious writings (Leonard, "On the Cuzco," 365–75; *Books*, 290–98).

Irving A. Leonard and others have explored the facts of this passage of the Spanish literary canon from "Old World" to "New" and observed its role in the colonizing process. My interest lies in some of the ambiguities of that process, even if these were symbolic rather than actual—they did not, after all, end exploitation, slaughter, and ruin. For what raises some of the questions with which I am concerned was an almost immediate dramatization of *Don Quijote* in the far-off parts to which the novel was now being brought. Such dramatizations quickly occurred, of course, in Spain and throughout western Europe. In a world of very restricted literacy, theater was the most popular of artistic forms; novels, too, and poetry were no doubt more frequently performed aloud in groups than were ever read in silent privacy. But this Andean story seems to involve more than these commonplaces, to say nothing of the speed with which Don Quijote passed into the popular imagination. For the dramatization in question was not even in Cuzco, which Sarria may have reached by late July or August 1606. It was in the far more remote mining camp of Pausa. Yet the performance took place just the next year.

The tale of this dramatization in Cuzco's region has been told at least three times, but it merits retelling beyond its simple facts. We can certainly suppose that the festive small-town event in which Don Quijote was included, played out in the still-Incan Andes, was intended to celebrate Spanish authority, and that the knight's setting his lance against the sort of everyday assumption in which that authority was grounded was meant to be comic. Nevertheless, the performance had aspects that allowed rather different, potentially more subversive, emphases. It set Don Quijote at a crossroads between histories, cultures, and geographies, vividly mocking aristocratic codes and symbols that the colonial authorities, if not the conquistadors, maintained, and overtly incorporating elements of indigenous culture, some of which these same authorities had expressly banned. This understanding of the performance implies how Don Quijote's lone, melancholic rejection of a world everyone around him accepted at its rational and material face value could make him a collective figure for the weaving of new patterns of culture. To be Don Quijote apparently did, as Carpentier proposed in the prologue to *Reino*, enable people (and thought) "to enter body and soul into" other worlds, be they "the world of *Amadis de Gaul* or *Tirant lo Blanc*," those of geographically distant cultures or those being or to be created (*Kingdom*, unpaginated).

Not long before young Sarria arrived in Lima in June 1606 with his crates of books, the conde de Monterrey, Spanish viceroy of Peru, had died. On receiving news of his death, Philip III designated Juan de Mendoza y Luna, marqués de Montesclaros, then viceroy of New Spain, to be his successor. News of Montesclaros' nomination got to Peru in mid-1607. The new viceroy himself would not reach Callao, Lima's port, until late December. Before he did so, Don Pedro de Salamanca, *corregidor* of the distant mining camp of Pausa, then the principal town of a Cuzco district, decided to hold a carnival in late Spring (October or November) fêting Montesclaros' nomination. The carnival was to be a *juego de sortija*, a popular festivity whose focus was a series of jousts involving setting a lance through a small ring from a galloping horse. Each competitor adopted a knightly role and was expected as well to organize a masquerade on his knightly theme or another. Prizes were given for both aspects of the merriment, as well as for the best costume and/or masquerade overall and the most "gallant" participant.

How much those chiefly involved in mounting these festivities could be considered "the authorities" is unclear. Most of the principals were certainly Spanish in origin, and the *corregidor* Salamanca was the crown agent in charge of the whole district, the *corregimiento*, whose official duty was to protect both royal and Indian interests. For the festival, Salamanca's aides included one Cristóbal de Mata, Román de Baños, described as a mestizo, the local priest Antonio Martínez, and Luis de Gálvez, a native of Córdoba. Don Pedro opened the affair with a comic performance involving himself as the first contender and his deputy Don Cristóbal as Bacchus. While the latter careened about the place riding a barrel carried by devotees of the vine, numbers of *indígenas* drummed and chanted. Later on, in a formal reminder of how authority had changed from Inca to Spanish in this mining town where 1500 indigenous slaves labored in the workings and whose indigenous population outnumbered their colonizers many scores—doubtless hundreds—of times, there was a full-scale parade and tableau showing the glories of Inca culture in which Don Román appeared as a European knight errant seated in an Inca's royal litter and surrounded by a hundred Inca musicians singing and dancing, as the contemporary *relación* described it (Rodríguez Marín, 107–9). But in the sequence of Spanish knights underscoring the change in authority, a climax was the appearance of "the Knight of the Sad Countenance," played by the ex-Cordoban Gálvez (known as something of a comedian), accompanied by Cervantes' parish priest, barber, Princess Micomicona, and Sancho Panza. This was not the last joust and performance before evening, but the contemporary account clearly held it the most interesting of its kind, and its protagonist won the prize for the best "*ynbençion*" of the afternoon (Rodríguez Marín, 75–93; Leonard, *Books*, 302–12; full text of contemporary account in Rodríguez Marín, 97–118).

Quijote was just one of many knights of romance, legend, and history in the parade, but his posture "on a decrepit nag quite similar to his Rocinante," his tattered clothing, antique high collar and rusty armor, helmet crowned with rooster's feathers, droll melancholic demeanor—all enacted an ironic derision that vanquished his more aristocratic, familiar competitors. Adding that to the repeated use, in this overwhelmingly indigenous milieu, of local cultural artifacts, drumming, clothing, song, and dance—memorializing Inca imperial power and defeat—one feels the occasion was less innocently comic than chroniclers claim, recycling the dictum that "the first readers of *Quixote* must have seen just comedy in this literary novelty" (Ortega, *Meditations*, 159). Pausa's high plain festival may *not* have echoed what Leonard calls "the contemporary failure in Spain itself to appreciate the profounder meanings inherent in these chief protagonists" (*Books*, 312). The move of Quijote and the others to the Andes, the addition of indigenous elements, the collective creation of *this* Quijote and his festival, and the prize awarded to the melancholy knight, signaling "defeat" of familiar fantastic or realistic characters—all emphasized that this was *not* the Spain of most of its principals' origin. Too, the theater and poetry of Inca popular spectacle typically played, said one late-sixteenth-century writer, "memories of their ancestors" (Lipschutz, 133). How could the Inca performers of Pausa *not* see this display as part of *their* tradition? Quijote was tied here not just to celebration of a new viceroy but to those of indigenous actuality and Pausa itself, founded like other such towns, Alexander von Humboldt observed in his *Political Essay on the Kingdom of New Spain*, to enable exploitation of the nearby mine, to permit establishment of Spanish-owned haciendas and exploitation of *their* agricultural production, and so to link town, mine, and land as a joint source of profit at the expense of the indigenous slaves whose labor produced it (quoted in Frank, *Latin America*, 235–36).

The ambiguity of these conditions was patent in a report an earlier viceroy, Francisco de Toledo, had sent Philip II in August 1571, during a five-year tour of the Andean interior begun ten months before. For a century and a half, the Cuzco region had been rent by huge pressures. Early fifteenth-century Inca conquest and Spanish invasion in the 1530s meant that "indigenous patterns of human organization and production had been dramatically altered by the time Toledo arrived to reform colonial government." Inca adaptations and appropriations of "traditional indigenous institutions" had in turn been forced into Spanish colonial patterns (Wightman, 1; and see Stern, 3–26). Toledo ignored such matters. He dwelt on "the ways in which Indians, their leaders, and private settlers were challenging the authority of the Spanish Crown. Toledo's staff had reported that throughout the Cuzco zone 'there were many Indians who neither paid tribute nor were supervised by an encomendero or any other person' ." The native community, he said, was "disorganized, dispersed, and demoralized from the Spanish conquest, the prolonged civil wars between opposing bands of conquistadores (1531–1547), and rumors of an uprising planned by the heir to the Incan Empire, Tupac Amaru. Toledo told Philip that the indigenous community was being exploited by local landowners and miners, harassed by the colonial judicial system and deceived by a false religion" (Wightman, 3; her citation is from the viceroy's report). By 1607, memories of civil wars and fear of Tupac Amaru (captured and killed by the Spanish in 1571) had faded. The other tensions had not.

By then, Toledo's "reforms" were in fact making things worse. Edicts moving Indians into settlements, regulating Spanish exploitation, instituting law courts to protect Indians, and banning religious objects sacred to indigenous peoples had harmful effects. Settlement "actually stimulated population dispersal and migration." It aggravated epidemics and increased Spanish demand for goods and services even as it decimated local populations—judged to have shrunk by at least 90 percent over the whole of Peru in the century after 1532, and perhaps by far more (Wolf, 134). New kinds of exploitation "drove Indians to abandon their home communities to seek protection from the Spanish employers." "Local court systems proved as efficiently predatory as their predecessors." Efforts to end "idolatry" reinforced native religious practices. Further, Toledo compelled all Indian men between ages 18 and 50 to pay heavy taxes—tribute—and to labor, supposedly for limited periods, in mine, hacienda, or personal service (Wightman, 3–4, 16, 18, 23, 54). Indian *caciques* and agents like the *corregidores* enforced both charges for a viceroyalty whose existence hung on them. Unsurprisingly, Indians proved as adept at working the justice system (Stern, 114–37) as colonists were at harassing royal officials and maximizing their own incomes (Wightman, 23). Indians were able "to modify, adapt, avoid, or utilize the institutions imposed by their conquerors, as well as preserve and adapt their own traditions" (Spalding, 47–48; cf. Stern, 80–183). By October 1604, the viceroy Luis de Velasco told Philip III that Toledo's system had utterly failed (cited in Wightman, 24). Under pitiless Spanish power, whose wider colonial oppression was naturally unaffected by any of this, ambiguities of these pressures of resistance and victimization, refusal and exploitation were marked in the Pausa festival by the mix of indigenous and Spanish cultural artifacts and processes and the presence of landowners, mine foremen, miners and fieldworkers, exploiters and exploited, conquerors and conquered, victimizers and victimized.

These facts suggest that the story and idea of Don Quijote, which already deeply questioned traditions from which they sprang, might readily acquire such associations with other cultures, histories, and forms of cultural creation as to make him a much more ambiguous figure than the celebrants of Pausa might have intended, unwittingly drawn by what Ortega called his "frontier nature" (*Meditations*, 136). Moving in indigenous colonized Pausa, run-down, sad-eyed Quijote is both the wanderer of La Mancha and a decrier of conquest and chivalric ideology in the high Andes. Diana de Armas Wilson shows how the opening of Cervantes' later *Persiles* (1617), set in a Europeanized American "island," "fashioned a cultural critique dependent not upon an inversion but a subversion of binary oppositions" (248). The same can be said of Don Quijote in Pausa, stepping from a novel by no means bereft of references to the Americas (de Armas Wilson, 236–37, 252 n. 11; for a full catalogue, see Campos, "Presencia") and from a creator who had yearned to make the Atlantic passage. Whether such associations *explain* the popularity of the story and the idea among these European invaders of the Americas, they surely allow us to use Don Quijote to follow the tense debates about history and cultural creation to which I alluded at the outset of this chapter and which have been a theme throughout the book.

For, like those colonizers of Pausa who associated him with "Indian" culture, not only was Don Quijote essentially out of step, out of kilter, with the world he inhabited, using pieces of its old history to make his own, new and unfamiliar, story, but he did so by embedding them in his travels across, through, and about the plains and hills of La Mancha, tying his history to place, forging it by binding his pieces of story to a geography, as Azorín, Maeztu, Ortega, and Unamuno all insisted. How much clearer could this bond become, how much more equivocal Quijote himself, transferred to the Andes and tied to indigenous cultural actualities? Such transfers as these, such questionings of familiar stories, and such minglings of culture put fundamental questions to the kind of authoritative imposition the colonizers thought they were celebrating, imposing their expansive story on others who would, of course, be made better by it. To some considerable extent, the performance of these questions and their prize undermined that very idea by expressing its real purposes with some clarity. Subsequent western historiography, developing from just these years, was no doubt organized to prevent these sorts of underminings and to certify the rectitude of its authority.

For later western literary and historiographic culture would of course not miss *Quijote*'s oppositional traits. But unlike their seventeenth-century colonial precursors in Pausa, who knew only its earliest beginnings, that culture's representatives have sought to tame these characteristics by translating them into the comforting terms of a "romantic" buttressing of its own norms—in full accord with the sequence, colonial brutality/"slavering apology," of which we saw Césaire speak. In its simplest and commonest version, the opposition has been put in terms of the deluded knight's "false realities" versus the "noble seriousness" of right history, as Nietzsche condemned Quijote (however tangled the idea of history at issue; "On the Uses," 84). Sciascia writes analogously of idealism versus materialism, illusion against reality, further remarking that this understanding of the novel was perfect for Unamuno, leading member of that "Generation of '98" that had its name from the traumatic defeat of the Spanish-American war in which, losing Cuba and the Philippines, Spain was deprived of the last little Caribbean and Asian pieces of "an empire on which, in Cervantes' time, the sun never set" (*Heures*, 40).

Nietzsche claimed nothing but scorn for what he considered the seventeenth-century and Enlightenment idea of a progressive history that raised the "latecomer . . . to godhood as the true meaning of all previous events [and as] completion of world-history," and thereby gave that late-comer a "right," even "duty," to direct the lives of those who inhabited his-tories supposed to have progressed less. He called for an "antidote to the historical" that took two forms. The "unhistorical" demanded "forgetting" and "enclosing oneself within a bounded *horizon*"; the "suprahistorical" re-quired working "towards that which bestows upon existence the character of the eternal and stable, towards *art* and *religion*." Their discovery would in fact be signaled by a new "natural instinct for" genuine "poetry" ("On the Uses," 104, 120, 116–17). If the one was a withdrawal into the recognizably local—even national—story requiring something like Renan's forgetting, the other proposed a kind of eschatological or moral teleology. The first de-manded the invention of fictions, the second of myth. For Hegel, both had been shapes of Absolute Spirit, unattainable for History as such; for Nietzsche, they became real and present alternatives to traditional history. Unamuno took these from Nietzsche in his *Vida de Don Quijote y Sancho Panza*, published exactly three centuries after the first part of Cervantes' novel. Taking up the challenge of the philosopher's simplification of Don Quijote, and in the aftermath of loss of empire, Unamuno rewrote the knight's story so that faith, illusion, and innocence were spiritual benefits of material defeat. The local—or perhaps here, rather, parochial—story was Spain's fiction of grandeur and loss. The myth transformed it into a dream of transhistorical faith. It is hard to see this as anything but an inversion of the history Nietzsche scorned. And what were his myth and fiction but avowals of what the progressive history had always been about?

Unamuno was not alone in turning Quijote into a tale of history and memory, nostalgia and geography. For others of his generation, writing in the gloom of 1898, Quijote's place was one of nostalgic loss, of disappearing horizons under a transparent sky. It was, wrote Azorín, a *paisaje* where "una luz clara, limpia, diáfana, llena la inmensa llanura amarillenta; la campiña se extiende a los lejos en suaves ondulaciones de terrenos y oteros," where "a clear, limpid, diaphanous light overwhelms the immense yellowish plain; the country stretches far away in gentle waves of fields and hills" (*Ruta*, 84). The knight and those after him rode and walked through limpid ruins of a Spain going or now long gone, fading through an infinitely "remote line of the horizon," over "la llanura ancha, la llanura infinita, la llanura desesper-ante," "the wide plain, infinite plain, hopeless plain" under a sky of brilliant blue (*Ruta*, 111; cf. 121, 123–24 and *passim*). Azorín's ever far-off "horizonte," immediately taking up the sound of "desesperante" and soon echoed in "el horizonte es el horizonte de siempre" (*Ruta*, 111–13), assonantly summoned up Quijote on Rocinante, firmly grounding him in his landscape and answering Nietzsche's bounded horizon. For Azorín thought Quijote still knew the mysterious deep waters of eternal Spain in the cave of Montesinos, Spain of "conquistadors, warriors and mystics" (*Ruta*, 127–30), than whom none "achieved greater deeds" and who "wrested a splendid civilization from a virgin world" ("Claro," 168–69). Against the little land of today, he was the vast Spain of empire, whose "single tongue stifled a multitude of indigenous tongues" ("Famosa," 172). With all its ambiguity, Quijote's countryside was timeless depth of greatness pitted against the "exhaustion, sadness and resignation" of city civilization. He marked the chasm between the two, where "passed a sigh of the Tragic" (*Ruta*, 77, 104). And yet this ruinous nostalgia was also part of the landscape he was dreaming, caught out of time, its people "unable to excel themselves"—"as Nietzsche the philosopher wanted" (*Ruta*, 108). Quijote was at once presence of Spain's imperial history and mark of its passing.

Maeztu claimed to be rejecting Azorín's view in asserting how Quijote signaled a moment of decadence and "exhaustion," "dream" and "energy" gone, the day "melancholy and grey," when a "golden age" had already yielded to "ours" of "iron" and Cervantes was "preparing minds to be resigned to giving up progress" ("Don Quijote," 42, 44, 50, 52, 61). But he saw him only as further along a line toward decadence: the time when "we understand ourselves to be defeated before the unattainable ideal . . . our means inadequate to our ends," lost "at the fall of evening" in melancholy realization "that we haven't done all we planned" ("Don Quijote," 21). We cannot read *Don Quijote*, Maeztu believed, "without being saturated with the melancholy felt by a man and a people when deceived of their ideal." It is "the voice of an exhausted race" seeking rest "after achieving its work in the world" (22). Maeztu opposed the novel to Camões' earlier Portuguese epic of empire, *The Lusiads* (1572), as an elegy of loss of empire foretelling the melancholic disasters of 1898 (46). Whether in Azorín's nostalgic timeless depths or Maeztu's "melancholy" and "vastly tired" emptiness (21), Don Quijote marked Spain's passage *out* of History (one that Maeztu saw now—in 1925—as needing to be reversed by Spain's "recovery of the historical initiative"; 61). Both counter this retreat from History by stressing Quijote's grounding in a *place* embodying the traits they gave him. His "gran figura dolorosa que es nuestro ídolo y nuestro espejo," image and "condensation" of the people and villages amid whom he rides, bears "toda la tristeza de la Mancha" (*Ruta*, 80, 144), a bond Azorín embedded in his very language. Fathomless loss or hope of renewal, Quijote's meanings lie in the landscapes of his travels. Their very ambiguity is tied to these landscapes: Castilian La Mancha, Incan Andes, modern Haiti. . . . This, whatever Maeztu or Azorín may have wanted to the contrary—unlike their contemporaries Machado and Pessoa—makes Quijote endlessly *disponible*, available to adopt and give back meanings according to the landscapes in which he moves.

Recovering from myth and fiction that its own story transformed, Spain was finding for itself, in an uncanny and historically telling way, what the colonized peoples of its now lost empire had always known: Europe was not the universal guide and maker of world History. It was just one place where histories were told. For his part, Unamuno recast the knight as a symbol of a different sort of new Spain. Quijote and Panza were translated into the still vital ideal Other of rational and imperial but vanquished Spain, victorious inside truth of defeated outside appearance, defeat itself letting Spain return to its true eternal soul. Like Quijote, we have seen Unamuno urge, Spain had to clear the undergrowth and rubbish hiding the mouth of the cave of Montesinos, the "crows and jackdaws" of nostalgias and dead histories, to go down and find one's traditions (*Our Lord*, 192–93). Azorín described his own visit to the cave in analogous terms, although he was more pessimistic about recovering the traditions (*Ruta*, 126–30). Don Quijote traveling back to Europe changed its claim on history, doing in symbol as did in angry event the Haitian Revolution of C. L. R. James' telling, showing how "men make their own history," how histories in different places "alter the fate of millions of men and shift the economic currents of . . . continents" (*Black*, 25)—like González Prada's infusorians named at the end of the last chapter—how histories are a dialectic of places not an imposition of one. But Unamuno, like Nietzsche, still used Quijote in terms fully adopting the cultural values of western history, self and other, here and there, victor and victim, dissonance and harmony. So did Unamuno's compatriots Azorín and Maeztu, pitting past against present, country against city, timeless ideal against historical decadence, individual grandeur against mass monotony, melancholy nostalgia for tradition against present metropolitan despair.

In his ironic commentary on Unamuno's adoption of Nietzsche's versions of history, Borges had "Pierre Menard" write a *Don Quijote* seemingly identical to Cervantes' but which, written in the early twentieth century, did not incorporate "a mere rhetorical eulogy of history." Instead, it advanced the "astounding" idea of history as "mother of truth," and so of "historical truth" as "not what took place" but as "what we think took place" (Borges, "Pierre Menard," 52–53; Sciascia, *Heures*, 42–44). Similarly, Nietzsche had cited Schiller criticizing the very notion of ordered historiography as creating a "harmonious whole . . . present only in [the historian's] imagination" and wholly "subjective" ("On the Uses," 92). It is not clear how this differed from his forgetting, from the forging of a history carefully bound by the nature of one's own "horizon," or from history as myth—which was no doubt, from the other side of the Atlantic, one of Borges' points. But another point aimed at this history's power and the truly vast difficulties of escaping its seizure. To get from criticism to refusal is one thing, but the ease with which critics fall back into its forms (not necessarily even as its inversion or its opposite) also shows how very hard it may be to achieve a real "alternative" to such history, a quite different composition of time, place, people, and culture.

Just so, speaking of Caribbean writers, Walcott once praised a rejection, analogous to that of Unamuno's use of Quijote, "of history as time for its original concept as myth" as a way for "New World" writers sardonically to appropriate European cultural traditions for their own ends even as they seemed, deceptively, to submit to them. For them, he asserted, "history is fiction, subject to a fitful muse, memory" ("Muse," 1–2). This was also to adopt same/other dichotomies, taken directly, these phrases imply, from Nietzsche's essay, which explains why Walcott, too, took renewal of poetry in the contemporary Caribbean as a sign of its writers' discovery of a new idea of history. The dangers of thinking one can live in some stable myth beyond history are now no less apparent than the idea of history as forgetful fiction. History may be a narrative of the fictive imagination, as Walcott then asserted, but it matters who tells it, how, and from whence. Temporalities evidently depend on this whence, how, and why they are told. "If we change the classification principle," Latour remarks, for example, "we get a different temporality on the basis of the same events" (*We Have*, 75). It was the ordered imposition of another's ordered history that Walcott was trying to reject, noting that Caribbean historiography (and culture more generally) was torn between despair and remorse, stories told by descendants of slaves and those told by descendants of masters, rage, and guilt—merely counter versions of the Old World narrative. But from this, the "way out" is not via claims of fiction, signals of however grand a poetry or leaps over history to some atemporal Adam ("Muse," 3; but contrast Breiner's view of Walcott's various Adams in "Tradition," 8–11).

A different kind of signal suggests a different kind of exit. For these different stories, their places, their times, and their protagonists may perhaps be combined in other ways. In Caribbean writing, Walcott urged, "its traces of melancholy are the chemical survivals of the blood which remains after the slave's and the indentured worker's convalescence. It will survive the malaria of nostalgia and the delirium of revenge just as it survived its self-contempt" ("Muse," 18). It may do so in a figure central to great poets of the Caribbean, Césaire or Saint-John Perse, whose "hero remains the wanderer, the man who moves through the ruins of great civilizations with all his worldly goods by caravan or pack mule, the poet carrying entire cultures in his head, bitter perhaps [or melancholic and sad-countenanced?], but unencumbered" (3). Quijote, we recall, wandered through just such ruins. His melancholy was just such disease and delirium to those who watched and accompanied him, a desiccation of the brain, said the novel's narrator as he began.

Disease and delirium signaled (to those others) Quijote's refusal of familiar histories. Here, now, they made "actual the quest of a medieval knight or the bulk of a white whale, because of the power of a shared imagination" ("Muse," 25). It is surely the "shared imagination" that matters, and that Quijote should mark this telling and retelling, *remaking*, of history puts a finger on one crucial care of Caribbean writing: the effort to escape the crushing angel of European history so as to write itself, make its own voice, elaborate its own history and geography of home. So, too, does Walcott's protagonist Makak of *Dream on Monkey Mountain* adopt for a moment Quijote's mask, his friend Moustique Sancho's: "Saddle my horse, if you love me, Moustique, and cut a sharp bamboo for me, and put me on that horse, for Makak will ride to the edge of the world, Makak will walk like he used to in Africa, when his name was lion." As Moustique mocks his taking "Berthilia the jackass" for a horse, a "beat-up tin pot" for a helmet (like Mambrino's), a bamboo "for a spear," and weeps for his madness, recalling Quijote in all these things, Makak responds with Quijote's gentle gravity: "I hurt you, little one? . . . I am not mad . . . I beg you now, come" (*Dream*, 240–41). The play's mysterious white-masked apparition is Dulcinea imagined in equivocal beauty; dream of return to Africa is imagined recovery of freedom from colonial and neocolonial History, if here a tilting at windmills.

Lamming proposed that these takings, these forgings of new histories, could not use an oppressor's History, making the Caribbean archipelago's history someone else's "vomit"—a reply to Césaire's earlier sarcasm: "nous vomissure de négrier," "we the vomit of slave-ships" (*Cahier*, 98/9; 60/1). It had to be history developed in the common imagination of "West Indians" together, a "great people" inhabiting the same topography (Lamming, *Emigrants*, 67–68). It would not be a history as Europe's other or as a Nietzschean rejection of its version and idea of "history." It had to incorporate and transform both version and idea. It would, as Césaire put it, embrace the cast-off river mud, the *raque*, of its own topography. Only in and through it, exclaims his Christophe, could the Caribbean forge its own "freedom":

You know what they call a *raque*: vast [*fondrière*], interminable stretch of mud. On the banks of the Arbonite, precisely, you're familiar with the *Maurepas raque*, that compacted, infinite mud, and this century is the rain, the long march through the long rain. Yes, in the *raque*, we're in the *raque* of history. (Césaire, *Tragédie*, 98)

The history forged in this struggle would embrace different rhythms and places and lives, not "other" but dwelling and happening, simply, in a different *home*: "for some time I have tried to master a time that keeps slipping away," writes Glissant, "to live a landscape that is constantly changing, to celebrate a history that is documented nowhere" (*Caribbean*, 245). It would tell of other heroes, struggles, cultures, and homes, of currents and happenings that for Ngũgĩ's colonially educated narrator of "A Mercedes Funeral" were "not history" and only to be "pitied," for "true and correct history" was that of "the Celts, the Anglo-Saxons, the Danes and Vikings" (*Secret*, 123), or the Gauls. But the dialectics of these histories mean that elements from others can *always* be turned to account, like Caliban or flowers, otherness or Don Quijote.

Walcott revisits his earlier thoughts in *Omeros*, where both sides, fiction and myth, the unhistorical and the suprahistorical, but also victory and defeat, here and there, become simply and clearly two versions of one history seen through the eyes of (Sergeant) Major Dennis Plunkett, expatriate Briton. For him as well, though, matters become more complicated. Once upon a time, he had seen the Antilles as a fairy tale, a "place where what they called history could not happen" (for all its echoes of a Greek Mediterranean; *Omeros*, 28) and simply opposed to Britain's "reasonable leaves shading reasonable earth" (61). In the Caribbean, Maud Plunkett, his wife, had them both feeling "like Adam and Eve all over. . . . /Before the snake. Without all the sin" (63). Facing actualities of different spirit of place and time, Plunkett comes to doubt his stories, though at first resistant: "History was fact,/History was a canon, not a lizard" (92). But these were no longer the days when "history was easy" (113). He finds that "History earns its own tenderness/in time; not for a naval victory, but for // the V of a velvet back in a yellow dress" (103). Now alien in London, "he began to hear/The surf of a dialect none would understand" (252). He had become "one with the farmers" of St. Lucia, "transplanted to the rich dirt/of their valleys" (268), even though he could still only ever try "to change History to a metaphor/in the name of a housemaid" (270). Perhaps at the last, though, he does close on the fisherman Achille's sense that "time is the metre, memory the only plot" (103, 129).

Of course, none of this yet answers the earlier problem of how to avoid the trammels of a history whose progressively causal order is taken to grasp and describe all the possibilities of events in time. But it casts on it a less adamant, hazier light even as it shows how the unhistorical and the suprahistorical, fictive and mythic, are two sides of a single historical coin ordering its straightforwardly linear universality by an Enlightenment schema of which Laplacean probability was only the most extreme form (if one knew the whole state and all motions of the universe now, one could predict its evolution to all eternity and know its past in smallest detail by a ready calculus of cause and effect). Each wants to teach those it seizes as its Other its own history as "a history of which [they] too are capable" (Walcott, *Omeros*, 197). Each erects moribund museums, where (in contrast to Nietzsche and earlier Walcott) "Art has surrendered/to History with its whiff of formaldehyde" (182), or makes a dull order where "Art is History's nostalgia" (228), divorced in either case from imagination and Achille's living memory. This memory, we shall see, is not only collective but one that tries to make cultural homes communicate with one another from places and times of each, not at the demand and behest of one.

Reworking Quijote clarifies this hard debate. Many Caribbean writers, refusing the sorts of self-congratulatory or dejected oppositions just set out, have woven the melancholy knight into a different pattern, one composed from the many sources into which these writers reach. For Caribbean writers, Don Quijote might be an instrument through which to make a history that involved a new way of telling. Carew describes this possibility in his portrait of one local voice:

In every large rural community in the Caribbean, one inevitably comes across an unusually eloquent and gifted storyteller, and Mardi Gras [on Grenada] was no exception. I met Marko one morning when he was on his way to milk his cows. He was tall, lean, grizzled and his dark and ageless face looked like that of a cadaver. His enormous and sad eyes were like those of a swarthy Don Quixote who had never ventured forth to fulfil his impossible dreams. (Carew, "Harvesting," 158)

Cadaverous Quijote appears as an ageless but deathlike angel whose "impossible dreams" are in fact fulfilled in the making of a new—the Caribbean's own—history first of all by *telling*. The knight of the sad countenance here becomes the repository of an oral history who, like his long-dead predecessor in the high mountains of the Incas, tells a story incorporating many pasts, a different land, and a rejection of purely western realities: "He talked with a hoarse eloquence, and sometimes he punctuated a statement with bitter laughter. Walking ahead of me on the trail with his cutlass in its scabbard at his side" ("Harvesting," 158). What he told was of the land's ruin by western farming practices and its chemical fertilizers, of hurricanes and landslides, of his discovery of the amaranth cultivated with immense care by the Aztecs of Tenochtitlán and others, of its endless uses by indigenous peoples, its immense importance in their cultures, its deliberate destruction by Cortés, and of the decay that started things growing again (158–62). What he told was the indissoluble imbrication of history and geography and through that perhaps an answer to impositions of singular history and its other.

A similar moment occurs in Schwarz-Bart's *Ti Jean l'Horizon* when old père Filao upbraids Gros Édouard for denigrating black people and accuses whites of having struck and kept them down, so that they no longer know whether "nous appartenons au monde des hommes ou à celui des vents, du vide et du néant" ("we belong to the world of humans or that of winds, void and nothingness"). He adds that whites have kept their dagger in hand ready to strike again. On this, Ti Jean says these "paroles étranges . . . sans qu'ils put les reconnaître" ("strange words . . . without being able to recognize them"):

Père Filao, avec tout le respect: *il n'y a plus d'oiseaux dans les nids de l'an dernier et moi qui n'ai pas peur de la mort, le poignard, je leur ôterai des mains.*

Père Filao, with all respect: there are no more birds in last year's nests and I, who aren't afraid of death, I'll take this dagger from their hands. (51)

Thus adapting Quijote's very words in which he recognizes his past madness at the end of *Don Quijote*, Ti Jean says, on the contrary, that just *because* that past is over and done, he will now *become* the knight and take on their enemies. He will do so out of his island's geography. And just as Ti Jean makes himself a mediator between times, places, and worlds, so there comes another such messenger from "En-haut," Eusèbe l'Ancien, "un homme d'un abord suprenant, long et maigre comme un jour sans pain, avec un grand chapeau bacoua qui lui battait millement les épaules . . . ("A man of surprising appearance, long and thin like a day of famine, with a great *bacoua* hat which constantly beat his shoulders . . ."; 53). Here Quijote is again mediator between times, places, and worlds. More particularly, he is the righter of wrong histories.

The image of Don Quijote is in fact only occasionally directly apparent in Caribbean imaginative writing, but one meets it often enough in the writing of Caribbean critics as to make it more than intriguing—and indirectly and obliquely the figure is widespread, half-effaced presence on a palimpsest, although we shall see him become considerably more than that on at least one occasion: in Depestre's *Le mât de cocagne*. Among critics, here is J. Michael Dash, for example:

In tracing [the writer's] concern with the expressiveness and redeeming force of language, we may well see the Caribbean writer as a modern Quixote, relying on his imagination in order to confer meaning on an elusive and complex reality. ("World," 115)

Such writers would have experienced two attitudes toward history, subordination, and refusal: a nineteenth-century one, putting "faith in the wrong books just as Quixote does in his chivalric romances," and a later one, in which "Quixote's books are ridiculed" (116). Dash adopts here Nietzsche's and Unamuno's view of Quijote as performing an illusory story.

But Quijote is always figured as something else and as something more intricate. It is surely suggestive that Carlos Franqui should have proposed *Don Quijote* as the first book published by the Imprenta Nacional in Fidel Castro's postrevolutionary Cuba, with a print run in the millions of copies and prefaced by Castro himself (*Retrato*, 156, a reference for which I am indebted to Christopher Winks). In Quijote, the *imagination* of which Dash speaks is never individualist. At stake for Dash and other Caribbean critics is not a private quest for personal space but common tales of exile, decisions of place, relations of people, reworking stones of Venice, houses of Kumasi or Zimbabwe, streets of Tenochtitlán, where the amaranth was

so grave. As in the response to Cortés' destruction, this imagination ineluctably incorporates those pieces of another's history. Quijote joins not
nostalgia and revenge but plural traditions in a new home place. So, writing of *Moby Dick*, C. L. R. James also chose Quijote as an "original character" signaling the possibility, and maybe in the contemporary outer
world, actuality (shades of Unamuno, Maeztu, and Borges) of a new start
(*Mariners*, 76–77). Walcott, we saw, seemingly recalled this association
with Ahab's great whale, although lasting ambivalences and ambiguities in
these signs—Borges' "abomination and love of the White Whale" ("Que-
vedo," *Other Inquisitions*, 37)—climax in his later savage rejection of Melville's search:

> Heah's Cap'n Melville on de whiteness ob de whale—
> *"Having for the imperial colour the same imperial hue . . .*
>
> *giving the white man ideal mastership over every dusky tribe."*
> Lawd, Lawd, Massa Melville, what could a nigger do
> but go down dem steps in de dusk you done describe?
> (Omeros, 184)

If Melville's search still hoisted the "redemptive white sail" of European rescue, things were never so clear-cut, and "there was Plunkett in my
father, much as there was/my mother in Maud," not just because they
lived in familiar Caribbean surroundings or because they and theirs had
supplied the stories on which one had been weaned, but because "there in
that khaki Ulysses,"

> there was a changing shadow of Telemachus
> in me, in his absent war, and an empire's guilt
> stitched in the one pattern of Maud's fabulous quilt. (263)

Maud Plunkett, herself having crossed lands and seas in quest of an
Adamic brave new world, become Penelope weaving a quilt, mixing the
flora, fauna, and stories of Europe and the Caribbean into a tissue not now
undone at night, is another version of our Quijote, trying unsuccessfully
here to find new composures of lives and cultures.

So it is that in Carpentier's story of a quest for an indigenous music
and a place whose plural history would replace the labeling of "the thinking, Cartesian, position," we twice meet Don Quijote at crucial moments
(*Lost Steps*, 219 [hereafter abbreviated L before the page number]; *Pasos*, 242
[hereafter abbreviated P before the page number]). The first occurs as the

narrator climbs the parodic Calvary of Los Altos, the town from whence he starts his trip into the interior. Here, one station is a museum displaying with other things "a grain of rice on which several paragraphs of *Don Quixote* had been copied" (L66; P66): the novel reduced to a tiny parody of itself for tourists in Venezuela. The Calvary also recalled an earlier one (implicit in the Spanish, explicit in translation), referring to the destitution of the poor in the capitalist world of surrounding consumerism (L29–30; P24). We might also incline to recall Unamuno's Quijote as "[a]quel Cristo castellano [que] fué triste hasta su muerte hermosísima," that Castilian Christ who was melancholy until his most lovely death ("Caballero," 83), or Ortega's as "the sad parody of a more divine and serene Christ" (*Meditations*, 51), as if in Los Altos *that* Quijote (of Nietzsche, Ortega, Unamuno, and their contemporaries) and what he parodied were reduced to the ironic debris of a civilization from which the narrator was fleeing, but which was here anyway, already of literally small matter.

For soon after, Quijote is transformed differently and more significantly. This involves the narrator's fusion of place and memory at the moment when he first meets Rosario, the woman who becomes his lover and the embodiment of everything that is not western dominance:

Suddenly a village emerged on a small round butte surrounded by swift streams. It seemed to me astoundingly Castilian in appearance despite its baroque church, its slope of roofs around the plaza into which winding, narrow mule paths debouched. The braying of an ass brought to my mind a picture of El Toboso—with an ass in the foreground—which illustrated a lesson in my third reader, and which had a striking resemblance to the hamlet that lay before me. "*In a village of La Mancha, whose name I prefer not to recall, there lived not long ago one of those hidalgos with lance in rack, ancient buckler, lean nag, and fleet hound. . . .*"

I was proud of my ability to remember a thing it had cost the teacher so much effort to teach the twenty of us. Once I had known the whole paragraph by heart, and now I could not remember beyond "*fleet hound.*" I was exasperated at my lapse, returning again and again to "*village of La Mancha*" to see if the second sentence would come back to me.

It does so when Rosario interrupts to say that the village is named "La Hoya," words pronounced almost exactly like the opening noun of the sentence in question, "*Una olla*" (L77; P79).

Locale here intervenes in a different way in the narrator's memory and his awareness and mixing of place than at the earlier Calvary. At issue is the working out not just of a new history, but of some new notion of the relation between history and culture, between culture and historical understanding, between history and place—that also remembers how Unamuno, Azorín, and Maeztu grounded Quijote in the land. Carpentier's narrator's forgetting of the familiar paragraph matters no less than the fact that it takes the indigenous to bring it back. He will learn that it is not enough to oppose what are too readily taken to be contrasting histories, that it is not enough for westerners "to use masks of Bandiagara, African *ibeyes*, fetishes studied with nails, without knowing their meaning, as battering-rams against the redoubts of the *Discourse of Method*." These things were not "barbarous" others. They had other meanings and places "when fulfilling their ritual function in the setting for which they were designed" (L219; P242). The history of old Europe, Heidelburg and Potsdam, Siena and Paris, its glories of Erasmus and Descartes destroyed by Inquisition and torture (L83–85; P86–88), transplanted to the Venezuelan rain forest, had its ruins transformed into undergrowth, reborn into flowers from decay (as told, too, by Carew's cadaverous Quijote), even as local songs and their familiar/unfamiliar rhythms brought back quests of medieval knights, Roland and Turpin, the Infantas of Lara (L106–8; P112–15), a medieval Ship of Fools absorbed into something new, as if "the role of these lands in human history might not be for the first time to make possible certain symbioses of cultures" (L109; P115–16). These knights marking Carpentier's fabrication of the Americas as a world of "marvelous" or "magical" realism may have a hitherto unacknowledged but intriguing source, embedding it in memories of Quijote in a different way.

In 1928, Machado published the ideas and poems of his apocryphal philosopher, proposing "una nueva dialectica, sin negaciones ni contrarios, que Abel Martín llama lirica y, otras veces, mágica, la lógica del cambio substancial o devenir inmóvil, del ser cambiando o el cambio siendo" ("a new dialectic, without negations or contraries, that Abel Martín called lyric and, sometimes, magical, the logic of substantial change or immobile becoming, of being changing or of change being; "De un cancionero"; 291). Critics have most often associated Carpentier's magical realism with the surrealists; and Depestre, who has often written of hearing Carpentier talk on the subject in Port-au-Prince in 1942, is typical in noting "the confluence of european surrealism with the currents of creole oneirism in the Caribbean" (*Métier*, 65). Like Depestre later, Carpentier had been a student opponent of his government and fled to Paris in 1928 to elude a different Machado, the Cuban dictator Gerardo Machado y Morales. In

Paris, he worked as a journalist and critic until 1939, frequenting surrealist circles on and off. Through his articles, writes González Echevarría, "the Cuban public had been kept abreast of the rapidly changing European artistic trends and fashions" (*Alejo Carpentier*, 34). He was in Madrid in 1933, 1934, and again in 1937 with the Cuban delegation to the antifascist Congress of Writers for the Defense of Culture, a group with whom Breton and his friends, as well as most leftist European writers, were associated (Hilden and Reiss). Machado was not only the celebrated poet of Quijote's eternal landscapes in *Campos de Castilla* (1912)—his Generation's breviary—he was also an ardent supporter of the Spanish Republic and had been a member of the Spanish committee to the Congress since 1935.

It would be impossible for Carpentier not to have known Machado's writing; and the latter's heteronymous *Juan de Mairena* and his celebrated lament for Federico García Lorca, "El crimen fue en Granada," had both been printed in Madrid at the end of 1936. The two could also have met. Carpentier recounted his stay in Valencia for the Congress's opening sessions in July 1937 in the second of his chronicles, "España bajo las bombas." Machado, already very ill, was brought by his brother to Valencia from Rocafort in southern France, where he was then staying, and gave a dramatic public speech to the Congress (Sésé, 2:818–19). The speech was published that August in the journal *Hora de España*, which had published some of the last pieces of *Juan de Mairena*. Certainly, Carpentier does not name him in the chronicle, and indeed I find no reference to the Spanish poet in his work other than Carpentier's signature on the 1978 public homage for the fortieth anniversary of Machado's death in exile (García-Carranza, 535).

Nonetheless, the real—or marvelous—connection suggests that as for Machado, so for Carpentier the notion of a magical or lyrical logic might have been tied more to issues of broad cultural and political change than to concerns with expanding consciousness. Perhaps, too, the Cuban's image of Quijote as a force for change moving through Caribbean landscapes, of which we shall see more, may have had a source here. Machado's magical dialectic would have been a *ratio* reacting to loss of empire given back to be expanded by those who had hoped to gain from Spain's loss.

While Quijote seldom appears as a character in novels (whether "literally" or by direct metaphor), his "essence" as Ortega's "frontier nature," as traveling and exiled creator of new realities, new histories, new homes, appears constantly. The knight plays out of an old history, making it first seem oppositional, but then enabling it to be turned in quite other directions, even when the opposition might have been, we have seen, ensconced in the Caribbean itself. In these terms, even Walcott's earlier medieval knight might bring some sort of balance:

Perse and Césaire, men of diametrically challenging backgrounds, racial opposites to use the language of politics, one patrician and conservative, the other proletarian and revolutionary, classic and romantic, Prospero and Caliban, all such opposites balance easily, but they balance on the axis of a shared sensibility, and this sensibility, with or deprived of a visible tradition, is the sensibility of walking to a New World. ("Muse," 16)

But sensibility is a vague thing, and these oppositions surely are Old World oppositions that exist by virtue of binary analytical thinking. They match *self/same* and *other*, *here* and *there*, *sun* and *ice*, *Gemeinschaft* and *Gesellschaft*, *animal* and *cogital*, in Nietzsche's phrase ("On the Uses," 119).

As we have already seen suggested in Carew, Carpentier, and Dash (and even in Walcott), Quijote argues that they may, must, be turned in some quite other way, a new weaving of events and places, not just sensibility dwelling in the rhythm of the transatlantic ocean passage—although that experience may be a source of some clearer new organizing of the imaginary and its makings:

across an ocean so calm, so much master of its rhythm, that the ship, gently cradled, seemed asleep on its course, suspended between a yesterday and a today which moved with us. Time caught between Pole Star, Great Bear and Southern Cross—I do not know, for it is not my job to know, whether such were the constellations, so numerous that their vertices, their lights of sidereal position, were jumbled and disordered, shuffling their allegories, in the brightness of a full moon made pale by the whiteness of the Milky Way. (Carpentier, *Explosion*, 7; *Siglo*, 7)

This opening of Carpentier's *El siglo de las luces*, itself "displaced" from later in the book (where it would fall, linearly, between sections xvi and xvii of Chapter 2), holds the protagonist at a crossroads between North and South, East and West, where rhythms of the ocean are caught with re-forming of the heavens. It shapes the novel to a reweaving of time and story, in a Caribbean "where words and phrases multiplied with surprising fertility" (E38; S39)—as, maybe, Quijote made realities from words catching his sense of time and honor and place. For Esteban and Sofía, two of *Siglo*'s main protagonists, are also Quijote. The first crosses lands, oceans, and seas from Cuba to France, Haiti to Guadeloupe, the second from Cuba to Haiti, Guadeloupe, Barbados, and Guiana, both finally set against a history that the mulatto Victor Hugues, entrepreneur of Revolution, wants to force on the Caribbean according to the changing rhythms of its French *parcours* and not at all to those of its unfurling through the archipelago and seas. And both cross the ocean "back" to Spain, there to disappear mysteriously in a new "revolutionary" clamor; no trace ever being found of them (E349; S358).

In their confrontation (which will return) and others like it, one starts to see something of the outcome of this quest: histories as a complex settlement of homes, secure in sense of place, and firm in urgencies of colloquy. These unfurling histories are necessarily hard to build. They will not turn to fiction or myth, still less to Ortega's notion of "European culture [as] the protagonist of history as long as a superior one does not exist" (*Meditations*, 76), or to its polar opposite, which Walcott saw commonly imposed on exiled Antilleans who viewed histories of Africa, Asia, or Americas as inferior: "we see how close we draw to madness here, for this sense qualifies not the significance of an event, but the event itself, the action of the event as second class" ("Muse," 21). For Ortega, Quijote would then be just a mediator between superior and inferior cultures. For Walcott, the melancholy quest would be blocked at its outset, giving only an exile's resignation and a next generation's "eugenic leap" to belief in rediscovery of some mythical "ancestral dignity of the wanderer-warrior" dwelling in an Africa of unflawed splendor ("Muse," 22).

The latter version of this melancholy quest is found in such characters as Selvon's Galahad, Trinidadian exile like his author, crossing the ocean to London to find himself doomed to "loneliness and fright" in a thoroughly racist world (*Lonely Londoners*, 41). At first, because he is able to use "the names of the places like they mean big romance," he seems to be "getting on well in the city" (83–84). Soon, determined fiction is rocked by "all the experiences . . . that come to him": "Lord, what it is we people do in this world that we have to suffer so? What is it we want that the white people and them find it so hard to give?" (88). Still, we saw earlier, he tries to fictionalize life by turning racism into abstraction:

So Galahad talking to the colour Black, as if is a person, telling it that is not *he* who causing botheration in the place, but Black, who is a worthless thing for making trouble all about. "Black, you see what you cause to happen yesterday?" . . . "Is not we the people don't like," he tell Moses, "is the colour Black." (88–89)

Through all this, even so, Galahad passes as if untouched by parochial superiorities that force him and his friends into direst poverty, as if bearing within him the miracle of his own place, even in the most "bitter season":

Galahad for one lose his work, and though it was winter—a real grim one . . . the old Galahad not much affected by the weather. Some miracle of metabolism was still keeping him warm at a time when normal people rattled with cold, and while they bawling and shivering he was able to walk about the streets in an ordinary suit of clothing. (123)

He even manages to turn Kensington Gardens into Trinidad's San Fernando by catching a pigeon to eat (123–26) and stays optimistic despite all. It takes Moses, the novel's focal character, to make clear how such fictive abstractions of inferiority and superiority hide reality: "he could see a great aimlessness, a great restless, swaying movement that leaving you standing in the same spot. As if a forlorn shadow of doom fall on all the spades in the country" (141); how they distort all experience: "As if the boys laughing, but they only laughing because they fraid to cry, they only laughing because to think so much about everything would be a big calamity—like how he here now, the thoughts so heavy like he unable to move his body" (142). Many are the traveling exiles of Caribbean fiction who have crossed the Atlantic from West to East to try and keep hope alive by seeking to make another's history theirs ("of which they too are capable"), faced with that history's claim either to superiority or uniqueness. "Don't you know," sarcastically cries the Antillean Veronica to her African relative Birame III in Maryse Condé's *Heremakhonon*,

that history never bothered about niggers? It's been proven they weren't worth the fuss. They had no part in building the Golden Gate Bridge or the Eiffel Tower. . . . It's with the lash they had to be civilized, given not just a history they needn't be ashamed of, but a *history*, period! You might think that everybody has a history. Well, no. These people had none. (11–12)

This is the negative counterpart to the positive Adamic myth, no more useful or valid than Galahad's fictions. In a woman author's novel, this perhaps makes it only the clearer that all are counters in another's story. Philip comments similarly on how western history deliberately sets Caribbean people out, "beka [the white] cutting them off in time, telling them they having no past and that their past not worth anything." How, too, this cuts the future: "Beka also stopping them from moving forward and making progress like everybody else doing and telling each other to do" (*Genealogy*, 222). These react to Césaire's celebrated irony about "those who invented neither powder or compass/those who could never harness steam or electricity" (*Cahier*, 110/1; 64/5). Added to the many we have already seen, they are further expressions of once-colonized people's endless dismay over Fuentes' "historical nightmare" of the imposition of an oppressor's history. But they are not simply negative. They lead to and draw in other histories, different stories—stories where once again Quijote steps in as a compiler of their places and needs.

I think particularly of Depestre's *Le mât de cocagne* (first published in Spanish in Castro's Havana in 1975, where the author had lived since 1959), with its story of Henri Postel proposing to set in motion a revolution against the Duvalieresque dictator, Zoocrate Zacharie. At the start, Postel decides not to leave his island and move to wealth in Canada but to participate in the three-day October festival of climbing the grease-besmeared *mât de cocagne*, whose winner would be especially fêted and celebrated. But Postel is an ex-senator, noted opponent of Zacharie's regime, banished to the small town of Tête-Boeuf to be zombified, after his family has been tortured and murdered. We first meet him just before he elects not to kill Zacharie's chief economic backer, Habib Moutamad, soon to be minister of commerce, but to enter the climbing competition, taking on this "moulin à vent," this windmill, pitting himself "against the risen wind" (*Mât de cocagne*, 23, 50 [hereafter abbreviated M before the page number]; *Festival*, 15, 36 [hereafter abbreviated F before the page number]). As un "petit chevalier à la triste figure mulâtre," a "little knight with a sad mulatto face" (M72, 83; F54, 64), Postel's identification with Quijote is made explicit as soon as he returns to his old shoemaker friend and neighbor, Horace Vermont, himself a local "legend," ex–school principal (M15; F8), of whom it is now said, "His face was haggard, his forehead was waxen black, his cheeks hollow—he looked like a Sancho Panza from an underdeveloped nation receiving his Don Quixote on the dawn of an uncertain campaign" (M40; F29). And such he is indeed.

"Maître Horace" had earlier thought him bound to undertake some "act that would have raised [him] back up in the esteem of [his] friends" (M25; F16). Soon Horace will be constantly calling him "Chief" and offering himself as "the stilt for him to mount" from (M40, 53; F29, 39). Like Sancho, he is a voice of popular common sense, as he is also that of hope for change. In the meantime, contemplating his decision, Postel thinks himself a victim of "always thinking, dreaming, talking too much. A bunch of words and airy thoughts that have ruined your life" (M39; F28). As Quijote's books led him into knight errantry, so do Postel's words transform him into "le sieur Henri Postel" (M61, 72; F45, 54). His opponent, Zacharie, is said by his chief minister, Clovis Barbotog, head of the National Office for the Electrification of Souls (NOFES), to be eager to take him on in "single combat with open visor" (M72; F54). The government's representative climber will "don greasy armour" to defeat Postel (M61; F45). This climbing enemy, changed for a time into the voudou *cheval* (horse) of Baron Samedi, *loa* of death (but also very much associated in the popular mind with Duvalier—an association he stressed), threatens Postel at the end of the first day of competition, telling him that he will inevitably fail if he does not have permission "from the supreme knight of violent death" (M94; F73), introducing a menace of evil that slowly changes the nature of this Quijote's enterprise. But Quijote, nonetheless, he is, and just as his predecessor was depicted by Cervantes' narrator as mad from a dried-out brain (i.e., clinically melancholic), so too, Postel suggests, Moutamad thinks him "cracked, loony, good for the booby hatch" (M30; F20), just before they arm wrestle—sinister if farcical precursor of the deadlier combat to come. Soon the Canadian sailor David Ritson agrees, calling him "timbré . . . sonné . . . dingue" (M33; F23). The NOFESian psychiatrist Dr. Primas judges him schizophrenic and worse (M50–52; F37–38). Unlike Quijote's madness, however, from which he awakens at the end and as he dies, Postel's is sanity. Rather is it the nation that must awaken from *its* madness.

This changes the cast of Quijote's quest: it becomes nothing less than transforming a history by telling and making it differently. "What's a man like you going after on the greasy pole?" Moutamad exclaims when Postel tells him his project (M30; F20). Bit by bit, the question gets its answer. Postel tells Ritson how Horace remarked that people expected more of him "than fading away in exile"; how he understands that the "pole is the only road left for" him (M34; F23–24). Later on, he will imply that his position as the "people's senator" (M45; F32) means that he is obliged to follow this path: "Who says my deed won't wake up the country?" He has, he adds to Ritson, no "magical conception of the struggle for freedom," simply a need to "make this half of the island see that there is no road left but a hard climb." Ritson berates him: that his "citizen fellow zombies won't decipher the coconut parable [he's] putting in [his] tree-trunk story," that he'll just make an ass of himself, be hissed out of town, and finally killed by a vengeful Moutamad. Postel responds that to the "egotistical adventure" of flight he prefers "the test of the pole" (M35–36; F24–25). Contrary perhaps to Cervantes' Don Quijote, the task is to turn symbol into fact, to bring the pole to life not as a symbolic ideal but as an actual revolution, to make the airy words of his early self-criticism into the gunpoint of his final victory. The pole must be brought to life, but to a particular life. Not at all surprisingly, this becomes a matter of struggle from the outset, and Postel will change the weight of Quijote with considerable aid from his enemies, who help embed the pole as a live tree and a living symbol in the land.

But it starts as something dead: as a "sinister tree—faithless and lawless, without entrails, without foliage or bird songs, the post or columnlike object most closely resembling the gallows or the cross." When he first comes across it lying in the square where it is being prepared, Postel wonders "how a tree that has lost its vegetable innocence, its sap and its song, could become a motionless, bald, and sticky monster, devouring and digesting the insolence and strength of those who aspired to conquer it" (M24; F15). Later on, as Postel prepares himself, he thinks of "the naked tree that is pulling you toward itself with all the sinister patience of its grease. It no longer remembers the wind and the sun, nor the song of rain and birds in its foliage, nor the joyful circulation of sap in its bark" (M59; F43). But one would do well to recall Césaire's land at the beginning of *Cahier*, "en rupture de faune et de flore," which by the end will be rich with hope of renewal and change, thanks to the poet's new sight. Something similar happens here. When Horace repeats the idea that the pole is nothing but a tree's "cadaver," sor Cisafleur (or Cisa), the good voudou *mambo*, angrily replies that he is talking rubbish and that "you only need to scratch this mast with a fingernail to find under the grease the true wood of life." A tree, she goes on, "always remains a *pied bois*—even without its roots and its branches, it remains a living being that has grown straight, an altar of repose for other living creatures that need its tenderness and peace (M66–67; F49–50). It is, in fact, a *pied bois*, or a *poteau mitan* (M67; F50), living road for the *loas*, good gods and spirits or bad, depending on who summons the most power. So when Postel, leaving Horace to go and sign up for the competition, assures him that "this is the only road left for me" (M42; F30), we may want to give the farewell more complex weight.

It is Quijote's road through La Mancha or Pausa, between Europe and the Americas. It is the *loa*'s path between worlds. Both need horses:

Horace, "little old horse of a shoemaker" (M55; F40); "carnival that came on its wild horses"; the horse that greets Postel with its neighing as he walks above the city preparing himself, a horse "emaciated" like Rocinante (M57–58; F42–43); the "expression of an innocent, tamed horse" that Postel recalled on the face of a person cured by a *mambo* as he is to be helped by sor Cisa (M108; F84); or the voudou "horses" that carry the *loas*, Espingel Nildevert as Baron Samedi's *cheval*, Cornélius Sébastien as that of the good papa Loko, the evil Siméon Sept-Jours-Ténébreux as that of Zacharie, who turns courtiers into their leader's *chevaux*, and tries to make the pole into one as well (M96–97, 105, 134–37; F74–75, 81–82, 106–7). This "mutualizing" of these elements is found elsewhere as well. As the winds, for example, are those of Quijote's mills, so are they those of the state that will blow him away or those of history that have to be changed. As Barbotog menaces Postel with "winds" of power that will destroy him, so Postel becomes his counter, Jean-Jacques Dessalines, defeated hope of the earlier revolution, but source here of many mutualities. Thus Postel reminds himself that the greasy pole is not the same as "that well-known bridge where one man alone was able to hold back an enemy army. Not a defile where a handful of blacks tries to stop the advance of this century's Persians" (M39; F27). The references are to local and ancient European history: Horatius Cocles' legendary defense of Rome against the Etruscans at the Sublician Bridge in the sixth century B.C.; Leonidas and his band of 300 defending Thermopylae gorge against the Persians in 480 B.C.; Dessalines ambushed and assassinated at the Pont Rouge by Alexandre Pétion and Christophe in October 1806. Postel lives at "111, avenue Dessalines, Tête-Boeuf" (M44; F32). Sor Cisa tells Horace that Dessalines died because papa Loko, who had protected him "during all the battles for independence," was not then "at his side, unfortunately." More successfully, he protected Simon Bolivar when Latin America's Liberator from colonialism was in Depestre's hometown of Jacmel in 1816 (M69; F52).

The word "unfortunately" is interesting. However dictatorial the historical Dessalines was, he is offered here as the good "head of the revolution" against the harmful dictator Christophe. So, at least, Christophe is depicted in *El reino de este mundo* by Carpentier, a writer whose influence Depestre has always acknowledged, and who may also be behind the narrator's later remark about the intricate *vèvè* that Cisa traces in honor of papa Loko when, calling on him to protect Postel as he had Dessalines, she performs the counterrite to Baron Samedi's: "inventing new motifs that corresponded to the mythical identity of the *loa* in a language born fresh from the spontaneous outflow of the marvelous and the real" (M106; F83). This intricately woven language matters (one coming perhaps as much from Machado as from Carpentier), not only because it is the new making of tongues that must restore and change Haiti's history, but because papa Loko—and with him papa Legba—is the *loa* called to save Postel and bring him victory (M108–15; F84–89). Loko it is who will elucidate the living pole's union "avec le soleil et la rosée," with the sun and the dew—perhaps another reference to Roumain's *Gouverneurs de la rosée*, story of an effort to remake Haiti. Loko is "the escort-chief for Atibon-Legba, the prince of *carrefours* and crossroads" (M67–68; F50–51). Legba is the powerful god of borders, trickster, messenger, tight bond between Africa and the Caribbean, *loa* of openings to change and difference. Associated directly with Dessalines through Legba's agent, Loko, Postel reincarnates the true revolutionary path, against Christophe/Zacharie/Duvalier's evil neocolonialism, which lives off selling its people's blood quite literally to the industrialized world. So the road open to Postel is also one of political opposition to Zacharie, one that aims actually to change history.

To do this, powerless in any concrete way, Postel/Quijote finds in the pole a potential metaphor for defeat of the state which along his road actually *becomes* the state. He gets help from his enemies as they struggle over who will control the symbol's meaning and the real action it will enable. First, it is Barbotog's NOFES that organizes the festival (M41; F30). Next, it is Barbotog's aide, Dr. Parfait Merdoie (Dr. Perfect Gooseshit), who accuses Postel of undertaking "an attack against the security of the NOFESo-Zacharian state" (M46; F33). Little by little, the Zacharians transform their pole not into a living tree, not even into an ineffective *pied bois*, but into something quite different. "What would you think," Barbotog asks Postel, "if we told you that the greasy pole, which can already be seen from that window, is a gigantic male organ splitting the sky of the capital in half?" "I'd say," replies Postel, "that the poor sky is the NOFESo-Zacharian system—and that it deserves to be slashed by that sword." Quijote's weapon is on its way to surpassing his predecessor's. Barbotog takes up the challenge by further insisting that "we shall make of this mast the symbol of our tutelary and upright power in this country." "Henri Postel," he then ends, "with your remnant of manhood, you are going to try to climb the back of the NOFESo-Zacharian state!" (M49; F35–36). In response to these exchanges, Dr. Primas writes up his very western, "freudian" psychiatric report on Postel, noting a "dual personality," a sense of "grandiosity . . . loss of a sense of reality . . . terrible adaptation to the social milieu and to the dynamism imparted to it by our Great Electrifier for Life," neurosis, a phallic fetish, paranoia, and divers other pathological tendencies (M51–52; F37–38). Parodying the individualism Postel rejects, this evaluation actually bares the grounds of the Zacharians' own sexualized and individualized neocolonial rule and interests—an individualism made patent in the private conflicts between the various members of Zacharie's coterie which will eventually cause their fall, and that of course opposes the collective voice of the people performed by Postel, Vermont, Cisa, and Elisa Valéry.

The Zacharians' fetishistic seizure of phallic power is itself mocked through the headlines of their own newspapers: "Zacharian Negritude Changes to Vertical Tigritude in Expectation of Sir Henri Postel's Arrival." Depestre himself eventually came to reject *négritude* as an essentialist inversion of the Eurocentric story, and that, I suggest, is what is depicted here through the pole as phallus: giant erection of Zacharian neocolonial dictatorship. Taking *négritude* to its essentialist limit, turning it with a vengeance into Soyinka's tigritude, the Zacharians invoke their dependency on and mediation of First World interests, wants, and demands. (Papa Doc Duvalier had always associated himself with the Griot writers and ethnologists and claimed to be champion of the "noirs" in Haiti's internal class and color politics.) The state's newspapers immediately embroider on this essentialism, depicting Postel's opposition as a pathological "racism" (M61–63; F45–47). Henceforth it will be the status of the government and its very idea of the state that will be in question. No wonder Postel has to say, "I haven't got the right to fail" (M53; F39). He has no right to fail before what a sympathetic journalist calls Zachary's "idea of erecting, on this October afternoon, his absolute power in the form of a 'Papa Phallus, a clear and evident organ defying the palm tree and the breadfruit tree in its glorious irruption towards the sky-vagina of Freedom!' as one local newspaper expressed it" (M82; F63). Barbotog had earlier said just the same. The violence here is exactly that with which the Zacharians have murdered Postel's wife and eldest daughter, with which they will murder sor Cisa, and with which they would like to murder Postel: inherent, one would say, in their sexualized individualism.

The morning after the competition's first day, after Nildevert's efforts to make the pole "the very backbone of death" (M98; F76), supported by Zacharie, who asserted him to be "one of our own (M90; F70), the people of the city of Port-au-Roi think they have seen the pole parading through the streets as "a general who has been crowned king, a certain Siegfried von Phallus, or Phalbus" (M127; F99). Nor are they so far wrong, for during the night, Zacharie has held his own ceremony, when the evil *bokor* Gloomy-Simon-Seven-Days tried to unite Zacharie and his pole, having him ride and masturbate on it, so as to infuse it with his soul and enable him to say, in echo of Louis XIV's claim in less insalubrious circumstance, "this greasy pole is my State, it is myself!" (M134–39; 151–54; F105–9, 119–21; citation on M135; F106)—paralleled in voudou religion, where Baron Samedi usually appears surrounded by obscenely gesturing subordinates. Again, thereby, Zacharie is identified with the colonizer. At the end of this ritual, the pole, now named "king-general Siegfried von Phalbus" had walked or been carried to the cathedral for blessing (F139, 153; M109, 121). This is the pole that Zacharie and Barbotog think is bound to defeat Postel/Quijote, path as it supposedly is for Baron Samedi, "knight of violent death" and even more now "the *poteau mitan* of the Spiritual-Chief-for-Life" (M99; F77) than it had been before the *bokor*'s nighttime ceremonies. But two of the climbers they think on their side are already on Postel's, Nildevert is worn out, and papa Loko and papa Legba, *loas* of life and of the living tree, prove altogether stronger. Zacharie and his cohorts failed to make their phallic symbol live and crush Postel. As Loko and Legba's *poteau mitain*, the pole brings Postel's body to youthful life, helping him move smoothly up the trunk and make his last great leap to the tripod crown.

This is the pole and the state that Postel defeats when he reaches the top at the second day's end, grabs the machine gun that is the prize at the summit, fires at the dignitaries on the rostrum, and is shot by a sniper. Quijote by now has changed: "the sadness had disappeared from his eyes . . . now shining with a kind of eager and joyful fury" (M86; F67). He has met Zaza Valéry and united with her, his "sun in all its glory," like Quijote's Dulcinea an imagined "*femme-jardin*"—garden-women, associated with the flowers we have seen and maybe, too, with the dew, *rosée*, of another Haitian history (M102; F79). He has convinced the doubters that he was not just an individualistic adventurer (M132, 155; F103, 122). He has even, on his second day's return to the pole, taken a ride to his own Calvary, through masses of beings of skin and bone, ragged, half-naked, and crippled (M157–58; F124–25). Preceding his death, this also precedes the country's fall "back into its usual silence and shadows" (M168; F133)—reminiscent of the vision of Spain held by so many of the '98 Generation. This i-mage of Postel/Quijote is nothing if not generous in its references, transplanted, says the narrator, "to the most fertile lands of my imagination" (M169; F134). And Postel did not die from the sniper's bullet or from his fall from the pole, but was picked up alive by his friends and raced away in their car, dying later: "No use, Zaza, it's the end for me. Do what I asked you a while ago. And stay on the mountain to . . ." (M172; F136). The tone altogether recalls Quijote's final melancholy "no hay pajaros . . . ," "there are no birds in yesterday's nests. . . ." But unlike his predecessor, Postel does not think he was mad, nor is it suggested that his act was in vain. On the contrary. The silence and shadows have been definitively disturbed.

Cisafleur and Elisa prepare Postel's body amidst "the hibiscus, the bougainvilleas, the amaranths, the lilacs, and the oleanders," washing it in "an infusion of orange flowers, soursop, and the physic nut tree." They felt not despair of death, says Elisa, but "after-pains of childbirth." "We are celebrating Christmas-Postel," rejoices Cisa*fleur,* the flower of whose complete name now gives fuller meaning to her earlier insistence on the living tree. It, too, marks those flowers which we have seen so much. Now as well: "we sang, danced, lived his departure, with the congo and tender movement of our bodies, to the rhythm of drums well in tune with the coursing of our blood." We have seen much, too, of these drums throbbing presence to place and culture. The women then prepare to put his body to the flames "that are going to incorporate him forever into the power of the trees in this country!" (M173–74; F138–39), irresistibly recalling Macandal, whose ambivalent burning begins Carpentier's *Reino,* whites thinking him dead, blacks finding him forever united with the fauna and flora of the land. So it is natural for Elisa to see Postel as "joyful cradle for everything good and beautiful that will be born in our land," supporting "the light, the hope, and the beauty of your people because, when you lived, you were able to enlarge their right to fight and to dream." His ashes they then mix with "the ceibas, mangoes, flamboyants, guavas, almonds, lemons, breadfruit, and other generous perfumes of our mountains" (M175; F139).

To be sure, silence and shadows take over at first. Most of the band of friends are killed horribly in the next months. Shortly, though, Zacharie and most of his cronies also die, either as a result of these events or of conflicts among themselves aggravated by them. The revolutionary days of October have after all had some effect—and Papa Doc Duvalier did die in April 1971, right after the novel's fictional October. At least in the fictive imagination, this Quijote *did* write a new history, grounded in mutuality of cultures as well as in local place, in Haiti's land, flowers, trees, religion, and culture, in "a language born fresh from the spontaneous outflow of the marvelous and the real" (M106; F83), put to use by a new Quijote. Depestre has suggested elsewhere how this language is itself embedded in Haitian traditions, recalling his childhood role as the "*audiencier* de service" and explaining "*audience*" as a "style of conversation and narration widespread among Haitians. *Audience* and '*audienciers*' impart to the unbridled story-telling of facts of life and death the liveliness of a picaresque carnival, in that reversible time and space where the Great toothed Mechanism of History turns in the Haitian manner" (*Métier*, 154, 154 n. 1). Such telling matches an idea of history as that "braid of histories" of which Bernabé, Chamoiseau, and Confiant write as of an experience and a practice needing recovery: "We had a taste of all kinds of languages, all kinds of idioms. Afraid of this uncomfortable muddle, we tried in vain to anchor it in mythical shores (exterior vision, Africa, Europe, and still today, India or America), to find shelter in the closed normality of millennial cultures, ignoring that we were the anticipation of the relations of cultures, of the future world whose signs are already showing" ("In Praise," 892), a view we have seen advanced by Glissant, Walcott, and others.

One's own history starts, then, with time springing from its own place. It may recognize others' places and times with "love," but it begins by separating itself from them. So Brathwaite's knight faces the ocean with new understanding. However decrepit, torn, tattered, and rusty he may at first seem, he assumes his place in pride:

> *ship was too early*
> *or was i too late . . .*
> running now
> one last rope stretch
> to the dockside
> tripping over a chain/chink
> in my armour
>
> but the white bows are turning
> stern coming round squat in the water
>
> and i
> older now
> more torn & tattered than my pride
> cd stand

stretch out my love to you across the morning
but cannot reach your hand
("Schooner," *Black + Blues*, 6–7)

Not surprisingly, perhaps, Brathwaite ties a later version of this poem directly to the complicated feelings of an American Quijote about the Europe whence he also brings part of himself: "I began to conceive of this encounter with Europe as a weird unexpected echo of the 'encounter' with my Father . . . with all the love doubts ambiguities + in this case of course the need for complex liberation" (*ConVERSations*, 111–12).

Old chains may get in the way, old habits impede, accusations of immaturity imply contempt, but times and places have their own rhythm, as Kincaid also insists, with "we," not "I":

The people in a small place can have no interest in the exact, or in completeness, for that would demand a careful weighing, careful consideration, careful judging, careful questioning. It would demand the invention of a silence, inside of which these things could be done. It would demand a reconsideration, an adjustment in the way they understand the existence of Time. To the people in a small place, the division of Time into the Past, the Present, and the Future does not exist. An event that occurred one hundred years ago might be as vivid to them as if it were happening at this very moment. And then, an event that is occurring at this very moment might pass before them with such dimness that it is as if it had happened one hundred years ago. No action in the present is an action planned with a view to its effect on the future. When the future, bearing its own events, arrives, its ancestry is then traced in a trancelike retrospect, at the end of which, their mouths and eyes wide with their astonishment, the people in a small place reveal themselves to be like children being shown the secrets of a magic trick. (*Small Place*, 53–54)

The magic trick is imposition of another's ordered story. To ignore that is to be turned into the other's "children," slaves or "Blacks." To know is to "reconsider," to be "older," enabled, like Quijote and his avatars, to turn unlost past into possibility of a present of one's own. These are not contraries. Perhaps, even, the one is somehow contained in the other, as particular order in what is a potential *for* order. For most of us, no doubt, just because we are born or educated to one or another, a passage or a bridge is needed to avoid falling back into familiarities. This, too, is to formulate badly a matter that concerns varieties of temporalities and the diversities of story they consequently enable—diversities, that is, in the very *conditions* of story: not *what* can be told, but how and why. One needs to understand times as composed differently by different cultures, by no means necessarily commutable (explored not only here but in Reiss, "Perioddity"). To pass between them, mediate them, a moment of suspension may be needed in which to sense these gaps and these overlappings. I shall give two concrete examples from Borges, the one of topographically noncommutable times, the other of repetitions that seem to contradict easy notions of historically linear time:

At the beginning of August, 1824, Captain Isidoro Suárez, leading a squadron of Peruvian Hussars, achieved the victory of Junín; at the beginning of August, 1824, De Quincey published a diatribe against *Wilhelm Meisters Lehrjahre*. These events were not simultaneous (they are now), for the two men died, Suárez in the city of Montevideo, De Quincey in Edinburgh, each without knowing of the other. ("New Refutation of Time," *Other Inquisitions*, 176)

The topographies need not be so distant. Of Mexico, Paz wrote, "a variety of epochs live side by side in the same areas or a very few miles apart, ignoring or devouring one another" (*Labyrinth*, 11).

My other example is from Borges' same text, after its author has queried the nature of a life abundant in repetitions of reaction and sensibility, each minutely or significantly varied by emphases of "temperature, light, general physiological state" and more, where Borges then quotes an earlier text of his where he had said just the same thing sixteen years earlier. It recounts his walking in an evening in an area of Buenos Aires familiar to him from his childhood, not so much his own neighborhood, but "the still mysterious fringe area beyond it." Arriving at a spot of such "typicality [as] made it unreal," he gazes over the simplicity of a street of ordinary poor houses, elemental clay edging on the pampa, scented with honeysuckle, limpid in the moonlight:

I thought, no doubt aloud, "this is the same as it was thirty years ago." I guessed at the date: a recent time in other countries, but already remote in this changing part of the world. . . . In the already vertiginous silence the only noise was the intemporal sound of the crickets. The easy thought, "I am in the eighteen hundreds" ceased to be a few careless words and deepened into reality. . . . I did not believe I had traveled across the presumptive waters of Time; rather I suspected I was the possessor of the reticent or absent meaning of the inconceivable word *eternity* . . . : that pure representation of homogenous facts . . . is not merely identical to the scene on that corner so many years ago; it is, without similarities or repetitions, the same. If we can perceive that identity, time is a delusion. (179–80)

The point is made as well by Gabriel García Márquez, when he says of his protagonist, José Arcadio Buendia, as all came to understand, "was the only one who had enough lucidity to sense the truth of the fact that time also stumbled and had accidents and could therefore splinter and leave an eternalized fragment in a room" (*One Hundred Years*, 283).

The issue is not "objectivity" or "subjectivity," two notions anyway inextricably entwined. And while we may think Borges' and García Márquez's examples concern individual perceptions and sensibilities (partly because of the very difficulty of grasping—even more of feeling—how time is *in* place and changes with it), they involve actualities of culture and belonging—as the second makes clear by writing of "lucidity" and "truth." Varieties of local tempo and rhythm and depth are not just matters of sensibility. They are the being of people's lives. The suspension tells us not that time is a delusion, but that its unicity is. It denies Andrés Bello's and others' thought that a "general philosophy of history . . . science of humanity" is possible (and certainly not with its source in one people) but agrees that even if it were, it could never speak to the "history of a people." Just as there can be no knowledge of geographical place without local observation, so to try to know a people's history from some general History "would be like a European geometrician trying, with the sole aid of Euclid's theorems, to draw a map of Chile from his study" ("Craft of History," 176). Whatever sort and sense of temporality inheres in a culture, the importance given to it may differ entirely from that given to it in another. Few seem to give it quite the overwhelming weight Europe's sense of linearly historical time has had in *its* culture. Even fewer have tried to give their time viceregal powers over others' stories. The knight had just cause for his sad countenance.

But the 1607, Pausa carnival put Quijote in a new story at his birth. I have been showing that that event just gave an early start to later reincarnations of the knight, nominally literal, like Depestre's recounting of his Haitian carnival, or only inferential. Two-thirds through Marshall's *The Chosen Place, the Timeless People*, another carnival lets further implications be drawn. This one occurs every year in the capital of Bourne Island, New Bristol. Here, groups from across the island create new floats every year and a great day-long festival fills the streets. One town only refuses to change its float, "backward" Bournehills. Each year its people show, over and over again, the island's only historical event of note: the violent and unsuccessful revolt of Cuffee Ned. Each year, they are duly ridiculed. Each year, however, as they repeat their display through the streets, they eventually take over the carnival in a great joyous outburst that possesses the whole town, and, this time, almost kills the clearest representative of western rectitude (280–98).

Later, the novel's main protagonists, Merle Kinbona and Saul Amron, she from Bournehills, he working in its parish to create some sort of cooperative agricultural project, discuss the float and its effects: "people," he concludes, "who've truly been wronged . . . must at some point, if they mean to come into their own, start using their history to their advantage" (315).

Bournehills faces New Bristol and the rest of the island not only as a disliked and feared oddity but as a "trapped quarry" (57) taking on a neo-colonized capital that lives and works wholly in the shadow of Britain and its history, never "trusting its own" and not believing "deep inside us that we can plan and do for ourselves": "I tell you," says Merle, "they colonized our minds but good in this place" (129). That is why in Bournehills she was fired from school for "telling the children about Cuffee Ned and things that happened in olden times, when the headmaster wanted her to teach the history that was down in the books, that told all about the English" (32). For Cuffee Ned, cries Ferguson with a "voice soaring like that of an Old testament prophet," is one

who's goin' to come again I tell you. . . . Ain't one of you ignoramuses ever heard of the second coming? Well, who the bloody hell you think they was talking about if not Cuffee? . . . "O ye of little faith!" . . . They couldn't kill off someone like Cuffee Ned. (134–35)

Cuffee Ned has something of the tattered Christ seen before, Quijote taking up and uniting many displaced pasts. In his "second com-ing," he is like the Indio-African Macandal of Carpentier's *Kingdom of This World* (or Postel at the end of Depestre's *Mât de cocagne*), who simul-taneously inhabits two histories, burned alive and dying in the European, saved and living in the Antillean, returning in any one of a whole myste-rious "cycle of metamorphoses" to plunge "into the black waves of the sea of slaves," to free them and make a new culture (*Kingdom*, 35–36). In a way, Merle *is* Cuffee Ned. She herself is the real figure of remaking, so nearly identified with the old revolutionary. Her most basic creed, pro-jected on and through Bournehills, lived out in the inn she has made from her decrepit and noble old house, is that "a person has to go back, really back—to have a sense, an understanding of all that's gone before to make them—before they can go forward" (468).

Through Saul's project, this historical imperative dwells in the very geography of the place. Unlike the impositions recounted by Carew's Quijote, Marshall's character seeks at every turn *not* to destroy the land as his predecessors have, tearing down whole hills to stop agricultural slip-page, just as Carew's outsiders killed the land with chemical fertilizers (66). "There are two kinds of projects," his Quijote had said:

There's that United Nations one at Mardi Gras, a big boss drives up in a jeep every now and then, and tells us poor folks what to do, then he drives back to his air-conditioned office and his drinks and social life . . . then there's the other kind where you work shoulder to shoulder.

For the last kind, "science, technology and culture[s are] fruit of the same tree." Geographies and histories intermingle, warp and weft of a single car-pet: "woven into the cultural matrix of peasant communities like threads into cloth" ("Harvesting," 159–60, 167).

Just so, Saul wants to grasp the symbiosis of land and life, of people and crops, time and place (141, 157) in this island lying in its sea like "one more in the line of steppingstones that might have been placed there long ago by some giant race to span the distance between the Americas, North and South" (13). Islands and broken seas shape the being, understanding, and living rhythms of those who inhabit them. They offer, too, a topogra-phy so particular as readily to escape seizure by histories of others' places. One is reminded of Brathwaite's reiterated figure of the islands as an arc made by skipping flat stones across the face of ocean ("Calypso," *Rights of Passage*, in *Arrivants*, 48). Bournehills comes to be the very place of a new forging of time:

a place in which had been stored the relics and remains of the era recorded in the faded prints on the walls, where one not only felt that other time existing intact, still alive, a palpable presence beneath the everyday reality, but saw it as well at every turn, often without realizing it. Bournehills, its shabby woebegone hills and spent land, its odd people who at times seemed older than themselves, might have been selected as the repository of the history which reached beyond it to include the hemisphere north and south. (402)

"Deep down, at a depth to which only a few would be permitted to pene-trate, it would remain fixed and rooted in that other time, . . . a lasting tes-timony," but bound tightly, in its "ravaged hills and . . . blight visible every-where," to a present whose form it also makes; again like that ravaged and tattered Quijote of old.

Some of the "few," the novel tells us, could come from that different place and time represented not just by Saul's presence, but by his active in-tervention. Although this proves calamitous to himself, it is absorbed into those new rhythms sought by so many, just as is the Revolution in Carpentier's *Siglo*, whose very symbol comes early in the novel, with Socrates' bust turned into the god of a mestizo curative garden (*Explosion*, 45; *Siglo*, 45–46). Crossing the Atlantic, Esteban eventually wants something similar to happen to the revolution itself, that it be "jumbled and disordered" by and into realities of a different place. As it is, the Revolution is an "Event" (*Acontecimiento*) which, moving from its own place, "was simplified in people's minds, . . . reduced to its basic elements [*esquemas*] and pared of contradictions" (E117; S120). This first change is precisely that fictional, even mythic, reduction we saw before. Later, it is no longer opposed to and imposed on an Other ("totemic" to "theological Man" in some "Auto Sacramental del Gran Teatro del Mundo" putting Europe, Christ, and the Cross violently in the Americas; E244; S251), but adjusted to a different sort of growth. Set adrift from Hugues' Revolution in Guadeloupe to sail as a privateer, Esteban experiences another kind of *Event*, one binding him otherwise and with other force to different time and place and rhythms.

Sailing through the islands, Esteban is first struck by the "pluralidad de las playas" and on them by how the sea reworks the varied glasses of Europe, fallen from ships, floating across oceans, becoming carved and shaped into local stones and minerals. The very "Idea of the Sea," with its abundant and ever varied life, its forging rhythms, and its swaying beauties, give Esteban a sense of living in "a world of symbiosis," where language grew from the multiplying forms of vegetation, marine creatures, rock formations, words making a fantastic bestiary whose reference was, though, real (E175; S179). Like "the plurality of beaches" and multiplicity of forms, these connections are actually many: *las simbiosis*. Their allegory was best caught by dolphins, that

would spiral in concert, integrating themselves into the wave's very existence, their lively movements, as they paused, leapt, fell back and rested, so closely identified with it, that they seemed to bear the wave on their bodies, to lend it their own rhythms and measure, their own tempo and sequence. . . .

Sometimes a great silence foreshadowing an Event [*Acontecimiento*] would fall over the water, and then some enormous, belated, obsolete fish would appear, a fish from another epoch. . . .

When it soon disappears, the sea seems to return to its everyday "Gran Teatro de la Universal Devoración." But, as it did the later Auto Sacramental, this *Acontecimiento* has also changed the place and time of the Revolution whose name it has taken (E177–79; S180–83)—like Bournehills in Bourne island, one might say.

Carpentier's spirals and waves suggest a different shaping of culture, one for which history, as González Echevarría has put it, is "not so much elucidation as cultural self-recognition" ("Socrates," 51). The novel's central image, the painting "Explosion in a Cathedral," with its shattered pillars suspended in space and others still intact, seems "a presage of resistence, endurance and reconstructions, after times of ruins and stars prophesying abysms" ("como un anuncio de resistencia, perdurabilidad y reconstrucciones, después de tiempos de estragos y de estrellas anunciadores de abismos"; E253; S259; my translation). This possibility, and pride of Brathwaite's quayside knight, is imaged not in oppositional constructs like line and circle, taken somehow to correspond to reason and emotion, same and other, closed and open, expansion and embrace. Rather does it take forms like Carpentier's mingling of stars. Or it is found by Walcott's Achille, come "home" to Africa (*Omeros*, 141), in the sense of what he calls "pre-history,/that itching instinct in the criss-crossed net/of their palms, its wickerwork" (150), not, it may be, without its correspondence in the "thudding metre" of the sea "on a morning beach" (249).

But by the end of *Omeros*, these images have slipped from its narrator's grasp. He finds he has been caught in an old myth, where Philoctete's cure makes him an "Adam" in a new "Eden" (248), or he has written the same old fictions: "What I had read and rewritten till literature/was guilty as History . . . mine to make what I wanted" (271–72). Perhaps he had too much wanted to skip "centuries, ocean and river, and Time itself" (134) to places not his own, here where "a quiet culture/is branching from the white ribs of each ancestor" (296), where "the mirror of History/has melted and, beneath it, a patient, hybrid organism/grows in his cruciform shadow" (297). In this, too, coral eyes or no, Adam still lies, who would unite, thinks the narrator still, an "East and West," a "New/World, made exactly like the Old, halves of one brain" (319). At least one critic, Jahan Ramazani, argues that Walcott has successfully "indigenized" Philoctete—as others have Caliban, as Brathwaite has Uncle Tom in *The Arrivants*, as Jean Rhys has Bertha Rochester in *Wide Sargasso Sea*, and as many have Don Quijote, I propose here (407). He shows how Philoctete's wound not only binds him to other wounded figures in *Omeros*, but ties Greece to Africa, Europe to the Caribbean, while at the same time embedding him in a familiar slave past:

> His knee was radiant iron,
> his chest was a sack of ice, and behind the bars
>
> of his rusted teeth, like a mongoose in a cage,
> a scream was mad to come out; his tongue tickled its claws
> on the roof of his mouth, rattling its bars in rage
>
> (*Omeros*, 21; "Wound," 406)

This certainly names conditions of black enslavement, portraying "the pain of the wound as colonizing Philoctete's entire body" ("Wound," 407). It also echoes Pope's, Eliot's, Saramago's disease, Venice's ghetto. How to tame these ambiguities? Perhaps one need not. Yet the "halves of one brain" united in a new Adam seem different from Harris' mutualities or Glissant's *relation*. But maybe Philoctete's cure by the combined "sibyl" and "obeah-woman" Ma Kilman *does* join Greece, Africa, and the Caribbean; perhaps it is a creolization of such a sort ("Wound," 411).

Yet now another nightmare (294) knight may come, led along hellish paths of volcanic Malebolge, where live "Hephaestus or Ogun" (289), "not for Omeros's gods, . . . but for the One that gathered his race/in the shoal of a net" (292). As Dante was guided by Vergil, the new poet is guided by dead Omeros. But God's grace in Dante's second guide, Beatrice, who momentarily left her foot prints in Hell to save the poet, sardonically disappears into the "charred face" of "Hector in hell" rising like the devil's: memory, perhaps, of Dürer's famed engraving, *Knight, Devil and Death*. For this very Christian knight does not join Quijote in embodying an idea of the fictive imagination overcoming deathly trammels of settled history. On the contrary, Walcott's knight affirms Unamuno's faith, imposing his place, time, and story on *his* world's most awful antagonists. This too renews fictive bonds with a European history "rewritten" into literature: not just Dürer and his contemporary Erasmus, whose 1524 *Enchiridion militaris christiani* depicted this Christian knight invulnerable in his armor, his faith and warrior's power, riding like Despestre's Zacharie with "visor raised seeing neither death nor the devil at his side" (Bataillon, 1:209) and imposing the Cross others planted on the Americas, but Sciascia's *Death and the Knight*, Dürrenmatt's *Judge and His Hangman* and *The Quarry*, Nooteboom's *Knight Has Died*. The crates of books keep coming. . . .

This cannot matter in one sense, even though it makes the poet feel deeply ill at ease. For unless these images and artifacts are embedded in different arenas, built, as the sea does Esteban's glass, into "hybrid" shapes whose meaning is made from its different time and place, one risks collapsing into a same history. The God who masters the shoals of *Omeros'* narrator's net is surely Dürer's, however reduced; "these Helens are different creatures" (313), but to have *begun* by naming differences the same (he says) is to have assured what seem the final hesitant regrets of *Omeros'* poet. The almost, but not quite, final carnival might have enacted such difference of place and reworking of time as we saw it do in Marshall—in Depestre, or at Pausa. Here, for all its mingling of geographies and genders (Philoctete and Achille play women in this carnival), it leads only to Philoctete "pick[ing] up the coins on the street" (273–77), pale echo of Carpentier's consumerist Calvary and that History whose time Borges sought to refute, as do Kincaid and Carpentier, Brathwaite and Marshall, Depestre and indeed Walcott—if not at this end.

Usually, for the fictive imagination and in life, carnival becomes a profounder celebration of cultural self-recognition and affirmation. It clearly does in Marshall's *Chosen Place*. There, it actually forges the union of what dwells in local memory and abides in the land with its people's manner of inhabiting place. It embeds culture's historical reason in its local habitation. This working has its image in little, when Merle tells a story of "Spider, the wily hero of the Anancy tales told throughout the islands":

who, though small and weak, always managed to outwit the larger and stronger creatures in this world, including man, by his wit and cunning. In the fretwork of sunlight and shade under the tree the children's eyes as they listened were enormous, huge wells, reservoirs they seemed to him, which were storing everything she was saying against some future use. (*Chosen Place*, 224)

Here, in fact, Marshall is picking up on another side of the people's history. The broad imaging of their vital soul in memories of Cuffee Ned and the deep continuity of cultural pasts kept alive by the storytellers' living voices join traces of earlier *literary* tradition. For Marshall is echoing lines from the early twentieth-century Jamaican poet, Tropica (Mary Adella Wolcott), telling how "the Nanas of past days" related:

> The strange "Anancy" stories,
> And legends weird and old
> Which after patient coaxing
> Were in the twilight told
> To breathless, wide-eyed children.
> ("Nana," 42–43)

These, she wrote in 1904, were "hardly hear[d] to—day;/A few faint echoes linger—/The rest have passed away."

That lament for lost cultures, write Marshall and others, begins to be put behind. Their stories can now be stored "against some *future* use." The cultures they embed are to be recovered and reset in new-built and new-found ways. The webbed fretwork of Anancy's activities meets Penelope's weaving and Achille's wickerwork. They do even more when one recalls how the indigenous spider woman of the Americas was brought to or dwelt in the islands. So in Schwarz-Bart's *Pluie et vent sur Télumée Miracle*, Toussine shows Télumée what village life is:

Picking up a dry branch, she started to draw a shape in the loose earth at her feet. It looked like a spider's web, with the threads intersecting to make ridiculously tiny little houses . . . That's Fond-Zombi. . . . You see, the houses are nothing without the threads that join them together. . . . And what you feel in the afternoon under your tree is nothing but a thread that the village weaves and throws out to you and to your cabin. (*Pluie*, 127 [hereafter abbreviated P before the page number]; *Bridge*, 84–85 [hereafter abbreviated B before the page number])

When Télumée's life is broken after her husband goes bad, she "saw there was no longer any thread linking my cabin to the others" (P153; B104). The villagers show her "that there couldn't be a gap in the weft," passing to and fro before her cabin, a woman approaching from time to time, calling to her, giving her "the strange feeling that she was throwing me a thread in the air, throwing a light, light thread toward my cabin" (P160–61; B109–10). At the last, the whole village of La Ramée recovers Télumée, its people giving her a plot of land and place in their life.

> Such is Anancy's weaving, too, squatting
> on the tips
>
> > of our language
> > black burr of conundrums
> > eye corner of ghosts, ancient his-
> > tories;
> >
> > he spins drum-
> > beats, silver skin
> > webs of sound
> > through the villages

He bears and makes stories of the poor and the islands, "black iron-eye'd eater, the many eye'd maker,/creator/dry stony world-maker, word-breaker,/ creator . . ." (Brathwaite, "Ananse," *Islands, Arrivants*, 165–67). He is, as Marshall says, a constant of these Caribbean tellings. Joining, not "opposing" line and circle, he is Carew's woven cultural matrix. He is Harris' web of rivers as God's spider's weaving (see Chapter 9). He is Brathwaite's vèvè in echo of sor Cisa's conjuring Loko and Legba, grounded in the island lands:

> and from this tennament
> this sipple spider space of land we hold
> we make this narrow thread of silver silver
> spin against the long time of sand
> ("Vèvè," *X/Self, Ancestors*)

He counters "erasures" of "reason" with "numinous glyphs of love" incised as Brathwaite's *timehri*. The whole landscape "*is* the central spider/ in our web of dreams/that weaves the net of Eldorado" (McWatt, "Heartland," *Language*, 27). Thus it meets the shuffling of Esteban's stars, spirals of his dolphins, criss-crossings of waves, and the ever-repeated image of the interweavings of the "mangrove's green and gold" amidst "the river's tidal swelling" (McWatt, "Ibis," *Language*, 17). Winding their roots through the swamps mangroves *are* this interwoven history and geography, whether Walcott's, with "their ankles in water" (*Omeros*, 133), Harris' imaging a landscape where water, earth, and sky intertwine as inextricable forms, Condé's, figuring the twisted bonds of an entire community, freeing if you fully know "their form, their nature, how far they dig to get water," deadly if you "get impaled on the roots" or "suffocated in the brackish mud" (*Traversée*, 170, 192), or Césaire's "bitter mangroves" whose roots pull together flora and fauna in a poem depicting the poet as one who joins and overcomes contraries ("Moi, laminaire," *Lyric and Dramatic Poetry*, 88). These "mangroves at the water's edge,/their plumbing exposed by the tide," McWatt meditates in turn, may not always be gentle to human imaginings,

> Yet roots and branches form the web
> woven by that spider sun
> to sift the alluvial souls of rivers
> and trap their sins as they run
> to the sea's salt, purgatorial troughs
> where soul and substance become one.
> ("Benediction," *Language*, 29)

Spider, mangrove, glyphs on rocks, countercurrents in waves, stars' spiraling are sources that knit a fictive imagination. They are evidence alive of Glissant's *poétique de la relation*, of a politics, too, and a culture. "The history of the diverse intonation of a few metaphors" may or may not be the "universal history" Borges proposes ("Pascal's Sphere," *Other Inquisitions*, 9). But that history may help forge bridges of understanding, and its metaphors, however imprecise at first telling, are sources of a single whole *imaginaire*, rooted in the curious operations and minutiae of local memory that blooms into new histories, the sort of history, maybe, that we saw Descartes and others probing and Seneca's bees constructing in Chapters 4 and 5. They are the flowers we saw in earlier chapters, the islands' fauna and flora reborn as histories' ground. These are the sources and weavers of mutualities, of that "cultural creolization" which "establishes a cross-cultural relationship," argues Glissant, "in an egalitarian and unprecedented way, between histories that we know today in the Caribbean are inter-related. The civilization of cassava, sweet potato, pepper, and tobacco points to the future of this cross-cultural process; this is why it struggles to repossess the memory of its fragmented past" (*Caribbean*, 249).

So I name these i-mages because they shape a different history, not one figured as oppositional or "other." Walcott once wrote, "the new poet enters a flux, as the weaver continues the pattern" ("Muse," 12). These "spinning songs of the spider," as Brathwaite has it, "Kwaku Ananse who gleams/in the darkness/and captures our underground fears" (*Barabajan Poems*, 79), does not proffer an "Africa of dreams" (76), nor a Europe to make one "plummet down full fathom five under" (41). It limns a poetry "more polytone and complex" (115) and draws a culture, as Marshall agrees, "from 'below'—from the ground from the underground coralwater . from these people from 'the poor'" (172). Quijote refurbishes his armor from tatters and tears of many memories and many places, standing firm and deep in the ground of *this* place, rejoicing in the light of her Antillean morning. People and geography, writing and history shape from trainbeat and jazz, from Legba and Pentecostalism, from Shango and Christian hymns, a wild web (187) whose glory is that even as it forms these into the recognition of a culture of *home*, drawn up from its own coralwater and its own seas and made from its own time, it recognizes them as rooted bonds with different places and times; not imposed, but absorbed and given back; not knocking down or forcing walls, but making a common story from a place and its many pasts.

11

Urban Imaginings: Histories and Geographies of Place

But different places made a different story from Quijote, even perhaps in the country of his first American performance. This other story will take us into a different confirmation of the last chapter's argument about the Caribbean, as to its writers' grounding of histories in geography. As I began that chapter with Quijote in Peru, it may not be amiss to begin this one with him still there, via Mariátegui's comments on the Peruvian poet Alberto Guillén's *Deucalión* (1920), a "song of embarkation," where "[t]his new knight errant does not watch over his arms in any inn. He has no horse, no squire, no armor. He walks naked and serious, like Rodin's John the Baptist":

> Yesterday I went out naked
> to challenge Fate:
> for a shield, my pride;
> for a helmet, Mambrino's.
> (Mariátegui, 258)

This time, the poet has only been "unlucky and ridiculous," and he knows he "carries the ironic Sancho crouched in his soul. He is not completely deluded or altogether mad. He sees the grotesque and comic side of his wanderings." All uncertainties have to be questioned in the light of an "imperious" search for definitive solution. Whatever doubt may arise, it can be cast off and replaced by "determination," "devil's temptation" or no. But as such doubt does nonetheless "work its way into his conscience, corrupting and weakening it," as the poet comes to agree "with the devil that 'we do not know who is right, Quixote or Panza,'" so he becomes "uncertain and mistrustful," moves toward Nietzsche's "Myth" and "chooses the road of faith. His quixotism has lost its candor and purity. It has become pragmatic" (Mariátegui, 259–60).

According to Mariátegui, we may say, Guillén had moved toward Dürer's knight. He then will find an echo in Zea and the philosopher's overriding idea that Latin America's task was to become the vanguard of a western History by retrieving its lost "Erasmian catholic spirituality" and by setting History back on that right track from which it had deviated (*Role*, 122–23, 220–24, 247). Zea did not think western history "universal" or history "par excellence," but he did argue that Latin America would be renewed by participating "in the empire established by the West but by giving it a different meaning from that intended by its founders" (*Role*, 247). On Europe, he found Spengler not entirely wrong, but urged that the West's decline could be halted if Latin America became its History's new vanguard. This is surely the idea of History that Spengler, like Azorín, Maeztu, and Unamuno, associated with the decadent western city? Guillén and Zea thought it potentially and ultimately good and renewing. For others, it will be as disastrous as the four just named thought it. This is not to say that Zea's—or others'—versions of history (or History) have been or are dominant. It is to propose that debates about cultural creation and constitution focus on concepts and experiences of history.

For whatever the core claim, central to much Latin American writing seems to have been not the "geographic" prism just explored, but a historical one very frequently focused on some version or experience of the city. In this, it can often be compared directly to the Caribbean fictive imagination, not as country to city—which would, as preceding chapters make clear, be foolish nonsense—nor as myth to history, but as two different kinds of historical imagining. No doubt the Caribbean's plantation legacy and an island sense of boundedness are both at least partly responsible for a sense of the importance of a geography of the land. Indeed, Glissant sees it as the very ground of his world of *Relation* where "Alejo Carpentier then meets Faulkner, Edward Kamau Brathwaite joins Lezama Lima, I recognize myself in Derek Walcott, we rejoice in the rollings-up of time [*les enroulés du temps*] in García Márquez's century of solitude. The ruined Plantation has touched all round the cultures of the Americas" (*Poétique*, 86). On the other hand, many Latin American writers have had much to say about the importance, there, of the city, as counter to and emulator of European metropolitan centers and as *historical* marker of the establishment of local authority and tradition.

In this regard, as Jean Franco shows in "Virtual Cities," Italo Calvino's *Invisible Cities* has become a favorite reference in Latin America for imagining changing forms of the urban in our increasingly globalized world. Having used Calvino's work to begin this book, this and Franco's point of departure in an earlier version of Chapter 1 seem now to turn these contemplations on the fictive imagination and its action in sociopolitical and cultural life into a kind of Calvinian *Castle of Crossed Destinies*. So it is appropriate to continue for a moment with some remarks about writing and the city drawn from this other novel of his. For, among other things, Calvino spoke to the grandiose western idea of literature as Angel Rama's lettered city in full *concertación* with political authority and Zea's History, reducing it to size with nice irony: "Of all this, writing warns like the oracle and purifies like the tragedy. So it is nothing to make a problem of. Writing, in short, has a subsoil which belongs to the species, or at least to civilization, or a least to certain income brackets" (*Castle*, 103–104). One may read this as a comment on Borges' literate city of immortals, casting its "famous" presence on Others, "barbarous regions, where the earth is mother of monsters" ("The Immortal," *Labyrinths*, 137). For cities of this sort are places of oppression, whose cinematic version would be Fritz Lang's fascist *Metropolis*, geometric parody of reason's imposition on space and people. Calvino, Rama, and Borges were all three tying the modern West's reason and "literature" directly to its institutions of power.

Rama argued that the conquerors' efforts to impose Europe's cities on the razed cities of the Americas—imagined and idealized as those "European" cities necessarily were, "technocratic fictions" of ordered law, society, politics, science, and culture, said Kusch, set over and against such fears of the primitive as Borges' "monsters" (*Ciudad*, 10, 13, 15–16)—and the various forms of writers' collusion with that dominion made for an association of letters and power unique to the Americas. I have proposed elsewhere that it was in fact less unique than might appear. Calvino's *Castle of Crossed Destinies* replied to a similar European association, replacing this view of the city of letters with a tavern of crossed destinies where a mute traveler chooses his tale at random from a pack of signs whose permutations may be finite, but whose meanings are limitless. Sense is lost in pursuit of permutation. Literature is no longer revelation but an outpouring of signs whose babble may be interpreted at will—if the traveler's muteness is not an absolute impediment. This undermines any claim not just to singular dominion, but to *any* dominion whatsoever.[1]

If the remark cited from Calvino invokes imposition of a Lima or a new Mexico City on geographies of different homelands, his dance of permutable signs recalls José Joaquín Brunner's use of his Tamara as the ideal postmodern city replying to and superseding such cities and their impositions, a city of "signs that dance without end, through which identities are made and unmade, constituting us as the changing subjects of modernity" ("Tradicionalismo," 189; cf. Franco, 429). But the dance of signs querying the Enlightenment city is not an alternative to it, nor has it anything in common with the weaving i-mages of the Caribbean writings we have been seeing. On the contrary, it is farce on tragedy, parodying, Borges wrote, its immortals' predecessor, "mad city" of inversions, irregularities, dead ends, and labyrinths, staining "the past and the future and in some way even jeopardiz[ing] the stars" (*Labyrinths*, 144, 141). Its immortal citizens, leaving the city to its own devices, have become troglodytes dwelling in coffin-size caves and given over entirely to abstract meditation, like the gods of another tale in whom "centuries of fell and fugitive life had atrophied the human element" ("Ragnarök," *Labyrinths*, 277).

Boundless megalopolis is not only a place whose citizens are alienated because they have no clear access to authority's core, but one whose rulers are unaccountable because the paths of that authority are so imprecise as to be rendered effectively invisible. As Ngũgĩ observes in a different context, they and the unspoken hidden terror that can accompany them create an aura of "mystery . . . suspense . . . secrecy," enabling a "culture of silence and fear" and depriving people of open lines of response to "coercive violence." There is nothing precise on which to focus (*Detained*, 19 and *passim*; cf. Taussig, *Shamanism*, 8). And what, to return to Brunner, could be less able to contest hidden lines of authority than an identity that can no longer be established? Brunner's own status as lettered intellectual turned government minister is surely an issue here. The dance of signs must be seen as a question (Franco implies in analyzing Brunner's use of Calvino), not a solution. Brunner's Tamara stands in fact as little more than the old lettered city's "other," not a real place but an idealized opposite of the colonial and then Enlightened city of ordered words—exactly as Borges had seen it. Further, Franco observes, this ideal "is possible only because of the amnesia that erases the violence of change" (429). We shall see how the

Chilean writer Diamela Eltit, in *Vaca sagrada*, relating narrative reaction to just such a city, where "all the signs began to disintegrate," comes close to a direct reply to Brunner's encomium of the brave new city putatively constituting its floating subjects of modernity (*Sacred Cow*, 15).

Suggesting some sort of new and original creation, this city actually reinscribes a familiar history: metropolitan and colonial imposition on its many varied and increasingly underdeveloped "peripheral" others (Frank, *Capitalism*, 17, 25, 53; *Latin America*, 5–6, 226). Its imagining now conceals the patterns of authority by, among other things, claiming to have moved away from its history, to have remade itself in a quite new form. But that is surely just one kind of mythmaking? For can it be true that "real cities no longer evoke any imaginable order" (Franco, 427)? They exist, after all, in specific geographies. They embody particular histories. They contain, hidden or not, specific forms of authority which use or put to use the "dance of signs." One thinks of Carlos Monsiváis' tale of Cantinflas, who first had success in Mexico City's vaudeville tents by managing accidentally to echo in words the proliferating city's "abyss of meaninglessness," and who last became fixed legend, mocked participant in games of the political elite and purveyor of repeated film versions of a rise from rags to riches and married happiness: "ferocious" dispossessed lumpen become "inoffensive" rogue at the service of the elites (*Mexican Postcards*, 95, 99; see also 88–105), subjugated and subjugating carnival in the service of order. *This* carnival is a very different one from Pausa's, Depestre's, or Marshall's.

The megalopolis with its proliferating barrios, industrial and semi-industrial wastelands and parklands typically surrounding financial and commercial cores, exactly depicts and manifests relations between owners of global capital, their local representatives, and the many different levels of workers producing it. This city remains an "instrument of conquest" (Frank, *Capitalism*, 123). It is one link in a chain of "metropolis/satellite structures" that starts with western "centres" and ends with the most distant producer from whom a surplus for expropriation/appropriation is available for extraction (Frank, *Capitalism*, 17–19; *Latin America*, 6). Calvino's cities may provide a "seductive parable" (Franco, 427), but they can do so only if one remains attentive to the risk of losing touch with realities on the ground. They hardly offer ungrounded models for establishing cities—geographical urban spaces and political civil societies—from scratch. This is not, of course, to suggest that analysis of the imaginary should fade before sociological studies such as Alan Gilbert's *The Latin*

American City, or *The Urban Caribbean*, by Alejandro Portes et al. (the reason for whose mention will become apparent). The stories people tell are part of their real world. But the imaginary and "facts on the ground" are in a dialectic in which the material is one boundary. Franco's essay to which I refer is exemplary in its efforts to maintain this dialectic.

Calvino himself was always conscious of the writer's responsibility to history—hence his sarcasm in the passage I quoted. It is not just that his cities are imaginary. It is that they are also, as Calvino's Polo said to the Khan, versions of Venice, versions not just of one western traveler's "home" but of that city central to the western imagination, archetype in many ways, we have seen, of western culture and western imperial, economic, and cultural pretensions (*Invisible Cities*, 86–87). Not for nothing did the conquistadors find and destroy Tenochtitlán, its Mexican counterpart, and then rebuild it as an even more glorious Venice in a "New World": imposing an imagined European history on an American geography. In this regard, Hernán Cortés was precise when he wrote to Charles I about the city's rebuilding:

I assure Your Majesty that each day it grows more noble, so that just as before it was capital and center of all these provinces so it shall be henceforth. And it is being so built that the Spaniards will be strong and secure and well in charge of the natives, who will be unable to harm them in any way. (*Cartas*, 185; *Letters*, 270)[2]

With Cortés' arrival, writes Frank, "a single and integral society was rapidly formed—totally integrated, furthermore, into the world system of mercantilist expansion and capitalist development." Elsewhere he cites the Secretary General of the Latin American Center for Research in the Social Sciences on the permanently "privileged position of the city" in Latin America: "It was founded by the Conqueror to serve the same ends that it still serves today; to incorporate the indigenous population into the economy brought and developed by that Conqueror and his descendants. The regional city was an instrument of conquest and is still today an instrument of domination" (*Latin America*, 321, 5–6).[3] Kusch proposes the affective counterpart to this reality in his critique of the imported European city as a technocratic fiction settled onto indigenous reality, ordered society and rational law set over the "vegetal" actuality of the land and its peoples, marking a "passage from shade to light," Renaissance city of power commanding but tempted by and incorporating the indigenous as "a dream" (*Ciudad*, 7, 21–26). Shades of Aeschylus' Athena founding her city's lawful polity, standing stone tall in and over the countryside. Symbolic and imaginary understandings do not just supplement economic and sociopolitical actuality, they are essential to their functioning.

Reacting to something like that imposition, Calvino himself already had the warning we saw in reply to Kublai's wish for a simple map, whether of a joyous utopia or a dystopic inferno:

> The inferno of the living is not something that will be; if there is one, it is what is already here, the inferno where we live every day, that we form by being together. There are two ways to escape suffering it. The first is easy for many: accept the inferno and become such a part of it that you no longer see it. The second is risky and demands constant vigilance and apprehension: seek and learn to recognize who and what, in the midst of the inferno, are not inferno, then make them endure, give them space. (*Invisible Cities*, 164–65)

Here too Ngũgĩ is pointed, analogously remarking "two types of political prisoners: those who finally succumbed and said 'yes' to an oppressive system; and those who defied and maintained 'Never!' " Of these, the first walk into "the abyss of despair to a valley of white bones" (*Detained*, 81). They do so because to recognize those "who are not inferno" depends on knowing particular histories and geographies and patterns of authority—no less than did Cortés. And these—especially the first two—remain among my principal themes in this last chapter. So, too, also continuing earlier chapters' concerns are some of the many ways in which history informs the present.

One of them may well make something like García Márquez's Macondo, included third between imaginary Enlightened Eldorado and the postmodern Tamara of Brunner's, not Calvino's, imagining. And it may have something to do with the Caribbean music of Edgardo Rodríguez Juliá's *El entierro de Cortijo*, a music weaving together multiple elements mostly found among the people (like González Prada's—or Bovelles'—proliferation of popular language). Both of these are central elements in Franco's argument about the "postmodern" city. But one of the things I want to suggest is a major difference between those Caribbean histories and geographies of which we have already seen much and Latin American ones.[4]

To this I'll return, but first I'd like to observe another moment of crossed destinies, speaking quite remarkably to the intersection of Franco's story with concrete actuality—and so, again, to the place of history, and particularly, here, to continuing effort to impose History.

Some sardonic ironist must have presided over my first reading Franco's essay on the same day as a *New York Times* story about Pope John Paul II's October 1997 visit to Latin America. She writes of "the grip of Catholic religion, traditional morality and the national imaginary," brought over and continued by European conquest and sustained by and for the lettered city, and of how these are now questioned by a "recycling of whatever is at hand" (Franco, 426). In the *New York Times*, Calvin Sims (and how to explain this new *Calvin*? more crossed destinies), in an article filed from Rio de Janeiro and bizarrely titled "Brazil Is Likely to Wink at Pope's Call to Behave," repeated the opposition. He noted the themes of the Pope's visit in startlingly similar terms. "Human life starting in the mother's belly" (*dixit* John Paul), family values, and humanity were set against "a different drummer," "secularization" of same-sex marriages, "steamy soap operas," "revealing bathing suits," "suggestive dances," and videos—shameful modern technology, one supposes—from Disney to porn. This catches precisely the contrast between the inflicted old and a new sought in the proliferated recycling of almost anything. Monsiváis has offered an equally remarkably similar version of this contrast. He observes on the one hand how "the Church verbalizes, amid homilies and absolutions [like the Pope's in Rio], the landowner's dream: that history and society do not change, and that respect for owners will be eternal." He writes on the other of the proliferating, overcrowded, polluted, catastrophic, apocalyptic city, where nonetheless "optimism wins out." "And the result is: *Mexico, the post-apocalyptic city* . . . [where] everyone takes from the resulting chaos the visual and vital rewards they need and which, in a way, compensate for whatever makes life unlivable" (*Mexican Postcards*, 4, 35)—leaving intact lines of authority marked by the first side of the contrast, wielding real power against the chaos of signs.

These analyses show just how *actual* the issue is, and why questions of history—and music—matter. For there is more to this than the opposition between Rama's lettered city and Brunner's city of signs.

This is where I want to come back to Rodríguez Juliá. For does it not matter that Puerto Rico has a Caribbean, not a Latin American history, whose fragments and ruins are very different? In the first, peoples and their cultures were indeed obliterated, "almost totally eradicated, eroded and destroyed . . . within thirty years of Columbus" (Brathwaite, *ConVERSations*, 199). Cortés was very aware that the near-total cultural and material destruction wrought by the Spanish invaders in the Caribbean islands required that he experiment with different colonizing methods in "New Spain."[5] His letters are full of remarks not only about the need to form and maintain suitable alliances, but also to settle, plant, and farm in an already populated land in appropriate ways—as he specifies was not done in Hispaniola or Fernandina (Cuba).[6] Cortés did not see the empire he was invading as a tabula rasa. On the contrary, it required military and political imposition, diplomatic jobbery, and cultural dominance. Césaire was exact in saying that "neither Cortez discovering Mexico from the top of the great teocalli, nor Pizarro before Cusco (much less Marco Polo before Cambaluc), claims that he is the harbinger of a superior order . . . they kill . . . they plunder . . . they have helmets, lances, cupidities" (*Discourse*, 10–11). We have seen Frank, too, lucid on the actualities of colonial expansion, whose "instruments were then, as they have been since, conquest, pillage, plantations, slavery, investment, unequal trade, and the use of armed force and political pressure" (*Capitalism*, 151). Taking account of local realities in this light, Cortés distinguished sharply between what had happened in the Antilles and what he hoped could occur in New Spain.

The difference—and its awareness—goes back, then, to invasion and conquest. Brathwaite is far from alone in writing of how Caribbean literatures—or, rather, cultures—are being created from the shreds of the many cultures whose remnants can be picked from the history of the past five hundred years and inflected by their placement in an island geography and home. In his Nobel lecture, Walcott spoke of recomposing shards and fragments of a broken vase. But the vase never existed before its present creation. It only ever was the "thousand conflictive fragments" of which Rodríguez Juliá writes (*Entierro*, 96); it only ever was the *permanencia* of the repeated musical phrase, culled from Cortijo's popular music and picked up and transformed by myriad voices, but also into the voice that sets the local worker into his own Borinquen, an Eldorado of, say, Harris' or McWatt's imagining, not Raleigh's: a point made many times, precisely in regard to music and writing, by Brathwaite and others, for whom jazz riffs and train blues provide fragmented rhythms echoing a broken past but also composing a vital present and future. Tourist T-shirt and Levi shoes become affirmation of being home.

Here, we come back to the kind of "bricolage" that the Pope saw as undermining real Catholic, western values. Perhaps it offers a way to build something anew. Rodríguez Juliá's description of a worker's incongruous wearing of a tourist T-shirt, with its palm trees and tropical sunset, both marks the yawning gap between the reality of poverty and the kitsch tourism that lives off that poverty and the worker's yearning for and self-association with "his Beautiful Borinquen" (*Entierro,* 18–19). I am reminded of Cobham's brief discussion of a poem by Lorna Goodison recording a similar appropriation in Jamaican form:

> For sometimes it would suit a one
> to write him name upon himself.
> In case Babylon stop you
> and fraid claim your tongue
> in which case you could just
> look down and remind you eye
> and say "Yes oppressor
>
> I name is Levi."
>
> (Goodison, *Selected Poems,* 92)

Cobham points out how Goodison is playing here with "'I and I,' 'the double first person of Dread Talk that appropriates and disables the subject 'I' of Standard English, reaching back to the self as and as part of a deeper essence. The last line of the poem can thus be heard as 'I name is—leave I,' which bears a symbolic valency quite distinct from that of the white authority 'Levi' 'originally' inscribed in the speaker's shoe" ("What's Real," 52–53).

The complex appropriation of supposedly dominant images creates new spaces and new cultural realities. Philip in turn takes up this way to question such images to create the potential of an altogether wider geographic determination, marking/making an i-mage for the possible break from a past of imposed histories. This double i signals a clear choice, she writes, for the Caribbean, in this case her home island of Tobago:

> A piece of land—a piece of real estate surrounded by water. Or, a piece of land floating—keeping itself afloat consciously, responsibly and responsively. Island, *I-land,* or *I an' I land.* Sycorax *and* Caliban or Caliban alone. That is the stark choice facing us on *I-land* today—it permeating every activity while Prospero continuing and working his white magic. (*Genealogy,* 173)

Whether or not this and other such figures—or their manner—mark a difference between geographical and historical arenas is itself something to consider. But that is surely the point. For something else—perhaps differently complex—may be the case for Latin America.

A difference between imagined Caribbean cities and those of main-

land Latin America may be suggested by an odd meeting of fictive imaginings. In his 1949 prologue to *El reino de este mundo*, Carpentier described
the seekers of "the Fountain of Eternal Youth, . . . the Golden City of
Manoa" and others as marking a new American reality (*Kingdom*, unpaginated [xii]). Elaborating the thought fifteen years later (1964), Carpentier
turned the earliest apologia for the conquistadors into the kind of mixing
of signs offered by Brunner's reading of Calvino:

Open Bernal Díaz del Castillo's great chronicle and you find the only real and be-
lievable book of chivalry that has been written—a book of chivalry where the cast-
ers of evil spells were visible and palpable *teules* [spirits or "gods"], where unknown
beasts were real, where unimagined [*ignotas*] cities were actually gazed upon, where
you saw dragons in their rivers and mountains strange with their snows and
smoke. ("De lo real," 72)[7]

It is no doubt the case that what Diana de Armas Wilson calls "perhaps the
hoariest example of this discursive drift" toward the chivalric is to be found
in Díaz's comment about their first sight of Mexico City: "Y decíamos que
parecía a las cosas de encantamiento que cuentan en el libro de Amadís, por
las grandes torres y cues y edificios que tenían dentro en el agua" ("and we
said that it seemed like the enchanted things told in the book of Amadis,
because of the great towers and temples and buildings standing in the
water"; *Historia*, 147; Wilson, 235). But the remark is really far more exception than rule. Don Quijote was not here riding through the *campos de
Castilla*.

  For this "Caribbeanized" version was on the whole *not* how Díaz
himself imagined Mexico and the Americas in the *Historia* first published
in Madrid in 1632. *His* story was Cortés' (or Césaire's), one of opposing
powers facing each other through an already urban landscape—which the
Spaniards took it upon themselves to transform. And they did so as a tale
of two cities. Díaz's conquistadors were using the might of superior military
technology (guns and horses) and the manipulation of political differences
to impose themselves on a landscape and its histories. From the very beginning of his narrative, Mexico/Tenochtitlán *was* Venice:

Some curious readers and other people who have been in New Spain have heard it
said in Spain that Mexico is a very great city and built in the water like Venice; and
it had a great lord who was king there over many provinces and ruled all these
lands of New Spain that are more than twice as large as our Castille.

Too, this prince, Montezuma, was always seeking to obtain greater power and rule over more lands (*Historia*, 23). He was, that is to say, ruler of an empire entirely comparable to that of Spain. Much later, Díaz was to wonder at the powers of the conquistadors just because so few had succeeded in capturing "una fuerta ciudad como es México, que es mayor que Venecia [so strong a city as Mexico, which is greater than Venice]" (185).

As a matter of simple fact, Díaz was quite correct. In the fifteenth century already, "built in the middle of the lake of Texcoco, Tenochtitlán, with its network of canals, became the largest agglomeration of the American world at that time, with more than 150,000, and possibly more than 200,000 residents" (Gruzinski, *Conquest*, 7). Inga Clendinnen puts the city's size by 1519 as "of perhaps 200,000 or more inhabitants" ("Cortés," 89). Carew holds that it was even bigger, with a population "at least three times larger" than the 120,000 of the neighboring city of Teotihuacán ("African Presence in the Americas," *Fulcrums*, 151). By comparison, Venice, with a population around 40,000 in the thirteenth century, never exceeded about 170,000 at the height of its power and prestige in the fifteenth century (at the time of its 1797 defeat by Bonaparte, its population was 139,000). Small wonder if "Cortés was sensitive to the physical beauty and social complexity of the great city of Tenochtitlán. It was the dream of the city which had fired his ambition and provided the focus for all his action. We must remember that Tenochtitlán was a marvel, eclipsing all other cities in Mesoamerica in size, elegance, order, and magnificence of spectacle" (Clendinnen, 119–20).

So Díaz told a story to be marveled at as a victory of David over Goliath, whose "magic" was Christianity and whose reality was one of justified conquest of an abusive, treacherous, and cruel imperial power. He justified their killing, pillage, and rapine on grounds that they were rescuing other indigenous peoples from the thievery and dominion of Montezuma and his Mexicans. He argued against Bartolomé de las Casas, for example, that their massacre of Mexicans in the city of Cholula was not, as the bishop of Chiapas had all too convincingly claimed, merely an amusement and pastime but punishment for a particular piece of Mexican treachery (*Historia*, 150). Díaz presupposed both the Spaniards' right to be in Mexico and that what was at stake was a confrontation between two different imperial forces. Certainly it was an unequal one. But it was unequal to the Mexicans' not the Spaniards' advantage.

As Díaz told it, the story of the invasion and conquest was one of reshaping an already urbanized landscape. Far from unimaginable or unknown, its towns and cities created familiar settings for military skirmishes and battles and a familiar framework for diplomatic maneuver. Díaz did not at all create any myth like the later North American one of an empty and deserted wilderness to be populated by Europeans as first comers—a myth, one may add, as alive now as greed made it almost from the start. Thus, Elizabeth Mankin Kornhauser, cocurator of a 1998 Hartford, Connecticut, exhibit of nineteenth-century American (and Australian) landscapes, can startlingly speak of "English and European" settler artists "confronting an alien wilderness and transforming that wilderness into a symbol of national identity"—this of a show and in a newspaper article both ruled by the myth, showing no sign and making no mention of the land's indigenous occupants (cited in Shulman). Díaz dwelt in no such myth.[8] On the contrary, he offered the very populousness of central American lands as justifying the play of power. The number of cities with their different populations showed Aztec power as itself an imposition. Paz observed that "the large number of cities and cultures" characteristic of Mexico "at the arrival of Cortés," with their "diversity" and "the rivalries that lacerated them," revealed "a complex of autonomous peoples, nations and cultures, each with its own traditions, exactly as in the Mediterranean and other cultural arenas. Mesoamerica was a historical world in itself" (*Labyrinth*, 90). Jacques Soustelle proposed that since the thirteenth-century Toltec era, conditions had been quite comparable to those of Renaissance Italian city-states (*Daily Life of the Aztecs*, cited in León-Portilla, 28–29). Mexican invasions from the north had not at all changed these conditions. Díaz and his companions found a world whose ground, if not its superstructure, was—or could easily be made—familiar.

Tenochtitlán emblematized Díaz's story of urban conquest and of renaming a landscape, its towns, and its cities into Europe. So he recounted Cortés' first great battle at the Mayan city of Potonchán (also called Champotón), which the victorious Spaniards then renamed Santa María de la Victoria (*Historia*, 55–56). Or they built new towns—like la Villa Rica de la Vera Cruz (81–82). These and others were not unimagined or unimaginable cities. Neither Díaz nor Cortés expressed any surprise at finding them, even if Tenochtitlán's magnificence was cause for amazement. They proved that Mexican societies functioned like European ones. Customs, geography, clothing, and food might differ. Use and operation of power and authority were the same. Cortés was precise about it, remarking apropos the city and province of Tlaxcala, for instance, that their form of government was "almost like that of the states of Venice and Genoa or Pisa" (*Cartas*, 45; *Letters*, 68). That was why sites of battles and diplomacy were without exception towns and cities, from Cempoal to Tlaxcala, from Cholula to Tenochtitlán itself. The final siege of Tenotchtitlán began with an encirclement achieved by a series of battles whose recounting insisted on its being from city to city, town to town. To build a city on top of an Aztec city or a Catholic church on an Indian temple was an extreme mark of coercive incorporation (Zea, 177). To rename or appropriate an earlier name for oneself (as the Spaniards did in Mexico/Tenochtitlán) signaled a change in dominion. To destroy the Aztecs' "idols" and replace them with the cross and figure of the Virgin, as Cortés did or tried to do everywhere, marked a change in political authority by imposing the narrative of a different history.

In that sense, Cortés and Díaz told similar stories. Early in his second letter, for example, Cortés explained how his first alliance with an indigenous people somehow allowed him to rename their home: "I set out from the city of Cempoal, which I named Sevilla." He soon did the same with another of their cities, Nautecal, "which is now called Almería" (*Cartas*, 34, 36; *Letters*, 50, 53). The practice was constant and an essential part and sign of conquest. Serge Gruzinski tells how between 1578 and 1585 throughout New Spain "*corregidores* and *alcaldes mayores* convened responsible officials of the Indian *pueblos*" to complete a vast questionnaire developed in 1577 by Philip II's chronicler and cosmographer, Juan López de Velasco. It asked "the Indians to account for . . . naming, ordering, geography, history, population, living conditions and way of life, languages, roads, distances, political regime and far more from as far back as the informants could go." Such a survey inevitably "imposed in the process a view of society, politics, religion and economy, in other words, a classification of reality with its prefabrication, its presuppositions, its explicit and implicit logic, its tacit axioms, its unconscious organization. It forced all indigenous informants to provide data sifted through categories and associations that were not necessarily theirs" ("Mémoires sur commande," *Colonisation*, 101–103, and see 101–37; *Conquest*, 70–71, 73, and see 70–97).[9] The claim of familiarity, the supposition that indigenous reality was—or could be—a version of the European self, however marked by exoticized *alteración*, grounded these forms and terms of imposition.[10]

The likeness between the powerful lake cities of Venice and Tenochtitlán was not lost, we have already seen, on other Renaissance Europeans. Differences in culture and fortune never hid identity of power.

That, no doubt, was why the mid-sixteenth-century humanists Fracastoro and Cornaro imagined and planned recreating Venice *as* Tenochtitlán (Tafuri, 152–53). As I wrote in Chapter 1, just to have destroyed the by then legendary lake-capital of Aztec civilization and to have built an imagined European city on top of it was not enough. It had to be absorbed, removed from its home, appropriated, made into a literally contained "other" of Europe's "same," familiar object of imposed History. Others, like Giulio Ballino in his *Disegni delle più illustri città et fortezze del mondo*, published in Venice in 1569, were satisfied to recount "Temistitan" and its "inhabi-tants' life, work and manners" as vanished ghosts from the past, available only to archeological reconstruction. This America "was accordingly a dead thing" (Ambrosini, *Paesi*, 171–72). Yet others simply made the Mexican capital disappear. In his 1575 dialogue *Il gentilhuomo*, Girolamo Muzio had a speaker say of Venice that "Of other cities one can say that one is like an-other . . . ; but of Venice one can give no other example." "Yet I have heard," another protested, "that in the new world there is a similar, named (if I remember aright) Temistitan." So many fables people scatter about, replied his interlocutor: "I'm talking to you about this sure old world, in which I've never heard either young or old say he's seen another city so miraculous" (*Gentilhuomo*, 53–54; cited in Ambrosini, *Paesi*, 187–88).

And these Venetians did not envy Tenochtitlan for nothing. Its power was real. In some ways, so it potentially remained. For what is now Latin America never lost its peoples and its cultures in the same way as did the Caribbean. Not until later (as Césaire observed to be the case in all such colonial instances) did las Casas' vehement criticisms of the sheer brutality of conquest give rise to the story of innocence betrayed, "childish world" ruined, healthy paradise sickened, and powerlessness overwhelmed, as told for example by Montaigne of Tenochtitlán, Cuzco, and their kings (*Essai*, III.6; *Oeuvres*, 886–94). Others still saw the contest between Tenochtitlán and Venice as one between equally strong powers. Thus in his *Licenciado Vidriera*, published with the other *Novelas ejemplares* in 1613, but written probably in 1605, Cervantes related how his protagonist, Tomás Rodaja, spent his youth traveling, going at one point by sea to Venice:

a city which if Columbus had not been born would have no equal in the world: thanks be to heaven and the great Hernando Cortés, who conquered the great city of Mexico, so that great Venice came to have something of a rival. These two fa-mous cities are alike in that their streets are all water; the European one wonder of the old world; the American one, marvel of the new. (*Novelas*, 2:50–51)

Of course, by this time, Tenochtitlán had become Spanish México, and its new inhabitants could take a view slightly different from the Venetians', seeing their capital city as greater than its European counterpart. Already in the dialogues he published in 1554 in emulation of Vives and in praise of the city and its university, Francisco Cervantes de Salazar had a wide-eyed visitor exclaim, "So great is the profusion of boats, so great that of freight canoes, splendid for business, that there is no reason to hold them less or fewer than those of Venice" (*México*, 52).[11] Twenty years later, in a verse *Epístola* to the city's *primer corregidor* (chief magistrate), another visitor, the poet Juan de la Cueva, compared México favorably with Venice as a city of equal opulence and greater delight (quoted in Reyes Cano, 73–75), although, we shall see, he later—once home in Spain—became rather indifferent. A year or two before Miguel de Cervantes and writing from Mexican Guadalajara, Bernardo de Balbuena again suggested the city's bustling size through the familiar Venetian comparison (and more):

This great city has paved roads built over the water, which despite their size become narrow for its many people; so that neither did the Greek horse make a bridge over the Trojan wall so full of weapons, nor did skillful Ulysses lead so many; nor, when cold Arcturus strips the trees, does he so cover the hard ground with dried leaves as always and ever on these roads and highways do masses of people intermingle. (*Grandeza mexicana*, 64, Capítulo [Cap.] I)

I shall later propose that Balbuena's purpose in his poem was precisely to offer Mexico City, twice named as greater than a Venice which could now no longer compete with it, as a European imposition on the Americas. Symbolically, here, Tenochtitlán *was* being absorbed by Venice, becoming a European construct in and on the indigenous world.

If the American world did not lose its cultures and its peoples as the Caribbean did, it still then had to fight against being caught in someone else's story, one turning it into the European other told by Montaigne and endlessly by many others since. A version of this is Murena's view of Latin Americans as fallen from the grace of a European Eden and Zea's close echo of it in his argument that Latin Americans feel themselves outcast Europeans, and so exiled from History, uninterested in making a new world (unlike the Protestants of North America) and eager only to recreate Europe in America—albeit eventually a better one (*Role*, 3–27)—hence their planting of European cities and symbols on Indian ones. Edmundo O'Gorman's America was invented from a European history (*Invención*). In the struggle against such entrapment, "Latin America" no doubt lost particular historical narratives. But it never lost them altogether, as one of Fuentes' expositors experiences in the midst of the hollow postmodernity of Mexico City, centuries since tumbled over and beyond the drained waters of Montezuma's, Cuauhtemoc's, and Cortés' Tenochtitlán:

Federico's knees buried themselves in the earth: surface-dry earth of forever-hidden lagoon, lagoon at the ancient, damp, froglike core, the place of meeting between men. He felt understanding through his body. Far from his bone and blood, in other lives which in this moment of defeat and rendered flesh were his own life, the mute lives which had fed him, he felt the true meaning. Those mute lives whose names he could not remember multiplied in mortal pantomime until they covered all Mexico with failures and downfalls and assassinations and battles. Then they came back again and spoke to him, recognized him, their own body. (*Where the Air Is Clear*, 341)

Mexico City, here, is a place of memory and forgetting, a place of *histories* which are always present to be recalled or to surface of their own accord. Indeed, Fuentes' novel deeply concerns a tension between fragmented "European" modernity and ever-present Aztec past (Van Delden, 11–32). So, too, does Macondo, also expressing a reality different from what seems possible in the Caribbean, where shards do have to be forged anew. But there, where the indigenous never disappeared, a different sort of *mestizaje* may be made from native and imposed. The indigenous remains in its histories and in the ways in which geography, place, serves and is ruled by those histories. The Mexican present is unimaginable, Fuentes remarks, without "the Indian past" (and its present), within which "we are historical beings" (Szanto, "Epilogue," 156, 158). "Any contact with the Mexican people," Paz agreed, "reveals that the ancient beliefs and customs are still in existence beneath western forms." Its "spirit," he added, "has not gone away, . . . it has gone into hiding" (*Labyrinth*, 89; *Other Mexico*, 286). But the extent to which debate is cast in terms only of *history* is noteworthy. For O'Gorman, wrote Paz, "America" was absolutely not "a geographical region" (*Labyrinth*, 170). Murena saw Americans as especially characterized by "a greater distance with regard to the world [una mayor distancia respecto al mundo]." Increased *distance* from geographical place marked historical progress ("Pecado," 201). Such views and feelings differ markedly from what one finds among Caribbean writers.

Rama seems accidentally to have caught just this in recalling how the

Venezuelan/Chilean intellectual, Andrés Bello, in his 1823 "Allocution to Poetry" (asking poetry to leave Europe and inhabit America), "had proposed two great American themes: Nature and History. But only history attracted wide attention from Latin American poets in the ensuing years," poets, precisely, of *la ciudad letrada*, raised in colonial and neocolonial practice. That they differed in this from those dwelling in Caribbean situations is implied by what follows: "the sumptuous descriptions of José María Heredia notwithstanding, their treatments of Nature remained mostly cosmetic imitations of the European schools from which they were copied, without the authentic accent attained by their treatment of other, heroic or amorous, themes." José Martí, he then adds,

was unusual in his tenacious defense of natural themes, even as they rapidly lost favor everywhere toward the end of the nineteenth century. During the course of that century, no Latin American Thoreau went to inhabit the solitude of nature and write a diary about its glories. Latin American writers lived and wrote in cities and, if possible, capital cities, remaining resolutely urban people, however much they sprinkled their works with the naturalistic details required by the literary vogue of local color. (*Lettered City*, 60–61)

Rama fails to mention that both Heredia and Martí were Cubans. This may go far to explain the difference between their writing and that of Latin Americans as to the imaginative weight of geography and history. This difference, I shall suggest toward the end of this chapter by looking at two celebrated seventeenth-century poems written by Cuban and Mexican contemporaries, goes back to beginnings of the postinvasion American imagination and to Cortés' earlier perception of material contrast between conquest in the Caribbean and conquest in the mainland.

Macondo is one kind of a "third" city between Venice's imaginary and the postmodern megalopolis, one that in its own history passes from newly created colonial town through neocolonial underdevelopment to city of proliferating mingled signs and last disappearance, a tale for which "history is the base," as José David Saldívar puts it (*Dialectics*, 27). The earliest version of García Márquez's town, *La hojarasca*, even while marking its passage through neocolonial dependence and destruction, ended on a note of optimism quite similar to that noted by Rodríguez Juliá at the end of *Entierro*: "Yo pienso: *Ahora sentirán el olor. Ahora todos los alcaravanes se pondrán a cantar*" ("I think: *Now they'll get the smell. Now all the curlews will start to sing*"; *Hojarasca*, 184, *Leaf Storm*, 97). It was as if the author, writing of Columbia's Caribbean coast, might allow some Caribbean sense of place to take over. By the end of *One Hundred Years of Solitude*, a more pessimistic tone has set in, there being "no second opportunity on earth" (336). *This* dystopic city, destroyed into apocalypse by the Banana Company, had passed through a phase in many ways common to Caribbean and Latin American experience: the neocolonial city of Babylon—to use a Caribbean noun describing it—a worsening of the Enlightenment city already oppressive in its displacement, one that, far from hiding its power, deploys it everywhere, forcing its inhabitants to "live," as Monsiváis puts it of a different case, "under the terrible weight of the rules of a game imposed and sustained by others" (*Mexican Postcards*, 61). Such a one is the Fort-de-France of Césaire's *Cahier*, the Kingston of Orlando Patterson's *Children of Sisyphus*, or of Brathwaite's *Trench Town Rock*, or the Santa Lucia of Namba Roy's *No Black Sparrows*. Unlike the last, at least, the Macondo of *One Hundred Years* has "no second opportunity."

Such a one, too, is the capital city of Carpentier's dictator in *El recurso del metodo*. But in that novel, it is only one of several cities. For *Recurso* ironically poses these complexities by playing five cities against one another. Carpentier's dictator often lives in the metropolis of Paris, for which Descartes' writing becomes a sardonic commentary on his protagonist's inversion, abuse, or just overelaboration of Enlightenment values (colonialism into neocolonialism, if you will). At the outset, the dictator returns home from Paris to put down a revolt in the course of which he attempts to destroy the old renamed indigenous city of Nueva Córdoba that will come back to haunt him as the place of origin of his eventual overthrow. Before that, however, he transforms his once-colonial capital city into a kitsch vision of the Enlightened city, one finally flooded by the forces of authority. As it crumbles around the dictator during his last years and months in power, it reveals itself, in fact, to be the megalopolis that Franco describes and that the Pope fears and scorns: a city of proliferating signs. Even "Macondo" has its place in Carpentier's equation, in the curiously mixed and hybrid coastal city of Puerto Araguato and its environs to which the dictator finds himself oddly and constantly attracted. This was perhaps Carpentier's version of Latin American histories. In *Recurso*, geography is always the victim of its rewriting into someone's history. In that, it is quite different from a novel like *El siglo de las luces*, centered in Cuba and telling a tale, we saw in Chapter 10, in which history is subordinated to geography.

The presence and absence of history may account for the intricacies of novels like those of the Argentinian Ricardo Piglia and the Chilean Eltit.

And this concern gives these novels a different sort of end. In his *Ciudad ausente*, as Franco observes (430–32), Piglia explores how the "city," one's place, is but the matter of the endless histories through which it can be told. If you can't recall the language for telling these histories, their place itself falls into oblivion (*Ciudad*, 124). Losing ability to recount a stable narrative produces an empty proliferation of signs. Unlike Rodríguez Juliá's Caribbean music, picked up as part of a *bricolage* to mark a *place's* continuing sense of itself, Piglia's Berenson insists on the futility of repeating broken bits of melody, precisely because they are deprived of place— "Humphry Chimden Earwicker's bar," in this instance (*Ciudad*, 127–28). The abstracting and aestheticizing Joycean reference is itself not indifferent here to the caustic loss, exactly, of a sense of place. One might read a novel like *La ciudad ausente* as a desperate attempt to find histories to counter the terrible violence of that authority whose source the megalopolis of proliferating signs manages to conceal. The novel's final narrator, deaf and blind as she is, represents herself as the singer of a song ("soy la cantora, la que canta") that is not a found shard, but the historical record of lost waters: "at the edge of the water I can still remember the old lost voices, I am alone in the sun, no one approaches, no one comes, but I shall keep going, the desert is before me, the sun burns the stones, sometimes I drag myself, but I shall keep going, up to the edges of the water, yes" (*Ciudad*, 178). Franco's comment is exact: "the 'yes' of Molly Bloom is here spoken by a Borgesian troglodyte. Yet, the ending resonates not only with Joyce and Beckett but with a very different novel, *Los vigilantes*, by the Chilean writer, Diamela Eltit" (432).

For Eltit also explores a city that is off (and *of*) the margin of the Enlightened city's Other, one that developed, however, *from* it—the megalopolitan and repressive postmodern city of alienating proliferations of signs. It may be that at the end of *Los vigilantes* her refuseniks go in search of different homes. But those homes are, potentially, there—Macondo perhaps or perhaps not—and they were theirs from the start. Eltit is overwhelmed by the sense of how the authoritative city of signs consumes its inhabitants, how its very signs (if it suffices so to call them), as her foreword to the English translation of *Lumpérica* suggests, at once hide and manifest "negative, sordid, prying power" (*E. Luminata*, 4). Yet manifestation *does* allow, however painfully and haltingly, a tracing of new histories from old—as for the novelist herself: "when one lives in a world that is collapsing, constructing a book perhaps may be one of the few survival tactics" (5).

Eltit's protagonists imagine their histories as she does herself, who not seldom appears as or fuses with those protagonists: as happens in *E. Luminata*. In this novel, authority has literal shape in an insistently intrusive interrogator. The protagonist's nighttime existence takes order from a neon sign fitfully illuminating the square where she is. This sign is in fact many signs. Its changing words and forms enable the protagonist to forge various means of struggle against the power whose nighttime curfew she (and other "pale people") is defying: not just protest by burning and cutting her body (as Eltit once did) but by rediscovering histories: of Incas, Romans, and the Bible from the past, of Mapuche Indians and writers like Stéphane Mallarmé, Joyce, Juan Rulfo, and Severo Sarduy from the present.[12] These are tips of histories whose deep and broad continuities offer diverse pasts as living resistance to the present interrogatories of power—which manipulate the same histories.

The city can consume its inhabitants by using particular histories. The difficult relation of *The Fourth World*'s narrators with the city in which they live and its inhabitants owes much to the place's labyrinthine form (its proliferating signs) and its ties to neocolonial forms of authority, its submission to and ordering by "the most powerful nation in the world" (Eltit, *Fourth World*, 87). This is a nation that may change "names every century" (84), but which nonetheless always directs its subalterns into similar historical paths, repeating Cortés' and Díaz's stories in one form or another. Eltit's incestuous twin narrators, breeding a deformed offspring, turn to one another in rejection of the horrors of deformations inflicted by neocolonial violence, which threatens here to take the city altogether out of its history and make it only the abstract of another's story:

> The city, fallen into collapse, already a fiction. Only the name of the city remains, because everything else has been sold on the open market. Amid the anarchy of supply and demand, the last items are auctioned off, amid accusations of sham and fraud. (113)

In this novel, while everyone else leaves, the two main protagonists remain trapped in their imploded city. But one wonders whether the protagonists' strugglingly difficult departure at the end of Eltit's *Los vigilantes* (Franco, 432–33) expresses very much more "hope." These cities do seem to consume their inhabitants just because they come from and lie in specific histories, histories that can be among the terrible signings of authority. But these are available as well to their victims.

This is clear in *Vaca sagrada*, a novel, as I said, that could be read almost as a reply to Brunner and his "changing subject of modernity" made by the dancing signs of his vaunted postmodern city. Here, the five comingled protagonists (Francisca, Manuel, Ana, Sergio, and Marta) all speak as versions of a single narrator, a narrator who—as one of her voices says—"always detested unnecessary attachment to places and particularly nostalgic attachment" (*Sacred Cow*, 3). She sets herself in "apprenticeship to the *map* of the city, the city's bodies, the city's features" (11; my italics), and tries to *read* the city and find herself in that reading. But the signs "disintegrate" (15). Far from offering a "changing subject" as a profound new "good," this opens the protagonists to rounds of terrible bloody violence, of men on women, of powerful on powerless. This subject is all too clearly the victim of entrenched forms of power, whether sexual or political.

There has to be another way to turn the "countless lines of energy" making up this "modern labyrinth" (65) into a story that would be something other than "one more repetition of [this] human agenda," of this submission to self destruction: "she passionately loathed the humility of this repetition, the meagreness of the scope of human conduct" (77). In memory and the demand to "remember" (92), the multiple narrator finds an alternative, one that does not just "invent . . . a combination of names," write "a history for myself," or be "nothing more than a mouth consumed by the clamour of the city centre" (103–104): Brunner's postmodern subject exactly. Summoning memory, the narrator—now almost fused with the author—begins "the agonising journey of retracing [her] own steps, decoding the hieroglyphics on the fringes of [her] mind." She can avoid the oppressive city's "history whose course was exceedingly dangerous" (105) by collecting together hers as part of different histories—here, for example, as the *machi*, Araucanian shamaness whose ritual support by a man reverses dominance (87).[13] So she "catalogues" her "boxful of artifacts" (106), her pieces of history, into the story we have just finished reading.

These are curiously abstract histories that mesh with Murena's, O'Gorman's, or Zea's idea of an America abstracted from what would be its own specific *place*. One might come back, here, to Calvino, remarking the hard end of a long story made by a western literary canon culminating in Macbeth's final lament and "ours": wishing "the syntax o' *The World* were now undone, that the playing cards were shuffled, the folios' pages, the mirror-shards of the disaster" (*Castle*, 120). These are the shards of a different history, albeit one that for five centuries sought to impose itself

globally—as it continues to wish to do in aged papal imaginings and is contested for doing in the Mexico of Fuentes' stories, the Chile of Eltit's, the
Argentina of Piglia's. And *if* by chance that history *has* been broken, its
shards can well enter new stories. But stories that are also different from
one another, to the precise extent that they belong to different (*not*
"Other") places and to different histories, indeed, to different *kinds* of history. What is remarkable about the stories just explored is the degree to
which telling and retelling subsume altogether anything like a sense of
place—or, indeed, make it, "*map*" it out of the very telling. Picking their
way through the multiple narratives of their cities, the protagonists of these
novels make those narratives the mark of their presence, forging their own
geography from narrative: "she was no decoration for the square [*la plaza*]
but just the reverse: the square was her page, only that" (Eltit, *E. Luminata*,
100). The city becomes a palimpsest on which to trace new stories. To a degree, that has been a main point in distinguishing between historical and
geographical imaginations. For as I have argued here and in other chapters,
the play of history and geography is quite different in Caribbean writing.
That difference tells us something about diversities of cultures in general
and in particular about how cultural instruments/*rationes* are fruitfully
turned into loci and ways of exchange, acquiring new meanings in the
precise sense that they cohere in processes belonging to quite different
cultures.

In this regard, I mentioned before two early seventeenth-century
poems, one written in Mexico, the other in Cuba. The first is again Balbuena's *La grandeza mexicana*, written in 1603 and published in 1604. The
second is Silvestre de Balboa's *Espejo de paciencia*, written between 1604 and
1608. Both made ample use of geographic context. Balbuena indeed pur-
ported to offer an exact description of Mexico City. He had come to the
country in 1584 at the age of twenty-two to join his father, who had come
twenty years before. After two years in the capital, he had gone to
Guadalajara to take orders and begin religious studies. In 1590, he had won
a prize in the poetry competition to celebrate the arrival of the new viceroy
Luis de Velasco in the capital, and, although living in Guadalajara, it appears that he continued to go as often as he could to Mexico City. So when
a friend asked him about the capital's wonders, he was well placed to recount them.[14]

González Echavarría follows Picón Salas in arguing that Balbuena
was remarkable for how, in his "great poem," he mingled elements taken

from "the Old and the New World," whose "plants, animals, and mythology" were incorporated in its descriptions ("Reflections," 144–45). They then quote:

> La plata del Pirú, de Chile el oro
> viene a parar aquí y de Terrenate
> clavo fino y canela de Tidoro.
>   De Cambray telas, de Quinsay rescate,
> de Sicilia coral, de Siria nardo,
> de Arabia encienso, y de Ormuz granate;
>   diamantes de la India, y del gallardo
> Scita balajes y esmeraldas finas,
> de Goa marfíl, de Siam ébano pardo. . . .
>
> Silver from Peru, and from Chile gold
> comes to lodge here and from Ternate
> fine clove and cinnamon from Tidore.
>   From Cambrai fabrics, from Kinsai contraband,
> from Sicily coral, from Syria nard,
> from Arabia incense, and from Ormuz garnet;
>   diamonds from India, and from valiant
> Scythia fine rubies and emeralds,
> From Goa ivory, from Siam dark ebony. . . .
>   (Balbuena, *Grandeza*, 77)

The list goes on for seven more tercets with the wealth brought to the city from around the world. After much more of like kind, this third Capítulo of the poem (as Balbuena called his Cantos) ended with several more tercets showing how Mexico City was at the center of the imperial trading world.

Actually, what is "remarkable" about this passage, contrary to what the two aforementioned critics urge, is that it contains *no* indigenous elements: silver and gold, specialties from the Spice Islands, fabric, money, perfumes, jewels and more from around the Mediterranean, the Middle East, Asia Minor, and the Far East. The city was a place, Balbuena did insist, that brought together peoples "diferentes en lenguas y naciones" (65, Cap. I), but their languages and nations were not indigenous. México was a trading center greater even than Venice (70, Cap. II; 80, Cap. IV). That may be why Kinsai, their Chinese counterpart, is recalled—the one place, further, whose trade is imprecise (*rescate*).[15] The poet excitedly sang his refrain of the city as a treasury of Indian ivory, Arabian perfumes, Biscayan steel, Dalmatian gold, Peruvian silver, Moluccan spices, Japanese silk, South Sea pearls, Chinese mother-of-pearl, Tyrian purple, North African dates. In México, "Spain joins with China,/Italy with Japan, and in sum/ a whole world in traffic and science [*disciplina*]" (90–91, Cap. V). Balbuena certainly recognized in his *Compendio apologético en alabanza de la poesía* (*Apologetic epitome in praise of poetry*) that the land's first peoples had their own histories, not lacking "poems and songs in which they preserve[d] from memory to memory the ancient and famous deeds of their ancestors." He saw these as equal in purpose to "the ancients romances of our Spain" (135). But they were of no further interest to him either in the *Compendio* or in *La grandeza mexicana*. México was a new center for that imperial Spain whose soldiers tramped (and trumped) the same world whence the city drew its global treasures, India, Malabar, Japan, China, the Moluccas, Africa . . . (122, Cap. Último). The poem erased any and all local memories, overlaid indigenous histories with its European one, telling Mexico City as a vast entrepôt outrivaling its European source and *being* a greater Venice in America.

In that spirit, it overlaid geography as well. Balbuena's Capítulo VI, on México's "eternal spring," catalogues the flora and fauna, from willows, poplars, and familiar reeds to fallow deer, hedgehogs (!), pheasants, nightingales (95), and on into a long list which Balbuena summarizes in a kind of paroxysm at the end of the Capítulo:

> palms, ivy, elms, walnuts,
> almonds, pines, poplars, laurels,
> beeches, grapevines, cypress, cedars, mulberries,
> fir, box, tamarisk, oaks, holm oaks,
> vines, strawberry trees, medlars, service trees,
> citrus flowers, poppies, carnations,
> roses, pinks, iris, lilies,
> rosemary, stocks, white roses, sloes,
> sandalwood, clover, lemon balm, verbenas,
> jasmines, sunflower, myrtle, broom,
> bayberry, camomile filled with gold,
> thyme, hay plant, watercress with sprouting branches,
> basils, jonquils and ferns,
> and all the many more flowers April scatters. (99)

Again, what surprises here is the *absence* of native plants. It is as if Balbuena sought to bury local geography under a frenzied torrent of Europe (one recalls Stuart Hall's remark about knowing only the names of Wordsworth's daffodils). In his introduction the edition I have used, Luis Adolfo Domínguez proposes that Balbuena was perhaps yielding to "nostalgia" or allowing for his readers' ignorance of local flora (xxvii). If so, these were the deliberate ignorance and purposeful nostalgia of which we have seen much.

Domínguez suggests that a slightly older contemporary of Balbuena came closer to making room for the geography of local habitation and place, Juan de la Cueva, whom we have already met. The critic stresses the poet's attention in one of his *Epístolas* to indigenous reaction to Spanish rule and his praise of local produce and food (xxi). Cueva wrote of the Indians' dancing and their chanted mourning for Montezuma's imprisonment and death, of their curses of *la Malinche*, their acceptance of Cortés' power, their grief over war and defeat.[16] Unlike Balbuena, he made something, too, of local flora, its appearance and use:

> Mirad a aquellas frutas naturales,
> el plátano, mamey, guayaba, anona,
> si en gusto a las de España son iguales.
>   Pues un chico zapote, a la persona
> del Rey le puede ser empresentado
> por el fruto mejor que cría Pomona.
>   El aguacate, a Venus consagrado
> por el efecto y trenas de colores,
> el capulí y zapote colorado;
>   la variedad de hierbas y de flores,
> de que hacen figuras estampadas
> en lienzo, con matices y labores,
>   sin otras cien mil cosas regaladas
> de que los indios y españoles usan,
> que de los indios fueron inventadas.

> Look at those native fruits,
> plantain, mamey, guava, soursop,
> how in taste they equal those of Spain.
>   Indeed a sapodilla to the very King
> in person can be presented
> as the finest fruit Pomona raises.
>   The avocado, sacred to Venus
> for the effect and its twists of color,
> the capulin and red sapote;
>   the variety of herbs and flowers,
> of which they make drawings printed

on linen, with blended colors and fancywork,
 besides myriad other pleasant things
that the Indians and the Spanish use,
which were discovered by the Indians.
      (quoted in Domínguez, xxvi)

But Cueva spent just three years in Mexico and its capital, from 1574 until he sailed back to the peninsula in 1577, yielding to a homesickness rued in his poetry. He was, Domínguez remarks, a "tourist" (xiii), and these passages have the air of a passion for the exoticizing item.[17] Certainly they had nothing of any effort to be in, let alone *of* a different geography. But then, he was not staying. And so little was he touched by his stay (although Reyes Cano notes that reminiscences did occur in his later poetry: 73–77) that in his allegorical epic, *El viage de Sannio*, finished in 1585, just eight years after his return to Spain, Cueva offered a bird's-eye view of the world composed of three continents, Europe, Asia, and Africa, without so much as a glance at the Americas (book 1, stanzas 34–52, *Poèmes inédits*, 6–8).

Balbuena's mercantile accumulation and, to a slightly lesser extent perhaps, Cueva's touristic exoticism actually reached their paroxysm in another country and another century in authors, some of whom we glimpsed in Chapter 8 and whom Pope again may epitomize, representing a capitalist expansionism and fetishized consumerism well captured in verses that although they may in fact hark back to close English predecessors could almost have been lifted straight out of Balbuena. In *The Rape of the Lock* (1712–1717), Pope depicted his heroine Belinda preparing her *toilette*:

Unnumber'd Treasures ope at once, and here
The various Off'rings of the World appear;
From each she nicely culls with curious Toil,
And decks the Goddess with the glitt'ring Spoil.
This Casket *India's* glowing Gems unlocks,
And all *Arabia* breathes from yonder box.
The Tortoise here and Elephant unite,
Transformed to *Combs*, the speckled and the white.
      (*Poems*, I.129–36)

Belinda, Laura Brown remarks in quoting this passage, "is adorned with the spoils of mercantile expansion: the gems of India, the perfumes of Arabia, tortoiseshell and ivory from Africa" (*Alexander Pope*, 9). In the early and mid-eighteenth century, such listings, however ironic Pope may have made his, were increasingly typical, establishing and dependent on a "rhetoric of the commodity" setting protagonists and poets alike in their context of imperialist conquest and mercantilist expansionism (*Alexander Pope*, 13; cf. Brown, *Ends*, 113–14).

One is not surprised to find this view of exotic otherness perfected by the poets of expansionist industrializing England, and I mention them here only to emphasize a particular approach to history and the "other." For in their imposition and their exoticizing, Balbuena's and Cueva's writings differ widely from Balboa's previously mentioned *Espejo de paciencia*. In this brief epic, José Lezama Lima sees the "birth of Cuban ways and styles of being, which in spite of Spanish influence must be understood as something Cuban working to attain its contour and essence" ("Prólogo," 1004). Following his lead, González Echavarría calls it "the beginning of Cuban literature" ("Reflections," 142) but evaluates the poem quite otherwise. Balboa himself was born in Gran Canaria in 1563. It is not known when he sailed to Cuba and settled in Santa María de Puerto Príncipe (today Camagüey), but the liminary verses before his poem imply that he was then long established by marriage and career. In two cantos, the poem recounts the true story of the kidnapping and ransom of the Cuban bishop, Juan de las Cabezas Altamiro, by a French pirate Gilberto Girón, and of the vengeance wreaked on the latter and his men by the locals of Bayamo, who ambush and kill them all, beheading their leader and exposing his head on a pike, events that occurred in mid-1604. The first canto tells of the bishop's capture and hardships en route to the pirate's ship, his "patience" and forbearance, his release and the celebration held in his honor—a joyous encomium of the island's tropical flora and fauna. The second relates the gathering of a troop of twenty-four men to avenge the crime (each given a stanza or half stanza for name and description), dwells on the Lutherans' evil, the ambush, the Cubans' bravery—above all that of the black slave Salvador who killed the pirate (and would be given his freedom in return; *Espejo*, 84–85), and ends with quieter celebrations and a church mass. Indeed, this canto concludes with a "Motete" which Balboa had almost certainly written in 1604 actually to be sung in the church in thanksgiving.

Lezama Lima was right to speak of "the Spanish influence" in this poem whose most "remarkable and frequently commented on" aspect, González Echevarría adds, is its "admixture of elements from classical mythology and the description of the Cuban landscape" ("Reflections," 128; in this, it may be an appropriate ancestor of Walcott's *Omeros*). Besides the familiarity of the mythological trappings, of the epic enumeration of weapons and clothing, and of the quasihagiographical account of the bishop's trials, tribulations, and goodness ("Reflections," 131), the poem opens in habitual style. We are told of the bishop's presence in Bayamo, "this illustrious and noble city, rich in fruits and livestock, delightful and pleasing for its flowers":

> Era en el mes de abril, cuando ya el prado
> se esmalta con el lirio y con la rosa;
> Y están Favonio y Flora en su teatro,
> año de mil y un seis con cero y cuatro.

> It was in the month of April, when already the meadow
> is brightly adorned with the lily and the rose;
> And Zephir and Flora are on their stage,
> in the year one thousand, six hundred aught four.
>   (*Espejo*, 56, stanza 11 of the first canto)

The tone is familiar, the style common to a thousand European lyric and pastoral poems. But the moment is unique in the poem, a beginning that leads the reader into something quite different. "Spanish influence" acquires new connotations.

In his prologue "Al lector," Balboa justified the celebration of tropical fruits that ends the first canto by saying that thus he described

the gladness and joy that the whole island had from [the bishop's] return and freedom, and the rejoicing with which not only the townspeople of Bayamo came out to greet him, but also the nymphs of mountains, springs and rivers, so as to emphasize the need of a good in a commonwealth and the joy and gladness that not only rational humans show at its coming, but also even brute animals and insensible things. (*Espejo*, 44)[18]

He urged a sort of social, political, moral, and geographical symbiosis. In the introduction to the cited edition, Angel Aparicio Laurencio rightly remarks that the poem's hero is "collective." While the bishop is in some sense at the center, his role is entirely passive, object of collective ransom, collective celebration, collective revenge, collective mass. *Nuestro*, the plural possessive pronoun, is always at the end of Balboa's pen, writing of "the twenty-four valiant islanders," "our people," "our islanders," "our squadrons," "our strong troop." And as Aparicio Laurencio also adds, among this collectivity the actual victor over Girón was the black Salvador, while the only Cuban soldier actually to die of "a penetrating wound" was an "indio de los nuestros" (*Espejo*, 86; Aparicio Laurencio, introduction,

24). This group is very much a mixed and *criollo* one. Indeed, the Cubanness of this "we," "our," "us" was emphasized even before the poem began. Lezama Lima noted how Balboa's friend, captain Pedro de las Torres Sifontes, referred to his own liminary poem as "este soneto criollo de la tierra," a sonnet native to the land, a Cuban sonnet written by a Cuban (the pleonasm of "criollo" and "de la tierra" merely stressing the fact). It was also the sonnet that Balboa placed first in order of the six that preceded the poem (*Espejo*, 47; Lezama Lima, "Prólogo," 1004).

In the poem itself, Girón's victor was praised as "¡Salvador criollo, negro honrado!", and the poet went out of his way to name Bayamo and its eponymous river as "el ameno lugar que tanto amo" ("the delightful place [*locus amoenus*] that I so love"; *Espejo*, 84, 89). It was this sense of *home*, of a *collective* and geographically embedded home, that Balboa set out to elaborate in the closing celebration of the first canto. Contrary to what one finds in Balbuena, where the flora is all European, or in Cueva's touristic exoticism, Balboa had prepared his reader to understand the festival's tropical fruits, trees, and flowers, animals, birds, and fish as central to "us," "our" being, and "our" place. In turn, they drew the reader into a second canto that emphasized this now clearly grounded collectivity. Balboa brought out not just the local citizens, but satyrs, fauns, wood nymphs, and deities to offer "soursops, *jijiras* and star-apples," baskets of "mehí y tabaco, /mameyes, piñas, tunas y aguacates,/plátanos, y mamones y tomates [*mehí* and tobacco, mameys, pineaples, prickly pears and avocados,/plantains and papayas and tomatoes]." The poet continued into his poem's most often discussed stanza:

> Bajaron de los árboles en naguas
> Las bellas amadríades hermosas,
> Con fruitas de siguapas y macaguas
> Y muchas pitajayas olorosas;
> De vijirí cargadas y de jaguas
> Salieron de los bosques cuatro diosas
> Dríadas de valor y fundamento
> Que dieron al pastor grande contento.

> From the trees came down in flowing skirts
> The lovely and beautiful hamadryads,
> With fruits of *siguapas* and *macaguas*
> And many fragrant *pitahaya* cactuses;
> Loaded down with *bijirí* and genipaps

Four goddesses emerged from the forest
Wood nymphs of prowess and plenty
Which gave the holy shepherd great delight.
(*Espejo*, 67–68)

River nymphs added varieties of local fish and a thousand other "*cosas peregrinas*," nymphs of the springs came simply crowned with sweet-smelling herbs, their hair waving and "more brilliant than Arabian gold," to welcome the bishop "with sweet and joyous conversation," yet others brought tortoises, "a thousand unusual kinds of game," various animals, and "many iguanas, hooved animals and *hutías*." After all this, the fiesta ends with a joyous dance to the sound of "flutes, panpipes and rebecs," "maracas, cymbals, drums, *tipinaguas* and tambourines" (*Espejo*, 68–71), a wild celebration that was to be repeated in the riotous jam session of Carpentier's *Concierto barroco*, whose Filomeno is a descendant of Salvador and who retells for his master the events of *Espejo de paciencia*, as his master relates for him the travels of Quijote—further echo of Balboa's cultural mingling. For Balboa was surely emphasizing, as we saw him say in his prologue to the reader, a new symbiosis of people and place, of cultures and geography. González Echevarria again urges how "remarkable" was "the curious mixture of figures from classical mythology and exotic tropical plants" ("Reflections," 131), but I insist that only its earliness, if anything, is "remarkable." The mixture itself, the gathering of what later writers call the shards and remnants of different histories and cultures into a localized geography, is utterly usual in Caribbean writing.

To compare Balboa's and Balbuena's poems is therefore instructive. González Echevarría writes of Balboa's "chaotic accumulation of fragments from different cultures" and of his poem's "motley multiplicity of fruits . . . [that] has its counterpart in the different origins of the characters. In Balboa's poem there are Spaniards from various regions, Africans, Italians, Frenchmen, and Indians" ("Reflections," 145, 148). Arguing against Lezama Lima, other eulogists and the poem's first discoverers (it was found among the bishop's papers in the early nineteenth century, apparently having been presented to him in a fair copy by Balboa) who saw *Espejo* as essentially "Cuban," González sees in this "chaos" only "artificial representations of the American cornucopia . . . ephemeral manifestations, superficial in the literal sense, of a carnivalesque explosion, of a baroque feast." He even goes so far as to claim that in emphasizing fruits rather than flowers, the end rather than the process, Balboa accentuated "a nature that is dead (a *naturaleza muerta*), fixed, completed, exotic; unusual, but not distinct" ("Reflections," 146, 147). These propositions deserve unpacking, although the last is notably bizarre, since fruit, in fact and in endless symbolic representations, is by definition *not* dead, but is and contains the revitalizing seeds of nature.

That mattered, of course, to Balboa's purpose. He offered the reader a culture and a place in process of building. Balbuena's Mexican poem certainly offered many places (though not their cultures), but explicitly only represented in manufactured goods, gems, and other such valuables, dead products brought as objects to traffic. It bespoke a European ideal of incorporating everyone else's wealth, Venice in the Americas, essentially a great trading depot. This differed utterly from Balboa's poem, expressing the use-value of gifts: fruits of the land to the people, people's labor and joy to the land ("this place that I love"), voluntary giving of the bishop's ransomers and of his avengers who, doing so, affirmed the wholeness of their community in its locality. These specifically *replaced* the European spring of the poem's opening and the theft and trade undertaken by the pirates. In a way, too, Balboa gifted European culture to the land rather than following Balbuena in doing the opposite. As Lezama Lima put it, "the European imagination, the Graeco-Latin no less than the medieval, passed in its entirety into a new circumstance" ("Prólogo," 997). In another essay, Lezama Lima described a contemporary chronicler's efforts to describe and explain local fruits to European readers, and perhaps to himself. He showed how in his very comparisons the writer found himself emphasizing what was "distinct and different," drawn into a "nueva naturaleza" (a new kind of nature) that obliged him to see things "con nuevos ojos fabulosos," his marveling eyes opening up on and to an entirely new geography ("Paralelos," 936–37). One could say much the same of Balboa: he does not make the land his; rather does the land make him its.

So the variety of flora, fauna, and peoples was not at all "motley," but directly marked a reality on the ground. Indeed, it did more than that. From his list of Indians, Europeans, and Africans, González Echevarría omitted creoles—who include many of those he calls Africans and "Spaniards from various regions." These peoples join flora, fauna, and varieties of musical instrument as combinations of those fragments of which I have so much spoken. They are symbol and presence of seeds vitalizing and growing together these multiple fragments. The poem's very presentation insisted on this, with its liminary poems showing how Balboa was part of an extended creole family and with its first "creole" sonnet. This "packaging" led the reader into the grounded collectivity the epic then went on to express, just as, perhaps, the poem inaugurated the poetry of a *different* place, one where a people could have a deeply internalized sense of *being there*. "After this poem was written," Lezama Lima added, "one could speak of Cubanness, more than in outward appearance in poetry's complex presence" ("Prólogo," 1003, 1004). This "Cubanness" of the poem is also its Caribbeanness, its creolity. It lies chiefly, I submit, in its embedding of culture in places where a particular European history has become one fragment of many, one shard to be joined to others in ways governed by memories embedded in and organized by local topographies.

It was exactly this, perhaps again in a memory of Balboa, that Carpentier captured as the protagonist of another of his novels, *El siglo de las luces*, wanders through Guadeloupe:

[Esteban] breathed in with delight the delicate fragrance of the anonas, the grey acidity of the tamarinds, the fleshy softness of all these fruits, with their red and purple pulp, concealing in their most recondite folds sumptuous seeds with the texture of tortoise-shell, ebony or polished mahogany. He buried his face in the white coolness of the xorozos; he tore at the amaranthine star-apple, searching with avid lips for the crystalline droplets secreted in the depths of its pulp. (*Siglo*, 164–65; *Explosion*, 161)

Thus does Esteban find himself again at home after his journey into European history. Marshall has her protagonists do the same in *The Chosen Place, the Timeless People*, a night of arrival in the island, gazing into the darkness, reconnecting with place: "they could smell the mixed fragrances of the flowers in the garden below and, faintly, the rich odor of the soil that fed them, and the smells were those of the night itself, the exhalation of its breath" (72).

One thinks, too, of J. Michael Dash commenting on Haitian cultural creation:

In this desire to write the new Haitian world into existence, nature played an important role in that it established a referential validity for the new republic. The idea of the Haitian landscape as the territory of the marvellous and the magical has its roots in early writing, where nature is endowed with a capacity to ground an authentic national identity. (Chapter Nine, 289).

Apropos of Puerto Ricans in New York and their nineteenth- and early twentieth-century efforts to set themselves in the specific history and place of Puerto Rico, as well as of the Caribbean more generally and of the United States, Bernardo Vega uses a version of Descartes familiar to us from earlier chapters, to assert an entirely analogous rooting in place: "Como si dijéramos: tenemos un origen, ¡luego, somos! [It is as if we were saying—we have roots, therefore we are!]." So he speaks a sense of collective identity rooted in particular places of origin (*Memorias*, 81; *Memoirs*, 43). Of a third island, Gilberto Perez (making a point of the difference in accents) reviews Louis Pérez Jr.'s *On Becoming Cuban: Identity, Nationality and Culture*, to note how the author misses "the sense of Cuba as a country with a quality of its own," emphasizing U.S. influence to the exclusion of African and Spanish (to say nothing of the rest of America), and above all, he observes, "there is also the question of place: the air one breathes, the terrain and the trees, the sea and the sun and the clouds, the way in which place informs the identity of a people" (G. Perez, "So Close").

The Cuban poet Heberto Padilla also tells this enlacement in actuality of place. "Historia" takes the form of an outside weight imposed on the loves, desires, and daily life of the ordinary human in his tropical locale, set against a history from outside (drawn in the poem "En tiempos difíciles," for example, from the "manual/de marxismoleninismo" of the "compañera de viaje"; *Legacies*, 22) that seeks to push the "tiempo" of a human life "al tiempo de la Historia" (24) and that can be only too successful in making even the sparrow turn against those weaker than itself ("Síntesis," *Legacies*, 68). Marxism-Leninism joins Carpentier's French Revolution, Balbuena's imperialist trade, and Cortés' Spanish squadrons as one more avatar of European history and power. In these circumstances, "Homenaje" (98) must be given to the "parra desobediente" that resists efforts to force it into History's ordered service. This grand narrative of history is always another's, the city of Babylon's, that seeks to colonize and capture all places as its own and make them into its own image. The poet's task is then not to accept the "magia" or the "maravilloso" of the purveyors of foreign histories, nor to copy or be copied in "los cristales cifrados," their mysteriously coded windows. The task is to offer

> palabras que acuden cuando hablo,
> neutras y desprovistas de ilusión.
> Centellean no porque yo las pula con trapos de metal,
> las encuentro a la diabla, entre las calles,
> tontas alegres como niños.

words that come to me when I speak,
>   neutral words, stripped of all fantasy.
They shine, not because I polish them with steel wool;
I find them all over the place, in the streets,
>   happy idiots, the way children are.
>   ("Nota," *Legacies*, 124/5)

These ordinary words are those of local rhythm and experience, of the everyday song and familiar acts on which Mariátegui quoted González Prada, which Bovelles bemoaned and praised, which Brathwaite and so many others drum in delight. To know these, you need not History, "Hegel's fingernail" ("una uña de Hegel"; "Síntesis," *Legacies*, 68). You find it "Con sólo abrir los ojos" (118) to the geography and spirit of place about you. Geography makes its own history, or, rather, is attached to local histories.

The Jamaican poet Olive Senior draws a similar picture in "Cockpit Country Dreams" (from her collection, *Talking of Trees*), where two versions of home and history seem to come into conflict, leaving a person torn between those things that have been set on maps and those other local mysteries that have not—and perhaps cannot be:

Our road led to places on maps
places that travelled people
knew. Our river, undocumented
was mystery.

My father said: lines on paper
cannot deny something that *is*.
(My mother said: such a wasted life
is his).

The mother then goes on to offer the child pictures of her ancestors and of their places: "Herein/your ancestry, your imagery, your pride./Choose *this* river, *this* rhythm, *this* road./Walk good in the footsteps of *these* fathers." The "well-worn grooves" still drew her mind in its familiar directions, says the child. But now the father advises that the first source of firm being is to be found in knowledge and spirit of place:

Study rivers. Learn everything.
Rivers may find beginnings
in the clefts of separate mountains

Yet all find their true homes
in the salt of one sea.

The child seems to begin to obtain some new stability: "Now my disorder
of ancestry/proves as stable as the many rivers/flowing round me.
Undocumented/I drown in the other's history." Between one's own and
others' histories, there is an abyss. But cross it one must. To have done so
may give one "terrible/knowledge," but the result is firmly one's own:
"wisps of smoke from cockpits crying lonely/lonely/But walking in the
woods alternating dark with/sunshine I knew/nothing then of cities or the
killing of children/in their dancing time" (in Markham, ed., *Hinterland*,
218–19).

Marshall brings many of these things together in *The Chosen Place,
the Timeless People*, a novel I explored at some length in the preceding chapter in regard to its play of history and geography. Its two principal protagonists, Merle Kinbona and Saul Amron, are both outsiders, in their different ways, to the western city, the first living in her "backward" Bournehills
on the Caribbean Bourne Island (a version of Barbados), the second being
a kind of wandering Jew. We saw Bournehills set in direct opposition to the
neocolonial capital of New Bristol, with its places named in and after a particular western history: Mayfair, Park Lane, Westminster . . . , eliciting
Merle's remark to Saul, "they colonized our minds but good in this place"
(*Chosen Place*, 129). But the "trapped quarry" (57) of Bournehills, we also
saw, has a powerful local history of its own, wholly bound to the place it is,
in the still-living story of Cuffee Ned's unsuccessful slave revolt, whose
leader those of Bournehills believe will finally come again to save them
from the imposition of another's history. Year after year, in the island's carnival, the district resolutely presents the same float of Cuffee Ned's revolt.
Year after year, they overcome the capital's scorn and end up absorbing the
entire carnival into their story, just as Cuba absorbed European mytholo-
gies and their figures in Balboa's epic, now "using their history," as Saul remarked to Merle, "to their advantage" (315).

I suggested that we could see Merle herself as Cuffee Ned, her work
in Bournehills being to revitalize the district's sense of its own local identity, by, as Carew has put it, harvesting history in its hills (*Fulcrums*, 155–
70). As in Senior's poem and Saul's remark about history, she emphasizes
that "a person has to go back, really back—to have a sense, an understanding of all that's gone before to make them—before they can go forward"

(468). This historical imperative is embedded deep in the geography and topography of Bournehills. It will be drawn from the land like Balboa's tropical fruits and animals, very signs and embodiments of a place and its histories. And here it is worth repeating a slightly longer passage I quoted before, in which, unlike the pale unhappy echo of another's history that is New Bristol, Bournehills is recognized as the repository of the island's own history,

a place in which had been stored the relics and remains of the era recorded in the faded prints on the walls, where one not only felt that other time existing intact, still alive, a palpable presence beneath the everyday reality, but saw it as well at every turn, often without realizing it. Bournehills, its shabby woebegone hills and spent land, its odd people who at times seemed older than themselves, might have been selected as the repository of the history which reached beyond it to include the hemisphere north and south.

Its local history is buried "deep down," "fixed and rooted in that other time," and bound in its "ravaged hills" (402). The carnival float that takes over New Bristol momentarily, before coming back to Bournehills, unites what lives in local memory and what abides in the land with its own people's way of inhabiting place. It embeds the culture's historical reason in its local habitation.

This expression of the fictive imagination seems particular to the Caribbean, a way of building shards of lost cultures into a whole whose cement is drawn from particular geographies. In all the Caribbean writers mentioned, Marshall and Senior no less than Balboa, Brathwaite, Carpentier, Dash, Padilla, Perez, Rodríguez Juliá, and Vega (not to speak of Heredia and Martí), the sense of real place is palpable. They tell their stories as coming *from* such place. In Eltit, Fuentes, and Piglia, one faces a swirl of narratives. Possible narratives confront the oppressive weight of the many historical tales that mark continual efforts to stamp another's dominion, down to and including those of whatever may be the present "most powerful nation in the world" (as Eltit had it) and of the forking paths of internal authority. Even Balbuena, who so effectively overlaid Indian stories with a European one as to cut them wholly from his poem, could not stop their appearance in his *Compendio apologético* even as full rivals of European ones. I explored Cortés and Díaz because their tales of impressing metropoles, whether Venice or Madrid, on the different geography of Tenochtitlán and its many companion cities resonate through these

Latin American writings. Their tensions are those of creating new histories out of and against old ones whose multitudes lie complete in memory, layered and intertwined ones on others, ones with others. They are *there*; and Eltit shows how they can be turned to "reimagining our world" (Tierney-Tello, 93). Caribbean writers face tensions in some ways similar, but they cope with them otherwise. Because their histories are still always fragments of many, shards of the indigenous, of Europe, of manifold Africa and Asia, geography—a deep sense of place—becomes the means to forge a new history of their own. Geography enables the many fragments to be joined into an unknown whole. At least in the imaginary, it does so not in the neo-colonial or "postmodern" city of New Bristol, but in locally rooted Bournehills. This way of fixing one's ground differs completely from one that "detests unnecessary attachment to places" and sets itself on deep grounded histories.

From the contrast between the poems of Balbuena and Balboa, one can see that this difference was established very early. It is not to say that one adopts a European mode of History while the other rejects it as an imposition of Babylon. It is to say that there are more ways than one to skin a cat. At least those Latin American writers looked at here propose, rather, that as imposed History disperses into a proliferation of signs, losing its clear source of authoritative agency (however much this itself may repeat the hidden harm of menacing Venice), older stories and different histories are laboriously freed, rise to the surface, become available as counters. So far they remain possibilities of telling rather than firm narratives, reminders of pasts disappeared that need recovery. But above all, they are stories—histories that turn, and turn against, History and its singular narrative. Caribbean writers have given Seneca's bees new wings and new flowers to fly to. They have brought out the collective being of those bees, emphasized entanglements, the weavings that already many ancients used to describe honeycomb building, the mutualities of cultural exchanges and the *relations* that put found shards together. These are not stories to be recovered but pieces that can be made into stories. They are bits of (potential) histories grounded in and projected by topography or, in terms, perhaps, of the teller rather than the told, histories trammeled in the body. Both turn others' cultural instruments, *rationes*, on their head, find diverse ones elsewhere, forge their own. They just do these things in different ways, according to local contexts and imperatives.

Notes

INTRODUCTION

1. Not the hypothesis but the earlier details are mostly from Geoffrey Elton, *England*, 331–34. He resisted linking things like "Reformation" and "capitalist spirit," and no doubt American invasion and structures of religion or American trade and European cultural forms (what in Chapters 4 and 5 I call "categorial correspondence" or "convertibility"), and while seeing *some* sort of link, would surely have rejected the hypothesis (see, e.g., Elton, *Reformation*, 311–18). Contemporary historians of the English Reformation ignore any such idea, and J. J. Scarisbrick, noting Henry's push in 1521 (and up to 1527), is typical in viewing him as having lost interest in such trade and ignored "the new worlds across the seas" (*Henry VIII*, 124, 507). An older writer, Oscar Albert Marti, gives *some* weight to commercial expansion and opening of transatlantic trade, implying then that the 1527 Proclamation of Calais may have aimed, as it said, at "extending the wealth, increasing, and enriching of all England" as much by wider trade as by European trade (*Economic*, 209, 212). With respect to Spain and its Venetian supporters, Federica Ambrosini finds many early sixteenth-century writers who saw a direct (divine) link between "Peruvian gold and the house of Austria's antimuslim crusade," Spain's "success" in the Indies prefiguring the empire's divinely inspired "*renovatio*" of "the whole of humanity" (*Paesi*, 59, 77). The counterreform, with its huge effect on European culture, would itself have been one element in a massive Spanish and Catholic renewal legitimated, enabled, and directed by the success of American invasion.

2. In *Theories of Africans*, Christopher Miller probes these issues. In *Nationalists and Nomads*, 152–70, he explores rather how different cultures' texts question these tools and their objects. These issues are not new or limited to literary critical matters. Writing of explorers in "the social and cultural disciplines" in nineteenth-century Bengal, Chatterjee observes how they raised these very queries: "Did the fact of the birth of the modern sciences of society in Europe rule out their applicability in societies that were fundamentally different? Could their methods be used in Indian conditions without modification? Were their fundamental concepts

applicable in India? Was it necessary to devise alternative theories? Or was science itself inappropriate in discussing matters of Indian society and culture? These are of course, questions that pervade the entire literature on modernity in India, and they acquired their problematic and contested disciplinary forms even at the time of their birth in the deliberations of the nineteenth-century [Bengali] learned societies" ("Disciplines," 16). Chatterjee explores these questions with particular regard to the idea of nationalism(s) in his *Nationalist Thought* and *The Nation and Its Fragments*.

3. Clearly, the fictive imagination does not only produce diverse practices and forms in different cultures. It is also manifested as verbal, pictorial, musical, cinematic, and so on. Throughout this book "fictive imagination" implies the verbal fictive imagination.

4. I refer to comments in Goethe's *Italienische Reise*, September 14, 1786; *Italian Journey*, 46. See the end of Chapter 1.

5. I am thinking here particularly of Hall's "The Local and the Global," but these debates are central to contemporary preoccupations with cultural globalization.

6. For the claim of value(s), consider the so-called moral majority; for that of empowerment, tricks like refusing affirmative action in favor of an imaginary level playing field and cutting Social Security in favor of work and self-help programs. The first seeks power in the name of imposing *its* universalist virtue on all; the second aims to pare taxes and other levies on those who can afford them (but who covet material overconsumption—including collecting/investing in/appropriating the artifacts and symbols of the deprived and colonized) on the pretense that all humans are equally favored, equally able, and have equal access to social, cultural, and educational benefits.

7. One could say much about the "English-only" movement. This is not the place for such a discussion, but for its connection with what I am saying here, one might consider the many remarks made by Édouard Glissant in *Poétique* concerning the "monolinguism" of colonial centers, its use, its history, and its opposition to an aesthetic of "*relation*" (27, 31, 35–48—esp. 40, 112, 117–23). The issue recurs later in this text, and see, too, my "History and Language."

8. Such efforts continue in Random House's Modern Library editorial board's naming of the twentieth century's hundred best English-language novels. The list starts with James Joyce's *Ulysses*, gets in nine novels by women (in competitive order, the women authors are Virginia Woolf, Carson McCullers, Edith Wharton—twice, Willa Cather, Muriel Spark, Elizabeth Bowen, Jean Rhys, and Iris Murdoch), three novels by African Americans (Ralph Ellison, Richard Wright, and James Baldwin), three by writers from the Caribbean (Rhys and two by V. S. Naipaul), and one novel by Salman Rushdie, before ending with Booth Tarkington's *Magnificent Ambersons*. The other eighty-four winners, some repeatedly, are the usual suspects, plus many whose inclusion shows the selectors desperate to keep them to England and the United States (including Vladimir

Nabokov's two). Paul Lewis, writing for the *New York Times*, notes minor dissent among judges but manages to underline the cultural illiteracy of reporter and reportees and to patronize as he criticizes the imperialist urge: "although India, Australia and South Africa all have flourishing literary traditions and have produced many distinguished authors" ("Ulysses," B4). The exercise is without artistic meaning but potent as a sign of links between desired cultural hegemony and the global market (from its German base, the Bertelsmann group owns Random House and Bantam Doubleday Bell in the United States and is "the largest commercial book publisher in the world"; "Ulysses," B1). With no tragic predecessor, this farce now has a parodic successor in the top hundred nonfiction books (Smith, "Another Top 100 List")!

9. Claims to victimhood of the World War II European Holocaust laid by reference to even proximate relatives can be as unsavory—often made for aggressive political or "moral" purpose, the first to justify even the ugliest Israeli state behavior, the second to claim a fundamental rectitude and preempt objection—the last then offensively categorized and dismissed as "anti-Semitic."

CHAPTER I

1. No one knows what city Kinsai was. Haun Saussy suggests it was either Hangzhou or Suzhou, both "at the southern end of the Grand Canal, dug to facilitate shipping of grain and tax money up to the capital at Beijing" and able to "qualify as the 'Venice of China'" (personal communication). The Grand Canal was opened in 1411, a century after Polo's death. Presumably this does not rule out the qualification. It doesn't help identification.

2. Habermas, *Structural Transformation*, 253 n. 32, and Morris, *World*, 20. The first argues that newsletter writers, *scrittori d'avvisi*, and the eventual commodification of news, were directly tied to the rise of capitalist modes of production (15–17). One could presumably say the same about the establishment of archives for the telling of its history (with no doubt ambiguous results)—of which more in later chapters.

3. For present argument, the claim is fascinating, but the book as a whole is a repellent mixture of pretentious mush about Venice, the senses and beauty, bedded in maunderings of irredeemable vulgarity.

4. It is further symptomatic, apropos of the "bond" between Venice and Tenochtitlán, Venice and Spain of which we will see more, that in his 1660 *Carta del navegar pitoresco*, Marco Boschini likened Tintoretto to Columbus discovering the true wealth of painting and Titian's artistic worth to the gold-bearing Indies (Ambrosini, *Paesi*, 165). In a recent study, Bruce Cole takes another aspect to express an analogous view, seeing such artists as epitomizing Jacob Burckhardt's virile Renaissance: "It was the Renaissance conception of man as the embodiment of command, power, and intelligence that most attracted Titian and his fellow artist's critical intellect and powers" (Cole, *Titian*, 108; quoted in Rowland, "Titian," 14).

5. See, too, our sharp debate: Cascardi and Reiss, "Poetry." Some of what immediately follows is taken or adjusted from my part of this argument.

6. Chatterjee shows just such a case of one nineteenth-century Bengali nationalist's adoption of free trade in this way as "a more developed form of economic organization than anything that had existed" in local sources (*Nationalist*, 62–63). Like others, Noam Chomsky points out that the "reasons of profit and power" behind the *doctrine* of free trade actually benefit by "radically violating approved free market doctrine" ("Free Trade," 367, 360). Again, autonomy of free trade discourse enables realities of tariff protectionism, violence, and state intervention to stay "hidden" or talked of in quite different terms ("Free Trade," 362–68).

7. In the arena of "history," Michel de Certeau has suggestively analyzed western historiography as founded on a series of splits enabling such abstracting universalism: of narrated past from present writing, of the masses whose history is supposedly told from the educated historian, of reality from thought, of oral from written, spatiality from temporality, otherness from identity, unconscious from conscious—the last four contraries, not incidentally, also separating the domain and "objects" of historiography from those of ethnography, peoples with from "peoples without history" (*Écriture*, 9, 215).

8. Stanley Corngold observes that the third *Critique* "takes back its tendency to autonomization" and "operates as its own best counter-example" in at least two ways. One regards how the "imputation" of *universal agreement* crucially validates the "autonomous judgment of a subject," the other how "it annexes to . . . aesthetic judgment collateral cognitive and moral interests" (personal communication, May 31, 1995). The first requires one to accept the imputation of universal agreement as itself valid and anyway does not affect the autonomization of aesthetic discourse itself. The second is persuasive to the degree it does touch that discursive autonomy. Again, my concern is not to examine Kant's *Critique* but its uses.

9. Despite the obeisance to western antiquity, the then-familiar spectrum of logic, dialectic, and rhetoric (for example) could find no place in an evaluation of this sort, any more than could a sequence such as mathematics, philosophy, and law. The diverse place and role of the fictive imagination in Greco-Roman antiquity's public spheres (at least two, doubtless several, certainly not one) cries out for detailed examination.

10. Hilden uses the phrase to refer mostly to that school of anthropology whose practitioners think that to confess their own psychic needs and lifelong marginality somehow meliorates their grasp on the indigenous peoples who are their objects of interest, "the off-centering of the ethnographer . . . becom[ing] the purpose of postmodern ethnography" (Prakash, "Writing," 388 n. 53). Here I mean a wider refusal of personal responsibility on grounds running from mental incapacity (some version of the fragmented psyche) to social alienation (individuals owe nothing to a collectivity whose demands impede personal freedom). The chaotic dualisms ruling misconceptions of person and community are here myriad, but they are endemic to late twentieth-century capitalist western cultures.

11. Some might want to argue that this passage has little to do with "a colonized situation," since it is from a lecture series that De delivered (in Chicago) in 1961. He was, though, summarizing a lifetime's work, published earlier in *Studies* (1923–1925) and *History* (1947).

12. Mphahlele, *Voices*, 4–5, 15. The first two citations are from Eric Heller and D. J. Enright, and the third from T. S. Eliot.

13. When quoting here and later from Kane's novel, I give references to the original as well as its translation because the latter is not always wholly accurate; I adjust it as necessary.

14. Soyinka sees Kane's novel as setting western secularism against "a new African consciousness shaped by the wisdom of Islam and a sensibility that occasionally, very occasionally, suggests the animism of African traditional beliefs" (*Myth*, 79). The novel signals "the will to break free" of "previous history or colonial culture" (67) but faces two colonial histories, European and Arab (*Myth*, 79–85). Mphahlele adopts a similar view, although he sees this duality—or more: occident, Islamic Africa, and perhaps Islam against Africa—as a ground of "anguish" (*African Image*, rev. ed., 46–47).

15. Mphahlele, "The Fabric of African Cultures," *Voices*, 169. This essay first appeared in *Foreign Affairs*, 22, no. 4 (July 1964): 614–27.

16. Identically, the aim of the nineteenth- and twentieth-century Indian boarding schools of the United States was succinctly expressed by General Richard Henry Pratt, founder of the first of them at Carlisle: "Kill the Indian and save the man" (Hilden, *Nickels*, 152).

17. The last is Ngũgĩ's phrase for what has *historically* been the choice (I refer to conversations, but see *Writers*, 75). The trap of either hearing all cultures on a sounding board of the European or seeing them through its lens is clearly as hard to avoid as the description of cultures in their own actuality is to achieve. Nor is this so just for those born to the European, although different conditions vary difficulties of flight and expression. Guha-Thakurta explores analogous Orientalist dilemmas in Bengali efforts to build an aesthetic in the nineteenth and early twentieth century: first efforts to use *Greek* and *materialist* aesthetic values yielded to claims of Hindu *spirituality*, reversed image of each other ("Recovering," 71–72, 78, 83, 86, and *Making*, 118–225, and 226–312 for Abanindranath Tagore; cf. Chatterjee, "Modern," 114; Prakash, "Writing," 355). Krishna Chaitanya's *Sanskrit Poetics* is a textbook case of these colonizing effects of discursive autonomy, whose adoption leads to the universalist abstraction that poetry, its meanings and aesthetic delight (*rasa*, emotional experience open to all humans, relished in poetry by those with educated sensibility), divorced from other human practices, everywhere have the same principles and aims: Sanskrit poets and critics share views with all conceivable western commentators. De (and others) share the universalist views, although De slots Sanskrit poetry and poetics into them as sounding board rather than lens (and see above, note 10, and corresponding text). V. K. Chari's *Sanskrit Criticism* still uses this sounding board, although it insists on Sanskrit sources.

These predicaments are central to what follows, specifically near the end of this chapter and in Chapter 2 and, of the fictive imagination, in Chapter 4. In a sense, they underlie this book.

18. The remarks became a basis for Chinweizu's seemingly pathological demonization of Soyinka (Chinweizu, *Decolonising*, 193–200; Chinweizu et al., *Toward*, 204, 234–38), to which Soyinka reacted appropriately, referring to this rabid criticism as "Neo-Tarzanism" (*Art*, 249–60, 293–305, and "Ethics"). In the context of exactly contemporary Nigerian militarized and increasingly dictatorial politics, of murderous ethnic and cultural fights, and of Soyinka's own imprisonment, exile and death sentence in absentia, Chinweizu's ranting aggression in writings from 1972 to 1987, reprinted during the Abacha years, had ugly overtones.

19. Appiah's essay has been reprinted in a longer version (treating also V. Y. Mudimbe) in *In My Father's House*, 137–57.

20. Autonomy and division are organizing principles of Fanon's *The Wretched of the Earth*. See also, e.g., arguments at 47, 50, 153, 156–62.

21. Silone, *Bread and Wine* (1937), 289 and *passim*. Silone's revised version (English, 1963), retaining the thought, rather abbreviated it (264 and *passim*).

22. Eagleton, *Criticism*, and Sinfield, *Faultlines*. I have discussed at length the first's play with autonomies in another context (*Uncertainty of Analysis*, 179–203, esp. 183–90) and the second's more briefly (Review of *Faultlines*).

23. The last sentence summarizes comments that Alain Locke quotes at some length. They are from Nancy Cunard's *Negro Anthology* (London, 1934), 346. Locke later offers the beginnings of a complex judgment about possible relations between, in this case, plastic arts of certain African cultures and those of African Americans (*Negro and His Music*, 4–5).

24. C. L. R. James set down the stakes and uses of this trap with clear-eyed anger: "For many hundreds of years . . . it has been the almost universal practice to treat African achievement, discoveries and creations as if Western civilisation was the norm and the African people spent their years in imitating, trying to reach or, worse still, if necessary going through the primitive early stages of the Western world" (*History*, 141).

25. Goethe, *Italian Journey* [1786–1788], 39 (September 11, [1786], early morning): "Und nun, wenn es Abend wird, bei der milden Luft wenige Wolken an den Bergen ruhen, am Himmel mehr stehen als ziehen, und gleich nach Sonnen-untergang das Geschrille der Heuschrecken laut zu werden anfängt, da fühlt man sich doch einmal in der Welt zu Hause und nicht wie geborgt oder im Exil. Ich lasse mir's gefallen, als wenn ich hier geboren und erzogen wäre und nun von einer Grönlandsfahrt, von einem Walfischfange zurückkäme" (*Italienische Reise*, 26).

26. *Italienische Reise*, 33: "Bürger einer Republik zu sein, welche zwar an Macht und Grösse dem erlauchten Staat von Venedig nicht verglichen werden kann, aber doch auch sich selbst regiert und an Handelstätigkeit, Reichtum und Weisheit ihrer Vorgesetzten keiner Stadt in Deutschland nachsteht. Ich bin nämlich von Frankfurt am Main gebürtig."

27. In a fine reading of *Le città invisibili* and *Il castello dei destini incrociati*, in the course of exploring what it means to imagine the unknown, Ladina Bezzola Lambert sees this passage as expressing "the arbitrariness of conceptual frameworks and . . . their multiplicity" and the leap from easily accepting imposed familiarity to risking the unknown ("Imagining," 140; for the whole chapter, 136–58). Such a reading readily ties the aesthetic to the political (as we shall see, again of this passage, in my final chapter).

28. Interestingly, Domenico Scarlatti has a similar role in another contemporary novel, where the intricacy of his piano playing forges bonds not so much across cultures as classes—peasants, citizens, and priests tied through his music to the royal houses of Portugal and Spain. Since one of the central characters, who makes Scarlatti so important, is Brazilian, one could argue that the cross-cultural is present too (Saramago, *Baltasar and Blimunda*, 147–59 and *passim*). Scarlatti also appears in Mphahlele's *Down Second Avenue* (182), where he figures the rejection, by the narrator and his friends, of a white South African's patronizing efforts to appropriate their performance, fearful that *they* have successfully appropriated "*his*" culture. What is it about Scarlatti?

CHAPTER 2

1. De Certeau's *L'écriture de l'histoire* explores implications and consequences of this assertion, of the fact that the historian uses a disciplinary order "to *translate* one cultural language into another," "to change elements [of nature] into culture," to set "the alien in a place *useful* to the discourse of intelligibility, exorcizing the unknown to make it a means of knowing"—even as it returns "surreptitiously" to menace historiography's sureties (82–83, 114–15). His analysis of Jean de Léry's 1578 *Histoire d'un voyage fait en la terre du Brésil* (215–48) is especially clear on modern historiography's self-establishment as a "hermeneutics of the other" (231). Léry indeed began by saying that he would "show how everything to be seen in America, its inhabitants' way of life, animals' form and generally everything the earth produces, being unlike what we have in Europe, Asia and Africa, can well be called a new world" (de Certeau, *Écriture*, 228; Léry, *Histoire*, 28).

2. These last comments come largely from my *Uncertainty of Analysis* (164), in which Sartre's lifelong concern for language in its relation to society and persons receives fairer attention to its complexity (153–78).

3. Unlike Todorov, Piedra complicates things considerably by seeing an ambiguous Columbus who *did* "transculturate" himself and play a go-between, if partly as a "deceit" ("Game," 41–42, 46–50, 56–57). In "I Cristóbal Kamau," Brathwaite also has Columbus knowingly between places.

4. Piedra counters that critics from different cultures can avoid this trap ("Game," 34–39, 58–60).

5. It matters that Ahmad expresses a similar curiosity "that the Urdu language, although one of the youngest linguistic formations in India, had nevertheless pro-

duced its first great poet, [Amir] Khusrow (1253–1325) in the thirteenth century" (*In Theory*, 113). It matters because what is at stake here is the wealths, the varieties, the forgings of cultures in their own beings, not as seized by someone else's.

6. Deane's depiction of colonized Irish culture as without a specific language may exemplify such an interiorized stereotype. The Irish-language poet Nuala Ní Dhomhnaill has much to say about such characterizations as all too readily accepting the colonizing culture's estimate.

7. Gourgouris criticizes Brennan's argument not on historical grounds but for its claim that the process of "narration" common in the realm of the imaginary to both nation and novel means that the latter best satisfies "the national longing for form" (*Dream*, 30). For Gourgouris, nation is *not* founded on narration.

8. These claims of usage are always dubious. With regard to the "nation" claim in Jusdanis (*Belated Modernity*) and all those others named earlier, for example, what does one do with Hakluyt's celebrated work of 1589, hugely expanded in 1598–1600: *Voyages and Discoveries: The Principal Navigations, Voyages, Traffiques and Discoveries of the English Nation*? The work was written to assert the mercantile authority and history of the English and establish political, social, and commercial parameters of their "Nation." And what of the English Parliamentarian Henry Parker's 1642 argument against Charles I, that "it is unnatural for any Nation to give away its owne proprietie in it selfe absolutely" (*Observations*, 186)? The terms *nature, Nation, property*, and *self* and their association were not meant to startle but to explain in ways that Parker clearly assumed his readers would recognize. I have explored "literature" in *Meaning*. The matter of "private" and "public" is hugely complex. I discuss it in *Mirages of the Selfe*.

9. The same is the case for literatures and cultures of Central/Eastern Europe, many of whose representatives have sought to understand them from inside *against* those of western Europe, seeing themselves in a relation of "periphery" to "center," "belated" to "modern," "universalist" to "nationalist" (as Sarmatian, pan-Slavic, or some other). Krystyna Lipinska-Illakowicz has fascinatingly explored aspects of this ("European Peripheries"). The issue returns, implicitly at least, in Chapter 7.

10. Apart from de Certeau (*Heterologies*, 67–79), Timothy Hampton on "Des coches" ("Subject") seems more accurate and judicious than Cheyfetz in interpreting Montaigne on these issues. His essay "Des cannibales" has of course been endlessly analyzed.

CHAPTER 3

1. Vassilis Lambropoulos points out to me (personal communication, November 16, 1997) such exceptions as Karl Jaspers and George Steiner. Debates over *Job* are a hard case, since it may readily be considered part of this "western" tradition.

2. Some still contest using the word "genocide" even of North America, on fal-

lacious grounds that it was not "deliberate" or not "government policy." Besides the perpetrators' many easily available remarks to the contrary, most responsible expositors agree that virtual total slaughter of native populations in the Caribbean and reduction of at least 18,000,000 North Americans *ca.* 1492 to 250,000 in 1900 are nothing else (these figures are from Hilden, "Ritchie Valens," 229, and note 24; see too Chapter 11 below, note 5). While far more indigenous peoples survive over-all in Latin America, their ongoing destruction and debilitated condition can hardly be more exactly named. One thinks of Mexico, ever conscious of its native and European *mestizaje* but in whose history a person in Audre Lorde's *Zami*, savoring "what was Zapotec, Toltec, Mixtec, Aztec in the culture" and knowing "how much of it had been so terribly destroyed by Europeans," surely also rightly sees a "genocide" (170). Anzaldúa recalls that Mexico's population of 25 million in 1492 was down to 7 million soon after conquest and 1 1/2 million pure-blooded inhabitants by 1650 (*Borderlands*, 5). (I use these writers for the case because this is a book mostly about fictive imaginations, but see too, e.g., Frank, *Capitalism*, 127, and more importantly Jennings, *Invasion*. In *ReOrient* [70], Frank gives a figure of population decline for the entire Americas of from 100 million to 5 million.)

3. Aeschylus, *The Eumenides*, in *Eschyle II*, 158 (ll. 681–706). With a few changes for greater literalness, the translation is that of Robert Fagles, *The Oresteia*, 262.

4. Heidegger, *Introduction*, 146–65. I thank Roberto Dainotto for recalling this reading, based in fact on readjustment in the Greek: Dainotto, "All Regions," 240–46. See also Dainotto, *Place*, 163–67.

5. Sophocles, *Sophocle I*, 89 (ll. 450–55). The English translation is that of Elizabeth Wyckoff in *Sophocles I*, 174.

6. I take the Hegel/Nietzsche opposition from a question asked by Christopher Prendergast after the original oral presentation of this essay's subject matter, when the Christian/Greek opposition was also much debated. He and others are more generally thanked in the Acknowledgments. The quoted phrase is Nuala Ní Dhomhnaill's, from a private letter about other, connected issues (April 11, 1995). I thank her too.

7. As a classicist, Nietzsche may well have had in mind the solitude and exclusion that Diogenes Laertius tied to tragedy, although Nietzsche would not have seen his isolated life as harmful: "All the curses of tragedy, [Diogenes the Cynic] used to say, had lighted upon him. At all events, he was 'Cityless, homeless, deprived of a homeland,/A beggar wandering, living life day by day' " (Diogenes, 2:38 [vi.38]; my translation of verses): Oedipus as the exemplar of a tragic solitude due to find its avatar not just in Nietzsche but also in Freud.

8. It may be worth recalling that d'Amico, to whom Pirandello wrote the quoted letter, also held fascist beliefs, while Tilgher was of the socialist opposition and long suffered censorship, ostracism, and police surveillance—until another fascist writer got Mussolini to lift his veto (Sciascia, *Pirandello*, 149–50).

9. My reference is to Sciascia's recall of a remark in Pirandello's *The Late*

Mathias Pascal, where the difference between "ancient" and "modern" tragedy is suggested by the image of an Orestes played in a marionette theater. If the paper sky were torn as he was about to avenge his father's murder on Ægisthus and Clytemnæstra, Orestes would look toward it and the "maleficent influences" bursting down through it. His arms would drop, he "would, in sum, become Hamlet." The difference is not in the fact or nature of the conflict, but in one's awareness of it and of self (Sciascia, *Pirandello*, 23–24).

10. It has been asserted that the Jews of Venice "were respected and esteemed for their craftsmen's skill and welcomed as useful to the city's economy" (*Invitation to Venice*, 110). They were certainly found useful, and were surely dunned for the city economy on all possible occasions. Signs of respect, esteem, or welcome are more tenuous. As Morris puts it, "They had to wear a special costume . . . ; they were relentlessly taxed on every conceivable pretext; they had to pay through the nose for permission, frequently renewable, to remain in the city at all." The Christian guards who forbade all access to or from the ghetto at night were naturally paid for by the Jews. Possibly physically safer than elsewhere in Europe, an official sixteenth-century inscription nonetheless threatened "with the cord, stocks, whip, galleys or prisons all [Jews] who are guilty of blasphemy" (Morris, *World*, 106, 108). All Jews being by definition so guilty, the edict was a Damocles' sword, a doomwatch giving authorities carte blanche. Useful they were, but the Jews were economically exploited, legally threatened, socially deprived, and physically oppressed, locked away in the "grey desolation" (127) of the "tall teeming houses of the ghetto . . . still poor and filthy" (107).

11. The apt phrase quoted was Prendergast's ironic characterization.

12. No edition of Nietzsche that I have found (in any language) explains these references, and I had difficulty tracking them down. I owe thanks to Mikhail Iampolski, who reminded me of Jean-Pierre Vernant's little book; Friedrich Ulfers, who suggested allegorical readings of the use of Heracles' ape; above all Peter N. Miller, who put me on to Janson. This led me to McDermott, who brought me to Lucian.

13. Some images of the monkey in postmedieval Japan seem similarly disjunctive, but the meanings are so many as to make any such claim at best ambiguous (Ohnuki-Tierney).

14. In Bhabha's view, "colonial" mimicry would be a kind of third site between colonizer and colonized, not quite the one not quite the other; a practice that "unhomes" both, estranging and unsettling fixed identities and securities of power ("Of Mimicry and Man," *Location*, 85–92). Walcott's argument seems the more radical, concerned not with "unhoming" (perhaps Bhabha's Walcottian mirroring of his own name) but with making the new. In a fine essay ("Mimesis and Catharsis"), Goldstein long ago argued that by poetic *mimesis*, Aristotle meant the actual human *process of making* the work as well as the rational internal organizing principles enabling it. This is very different from just about every other post–European Renaissance interpretation.

15. I'm not sure where Césaire made the comments on *Saison*; they are quoted as his on the back of the American Grove edition. These two plays would differ from *Et les chiens se taisaient*, at least according to A. James Arnold, who remarks of it: "In Césaire's vision of tragic myth there is a gulf between the order of nature—to which the Rebel and his ritual sacrifice belong, hallowing his relationship to the black world—and the order of contemporary culture, however perverse, that Césaire represents as belonging to the masters of colonial empire" (introduction, xxvii). Here, then, Césaire would use tragedy to depict a fundamental division between *Gemeinschaft* and *Gesellschaft*—a view cohering with some of Chapter 1's arguments about *négritude*. The penultimate scene of Walcott's *Dream on Monkey Mountain* manifests the problematic poverty of this view (see in Chapter 1, above), but so, too, do Césaire's own *La tragédie du roi Christophe* and *Saison*; a closer reading of *Chiens* might actually suggest something similar.

16. For Japan, see Ohnuki-Tierney, 46–54; for Esu, Legba, and associated figures in West Africa, see Pelton—and Piedra, "Monkey Tales," 129–33, 136–37; for the Caribbean, Brazil, and African America, see Gates, *Signifying*, esp. 3–88; for Cuba, see Piedra as well as Cabrera, *El monte*; for Barbados, Brathwaite, *Barabajan*, 152, 172–73, 180, 188.

17. These points are needed in reply to a questioner at the original lecture who did think an East–West polarity was in hand (an apprehension implying larger blindness) and that I was "laying claim" to a "liminal" space between them. I'm unsure what it *means* to think oneself as "marginal" or as occupying the "limen," under *any* situation (although Bhabha and Mignolo are surer). My own home is anyway inevitably in western culture—as Césaire reminded his 1950s audience: "we do not choose our cultures, we belong to them" (Baldwin, *Nobody*, 53). But living in an ever more global exchange of cultures makes for at least two main tasks: to analyze from within the categories and consequences of one's own culture, and to enable interweavings of cultures by "a process of embedded exchange, . . . a knowing of homes from home" (67 above).

18. That Darwin used such Latin *nowhere* else in the work suggests he was fully aware of his note's offensiveness. No doubt unsurprisingly, Ortega y Gasset allows himself a similarly telling comment on the Spaniard's "ambiguous destiny": "Behind his Mediterranean features there seems to lurk the Asiatic or African gesture, and in the latter—in the Asiatic or African eyes and lips—lies the subhuman animal, as if only dozing, ready to invade the whole face" (*Meditations*, 98). Written in 1914, this is of a piece with Maeztu's and Unamuno's political tendencies. But such telling moments are legion. Philip offers several apropos of modernist western artists disavowing in usually ugly terms an earlier avowed—or anyway not denied—African influence in their art, Constantin Brancusi referring for instance to "demonic forces" and even destroying some of his earliest work in disgust (*Frontiers*, 94–95).

19. The "Double Mistress Episode" is usually ascribed to Pope. David Barton, to whom I owe renewed acquaintance with it, feels it smacks more of Jonathan Swift.

20. This may say more about the universalizing *Weltliteratur* of my Introduction and its intended controlling place and role. With minor changes, I have followed John Oxenford's translation of Goethe's *Autobiography* (1st ed., 1848), rather than the more recent one by Robert R. Heitner. The latter tones down Goethe's phrase: "diese kunstwidrigen Gespenster" become "these inartistic fancies" (397). On the other hand, Oxenford heightens it: "these goblins, so repulsive to art."

21. I thank Kamau Brathwaite for reminding me of this.

22. Carlos Fuentes has analyzed Faulkner's writing as signaling a "tragic" divided relation to nature ("Yoknapatawpha" itself being a Chickasaw word meaning "the divided earth"; Fuentes, *Casa*, 64–78; Van Delden, 53–54). Apropos of Baldwin's anger, one might ponder the description of Toomer quoted earlier. In Toomer's *Cane* (1923), at stake was the stunting and destruction of black lives and life by poverty, hopelessness, violence, blighted opiate religion, racism, and endless fear. Equating Toomer (and other black writers) with poet "exiles" like Robert Duncan, Robert Creeley, and Charles Olson, as Mackey does in the book cited, takes his work from its concrete embedding in actual horror. The others' self-proclaimed "marginality" concerned poetry and a mainstream their relation to which they could *choose*. Neither aestheticism nor such choice could be Toomer's. To write of a "tragic" sense of "the soul's passage through an unsoulful world" urges, we now see, that evacuation of reality.

CHAPTER 4

1. Like so many others we have seen, Dallal adds that just as these standards and modes "could be alien . . . to western literary traditions," so they would also be "ideally stimulating" ("Perils," 8): a necessity of a culture's life, indeed.

2. I recall Anzaldúa's comments recorded in Chapter 1, where she adds: "An Indian mask in an American museum is transposed into an alien aesthetic system where what is missing is the presence of power invoked through performance ritual" (*Borderlands*, 68). Patricia Penn Hilden and Shari Huhndorf explore how native Americans are exhibited in U.S. museums—notably in the Smithsonian National Museum of the American Indian [sic]("Performing"). Their conclusions add layers of complexity to Anzaldúa's remark but confirm its accuracy. See, too, Philip: "For Africans, the museum has always been a significant site of their racial oppression . . . pivotal in the expansion of the West's knowledge base about the world . . . seminal in the founding of its disciplines ethnography, archeology and anthropology . . . indispensable in Europe's attempt to measure, categorize and hierarchize the world" (*Frontiers*, 104). Of his "alleged" remark, Bellow protested that he made it during a now "forgotten" interview apropos "the distinction between literate and preliterate societies," and that *he* never put it in print ("Papuans"). This hardly changes its implications.

3. *Nietzsche* (Pfullingen: Neste, 1961), 1. 215, as quoted in Melberg, *Theories*, 4.

4. Iulian K. Shchutskii, *Researches on the I Ching*, translated by William L. MacDonald and Tsuyoshi Hasegawa with Helmut Wilhelm, Bollingen Series 62:2 (Princeton, N.J.: Princeton University Press, 1979), 84; quoted by Yu (40).

5. Owen offers, too, a useful "summary" of fundamental elements of "the Chinese literary tradition" (*Traditional*, 34). On the poem as "enactment" and limited "manifestation" of "a full world," see, too, 62–63.

6. Liu Hsieh was taken to sum up some thousand years of tradition and was still quoted as a principal authority into the second half of the twentieth century.

7. These two sentences are largely Haun Saussy's, to whom I owe this reminder.

8. I am indebted to Daniel Javitch for reminding me of this (as of much more), as well as for sending me to divers sources. To be pedantic, McKeon does mention Seneca twice in "Imitation," once to note the uninformative remark that "all art is an imitation of nature" (*Ep*, lxv.3), once to recall, *sans plus*, Nicolas Malebranche's analysis of his prose ("Imitation," 123, 137).

9. Plato, *Ion*, 534a–b (Loeb edition, 420–23). Lamb reminds us that Aristophanes used the idea of the tragedian Phrynichos: "he sipped the fruits of ambrosial lays, ever bringing away sweet song" (*Birds*, 750; *Ion*, 422–43 n. 1; cf. von Stackelberg, 273–74).

10. The tradition has been traced by von Stackelberg, who finds its beginnings in Sanskrit, its endings in the western European eighteenth–nineteenth centuries ("Bienengleichnis," 272). For the Renaissance, see especially Hermann Gmelins and Michel Jeanneret. For an older, still useful, compendium of ancient use of bee imagery, see Robert-Tornow. The exclusive later reading of Seneca as speaking of imitating previous writers may owe much to Lucretius, whose most notable use of the image was to refer to himself as a bee reading the flowers of Epicurus (*De rerum natura*, III, 11–12).

11. These terms are named by George W. Pigman, "Versions." His essay is important for the Renaissance and also provides excellent bibliographical information up to its date of publication (1980). For general analyses of the western mimetic tradition in history, see Beardsley, *Aesthetics*, and McKeon, "Imitation." For the literature on metaphor (and, to a degree, on mimesis), see Shibles, *Metaphor*, and van Noppen and Hols, *Metaphor II*; the first text is fully annotated, the second partially.

12. The same seems the case for Horace's equation of the poet who finds it as hard to write poetry as a "Matinian bee" gathering thyme does to make a honeycomb (*Odes*, IV.2.27–32). Most ancient uses of the image (e.g., Pindar, *Pythian*, 10:53–56; Lucretius, *De rerum natura*, IV.21–22) seem so brief as to allow no clear interpretation, but John Hamilton has made some wonderful readings of Pindar in this regard ("Soliciting Darkness"). Susan Scheinberg notes that the relation between bees, honey, truth-telling prophecy, and poetry was traditional from archaic Greek times, but she is unable to say much about its meaning (16–26).

13. Contrary to W. B. Stanford, who argued that Homer hardly used metaphor

because he could not undermine accepted meaning so early in the creation of a language (*Greek Metaphor*, 118–43)—a curiously Whiggish understanding of cultural creation. He did, however, try to make a space for a different idea of metaphor much later: in Hermogenes' thought that metaphor united subject and "extraneous reference" into some "composite concept" where all three somehow remained alive in an ongoing dialectic (*Greek Metaphor*, 14). One may or may not agree with this interpretation of Hermogenes; Stanford, anyway, took him to be a uniquely isolated case.

14. Fascinatingly, Owen analyzes a poem ("Facing the Snow") in which Tu Fu, lamenting recent military defeat and gazing out in sorrow on the winter weather, also associated snow with battle, a "'swift and urgent' snow that moves with the 'alarums' of war, with the 'hard-pressed' advance of levies to the front; troops moving hastily, snow driven whirling in the wind—the hidden pattern of battle and dissolution" (*Traditional*, 38). I suspect the cases indicate two very different workings of the fictive imagination (or, if they don't, show how different ancient Greek culture was from later western ones). They would offer a wonderful case study for someone deeply at home in both cultures.

15. The same text is given in Cabral, *Return*, 39–56. The translation is different and omits Cabral's introductory material about Eduardo Mondlane, the assassinated (1969) president of FRELIMO.

16. Mphahlele has a strong point in observing that Eliot saw "conflict and diversity between cultures . . . as essential so that allegiances and alliances in other areas may bring about cohesion in larger relationships" and that he "abdicated" his stand on the need for cultural exchanges "by later advocating a general re-grouping under a Christian banner" (*African Image*, original ed., 94).

17. I. A. Richards, inventor of the tenor/vehicle doublet, actually seems to support such a view as this (*Philosophy*, 94–96). He and Black call it "an *interaction view*" of metaphor (Black, "Metaphor," 38), but their descriptions are watered-down versions of the kind of "mimetic" power of which Seneca wrote (see, too, Beardsley, *Aesthetics: Problems*, 134–47).

18. I am grateful to Ladina Bezzola Lambert for recalling these remarks on Seneca's bees.

19. This makes Martin Foss' 1949 remark as curiously prophetic as it is wrongheaded: "It would be a sad day for humanity, if philosophy were proved to have emerged out of an impulse to confuse and to hide, out of an inclination to create disorder. The enemies of metaphysics might have reason to rejoice, but no serious scholar would" (*Symbol*, 3). At issue is not disorder but the choice and universalization of certain kinds of order. Some, of course, would call that disorder (but not in Foss' sense).

20. Kendall Walton's *Mimesis as Make-Believe* seems to approach such a view. He argues that "representations" are "props in games of make-believe, although they also *prompt* imaginings and are sometimes *objects* of them as well. A prop is something which, by virtue of conditional *principles of generation*, mandates imag-

inings. Propositions whose imaginings are mandated are *fictional*, and the fact that a given proposition is fictional is a *fictional truth*. *Fictional worlds* are associated with collections of fictional truths; what is fictional is fictional in a given world—the world of a game of make-believe, for example, or that of a representational work of art" (69). Roman Ingarden thought Aristotle offered a similar idea of poetry as "*mimesis*" rationally creating "*appearances of reality*" not subject to judgments of true or false and meant to produce emotional experiences. Mimesis cuts "poetic work" from the real world and from all "nonartistic writing" ("Marginal Commentary," 275–78, 284). Both views clearly presuppose division, and perhaps even sharpen it.

21. McKeon records Philostratus as making an apparently quite different claim, holding that "imagination" far surpasses "imitation," because the first creates while the second copies (VI.xix: McKeon, "Imitation," 146). One can only say that the meaning Philostratus is here giving *mimesis* differs entirely from that of the earlier passage, where imagination and mimesis are anything but opposed. Gerard Watson ("Discovering") also gives a different view of Philostratus, tracing his philosophical contexts and providing a good overview of modern critical writing on him.

22. Personal communication, April 30, 1998. I am indebted to Jenine Abboushi Dallal for conversation and for pointing me to writings named here and elsewhere, following my initial query about Adonis.

23. I also owe thanks to Ngũgĩ for conversations about the idea and practice of *kĩrĩra*.

24. I have again changed the published English translation somewhat.

CHAPTER 5

1. Among myriads, I mention Gilbert Ryle, *Concept*, and Bernard Williams, *Descartes*. Most current works in "neural philosophy" make Descartes the villain of their piece; indeed, it is largely of these that Sutton is writing when he speaks of Descartes' "talismanic place in philosophy and cultural studies alike as the demonic source of modern alienation" (*Philosophy*, 24). Two essays by Margaret Dauler Wilson summarize this philosophical view, "Cartesian Dualism" and "Body and Mind," but at least as far as memory is concerned, Sutton's volume takes it apart.

2. This is Theodore M. Brown's term ("Descartes," 41). He argues that in the medical literature, neither Descartes himself nor avowed followers claimed dualism. Only in the nineteenth century did "anatomical localism, cellular pathology, and microbiological etiology" rupture "organismic totality" (52). Sylvana Tomaselli also shows Descartes' paternity of the mind/body split to be a later myth. Like all myths, it came to rule subsequent belief and created "nostalgia" for a wholeness its forms supposedly displaced ("First Person," 185–86, 192).

3. With slight changes, I use Descartes, *Philosophical Writings* (indicated as

CSM). This edition is keyed to *Oeuvres* (indicated as AT): here AT, 11:351; CSM, 1:339–40 (*Passions*, I.30). When CSM is not indicated, either the text is not there or my changes are significant.

4. *Traité de l'homme* (AT, 9:119–202; CSM, 1:99–108); *Discours de la méthode*, part 5 (AT, 6:55–56; CSM, 1:139); *Description du corps humain* (AT, 11:223–57; CSM, 1:314–24); *Passions*, I.7 (AT, 11:331–32; CSM, 1:330). See Sutton, *Philosophy*, 74–81, 90–95, for especially lucid discussion. Of this point, he correctly observes that Descartes' automata "*are* organic" (76). *My* point is that Descartes wanted to be able to analyze them as limit cases whose organicity did not impede understanding the logical or "geometric" functioning of their body parts.

5. The thought that comparing the arts across cultures shows "not the influence of one system of thought upon another, but the coherence of the metaphysical tradition in the world and at all times" (Coomaraswamy, *Transformation*, 150 n. 56) is basic to Coomaraswamy's writings; see especially *Transformation*. The view tends to assimilate "traditional societies" to one another (although Coomaraswamy himself is very conscious of differences and details traditions, as for example in "Hindu View of Art: Historical," "Hindu View of Art: Theory of Beauty," "That Beauty Is a State," collected in *Dance*, 18–45). For brief statements that modern western art has lost sight "of the only universal language of culture" ("Gradation and Evolution II," *What Is Civilisation?*, 80) and suggestions as to how, see "Mind and Myth," "Symbols," "The Interpretation of Symbols," and "The Symbolism of Archery," collected in *What Is Civilisation?* (120–56).

6. As played out in Fuentes' *Cambio de piel*, this relation between architecture and order is embodied in the novel's principal Nazi character, Franz Jellinek, an architect who builds a concentration camp and who sees the architect as the symbolic representative of the modern world's rational order. This is an extreme echo of many writers already mentioned.

7. De Certeau holds that history as simultaneity *is* found in modern western experience. The discourse analyzing it is called not historiography but psychoanalysis: "Psychoanalysis and historiography thus have two different ways of distributing the *space of memory*. They conceive of the relation between the past and the present differently. Psychoanalysis recognizes the past *in* the present; historiography places them one *beside* the other" (*Heterologies*, 4). If this is right, the displacement of the first into the individual psyche is itself a principal mark of a change in the understanding (and ordering) of a collective history—and indeed in what is comprehensible *as history*.

8. Nandy argues that "those living outside" Enlightenment ideas of history, "especially in societies where myths are the predominant mode of organizing experiences of the past," function by "the principle of principled forgetfulness." Their myths are vital "morality tales" involving "a refusal to separate the remembered past from its ethical meaning in the present. For this refusal, it is often important not to remember the past, objectively, clearly or in its entirety" ("History's," 5). Nandy insists on the limitless variety of "ahistorical societies" (so

named by cultures defining themselves in some version of Enlightened history), but Descartes' adoption of this "principle of forgetfulness" is striking. (I was unaware of Nandy's argument until years after mine was in print; I first saw this paper in 1998, thanks to Patricia Penn Hilden. His argument here, though, summarizes a more detailed discussion advanced, for example, in *Intimate Enemy*, 57–59.) If Nandy is right, then what Descartes did—familiarly—was radically extend a familiar technique: provisionally trying to forget—or bracket—the past as totalizing prejudice. Too, an older European sense of "history as encroachment" was quite different from the kind of "history in the present" of which Nandy speaks, and Descartes' aimed his "forgetting" at its totality, not at selected elements.

9. "Supponis *posse mentem liberam fieri a præjudiciis omnibus*: at impossibilis res videtur. Imprimis, quia memoria judiciorum prius factorum, penesque ipsam depositorum thesaurus cum sit, excuti a nobis pro votis non potest. Id in se quisque experitur, et ille norat optime, qui artem non tam memorandi, quam obliviscendi optabat. Videlicet facta judicia ita habitu perseverant, et sigillorum instar impressa sic haerent, ut illa ad placitum eluere, aut eradere in potestate nostra non sit"; Gassendi, *Disquisitio*, 36/37 (Gassendi, *Opera omnia*, 6 vols. [Lyon, 1658], 3:279a–b). *Habitus* is a scholastic (Aristotelian) term of art for an ability or capacity, in a given physiological-intellectual domain, that is imprinted in the mind or soul, *animus*, or *anima*. It is, as it were, a mode of functioning stamped in the brain, enabling—producing—actions within its particular area of concern according to expected habit. It can be innate or learned.

10. Cicero, *De oratore*, 1:426 : "si se oblivisci quae vellet quam si meminisse docuisset" (II.lxxiv.299). Compare 1:464, where Antonius says he is less clever that Themistocles and so unable to desire rather "oblivionis artem quam memoriae" (II.lxxxvi.351). Cicero also used the thought in *Academica*, II.i.2, and in *De finibus*, II.xxxii.104. Quintilian rang a variant with the musician Timotheus charging double to teach those who had been taught before because they had to be made to forget what they had learned (1:218; II.iii.3). The idea was something of an ancient and modern tag: Baldesar Castiglione recalled Themistocles at the start of the second book of his 1528 *Book of the Courtier* (108), as Vives did both ancients in his 1520 *In Pseudodialecticos*: "there are some things I would do as much to unlearn [*dediscere*] as I would to learn [*addiscere*] many others" (Vives, *Against*, 50/51).

11. Sorabji, *Aristotle*, 37. The opposition comes from Plato: *Meno*, 85d; *Phaedo*, 75e; and *Philebus*, 34b–c. For the other concepts, see especially *Theaetetus* 191d, 193b–c, 194c–195a.

12. It is worth stressing that memory as a seal's imprint was *not* a metaphor. For Descartes and his predecessors back to Aristotle and Plato, memory was literally experience physically impressed on the brain. With others, Ortega urged that from Greek antiquity through the European middle ages, "the *metaphor* of the seal that prints its impress in wax" was the central figure encapsulating human mental experience and "orienting . . . all men's ideas" ("Las dos," 258; my italics). The argument matters because that it was *not* in fact a metaphor emphasizes how mind was

embedded in the world (and helps us understand both history as encroachment and the person as embedded in the physical world and its history). To see only a metaphor is to see not an experience of the human in the world but a way of rationally overcoming a supposed awareness (again) of *distance* and *division* between the world and the human. Ortega also argued that the metaphor changed for European modernity, becoming that of "the container and its contents" ("Las dos," 261). But that, too, goes back to antiquity. This chapter suggests a different sort of debate.

13. Sutton is very fine as well on intellectual memory (*Philosophy*, 67–73). In general, he argues that such overlappings as those mentioned here (and more) show that Descartes was not thinking just of permanent imprints, but of memory as a *process*. I don't think this affects my point here, for what I suggest as his way around the imprinted figure problem certainly *is* a process. Part of the problem is that Descartes did not easily separate physiology and epistemology (and perhaps ontology), and it may be that he *was* trying to find a way to describe memory as a (potentially controllable) process—this itself being part of a reorganization of the relations between mind and history, body and memory. At issue were indeed reformulations of history and identity.

14. After discussing Descartes' "solipsism," Nkrumah (*Consciencism*, 20–21) argued the need to understand "categorial convertibility": "such a thing as the emergence of self-consciousness from that which is not self-conscious; such a thing as the emergence of mind from matter, of quality from quantity." This had been hopeless until science offered models like the convertibility of matter and energy or the emergence of qualities from physical quantities in chemical change. This puts the issue in binary western terms, but it matters that Nkrumah raised it just when writing of the normative view of Descartes. It matters too that Unamuno raised the same issue of categorial "*convertibilidad*" apropos of Quijote, here between body and actions ("facciones . . . color . . . estatura" and "hazañas"), between these and spirit and, with regard to them all, between idealism and realism ("convertibles también") and individual and social, as if Quijote offered a quite different model of understanding ("Caballero," 77; cf. 81).

15. "Addo, existimare mentem capaciorem fieri verae perceptionis ex deflexione ad falsitatem, perinde videri, ac existimare, debere quampiam, ut dealbetur, fieri prius Æthiopem" (Gassendi, *Disquisitio*, 42 [*Opera omnia*, 3:280b: Dub. I, Inst. III, adv. Med. I]).

16. Like the art of forgetting tag (note 10 above), the reference was proverbial. In *Adages*, i.iv.50, Erasmus cited Lucian's *Adversus indoctum* (§28: "Αἰθίοπα σμήχειν ἐπιχειρέω": "I am trying to wash an Ethiopian white"), calling it a cliché that started in Aesop's fable, "The Ethiopian," about a man who bought a black slave and tried to wash away the "dirt." *Adages* iii.x.88 has ("Αἰθίοπα οὐ λευκαίνεται": "the Ethiopian cannot be whitened") and adds the Latin: "Aethiope non albescit." All this is to say that, as with the art of forgetting, Descartes could

well take Gassendi to be trapped in just the sort of prejudice, historical imposition, that he, Descartes, was seeking the means to get past. It may be said that Griffin *wrote* more like Gassendi than Descartes: "If a white man *became* a Negro in the Deep South, what adjustment would he have to make" (*Black Like Me*, 1; my italics). But his object was to implant new knowings in order to change his own and others' prejudices.

17. "Non posse mentem in isto quasi æquilibrio constitutam a recta rerum perceptione detorqueri" (Descartes, cited by Gassendi, *Disquisitio*, 42 [*Opera omnia*, 3:280b]).

18. AT, 7:23; CSM, 2:16: "In tantas dubitationes hesternâ meditatione conjectus sum, ut nequeam ampliùs earum oblivisci nec videam tamen quâ ratione solvendae sint."

19. I mention Kusch because he opposes this western history to myths of cultures that Nandy terms, by contrast, "ahistorical" (note 8 above; Nandy, "History's," 5)—here, those of Quechua and Aymara peoples (Kusch, *América*, 19–111), whose differences make western minds "fearful" (9–18). Kusch offers the solution of "*fagocitación*"—dialectical and mutual absorption (17 and *passim*) of what he calls—ironically?—Western "beauty" and American "stench." He aimed his ambiguous irony at Latin American traditions opposing European civilization to American barbarism (one of their best-known illustrations being Kusch's compatriot Sarmiento's 1845 *Facundo: Civilización y barbarie*). Comparison of Kusch's analyses with those of (subcontinental) Indian epics and their historical meaning (by Girindrasekhar Bose as noted by Nandy, "History's," 17–20, who then draws more recent implications, 21–28) would show workings of the different "ahistoricities" of which Nandy writes—and of which, in other terms, previous chapters tried to be so conscious. Like Nandy, however, Kusch also envisages the pasts of such cultures as always still "present" (*América, passim*; Nandy, "History's," 5, 26)—and see my own comment about the sixteenth century early in this chapter. Like America, India would have "many pasts," and "to absolutize them with the help of the European concept of history is to attack the organizing principles of [their] civilization." "It is doubtful," writes Nandy, "if [traditional India] finds objective, hard history a reliable, ethical or reasonable way of constructing the past." "Time" itself "is not given or preformatted" but "is an open-ended enterprise" able to be reforged by different stories made present ("History's," 27, 25). These issues will return.

20. Cf. *Discours de la méthode*, part 5: AT, 6:55–56; CSM, 1:139.

21. For the first, see More's letter of April 2, 1650, to Samuel Hartlib (AT, 5:636); for the second, *Naudaeana*, 125–26. I have made this argument at length in "Descartes, the Palatinate."

22. AT, 7:228; CSM, 2:160: "ususque sum rationibus, quibus non memini me ullas ad idem probandum fortiores alibi legisse."

23. In "Anna Liffey," a poem concluding this essay, Boland writes (22a; now in *In a Time of Violence*, 57):

I am sure
The body of an ageing woman
Is a memory
And to find a language for it
Is as hard
As weeping and requiring
These birds to cry out as if they could
Recognize their element
Remembered and distinguished in
A single tear. (22a)

CHAPTER 6

1. This is why Nandy argues that the impact of Freudian psychoanalysis in India was muted. In Europe, at first psychoanalysis *seemed* to challenge western "scientific rationalism" in its service not only as "a tool of knowledge and power" but "as moral fulcrum." In India, for the most part, it was taken as just another case of European rationalism whose notions of sexuality and the self were anyway largely incompatible with Indian traditions (*Savage Freud*, 111–12 ff.).

2. Given what I have said about time and space, motion and stasis (even writing and visuality), I quote the editors' note: "'Innervation' is a highly ambiguous term. It is very frequently used in a structural sense, to mean the anatomical distribution of nerves in some organism or bodily region. Freud uses it more often (though not invariably) to mean the transmission of energy into a system of nerves" (SE, 5:537 n. 2). I cannot henceforth note all these constant ambiguities.

3. Sherry Turkle, in *Psychoanalytic Politics*, wonders if this will not bring psychoanalysis to self-destruct from this constant questioning—undermining?—of its own status and practice: western science revealing its limits.

4. In their translation of Schiller's *On the Aesthetic Education of Man*, Wilkinson and Willoughby explain two important points in their translation by saying that "wenn nicht ... Subjekten" cannot meaning something like "in the various branches of knowledge" (which is how Snell translates it) because *Subjekt* can never mean "a particular department of art or science" as "subject" can in English. They explain their final "armed their eyes with a glass" (which Snell waters down as, "Reason ... strengthened its gaze") as a metaphor from the physical sciences, "mit bewaffnetem Auge," meaning "to aid the eye with a glass (*Aesthetic*, 235).

5. Roy also writes of this fall or disappearance of the chief found in both Hobbes and Freud, but without considering the meaning of this return to a state of nature (*Hobbes*, 20). Several of Rieff's writings look at these aspects of Freud, notably *Freud: The Mind of the Moralist* (which incorporates earlier arguments).

6. Derrida has constantly returned to Freud, especially in *La dissemination* (notably "Hors livre" and "La double séance") and the entire second half of *La carte*

postale, 277–549. On the "passage" from the "Projet" to the *Interpretation*, see Green, "De l'*Esquisse*."

7. Derrida criticizes Lacan's reading of Freud (through Edgar Allan Poe) as a "rediscovery" of singularizable truth and a misguided use of both Freud and Poe ("Le facteur de vérité," *Carte*, 441–524). I disagree. Freud certainly *thought* he was offering singular truths about the psyche.

8. The first remark is Jenkins'; the rest are Arnold's as quoted from the book under review: Ian Hamilton, *A Gift Imprisoned: The Poetic Life of Matthew Arnold* (New York: Basic Books, 1999).

CHAPTER 7

1. Gombrowicz started writing *Trans-Atlantyk* in 1948. It was serialized in 1951 in the Parisian Polish émigré review *Kultura* (R. Gombrowicz, *Gombrowicz*, 112), outraging its community. Nonetheless, it appeared as a book in 1953, while the diary had its life in regular contributions to the same review from 1952 until the author's death in 1969. Besides these and many short pieces, in Argentina Gombrowicz wrote two plays (*The Marriage*, 1948, and *Ivona*, 1957) and two other novels (*Ferdydurke*, 1947, and *Pornografia*, 1960).

2. Krystyna Lipinska-Illakowicz analyzes these issues especially through Gombrowicz's earlier novel *Ferdydurke* ("European Peripheries," 110–57; for a capsule "definition" of "immaturity" and its specific opposition to Kant's reflection on Enlightenment, see especially 113–17).

3. I do not read Polish. References are to the inaccurate English version made from French and German translations, the fine French translation, and the Polish original. I indicate these by E, F, and P, respectively. I am grateful to Sophie Janik and Wladimir Krysinski for good-humoredly answering endless queries about words, phrases, sentences, and meaning in the Polish. Lipinska-Illakowicz was similarly gracious at a later time. Square brackets in the next quotation signal additions and alterations made in the published English version; removal of their content gives a text nearer to the Polish. Thereafter, I make the changes without this cumbersome apparatus. The English version moves the novel toward "traditional" analytico-referential form.

4. Science has familiar cases of that sort of exclusion: comets as supralunar bodies and the moon (and planets) as earthlike ones for Ptolemaic cosmology or all quantum phenomena for the Newtonian system. Examples are evidently legion and the bibliography vast.

5. Joanne Rappaport, in *The Politics of Memory*, explores what seems an analogous historico-political consciousness among the Nasa people of the Colombian Andes, but she does not altogether avoid the myth/history/legend vocabulary that willy-nilly makes difference "difference from" western historiographical modes. Not to get caught by vocabulary is of course extraordinarily difficult, demanding

a vigilance that most of us cannot sustain and not seldom an outsider's position to our own culture that most cannot have.

6. Like the second citation above, this is Searle's quotation from Kurzweil, *The Age of Spiritual Machines: When Computers Exceed Human Intelligence* (New York: Viking, 1999). The view echoes a hope for an underlying grammar of mind that runs from the European sixteenth century to contemporary structural grammarians, philosophers of mind, and divers cyberneticists. The case for deep rules in biology is taken from Philip Kitcher's review of Ian Stewart, *Life's Other Secret: The New Mathematics of the Living World* (London: Penguin, 1998).

7. For these comments on *ptak*, I am indebted to Sophie Janik.

8. Since Marx, much has been written on the dialectic of consciousness and society, especially by Lev S. Vygotsky, Alexander Luria, and their colleagues. See too Vološinov, *Freudianism*.

9. The Mighty Sparrow is the name taken by the Grenadan-born (1935) Trinidad calypsonian Slinger Francisco, acknowledged calypso champion from the mid-1950s and winning the title of monarch seven times from 1956.

CHAPTER 8

1. Gomez has collated the most reliable figures concerning the geographical origins of slaves imported to north America, many of whom came via Caribbean islands. Parts of Africa were exploited differently at different times, but overall, between the 1620s and 1830s, nearly a quarter of the slaves came from the Bight of Biafra, mostly Igbo—a proportion virtually even with that of slaves brought from the whole of West Central Africa, which included peoples from all down the coast and inland from modern Cameroon, Equatorial Guinea, and Gabon through Congo to Angola (*Exchanging*, 29, 114–15). Since the Bight of Biafra was a principal British trading area, these proportions could well be more lopsided for the British Caribbean.

2. Depestre, "Lettre à Dobzynski," *Optique* 18 (August 1955): 46–50, here 48, quoted by Joan Dayan, introduction to *Rainbow*, 32. Césaire offered a sharp "Réponse à Depestre" in the same *Optique* (50–52). In a further "Réponse à Césaire" (*Optique* 24 [February 1956]: 5–33), Depestre asked how colonized peoples, "American, and even Negro American," could take on "the adventure of English verse without a preliminary meditation on the forms utilized in Great Britain, from Chaucer to Dylan Thomas? Can one believe that Whitman rushed into the luminous swell of verse without having reflected upon that of Shakespeare? . . . In a word, does a revolutionary and human content really make a work of art? What would Rimbaud be without the carnal triumph of his verse?" ("Réponse à Césaire," 16–17; Dayan, 29, her translation). Brathwaite might agree but argue (as does Philip and others) that just because form *is* inseparable from "revolutionary" content is why "the adventure" is one that demands that poets find forms embedded in their own cultural reality.

3. T. S. Eliot, "Scylla and Charybdis," *Agenda* 23 (1985): 11. Quoted by Ronald Schuchard in Eliot, *Varieties*, 53 n. 20.

4. First page references are to the 1971 edition, the second to the 1983 *Collected Poetry* (32–83); translations are mine, but I draw heavily on Goll/Abel/Snyder (1947/1971) and Eshleman/Smith (1983).

5. To friends in the incipient Caribbean Artists Movement, Ramchand had written in January 1967 that Caribbean writers and artists should do their best to get home to the West Indies and do their cultural work there (as he did in 1968, right away starting with Brathwaite the journal *Savacou* for this proselytizing goal (Walmsley, 53–54, 190). He had been in Britain for some years, working on his doctorate at Edinburgh University (Walmsley, 28), and even after leaving, it was perhaps a lingering sense of being in a tradition without *home* support, with exile inevitable, that imposed pride in Caribbean achievement abroad (Walmsley, 105, 172–73, 200–206).

6. Another version of "Clips" is in Brathwaite, *ConVERSations* (60–78). I find it gentler than that of *Ancestors*. If this is so, it may be largely because the poet addresses it more directly to an *actual* father.

CHAPTER 9

1. Eugenio Ascensio has shown that Nebrija did not originate the equation. He was preceded by Lorenzo Valla (who had close ties with the court of Aragon) in his *Elegantiae* (1471) and by Gonzalo García de Santa María in the prologue (ca. 1486) to his *Lives of the Fathers* ("La lengua"). I don't know to what work Ascensio is alluding in the last case, unless to the *Evangelios*, of which a 1485 edition supposedly existed of which no copies are now known; otherwise it is contemporary with Nebrija—whose view was quickly followed by others.

2. Soyinka (with others) notes that "the original owner" of the "colonial language" very well "understood the fatal consequence of this acquisition of his own weapon of oppression, a fear, often disguised under the veneer of the benevolent policy of separate development, lest the oppressed peoples prove as skilled as the oppressor had been in the exploitation of the now common medium" (*Art*, 89). And this says nothing, of course, about access to common sources.

CHAPTER 11

1. I quote here, more or less, from my *Meaning of Literature*, 345. The whole book argues the relation between "literature" and political authority (among other complex relations).

2. In the fourth letter, Cortés explained how they had built the Spanish section so that it was "separate from that of the natives and divided from it by a stretch of water, although there are wooden bridges on all the roads joining the two districts." Anthony Pagden, who translated and edited Cortés' *Letters from Mexico*,

notes that the Spanish section was in fact surrounded in the water by four native barrios (*Cartas*, 219; *Letters*, 323, 507 n. 55). (The draining of the lake came later.)

3. In *ReOrient*, Frank alters the focus, seeing European invasion of the Americas as an essential element in Europe's "integration" into a centrally *Asian* economy.

4. "Latin America" is not one place. Brunner notes that efforts so to speak of it risk being "a genuine Tower of Babel" ("Tradicionalismo," 151). But he agrees with Franco that "although each national case is different, the narratives have a certain similarity" (423). "Men and women of the continent," says Brunner, "come to share the same experiences, enabled by the current organization of cultural production/communication/consumption." They do so, he adds, because they now "participate in the same city-labyrinth" (185). More specifically, speaking of actuality on the ground, one may say that for all their material and geographical differences, Latin American cities share vast similarities in organization of center and barrio (as Alan Gilbert shows in *The Latin American City*) and as links in that "metropolitan centre–peripheral satellite" chain of which Frank has so much written as enabling massive surplus "expropriation/appropriation" from Latin America since the sixteenth century (*Capitalism*, 20).

5. The destruction had been appallingly rapid. In 1525, Gasparo Contarini, Venetian ambassador to Charles V's court, reported that Peter Martyr had told him that the islands of Hispaniola and Jamaica had gone "from a million souls and more" in Columbus' time to not even seven thousand and that the destruction continued. A later ambassador, Paolo Tiepolo, reported in 1563 that the Antillean archipelago had been "reduced to a wasteland whose indigenous people's unique passion was stubborn refusal of procreation and of life itself, a heart-broken will for annihilation." Others held that by then Hispaniola's Indians were extinct (Ambrosini, *Paesi*, 94–96). This was correct. Modern estimates are that Hispaniola went from 8 million in 1492 to less than 4 million by 1496 and to 250 by 1540 (Cook and Borah, 1:376–410).

6. Pagden remarks, too, of the ordinances issued by Cortés in New Spain (published in, e.g., Cortés' *Escritos sueltos*, 26–39), which the conquistador names at the end of his fourth letter, that "they make an interesting document which shows just how aware Cortés was of the damage done in the Antilles by the uncontrolled exploitation of the land and its inhabitants" (*Letters*, 336, 511 n. 69; *Cartas*, 228).

7. I am indebted to José David Saldívar for the reference and divers clarifications. On this, compare his *Dialectics*, 93.

8. Widespread views of indigenous "barbarism" versus European "civilization" are not the same, but that is not to say that some did not adopt such a myth. Thus Hector A. Murena began "El pecado original de América" by writing that those "expelled" from Europe "fell on another land, an uncivilized land, a vacuum of spirit, a land we came to call America." They had been "expelled from a spiritualized land to another without spirit ("Pecado," 163, 167). Murena saw arrival in the Americas as a fall from a European Eden, which, however, with faith and divine

help, might be turned to new creativity (if not creation); "Pecado," 196–232. And Andrés Bello certainly adopted another aspect of the myth, the idea that if the land was not empty to start with, it was becoming so as its peoples died or were absorbed: "The indigenous races are disappearing, and in the long run will be lost among the colonies of transatlantic peoples, leaving no more traces than a few words that have crept into the newly brought languages, and scattered monuments where curious travelers will ask in vain the name and description of the civilizations that brought them into being" ("Commentary," 164). Overall, though, such myths are rare south of the Mexican border. Paz was right to contrast north and south in just these terms (*Mexico and the United States*, 362).

9. I have changed the published English translation, which is marred by inaccuracies. Gruzinski adds that "the process was not one way, since the Spanish investigators were forced not only to translate in the literal sense of the term, but also to interpret what the Indians were willing to tell them" (*Colonisation*, 106). In a survey so organized, what could "interpretation" be?

10. We have earlier seen how concepts like tragedy and mimesis also permitted imposition of such an overlay, creating their own classification ("*découpage*") of a different reality.

11. Cervantes, an Erasmian disciple and friend of Vives, professor of rhetoric at the University of Osuna, went to Mexico in mid-1550 at his cousin's invitation. For years, the viceroy Antonio de Mendoza had been a strong proponent of building a university in the capital. The matter had been under consideration for twenty-five years, and the process was now reaching a head. Mendoza was eager to have qualified scholars available. A royal order for the creation of the University of Mexico was issued on September 21, 1551, and it was officially established in late January 1553, with courses inaugurated in June at a ceremony at which Cervantes delivered an oration in Latin. In July, he gave his first rhetoric class. By November of the next year, he was the University's treasurer. Later on, he would twice be rector (1567 and 1572). He died on November 14, 1575.

12. Ronald Christ inventories these and others in his afterword to Eltit's *E. Luminata*, 205–34. Djelal Kadir has an illuminating discussion of the way in which Eltit uses these literary histories in this novel and some suggestive remarks on her use of Inca history in another, *Por la patria* (*The Other Writing*), 186–90, 193–200.

13. For this aspect of *Lumpérica*, see Christ's afterword, 224–25.

14. Balbuena returned to Spain in 1606, became a doctor of theology in 1607, and published a pastoral novel in 1608. That same year, he was elected *abad mayor* of Jamaica, going there in 1610. Named bishop of Puerto Rico in 1620, he arrived there in 1623 after participating for two years in a provincial council held in Santo Domingo. His epic poem *El Bernardo*, completed in 1602, was published in Madrid in 1624. The next year, Dutch pirates burned San Juan, and his house and library were destroyed. He died in 1627.

15. Saussy suggests that Frank's *ReOrient* helps explain this imprecision. Frank

observes that from soon after the mid-sixteenth century, American silver (from Peruvian Potosí from 1545 and Mexican Zacatecas from 1548; *ReOrient*, 132) enabled European merchants to profit by participating in internal Asian trade, since Asians were uninterested in inferior western goods. A result would be that no actual goods found their way back. But what was the *rescate*? unless just a reference to westerners' awareness of the prevalence of piracy off Asian coasts.

16. Dos mil indios [¡oh extraña maravilla!]
     bailan por un compás a un tamborino,
     sin mudar voz, aunque es cansancio oílla;
     en sus cantos endechan el destino
     de Moctezuma, la prisión y la muerte,
     maldiciendo a *Malinche* y su camino:
     al gran Marqués del Valle llaman fuerte,
     que los venció; llorando desto cuentan
     toda la guerra y su contraria suerte.

     Two thousand Indians [o strange marvel!]
     dance to the beat of a tambour,
     without changing their tune, although it's wearisome to hear it;
     in their songs they lament the fate
     of Montezuma, his prison and death,
     cursing la *Malinche* and her course:
     they call great Cortés powerful
     for he defeated them; weeping over it they tell
     the whole war and its adverse fortune.

17. In fact, this *Epístola* was, in a sense, precisely that. Its full title is "Al licenciado Laurencio Sánchez de Obrégon, Primer Corregidor de México. Descrívesse el assiento de la ciudad, el trato i costumbres de la tierra i condiciones de los naturales della" (cited in Reyes Cano, 73). I have mostly drawn my information about Cueva's life from José Cebrián García's introduction to his edition of Cueva's *Fábulas mitológicas* and from the first chapter of Cebrián's *Estudios*, which somewhat rewrites the intellectual–biographical part of the earlier introduction. I am assuming that the cited passages are all from the same poem. I don't think it matters, but I have been unable to verify it.

18. "Escribo la alegría y contento que recibió todo la isla con su venida y libertad, el júbilo, con que le salieron á recibir no solo los vecinos del Bayamo, sino tambien las ninfas de los montes, fuentes y ríos, para que se note la falta que hace un bueno en una república, y el contento y alegría que muestran en su venida, no solo los hombres racionales, pero aun hasta los animales brutos y cosas insensibles."

Works Cited

Abanda Ndengue, Jean-Marie. *De la Négritude au Négrisme: Essais polyphoniques.* Yaoundé: Éditions CLE, 1970.

Abu Deeb, Kamal. "Al-Jurjānī's Classification of *Isti'āra* (Metaphor) with Special Reference to Aristotle's Classification of Metaphor." *Journal of Arabic Literature* 2 (1971): 48–75.

Achebe, Chinua. *Conversations with Chinua Achebe.* Edited by Bernth Lindfors. Jackson: University Press of Mississippi, 1997.

———. *Home and Exile.* Oxford: Oxford University Press, 2000.

———. *Hopes and Impediments: Selected Essays.* 1988. Reprint, New York: Doubleday Anchor, 1990.

———. *Morning Yet on Creation Day: Essays.* 1975. Reprint, Garden City, N.Y.: Doubleday Anchor, 1976.

Addison, Joseph. *The Freeholder.* Edited by James Leheny. Oxford: Clarendon, 1979.

Adonis [Ali Ahmed Said]. *An Introduction to Arab Poetics.* Translated by Catherine Cobham. Austin: University of Texas Press, 1990.

Aeschylus. *Eschyle II: Agamemnon, Les Choéphores, Les Euménides.* Edited and translated by Paul Mazon. Paris: Belles Lettres, 1925.

———. *The Oresteia: Agamemnon, The Libation Bearers, The Eumenides.* Translated by Robert Fagles. Introductory essay, notes, and glossary by Robert Fagles and W. B. Stanford. 1975. Revised and reprinted, Harmondsworth: Penguin, 1979.

Agamben, Giorgio. *Language and Death: The Place of Negativity.* Translated by Karen E. Pinkus with Michael Hardt. Minneapolis: University of Minnesota Press, 1991.

Ahmad, Aijaz. *In Theory: Classes, Nations, Literatures.* London: Verso, 1992.

Ajami, Mansour. *The Neckveins of Winter: The Controversy over Natural and Artificial Poetry in Medieval Arabic Literary Criticism.* Leiden: E. J. Brill, 1984.

Althusser, Louis. *Positions (1964–1975).* Paris: Éditions Sociales, 1976.

Ambrosini, Federica. *Paesi e mari ignoti: America e colonialismo europeo nella cultura veneziana (secoli xvi–xvii).* Deputazione di Storia Patria per le Venezie: Miscellanea di Studi e Memorie 20. Venice: Deputazione, 1982.

Antoni, Robert. *Divina Trace*. 1991. Reprint, Woodstock, N.Y.: Overlook Press, 1992.

Anzaldúa, Gloria. *Borderlands/La Frontera: The New Mestiza*. San Francisco: Aunt Lute, 1987.

Aparicio Laurencio, Angel. Introduction to *Espejo de paciencia*, by Silvestre de Balboa y Troya de Quesada, 7–37. Miami: Universal, 1970.

Appiah, Kwame Anthony. *In My Father's House: Africa in the Philosophy of Culture*. New York: Oxford University Press, 1992.

———. "Is the Post- in Postmodernism the Post- in Postcolonial?" *Critical Inquiry* 17 (winter 1991): 336–57.

Arbuthnot, John, Alexander Pope, et al. *Memoirs of the Extraordinary Life, Works, and Discoveries of Martinus Scriblerus*. Edited by Charles Kerby-Miller. New Haven, Conn.: Yale University Press for Wellesley College, 1950.

Aristotle. *The Complete Works*. Revised Oxford translation. Edited by Jonathan Barnes. 2 vols. Princeton, N.J.: Princeton University Press, 1984.

———. *Poetics*. Edited and translated by Stephen Halliwell; Longinus. *On the Sublime*. Edited and translated by W. H. Fyfe. Rev. Donald Russell; Demetrius. *On Style*. Edited and translated by Doreen C. Innes. Based on W. Rhys Roberts. Cambridge, Mass.: Harvard University Press, 1995.

———. See also: Gravel.

Arnold, A. James. Introduction to *Lyric and Dramatic Poetry 1946–82*, by Aimé Césaire, xi–xli. Translated by Clayton Eshleman and Annette Smith. Charlottesville: University Press of Virginia, 1990.

Asante, Molefi Kete. *The Afrocentric Idea*. Philadelphia, Penn.: Temple University Press, 1987.

Ascensio, Eugenio. "La lengua compañera del imperio: Historia de una idea de Nebrija en España y Portugal." *Revista de Filología Española* 43, no. 3–4 (1960): 399–413.

Assoun, Paul-Laurent. *Introduction à l'épistémologie freudienne*. Paris: Payot, 1981.

Aubenque, Pierre. *Le problème de l'être chez Aristote: Essai sur la problématique aristotélicienne*. 3rd ed. Paris: PUF, 1972.

Auerbach, Erich. *Mimesis: The Representation of Reality in Western Literature*. Translated by Willard Trask. 1953. Reprint, Garden City, N.Y.: Doubleday Anchor, 1957.

Azorín (José Martínez Ruíz). "Claro en el bosque." In *Hora*, 168–70.

———. "La famosa decadencia." In *Hora*, 171–74.

———. *Una hora de España*. Edited by José Montero Padilla. Madrid: Editorial Castalia, 1993.

———. *La ruta de Don Quijote*. Edited by José María Martínez Cachero. Madrid: Catedra, 1984.

Bacon, Sir Francis. *The Advancement of Learning* [1605]. In *Essays*, edited by Jones, 169–235.

————. *Description of a Natural and Experimental History*, in *The Works*, vol. 8. Edited by James Spedding, Robert Leslie Ellis, and Douglas Denon Heath. 15 vols. Boston: Taggard & Thomson, 1861–1864.

————. *The Essayes or Counsels, Civill and Morall*. Edited by Michael Kiernan. Cambridge, Mass.: Harvard University Press, 1985.

————. *Essays, Advancement of Learning, New Atlantis, and Other Pieces*. Selected and edited by Richard Foster Jones. New York: Odyssey Press, 1937.

————. *Magna Instauratio* [1620]. In *Essays*, edited by Jones, 237–363.

————. "The Refutation of Philosophies" ["Redargutio philosophiarum"]. In *The Philosophy of Francis Bacon. An Essay on Its Development from 1603 to 1609 with New Translations of Fundamental Texts*, by Benjamin Farrington, 103–33. Chicago: University of Chicago Press, 1964.

Baillet, Adrien. *Vie de Monsieur Des-Cartes*. 2 vols. Paris: Hortemels, 1691.

Balboa y Troya de Quesada, Silvestre de. *Espejo de paciencia*. Edited, introduction, and notes by Angel Aparicio Laurencio. Miami: Universal, 1970.

Balbuena, Bernardo de. *La grandeza mexicana y Compendio apologético en alabanza de la poesía*. Estudio preliminar de Luis Adolfo Domínguez. 1971. Reprint, Mexico City: Porrúa, 1990.

Baldwin, James. *Nobody Knows My Name*. New York: Delta, 1962.

————. *Notes of a Native Son*. 2nd ed. Boston: Beacon, 1984.

Baranzcak, Stanislaw. Introduction to *Trans-Atlantyk*, by Witold Gombrowicz, ix–xxi. New Haven, Conn.: Yale University Press, 1994.

Bataillon, Marcel. *Érasme et l'Espagne*. New ed. in 3 vols. Text established by Daniel Devoto. Edited by Charles Amiel. Geneva: Droz, 1991.

Beardsley, Monroe C. *Aesthetics from Classical Greece to the Present: A Short History*. 1966. Reprint, University: University of Alabama Press, 1975.

————. *Aesthetics: Problems in the Philosophy of Criticism*. 2nd ed. 1958. Reprint, Indianapolis, Ind.: Hackett, 1981.

————. "Metaphor." In *The Encyclopaedia of Philosophy*, 5:284–89. Edited by Paul Edwards. New York: Macmillan, 1967.

————. "The Metaphorical Twist." *Philosophical and Phenomenological Research* 22 (March 1962): 293–307.

Begley, Adam. "Harold Bloom: Colossus among Critics." *New York Times Magazine*, September 25, 1994, 32, 34–35.

Bello, Andrés. "Commentary on 'Investigations on the Social Influence of the Spanish Conquest and Colonial Regime in Chile' by José Victorino Lastarria (1844)." In *Selected Writings*, 154–68.

————. "The Craft of History (1848)." In *Selected Writings*, 175–84.

————. *Selected Writings of Andrés Bello*. Translated by Frances M. López-Morilas. Edited, introduction, and notes by Iván Jaksić. New York: Oxford University Press, 1997.

Bellow, Saul. "Papuans and Zulus." *New York Times*, March 10, 1994, A25.

Benítez-Rojo, Antonio. "Alejo Carpentier: Between *Here* and Over *There*." In *Sisyphus and Eldorado*, edited by Brathwaite and Reiss, 75–84.

———. *The Repeating Island: The Caribbean and the Postmodern Perspective*. Translated by James E. Maraniss. Durham, N.C.: Duke University Press, 1992.

Bernabé, Jean, Patrick Chamoiseau, and Raphaël Confiant. "In Praise of Creoleness." Translated by Mohamed B. Taleb Khyar. *Callaloo* 13 (1990): 886–909.

———. See also: Chamoiseau and Confiant.

Bezzola Lambert, Ladina. "Imagining the Unimaginable." Ph.D. diss., Universität Zürich, 1999.

Bhabha, Homi. *The Location of Culture*. London: Routledge, 1994.

———, ed. *Nation and Narration*. London: Routledge, 1990.

Binet, Étienne. *Essay des merveilles de nature, et des plus nobles artifices*. Preface by Marc Fumaroli. Évreux: Des Opérations, Association du Théâtre de la ville d'Évreux, 1987.

Black, Max. "Metaphor." In *Models and Metaphors: Studies in Language and Philosophy*, 25–47. Ithaca: Cornell University Press, 1962.

Bloom, Allan David. *The Closing of the American Mind*. New York: Simon & Schuster, 1987.

Bloom, Harold. *The Western Canon: The Books and School of the Ages*. New York: Harcourt Brace, 1994.

———. See also: Begley.

Boland, Eavan. "Making the Difference: Eroticism and Ageing in the Work of the Woman Poet." *P. N. Review* 96 (20, no. 4, March–April 1994): 13–23.

———. "The Water Clock." In *In a Time of Violence*, 36–37. New York: Norton, 1994.

Borges, Jorge Luis. *Labyrinths: Selected Stories and Other Writings*. Edited and translated by Donald A. Yates and James E. Irby, et al. Preface by André Maurois. 1964. Reprint, Harmondsworth: Penguin, 1970.

———. *Other Inquisitions 1937–1952*. Translated by Ruth L. C. Simms. Introduction by James E. Irby. 1964. Reprint, Austin: University of Texas Press, 1995.

———. "Pierre Menard, Author of the Don Quixote." Translated by Anthony Bonner. *Ficciones*. Edited and introduction by Anthony Kerrigan. New York: Grove, 1962. 45–55.

Bouveresse, Jacques. *Wittgenstein Reads Freud: The Myth of the Unconscious*. Translated by Carol Cosman. Foreword by Vincent Descombes. Princeton, N.J.: Princeton University Press, 1995.

Bovelles, Charles de. *Liber de differentia vulgarium linguarum, & Gallici sermonis varietate . . . ; Que voces apud Gallos sint factitiae & arbitrariae, vel barbariae . . . ; De hallucinatione Gallicanorum nominum*. Paris: Robertus Stephanus, 1533.

Brathwaite, [Edward] Kamau. *Ancestors*. New York: New Directions, 2001.

———. *The Arrivants: A New World Trilogy*. Oxford: Oxford University Press, 1973.

———. *Barabajan Poems 1492–1992*. Kingston: Savacou North, 1994.

———. *Black + Blues*. Havana: Casa de las Américas, 1976.

———. *Contradictory Omens: Cultural Diversity and Integration in the Caribbean.* 1974. Reprint, Mona, Jamaica: Savacou, 1985.

———. *ConVERSations with Nathaniel Mackey.* Staten Island, N.Y.: We Press; Minneapolis, Minn.: Xcp: Cross-Cultural Poetics, 1999.

———. *The Development of Creole Society in Jamaica, 1770–1820.* Oxford: Oxford University Press, 1971.

———. *Dream Haiti.* New York: Savacou North Limited Editions, 1995.

———. *DreamStories.* Harlow: Longman, 1994.

———. Editor's note to a special issue on English Caribbean Literature and Arts. *Review: Latin American Literature and Arts* 50 (spring 1995): 4.

———. *History of the Voice: The Development of Nation Language in Anglophone Caribbean Poetry.* London: New Beacon, 1984.

———. "I Cristóbal Kamau." *Review: Latin American Literature and Arts* 50 (spring 1995): 5–11.

———. *Jah Music.* Mona, Jamaica: Savacou Cooperative, 1986.

———. *Love Axe/l.* Leeds: Peepal Tree Press. Forthcoming.

———. "Metaphors of Underdevelopment: A Proem for Hernan Cortez." *New England Review and Bread Loaf Quarterly* 7, no. 4 (summer 1985): 453–76.

———. *Middle Passages.* Newcastle: Bloodaxe, 1992.

———. *Middle Passages.* New ed. New York: New Directions, 1993.

———. *Mother Poem.* Oxford: Oxford University Press, 1977.

———. "A Post-Cautionary Tale of the Helen of Our Wars." *Wasafiri* 22 (autumn 1995): 69–81.

———. *Roots: Essay.* Havana: Casa de las Américas, 1986.

———. "Sir Galahad and the Islands." In *Roots: Essay,* 7–27. Havana: Casa de las Américas, 1986.

———. *Sun Poem.* Oxford: Oxford University Press, 1982.

———. "Timehri." In *Is Massa Day Dead? Black Moods in the Caribbean,* 29–44. Edited by Orde Coombs. Garden City, N.Y.: Doubleday Anchor, 1974.

———. *Trench Town Rock.* Providence, R.I.: Lost Road, 1994.

———. *X/Self.* Oxford: Oxford University Press, 1987.

———. *The Zea Mexican Diary, 7 Sept 1926–7 Sept 1986.* Madison: University of Wisconsin Press, 1993.

———, general editor and author. *The People Who Came.* 3 vols. London: Longman, 1968–1972.

———, and Timothy J. Reiss, eds. *Sisyphus and Eldorado: Magical and Other Realisms in Caribbean Literature. Annals of Scholarship* 12, no. 1–2 (1997).

Breeze, Jean "Binta." *Spring Cleaning.* London: Virago Press, 1992.

Breiner, Laurence. "Tradition, Society, the Figure of the Poet." *Caribbean Quarterly* 26, no. 1–2 (March–June 1980): 1–12.

Briosi, Sandro. *Il senso della metafora.* Naples: Liguori, 1985.

———. *Il simbolo e il segno.* Modena: Mucchi, 1993.

Brodsky, Joseph. *Watermark.* New York: Farrar, Straus & Giroux, 1992.

Brown, Laura. *Alexander Pope.* Oxford: Basil Blackwell, 1985.

———. *Ends of Empire: Women and Ideology in Early Eighteenth-Century English Literature.* Ithaca, N.Y.: Cornell University Press, 1993.

Brown, Patricia Fortini. *Venice and Antiquity: The Venetian Sense of the Past.* New Haven, Conn.: Yale University Press, 1996.

Brown, Theodore M. "Descartes, Dualism, and Psychosomatic Medicine." In *The Anatomy of Madness: Essays in the History of Psychiatry,* edited by W. F. Bynum, Roy Porter, and Michael Shepherd, 1:40–62. London: Tavistock, 1985.

Brunner, José Joaquín. "Tradicionalismo y modernidad en la cultura." In *Cartografías de la modernidad,* 151–90. Santiago: Dolmen, 1994.

Buell, Frederick. *National Culture and the New Global System.* Baltimore, Md.: Johns Hopkins University Press, 1994.

Burton, Robert. *The Anatomy of Melancholy.* 3 vols. Edited and introduction by Holbrook Jackson. 1932. Reprint, London: Dent, 1968.

Cabral, Amilcar. "National Liberation and Culture." In *Unity and Struggle: Speeches and Writings,* 138–54. Texts selected by the PAIGC. Translated by Michael Wolfers. London: Heinemann, 1980.

———. *Return to the Source: Selected Speeches.* Edited by Africa Information Service. New York: Monthly Review Press, 1973.

Cabrera, Lydia. *El monte, Igbo-Finda-Ewe Orisha-Vititi Nfinda (Notas sobre las religiones, la magia, las supersticiones y el folklore de los negros criollos y del pueblo de Cuba).* 1954. Reprint, Miami: Ediciones Universal, 1975.

Cabrera Infante, Guillermo. *Mea Cuba.* Translated by Kenneth Hall and the author. 1994. Reprint, New York: Noonday, 1995.

Calvino, Italo. *The Castle of Crossed Destinies.* Translated by William Weaver. 1977. Reprint, New York: Harcourt Brace Jovanovich, 1979.

———. *Invisible Cities.* Translated by William Weaver. 1974. Reprint, New York: Harvest/HBJ, 1978.

———. *Numbers in the Dark and Other Stories.* Translated by Tim Parks. 1995. Reprint, New York: Vintage International, 1996.

Campos, Jorge. "Presencia de América en la obra de Cervantes." *Revista de Indias* 8, no. 28–29 (April–September 1947): 371–404.

Carew, Jan. *Fulcrums of Change.* Trenton, N.J.: Africa World Press, 1988.

———. "Harvesting History in the Hills of Bacolet." In *Fulcrums of Change,* 155–70. Trenton, N.J.: Africa World Press, 1988.

Carpentier y Valmont, Alejo. *Baroque Concerto.* Translated by Asa Zatz. 1988. Reprint, London: André Deutsch, 1991.

———. *Concierto barroco. Novela.* 1974. Reprint, Mexico City: Siglo Veintiuno, 1989.

———. "La cultura de los pueblos que habitan en las tierras del mar Caribe." In *La novela latinoamericana en vísperas de un nuevo siglo y otros ensayos,* 177–89. Mexico City: Siglo Veintiuno, 1981.

———. "De lo real maravilloso americano." In *Tientos, diferencias y otros ensayos*, 66–77. Barcelona: Plaza & Janés, 1987.

———. *Explosion in a Cathedral*. Translated by John Sturrock. 1963. Reprint, New York: Noonday, 1989.

———. *The Kingdom of This World*. Translated by Harriet de Onís; prologue translated by Heather Martin. 1957. Reprint, London: André Deutsch, 1967.

———. *The Lost Steps*. Translated by Harriet de Onís. Introduction J. B. Priestley. 1967. Reprint, New York: Bard/Avon, 1979.

———. *Los pasos perdidos*. 1953. Reprint, Montevideo: Arca, 1968.

———. *El recurso del metodo*. 1974. Reprint, Havana: Letras Cubanas, 1979.

———. *El siglo de las luces*. 1962. Reprint, Barcelona: Bolsillo, 1983.

Carr, Raymond. "Tonics for a Weak Nation: How Spain's Fragile Stability Was Shattered by Defeat in Cuba." *Times Literary Supplement*, August 7, 1998, 3–4.

Cascardi, Anthony J. *The Subject of Modernity*. Cambridge: Cambridge University Press, 1992.

———, and Timothy J. Reiss. "Poetry as Political Foundationalism/The Limits of Discursive Idealism." *Modern Language Quarterly* 54 (1993): 393–418.

Castellanos, Rosario. *The Nine Guardians [Balún-Canán]* [1957]. Translated by Irene Nicholson. 1959. Reprint, London: Readers International, 1992.

Castiglione, Baldesar. *The Book of the Courtier*. Translated and introduction by George Bull. Harmondsworth: Penguin, 1967.

Cavarero, Adriana. *In Spite of Plato: A Feminist Reworking of Ancient Philosophy*. Foreword by Rosi Braidotti. Translated by Serena Anderlini-D'Onofrio and Áine O'Healy. New York: Routledge, 1999.

Cebrián García, José. *Estudios sobre Juan de la Cueva*. Seville: Publicaciones de la Universidad de Sevilla, 1991.

———. See also: Cueva.

Cervantes de Salazar, Francisco. *México en 1554 y Túmulo imperial*. Edited by Edmundo O'Gorman. 1963. Reprint, Mexico City: Porrúa, 1985.

Cervantes Saavedra, Miguel de. *Novelas ejemplares*. Edited by Harry Sieber. 2 vols. Madrid: Cátedra, 1992.

Césaire, Aimé. *Cahier d'un retour au pays natal/Return to My Native Land* [rev. ed., 1956]. Translated by Émile Snyder, after Lionel Abel and Yvan Goll. Preface by André Breton. Paris: Présence Africaine, 1971.

———. *The Collected Poetry*. Translated, introduction, and notes by Clayton Eshleman and Annette Smith. Berkeley: University of California Press, 1983.

———. *Discourse on Colonialism* [1955]. Translated by Joan Pinkham. New York: Monthly Review Press, 1972.

———. *Lyric and Dramatic Poetry 1946–82*. Translated by Clayton Eshleman and Annette Smith. Introduction by A. James Arnold. Charlottesville: University Press of Virginia, 1990.

———. *Une saison au Congo*. Paris: Seuil, Points, 1973.

———. *A Season in the Congo.* Translated by Ralph Manheim. New York: Grove Press, 1968.

———. *A Tempest* [1969]. Translated by Richard Miller. 1985. Reprint, New York: Ubu Repertory Theater, 1992.

———. *La tragédie du roi Christophe: Théâtre.* Rev. ed. Paris: Présence Africaine, 1970.

Chaitanya, Krishna [Krishnapilli Krishnan Nair]. *Sanskrit Poetics: A Critical and Comparative Study.* London: Asia Publishing House, 1965.

Chamberlin, J. Edward. *Come Back to Me My Language: Poetry and the West Indies.* Urbana: University of Illinois Press, 1993.

Chamoiseau, Patrick, and Raphaël Confiant. *Lettres créoles: Tracées antillaises et continentales de la littérature. Haïti, Guadeloupe, Martinique, Guyane 1635–1975.* Paris: Hatier, 1991.

———. See also: Bernabé, Chamoiseau, and Confiant.

Chandra, Bipan. "Colonialism and Modernization." In *Nationalism and Colonialism in Modern India,* 1–37. 1979. Reprint, Hyderabad: Orient Longman, 1981.

———. "Historians of Modern India and Communalism." In Thapar, Mukhia, and Chandra, *Communalism,* 22–35.

———. *Nationalism and Colonialism in Modern India.* 1979. Reprint, Hyderabad: Orient Longman, 1981.

Chari, V. K. *Sanskrit Criticism.* Honolulu: University of Hawaii Press, 1990.

Chatterjee, Partha. "The Disciplines in Colonial Bengal." In *Texts of Power,* edited by Partha Chatterjee, 1–29.

———. "A Modern Science of Politics for the Colonized." In *Texts of Power,* edited by Partha Chatterjee, 93–117.

———. *The Nation and Its Fragments: Colonial and Postcolonial Histories.* Princeton, N.J.: Princeton University Press, 1993.

———. *Nationalist Thought and the Colonial World: A Derivative Discourse?* London: Zed, for the United Nations University; Delhi: Oxford University Press, 1986.

———, ed. *Texts of Power: Emerging Disciplines in Colonial Bengal.* Minneapolis: University of Minnesota Press, 1995.

Chinweizu [Chinweizu Ibekwe]. *Decolonising the African Mind.* Lagos: Pero Press, 1987.

———, Onwuchekwa Jemie, and Ihechukwu Madubuike. *Toward the Decolonization of African Literature.* Vol. 1, *African Fiction and Poetry and Their Critics.* 1980. Reprint, Washington, D.C.: Howard University Press, 1983.

Cheyfetz, Eric. *The Poetics of Imperialism: Translation and Colonization from "The Tempest" to "Tarzan."* Oxford: Oxford University Press, 1991.

Chomsky, Noam. "Free Trade and Free Market: Pretense and Practice." In Jameson and Miyoshi, *Cultures of Globalization,* 356–70.

Christie, Agatha. *Murder after Hours* (originally titled *The Hollow*). 1916. Reprint, New York: Dell, 1976.

———. *The Mysterious Affair at Styles* [1920]. In *Agatha Christie Omnibus. 1920s: Volume 1*, 1–189. London: Harper Collins, 1995.

Cicero, Marcus Tullius. *Brutus*. Edited and translated by G. L. Hendrickson. *Orator*. Edited and translated by H. M. Hubbell. Rev. ed. 1962. Reprint, Cambridge, Mass.: Harvard University Press; London: Heinemann, 1971.

———. *De oratore*. Edited and translated by E. W. Sutton and H. Rackham. 2 vols. 1942. Reprint, Cambridge, Mass.: Harvard University Press; London: Heinemann, 1967–1968.

Clark-Bekederemo, John Pepper. *Collected Plays 1964–1988*. Introduction by Abiola Irele. Washington, D.C.: Howard University Press, 1991.

———. *Masquerade* [1964]. In *Collected Plays*, 40–70.

———. *Song of a Goat* [1961]. In *Collected Plays*, 3–39.

Clendinnen, Inga. "Cortés, Signs, and the Conquest of Mexico." In *The Transmission of Culture in Early Modern Europe*, 87–130. Edited by Anthony Grafton and Ann Blair. Philadelphia: University of Pennsylvania Press, 1990.

Cobham-Sander, Rhonda. Introduction to *Contemporary Caribbean Culture and Art*, edited by Rhonda Cobham-Sander. Special issue of *Massachusetts Review* 35, no. 3–4 (autumn–winter 1994): 336–40.

———. "What's Real and What's Not in Robert Antoni's *Divina Trace*." In *Sisyphus and Eldorado*, edited by Brathwaite and Reiss, 49–73.

Cole, Bruce. *Titian and Venetian Painting, 1450–1590*. Westview: Icon Editions, 1999.

Coleridge, Samuel Taylor. *Biographia Literaria or Biographical Sketches of My Literary Life and Opinions*. Edited by James Engell and W. Jackson Bate. 2 vols. (*Collected Works*, Vol. 7, tomes 1–2.) Princeton, N.J.: Princeton University Press; London: Routledge & Kegan Paul, 1983.

———. *The Notebooks*. Edited by Kathleen Coburn. 4 vols. to date. New York: Pantheon; Princeton, N.J.: Princeton University Press; London: Routledge & Kegan Paul, 1957–1990.

Condé, Maryse. *Traversée de la mangrove*. 1989. Reprint, Paris: Folio, 1997.

———. *Heremakhonon*. Translated by Richard Philcox. 1982. Reprint, Colorado Springs, Colo.: Three Continents, 1994.

———. "Tracés de la littérature antillaise"/"Sketching a Literature from the French Antilles: From Negritude to *Créolité*." Translated by Richard Philcox. *Black Renaissance/Renaissance Noire* 1, no. 1 (fall 1996): 138–63.

Connerton, Paul. *The Tragedy of Enlightenment: An Essay on the Frankfurt School*. Cambridge: Cambridge University Press, 1980.

Constant, Benjamin. *Oeuvres*. Edited by Alfred Roulin. Paris: Gallimard, 1957.

Cook, Sherburne F., and Woodrow W. Borah. *Essays in Population History: Mexico and the Caribbean*. 3 vols. Berkeley: University of California Press, 1971–1979.

Coomaraswamy, Ananda Kentish. *The Dance of Śiva: Fourteen Indian Essays*. New York: Sunwise Turn, 1918.

———. *The Transformation of Nature in Art*. Edited and introduction by Kapila

Vatsyayan. New Delhi: Indira Gandhi National Centre for the Arts and Sterling Publishers, 1995.

——. *What Is Civilisation? and Other Essays.* Edited by Brian Keeble. Foreword by Seyyed Hossein Nasr. New Delhi: Indira Gandhi National Centre for the Arts; Delhi: Oxford University Press, 1989.

Copplestone, Fenella. Review of Kamau Brathwaite, *Middle Passages* (1992). *P. N. Review* 89 (19, no. 3: January–February 1993): 61.

Coronil, Fernando. "Discovering America Again: The Politics of Selfhood in the Age of Post-Colonial Empires." *Dispositio* 14, no. 36–38 (1989): 315–31.

Cortés, Hernán. *Cartas de relación de la conquista de México.* 1945. Reprint, Madrid: Espasa-Calpe, 1970.

——. *Escritos sueltos de Hernán Cortés.* Biblioteca Histórica de la Iberia 12. Mexico City: I. Escalante, 1871.

——. *Letters from Mexico.* Translated and edited by Anthony Pagden. Introduction by J. H. Elliott. New ed. New Haven, Conn.: Yale University Press, 1989.

Cueva, Juan de la. *Fábulas mitológicas y epica burlesca.* Edited by José Cebrián García. Madrid: Editora Nacional, 1984.

——. *Poèmes inédits.* Edited by Fredrik-A. Wulff. Introductory study followed by full text of *El viage de Sannio i de la Virtud al Cielo de Iupiter.* Acta Universitatis Lundensis/Lunds Universitets Ars-Skrift 23 (1886–1887). Lund: Malmström & Komp, 1887–1888.

Dainotto, Roberto Maria. "All Regions Do Smilingly Revolt: Region, Place, Literature." Ph.D. diss., New York University, 1995.

——. *Place in Literature: Regions, Cultures, Communities.* Ithaca, N.Y.: Cornell University Press, 2000.

Dallal, Jenine Abboushi. "The Perils of Occidentalism: How Arab Novelists Are Driven to Write for Western Readers." *Times Literary Supplement,* April 24, 1998, 8–9.

Damon, Phillip. *Modes of Analogy in Ancient and Medieval Verse.* University of California Publications in Classical Philology 15, no. 6 (1961): 261–334. Reprint, Berkeley: University of California Press, 1973.

Darwin, Charles. *The Origin of Species by Means of Natural Selection . . .* and *The Descent of Man and Selection in Relation to Sex.* New York: Modern Library, n.d.

Dash, J. Michael. "Literature and Language." In *Libète: A Haitian Anthology,* 289–314. Edited by Charles Arthur and Michael Dash. London: Latin American Bureau; Princeton, N.J.: Marcus Wiener; Kingston: Ian Randle, 1999.

——. "The World and the Word: French Caribbean Writing in the Twentieth Century." *Callaloo* 11 (winter 1988): 112–30.

——. See also: Glissant, *Caribbean Discourse.*

Davidson, Basil. *The African Genius: An Introduction to African Social and Cultural History.* Boston: Little, Brown, 1969.

Dayan, Joan. Introduction to *Rainbow,* by René Depestre, 1–106. Amherst: University of Massachusetts Press, 1977.

————. "Paul Gilroy's Slaves, Ships, and Routes: The Middle Passage as Metaphor." In *Sisyphus and Eldorado*, edited by Brathwaite and Reiss, 42–63.

De, Sushil Kumar. *A History of Sanskrit Literature (Prose, Poetry and Drama)*. Calcutta: University of Calcutta, 1947.

————. *Sanskrit Poetics as a Study of Aesthetic*. Notes by Edwin Gerow. Berkeley: University of California Press, 1963.

————. *Studies in the History of Sanskrit Poetics*. 2 vols. London: Luzac, 1923–1925.

de Certeau, Michel. *L'écriture de l'histoire*. Paris: Gallimard, 1975.

————. *Heterologies: Discourse on the Other*. Translated by Brian Massumi. Foreword by Wlad Godzich. Minneapolis: University of Minnesota Press, 1986.

————. *The Practice of Everyday Life*. Translated by Steven F. Rendall. Berkeley: University of California Press, 1984.

Depestre, René. *Bonjour et adieu à la négritude*. Paris: Robert Laffont, 1980.

————. *The Festival of the Greasy Pole*. Translation of *Le mât de cocagne* and introduction by Carrol F. Coates. Charlottesville: University Press of Virginia, 1990.

————. "Jean Price-Mars y el mito del Orfeo negro." In *Por la revolución, por la poesía*, 51–73. 1969. Reprint, Montevideo: Biblioteca de Marcha, 1970.

————. *Journal d'un animal marin*. Paris: P. Seghers, 1964.

————. *Le mât de cocagne* [1975]. Paris: Gallimard, 1979.

————. *Le métier à métisser. Essai*. Paris: Stock, 1998.

————. *Minerai noir. Poèmes*. Paris: Présence Africaine, 1956.

————. *Por la revolución, por la poesía*. 1969. Reprint, Montevideo: Biblioteca de Marcha, 1970.

————. *A Rainbow for the Christian West*. Translated and introduction by Joan Dayan. Amherst: University of Massachusetts Press, 1977.

De Roux, Dominique. See: Gombrowicz, *Entretiens*.

Derrida, Jacques. *La carte postale, de Socrate à Freud et au-delà*. Paris: Flammarion, 1980.

————. *La dissémination*. Paris: Seuil, 1972.

————. "Freud and the Scene of Writing." In *Writing and Difference*, 196–231. Translated and edited by Alan Bass. Chicago: University of Chicago Press, 1978.

————. "La mythologie blanche: La métaphore dans le texte philosophique." *Marges de la philosophie*, 247–324. Paris: Minuit, 1972.

Descartes, René. *Oeuvres*. Edited by Charles Adam and Paul Tannery. New ed. 11 vols. Paris: Vrin/C.N.R.S., 1964–1976.

————. *The Philosophical Writings*. Translated and edited by John Cottingham, Robert Stoothoff, and Dugald Murdoch, with Anthony Kenny for vol. 3. 3 vols. Cambridge: Cambridge University Press, 1985–1991.

Díaz del Castillo, Bernal. *Historia de la conquista de Nueva España*. Edited by Joaquín Ramírez Cabañas. 1955. Reprint, Mexico City: Porrúa, 1994.

Diogenes Laertius. *Lives of Eminent Philosophers*. Edited and translated by R. D. Hicks. 2 vols. 1925. Reprint, Cambridge, Mass.: Harvard University Press, 1991.

Diop, Cheikh Anta. *The African Origin of Civilization: Myth or Reality*. Edited translated by Mercer Cook. Chicago: Lawrence Hill, 1974.

Dirks, Nicholas B. Introduction to *Colonialism and Culture*, edited by Nicholas B. Dirks, 1–25. Ann Arbor: University of Michigan Press, 1992.

———, ed. *Colonialism and Culture*. Ann Arbor: University of Michigan Press, 1992.

Domínguez, Adolfo Luis. "Estudio preliminar." In Bernardo de Balbuena, *La grandeza mexicana y Compendio apologético en alabanza de la poesía*, xiii–xxxi. 1971. Reprint, Mexico City: Porrúa, 1990.

Donoghue, Denis. "Fretting in the Other's Shadow." Review of *The Penguin Book of Irish Fiction*, edited by Colm Tóibín. *Times Literary Supplement*, November 19, 1999, 21.

Douglas, Ann. Introduction to *Uncle Tom's Cabin or, Life Among the Lowly*, by Harriet Beecher Stowe, 7–34. 1981. Reprint, Harmondsworth: Penguin, 1986.

Dürrenmatt, Friedrich. "Problems of the Theatre." In *Problems of the Theatre, An Essay, and The Marriage of Mr Mississippi, A Play*, translated by Gerhard Nellhaus, 7–39. New York: Grove, 1964.

Dürer, Albrecht. *The Writings*. Translated and edited by William Martin Conway. Introduction by Alfred Werner. New York: Philosophical Library, 1958.

Eagleton, Terry. *Criticism and Ideology: A Study in Marxist Literary Theory*. London: NLB, 1976.

———. *The Function of Criticism: From "The Spectator" to Post-Structuralism*. London: Verso, 1984.

———. *Ideology: An Introduction*. London: Verso, 1991.

———. *Marxism and Literary Criticism*. London: Methuen, 1976.

———, Fredric Jameson, and Edward W. Said. *Nationalism, Colonialism, and Literature*. Introduction by Seamus Deane. Minneapolis: University of Minnesota Press, 1990.

Eliot, Thomas Stearns. *Four Quartets*. 1944. Reprint, London: Faber & Faber, 1995.

———. "The Metaphysical Poets." In *Homage to John Dryden: Three Essays on Poetry of the Seventeenth Century*, 24–33. London: Leonard & Virginia Woolf at the Hogarth Press, 1927.

———. *Notes Towards the Definition of Culture*. New York: Harcourt, Brace, 1949.

———. *The Sacred Wood*. New York: Knopf, 1921.

———. *The Varieties of Metaphysical Poetry. The Clark Lectures at Trinity College, Cambridge, 1926, and The Turnbull Lectures at The Johns Hopkins University, 1933*. Edited and introduction by Ronald Schuchard. New York: Harcourt Brace, 1993.

Else, Gerald F. *Aristotle's Poetics: The Argument*. 2nd ed. Cambridge, Mass.: Harvard University Press, 1963.

Eltit, Diamela. *E. Luminata [Lumpérica]*. Translated by Ronald Christ, with Gene Bell-Villada, Helen Lane, and Catalina Parra. Santa Fe, N.M.: Lumen, 1997.

———. *The Fourth World; El cuarto mundo*. Translated by Dick Gerdes. Lincoln: University of Nebraska Press, 1995.

———. *Sacred Cow*. Translated by Amanda Hopkinson. London: Serpent's Tail, 1995.

———. *Los vigilantes*. Santiago: Sudamerica, 1994.

Elton, Geoffrey R. *England under the Tudors*. Reprint of 2nd ed. London: Methuen, 1983.

———. *Reformation Europe 1517–1559*. London: Fontana, 1963.

Encyclopédie, ou dictionnaire raisonné des sciences, des arts et des métiers. Edited by Denis Diderot and Jean Le Rond d'Alembert. 36 vols. Berne: Sociétés Typographiques, 1778–1782.

Erasmus, Desiderius. *Adages*. Translated by Margaret Mann Phillips. Annotated by R. A. B. Mynors. 4 vols. *Collected Works of Erasmus*, Vols. 31–34. Toronto: University of Toronto Press, 1982–1992.

———. *Ciceronianus or, A Dialogue on the Best Style of Speaking*. In *Controversies over the Imitation of Cicero in the Renaissance*, with texts translated by Izora Scott, 19–130. Part 2. 1910. Reprint, Davis, Calif.: Hermagoras Press, 1991.

———. *On Copia of Words and Ideas (De utraque verborum ac rerum copia)*. Translated and introduction by Donald B. King and H. David Rix. Milwaukee, Wis.: Marquette University Press, 1963.

Euben, J. Peter. *The Tragedy of Political Theory*. Princeton, N.J.: Princeton University Press, 1990.

———, ed. *Greek Tragedy and Political Theory*. Berkeley: University of California Press, 1986.

Ezenwa-Ohaeto. "The Nature of Tragedy in Modern African Drama." *Literary Half-Yearly* 23, no. 2 (July 1982): 3–17.

Fanon, Frantz. *Black Skin, White Masks*. Translated by Charles Lam Markmann. 1967. Reprint, New York: Grove Weidenfeld, 1968.

———. *Les damnés de la terre*. Preface by Jean-Paul Sartre. Paris: Maspero, 1961.

———. *Peau noire, masques blancs*. Paris: Seuil, 1952.

———. *The Wretched of the Earth*. Preface by Jean-Paul Sartre. Translated by Constance Farrington. New York: Grove, 1963.

Farah, Nuruddin. *Maps*. New York: Pantheon, 1986.

Fein, Esther B. "Günter Grass Considers the Inescapable: Politics." *New York Times*, December 29, 1992, C16.

Fernández Retamar, Roberto. "Caliban: Notes toward a Discussion of Culture in Our America." Translated by Lynn Garafola, David Arthur MacMurray, and Roberto Marquez. In *Caliban and Other Essays*, 3–45. Translated by Edward Baker. Minneapolis: University of Minnesota Press, 1989.

Fonte, Moderata [Modesta Pozzo]. *Tredici canti del Floridoro*. Edited by Valeria Finucci. Modena: Mucchi, 1995.

Foss, Martin. *Symbol and Metaphor in Human Experience*. 1949. Reprint, Lincoln: University of Nebraska Press, 1964.

Foucault, Michel. "The Confession of the Flesh." In *Power/Knowledge: Selected Interviews and Other Writings, 1972–1977*, edited by Colin Gordon, translated by C. Gordon, Leo Marshall, John Mepham, and Kate Soper, 194–228. New York: Pantheon, 1980.

———. "Dream, Imagination and Existence." Translated by Forrest Williams. In *Dream and Existence*, by Michel Foucault and Ludwig Binswanger, edited by Keith Hoeller, 31–78. 1993. Reprint, Atlantic Highlands, N.J.: Humanities Press, 1994.

———. *Language, Counter-Memory, Practice: Selected Essays and Interviews*. Edited by Donald F. Bouchard. Translated by D. F. Bouchard and Sherry Simon. Ithaca: Cornell University Press, 1977.

———. *Les mots et les choses: Une archéologie des sciences humaines*. Paris: Gallimard, 1966.

Franco, Jean. "Virtual Cities." *Centennial Review* 42, no. 3 (fall 1998): 419–36.

Frank, Andre Gunder. *Capitalism and Underdevelopment in Latin America: Historical Studies of Chile and Brazil*. New York: Monthly Review Press, 1967.

———. *Latin America: Underdevelopment or Revolution. Essays on the Development of Underdevelopment and the Immediate Enemy*. New York: Monthly Review Press, 1969.

———. *ReOrient: Global Economy in the Asian Age*. Berkeley: University of California Press, 1998.

Franqui, Carlos. *Retrato de familia con Fidel*. Barcelona: Seix Barral, 1981.

Frege, Gottlob. "On Sense and Meaning" ["Über Sinn und Bedeutung"]. Translated by Max Black. In *Translations from the Philosophical Writings of Gottlob Frege*, Edited by Peter Geach and Max Black, 56–78. 3rd ed. Oxford: Blackwell, 1980.

Freud, Sigmund. *Die Traumdeutung*. In *Studienausgabe*, vol. 2. Frankfurt: Fischer, 1972.

———. *La naissance de la psychanalyse: Lettres à Wilhelm Fliess, notes et plans (1887–1902)*. Edited by Marie Bonaparte, Anna Freud, and Ernst Kris. Translated by Anne Berman. Paris: PUF, 1956.

———. *The Standard Edition of the Complete Psychological Works*. Translated and edited by James Strachey, with Anna Freud, Alix Strachey, Alan Tyson, and Angela Richards. 24 vols. London: Hogarth Press and the Institute of Psycho-Analysis, 1966–1974.

———, and Carl Gustav Jung. *The Freud/Jung Letters: The Correspondence between Sigmund Freud and C. G. Jung*. Edited by William McGuire. Translated by Ralph Manheim and R. F. C. Hull. Princeton, N.J.: Princeton University Press, 1974.

Froude, James Anthony. *The English and the West Indies or, The Bow of Ulysses*. 1888. Reprint, New York: Charles Scribner's Sons, 1892.

Fuentes, Carlos. *Cambio de piel*. Mexico City: Joaquín Mortiz, 1967.

———. *Casa con dos puertos*. Mexico City: Joaquín Mortiz, 1970.

———. "A Harvard Commencement." In *Myself with Others: Selected Essays*, 199–214. New York: Farrar, Straus & Giroux, 1988.

———. *La nueva novela hispanoamericana*. Mexico City: Joaquín Mortiz, 1969.

———. *Where the Air Is Clear*. Translated by Sam Hileman. 1960. Reprint, New York: Farrar, Straus and Giroux, 1984.

———. See also: Rodó; Szanto.

Fukuyama, Francis. *The End of History and the Last Man*. New York: Free Press, 1992.

Galeano, Eduardo. *We Say No: Chronicles 1963–1991*. Translated by Mark Fried et al. New York: Norton, 1992.

García-Carranza, Araceli. *Biobibliographía de Alejo Carpentier*. Havana: Letras Cubanas, 1984.

García Márquez, Gabriel. *La hojarasca*. 1955. Reprint, Buenos Aires: Sudamericana, 1997.

———. *Leaf Storm and Other Stories*. Translated by Gregory Rabassa. 1972. Reprint, New York: Harper Colophon, 1979.

———. *One Hundred Years of Solitude*. Translated by Gregory Rabassa. 1970. Reprint, London: Picador, 1978.

Gassendi, Pierre. *Disquisitio metaphysica, seu dubitationes et instantiae adversus Renati Cartesii metaphysicam et responsa. Recherches métaphysiques, ou doutes et instances contre la métaphysique de R. Descartes et ses réponses*. Edited by Bernard Rochot. Paris: Vrin, 1962.

Gates, Henry Louis, Jr. *Figures in Black: Words, Signs, and the "Racial" Self*. New York: Oxford University Press, 1989.

———. *The Signifying Monkey: A Theory of African American Literary Criticism*. New York: Oxford University Press, 1988.

Gebauer, Gunter, and Christoph Wulf. *Mimesis: Culture–Art–Society*. Translated by Don Reneau. Berkeley: University of California Press, 1995.

Gibbon, Edward. *An Essay on the Study of Literature*. In *The Miscellaneous Works. . . . with Memoirs of His Life and Writings, Composed by Himself; Illustrated from His Letters, with Occasional Notes and Narrative*, by John, Lord Sheffield, 631–70. London: B. Blake, 1837.

Gilbert, Alan. *The Latin American City*. 2nd ed. London: Latin American Bureau, 1998.

Glissant, Édouard. *Caribbean Discourse: Selected Essays*. Translated by J. Michael Dash. 1989. Reprint, Charlottesville: University Press of Virginia, 1992.

———. *Poétique de la relation*. Paris: Gallimard, 1990.

Gmelins, Hermann. "Das Prinzip der Imitatio in den romanischen Literaturen der Renaissance." *Romanische Forschungen* 46 (1932): 83–360.

Goethe, Johann Wolfgang von. *The Autobiography of Johann Wolfgang von Goethe*. Translated by John Oxenford. Introduction by Karl J. Weintraub. 2 vols. Chicago: University of Chicago Press, 1974.

———. *Dichtung und Wahrheit*. Edited by Lieselotte Blumenthal. Commentary by

Erich Trunz. In *Goethes Werke*, vols. 9–10. Edited by Erich Trunz. Hamburg: Christian Wegner, 1949–1960.

———. *Faust. Part One*. Translated and introduction by David Luke. Oxford: Oxford University Press, 1987.

———. *From My Life: Poetry and Truth. Parts One to Three*. In *Collected Works*, vol. 4. Translated Robert R. Heitner. Introduction and notes Thomas P. Saine. Edited by Thomas P. Saine and Jeffrey L. Sammons. 1987. Reprint, Princeton, N.J.: Princeton University Press, 1994.

———. *Italienische Reise*. In *Goethes Werke*, vol. 11. Edited by Erich Trunz. Commentary by Herbert v. Einem. 14 vols. Hamburg: Christian Wegner, 1949–1960.

———. *Italian Journey [1786–1788]*. Translated by W. H. Auden and Elizabeth Mayer. 1962. Reprint, Harmondsworth: Penguin, 1970.

———. "On Interpreting Aristotle's *Poetics*" ["Nachlese zu Aristoteles' Poetik"]. [1827]. In *Essays on Art and Literature, Collected Works*, edited by John Gearey, translated by Ellen von Nardroff and Ernest H. von Nardroff, 3:197–99. 1986. Reprint, Princeton, N.J.: Princeton University Press, 1994.

———. "On Realism in Art" ["Wahrheit und Wahrscheinlichkeit der Kunstwerke"] [1798]. *Collected Works*, 3:74–78.

———. "On World Literature." In *Collected Works*, 3:224–28.

———. "Shakespeare Once Again" ["Shakespeare und kein Ende"] [1826]. *Collected Works*, 3:166–74.

Goldstein, Harvey D. "Mimesis and Catharsis Reëxamined." *Journal of Aesthetics and Art Criticism* 24, no. 4 (summer 1966): 567–77.

Gombrowicz, Rita. *Gombrowicz en Argentine 1939–1963*. Preface by Constantin Jelinski. Paris: Denoël, 1984.

Gombrowicz, Witold. *Cosmos*. Translated by Eric Mosbacher. New York: Grove, 1970.

———. *Cosmos*. Translated by Georges Sédir. 1966. Reprint, Paris: Gallimard, Folio, 1973.

———. *Diary*. Edited by Jan Kott. Translated by Lillian Vallee. 3 vols. Evanston: Northwestern University Press, 1988–1993.

———. *Entretiens avec Gombrowicz*. By "Dominique de Roux." Paris: Pierre Belfond, 1968. [This is actually entirely by Gombrowicz.]

———. *Kosmos*. 1965. Reprint, Paris: Instytut Literacki, 1970.

———. *The Marriage*. Translated by Louis Iribarne. New York: Grove, 1969.

———. *Pérégrinations argentines*. Translated by Allan Kosko. Paris: Christian Bourgois, 1984.

———. *Trans-Atlantyk*. Translated by Carolyn French and Nina Karsov. Introduction by Stanislaw Baranczak. New Haven, Conn.: Yale University Press, 1994.

Gomez, Michael A. *Exchanging Our Country Marks: The Transformation of African Identities in the Colonial and Antebellum South*. Chapel Hill: University of North Carolina Press, 1998.

González Echevarria, Roberto. *Alejo Carpentier: The Pilgrim at Home.* 1977. Reprint, Austin: University of Texas Press, 1990.

———. "Reflections on the *Espejo de paciencia.*" In *Celestina's Brood: Continuities of the Baroque in Spanish and Latin American Literatures,* 128–48. Durham, N.C.: Duke University Press, 1993.

———. "Socrates Among the Weeds: Blacks and History in Carpentier's *Explosion in a Cathedral.*" In *Voices from Under: Black Narrative in Latin America and the Caribbean,* 35–53. Edited by William Luis. Westport, Conn.: Greenwood Press, 1984.

González Prada, Manuel. *Pájinas libres.* Paris: P. Dupont, 1894.

Goodison, Lorna. *Selected Poems.* Ann Arbor: University of Michigan Press, 1992.

Gordon, Lewis R. *Fanon and the Crisis of European Man: An Essay on Philosophy and the Human Sciences.* New York: Routledge, 1995.

Gouhier, Henri. *La pensée métaphysique de Descartes.* 2nd ed. Paris: Vrin, 1969.

Gourgouris, Stathis. *Dream Nation: Enlightenment, Colonization and the Institution of Modern Greece.* Stanford, Calif.: Stanford University Press, 1996.

Gravel, Pierre, trans. and ed. *Aristote. La poétique,* followed by *La comédie (Tractatus Coislinianus).* Montreal: Éditions du silence, 1995.

———. *Accompagnements pour la Poétique suivi de Mélancholie.* Montreal: Éditions du Silence, 1998.

Gray, Thomas. *An Elegy Written in a Country Church Yard.* London: R. Dodsley, 1751.

Green, André. "De l'*Esquisse* à l'*Interprétation des rêves*: Coupure et clôture." *Nouvelle Revue de Psychanalyse* 5 (spring 1972): 155–80.

Griffin, John Howard. *Black Like Me.* Boston: Houghton Mifflin; Cambridge: Riverside Press, 1961.

Gruzinski, Serge. *La colonisation de l'imaginaire: Sociétés indigènes et occidentalisation dans le Mexique espagnol xvie–xviiie siècles.* Paris: Gallimard, 1988.

———. *The Conquest of Mexico: The Incorporation of Indian Societies into the Western World, 16th–18th Centuries.* Translated by Eileen Corrigan. Cambridge: Polity, 1993.

Guha, Ranajit. *A Rule of Property for Bengal: An Essay on the Idea of Permanent Settlement.* 2nd ed. Foreword by Amartya Sen. Durham, N.C.: Duke University Press, 1996.

Guha-Thakurta, Tapati. *The Making of a New "Indian" Art: Artists, Aesthetics and Nationalism in Bengal, c. 1850–1920.* Cambridge: Cambridge University Press, 1992.

———. "Recovering the Nation's Art." In *Texts of Power,* edited by Partha Chatterjee, 63–92.

Habermas, Jürgen. *The Past as Future. Vergangenheit als Zukunft.* Interviewed by Michael Haller. Translated and edited by Max Pensky. Lincoln: University of Nebraska Press, 1994.

———. *The Structural Transformation of the Public Sphere: An Inquiry into a Cate-*

gory of Bourgeois Society. Translated by Thomas Burger with Frederick Lawrence. Cambridge, Mass.: MIT Press, 1989.

Haidu, Peter. "The Politics of Text and Discourse in Medieval France." Unpublished lecture. New York University, April 1998.

Hakluyt, Richard. *Voyages and Discoveries: The Principal Navigations, Voyages, Traffiques and Discoveries of the English Nation.* Edited, abridged, and introduction by Jack Beeching. Harmondsworth: Penguin, 1972.

Hall, Stuart. "The Local and the Global: Globalization and Ethnicity." In *Culture, Globalization and the World System: Contemporary Conditions for the Representation of Identity,* edited by Anthony D. King, 19–39. Rev. ed. Minneapolis: University of Minnesota Press, 1997.

Hamilton, John T. "Soliciting Darkness: Pindar, Obscurity and the Classical Tradition." Ph.D. diss., New York University, 1999.

Hampton, Timothy. "The Subject of America: History and Alterity in Montaigne's 'Des Coches.'" In *The Project of Prose in Early Modern Europe and the New World,* edited by Elizabeth Fowler and Roland Greene, 80–103. Cambridge: Cambridge University Press, 1997.

Harris, Wilson. *Eternity to Season.* 2nd ed. London: New Beacon, 1978.

———. *The Far Journey of Oudin* [1961]. In *The Guyana Quartet,* 119–238.

———. *The Guyana Quartet.* London: Faber & Faber, 1985.

———. *Palace of the Peacock* [1960]. In *The Guyana Quartet,* 15–117.

———. "Quetzalcoatl and the Smoking Mirror (Reflections on Originality and Tradition): Address to the Temenos Academy, London 7 February 1994." Rev. ed. In *Sisyphus and Eldorado,* edited by Brathwaite and Reiss, 29–39.

———. *Resurrection at Sorrow Hill.* London: Faber & Faber, 1993.

———. *Tradition, the Writer and Society: Critical Essays.* London: New Beacon, 1967.

———. *The Womb of Space: The Cross-Cultural Imagination.* Westport, Conn.: Greenwood Press, 1983.

Hartman, Geoffrey H. *The Fate of Reading and Other Essays.* Chicago: University of Chicago Press, 1975.

Hartmann, Heinz. "Psychoanalysis as a Scientific Theory." In *Psychoanalysis, Scientific Method, and Philosophy: A Symposium,* edited by Sidney Hook, 3–37. New York: New York University Press, 1959.

Heelan, Patrick J. *Quantum Mechanics and Objectivity: A Study of the Physical Philosophy of Werner Heisenberg.* The Hague: Martinus Nijhoff, 1965.

Hegel, Georg Wilhelm Friedrich. *Aesthetics: Lectures on Fine Art.* Translated by T. Malcolm Knox. 2 vols. Oxford: Clarendon, 1975.

———. *Phänomenologie des Geistes.* Edited by Wolfgang Bonsiepen and Reinhard Heede. Vol. 9 of *Gesammelte Werke.* Hamburg: Felix Meiner, 1980.

———. *Phenomenology of Spirit.* Translated by A. V. Miller. Analysis of the text and foreword by J. N. Findlay. 1977. Reprint, Oxford: Oxford University Press, 1979.

Heidegger, Martin. *An Introduction to Metaphysics*. Translated by Ralph Manheim. 1959. Reprint, New Haven, Conn.: Yale University Press, 1973.

Heinrichs, Wolfhart. *The Hand of the Northwind: Opinions on Metaphor and the Early Meaning of Istiʿāra in Arabic Poetics*. Abhandlungen für die Kunde des Morgenlandes 44.2. Wiesbaden: Deutsche Morgenländische Gesellschaft/Franz Steiner, 1977.

Helgerson, Richard. *Forms of Nationhood: The Elizabethan Writing of England*. Chicago: University of Chicago Press, 1992.

Hilden, Patricia Penn. "Ritchie Valens Is Dead: E pluribus unum." In *As We Are Now: Mixblood Essays on Race and Identity*, edited by William S. Penn, 219–52. Berkeley: University of California Press, 1997.

———. "What Happens When People Move?" History-Social Project Summer Institute for Teachers. Unpublished seminar. University of California, Berkeley, July 24, 1997.

———. *When Nickels Were Indians: An Urban, Mixed-Blood Story*. Washington, D.C.: Smithsonian Institution Press, 1995.

———, and Shari M. Huhndorf. "Performing 'Indian' in the National Museum of the American Indian." *Social Identities* 5, no. 2 (1999): 161–83.

———, and Timothy J. Reiss. "Discourse, Politics, and the Temptation of Enlightenment: Paris 1935." *Annals of Scholarship* 8, no. 1 (1991): 61–78.

Hobbes, Thomas. *Leviathan*. Edited by Richard Tuck. Cambridge: Cambridge University Press, 1991.

Hodge, Merle. *Crick Crack, Monkey* [1970]. Introduction by Roy Narinesingh. 1981. Reprint, Oxford: Heinemann, 1995.

The Homeric Hymns. Translated by Apostolos N. Athanassakis. Baltimore, Md.: Johns Hopkins University Press, 1976.

Horace [Quintus Horatius Flaccus]. "De arte poetica." In *Satires, Epistles and Ars poetica*, edited and translated by H. Rushton Fairclough, 450–88. 1926. Reprint, London: Heinemann; New York: Putnam, 1932.

———. *The Odes and Epodes*. Edited and translated by C. E. Bennett. 1914. Reprint, Cambridge, Mass.: Harvard University Press; London: Heinemann, 1947.

Horkheimer, Max. *Eclipse of Reason*. 1947. Reprint, New York: Seabury, 1974.

———, and Theodor Wiesengrund Adorno. *Dialectic of Enlightenment*. Translated by John Cumming. New York: Seabury, 1972.

Huarte de San Juan, Dr. Juan. *Examen de ingenios* [1575]. In *Biblioteca de Autores Españoles* 65, edited by Adolfo de Castro, 403–520. Madrid: Rivadeneyra, 1873.

Huhndorf, Shari M. See: Hilden and Huhndorf.

Hull, Gordon. "Hobbes, Marx, and the Foundations of Modern Political Thought." Ph.D. diss., Vanderbilt University, 1999.

Huntington, Samuel P. *The Clash of Civilizations and the Remaking of World Order*. New York: Simon & Schuster, 1996.

Ingarden, Roman. "A Marginal Commentary on Aristotle's *Poetics*." *Journal of Aes-*

thetics and Art Criticism 20, no. 2–3 (winter–spring 1961–1962): 163–73, 273–
85.

Invitation to Venice. Introduction by Peggy Guggenheim. Text by Michelangelo
Muraro. Photographs Ugo Mulas. Translated by Isabel Quigly. New York: Tri-
dent, 1963.

James, Adeola, ed. *In Their Own Voices: African Women Writers Talk.* London:
James Currey; Portsmouth, N.H.: Heinemann, 1990.

James, C. L. R. *The Black Jacobins: Toussaint L'Ouverture and the San Domingo
Revolution.* 2nd rev. ed. New York: Vintage, 1963.

——. *A History of Pan-African Revolt.* Introduction by Robin D. G. Kelley.
Chicago: Kerr, 1995.

——. *Mariners, Renegades and Castaways: The Story of Herman Melville and the
World We Live In* [1953]. London: Allison & Busby, 1985.

——. *Minty Alley* [1936]. Introduction by Kenneth Ramchand. London: New
Beacon, 1971.

——. *Spheres of Existence: Selected Writings.* London: Allison & Busby, 1980.

James, Henry. *The Aspern Papers.* In *The Great Short Novels*, edited by Philip Rahv,
469–564. New York: Dial, 1944.

Jameson, Fredric. *The Political Unconscious: Narrative as a Socially Symbolic Act.*
Ithaca, N.Y.: Cornell University Press, 1981.

——. Preface to *The Cultures of Globalization*, edited by Fredric Jameson and
Masao Miyoshi, xi–xvii. Durham, N.C.: Duke University Press, 1998.

——. "Third World Literature in the Era of Multinational Capitalism." *Social
Text* 5, no. 3 (fall 1986): 65–88.

——. See also: Eagleton.

——, and Masao Miyoshi, eds. *The Cultures of Globalization.* Durham, N.C.:
Duke University Press, 1998.

Janik, Sofie. "Gombrowicz: De la logique au carnaval." Ph.D. diss., Université de
Montréal, 1977.

Janson, Horst Woldemar. *Apes and Ape Lore in the Middle Ages and the Renaissance.*
London: Warburg Institute, 1952.

Jeanneret, Michel. *Des mets et des mots: Banquets et propos de table à la Renaissance.*
Paris: Corti, 1987.

Jenkins, Nicholas. "The Story of A." *New York Times Book Review*, June 20, 1999,
12–13.

Jennings, Francis. *The Invasion of America: Indians, Colonialism, and the Cant of
Conquest.* 1975. Reprint, New York: Norton, 1976.

Johnson, Samuel. *Lives of the Poets: A Selection.* Edited by J. P. Hardy. Oxford:
Clarendon, 1971.

Jones, Eldred D. "The Price of Independence: The Writer's Agony." In *Criticism
and Ideology*, edited by Kirsten Holst Petersen, 60–66.

Jones, LeRoi [Amiri Baraka]. *Blues People: Negro Music in White America.* New
York: Morrow, 1963.

Joyce, James. *Portrait of the Artist as a Young Man*. 1916. Reprint, New York: Viking, 1960.

Jung, Carl Gustav. *The Collected Works*. Edited by William McGuire, Sir Herbert Read, Michael Fordham, and Gerhard Adler. Translated by R. F. C. Hull. 19 vols. Princeton, N.J.: Princeton University Press; London: Routledge & Kegan Paul, 1953–1979.

———. See also: Freud and Jung.

Jusdanis, Gregory. *Belated Modernity and Aesthetic Culture: Inventing National Literature*. Minneapolis: University of Minnesota Press, 1991.

Kadir, Djelal. *The Other Writing: Postcolonial Essays in Latin America's Writing Culture*. West Lafayette, Ind.: Purdue University Press, 1993.

Kahler, Erich. *The Disintegration of Form in the Arts*. New York: George Braziller, 1968.

———. *The Inward Turn of Narrative*. Translated by Richard and Clara Winston. Princeton, N.J.: Princeton University Press, 1973.

Kane, Cheikh Hamidou. *Ambiguous Adventure*. Translated by Katherine Woods. 1963. Reprint, London: Heinemann, 1972.

———. *L'aventure ambiguë*. Preface by Vincent Monteil. 1961. Reprint, Paris: 10/18, 1979.

Kant, Immanuel. *Kant's Political Writings*. Edited by Hans Reiss. Translated by H. B. Nisbet. Cambridge: Cambridge University Press, 1970.

Kenyatta, Jomo. *Facing Mount Kenya: The Traditional Life of the Gikuyu*. Introduction B. Malinowski. 1938. Reprint, London, Nairobi and Ibadan: Heinemann, 1979.

Kincaid, Jamaica. *At the Bottom of the River*. 1983. Reprint, New York: Aventura, 1985.

———. *Lucy*. 1990. Reprint, New York: Plume, 1991.

———. *A Small Place*. 1988. Reprint, New York: Plume, 1989.

King, Anthony D., ed. *Culture, Globalization and the World System: Contemporary Conditions for the Representation of Identity*. Rev. ed. Minneapolis: University of Minnesota Press, 1997.

Kingston, Maxine Hong. *Tripmaster Monkey: His Fake Book*. 1989. Reprint, New York: Vintage, 1990.

Kipling, Rudyard. *Kim*. Introduction by Edward Said. Harmondsworth: Penguin, 1987.

Kirby, David. "The Survivor." Review of *Heaven's Coast: A Memoir*, by Mark Doty. *York Times Book Review*, March 10, 1996, 10.

Kitcher, Philip. "Sea-Shells and Tigers." *London Review of Books*, March 18, 1999, 31–32.

Kris, Ernst. "The Nature of Psychoanalytic Propositions and Their Validation." In *Freedom and Experience: Essays Presented to Horace M. Kallen*, edited by Sidney Hook and Milton R. Konvitz, 239–59. Ithaca: Cornell University Press, 1947.

Kristof, Nicholas D., and David E. Sanger. "How U.S. Wooed Asia To Let Cash Flow In." *New York Times*, February 16, 1999, A1, 10–11.

Krupat, Arnold. "Ideology and the Native American Novel." *Centennial Review* 39, no. 3 (fall 1995): 559–74.

Kusch, Rodolfo. *América profunda*. Buenos Aires: Hachette, 1962.

———. *La ciudad mestiza*. Buenos Aires: Collección Quetzal, 1952.

Labriola, Arturo. *Le crépuscule de la civilisation: L'occident et les peuples de couleur*. Paris: Mignolet & Storz, 1936.

Lamming, George. *Coming Coming Home: Conversations II. Western Education and the Caribbean Intellectual; Coming, Coming, Coming Home*. Introduction by Rex Nettleford. French translation by Daniella Jeffry. Philipsburg, St. Martin: House of Nehesi, 1995.

———. *The Emigrants*. 1954. Reprint, London: Allison & Busby, 1980.

———. *In the Castle of My Skin*. 1953. Reprint, New York: Schocken, 1983.

———. *The Pleasures of Exile* [1960]. Foreword by Sandra Pouchet Paquet. Ann Arbor: University of Michigan Press, 1992.

Lanham, Richard A. *A Handlist of Rhetorical Terms*. 2nd ed. Berkeley: University of California Press, 1991.

Latour, Bruno. *We Have Never Been Modern*. Translated by Catherine Porter. Cambridge, Mass.: Harvard University Press, 1993.

Leonard, Irving A. *Books of the Brave: Being an Account of Books and of Men in the Spanish Conquest and Settlement of the Sixteenth-Century New World*. Introduction by Rolena Adorno. Berkeley: University of Californa Press, 1992.

———. "*Don Quixote* and the Book Trade in Lima, 1606." *Hispanic Review* 8, no. 4 (October 1940): 285–304.

———. "On the Cuzco Book Trade, 1606." *Hispanic Review* 9, no. 3 (July 1941): 359–75.

León-Portilla, Miguel. *The Aztec Image of Self and Society*. Translated by Charles E. Bowen and J. Jorge Klor de Alva. Edited and introduction by J. Jorge Klor de Alva. Salt Lake City: University of Utah Press, 1992.

Léry, Jean de. *Histoire d'un voyage fait en la terre du Brésil autrement dit Amérique*. . . . Edited by Michel Contat. Afterword by Jean-Claude Wagnières. Lausanne: Bibliothèque Romande, 1972.

Levi, Primo. *The Drowned and the Saved*. Translated by Raymond Rosenthal. 1988. Reprint, New York: Vintage, 1989.

———. "A Mystery in the *Lager*." In *The Mirror Maker: Stories and Essays*, translated by Raymond Rosenthal, 66–70. New York: Schocken, 1989.

Lévi-Strauss, Claude. *Mythologiques*. 4 vols. Paris: Plon, 1964–1971.

———. *La pensée sauvage*. Paris: Plon, 1962.

Lewis, Paul. "'Ulysses' at Top as Panel Picks 100 Best Novels." *New York Times*, July 20, 1998, B1, 4.

Lezama Lima, José. *Obras completas*. 2 vols. Mexico City: Aguilar, 1977.

———. "Paralelos: La pintura y poesía en Cuba (siglos XVIII y XIX)." In *Obras completas*, 2:929–71.

———. "Prólogo a una antología." In *Obras completas*, 2:995–1038.

Ligon, Richard. *A True and Exact History of the Island of Barbados* (1657). In Excerpts from *Caribbeana: An Anthology of English Literature of the West Indies 1657–1777*, edited and introduction by Thomas W. Krise, 17–30. Chicago: University of Chicago Press, 1999.

Lipinska-Illakowicz, Krystyna. "European Peripheries: Poetics and Politics of Eastern Europe." Ph.D. diss., New York University, 1999.

Lipschutz, Alejandro. *El problema racial en la conquista de América, y el mestizaje*. 2nd ed. Santiago de Chile: Editorial Andrés Bello, 1967.

Liu Hsieh. *The Literary Mind and the Carving of Dragons*. Translated and annotated by Vincent Yu-chung Shih. Bilingual ed. Taipei: Chung Hwa Book Company, 1970.

Locke, Alain LeRoy. *The Negro and His Music. Negro Art: Past and Present*. 1936; Facsimile reprint, Salem, N.H.: Ayre, 1988.

Locke, John. *An Essay Concerning Human Understanding*. Edited by Peter H. Nidditch. Oxford: Clarendon, 1975.

Lorde, Audre. *Zami: A New Spelling of My Name*. Freedom, Calif.: Crossing Press, 1982.

Lotman, Yuri Mikhailovich. "La réduction et le déploiement des systèmes sémiotiques (Introduction au problème: Le freudisme et la culturologie sémiotique)." In *Travaux sur les systèmes de signes: École de Tartu*, edited by Yuri M. Lotman and Boris A. Ouspenski, translated by Anne Zouboff, 44–51. Brussels: Complexe, 1976.

Lovelace, Earl. *The Wine of Astonishment* [1982]. Introduction by Marjorie Thorpe. London: Heinemann, 1986.

Lucian of Samosata. "The Dead Come to Life, or the Fisherman (Piscator)." In *The Works*, edited and translated by Austin Morris Harmon, 3:1–81. 1921–1936. Reprint, Cambridge, Mass.: Harvard University Press; London: Heinemann, 1969.

Lucretius Carus, Titus. *De rerum natura*. Edited by Martin Ferguson Smith. Translated by W. H. D. Rouse; revised by M. F. Smith. 1975, 1992. Reprint, Cambridge, Mass.: Harvard University Press, 1997.

Lukács, György. *The Destruction of Reason*. Translated by Peter Palmer. London: Merlin, 1980.

Machado y Ruiz, Antonio. "De un cancionero apócrifa. CLXVII (Abel Martín)." In *Poesías completas*, 268–94. Buenos Aires: Espasa-Calpe, 1940.

———. *Juan de Mairena*. Edited by Antonio Fernández Ferrer. 2 vols. Madrid: Cátedra, 1986.

MacIntyre, Alasdair C. *After Virtue: A Study in Moral Theory*. 2nd ed. Notre Dame, Ind.: University of Notre Dame Press, 1984.

Mackey, Nathaniel. *Discrepant Engagement: Dissonance, Cross-Culturality, and Experimental Writing.* Cambridge: Cambridge University Press, 1993.

Maeztu, Ramiro de. "El decadencia del occidente." In *Ensayos*, 109–45. Buenos Aires: Emecé, 1948.

———. "Don Quijote o el amor." In *Don Quijote, Don Juan y La Celestina: Ensayos en simpatía*, 19–69. 1938. Reprint, Madrid: Espasa-Calpe, 1963.

Mannoni, Octave. *Caliban and Prospero: The Psychology of Colonization.* 2nd ed. Translated by Pamela Powesland. New York and Washington: Praeger, 1964.

Mariátegui, José Carlos. *Seven Interpretive Essays on Peruvian Reality.* Translated by Marjory Urquidi. Introduction by Jorge Basadre. 1971. Reprint, Austin: University of Texas Press, 1990.

Markham, E. A., ed. *Hinterland: Caribbean Poetry from the West Indies and Britain.* Newcastle upon Tyne: Bloodaxe, 1989.

Marks, Emerson R. *Taming the Chaos: English Poetic Diction Theory since the Renaissance.* Detroit: Wayne State University Press, 1998.

Marshall, Paule. *Brown Girl, Brownstones* [1959]. Afterword Mary Helen Washington. Old Westbury, N.Y.: Feminist Press, 1981.

———. *The Chosen Place, the Timeless People.* 1969. Reprint, New York: Vintage, 1984.

———. *Merle, a Novella, and Other Stories.* 1983. Reprint, London: Virago, 1985.

Marti, Oscar Albert. *Economic Causes of the Reformation in England.* New York: Macmillan, 1929.

Mattern, Ruth. "Descartes's Correspondence with Elizabeth: Conceiving Both the Union and the Distinction of Mind and Body." In *Descartes: Critical and Interpretive Essays*, edited by Michael Hooker, 212–22. Baltimore, Md.: Johns Hopkins University Press, 1978.

Maty, Matthew. "Letter to the Author." In Gibbon, *The Miscellaneous Works. . . . with Memoirs of His Life and Writings, Composed by Himself; Illustrated from His Letters, with Occasional Notes and Narrative*, by John, Lord Sheffield, 627–31. London: B. Blake, 1837.

Mazrui, Ali A. *Ancient Greece in African Political Thought. An Inaugural Lecture Delivered on 25 August 1966 at Makerere University College.* Nairobi: East African Publishing House, 1967.

———. *The Trial of Christopher Okigbo.* New York: Third Press, 1971.

McDermott, William Coffman. *The Ape in Antiquity.* Johns Hopkins University Studies in Archeology 27. Baltimore, Md.: Johns Hopkins University Press, 1938.

McKay, Claude. *Selected Poems.* New York: Bookman Associates, 1953.

McKeon, Richard P. "Imitation and Poetry." In *Thought, Action and Passion*, 102–221, 239–85. Chicago: University of Chicago Press, 1954.

———. "Literary Criticism and the Concept of Imitation in Antiquity." In *Critics and Criticism Ancient and Modern*, edited by Ronald Salmon Crane, 147–75. Chicago: University of Chicago Press, 1952.

McWatt, Mark A. *The Language of Eldorado*. Sydney: Dangaroo Press, 1994.

———. "The Two Faces of Eldorado: Contrasting Attitudes towards History and Identity in West Indian Literature." In *West Indian Literature and Its Social Context: Proceedings of the Fourth Annual Conference on West Indian Literature*, edited by Mark A. McWatt, 33–47. Cave Hill, Barbados: Department of English, University of the West Indies, 1985.

Melberg, Arne. *Theories of Mimesis*. Cambridge: Cambridge University Press, 1995.

Melville, Herman. *Selected Poems*. Edited by Hennig Cohen. Garden City, N.Y.: Doubleday, 1964.

———. *Typee: A Peep at Polynesian Life*. In *Typee; Omoo; Mardi*, 1–315. Edited by G. Thomas Tanselle. New York: Library of America, 1982.

Merleau-Ponty, Maurice. *The Prose of the World* [1969]. Edited by Claude Lefort. Translated by John O'Neill. Evanston: Northwestern University Press, 1973.

Messer-Davidow, Ellen, David R. Shumway, and David J. Sylvan, eds. *Knowledges: Historical and Critical Studies in Disciplinarity*. Charlottesville: University of Virginia Press, 1993.

Mignolo, Walter D. *The Darker Side of the Renaissance: Literacy, Territoriality, and Colonization*. Ann Arbor: University of Michigan Press, 1995.

Mill, John Stuart. *Philosophy of Scientific Method*. Edited by Ernst Nagel. New York: Hafner, 1950.

Miller, Christopher L. *Blank Darkness: Africanist Discourse in French*. Chicago: University of Chicago Press, 1985.

———. *Nationalists and Nomads: Essays on Francophone African Literature and Culture*. Chicago: University of Chicago Press, 1998.

———. *Theories of Africans: Francophone Literature and Anthropology in Africa*. Chicago: University of Chicago Press, 1990.

Miller, Peter N. *Defining the Common Good: Empire, Religion and Philosophy in Eighteenth-Century Britain*. Cambridge: Cambridge University Press, 1994.

Minnis, A. J., and A. B. Scott, with David Wallace, eds. *Medieval Literary Theory and Criticism c. 1100–c. 1375: The Commentary Tradition*. Oxford: Clarendon, 1988.

Miyoshi, Masao. See: Jameson, Fredric, and Masao Miyoshi, eds.

Mo, Timothy. *The Monkey King*. 1978. Reprint, London: Abacus, 1984.

Molloy, Sylvia. *At Face Value: Autobiographical Writing in Spanish America*. Cambridge: Cambridge University Press, 1991.

———. *Certificate of Absence*. Translated by Daniel Balderston with the author from *Un breve cárcel*. Austin: University of Texas Press, 1989.

Monsiváis, Carlos. *Mexican Postcards*. Edited, translated, and introduction by John Kraniauskas. London: Verso, 1997.

Montaigne, Michel Eyquem de. *Oeuvres complètes*. Edited by Albert Thibaudet and Maurice Rat. Paris: Gallimard, 1962.

Moore, Gerald. *The Chosen Tongue: English Writing in the Tropical World*. 1969. Reprint, New York: Harper & Row, 1970.

Morris, James. *The World of Venice.* New York: Pantheon, 1960.

Morris, Mervyn. *"Is English We Speaking" and Other Essays.* Kingston: Ian Randle Publishers, 1999.

Morris, Roderick Conway. "The Great Publisher." *Times Literary Supplement,* September 23, 1994, 20.

Moses, Michael Valdez. *The Novel and the Globalization of Culture.* Oxford: Oxford University Press, 1996.

Mphahlele, Ezekiel [Es'kia]. *Afrika My Music: An Autobiography 1957–1983.* Johannesburg: Ravan Press, 1984.

——. *The African Image.* London: Faber & Faber, 1962.

——. *The African Image.* Rev. ed. London: Faber & Faber, 1974.

——. *Down Second Avenue.* 1959. Reprint, London and Boston: Faber & Faber, 1980.

——. "Negritude Revisited." In *The African Image,* rev. ed., 79–95. London: Faber & Faber, 1974.

——. "Remarks on *Négritude.*" In *African Writing Today,* edited by Ezekiel Mphahlele, 247–53. Harmondsworth: Penguin, 1967.

——. *Voices in the Whirlwind and Other Essays.* New York: Hill & Wang, 1972.

——, ed. *African Writing Today.* Harmondsworth: Penguin, 1967.

Mugo, Micere Githae. *African Orature and Human Rights.* Human and Peoples' Rights Monograph Series 13. Roma, Lesotho: Institute of Southern African Studies, National University of Lesotho, 1991.

Muir, Edward. *Civic Ritual in Renaissance Venice.* Princeton, N.J.: Princeton University Press, 1981.

Murena, Hector A. "El pecado original de América." In *El pecado original de América,* 161–232. Buenos Aires: Sur, 1954.

Nagy, Gregory. "Early Greek Views of Poets and Poetry." In *The Cambridge History of Literary Criticism, I: Classical Criticism,* edited by George A. Kennedy, 1–77. 1989. Reprint, Cambridge: Cambridge University Press, 1993.

Naipaul, V. S. *A House for Mr. Biswas.* 1961. Reprint, Harmondsworth: Penguin, 1981.

——. *The Mimic Men.* 1967. Reprint, Harmondsworth: Penguin, 1969.

Nandy, Ashis. *Alternative Sciences: Creativity and Authenticity in Two Indian Scientists.* New Delhi: Allied Publishers, 1980.

——. "History's Forgotten Doubles." Unpublished draft of opening address at the Conference on World History, organized by *History and Theory,* Wesleyan University, March 25–26, 1994.

——. *The Intimate Enemy: Loss and Recovery of Self under Colonialism.* Delhi: Oxford University Press, 1983.

——. *The Savage Freud and Other Essays on Possible and Retrievable Selves.* Princeton, N.J.: Princeton University Press, 1995.

Naudaeana et Patiniana. Ou singularitez remarquables, prises des conversations de Mess. Naudé & Patin. 2nd ed. Amsterdam: François vander Plaats, 1703.

Nebrija, Elio Antonio de. *Gramática de la lengua castellana.* Edited by Antonio Quilis. Madrid: Editora Nacional, 1980.

Neier, Aryeh. "Watching Rights." *Nation,* July 31–August 7, 1995, 119.

Ngũgĩ wa Thiong'o. *Decolonising the Mind: The Politics of Language in African Literature.* London: James Currey, 1986.

———. *Detained: A Writer's Prison Diary.* London: Heinemann, 1981.

———. *Homecoming: Essays on African and Caribbean Literature, Culture and Politics.* London: Heinemann, 1972.

———. *Moving the Centre: The Struggle for Cultural Freedoms.* London: James Currey, 1993.

———. *Penpoints, Gunpoints and Dreams: Towards a Critical Theory of the Arts and the State in Africa.* Oxford: Clarendon, 1998.

———. *Secret Lives and Other Stories.* London: Heinemann, 1975.

———. *Writers in Politics: A Re-Engagement with Issues of Literature and Society.* Rev. ed. Oxford: James Currey; Nairobi: EAEP; Portsmouth, N.H.: Heinemann, 1997.

Nietzsche, Friedrich. *The Birth of Tragedy and the Genealogy of Morals.* Translated by Francis Golffing. Garden City, N.J.: Doubleday Anchor, 1956.

———. *Die Geburt der Tragödie.* In *Werke. Kritische Gesamtausgabe,* edited by Giorgio Colli and Mazzino Montinari, 3^1:5–152. 32 vols. to date. Berlin: Walter de Gruyter, 1967–2000.

———. *Die Philosophie im tragischen Zeitalter der Griechen.* In *Werke. Kritische Gesamtausgabe,* edited by Giorgio Colli and Mazzino Montinari, 3^2:293–366. Berlin: Walter de Gruyter, 1967–2000.

———. "On the Uses and Disadvantages of History for Life." *Untimely Meditations.* Translated by R. J. Hollingdale. Introduction by J. P. Stern. Cambridge: Cambridge University Press, 1983. 59–123.

———. *Philosophy in the Tragic Age of the Greeks.* Translated and introduction by Marianne Cowan. Chicago: Gateway, 1962.

———. *Thus Spoke Zarathustra: A Book for Everyone and No One.* Translated by R. J. Hollingdale. Harmondsworth: Penguin, 1961.

Nkrumah, Kwame. *Consciencism: Philosophy and Ideology for Decolonization.* Rev. ed. New York: Monthly Review Press, 1970.

Nooteboom, Cees. *Une année allemande: Chronique berlinoise 1989–1990.* Translated by Philippe Noble et al. Arles: Actes Sud, 1990.

———. *Désir d'Espagne: Mes détours vers Santiago.* Translated by Anne-Marie de Both-Diez. Arles: Actes Sud, 1993.

———. *In the Dutch Mountains.* Translated by Adrienne Dixon. Baton Rouge: Louisiana State University Press, 1987.

Norris, John. *Christian Blessedness: or, Discourses upon the Beatitudes Of our Lord and Saviour Jesus Christ. . . . to which are Added, Reflections upon a late Essay concerning Human Understanding. . . .* London: Rob. Midgely for S. Manship, 1690.

———. *An Essay Towards the Theory of the Ideal or Intelligible World. Design'd for Two Parts. The First Considering it Absolutely in itself, and the Second in Relation to Human Understanding.* . . . 2 parts. London: S. Manship . . . and W. Hawes, 1701–1704.

O'Gorman, Edmundo. *La invención de America. La universalisación de la cultura occidental.* Mexico City: Universidad Nacional Autónoma de México, 1959.

———. See also: Cervantes de Salazar, Francisco.

Ohnuki-Tierney, Emiko. *The Monkey as Mirror: Symbolic Transformations in Japanese History and Ritual.* 1987. Reprint, Princeton, N.J.: Princeton University Press, 1989.

Okot p'Bitek. *Artist, the Ruler: Essays on Art, Culture and Values,* including extracts from *Song of Soldier* and *White Teeth Make People Laugh on Earth.* Foreword and biographical sketch by Lubwa p'Chong. Nairobi: Heinemann Kenya, 1986.

———. *Song of Lawina and Song of Ocol.* Introduction by G. A. Heron. 1972. Reprint, Oxford: Heinemann, 1984.

Ortega y Gasset, José. *The Dehumanization of Art and Other Writings on Art and Culture.* Translated by Willard R. Trask et al. Garden City, N.Y.: Doubleday Anchor, 1956.

———. "Las dos grandes metáforas." In *El espectador, Tomo III y IV,* 241–62. 1923, 1925. Reprint, Madrid: Revista de Occidente, 1961.

———. *Meditations on Quixote.* Introduction and notes Julián Marías. Translated by Evelyn Rugg and Diego Marín. 1961. Reprint, New York: Norton, 1963.

———. "The Self and the Other." In *The Dehumanization of Art and Other Writings on Art and Culture,* by José Ortega y Gasset, 163–87. Translated by Willard R. Trask et al. Garden City, N.Y.: Doubleday Anchor, 1956.

Ouologuem, Yambo. *Bound to Violence* [1968]. Translated by Ralph Manheim. London: Heinemann, 1971.

Owen, Stephen. *Traditional Chinese Poetry and Poetics: Omen of the World.* Madison: University of Wisconsin Press, 1985.

Padilla, Heberto. *Legacies. Selected Poems.* Bilingual ed. Translated by Alastair Reid and Andrew Hurley. New York: Farrar Straus Giroux, 1982.

[Parker, Henry.] *Observations upon Some of His Majesties Later Answers and Expresses 1642.* In *Tracts on Liberty in the Puritan Revolution 1638–1647,* edited and with commentary by William Haller, 2:165–213. New York: Columbia University Press, 1934.

Patterson, Orlando. *The Children of Sisyphus.* London: New Authors, 1964.

Paz, Octavio. *The Labyrinth of Solitude; The Other Mexico; Return to the Labyrinth of Solitude; Mexico and the United States; The Philanthropic Ogre.* Translated by Lysander Kemp, Yara Milos, and Rachel Phillips Belash. 1985. Reprint, London: Penguin, 1990.

———. *The Monkey Grammarian.* Translated by Helen Lane. 1981. Reprint, New York: Arcade, 1990.

Pelton, Robert D. *The Trickster in West Africa: A Study of Mythic Irony and Sacred Delight.* 1980. Reprint, Berkeley: University of California Press, 1989.

Pemble, John. *Venice Rediscovered.* Oxford: Clarendon, 1995.

Perez, Gilberto. "So Close to the Monster." Review of Louis Pérez Jr., *On Becoming Cuban: Identity, Nationality and Culture. London Review of Books,* June 22, 2000, 12–14.

Pessoa, Fernando. *The Keeper of Sheep.* Bilingual ed. Translated by Edwin Honig and Susan M. Brown. Riverdale-on-Hudson, N.Y.: Sheep Meadow Press, 1985.

———. *Poems.* Translated and edited by Edwin Honig and Susan M. Brown. 1986. Reprint, San Francisco: City Lights, 1998.

Petersen, Kirsten Holst, ed. *Criticism and Ideology: Second African Writers' Conference. Stockholm 1986.* Introduction by Per Wästberg. Uppsala: Scandinavian Institute of African Studies, 1988.

Petrarch [Francesco Petrarca]. *Le familiari.* Edited by Vittorio Rossi. 4 vols. Florence: Sansoni, 1933–1942.

———. *Letters of Old Age/Rerum senilium libri I–XVIII.* Translated by Aldo S. Bernardo, Saul Levin, and Reta A. Bernardo. 2 vols. Baltimore, Md.: Johns Hopkins University Press, 1992.

———. *Letters on Familiar Matters/Rerum familiarum libri I–XXIV.* Translated by Aldo S. Bernardo. 3 vols. Albany, N.Y.: State University of New York Press; Baltimore, Md.: Johns Hopkins University Press, 1975–1985.

Philip, Marlene NourbeSe. *Frontiers: Essays and Writings on Racism and Culture 1984–1992.* Stratford, Ontario: Mercury Press, 1992.

———. *A Genealogy of Resistance and Other Essays.* Toronto: Mercury Press, 1997.

———. *Looking for Livingstone: An Odyssey of Silence.* Toronto: Mercury Press, 1991.

———. *She Tries Her Tongue, Her Silence Softly Breaks.* Charlottetown, P.E.I.: Ragweed Press, 1989.

Phillips, Caryl. *The Final Passage.* Harmondsworth: Penguin, 1985.

Phillips, Thomas [or John?]. "A Journal of the Voyage in the Hannibal of London, Ann. 1693, 1694, from England, to Cape Monseradoe, in Africa; and thence along the Coast of Guiney to Whidaw, the Island of St. Thomas, and so forward to Barbadoes. . . ." In *A Collection of Voyages and Travels. . . . ,* edited by Awnsham Churhill and John Churchill, 6:187–255. London: Thomas Osborne, 1752.

Philostratus, Flavius. *Life of Apollonius of Tyana.* Edited and translated by F. C. Conybeare. 2 vols. London: Heinemann; New York: Putnam, 1912.

Piedra, José. "From Monkey Tales to Cuban Songs: On Signification." In *Sacred Possessions: Vodou, Santería, Obeah, and the Caribbean,* edited by Margarite Fernández Olmos and Lizabeth Paravisini-Gebert, 122–50. New Brunswick, N.J.: Rutgers University Press, 1997.

———. "The Game of Critical Arrival." *Diacritics* 19, no. 1 (spring 1989): 34–61.

———. "A Return to Africa with a Carpentier Tale." *Modern Language Notes* 97 (1982): 401–10.

Piglia, Ricardo. *La ciudad ausente.* Buenos Aires: Sudamericana, 1992.

Pigman, George W., III. "Versions of Imitation in the Renaissance." *Renaissance Quarterly* 33, no. 1 (spring 1980): 1–32.

Plato. *Complete Works.* Edited, introduction, and notes by John M. Cooper. Associate edited by D. S. Hutchinson. Indianapolis, Ind.: Hackett, 1997.

———. *Ion.* In *The Statesman*; *Philebus*, edited and translated by Harold N. Fowler. *Ion.* Edited and translated by W. R. M. Lamb. 1925. Reprint, Cambridge, Mass.: Harvard University Press, 1990.

Pollard, Velma. *Considering Woman.* London: Women's Press, 1989.

Pollitt, Katha. "Subject to Debate." *Nation*, July 3, 1995, 9.

Polo, Marco. *The Travels.* Translated and introduction by Ronald Latham. Harmondsworth: Penguin, 1958.

Pope, Alexander. *The Poems.* Edited by John Butt. New Haven: Yale University Press, 1963.

———. See also: Arbuthnot, John.

Popper, Karl R. *The Poverty of Historicism.* 1957. Reprint, New York: Harper, 1964.

Portes, Alejandro, Carlos Dore-Cabral, and Patricia Landolt, eds. *The Urban Caribbean: Transition to the New Global Economy.* Baltimore, Md.: Johns Hopkins University Press, 1997.

Prakash, Gyan. "Writing Post-Orientalist Histories of the Third World: Indian Historiography Is Good to Think." In *Colonialism and Culture*, edited by Nicholas B. Dirks, 353–88. Ann Arbor: University of Michigan Press, 1992.

Prendergast, Christopher. *The Order of Mimesis: Balzac, Stendhal, Nerval, Flaubert.* 1986. Reprint, Cambridge: Cambridge University Press, 1988.

Quint, David. *Epic and Empire: Politics and Generic Form from Virgil to Milton.* Princeton, N.J.: Princeton University Press, 1993.

Quintilian[us], Marcus Fabius. *The Institutio oratoria.* Edited and translated by H. E. Butler. 4 vols. 1920–1922. Reprint, London: Heinemann; Cambridge, Mass.: Harvard University Press, 1963.

Rama, Angel. *The Lettered City.* Translated by John Charles Chasteen. Durham, N.C.: Duke University Press, 1996.

Ramazani, Jahan. "The Wound of History: Walcott's *Omeros* and the Postcolonial Poetics of Affliction." *PMLA* 112, no. 3 (May 1997): 405–17.

Ramchand, Kenneth. Introduction to *Minty Alley*, by C. L. R. James, 5–15. London: New Beacon, 1971.

Rappaport, Joanne. *The Politics of Memory: Native Historical Interpretation in the Colombian Andes.* 2nd ed. Durham, N.C.: Duke University Press, 1998.

Reiss, Timothy J. "Cartesian Discourse and Classical Ideology." *Diacritics* 6, no. 4 (winter 1976): 19–27.

———. "The *concevoir* Motif in Descartes." In *La cohérence intérieure: Études sur la littérature française du XVIIᵉ siècle, présentées en hommage à Judd D. Hubert*, edited by Jacqueline Van Baelen and David Lee Rubin, 203–22. Paris: Jean-Michel Place, 1977.

————. "Descartes, the Palatinate, and the Thirty Years' War: Political Theory and Political Practice." In *Baroque Topographies: Literature/History/Philosophy*, edited by Timothy Hampton, 108–45. Yale French Studies 80. New Haven: Yale University Press, 1991.

————. *The Discourse of Modernism*. Ithaca, N.Y.: Cornell University Press, 1982.

————. "Espaces de la pensée discursive: Le cas Galilée et la science classique." *Revue de Synthèse* 85–86 (January–July 1977): 5–47.

————. "History and Language against Cultural Essences: Netmaking with Mphahlele and Ngũgĩ." In *Relocating Literature: Africa and India. University of the Witwatersrand (English and African Literature Departments) Conference Papers, September 1999. Acts of 1st International South–South Conference, University of the Witwatersrand, Johannesburg September 9–13, 1999*, edited by Shaun Viljoen, 1–37. Johannesburg: English Department, University of the Witwatersrand, 2001.

————. "History, Criticism, and Theory: Fact and Fantasy." *Canadian Review of Comparative Literature* 16, no. 1–2 (January–March 1989): 136–53.

————. *Knowledge, Discovery and Imagination in Early Modern Europe: The Rise of Aesthetic Rationalism*. Cambridge: Cambridge University Press, 1997.

————. *The Meaning of Literature*. Ithaca, N.Y.: Cornell University Press, 1992.

————. *Mirages of the Selfe: Patterns of Personhood in Ancient and Early Modern Europe*. Forthcoming.

————. "Neo-Aristotle and Method: Between Zabarella and Descartes." In *Descartes' Natural Philosophy*, edited by Stephen Gaukroger, John Schuster, and John Sutton, 195–227. London: Routledge, 2000.

————. "The Origin and Development of French Tragedy." In *A New History of French Literature*, edited by Denis Hollier et al., 205–209. Cambridge, Mass.: Harvard University Press, 1989.

————. "Perioddity: Considerations on the Geography of Histories." *Modern Language Quarterly* 62, no. 4 (December 2001).

————. "Renaissance Theatre and the Theory of Tragedy." In *The Cambridge History of Literary Criticism, III: Renaissance to Late Seventeenth Century*, edited by Glyn P. Norton, 229–47. Cambridge: Cambridge University Press, 1999.

————. Review of *Faultlines: Cultural Materialism and the Politics of Dissident Reading*, by Alan Sinfield. *Renaissance Quarterly* 47, no. 4 (winter 1994): 967–71.

————. "Revising Descartes: 'Passage Techniques,' Subject, and Community." In *Life Writing in the Age of Reason*, edited by Patrick Coleman, Jill Kowalik, and Jayne Lewis, 16–38. Cambridge: Cambridge University Press, 1999.

————. "Significs: The Analysis of Meaning as Critique of Modernist Culture." In *Essays in Significs. Papers Presented on the Occasion of the 150th Anniversary of the Birth of Victoria Lady Welby (1837–1912)*, edited by H. Walter Schmitz, 63–82. Amsterdam and Philadelphia: John Benjamins, 1990.

————. *Tragedy and Truth: Studies in the Development of a Renaissance and Neoclassical Discourse*. New Haven, Conn.: Yale University Press, 1980.

———. "Tragedy." In *The New Princeton Encyclopedia of Poetry and Poetics,* edited by Alex Preminger et al., 1296–1302. Princeton, N.J.: Princeton University Press, 1993.

———. *The Uncertainty of Analysis: Problems in Truth, Meaning, and Culture.* Ithaca, N.Y.: Cornell University Press, 1988.

———. See also: Brathwaite and Reiss, eds.; Cascardi and Reiss; Hilden and Reiss.

Reyes Cano, José María. *La poesía lírica de Juan de la Cueva.* Seville: Publicaciones de la Excma, Diputación Provincial de Sevilla, 1980.

Richards, I. A. *The Philosophy of Rhetoric.* 1936. Reprint, New York: Oxford University Press, 1965.

Ricoeur, Paul. *Freud and Philosophy: An Essay on Interpretation.* Translated by Denis Savage. New Haven, Conn.: Yale University Press, 1970.

———. *La métaphore vive.* Paris: Seuil, 1975.

Rieff, Philip. *Freud: The Mind of the Moralist.* 1959. Reprint, Garden City, N.Y.: Doubleday, 1961.

———. "The Origins of Freud's Political Psychology." *Journal of the History of Ideas* 17, no. 2 (April 1956): 235–49.

———. "Psychology and Politics: The Freudian Connection." *World Politics* 7, no. 2 (January 1955): 293–305.

Roazen, Paul. *Freud: Political and Social Thought.* New York: Knopf, 1968.

Robert-Tornow, Walter Heinrich. *De apium mellisque apud veteres significatione et symbolica et mythologica.* Berlin: Weidmann, 1893.

Rodney, Walter. *How Europe Underdeveloped Africa.* Rev. ed. Introduction by Vincent Harding, William Strickland, and Robert Hill. Washington, D.C.: Howard University Press, 1981.

Rodó, José Enrique. *Ariel.* Translated by Margaret Sayers Peden. Foreword by James W. Symington. Prologue by Carlos Fuentes. 1988. Reprint, Austin: University of Texas Press, 1989.

Rodríguez Juliá, Edgardo. *El entierro de Cortijo (6 de octubre de 1982).* Río Piedras: Huracán, 1983.

Rodríguez Marín, Francisco. *El "Quijote" y Don Quijote en América.* Madrid: Hernando, 1911.

Rousseau, Jean-Jacques. "Discours sur . . . l'origine de l'inégalité parmi les hommes. . . ." In *Du contrat social ou, Principes du droit politique* [and other political writings], 25–122. Paris: Garnier, 1962.

Rowland, Ingrid. "Titian: The Sacred and Profane." *New York Review of Books,* March 18, 1999, 14–17.

Roy, Jean. *Hobbes et Freud.* Halifax, N.S.: Dalhousie University Press, 1976.

Roy, Namba. *No Black Sparrows.* Edited by Jacqueline Roy. Oxford: Heinemann, 1989.

Ruskin, John. "Traffic [from *The Crown of Wild Olive*]." In *Unto This Last and Other Writings,* edited by Clive Wilmer, 233–49. Harmondsworth: Penguin, 1985.

———. *Unto This Last and Other Writings*. Edited by Clive Wilmer. Harmondsworth: Penguin, 1985.

Russell, Bertrand. *An Inquiry into Meaning and Truth*. 1940. Reprint, Harmondsworth: Penguin, 1969.

Ryle, Gilbert. *The Concept of Mind*. London: Hutchinson, 1949.

Sabuco de Nántes Barrera, Luisa Oliva. *Obras [Nueva filosofía de la naturaleza del hombre]*. Introduction by Octavio Cuartero. Madrid: Ricardo Fé, 1888.

Said, Edward William. *Culture and Imperialism*. New York: Knopf, 1993.

———. "East Isn't East." *Times Literary Supplement*, February 3, 1995, 3–6.

———. Introduction to *Kim*, by Rudyard Kipling, 7–46. Harmondsworth: Penguin, 1987.

———. *Orientalism*. New York: Vintage, 1979.

———. See also: Eagleton, Terry.

Saint-John Perse [Alexis Saint-Léger Léger]. *Collected Poems*. Rev. ed. Translations by W. H. Auden, Hugh Chisholm, Denis Devlin, T. S. Eliot, Robert Fitzgerald, Wallace Fowlie, Richard Howard, and Louise Varèse. Princeton, N.J.: Princeton University Press, 1983.

Saldívar, José David. *The Dialectics of Our America: Genealogy, Cultural Critique, and Literary History*. 1991. Reprint, Durham, N.C.: Duke University Press, 1995.

Sanger, David E. See: Kristof and Sanger.

Saramago, José. *Baltasar and Blimunda*. Translated by Giovanni Pontiero. 1987. Reprint, New York: Ballantine, 1988.

———. *The History of the Siege of Lisbon*. Translated by Giovanni Pontiero. 1996. Reprint, San Diego: Harvest, 1998.

———. *The Stone Raft*. Translated by Giovanni Pontiero. London: Harvill, 1994.

———. *The Year of the Death of Ricardo Reis*. Translated by Giovanni Pontiero. 1991. Reprint, San Diego: Harvest/HBJ, 1992.

Sarmiento, Domingo Faustino. *Facundo: Civilización y barbarie*. Madrid: Espasa-Calpe, 1932.

Sartre, Jean-Paul. "Orphée noir." In *Anthologie de la nouvelle poésie nègre et malgache de langue française*, edited by Léopold Sédar Senghor, ix–xliv. 1948. Reprint, Paris: PUF, 1969.

———. See also: Fanon.

Saussy, Haun. *The Problem of a Chinese Aesthetic*. Stanford, Calif.: Stanford University Press, 1993.

Scarisbrick, J. J. *Henry VIII*. Berkeley: University of California Press, 1968.

Scheinberg, Susan. "The Bee Maidens of the Homeric *Hymn to Hermes*." *Harvard Studies in Classical Philology* 83 (1979): 1–28.

Schiller, Johann Friedrich von. *On the Aesthetic Education of Man, in a Series of Letters*. Edited and translated by Elizabeth M. Wilkinson and L. A. Willoughby. Oxford: Clarendon, 1967.

——. *On the Esthetic Education of Man, in a Series of Letters.* Translated and introduction by Reginald Snell. 1954. Reprint, New York: Ungar, 1965.

——. "On the Nature of Tragedy" ["Ueber den Grund des Vergnügens an tragischen Gegenständen"]. In *German and Dutch Theatre, 1600–1848*, compiled by George W. Brandt and Wiebe Hogendoorn and edited by G. W. Brandt, 221–25. Cambridge: Cambridge University Press, 1993.

Schopenhauer, Arthur. *The World as Will and Representation.* Translated by E. F. J. Payne. 2 vols. 1958. Reprint, New York: Dover, 1966.

Schwarz-Bart, Simone. *The Bridge of Beyond.* Translated by Barbara Bray. Introduction by Bridget Jones. Oxford: Heinemann, 1982.

——. *Pluie et vent sur Télumée Miracle.* Paris: Seuil, 1972.

——. *Ti Jean l'Horizon.* 1979. Reprint, Paris: Seuil, Points, 1981.

Sciascia, Leonardo. *Heures d'Espagne* [*Ore di Spagna*]. Translated by Maurice Darmon. Paris: Fayard, 1992.

——. *Pirandello et la Sicile* [*Pirandello e la Sicilia*]. Translated by Jean-Noël Schifano. Paris: Grasset, 1980.

Scott, Joan. *Gender and the Politics of History.* New York: Columbia University Press, 1988.

Searle, John R. "I Married a Computer." Review of Ray Kurzweil, *The Age of Spiritual Machines: When Computers Exceed Human Intelligence. New York Review of Books*, April 8, 1999, 34–38.

Selvon, Samuel. *The Lonely Londoners* [1956]. Introduction by Kenneth Ramchand. 1985. Reprint, Harlow: Longman, 1995.

Seneca, Lucius Annaeus. *Ad Lucilium epistulae morales.* Translated and edited by Richard M. Gummere. 3 vols. London: Heinemann; New York: Putnam: 1917–1925.

Senghor, Léopold Sédar. "The African Road to Socialism [1960]." In *On African Socialism*, translated and introduction by Mercer Cook, 67–103. New York: Praeger, 1964.

——. *Négritude et humanisme.* Paris: Seuil, 1964.

——, ed. *Anthologie de la nouvelle poésie nègre et malgache de langue française.* Précédée de "Orphée noir" par Jean-Paul Sartre. 1948. Reprint, Paris: PUF, 1969.

Senior, Olive. *Talking of Trees.* Kingston: Calabash, 1985.

Sésé, Bernard. *Antonio Machado (1875–1939): El hombre, el poeta, el pensador.* Prologue by Jorge Guillén. Translated by Soledad García Monton. 2 vols. Madrid: Gredos, 1980.

Shaftesbury, Anthony Ashley Cooper, 3rd earl of. *Several Letters Written by a Noble Lord to a Young Man at the University.* London: Printed for J. Roberts, 1716.

Shakespeare, William. *The Complete Works.* Rev. Pelican text. General editor, Alfred Harbage. New York: Viking, 1969.

Shelley, Percy Bysshe. "Mont Blanc" [1814–1817]. In *The Complete Poetical Works*, edited by Neville Rogers, 2:75–80. Oxford: Clarendon, 1975.

Sherrington, Charles. *The Endeavour of Jean Fernel.* Cambridge: University Press, 1946.

Shibles, Warren A. *An Analysis of Metaphor in the Light of J. M. Urban's Theories.* The Hague: Mouton, 1971.

———. *Metaphor: An Annotated Bibliography and History.* Whitewater, Wis.: Language Press, 1971.

———. See also: Van Noppen, Jean-Pierre, et al.

Shulman, Ken. "New Worlds an Ocean Apart, Seen Side by Side." *New York Times,* October 18, 1998, AR37.

Sidney, Sir Philip. *Astrophel and Stella.* Edited by Mona Wilson. London: Nonsuch Press, 1931.

———. *Defence of Poetry.* Edited by J. A. Van Dorsten. Oxford: Oxford University Press, 1966.

Silko, Leslie Marmon. *Ceremony.* 1977. Reprint, Harmondsworth: Penguin, 1986.

———. *Storyteller.* New York: Arcade, 1981.

Silone, Ignazio. *Bread and Wine.* Translated by Gwenda David and Eric Mosbacher. New York: Harper, 1937.

———. *Bread and Wine.* Rev. ed. Translated by Harvey Fergusson II. New York: Signet, 1963.

Sims, Calvin. "Brazil Is Likely to Wink at Pope's Call to Behave." *New York Times,* October 5, 1997, A8.

Sinfield, Alan. *Faultlines: Cultural Materialism and the Politics of Dissident Reading.* Berkeley: University of California Press, 1992.

Ṣofọla, ·Zulu. *Old Wines Are Tasty. A Play.* 1979. Reprint, Ibadan: University Press, 1981.

———. *Wedlock of the Gods.* London: Evans, 1972.

Sophocles. *Antigone.* Translated by Elizabeth Wyckoff. In *The Complete Greek Tragedies: Sophocles I.* Edited by David Grene and Richmond Lattimore. 1954. Reprint, Chicago: University of Chicago Press, 1967.

———. *Sophocle I: Les Trachiniennes, Antigone.* Edited by Alphonse Dain. Translated by Paul Mazon. Paris: Belles Lettres, 1955.

Sorabji, Richard. *Aristotle on Memory.* London: Duckworth, 1972.

Soyinka, Wole. *Art, Dialogue, and Outrage: Essays on Literature and Culture.* Edited and introduction by Biodun Jeyifo. 1988. Reprint, New York: Pantheon, 1993.

———. *The Bacchae of Euripides: A Communion Rite.* 1973. Reprint, New York: Norton, 1974.

———. "Ethics, Ideology and the Critic." In *Criticism and Ideology,* edited by Kirsten Holst Petersen, 26–51.

———. *Myth, Literature and the African World.* Cambridge: Cambridge University Press, 1976.

Smith, Dinitia. "Another Top 100 List: Now It's Nonfiction." *New York Times,* April 30, 1999, B44.

Spalding, Karen. "The Colonial Indian: Past and Future Research Perspectives." *Latin American Research Review* 7, no. 1 (spring 1972): 47–76.

Spengler, Oswald. *The Decline of the West [Der Untergang des Abendlandes]* [1926–1928]. Translated by Charles Francis Atkinson. 2 vols. Reprint, New York: Knopf, 1950.

Stanford, W. B. *Greek Metaphor: Studies in Theory and Practice*. 1936. Reprint, New York: Johnson Reprint, 1972.

Steele, Timothy. *All the Fun's in How You Say a Thing: An Explanation of Meter and Versification*. Athens: Ohio University Press, 1999.

Steiner, George. *The Death of Tragedy*. 1961. Reprint, New York: Hill & Wang, 1968.

Stern, Steve J. *Peru's Indian Peoples and the Challenge of Spanish Conquest: Huamanga to 1640*. Madison: University of Wisconsin Press, 1982.

Stillman, Robert E. "Hobbes's *Leviathan*: Monsters, Metaphors, and Magic." *English Literary History* 62 (1995): 791–819.

Sullivan, Margaret A. *Bruegel's Peasants: Art and Audience in the Northern Renaissance*. Cambridge: Cambridge University Press, 1994.

Sutherland, Efua Theodara. *The Marriage of Anansewa and Edufa*. 1975. Reprint, Harlow: Longman, 1987.

Sutton, John. *Philosophy and Memory Traces: Descartes to Connectionism*. Cambridge: Cambridge University Press, 1998.

Swift, Jonathan. *The Battel of the Books* [1710]. In *The Writings of Jonathan Swift: Authoritative Texts, Backgrounds, Criticism*, edited by Robert A. Greenberg and William Bowman Piper, 372–96. New York: Norton, 1973.

Szanto, George. "Epilogue: Our Personal Frontier with Latin America: An Interview with Carlos Fuentes." In *Inside the Statues of Saints: Mexican Writers on Culture and Corruption, Politics and Daily Life*, 151–60. Montreal: Véhicule Press, 1996.

Tafuri, Manfredo. *Venice and the Renaissance*. Translated by Jessica Levine. 1989. Reprint, Cambridge, Mass.: MIT Press, 1995.

Tanner, Tony. *Venice Desired*. Cambridge, Mass.: Harvard University Press, 1992.

Taussig, Michael T. *Mimesis and Alterity: A Particular History of the Senses*. New York: Routledge, 1993.

———. *Shamanism, Colonialism, and the Wild Man: A Study in Terror and Healing*. 1987. Reprint, Chicago: University of Chicago Press, 1991.

Taylor, Charles, et al. *Multiculturalism: Examining the Politics of Recognition*. Edited by Amy Gutmann. Princeton, N.J.: Princeton University Press, 1994.

Tesauro, Emanuale. *Il cannocchiale aristotelico*. Facsimile reprint of 1670 edition. Introduction by August Buck. Bad Homburg: Gehlen, 1968.

———. *Il cannocchiale aristotelico: Scelta*. Edited by Ezio Raimondi. Turin: Einaudi, 1978.

Thapar, Romila. "Communalism and the Writing of Indian History." In Thapar, Mukhia, and Chandra, *Communalism*, 1–21.

———. *The Past and Prejudice*. New Delhi: Publications Division, Ministry of Information and Broadcasting, Government of India, 1973.

———, Harban Mukhia, and Bipan Chandra. *Communalism and the Writing of Indian History*. New Delhi: People's Publishing House, 1969.

Thelwell, Michael. *Duties, Pleasure, and Conflicts: Essays in Struggle*. Introduction by James Baldwin. Amherst, Mass.: University of Massachusetts Press, 1987.

Thomas, J. J. *Froudacity: West Indian Fables Explained*. 2nd ed. London: J. Fisher Unwin, 1889.

Thomson, James. *The Seasons and the Castle of Indolence*. Edited by James Sambrook. 1972. Reprint, Oxford: Oxford University Press, 1984.

Thornton, John. *Africa and Africans in the Making of the Atlantic World, 1400–1800*. 2nd ed. Cambridge: Cambridge University Press, 1998.

Tierney-Tello, Mary Beth. "Testimony, Ethics, and the Aesthetic in Diamela Eltit." *PMLA* 114, no. 1 (January 1999): 78–96.

Todorov, Tzvetan. *The Conquest of America: The Question of the Other*. Translated by Richard Howard. New York: Harper & Row, 1984.

Tomaselli, Sylvana. "The First Person: Descartes, Locke and Mind–Body Dualism." *History of Science* 22 (1984): 185–205.

Tönnies, Ferdinand. *Community and Society [Gemeinschaft und Gesellschaft]*. Translated and edited by Charles P. Loomis. 1957. Reprint, New York: Harper & Row, 1963.

Toomer, Jean. *Cane*. Introduction by Darwin T. Turner. New York: Liveright, 1975.

Torres-Saillant, Silvio. "The Unity of Caribbean Literature: A Position." In *Sisyphus and Eldorado*, edited by Brathwaite and Reiss, 197–215.

Tropica (Mary Adella Wolcott). "Nana." In *The Routledge Reader in Caribbean Literature*, edited by Alison Donnell and Sarah Lawson Welsh, 42–43. London: Routledge, 1996.

Turbayne, Colin Murray. *The Myth of Metaphor*. Rev. ed. Forewords by Morse Peckham and Foster Tait. Appendix by Rolf Eberle. Columbia: University of South Carolina Press, 1970.

Turkle, Sherry. *Psychoanalytic Politics: Freud's French Revolution*. 1978. Reprint, Cambridge, Mass.: MIT Press, 1981.

Ulreich, John C., Jr. "'The Poets Only Deliver': Sidney's Conception of *Mimesis*." In *Essential Articles for the Study of Sir Philip Sidney*, edited by Arthur F. Kinney, 135–54. Hamden, Conn.: Archon Books, 1986.

Unamuno y Jugo, Miguel. "El caballero de la triste figura: Ensayo iconológico" [1896]. In *El caballero de la triste figura [y otros ensayos]*, 69–91. Buenos Aires: Espasa-Calpe Argentina, 1944.

———. *Del sentimiento trágico de la vida*. 1937. Reprint, México: Espasa Calpe Mexicana, 1992.

———. *Our Lord Don Quijote: The Life of Don Quixote and Sancho with Related*

Essays. Translated by Anthony Kerrigan. Introduction by Walter Starkie. Princeton, N.J.: Princeton University Press, 1967.

———. *Tragic Sense of Life.* Translated by J. E. Crawford Flitch. 1921. Reprint, New York: Dover, 1954.

———. *Vida de Don Quijote y Sancho* [1905]. Edited by Alberto Navarro. 1988. Reprint, México: Rei-México, 1990.

Van Delden, Maarten. *Carlos Fuentes, Mexico, and Modernity.* Nashville, Tenn.: Vanderbilt University Press, 1998.

Van Noppen, Jean-Pierre, S. de Knop and R. Jongen, with B. Nitelet, A. Nysenholc, and W. Shibles, comp. *Metaphor: A Bibliography of Post-1970 Publications.* Amsterdam: John Benjamins, 1985.

Van Noppen, Jean-Pierre, and Edith Hols, comp. *Metaphor II: A Classified Bibliography of Publications 1985 to 1990.* Amsterdam: John Benjamins, 1990.

Vasconselos, José. *The Cosmic Race: A Bilingual Edition.* Translated and annotated by Didier T. Jaén. Afterword by Joseba Gabilonda. Baltimore, Md.: Johns Hopkins University Press, 1997.

Vega, Bernardo. *Memoirs of Bernardo Vega: A Contribution to the History of the Puerto Rican Community in New York.* Edited by César Andreu Iglesias. Translated by Juan Flores. New York: Monthly Review Press, 1984.

———. *Memorias de Bernardo Vega (Contribución a la historia de la comunidad puertorriqueña en nueva york).* Edited by César Andreu Iglesias. Río Piedras: Huracán, 1977.

Vergil[ius] Maro, Publius. *The Works.* Edited by H. Rushton Fairclough. 2 vols. Rev. ed. 1934–1935. Reprint, Cambridge, Mass.: Harvard University Press; London: Heinemann, 1986.

Vernant, Jean-Pierre. *Entre mythe et politique.* Paris: Seuil, 1996.

———. "De la présentification de l'invisible à l'imitation de l'apparence." In *Entre mythe et politique,* 359–77.

———. "Figuration et image." In *Entre mythe et politique,* 378–95.

———. *La mort dans les yeux: Figures de l'autre en Grèce ancienne.* Paris: Hachette, 1985.

———. "Naissance d'images." *Religions, histoires, raisons.* Paris: Maspero, 1979. 105–37.

Veyne, Paul. *Comment on écrit l'histoire, suivi de Foucault révolutionne l'histoire.* Paris: Seuil, 1978.

Vives, Juan Luis. *Against the Pseudodialecticians: A Humanist Attack on Medieval Logic. . . .* Texts, Translated, edited, and notes by Rita Guerlac. Dordrecht: D. Reidel, 1979.

Vološinov, Valentin Nikolaevich. *Freudianism: A Marxist Critique.* Translated by I. R. Titunik. Edited in collaboration with Neal H. Bruss. New York: Academic Press, 1976.

———. *Marxism and the Philosophy of Language.* Translated by Ladislav Matejka and I. R. Titunik. New York: Academic Press, 1973.

Von Stackelberg, Jürgen. "Das Bienengleichnis: Ein Beitrag zur Geschichte der literarischen *Imitatio.*" *Romanische Forschungen* 68, no. 3–4 (1956): 271–93.

Walcott, Derek. *The Antilles: Fragments of Epic Memory. The Nobel Lecture.* New York: Farrar, Straus & Giroux, 1993.

———. "The Caribbean: Culture or Mimicry?" *Journal of Interamerican Studies and World Affairs* 16, no. 1 (February 1974): 3–13.

———. *Collected Poems 1948–1984.* New York: Farrar, Straus & Giroux, 1986.

———. *Dream on Monkey Mountain and Other Plays.* New York: Farrar, Straus & Giroux, 1970.

———. "History and Picong . . . in the Middle Passage (1962)." In *Critical Perspectives on Derek Walcott,* edited by Robert D. Hamner, 18–19. Washington, D.C.: Three Continents Press, 1993.

———. "The Muse of History: An Essay." In *Is Massa Day Dead? Black Moods in the Caribbean,* edited by Orde Coombs, 1–27. Garden City, N.Y.: Doubleday Anchor, 1974.

———. *Omeros.* 1990. Reprint, New York: Noonday, 1992.

———. "What the Twilight Says: An Overture." In *Dream on Monkey Mountain and Other Plays,* 3–40. New York: Farrar, Straus & Giroux, 1970.

Walmsley, Anne. *The Caribbean Artists Movement 1966–1972: A Literary and Cultural History.* London: New Beacon, 1992.

Walton, Kendall L. *Mimesis as Make-Believe: On the Foundations of the Representational Arts.* Cambridge, Mass.: Harvard University Press, 1990.

Watson, G. "Discovering the Imagination: Platonists and Stoics on *phantasia.*" In *The Question of "Eclecticism": Studies in Later Greek Philosophy,* edited by John M. Dillon and A. A. Long, 208–33. Berkeley: University of California Press, 1988.

Watts, David. *The West Indies: Patterns of Development, Culture and Environmental Change since 1492.* Cambridge: Cambridge University Press, 1987.

Weber, Samuel. *The Legend of Freud.* Minneapolis: University of Minnesota Press, 1982.

Wellek, René, and Austin Warren. *Theory of Literature.* 3rd ed. Harmondsworth: Penguin, 1963.

Werner, Heinz. *Die Ursprünge der Metapher.* Leipzig: Engelmann, 1919.

Weyer, Johann. *Witches, Devils, and Doctors in the Renaissance: Johann Weyer, De praestigiis daemonum* [1563]. Edited by George Mora et al. Translated by John Shea. Binghamton, N.Y.: Medieval & Renaissance Texts & Studies, 1991.

Wightman, Ann M. *Indigenous Migration and Social Change: The Forasteros of Cuzco, 1570–1720.* Durham, N.C.: Duke University Press, 1990.

Williams, Bernard. *Descartes: The Project of Pure Enquiry.* Harmondsworth: Penguin, 1978.

———. *Shame and Necessity.* Berkeley: University of California Press, 1993.

Williams, Chancellor. *The Destruction of Black Civilization: Great Issues of a Race from 4500 B.C. to 2000 A.D..* 3rd ed. Chicago: Third World Press, 1987.

Williams, Raymond. *Marxism and Literature*. Oxford: Oxford University Press, 1977.

———. *Modern Tragedy*. Stanford, Calif.: Stanford University Press, 1966.

Wilson, Diana de Armas. "'*The Matter of America*': Cervantes Romances Inca Garcilaso de la Vega." In *Cultural Authority in Golden Age Spain*, edited by Marina S. Brownlee and Hans Ulrich Gumbrecht, 234–59. Baltimore, Md.: Johns Hopkins University Press, 1995.

Wilson, Margaret Dauler. "Body and Mind from the Cartesian Point of View." In *Body and Mind: Past, Present, and Future*, edited by Robert W. Rieber, 35–55. New York: Academic Press, 1980.

———. "Cartesian Dualism." In *Descartes: Critical and Interpretive Essays*, edited by Michael Hooker, 197–211. Baltimore, Md.: Johns Hopkins University Press, 1978.

Wines, Michael. "Struggling Ukraine Teeters between East and West." *New York Times*, February 26, 1999, A1, A4.

Wittgenstein, Ludwig. *Culture and Value*. Edited by G. H. von Wright, with Heikki Nyman. Translated by Peter Winch. Chicago: University of Chicago Press, 1980.

———. *Philosophical Investigations*. Translated by G. E. M. Anscombe. 1953. Reprint, Oxford: Blackwell, 1972.

———. *Tractatus logico-philosophicus*. Translated by D. F. Pears and B. F. McGuinness. Introduction by Bertrand Russell. London: Routledge & Kegan Paul, 1961.

Wolcott, Mary Adella. See: Tropica.

Wolf, Eric R. *Europe and the People without History*. Berkeley: University of California Press, 1982.

Woolf, Virginia. *Orlando: A Biography*. 1928. Reprint, New York: Harcourt, Brace, 1946.

———. *To the Lighthouse*. 1927. Reprint, New York: Modern Library, 1937.

Wright, Richard. *Native Son*. New York: Harper, 1940.

Xenophon. *Memorabilia and Oeconomicus*. Edited and translated by E. C. Marchant. Cambridge, Mass.: Harvard University Press; London: Heinemann, 1953.

Yu, Pauline. *The Reading of Imagery in the Chinese Poetic Tradition*. Princeton, N.J.: Princeton University Press, 1987.

Zea, Leopoldo. *The Role of the Americas in History [América en la historia]*. Edited and introduction by Amy A. Oliver. Translated by Sonja Karsen. Savage, Md.: Rowman & Littlefield, 1992.

Index

In this index, "f" after a number indicates a separate reference on the next page; "ff" indicates separate references on the next two pages. A continuous discussion over two or more pages is indicated by a span of page numbers. An "f" or "ff" after a span indicates subsequent separate reference or references. *Passim* is used for a cluster of references in close but not consecutive sequence. Some central terms are not indexed: "colonization" and "decolonizing," for instance, or "imperialism," *mestizaje*, and their cognates. These are the book's constant object. Contemporary writers are indexed only when named for more than a straightforward bibliographical reference. People named in an enumeration or in another's quotation are not normally indexed unless also named elsewhere. Dates are given for people born through 1900.

Abacha, Sani, 448
Abanda Ndengue, Jean-Marie, 50
Abu Deeb, Kamal, 174
Achebe, Chinua, 20, 35, 43, 72, 105, 324, 339–42 *passim*; on the Caribbean, 18, 345–46; on Conrad, 52, 57, 61; on culture, 15, 17, 60ff, 148; on Descartes, 176–77, 186, 192f, 214; on history, 70; on Igbo culture, 60, 82–83, 176; on negritude, 50–54, 63; *No Longer at Ease*, 13; *Things Fall Apart* 13; on western anxieties, 79, 123–24, 151
Addison, Joseph (1672–1719), 254
Adonis (Ali Ahmed Said), 173–74, 183
Adorno, Theodor Wiesengrund, 39, 78, 122ff, 128, 192, 249, 303
Aeschylus (525–456 B.C.), 112–15; *Eumenides* 112–14, 126, 129, 410–11, 452n9

aesthetics, aesthetic judgment: autonomous, 36–37, 41–48, 67; as cultural instrument, 2; not autonomous, 56–62; western norms of, 31
"Aethiop," 206–7, 460–61
Africa, 4–6, 58, 61–2, 80, 105; art forms of, 152; and Caribbean, 135, 139, 181, 296, 306, 312–28 *passim*, 340–43, 359, 383, 464n1; as other, 333–35. *See also countries and authors by name*; *Négritude*
afrocentrism, 2, 47–48, 178
Agamben, Giorgio, 124, 128
Agīkūyū (Gikuyu people of Kenya), 83, 99, 104, 174–75, 178
Ahmad, Aijaz, 8, 34, 71, 77, 94, 449–50
Albertus Magnus, St. (c.1200–1280), 235
Alcalá de Henares, 360

Alexander VI, pope (Rodrigo de Borja/
Borgia, 1431–1503), 6
Al-Jurjānī, ʿAbd al-Qāhir (d.471 A.H./
1078 A.D.), 173–74
Allada, 5
Allen, Paula Gunn, 101, 155, 182
Allen, Philip Mark, 53–54
Althusser, Louis, 220
Amadis de Gaul, 363, 415
Ambrosini, Federica, 33, 443
Americas, 172, 188, 258, 278, 281, 334,
359–442; art forms of, 152 (*see also*
Iroquois); invasion of, 3, 7, 100, 111,
155, 322, 332, 335, 450–51n2 (*and see*
Myth of empty America); invention
of, 208, 360–405 *passim*, 420; as new
world, 32, 449n1; wealth of, 302, 428,
445. *See also* Genocide
American Indians, 82, 90, 144, 155, 188,
267, 430, 441, 467n16; and Caribbean,
296, 433; in Montaigne, 101–2, 185,
419f; as others, 17, 68, 86, 146, 252,
263. *See also* Allen, Paula Gunn;
Aymara; Aztec; Cherokee; Chickasaw;
Inca; Iroquois; Nasa; Nez Perce;
Quechua; Warraou; *and under*
Hilden, Patricia J. Penn
Amsterdam, 318
anagnōrisis (recognition, in tragedy),
118
analytico-referentiality, 222–24, 227–
28, 233–37 *passim*, 242–50, 253–57
passim; collapse of, 262–95; defini-
tions of, 221, 252, 271, 274–75, 302.
See also Process/stasis; *references under*
Reason
Anancy (West African and Caribbean
trickster figure), 354, 401–4
Anderson, Benedict, 78
Andes, 362, 365–67
Angola, 5
Antheil, George (1900–59), 61
"*Antillanité*," 338, 340
Antoni, Robert, 143, 337, 343, 347

Anzaldúa, Gloria, 42f, 107, 451f, 186;
against autonomous art, 59f, 62f, 175
Aparicio Laurencio, Angel, 433
ape: as pejorative term for not-western,
133–34, 141–43, 146. *See also* Monkey
Apollo, Apollonian, 165–66, 334; and
tragedy, 117, 121, 133
Apollonius of Tyana (*c.*4 B.C.–*c.*98 A.D.),
171–72
Appiah, Kwame Anthony, 53, 448
Arabic poetics, 173–74, 178
Arendt, Hannah, 187
Argentina, 90, 92, 427; Gombrowicz
and, 252, 261–63, 279, 281, 284, 294,
463n1
Ariel, 100, 319–20
Aristophanes (*c.*445–*c.*388 B.C.), 455n9
Aristotle of Stageira (383–322 B.C.), 116,
124, 191; on memory, 199, 459n12; on
metaphor, 100, 174; on mimesis, 136,
151, 154–55, 159–64 *passim*, 168–69,
171, 457n20; *Poetics*, 109, 117–18, 133,
151, 154, 159f; and tragedy, 117
Arnauld, Antoine, "le grand" (1612–94),
209
Arnold, Albert James, 453
Arnold, Matthew (1822–88), 249–50,
463n8
Asante, Molefi Kete, 47–48, 52, 178
Ascensio, Eugenio, 332, 465
Aschaffenburg, Gustav (1866–1944),
231–32
Aubenque, Pierre, 169
Auden, Wystan Hugh, 19
Auerbach, Erich (1892–1957), 155
Augustine, Saint, bishop of Hippo
(Aurelius Augustinus, 354–430), 176–
77, 274, 347
Aurobindo, Sri (Aurobindo Ackroyd
Ghose, 1872–1950), 97
autobiography, 90–92; cultures with-
out, 82, 90
automata, in Descartes, 191–92, 203,
208–9, 458n4

autonomy, 24–6, 29, 36–68, 184; in
Fanon, 54, 447n20; and literature, 31,
41–48, 56, 87; instrumental uses of,
99–100
Averroes (Abū-l-Walīd Muhammad ibn
Ahmad ibn Muhammad ibn Rushd,
1126–98), 109, 144
Aymara, 461n19
Azorín (José Martínez Ruíz, 1873–
1967), 127, 367–70, 379, 406
Aztec, 33, 376, 417–21 *passim*, 451n2

Babylon (as metaphor for imperial
center), 318, 326, 414, 423, 438, 442
Bachelard, Gaston (1884–1962), 268
Bacon, Francis, Lord Verulam (1561–
1626), 219, 234f, 255, 304; and bees,
259–61; and flowers, 259, 349, 357;
and new science, 40, 224, 226, 243–
44, 246; and spiders' webs, 258–61;
on war, 301–2
Baillet, Adrien (1649–1706), 203
Bakhtin, Mikhail Mikhailovich (1895–
1975), 78, 286, 291, 294
Balboa y Troya de Quesada, Silvestre de
(1563–[after 1608]), 427, 432–37,
440–41f
Balbuena, Bernardo de (1562–1627),
420, 427–30ff, 434–36, 438, 441f,
467n14
Baldwin, James, 20, 35, 43, 145ff, 444,
454; on alienation, 340–44f; on cultural understanding, 17, 90, 103, 215;
on cultural difference, 60, 68, 177
Ballino, Giulio (before 1530–*c*.1592), 419
Baños, Román de (16th–17th century),
363–64
Barbados, 185, 300, 311, 440; Brathwaite
on, 181, 296–97, 306, 312, 315f, 319,
322f, 327, 340, 343, 357; in Carpentier,
66, 382; cloth trade in, 5; Legba in, 140
Baron Samedi (voudou *loa* of death),
385, 387, 390

Barrell, John, 77f
Barthes, Roland, 43, 71
Barton, David, 453
Bayamo, 432–34, 468n18
Beckett, Samuel, 424
Beeckman, Isaac (1588–1637),
bee: as image of *ratio*, 21, 442; and
knowledge, 259–61; as metaphor for
poet, 161–63, 455n10; and mimesis,
161–67, 170, 174, 179–80, 345, 348–
50, 359, 404
Beer, Gillian, 77
Beethoven, Ludwig van (1770–1827),
304ff
Bellini, Giovanni (*c*.1426–1516), 33
Bello, Andrés (1781–1865), 395, 422,
467n8
Bellow, Saul, 152, 182, 452
Bengal, 5, 38, 443–44, 446; literature in,
447n17
Benin, 5
Benítez Rojo, Antonio, 220, 333, 335ff
Benjamin, Walter (1892–1940), 39, 102
Bennett, William, 11, 41
Bennington, Geoffrey, 77f
Berlin, 137, 212, 258; as European
center, 263, 290, 293
Bernabé, Jean, 339, 392
Bezzola Lambert, Ladina, 449n27,
456n18
Bhabha, Homi, 71f, 74, 77–80 *passim*,
97, 452f
Bible, The. See *under* Sparrow
Binet, Étienne (1569–1639), 209
Bismarck, Otto Eduard Leopold, Fürst
von (1815–98), 116
Black, Max, 163, 456n17
Bloom, Allan David, 11–12, 41, 152
Bloom, Harold, 13, 41–42, 43–44
Boccaccio, Giovanni (1313–75), 163, 349
Bohr, Niels Henrik David (1885–1962),
228
Boileau, Nicolas (1636–1711), 43, 161
Boland, Eavan, 206, 213, 461–62

Bolivar, Simon (1783–1830), 387

Bonaparte, Josephine (empress of the French, 1804–10; Marie-Josèphe-Rose Tascher de La Pagerie, vicomtesse de Beauharnais, 1763–1814), 306–7

Bonaparte, Napoleon (Napoleon I, emperor of the French, 1769–1821), 304, 306, 416

Bonaparte, Pauline (1780–1825): as character in Carpentier, 333–34

Borges, Jorge Luis (1899–1986), 109, 121, 143f, 147; on cities, 407–8, 424; on history, 394–95, 401, 404; on Quijote, 370–71, 76

Boschini, Marco (1613–78, or possibly still living in 1704), 445

Boswell, James (1740–95), 303

Bourdin, Pierre (1595–1653), 209

Bouveresse, Jacques, 224–25

Bovelles, Charles de (1479–1567), 330–32, 338, 356, 359, 411, 439

Bowlby, Rachel, 77

Brancusi, Constantin (1876–1957), 453n18

Brathwaite, [Edward] Kamau, 35, 43, 175, 296–328, 406, 423, 441, 449n3, 454; Anancy in, 402–4; *Ancestors*, 319, 324–26; *Arrivants*, 297, 313–17, 319, 322–23, 399; *Barabajan Poems*, 306, 320, 322–24, 343, 404; *Black + Blues*, 318–19f, 324; on Caribbean culture, 18, 66–67, 100, 104, 314–17, 335; and Césaire, 306–9, 314, 320–21; *ConVERSations*, 297, 307, 312, 325, 328, 393, 412, 465n6; on cultural creation, 28, 34, 183, 338, 340, 347, 350, 356–57, 413; *Dream Haiti*, 335; flowers in, 318–19, 353–54, 358f; *History of the Voice*, 297–98; on "home," 327–28, 330; on language, 310–12, 342; on metaphor, 179–82, 306; *Middle Passages*, 319–20f; *Mother Poem*, 319f, 323–25; on nation language, 27, 103,

178, 298, 306, 330, 338; and Quijote, 392–93, 399, 401; *Sun Poem*, 318–19, 323, 325; on Venice, 32, 66, 178–79; *X/Self*, 178–79, 319–21f, 324, 343. *See also* Drums; Sycorax; *and under* Barbados; Caliban; Colón, Cristóbal; Legba; Metaphor; Ogun; Shango

Borinquen, 413–14

Brazil, 140

Breeze, Jean "Binta," 322

Breiner, Laurence, 372

Brennan, Timothy, 78–79, 103, 450

Breton, André (1896–1966), 225, 380

Breuer, Josef (1842–1925), 225–26, 245

Bridgetown (Barbados), 306, 322

Briosi, Alessandro, 152

Brodber, Erna, 344

Brodsky, Joseph, 32

Brown, Laura, 431–32

Brown, Theodore Morris, 457

Brueghel, Pieter, the elder (c.1525–1569), 193–96 *passim*, 212, 218

Brunner, José Joaquín, 408, 411f, 415, 426, 466n4

Buenos Aires, 394

Burckhardt, Jacob Christoph (1818–97), 250, 445

Burke, Kenneth (1897–1993), 43

Burton, Robert (1577–1640), 167f, 193, 195, 212

Byzantium, 32

Cabezas Altamirano, Juan de las (d.1615), 432f, 435

Cabot, John (Zuan Caboto, c.1450–1498), 6

Cabral, Amilcar, 166, 175–76, 182f, 217, 456n15

Cabrera Infante, Guillermo, 357

Calais, Proclamation of (1527), 443

Calcutta, 5

Calderón de la Barca, Pedro (1600–81),

Caliban, 100, 337, 349, 373, 399, 414; in Brathwaite, 318, 320–21, 354–55, 359;

Lamming on, 97–98, 338, 342–43; in
   Mannoni, 141; in Walcott, 135, 381
Callao, 363
Calvino, Italo, 43, 94, 272, 282, 407–9,
   415, 426; *Invisible Cities*, 29–31, 33–
   36, 63, 65, 407, 410–11
Calypso, 297, 354, 464n9
Camões, Luis Vaz de (Camoens, 1524/
   5–80), 306, 369
Cantinflas (Mario Moreno, called), 409
capitalism, as cultural instrument, 2, 8;
   in literary criticism, 69, 76, 78
Cardano, Girolamo (Hieronymus
   Cardanus, 1501–76), 32
Carew, Jan, 20, 22, 332–33, 335f, 416,
   403; on Quijote and land, 375, 379,
   381, 396–97, 440
Caribbean, 5, 61, 66, 295; alienation of,
   52, 135; genocide in, 450–51n2; and
   geography, 139, 180, 296, 316–19
   passim, 337–40, 356–59, 306–404
   passim, 421–23, 432–42; writing of,
   18, 27–28, 32, 178–183, 295–359, 444.
   See also countries and authors by name
carnival, 135–36, 409; in Marshall, 395–
   96, 401, 440f; in Pausa, 363–64, 366,
   395, 401
Carpentier y Valmont, Alejo, 43, 94,
   143, 359, 406, 441; *Concierto*, 33, 65–
   66, 107, 435; on Descartes, 347, 377,
   379, 423; on Don Quijote, 363, 377–
   78, 435; and European other, 34, 333,
   337; and flowers, 353, 355, 437; and
   geography, 356; and magical realism,
   379–80; *Pasos*, 346–47, 377–79, 401;
   Recurso, 347, 423; *Reino*, 316, 319, 333–
   4, 387–88, 391, 396, 415; *Siglo*, 333,
   353, 356, 381–82, 398–99, 423, 438
Cartagena, 360
Cascardi, Anthony Joseph, 37, 39ff,
   446
Cassirer, Ernst (1874–1945), 267
Castellanos, Rosario, 330
Castelvetro, Lodovico (1505–71), 118

Castiglione, Baldassare [Baldesar],
   conde (1478–1529), 459n10
Castoriadis, Cornelius, 3
Castro, Fidel, 376, 384
categorial convertibility or correspondence, 206; in images, 157–58, 163–
   65, 169; of mind, 460n14
catharsis (in Aristotle), 117–18
Catherine of Aragon (1485–1536), 6
Cavarero, Adriana, 187
Cebrián García, José, 468n16
Cempoal: renamed Sevilla, 418
Cervantes de Salazar, Francisco (1513/
   18–1575), 420, 467n11
Cervantes Saavedra, Miguel de (1547–
   1616), 39, 360–61, 366f, 369, 419
Césaire, Aimé, 147, 186, 196, 225, 328,
   334, 372, 381, 464n2; *Cahier d'un
   retour*, 51, 306–9, 314, 319–21, 345,
   384, 423; on cultural belonging, 23,
   182, 359, 453; on cultural destruction,
   15, 98–99, 145, 313, 348, 373, 386; on
   cultural exchange, 89, 103, 148, 166,
   182f, 403; *Et les chiens se taisaient*, 110,
   453; and flowers, 351–52, 355f, 358; on
   invasion, 99, 112, 301, 331, 334, 347,
   367, 413, 415, 419; on negritude, 49–
   52; *Une Saison au Congo*, 50, 110, 139,
   215, 453; *Une tempête*, 100; *La tragédie
   du roi Christophe*, 49f, 57, 67, 110, 139,
   170, 373, 453. *See also under*
   Brathwaite, Kamau; History
Chaitanya, Krishna [Krishnapilli Krishnan Nair], 447
Chamoiseau, Patrick, 52, 339, 392
Chandra, Bipan, 2, 13, 51
Chapman, George (1559–1634), 193,
   195
Chari, Vinjamuri Krishna, 182, 447
Charles I, king of England, Scotland,
   and Ireland (1600–49), 450
Charles V, Holy Roman emperor, king
   of Spain as Charles I (1500–58), 410,
   466n5

Chateaubriand, François-Auguste-René, vicomte de (1768–1848), 334

Chatterjee, Partha, 3, 5, 37–38, 55, 96–97, 443–44, 446

Chaucer, Geoffrey (c.1340–1400), 297, 464n2

Cherokee, 144

Cheyfetz, Eric, 71, 85, 99–102 *passim*, 155

Chiapas, 330, 416

Chickasaw, 454

Chile, 395, 409, 427f

China, 6, 54; "literature" and "aesthetics" in, 8, 20, 156–58, 181. *See also* Sun Wu Kong

Chinweizu (Chinweizu Ibekwe), 47–48, 54, 82, 196, 448

Cholula, 416, 418

Chomsky, Noam, 291, 446

Christ, Ronald, 467n12

Christie, Agatha Mary Clarissa Miller (1891–1976), 259–63 *passim*, 272–73, 288–89

Christophe, Henri, king of Haiti (1767–1820), 135, 387–88; as character in Césaire, 49f, 139; in Carpentier, 316, 387

Cicero, Marcus Tullius (106–43 B.C.), 42, 197–98, 459n10; on metaphor, 152–53, 155

city (Latin American), 208, 406–42 *passim*, 466n4; colonial/neocolonial, 408–9, 422–23, 425, 440, 442; of Enlightenment (lettered), 407f, 411, 422–23f; of signs (as megalopolis), 407–9, 412, 424–27. *See also* Babylon; *and under* García Márquez, Gabriel

Clark-Bekederemo, John Pepper, 110, 137–38, 140

Clendinnen, Inga, 416

Clerselier, Claude (1614–84), 198

Cobham[-Sander], Rhonda, 329–30, 337, 413

cogito, 40, 176–77, 188, 221, 290; opposed to negritude, 47; "turned," 438

Cole, Bruce, 445

Coleridge, Samuel Taylor (1772–1834), 153, 169, 262, 269–70, 275, 297–99, 305

Colón, Cristóbal (1451?–1506), 278, 305, 419, 449n3, 466n5; in Brathwaite, 305–6, 322, 412; on conquest, 332; as image, 33, 445n4

Columbia, 422

Columbus, Christopher. *See* Colón, Cristóbal.

Comte, Auguste (1798–1857), 269

Condé, Maryse, 225, 383, 403

Confiant, Raphaël, 52, 339, 392

Congress of Writers for the Defense of Culture, 380

Conrad, Joseph (Teodor Jozef Konrad Korzeniowski, 1857–1924), 52, 57, 61; *Lord Jim*, 13

consciousness, 227–28, 237; differences in, 82–83; divine, 122; false, 182; individualist, 45, 81, 104–5, 123–24, 130, 238–44 *passim*, 255–57; new, 251, 306, 316, 349, 447n14, 460n14; racial, 50, 52; and society, 18, 286, 464n8. *See also* Self; Subject

Constant (de Rebecque), Benjamin (1767–1830), 119

Constantinople. *See* Byzantium

Contarini, Gasparo (1483–1542), 466n5

Coomaraswamy, Ananda Kentish (1877–1947), 11, 20, 35, 143, 192, 458

Copplestone, Fenella, 321

Corn, Alfred, 356

Cornaro, Alvise (1475–1566), 33, 419

Corneille, Pierre (1606–84), 118

Corngold, Stanley, 446

Coronil, Fernando, 71

Cortés, Hernán, marqués del Valle (1485–1547), 305, 411, 417–18f, 425, 430, 438, 441, 468n16; on Caribbean, 412–13, 422, 466n6; Césaire on, 99,

331, 413; destroying culture, 112, 333, 375, 377, 418; on Tenochtitlán, 410, 416, 465–66; on wealth, 332

Cournot, Antoine-Augustin (1801–77), 103

Creeley, Robert, 454

Cremonini, Cesare (1550–1631), 228–33 *passim*, 244, 246

Creole (languages), 330

"*créolité*," 336

Cristiani, Luca (*c.*1300/5–after 1352), 33

Croce, Benedetto (1866–1952), 168

Cromwell, Oliver (1599–1658), 299–300, 303

Crusoe, 185–86

Cuauhtemoc (*c.*1497–1525), 421

Cuba (Fernandina), 126, 307 [Philip**], 376; in Brathwaite, 297; in Carpentier, 381, 423; Cortés on, 413; and geography, 357, 432–38, 440; poetry of, 422, 427, 432–37; Spain's loss of, 367

Cueva, Juan de la (1543–1612), 420, 430–32, 434, 468n16

cultural instruments, 31, 97, 107–10, 141, 300, 327, 337; definition of, 2–8, 150; simplification in, 216; turned, 345–442. *See also* Ratio, Rationes; *and under* Tragedy *and separate instruments*

cummings, e(dward), e(stlin) (1894–1962), 297

Cunard, Nancy (1896–1965), 448

Cuzco, 99, 331, 362–63, 365, 413, 419

Dahomey (Benin), 320, 323

Dainotto, Roberto Maria, 451

Dallal, Jenine Abboushi, 150, 173–74, 454n1, 457n22

Damas, Léon-Gontran, 51

Damballah (Dahomeyan/Haitian python god/*loa*), 320

Damon, Phillip, 163–64, 169

D'Amico, Silvio (1887–1955), 125, 451

Dante Alighieri (1265–1321), 42, 313, 400

Darwin, Charles Robert (1809–82), 141, 453; and social Darwinism, 6

Dash, Jean Michael, 376, 381, 437, 441

Davidson, Basil, 60

Dayan, Joan, 335f, 464n2

Deane, Seamus, 75–77f, 450

De, Suchil Kumar, 44, 447nn11 and 17

De Certeau, Michel, 73, 102, 223, 238–39, 446, 458; on otherness, 68–9, 185, 449

De Man, Paul, 43

Demetrius of Phalerum (*c.*345–*c.*283 B.C.), 152

Depestre, René, 137, 319, 349, 359, 379, 409; and flowers, 391–92; *Mât de cocagne*, 384–92, 396, 400–401; on negritude, 47, 50ff, 389; on poetic language, 301, 313–14, 464n2; on Quijote, 384–92, 395

Derrida, Jacques, 71, 123, 169–70, 192, , 245–46, 248, 255, 462–63

Descartes, René (1596–1650), 26, 183, 184–218, 234, 255, 274–75; on blackness, 206–7, 460–61; as European reason, 47–48, 50–51, 59, 176–77, 347, 379; efforts to deny history, 191, 204, 208–10; varieties of history in, 40–1, 186, 192–99, 204–5, 208, 404; *Meditations* of, 63, 190, 197–98, 207–8, 215; and origins of modernity, 21, 39–40, 209–10, 224–27 *passim*, 243, 259, 268, 457n1; and memory, 40, 198–214, 232, 245–48, 268; and method, 40, 47–48, 176, 191f, 196, 205–6; on passions, 40, 190, 199–200, 202, 207, 209f, 247; and self, 26, 186, 210–18 *passim*, 250–51; and universality, 191, 198–99. *See also* Automata; *Cogito*; Mind/Body; *and under* Forgetting; History

Dessalines, Jean-Jacques (*c.*1758–1896; Emperor of Haiti, 1804–6), 387

Devil's Island, 307
Díaz del Castillo, Bernal (*c*.1498–*c*.1580), 415–18, 425, 441
Dickens, Charles (1812–70), 79, 259
Diderot, Denis (1713–84), 249
Diogenes the Cynic (*c*.412–323 B.C.), 451
Diogenes Laertius (2nd or 3rd century A.D.), 451
Dionysos, Dionysian, 117, 121, 133, 334
Diop, Cheikh Anta, 51f, 54
Dirks, Nicholas Bernard, 6
disciplines (discourses) of knowledge (as cultural instruments), 3. *See also under* Analytico- referentiality; Europe (and discursive collapse); History; Literature; Science
dissonance (scission; division): as cultural category, 110–50, 214; in literature and aesthetics, 150–52, 263; mimesis and metaphor as, 151–56, 169–70; as patriarchy, 270, 280, 282–83; in self, 233, 248–52. *See also* Autonomy; Mind/Body
Domínguez, Luis Adolfo, 430
Donoghue, Denis, 310
Don Quijote, 15–17, 165, 360–62, 364, 375–76, 378. *See also* Cervantes Saavedra, Miguel de
Don Quijote (character), 361–406, 415; colonized (in Peru), 405–6; as "frontier" image, 21, 27, 125, 362–63, 366; for Generation of '98, 367–71; and history, 127, 359; as European other, 370; Unamuno on, 122, 143, 367–71, 376–79, 460n14. *See also under* Nostalgia
Donne, John (1572–1631), 193
Doty, Mark, 356
Dreyfus, Alfred (1859–1935), 309
drums (as metaphor for new, Afro-Caribbean, language), 314–17ff, 326, 350, 354, 359, 391, 402, 439
Dryden, John (1631–1700), 118, 269, 286

D'Souza, Dinesh, 11
Duncan, Robert, 454
Dürer, Albrecht (1471–1528), 193ff, 212, 349, 400–401, 406
During, Simon, 77f
Durkheim, Émile (1858–1917), 45, 125
Dürrenmatt, Friedrich, 115, 119, 130, 146, 400
Duvalier, Dr. François ("Papa Doc," president of Haiti, 1958–71), 384–85, 388–89, 391

Eagleton, Terry, 43, 79, 89, 448; and otherness, 69, 71, 100; and colonialism, 76–77, 93; on Foucault, 80–82, 84–86
Edda (old Icelandic prose commentary and poetic lays), 142
Eldorado, 329, 345–48, 352, 357, 359, 413; as European nostalgia, 193, 303, 336, 411
Eliot, George (Mary Ann Evans, 1819–80), 92–93
Eliot, Thomas Stearns (1888–1965), 23, 447; on cultural exchange, 15, 167, 456n16; on diseased reason, 123, 191, 249, 286, 400; on metaphysical poets, 168, 193; on poetic language, 297–98, 300, 305
Else, Gerald Frank, 117
Elson, Henry William (1857–1954), 146
Eltit, Diamela, 409, 423–27, 441–42
Elton, Geoffrey Rudolph, 443
England, English, 75, 93–94, 99, 263, 339, 346; civil wars of, 116, 168; and cultural competition, 9, 27, 431–32; early trade and exploration of, 5–7, 443, 464n1; literary tradition, 79, 84, 88–89; nostalgia of, 299–305
Enlightenment, 4, 70, 76, 86, 94, 258; and autonomy, 38–40, 42, 54, 170; dismay with, 45, 56–57, 78, 192, 213–14, 262; and history, 367–68, 458n8; Kant on, 239–40, 263, 277, 463n2; as

imposition, 333, 340, 348; and language, 331; as maturity, 236, 252–53, 263, 277 (*see also under* Maturity); reason in, 2–3, 13–14, 39–40, 100, 125, 242; and science, 218; subversion of, 263–65; and tragedy, 118; universality of its reason, 13, 239–40, 269–72, 374

Enright, Dennis Joseph, 447

epic, 78–79, 301

Epicurus (341–270 B.C.), 455n10

Erasmus, Desiderius (1466/9–1536), 379, 400, 406, 420; on history and forgetting, 193, 195, 460n16; on metaphor, 153, 161, 349

Ethiopia, 74

Euben, J. Peter, 117

Euclid (fl. 323–283 B.C.), euclidian, 40–41, 269, 395

Euripides (485/80–407/6 B.C.), 113, 134, 136–37; *Alcestis*,112

Eurocentrism, 1, 127

Europa, 34, 51

Europe, 91, 127f, 189; and discursive collapse, 261–95; and dissonance, 122–33; and history, 184–218, 332–40 *passim*, 395; as other (to Africa or Americas), 31–36, 98, 185, 334–35, 352–53, 398, 407–42 *passim*. *See also* Eurocentrism; Reason; *and under* Latin America; Venice

Ezenwa-Ohaetu, 138–39

Fanon, Frantz, 12, 14, 100, 220; on colonialism, 55f, 75, 339–41; and Descartes, 190; on national culture, 60ff, 175, 216–17f; and Mannoni, 141, 144, 320; on negritude, 50–54 *passim*; and Sartre, 69–71f, 104–6; on western society, 217, 244

Farah, Nuruddin, 74–75f, 81, 91, 94, 104

Fashoda, 106

Faulkner, William (1897–1962), 146, 406

Faust, 142, 167

Fénelon, François de Salignac de la Motte- (1651–1715), 79

Fernández Retamar, Roberto, 100, 319

Fernandina. *See* Cuba

Fernel, Jean (1497–1558), 338

Fiat (inception of discourse): in Freud, 230–31; in Hobbes, 211–12, 264–65

fiction (versus real), 2, 42ff

fictive imagination, 25, 108, 444; against autonomy, 265, 336; in China, 156–58; different functionings of, 24, 152, 174–77, 182–3, 441, 446n9; idea of, 3–4, 8–9; as mimicry/mimesis, 135, 162, 164–65, 170–71; and social role, 27–29, 97, 107, 143–44. *See also* Literature

Fliess, Wilhelm (1858–1928), 226, 230, 232, 245

Florida, 296

flowers: as Caribbean cultural creation, 180–2, 318–19, 345, 347–59, 373, 391, 404, 442; as image of local place, 166–67, 259, 432–37; language as, 170, 300–301

Fonte, Moderata (Modesta Pozzo, 1555–92), 32f

Fontenelle, Bernard Le Bovier de (1657–1757), 269, 274

forgetting: of Africa, 318; Descartes on, 459n10; 186, 192, 197–212, 458–59; Freud on, 234–35; and the nation, 80, 89, 368; in Pessoa, 211

Forster, Edward Morgan (1879–1970), 76, 92

Fort-de-France, 306, 345, 423

Fortlage, Karl (1806–81), 256

Foss, Martin (1889–1969), 456

Foucault, Michel, 72, 80–81, 83–85, 220; on otherness, 95, 98; and self, 242, 244, 251–52

Fracastoro, Girolamo (1483–1553), 33, 419

France, 116, 261, 263, 381; and cultural competition, 9–10; early trade of, 5; and literary tradition, 27, 88–89

Franco, Jean, 407–12, 423f, 466n4
Frank, André Gunder, 7, 13, 332, 466n3; on capitalism, 2, 38, 55, 409–10, 466n4; on Europe and Americas, 99, 413, 451
Franqui, Carlos, 376
free trade, 14; as cultural instrument, 2, 8, 38, 446
Frege, Friedrich Ludwig Gottlob (1848–1925), 243, 248, 262; and science, 222f, 225–29 *passim*. *See also Vorstellung*
French Guiana, 309, 382
Freud, Sigmund (1856–1939), 219–57, 284–85, 462–63; on dreams, 222–25, 230, 234–35, 243–48, 251, 256; and Oedipus, 242, 451; in other cultures, 333, 337, 344, 388–89; and self, 26, 186, 219–20, 223–57 *passim*, 333. *See also* Process/stasis; *and under Fiat*
Friday. *See* Crusoe
Froude, James Anthony (1818–94), 7, 299–303, 324, 334, 345, 349
Fuentes, Carlos, 187, 340, 384, 421, 441, 454, 458n6; on cultural mixing, 103–4
Fukuyama, Francis, 13, 122, 128
Furet, François, 122

Galeano, Eduardo, 56, 62, 317–18, 320, 326
Galileo Galilei (1564–1642), 33, 178, 275; and new science, 40, 219, 226f, 243–44; and telescope, 221, 228, 231f, 246, 248, 255
Gálvez, Luis de (16th–17th century), 363–64
Gandhi, Mohanda Karamchand (Mahatma G., 1869–1948), 97
García de Santa María, Gónzalo (*fl.*1485–97), 465
García Lorca, Federico (1898–1936), 380
García Márquez, Gabriel, 394–95, 406, 411; and Macondo (historicizing different cities), 411, 422–23f

Gassendi, Pierre (1592–1655), 197–99, 204, 206–7, 460–61
Gates, Henry Louis, Jr., 48, 343
Gemeinschaft/Gesellschaft, 2, 45, 52, 57, 100, 102, 117, 125f, 194, 336, 381. *See also under Négritude*
Generation of '98 (Spanish), 21, 126, 367–68, 390. *See also* Machado, Antonio; Maeztu, Ramiro de; Ortega y Gasset, José; Unamuno, Miguel de
genocide, 38, 111, 135, 147, 365, 450–51n2, 466n5
George I, king of Great Britain and Ireland (1660–1727), 254
Geography. *See under* Caribbean
Germany/German lands, 27, 116, 127; culturally splintered, 9, 64; and Greece, 87–88; literature of, 10, 27, 89
Ghana, 315
ghetto (Venetian), 32, 131, 194, 400
Gibbon, Edward (1737–94), 10, 97–98, 100, 102, 278
Gĩkũyũ. *See* Agĩkũyũ
Gilbert, Alan, 409–10, 466n4
Gilroy, Paul, 335f
Girón, Gilberto (d.1604), 432–34
Glissant, Édouard, 26–27, 66, 158; on monolinguism, 103; on colonial impositions, 52, 55, 156, 339; on flowers, 348, 350, 353; on history, 108, 337, 373; on relation, 338, 340, 392, 400, 404, 406; and tragedy, 144f, 147
Gmelins, Hermann, 455n10
Goethe, Johann Wolfgang von (1749–1832), 43, 88, 146, 167, 208, 394; on home, 64–65f; on world literature, 9–10, 13, 16; on tragedy, 118f. *See also under* India
Goldsmith, Oliver (1728–74), 303
Goldstein, Harvey David, 117, 159–60, 452
Gombrowicz, Witold, 27, 259–62, 304, 463; *Cosmos*, 92, 261–94; on maturity

/immaturity, 252–53, 263, 277, 281, 294, 463n2. *See also under* Argentina

Gomez, Michael Angelo, 267, 272, 280, 310–11

González Echevarría, Roberto, 333–34, 380, 399, 427, 432–33, 435–36

González Prada, Manuel (1844–1918), 359, 370, 411, 439

González Refolio, Pedro (16th–17th century), 360

Goodison, Lorna, 414

Goodman, Nelson, 153, 169

Gordon, Lewis Ricardo, 105, 190

Gouhier, Henri Gaston (1898–1994), 204

Gourgouris, Stathis, 3, 78, 87, 89, 450

Grass, Günter, 28, 62, 86

Gravel, Pierre, 159

Gray, Thomas (1716–71), 297–99f, 302–5 *passim*, 324

Greece, 87–90; tragedy in, 112–14

Grenada, 464n9; in Brathwaite, 297

Griffin, John Howard, 207, 461n16

Grillparzer, Franz (1791–1872), 116

Groto, Luigi (1541–85), 33

Gruzinski, Serge, 418, 467n9

Guadalajara (Mexico), 427

Guadeloupe, 297, 352, 381, 398

Guha, Ranajit, 3

Guha-Thakurta, Tapati, 5, 54, 447

Guinea Coast, 5

Guillén, Alberto (1897–1935), 405–6

Guillén, Nicolás, 143

Gunew, Sneja, 77, 84

Guyana, 296, 307, 327, 338

Habermas, Jürgen, 67, 77, 129–30f, 143, 445; against autonomy, 64–65; on autonomy, 37, 39, 42; and public sphere, 84, 89

habitus, 197, 459n9

Haidu, Peter, 8, 24

Haiti, 349, 370, 437; in Carpentier, 316, 319, 381; in Césaire, 135, 139f; in

Depestre, 315–16, 319, 384–92, 395; Froude on, 300–301, 303

Hakluyt, Richard (1552?–1616), 7, 450

Hall, Stuart, 9, 180, 430

hamartia (in Aristotle), 117, 145

Hamilton, John Thomas, 163, 455n12

Hampden, John (1594–1643), 299–300, 303

Hampton, Timothy, 450

Händel, George Frideric (1685–1759), 65f

Hanuman (Hindu god of borders and transformations), 140, 142–43, 148, 172

Harris, Wilson, 183, 213, 218, 344, 413; concept of mutuality in, 4, 6, 15, 23, 104, 144–48 *passim*, 170, 186, 327–28, 400; and cultural creation, 344, 347–48; against Descartes, 187–88f, 192, 214; and flowers, 347, 352–53, 357; on language and culture, 16, 317, 319; on "web" of geography, 326, 337, 347, 403

Hartlib, Samuel (c.1600–1662), 461n21

Hartman, Geoffrey H., 44

Hartmann, Heinz (1894–1970), 228, 230

Hawkins, William (d.1554?), 7

Hegel, Georg Wilhelm Friedrich (1770–1831), and Hegelianism, 88, 116, 217; on Africa, 54, 70, 105, 341; and *Aufhebung* (sublation), 69–70,137, 139, 174; and history, 13, 39, 55, 128, 212, 238–40, 368, 439; on instrumentality, 229–30f, 233, 246, 248; and negation, 104, 124; and tragedy, 113, 115, 119, 451

Heidegger, Martin (1889–1976), 39, 113f, 154–55, 290; against technological reason, 122, 125f, 277, 303; on negation, 124

Heinsius, Daniel (1580–1665), 118

Heisenberg, Werner, 228, 274–75, 277

Heitner, Robert Richard, 454n20

Heller, Erich, 447
Henry VII, king of England (1457–
1509), 6
Henry VIII, king of England (1491–
1547), 6–7, 443
Heraclitus of Ephesus (*c.*535–*c.*475
B.C.), 121
Hercules (Heracles), 134, 141, 452
Heredia, José María (1803–39), 422,
441
Hermann the German (before 1240–
1272), 109
Hermes, 165–66, 174
Hermogenes of Tarsus (*c.*160–? A.D.),
456n13
Hilden, Patricia J. Penn, 17, 44, 446,
454, 459n8; on cultural understanding, 61f, 107; on oppressions of American Indians, 144, 146f, 447, 451
Hispaniola (modern Haiti and San
Domingo), 413, 466n5
Historikerstreit, 38, 41
history, 2, 35, 155–56, 185–218, 446; in
Caribbean, 337–40 *passim*, 345, 366–
404 *passim*; as encroachment ("presence"), 183, 194–96, 204–5; "end" of,
12–14, 55; as imposition, 70–71, 108,
132, 143–46, 211, 278, 372 (*and see*
History); in Latin America, 406–442
passim; as linear narration, 38, 196,
239, 262–95 *passim*, 395; as (cartesian)
method, 196, 208, 216; as new, 211–
12, 330, 371–76, 394–95. *See also* Forgetting; Memory; Nostalgia; Process/
stasis; *and under* Descartes; Don
Quijote; India
History (as the West's narrative), 4, 55–
56, 108, 127, 183, 369–70, 373, 395,
406–7, 419, 438; Césaire on, 49–50,
67, 139, 352; Fanon on, 105
Hjelmslev, Louis (1899–1965), 263
Hobbes, Thomas (1588–1679), 39–40,
116, 217, 220, 243, 245, 302; and
Freud, 226–27, 235–36f, 242–43,

462; and Hobbesianism, 54; and
metaphor, 162, 168, 174, 211–12; and
state of nature, 226–27, 241, 286. *See
also under Fiat*
Hobsbawm, Eric, 78
Hodge, Merle, 339, 358
Holland: early trade of, 5
Hölderlin, Friedrich (1770–1843), 116,
170
"home," 63–67, 74, 85, 89, 96, 184–85,
357–58; against "other," 34–36, 177–
78; in afrocentrism, 52; Caribbean as,
296, 306, 315, 327–30, 344, 358, 404,
434–42; forcible entry into, 57, 64,
329–30; and memory, 374; and
"unhoming," 452n14
Homer (8th century B.C.), 41f, 143, 301,
349; metaphor in, 163–65, 455–56
The Homeric Hymns, 163, 165–66, 349
Horace (Quintus Horatius Flaccus, 65–
8 B.C.), 42f, 260, 455n12
Horatius Cocles (legendary, 6th century
B.C.), 387
Horkheimer, Max (1895–1973), 39, 78,
122ff, 128, 192, 249, 303
Huarte de San Juan, Juan (*c.*1529–1588/
9), 191, 193, 195, 212
Hugues, Victor (1761/70–1826): as
character in Carpentier, 382, 398
Huhndorf, Shari Michelle, 452
Hull, Gordon, 168, 212
Humboldt, Alexander, Freiherr von
(1769–1859), 364–65
Huntington, Samuel Phillips, 11, 182
Husserl, Edmund (1859–1938), 39, 45,
122, 125, 277, 303

iambic pentameter, 296–99, 301–2,
304–5, 317, 321, 323, 326
Iampolski, Mikhail, 452
identity. *See* Mapping; Nationalism;
Self; Subject
identity, individualist. *See* Self; Subject
ideology, 31, 80–82; and autonomy, 38–

39, 56; concealment of, 44–45; as grip on the other, 34–35

Igbo, 60, 82–83, 90; in Caribbean, 296, 343, 464n1

Ijaw, 138

imitation. *See under* mimesis; mimicry

Inca, 362–66, 376, 425, 467n12

India, 6, 93–97, 428, 431, 462n1; Goethe and, 10, 142–43; and Caribbean, 343; and history, 458–59, 461n19; literature and aesthetics in, 8, 44, 447n17, 449–50; as West's other, 2, 10, 54, 443–44. *See also* Hanuman; Macaulay, Thomas

Indies. *See* Americas

Ingarden, Roman (1893–1970), 457n20

Ireland, Irish, 75–76, 79

Iroquois, 10, 97f, 102, 278

Isabella I, queen of Castile and Leon (Isabella the Catholic, 1451–1504), 331

Isocrates (436–338 B.C.), 151, 161, 176

Jamaica, 180, 313, 326, 414, 466n5, 467n14; in Brathwaite, 297–98, 327

James, Cyril Lionel Robert, 24, 62, 301, 312, 339, 341f, 359, 370, 377

James, Henry (1843–1916), 66, 93

Jameson, Fredric, 71, 76–77, 92f, 175, 257

Janik, Sophie, 293–94, 463n3, 464n7

Japan, Japanese, 71; monkey figure in, 140, 452n13; and tragedy, 110, 132

Jaspers, Karl (1883–1969), 450

Javitch, Daniel, 455n8

Jeanneret, Michel, 455n9

Jefferson, Thomas (1743–1826), 134, 141

Jenkins, Nicholas, 249, 463n8

Jerusalem: Venice as, 32

Job (Biblical book of), 450

John Paul II, pope (Karol Wojtyla), 412f, 423, 427

Johnson, Samuel (1709–84), 89, 286, 303

Jones, Eldred Durosimi, 58

Jones, Everett LeRoi (Imamu Amiri Baraka), 343

Joyce, James (1882–1941), 76, 93, 250–51, 309–11, 342, 424f, 444n8

Jung, Carl Gustav (1875–1961), 192, 231–32

Jusdanis, Gregory, 71, 78f, 84, 87–90, 450

Kadir, Djelal, 467n12

Kafka, Franz (1883–1924), 250–51

Kahler, Erich (1885–1970), 45

Kane, Cheikh Hamidou, 447n13; against autonomy, 62, 72, 103, 193; against Descartes, 63, 192, 214–16; on "cartesian" self, 176–77, 186; on constructing colonies, 48, 196; on new consciousness, 447n14

Kant, Immanuel (1724–1804), 43, 237–39, 253f; and autonomy, 36f, 41; *Critique of Judgment*, 41, 446; and Kantianism, 42; and subject, 119f, 252. *See also under* Enlightenment

Keats, John (1795–1821), 305,

Kenyatta, Jomo (Kamau wa Ngengi, c.1894–1978), 83

Khusrow, Amir (1253–1325), 450

Kierkegaard, Søren (1813–55), 249

Kilimanjaro, 179

Kimball, Roger, 11, 41

Kincaid, Jamaica, 19, 180, 333, 335, 339–40, 356; and flowers, 348, 350–51, 355; and history, 393, 401

Kingston (Jamaica), 345, 423

Kingston, Maxine Hong, 143, 148–49

Kinsai, 31, 428, 445, 467–68

Kipling, Rudyard (1865–1936), 93, 97, 100; *Kim*, 92–97f, 101, 107

kīrīra, 174–75, 178

Kitcher, Philip, 464n6

"kitsch memory," 45–46, 335; as fetishism, 193–94

knowledge. *See under* disciplines (discourses) of knowledge

Kornhauser, Elizabeth Mankin, 417
Koussevitzky, Serge (1874–1951), 61
Kris, Ernst (1900–57), 223
Krupat, Arnold, 53
Krysinski, Wladimir, 463n3
Kublai Kahn (1215?–1294), 31; as character in Calvino, 30–31, 35, 65, 410f
Kumasi, 376
Kurzweil, Ray, 274, 464n6
Kusch, Rodolfo, 208, 211, 214, 407, 410–11, 461

Labriola, Arturo (1874–1959), 128, 132, 147
Lacan, Jacques (and lacanian), 224f, 228, 242, 246, 250, 284, 337, 462–63
Lamb, Walter Rangeley Maitland (1882–1961), 455n9
Lambropoulos, Vassilios, 111, 450
Lamming, George, 64f, 100; on colonized minds, 144, 340–43; *The Emigrants*, 357, 373; *In the Castle*, 316; on Naipaul, 343, 346; on Prospero and Caliban, 97–98, 338, 342–43, 355
Lang, Fritz (1890–1976), 407
Lange, Norah, 91
language: creation of, 102–4, 135, 330–31, 338, 359, 455–56, 392; decolonizing of, 59, 73, 76, 87, 184; in literature/orature, 42, 174–75, 302–3; misuse of, 19–20; in negritude, 47, 49, 70; as oppression, 20, 101–2, 111, 305–6, 309–11, 331–33; of poetry, 173–74, 298–306 *passim*, 325; unsettling of, 263–94 *passim*, 407–9. *See also under* Brathwaite, Kamau ("language" and "nation language")
language games, 258, 263–65, 273–74, 277–79. *See also under* Wittgenstein, Ludwig
Lanham, Richard Alan, 153, 156
Laplace, Pierre-Simon, marquis de (1749–1827), 269, 374
La Rose, John, 309, 318

Las Casas, Bartolomé de (1474–1566), 416, 419
Latin America, 5, 27, 91, 466n4; against Europe, 252, 293, 461n19, 466–67; genocide in, 365, 451n2; and nationalism, 5; and revival of western values, 127–28, 131–32, 406, 420; and underdevelopment, 13–14. *See also countries and authors by name and under* history
Latour, Bruno, 194, 371
Legba (Esu-Elegbara, Yoruba and African diaspora trickster god), 136, 140, 359, 388, 390, 403–4; in Brathwaite, 305, 323–4, 327, 354
Leibniz, Gottfried Wilhelm, Freiherr von (1646–1716), 118
Leonard, Irving Albert (1896–1996), 362
Leonidas (d. 480 B.C.), 387
Léry, Jean de (1534–1611), 449
Lessing, Gotthold Ephraim (1729–81), 88, 116
Lezama Lima, José, 406, 432, 434–37
Levi, Primo, 45–46, 89, 105, 136, 211, 214
Lévi-Strauss, Claude, 267, 282; on diseased reason, 123, 192, 213, 249
Lewis, Paul, 445
liberalism (as cultural instrument), 2, 8, 37–38, 129–30, 241–42, 253–54
Lincoln, Abraham (1809–1865), 107
Ligon, Richard (1634–1703), 311
Lima, 359–63, 408
Lion King, The (1994 Disney film), 142
Lipinska-Illakowicz, Krystyna, 253, 450n9, 463nn2 and 3
literature: as cultural instrument, 2–4, 41–48, 182f, 326, 407–8; definitions of, 8–13, 89 260, 302; invention of, 4, 9–10, 27–29, 80, 357–59; and nation, 88; not autonomous, 151; supposed universality of, 10–13, 17. *See also* Autonomy; Fictive imagination; Novel

Liu Hsieh (465–522 A.D.), 158, 455n6

Locke, Alain LeRoy (1886–1954), 448n23

Locke, John (1632–1704), 116, 237, 241, 302; on property, 38, 56, 101, 146; on self and society, 249, 253, 255–56

Loko (escort for *loa* Atibon-Legba), 388, 390, 403

London, 312, 382; as imperial center, 76, 299, 303, 318

Lope de Vega. *See* Vega Carpio, Lope Félix de

López de Velasco, Juan (1530–98), 418

Lorde, Audre, 351, 451

Lotman, Yuri Mikhailovich, 237, 242–43

Louverture, Toussaint (1743–1803), 359; in Brathwaite, 323

Lovelace, Earl, 356–57

Lucian of Samosata (2nd century A.D.), 134, 140, 452, 460n16

Lucretius Carus, Titus (*c.*99–*c.*55 B.C.), 455nn10 and 12

Lukács, György (1885–1971), 39, 78, 122, 125, 303

Lumumba, Patrice (Emergy): as character in Césaire, 50, 139

Luria, Alexander (Aleksandr Romanovich), 464n8

Lyotard, François, 39, 71

Macandal, 391, 396

Macaulay, Thomas Babbington (1800–59), 112

McDermott, William Coffman, 136, 452

Machado y Morales, Gerardo (1871–1939; president, then dictator of Cuba, 1924–33), 379

Machado y Ruíz, Antonio (1875–1939), 126, 252, 256, 305, 370; and fragmented self, 250–51, 314; and magical realism, 379–80, 388; and other, 86, 92, 108

Machiavelli, Niccolò (1469–1527), 220, 234ff, 301

MacIntyre, Alasdair Chalmers, 41, 249, 285

McKay, Claude (1889–1948), 326–27

McKeon, Richard Peter (1900–85), 455n8, 457n21

Mackey, Nathaniel, 143, 454

Macrobius, Ambrosius Aurelius Theodosius (late 4th–first half 5th century A.D.), 161f

McWatt, Mark Andrew, 107, 211, 214, 304, 332, 347, 403, 413

Madrid, 33, 127, 318, 380, 441

Maeztu, Ramiro de (1875–1936), 126–28, 143, 367, 369–70, 377, 379, 406, 453

Malebranche, Nicolas (1638–1715), 455n8

Malinche, la, 430, 468n16

Malraux, André, 90

mangrove (metaphor mingling geography and history), 403–4

Mann, Thomas (1875–1955), 33, 66

Mannoni, Octave, 141, 145f, 220, 320

Mansilla, Lucio Victorio (1831–1913), 91

Manzano, Juan Francisco (1797–1854), 90

mapping (cultures), 15, 34, 55, 64–5, 72–75, 91–100 *passim*, 104, 135; in Eltit, 426–27; in Gombrowicz, 288

Mariátegui, José Carlos (1894–1930), 335, 359, 405–6, 439

Marks, Emerson Robert, 153, 169

Marley, Bob, 107, 307

Marmontel, Jean-François (1723–99), 271–72

Marshall, Paule, 147, 192, 213; against autonomy, 59, 62, 175, 184–85f, 189; on cultural destruction, 145; and flowers, 353, 355, 437; *Chosen Place*, 395–97, 401–4 *passim*, 440–41. *See also under* Carnival

Marsyas, 133

Martí, José (1853–95), 422, 441
Marti, Oscar Albert (1882–1955), 443
Martínez, Antonio (16th–17th century), 363
Martinique, 103
Martyr, Peter (Pietro Martire d'Anghiera, 1457?–1526), 466n5
Marx, Karl (1818–83), 84–85, 116f, 212, 236–40 *passim*, 286
marxism, 24, 39, 56, 438
mask, 138, 454n2; Nietzsche on, 133–34
Mata, Cristóbal de (16th–17th century), 363
Matteotti, Giacomo (1885–1924), 125
maturity (and immaturity), 237–39, 242. *See also under* Enlightenment; Gombrowicz, Witold
Maty, Matthew (1718–76), 102–3
Mazrui, Ali Amin, 57–58, 62, 196; on negritude, 51
mbari (Igbo ceremony), 60, 176, 178
Melville, Herman (1819–91), 131f, 377
memory, 2, 30, 339; cultural, 33, 296, 316–17, 335, 338, 374; minutiae of, 35, 404; in science, 222, 225–26, 232, 245–48; as solution to dissonance or chaos, 128–29, 147, 268, 426. *See also* Forgetting; history; "Kitsch memory"; Levi; Nostalgia; *and under* Descartes; Saramago
Méndez, Miguel (16th–17th century), 360
Mendoza, Antonio de (1490?–1552), 467n11
Merleau-Ponty, Maurice, 293
Merlin, Maria de las Mercedes Santa Cruz y Montalvo, condesa de (1789–1852), 90
Mersenne, Marin (1588–1648), 203
Mesland, Denis (1616–72), 203
Messer-Davidow, Ellen, 3
Messina, Tommaso Caloiro da (1302–41), 162–3
metaphor, 100–101, 151–56, 163–65,

167–70, 182; in Arabic poetics, 173–74; in Brathwaite, 296–98, 324, 343; Caribbean use of, 181–82. *See also* Drums; Flower; Mangrove; Sparrow; Spider; Telescope; *Translatio; and under* Bee; Hobbes, Thomas
Meyssonier, Lazare (1602–72), 202–3
Mexico, 112, 333, 415–21, 427, 430–31, 451n2, 467–68; comments on Cortés and, 99, 331f, 410; history in, 394
Mexico City, 360f, 408, 412, 415, 421; Balbuena on, 427–30ff. *See also* Tenochtitlán
Mexico, University of (1553), 467n11
Middle Passage, 49, 315, 341f, 354, 359
Mighty Sparrow, The (Slinger Francisco), 295, 464n9
Mignolo, Walter D., 34, 332, 453
Mill, John Stuart (1806–73), 269, 280
Millán Astray, José (1879–1954), 16, 125
Miller, Christopher L., 3, 54, 443
Miller, Peter Neal, 452
Milton, John (1608–74), 299–300, 303f
mimesis: as cultural instrument, 2, 150–83, 467n10; as "mutual" making, 154, 159–72, 452n14. *See also under* Bee
mimicry, 57, 133–36, 151, 167, 452n14
mind/body, 2, 184–92, 196–210, 213–14, 457nn1 and 2, 459–60
Mo, Timothy, 143a
Molloy, Sylvia, 71, 90–92, 93f, 104
Mondlane, Eduardo Chivambo, 456n15
monkey (trickster figure), 133–35, 140–43, 452n13, 453n16; in Walcott, 57, 135–36, 148, 173. *See also* Hanuman; Nietzsche; Sun Wu Kong
Monsiváis, Carlos, 409, 412, 423
Montaigne, Michel Eyquem de (1533–92), 42, 191, 193, 195, 212, 450. *See also under* American Indians
Mont Blanc, 179
Monterrey, Gaspar de Acevedo y Zuñiga, conde de (1548–1606), 363
Montesclaros, Juan Manuel de

Mendoza y Luna, marqués de (1571–1628), 363

Montezuma (or Moctezuma, 1480?–1520), 131–32, 415–16, 421, 430, 458n16; as character in Calvino, 272, 282

Moore, Gerald, 138

Moore, Marianne (1887–1972), 297

More, Henry (1614–87), 190, 209, 461n21

Morris, James (Jan), 131, 452

Morris, Mervyn, 326

Moses, Michael Valdez, 13

Mota y Escobar, Alonso de la, bishop (1546–1625), 332

Mphahlele, Es'kia (Ezekiel), 249, 319, 447, 449; on cultural understanding, 17, 20, 456n16, 215; on language, 111, 342; on negritude, 47–53; on "poetry," 45–46, 56–62 *passim*; on western oppression, 70, 140, 310b

Mugo, Micere Githae, 178, 183

Muhando, Penina, 139–40

Mulhern, Francis, 77

multiculturalism, 1, 78

Murena, Hector Alvarez, 127, 420f, 426, 466–67

museums, 152, 454n2

Mussolini, Benito (1883–1945), 451

mutuality (as cultural exchange), 4, 18, 170, 345, 391–92, 442; against autonomy, 37, 45, 73, 98–99; and fictive imagination, 29, 58, 160, 163, 166–68; and language, 102–4, 179–80, 184–85. *See also under* Harris, Wilson; Mimesis

Muzio, Girolamo (1496–1576), 32, 419

myth (as different discursive logic), 267–68, 282, 458–59, 461n19, 463–64; and history, 368–72, 406

myth of empty Americas, 417, 466–67

Naipaul, Vidiadhar Surajprasad, 143, 444; on Caribbean culture, 135, 343, 345–46

Nandy, Ashis, 6, 18, 94–97 *passim*, 217;

on history and myth, 267, 458–59, 272–73, 461; on psychoanalysis, 218, 220, 253, 462

Napoleon I. *See* Bonaparte, Napoleon

narrative. *See under* history

Nasa, 463n5

nationalism and nation, 51, 89, 450n8; as cultural instrument, 2, 5, 8, 80, 444n2; in literary criticism, 78–80, 87–89. *See also* Forgetting

natural rights, 7, 37, 254

nature, state of, 101, 226–27, 237, 241–42, 253. *See also under* Rousseau, Jean-Jacques

Naudé, Gabriel (1600–53), 209

Nautecal: renamed Almería, 418

Nebrija, Elio Antonio de (1444?–1522), 331–32, 334, 465

negativity, negation (in European thought), 123–25, 131. *See also under* Reason

négritude (negritude), 2, 24–25, 46–54, 68–71, 104–6, 336, 389; as *Gemeinschaft*, 47, 52f, 452n15

Neier, Aryeh, 19

Nelson, viscount Horatio (1758–1805), 306

"New Age," 57, 335

New Spain, viceroyalty of (Mexico), 363, 413, 415, 418, 466n6

Nez Perce, 99

Ngũgĩ wa Thiong'o, 13, 111, 178, 183, 319; on the Caribbean, 18, 180; on culture, 15, 24–5, 61f, 176; on history and land, 28, 70, 74, 83, 373; on language, 103–4, 175, 310, 342; on literature and art, 8, 27, 58, 174–75, 457n23; on moving centers, 103–4, 166, 345; on negritude, 51f, 447; on power and violence, 408, 411

Nicaragua, 332

Ní Dhomhnaill, Nuala, 450f

Nietzsche, Friedrich Wilhelm (1844–1900), 143, 145, 376, 378, 381, 406; on

Nietzsche (*continued*)
  apes and mimicry, 133–35f, 140f, 146;
  on history, 367–71, 374; and tragedy,
  114f, 119, 121–22, 126, 132–35, 451. *See
  also under* Venice
Nigeria, 448; Biafran war in, 57–8
Nkrumah, Kwame, 176–77, 186, 215–
  16f; on categorial convertibility,
  460n14
Noh theater, 110
Nooteboom, Cees, 59, 62, 175, 212–14,
  336, 400
Norris, John (1657–1712), 255–56
nostalgia, 56, 63, 67, 87, 135; in Americas, 335, 339, 426, 430; definitions of,
  45, 146f; as sentimentalized memory,
  35–36, 175, 182; in fascism, 125–27; as
  fetishism, 193–94, 217–18; in negritude, 46–47, 53; and Quijote, 122,
  126–27, 368–70, 377. *See also* history,
  "Kitsch memory," Memory; *and
  under* Eldorado; England
novel: detective, 268–69, 271–73, 283–
  84, 288–89; function of, 97, 107; and
  nation, 78–79, 88; as *ratio*, 273

obeah, 301
Ocampo, Victoria (1890–1979), 90
Ogaden (region of Somalia), 74
Ogden, Charles Kay (1889–1957), 280
O'Gorman, Edmundo, 420f, 426
Ogun (West African/Caribbean god of
  thunder, iron, war), 323, 400
Okigbo, Christopher, 58; as character in
  Mazrui, 57–8
Okot p'Bitek, 49, 52, 62, 170
Olsen, Charles, 454
Onuora, Oku, 326
orature, 8, 24, 175
organic (versus mechanistic), 2, 45,
  125
Ortega y Gasset, José (1883–1955), 73,
  126, 382, 453; on culture, 15, 23; on
  metaphor, 153, 156, 169f, 459–60; on

Quijote, 366f, 378, 380; on self, 86,
  108
Ortiz, Simon, 61f
Oshumare (Yoruba god, symbolized by
  python/rainbow), 320
Ossian (legendary Gaelic poet), 142
otherness, 54, 158, 186, 337; as cultural
  instrument 2, 13–14, 68–9, 81, 108–9,
  175, 373; negritude as, 48, 51, 70–71;
  in western literary criticism, 68–107,
  177–78. *See also* "home"
Otway, Thomas (1652–85), 33
Ouologuem, Yambo, 53–54, 62, 64f
Owen, Stephen, 165, 177, 455n5, 456n14;
  on cultural understanding, 20, 35; on
  dissonant culture, 152; on nondivisive
  cultures, 132, 146, 157–58
Oxenford, John, 454n20

Padilla, Heberto, 181, 353, 355, 438–39,
  441
Pagden, Anthony, 465–66
Paris, 9, 49, 258, 262, 344, 379–80; and
  western reason, 47, 106, 216, 263, 293,
  318, 347, 423
Parker, Henry (1604–52), 450
Pascal, Blaise (1623–62), 41, 124, 176
Patterson, Orlando, 345, 423
Pausa, 362–64, 366–67, 386
Paz, Octavio, 86, 140, 143, 172, 394, 417,
  421, 467n8
Peirce, Charles Sanders (1839–1914), 287
Pelton, Robert Doane, 136
Perez, Gilberto, 438, 441
peripeteia (reversal, in tragedy), 118
Peru, 359, 362–63, 365, 405, 428, 467–
  68
Pessoa, Fernando António Nogueira
  (1888–1935), 211, 213, 250–51, 305–6,
  314, 370
Pétion, Alexandre Sabès (1770–1818),
Petrarch (Francesco Petrarca, 1304–74),
  on mimesis, 161, 162–63, 167, 349; on
  Venice, 33

Philip II, king of Spain (1527–98), 365, 418

Philip III, king of Spain (1578–1621), 363, 366

Philip, Marlene NourbeSe, 38, 310, 316, 356, 453; on being "other," 11, 17, 19–20, 52; on culture, 111; on exile, 22, 312, 318; on "facts," 273, 278; on history, 338, 356, 359, 383–84; "I-mage" of, 178, 294–96, 327, 390, 404, 407, 414; on language, 19–20, 287–88, 298, 311, 313, 332–33, 341f; on literature, 8, 24; on memory, 63, 214; on Naipaul, 346; on oppressions, 46, 180, 186, 192, 277, 307, 454n2; on silence, 20, 280, 311, 314

Philippines, 126, 367

Phillips, Caryl, 312, 347

Phillips, captain John, or Thomas (*fl.*1690s), 5

Philostratus, Flavius (*c.*172–after 244), 171–72, 177, 457n21

Phrynichos (*fl. c.*512–476 B.C.), 455n9

Pico della Mirandola, Giovanni (1463–94), 353

Picón Salas, Mariano, 91, 427

Piedra, José, 71, 111, 134, 143, 449

Piglia, Ricardo, 423, 427, 441

Pigman, George Wood, III, 455n11

Pindar (518–*c.*438 B.C.), 163, 455n12

Pirandello, Luigi (1867–1936), 124–25, 128, 451–52

Pizarro, Francisco (*c.*1476–1541), 99, 331

Plato (427–347 B.C.), 43, 116, 121, 134, 171, 187, 359, 459; *Cratylus*, 153–54; *Ion*, 161, 165; on memory, 459nn11 and 12; on mimesis, 151–55; *Phaedrus*, 154; *Republic*, 153f, 252; *Sophist*, 153; and tragedy, 117

Plutarch of Chaeroneia (*c.*50–*c.*120 A.D.), 142

Poe, Edgar Allan (1809–49), 272, 463n7

poetic justice, 118

Pollard, Velma, 312–13

Pollitt, Katha, 142

Poland, 261–63, 284

Polo, Marco (1254–1323?), 31, 99, 331, 413; as character in Calvino, 30–31, 34, 36, 65, 67, 410

Pope, Alexander (1688–1744), 43, 146, 294, 324, 453n19; on diseased reason, 119, 123, 141–42, 191, 249, 286, 303, 400; *Dunciad* 134; on Hanuman, 141–43; *Rape of the Lock*, 431

Popper, Karl Raimond, 81, 269

Port-au-Prince, 301, 379

Portes, Alejandro, 410

Port-Royal, 205

Portugal, 6; early trade of, 5

Postlethwayt, Malachi (1707?–1767), 357–58

postmodernism, 1, 421

Potonchán (Champotón): renamed Santa María de la Victoria, 417

Powell, John Enoch, 334

Prakash, Gyan, 13, 51

Pratt, Richard Henry (1840–1924), 447

Prendergast, Christopher, 152, 451, 452

process/stasis (or history vs. reason: characterizing western science), 191–92, 197–210, 224–32, 243, 248–49, 462n2

progress: as cultural instrument, 2–3, 6, 8, 238–42, 269; as disease, 123f; and literature, 10, 29

property, private (as cultural instrument), 3, 37–38, 56, 146, 236; body as, 186; in North America, 100–101, 155

Prospero, 340, 381, 414; in Brathwaite, 339, 354–55; Lamming on, 97–98, 338, 342, 355

psychoanalysis (as cultural instrument), *see* Freud, Sigmund; *and under* Nandy, Ashis; Science

psychological insecurity (of western culture), 11, 21, 79, 123–24, 151

Puerto Rico, 297, 412, 437–38, 467n14

Quechua, 461n19
Quijote. *See* Don Quijote
Quintilian (Marcus Fabius
    Quintilianus, *c.*35–*c.*95), 155, 356f,
    459n10

Rabelais, François (1490/4–1553), 193,
    195, 212
Racine, Jean (1639–99), 119, 334
Raleigh, Sir Walter (1552–1618), 181,
    413
Rama, Angel, 407, 412, 421–22
Ramazani, Jahan, 399
Ramchand, Kenneth, 312, 465n5
Ranke, Leopold von (1795–1886), 33
Rappaport, Joanne, 463n5
Rastafari, 307, 326f
ratio, rationes, 110, 112; definition of, 2–
    8. *See also* Cultural instrument(s)
Rawls, John, 39
reason: internal negation of, 119, 123–
    25, 251, 303, 321; and history, 40–41.
    See also under Eliot, Thomas Stearns;
    Heidegger, Martin; Lévi-Strauss,
    Claude; Pope, Alexander; Saramago,
    José; Unamuno, Miguel de
Reformation, English, 6–7, 443
Renan, Ernest (1823–92), 80, 89, 368
Retamar, Roberto Fernández. *See*
    Fernández Retamar, Roberto
Reyes Cano, José María, 431
Rhys, Jean, 399, 444n8
Richards, Ivor Armstrong (1893–1979),
    8, 24, 169, 456n17
Ricoeur, Paul, 103, 154, 169, 220
Rieff, Philip, 236, 462
Rimbaud, Arthur (1854–91), 347, 464n2
Roazen, Paul, 235–37f
Robbins, Bruce, 79
Robert-Tornow, Walter Heinrich (1852–
    95), 455n10
Rodney, Walter, 13, 307

Rodó, José Enrique (1872–1917), 72f,
    98, 100, 320
Rodríguez Julía, Edgardo, 411–15, 422,
    424, 441
Rodríguez Marín, Francisco (1855–
    1943), 360
Romanus Pontifex (papal bull of 1455),
    6
Rome, 127, 140; Venice as, 32, 178; as
    western reason, 117, 320
Ronsard, Pierre de (1525–85), 161
Rorty, Richard, 39
Rotimi, Ola, 112
Roumain, Jacques, 315, 388
Rousseau, Jean-Jacques (1712–78), 126,
    236, 238, 254, 334; and idealized
    nature, 77, 237, 278
Roy, Jean, 235, 462
Roy, Namba, 345, 423
Rushdie, Salman, 13, 34, 103, 444
Ruskin, John (1819–1900), 33, 36, 46,
    66, 130–1f
Russell, Bertrand Arthur William, 3rd
    earl (1872–1970), 279–80
Ryle, Gilbert (1900–76), 457
Rymer, Thomas (1641–1713), 118, 269,
    274

Sá Carneiro, Mário de (1890–1916),
    305–6
Sabuco de Nántes Barrera, Luisa Oliva
    (1562–*c.*1622), 193, 195, 212
Saint-John Perse (Marie-René-Auguste-
    Aléxis Saint-Léger Léger, 1887–1975),
    9, 54–5, 185–86, 328; on language,
    313; and figure of Quijote, 372, 381
Saint-Pierre, Bernardin de (1737–1814),
    334
Salamanca, Pedro de (16th–17th
    century), 363
Saldívar, José David, 422, 466n7
Saussure, Ferdinand de (1857–1913),
    263, 277, 291
Saussy, Haun, 178, 349, 445, 455n7

Said, Edward William, 3, 35–36, 71–81
  passim, 91–96 *passim*, 101
Saint Domingue, 323; in Carpentier,
  334. *See also* Haiti
San(to) Domingo, 297, 467n14
Saramago, José, 16, 25, 64, 131, 265,
  305–6, 329; 449; on diseased reason,
  123, 249, 400; on memory, 35, 45, 50,
  211, 214
Sarmiento, Domingo Faustino (1811–
  88), 90f, 334, 461n19
Sarria, Juan de (father, 16th–17th
  century), 360
Sarria, Juan de (son, 1582–?), 361–62f
Sartre, Jean-Paul, 51–52, 72, 123, 449;
  and negritude, 69–71, 104–6
Scaliger, Julius Caesar (1484–1558), 43
Scarisbrick, John Joseph, 443
Scarlatti, Giuseppe Domenico (1685–
  1757), 65–66, 449
Scheinberg, Susan, 455n12
Schiller, Friedrich von (1759–1805), 88,
  118, 239–40ff, 246, 248, 253, 371; on
  tragedy, 119
Schopenhauer, Arthur (1788–1860),
  124, 240; and tragedy, 114, 119–22
Schwarz-Bart, Simone, 358, 375–76,
  402
Sciascia, Leonardo, 125, 143f, 147f, 367,
  451–52, 400
science (as cultural instrument), 2, 26,
  43, 218, 460n14; critique of, 125, 214;
  different kinds of, 96– 97; exclusions
  of, 266, 463n4; instauration of, 40–
  41, 168, 192, 195, 210; nature of, 216,
  219–20; possibility of, 443–44; psychoanalysis as, 219–57, 462n1. *See also*
  process/stasis
Scott, Joan, 81–82
Searle, John Rogers, 274, 464n6
self, 2, 26, 81f, 344, 418; and anti-self/
  other, 57, 84, 86, 108, 128–32, 214–18;
  artist as, 57–8; as cultural instrument,
  333; in Descartes, 176–77; destruction/

alienation of, 50–52, 75, 343, 447n16;
  and political community, 90–92; in
  tragedy, 120–26. *See also* Autobio-
  graphy; Consciousness; Descartes;
  Subject; *and under* Freud
Selvon, Samuel, 334, 336, 346, 382–83
Seneca, Lucius Annaeus (*c.*3 B.C.–65
  A.D.), 177, 357, 359, 455nn8 and 10,
  456n18; on art, 16; on mimesis, 161–
  74, 181, 259f, 348–49, 404, 456n17,
  442
Senegal, 5
Senghor, Léopold Sédar, 24, 60, 70, 186,
  207; on negritude, 46–47, 50–53, 63
Senior, Olive, 107, 439–40f
Seville, 360
Shaftesbury, Anthony Ashley Cooper,
  3rd earl of (1671–1713), 254
Shakespeare, William (1564–1616), 41f,
  98, 147, 298, 341, 354, 464n2; *Hamlet*,
  129, 289, 294, 452n9; *King Lear*, 194f;
  Macbeth, 145–46, 426–27; *Othello*,
  178, 187; *The Tempest*, 100f, 354; and
  Venice, 33, 187. *See also* Ariel;
  Caliban; Prospero; Sycorax
Shango (or Xango: West African and
  Caribbean god of thunder, iron, and
  war), 139, 404; in Brathwaite, 305,
  320–24 *passim*, 327, 354, 357
Shchutskii, Iulian Konstantinovich
  (1897–?), 157, 455n4.
Shelley, Percy Bysshe (1792–1822), 179
Shumway, David, 3
Sidney, Sir Philip (1554–86), 164–65,
  167, 169, 187; on tragedy, 147
Silko, Leslie Marmon, 104ff, 261
Silone, Ignazio (1900–1978), 56, 58f, 62,
  64
Simmel, Georg (1858–1918), 124, 128
Simpson, David, 77
Sims, Calvin, 412
Sinfield, Alan, 448
Sisyphus (as symbol of oppression), 329,
  333, 345, 347, 359

slaves, slavery, 37f, 49, 363, 365, 399–400, 432, 440464n1; and language, 310–11
Snead, James, 102f
Snell, Reginald, 462n4
Socrates (*c.* 470–399 B.C.), 161, 191
Şofọla, ·Zulu, 110, 138, 140
Somalia, 74
Sophocles (496–406/5 B.C.), 113–14, 121, 126; *Oedipus rex*, 112, 114, 137, 272, 451
Soustelle, Jacques, 417
Soyinka, Wole, 61, 138, 140, 447, 448, 465; against autonomy, 8, 24–25, 59, 62, 136–37, 186; *The Bacchae*, 110, 113, 136–37, 139; on negritude, 46–48, 50–55 *passim*, 63, 70, 389
Spain, 6, 116; Don Quijote as, 143; and loss of empire, 21, 126f, 367–70; remade by invasion of Americas, 443
sparrow, 21, 320, 345, 438; in Gombrowicz, 262–3, 265–68, 270–71, 275–95 *passim*; in Bible, 290, 294; in Shakespeare, 289, 294. *See also* Mighty Sparrow
Spengler, Oswald (1880–1936), 39, 122, 125–28, 406
spider, as image of *ratio*, 21, 258–61, 270, 273, 338, 401–2. *See also* Anancy
Spinoza, Baruch or Benedict (1632–77), 245, 251
Spivak, Gayatri Chakravorty, 71
Stackelberg, Jürgen von, 455n10
Stanford, William Bedell, 455–56
stasis. *See* process/stasis
Steiner, George, 114f, 146, 450
Stewart, Ian, 464n6
Stillman, Robert Ernest, 168
Stowe, Harriet Beecher (1811–96), 107
subject (willful), 37, 42; as fragmented, 44f, 92, 248–52, 257, 289–94, 446n10; and history, 40–41, 216; and meaning, 265–66, 271–73, 288; of tragedy, 119. *See also* consciousness; self

Sun Wu Kong (Chinese trickster monkey), 140, 143, 148
Sutherland, Efua Theodara, 110, 112
Sutton, John, 186, 201–2, 204, 209, 457, 458, 460
Swift, Jonathan (1667–1745), 259–60f, 453n19
Sycorax, 414; in Brathwaite, 305, 319–20, 323ff, 328, 337, 355
Sylvan, David, 3

Tagore, Abanindranath (1871–1951), 447
Tanner, Tony, 131
Taussig, Michael Thomas, 18, 57
Tawney, Richard Henry (1880–1962), 7
Taylor, Charles, 129
telescope (as discursive "metaphor"), 221–35, 240, 242–49, 265, 462n4
Tenochtitlán (Temistitan, México, Mexico City), 132, 375f, 417–20; in Harris, 352; as new Venice, 410, 415–16, 420, 428–30, 436, 441; Venice as, 33, 64, 66, 418–20, 445
Teotihuacán, 416
Tesauro, Emanuele, conte (1592–1675), 168, 221–22, 243, 248
Texcoco, lake (of Tenochtitlán/Mexico City), 416, 421
Thapar, Romila, 2, 10, 51
Thelwell, Michael, 346
Themistocles (*c.*525–*c.*460 B.C.), 197–98, 459n10
Thomas, John Jacob (*c.*1840–1889), 27, 299–300, 349
Thomson, James (1700–48), 303–4, 324
Thornton, John Kelly, 5
Thucydides (*c.*460–400 B.C.), 19, 168
Tiepolo, Paolo di Stefano (d.1585), 466n5
Tilgher, Adriano (1887–1941), 124–25, 451
timehri, 327, 403
Tintoretto (Jacopo Robusti, 1518–94), 33, 445

Titian (Tiziano Vecellio, 1477–1576), 33–34, 445

Tlaxcala, 417–18

Todorov, Tzvetan, 71, 449

Toledo, Francisco de (1515–82), 365–66

Toltec, 417, 451n2

Tomaselli, Sylvana, 457

Tönnies, Ferdinand (1855–1936), 39, 45, 122, 125

Toomer, Jean (1894–1967), 143, 454

Tordesillas, Treaty of (1494), 6

Toro, Antonio de (16th–17th century), 360

Torres-Saillant, Silvio, 335ff, 353

tragedy, 154; as cultural instrument, 2, 109–51, 467n10; and political thought, 116–18

tragic: as way of naming (and making) victims, 109, 143–48, 369, 454n22

translatio, 152–53, 155; and violence, 99–102

translation: of cultures, 34, 145, 178, 252, 449n1, 467n9; as reordering, 266, 283, 463n3

Trinidad, 300, 343, 358, 382–83, 464n9

Tropica (Mary Adella Wolcott, c.1874–?), 401

Troy: Venice as, 32

truth: as cultural instrument, 2, 9, 127, 258, 278–79, 284; in Descartes, 191–92, 204–6, 211, 215; different kinds of, 43, 74, 149; difficulty of knowing, 228–30, 244; dissolution of, 263, 292; local, 166, 349; as willful, 272–73, 371; in West, 25, 121, 142, 169, 240, 259–60, 463n7

Tu Fu (712–70 A.D.), 157, 456n14

Tupac Amaru, king of the Incas (d.1571), 365

Turkle, Sherry, 462

Ukraine, 14

Ulfers, Friedrich, 452

Ulreich, John Charles, Jr., 164

Unamuno y Jugo, Miguel (1864–1936), 11, 15–16, 125ff, 214, 453, 400, 406; on categorial convertibility, 460n14; on diseased reason, 123, 249; and tragedy, 114, 119, 121; on tragic self and community, 122–24, 128–30. *See also under* Don Quijote

underdevelopment, 13–14, 38, 53

Uruguay, 262

Urhobo, 138

Valdés, Clemente de (16th–17th century), 360

Valla, Lorenzo (1407–57), 465

Vasconselos, José (1882–1959), 91, 127

Vega, Bernardo (1885–1965), 438, 441

Vega Carpio, Lope Félix de (1562–1635), 362

Velasco, Luis de, marqués de Salinas (1534–1617), 366, 427

Venice, 9, 64, 418; as image of Europe/the West, 21, 30–36, 44, 65f, 130–32, 187, 410, 422, 442; Jews in, 131, 452n10; lesser than Tenochtitlán, 415–16, 418–20, 428; Nietzsche on, 121, 131; as supporter of Spain, 33, 443, 445; image turned against the West, 178–79, 376. *See also* ghetto

Vera Cruz, la Villa Rica de la, 417

Vergil (Publius Vergilius Maro, 70–19 B.C.), 162, 400

Verme di Verona, Luchino dal (c.1320–1372), 33

Vernant, Jean-Pierre, 133, 158–59, 452

Veronese, Paolo (1528–88), 34

Vespucci, Amerigo (Alberigo V., 1454–1512), 332–33

Vivaldi, Antonio (c.1675–1743): as character in Carpentier, 65

Vives, Juan Luis (1493–1540), 161, 193, 420, 459n10

Vološinov, Valentin Nikolaevich (1895–?), 275, 286, 294

Vorstellung (immediate perceptual image in Frege), difficulty for meaning, 222, 262, 268–69, 282, 286

voudou, 321, 385–90

Vygotsky, Lev Semenovich (1896–1934), 464n8

Walcott, Derek, 73, 141, 336, 381, 404, 406; on cultural creation, 328, 338, 344, 347, 355, 377, 392, 413; *Dream on Monkey Mountain* 57, 143, 148; and flowers, 356f; on imposition of history, 131–32, 140, 147, 382, 399–401; on mangroves, 403; on mimicry, 135–36, 151, 452; on Naipaul, 346; on new history, 371–74; *Omeros*, 343, 356, 373–74, 377, 399–401, 432; and Quijote, 372, 377, 381. *See also under* Monkey

Wallis, John (1616–1703), 245

Walton, Kendall Lewis, 172, 456–57

Warraou, 327

Warren, Austin (1899–1986), 42–43, 44, 58, 260

Warsaw (as "mature" Europe), 293

Watson, Gerard, 457n21

Weber, Max (1864–1920), 7, 39, 45, 122

Weimar, 9, 39

Weizsäcker, Richard von, 212

Welby, Victoria Lady (1837–1912), 103, 280

Wellek, René, 42, 44, 58

Werner, Heinz (1890–1964), 156, 170

Westphalia, Treaty of (1648), 210

Wheatley, Phillis (1753?–1784), 134, 141

Wheelwright, Philip Ellis, 153, 169

Whitman, Walt(er) (1819–92), 297, 464n2

Wilkinson, Elizabeth M., 462n4

Williams, Aubrey, 327

Williams, Bernard Arthur Owen, 113f, 146, 457

Williams, Chancellor, 54

Williams, Raymond, 79, 85, 114–15

Willoughby, L. A., 462n4

Wilson, Diana de Armas, 366, 415

Wilson, Margaret Dauler, 457

Wines, Michael, 14

Winks, Christopher, 376

Wittgenstein, Ludwig (1889–1951), 259, 261, 284–85; on language, 264–65, 273–74, 277–78, 287, 290–92; on mythmaking, 225, 229, 234

Woolf, Virginia (1882–1941), 44, 270–71, 280, 282–83, 339

Wordsworth, William (1770–1850), 180, 325, 430

Wright, Richard, 106, 444

Xenophon (*c.*428/7–*c.*354 B.C.), 161

Yeats, William Butler (1865–1939), 73, 76, 93

Yoruba, 110, 320; drama of, 137, 140

Yu, Pauline, 156–58, 165, 169, 177

Zea, Leopoldo, 5, 127–28, 406, 420, 426

Zephaniah, Benjamin, 346

Zimbabwe, 376

Zirimu, Pio, 8

Zola, Émile (1840–1902), 309

Cultural Memory | *in the Present*

Timothy J. Reiss, *Against Autonomy: Global Dialectics of Cultural Exchange*

Hent de Vries and Samuel Weber, eds., *Religion and Media*

Niklas Luhmann, *Theories of Distinction: Re-Describing the Descriptions of Modernity*, ed. and introd. by William Rasch

Johannes Fabian, *Anthropology with an Attitude: Critical Essays*

Michel Henry, *I am the Truth: Toward a Philosophy of Christianity*

Gil Anidjar, *"Our Place in al-Andalus": Kabbalah, Philosophy, Literature in Arab Jewish Letters*

Hélène Cixous and Jacques Derrida, *Veils*

F. R. Ankersmit, *Historical Representation*

F. R. Ankersmit, *Political Representation*

Elissa Marder, *Dead Time: Temporal Disorders in the Wake of Modernity (Baudelaire and Flaubert)*

Reinhart Koselleck, *Timing History, Spacing Concepts: The Practice of Conceptual History*

Niklas Luhmann, *The Reality of the Mass Media*

Hubert Damisch, *A Childhood Memory by Piero della Francesca*

Hubert Damisch, *A Theory of /Cloud/: Toward a History of Painting*

Jean-Luc Nancy, *The Speculative Remark: (One of Hegel's Bons Mots)*

Jean-François Lyotard, *Soundproof Room: Malraux's Anti-Aesthetics*

Jan Patočka, *Plato and Europe*

Hubert Damisch, *Skyline: The Narcissistic City*

Isabel Hoving, *In Praise of New Travelers: Reading Caribbean Migrant Women Writers*

Richard Rand, ed., *Futures: Of Jacques Derrida*

William Rasch, *Niklas Luhmann's Modernity: The Paradoxes of Differentiation*

Jacques Derrida and Anne Dufourmantelle, *Of Hospitality*

Jean-François Lyotard, *The Confession of Augustine*

Kaja Silverman, *World Spectators*

Samuel Weber, *Institution and Interpretation: Expanded Edition*

Jeffrey S. Librett, *The Rhetoric of Cultural Dialogue: Jews and Germans in the Epoch of Emancipation*

Ulrich Baer, *Remnants of Song: Trauma and the Experience of Modernity in Charles Baudelaire and Paul Celan*

Samuel C. Wheeler III, *Deconstruction as Analytic Philosophy*

David S. Ferris, *Silent Urns: Romanticism, Hellenism, Modernity*

Rodolphe Gasché, *Of Minimal Things: Studies on the Notion of Relation*

Sarah Winter, *Freud and the Institution of Psychoanalytic Knowledge*

Samuel Weber, *The Legend of Freud: Expanded Edition*

Aris Fioretos, ed., *The Solid Letter: Readings of Friedrich Hölderlin*

J. Hillis Miller / Manuel Asensi, *Black Holes / J. Hillis Miller; or, Boustrophedonic Reading*

Miryam Sas, *Fault Lines: Cultural Memory and Japanese Surrealism*

Peter Schwenger, *Fantasm and Fiction: On Textual Envisioning*

Didier Maleuvre, *Museum Memories: History, Technology, Art*

Jacques Derrida, *Monolingualism of the Other; or, The Prosthesis of Origin*

Andrew Baruch Wachtel, *Making a Nation, Breaking a Nation: Literature and Cultural Politics in Yugoslavia*

Niklas Luhmann, *Love as Passion: The Codification of Intimacy*

Mieke Bal, ed., *The Practice of Cultural Analysis: Exposing Interdisciplinary Interpretation*

Jacques Derrida and Gianni Vattimo, eds., *Religion*